The Political Economy
of China's Financial Reforms

Transitions: Asia and the Pacific

Series Editor, *Mark Selden*

The Political Economy of China's Financial Reforms:
Finance in Late Development, Paul Bowles and Gordon White

Reinventing Vietnamese Socialism:
Doi Moi *in Comparative Perspective*,
edited by William S. Turley and Mark Selden

FORTHCOMING

The Politics of Democratization:
Vicissitudes and Universals in the East Asian Experience,
edited by Edward Friedman

The World of the Ainu, Kayano Shigeru

The Origins of the Great Leap Forward,
Jean-Luc Domenach

Unofficial Histories: Chinese Reportage from the Era of Reform,
edited by Thomas Moran

Moving Mountains: Women and Feminism
in Contemporary Japan, Kanai Yoshiko

Japanese Labor, Kumazawa Makoto

The Political Economy of China's Financial Reforms

Finance in Late Development

Paul Bowles
and Gordon White

Westview Press

BOULDER • SAN FRANCISCO • OXFORD

Transitions: Asia and the Pacific

Copyright © 1993 by Westview Press, Inc.

Published in 1993 in the United States of America by Westview Press, Inc., 5500 Central Avenue, Boulder, Colorado 80301-2877, and in the United Kingdom by Westview Press, 36 Lonsdale Road, Summertown, Oxford OX2 7EW

Library of Congress Cataloging-in-Publication Data
Bowles, Paul.
  The political economy of China's financial reforms : finance in late development / Paul Bowles and Gordon White.
    p. cm. — (Transitions: Asia and the Pacific)
  Includes bibliographical references and index.
  ISBN 0-8133-8713-2
  1. Finance—China. 2. Financial institutions—China. 3. China—Economic policy—1976–   . I. White, Gordon, 1942–   . II. Title.
III. Series.
HG187.C6B69 1993
332'.0951—dc20   93-28620
                                                                            CIP

Printed and bound in the United States of America

        The paper used in this publication meets the requirements
  (∞)   of the American National Standard for Permanence of Paper
        for Printed Library Materials Z39.48-1984.

10   9   8   7   6   5   4   3   2   1

To Fiona and Barbara

Contents

List of Tables and Figures   xi
Acknowledgments   xiii

1   Introduction   1

Intention, 2
Approach, 4

**2   Market Socialism, Financial Liberalisation
          and Late Development**   12

Market Socialism: Towards a "Planned
    Commodity Economy," 14
Finance and Development: The Case
    for Liberalisation, 25
The East Asian NIC Model of Late Development, 33
Concluding Remarks, 45

**3   The Pre-Reform System: The Financial
          Institutions of Centrally Planned Socialism**   47

The Role of Banking Institutions Under
    Central Planning, 49
The Chinese Case, 55
Economic Performance in the Pre-Reform Era, 68
Concluding Remarks, 70

4   The Process of Financial Reform   72

Policy Process Phase I, 1979–1984: Financial
    Liberalisation Without Financial Markets, 73

Policy Process Phase II, 1985–1988:
  The Move Towards Financial Markets, 84
Retrenchment, Reversal and Renewal:
  The Financial Scene, 1988–1992, 94

5 **Policy Outcomes: The Macroeconomic and
Microeconomic Impact of Financial Reform**   98

Inflation, 98
The Relationship Between Banks and Enterprises
  in Practice, 112
Concluding Remarks, 120

6 **Towards a Socialist Capital Market?**   121

The Introduction of Bonds in the 1980s, 122
Bonds and the Politico-Economic Struggle
  for Resources, 132
The Introduction of Shares, 140
Debate on the Economic Impact of Shares, 147
Ownership Reform in a "Socialist" Economy, 150
Concluding Remarks, 157

7 **Conclusion: Future Trajectories**   160

Desirable and Feasible Reform: A Scenario, 162
An Alternative Scenario, 179

Bibliography   183
About the Book and Authors   196
Index   197

Tables and Figures

Tables

2.1 Three paradigms of financial systems: Summary   46

3.1 Inflation in China, 1951–1978   66
3.2 Domestic bond issues, 1950–1958   67
3.3 Average nominal wage in state-owned enterprises,
     1952–1978   68

4.1 Financial deepening: Selected ratios, 1979–1989   79
4.2 Domestic savings as a percentage of GDP, 1978–1988   81
4.3 Composition of savings, 1978–1988   82
4.4 Urban and rural savings in national banks, 1978–1990   82

5.1 Inflation, 1978–1990   99
5.2 Growth rates of monetary aggregates, 1978–1991   103
5.3 Composition of nominal wages for workers in
     state-owned units, 1978–1990   104
5.4 Annual average nominal wage levels, 1979–1990   104
5.5 Gross domestic investment as percentage of GDP,
     1970–1989   106
5.6 Central government revenue, expenditure and budget
     deficits, 1978–1989   108
5.7 Real growth of net national income, 1978–1990   111
5.8 Subsidies of losses of state-owned enterprises,
     1978–1991   118

6.1 Issues of bonds and shares, 1981–1989, by category   124
6.2 Issues of bonds and shares, 1981–1989, by year   125
6.3 State treasury bond issues, 1981–1988   125
6.4 Government budgetary and extra-budgetary revenues,
     1979–1989   135

6.5 Government debt revenue, 1979–1990   136
6.6 Shares in gross industrial output value by form
of ownership, 1979–1990   143

Figures

3.1 The organization of the People's Bank   57

Acknowledgments

W E WOULD LIKE TO THANK the British Academy for funding a research visit to China in 1987 to initiate research on the financial reforms. We would also like to thank Maisie Gray for making available to us her research files and Julie McWilliam and Bernadine Halliday for their assistance in the preparation of the manuscript.

Paul Bowles
Gordon White

1

Introduction

CHINA'S PROGRAMME of market-oriented economic reform has been under way since 1979. During the past thirteen years, there have been some remarkable changes in the structure and operation of the economy, particularly in the rural sector and in more "open" south-eastern coastal provinces such as Guangdong, Fujian and Zhejiang. In terms of welfare and productivity, the reforms have proven to be very successful. Continuing high growth rates have been accompanied by dramatic increases in per capita real incomes for both the urban and rural population and by significant improvements in factor productivity in both state and non-state sectors.

The reforms were premised on the need to introduce "market regulation" into the economy, partially to replace the centrally planned and administered allocation of resources. In comparison to former state socialist counterparts in east and central Europe, China started reforms both late and early: late in relation, say, to Hungary, which had been experimenting with a comparably market-oriented "New Economic Mechanism" since 1968, and early in relation to the Soviet Union, which did not begin until the late-1980s. Compared to east-central European developments, the Chinese experience of reform has been distinctive in several respects: The reforms have been pushed much faster and further; they have not been accompanied or preceded by substantial political reforms, as in the Soviet case; in economic terms, they have been far more successful; and as of the time of writing in late 1992, they have not culminated in a spectacular and comprehensive collapse of the pre-existing state socialist political and economic system. The dramatic events of 1989–1991 have left China as virtually the only socialist country (with the exception of Vietnam) which is still engaged in a "market socialist" project, theoretically in transition from an old to a new form of "socialist" economy, in contrast to the post-socialist countries of east/central

Europe, which are now involved in a seemingly ineluctable yet highly tortuous transition to some form of capitalism.

A central element of the reform programme in China has been a wide-ranging attempt to construct a new financial system. We use the term *financial* to denote financial institutions and flows outside of the state budgetary system, where a parallel process of fiscal reform has been under way since 1979.[1] The financial system channels financial resources, representing generalised command over physical resources, between savers and lenders, influences the rate of saving and the forms which it can take, and allocates purchasing power between lenders and thereby influences both the overall developmental process and the behaviour of micro-economic actors within it. The central thrust of reform has been towards a more flexible, variegated and competitive financial system, premised on the view that organising financial resources more effectively and allocating them more efficiently can bring substantial productivity benefits to the real economy.

While the monobanking system which was used in all Soviet-type economies is now discredited in China, the nature of an alternative financial system has been a matter of much dispute, raising a complex set of thorny issues: What range of financial assets should be available to savers? How should the banking system be organised? On what basis should resources be allocated to lenders? What role should the state play and what should be left to financial markets? What methods can be used to ensure macroeconomic balance? What impact do the reforms in the financial system have on other reforms—are they complementary or contradictory? How best should financial reforms be introduced and how can any potentially problematic consequences of the reform process, such as inflation, be avoided or contained? This is the territory we aim to explore.

Intention

There has been many a scholarly treatise written on the Chinese economic reform process as a whole as well as on particular sectors of the economy—especially agriculture, industry and foreign trade—and on specific policy areas such as labour, wage and price reform. The financial sector has, however, been relatively neglected in the academic literature until very recently (Byrd 1983 was a notable exception);

---

1. In Chinese, the words *caizheng* (fiscal) and *jinrong* (financial) are used to distinguish these spheres, but both words are often translated into English as *financial*.

however, the World Bank has produced a large volume of relevant literature in successive mission reports (for example, World Bank 1988 and 1990b). This relative neglect may partly reflect an implicit desire to focus on what is perceived as the "real" economy, a perspective which assigns a relatively marginal role to finance; it may also reflect a view that financial economics and financial systems are highly arcane and technical areas which are the province of a relatively small group of "money doctors" whose experience, expertise and conceptual universe are somewhat alien to the more mundane world of applied development economics. It is our belief, however, that the financial system plays a critical role in the development process, dealing centrally as it does with the mobilisation and allocation of resources, and deserves closer examination. Our objectives in this study are three: first, to understand the origins of, and rationale for, financial reform in the Chinese context; second, to sketch the specific character and impact of the reforms during the period 1979 to 1992 using a fairly broad brush; and third, to assess the likely evolution of the reforms in future. In so doing, we should stress that we do not believe that the financial reforms can be "separated" from other parts of the reform programme or the forces shaping the reform process as a whole. Thus, while our focus is on the financial reforms, we shall also refer to the evolving political economy of the reforms as a whole.

It is also important to say at the outset what we are not going to do. We do not intend to attempt any elegant econometric exercises on Chinese financial data, such as they are; nor will we try to provide a detailed chronological catalogue of specific aspects of the financial reforms or some kind of technical primer on the specific technical issues involved. As the bibliography demonstrates, these kinds of studies already exist. Rather we seek to fill a gap in the literature, first, by drawing on intellectual insights generated by contemporary comparative work in development studies and second, by using an analytical approach which seeks to understand financial processes in terms of an interplay of political and economic forces—hence the term *political economy* in the book's title. We shall focus primarily on the domestic financial system; though there have been important changes in China's external financial relations since 1979, this is a complex area and needs a separate and extended study. The study will also focus primarily on the "commanding heights" of the financial system in the state/urban/industrial system; there have also been important changes in the rural financial system, to which we will make only passing reference. This is an important subject in its own right and deserves separate attention.

Approach

Our approach to the Chinese financial reforms will be both "choice-theoretic" and "power-theoretic". The former engages the familiar mode of policy analysis which analyses a given situation in terms of its implications for policy choices; the latter focuses on the political factors, in both state and economy, which condition the feasibility of policy alternatives. We start from the assumption that any sensible analysis of the Chinese reform process must address both these questions, both what is desirable and what is (or what can be made) possible.

In our 'choice-theoretic' mode, we have been guided, first, by three broad analytical frameworks, or paradigms, each of which we feel throws considerable light on the theoretical and practical issues at hand, albeit from different directions and with different results. These paradigms have been available to, and influential in, Chinese policy-making circles in the 1980s. We are labelling these "market socialism", "finance and development" and "the NIC model of late development". Though these paradigms will be developed in detail in Chapter 2, a brief outline is in order here.

By 'market socialism' we mean a specific paradigm of economic reform which emerged in the state socialist countries of east/central Europe in the 1950s and 1960s (though its ancestry goes back to pre-war intellectual debates in Western Europe). This paradigm provided a critique of the traditional Soviet-type system of directive central planning and represented an attempt to move socialist economies in a more rational and productive direction by introducing market mechanisms of various kinds. The paradigm was broadly adopted by Chinese reformers in the late 1970s (though there had been interest much earlier, in the early 1960s) in their attempt to construct a "socialist commodity economy". Situating our study of China within this paradigm directs our attention to the state socialist countries as a comparable family of cases and to the experience of similar attempts at theorising and attempting reform in other socialist contexts (though with the exception of Hungary and the very special case of Yugoslavia, 'market socialism' did not get much of an airing in east/central Europe until it was far too late). In relation to financial reform, the advocates of 'market socialism' have varied in their notions of policy innovation, but the general thrust has been towards some form of financial liberalisation involving the freeing of financial flows from state controls. In place of state controls, an increasingly diversified system of financial institutions and assets was advocated together with an increasing use of market mechanisms and competition to stimulate greater efficiency and effectiveness in the generation, circulation and use of financial resources. Greater openness to, and integration with, the international financial system was also advocated.

The term 'finance and development' refers to that paradigm which has guided thought and action in international development circles and agencies on the question of the relationship between financial systems and economic development over the past decade or more. Its exponents drew on the intellectual tradition of neo-classical economics to develop a critique of policies and institutions adopted by many Third World governments in the 1960s and 1970s which, they argued, created "financial repression" with damaging effects on developmental performance. The solution was some form of thoroughgoing financial liberalisation, a programmatic prescription which became virtual orthodoxy in the 1980s and part of the stock-in-trade of the international financial institutions and major Western aid donors in their advice and ministrations to Third World countries. Though this paradigm shares many policy prescriptions with 'market socialism', it is distinctive in that first, it reflects the outlook, experience and interests of the major Western economies, particularly the U.S. and the U.K.; second, and in consequence, it explicitly or implicitly operates in terms of some kind of 'transition' to financial systems which share the characteristics of those in the advanced capitalist nations; third, and in consequence, in a context of a state socialist country, its policy prescriptions would be more radical than those of most advocates of 'market socialism', ultimately involving large-scale privatisation of financial institutions, the establishment of fully fledged markets in credit and capital and the eradication of barriers between the domestic and international financial systems.

The 'NIC model of late development' refers to the analytical tradition of 'late development', which is seen most clearly in the work of Gerschenkron (1962) but also in the earlier work of Friedrich List (1885) and is derived from the experience of the first generation of late industrialisers in continental Europe in the latter half of the nineteenth century. The argument is that 'late developers' and even more so the 'late late developers' of the post–World War II post-colonial world have adopted, and indeed should adopt, certain strategic policies and distinctive political/economic institutions if they wish to develop in an international context already dominated by earlier waves of developers. This implies the explicit adoption of policies which displace, shape or otherwise manage markets in pursuit of a strategic national economic interest in an institutional context in which the degree of state involvement in the economy is high and the relationship between state and economy is much more organic, more 'hands on' than that prescribed by liberal economics. In practical terms, the most recent expression of successful 'late development' is that of the East Asian newly industrialising countries (NICs), notably Taiwan and South Korea, which have adopted in different forms the central institutional and policy features of the 'late development' model, to spectacular effect. Though this model shares some characteristics with 'market socialism' to the extent that the latter allows for the continuation of national planning, it differs decisively from the finance and development paradigm in that it insists on the responsibility of the state to intervene massively and directly in the domestic financial system to direct flows of capital in strategically desired directions and to mediate between the domestic and international financial systems in ways which maximise the benefits and minimise the costs of the latter in relation to the national economic interest.

Thus a choice between financial systems reflects a broader choice between alternative development strategies. The logical culmination of prescriptions derived from the finance and development paradigm is a market-based developmental path which drastically curtails the role of the state in the allocation of domestic financial resources and allows increasing and unimpeded interdependence with the international economy. In their different ways, the other two paradigms point to strategies which embody a crucial steering role for the state in the context of a synergetic relationship between state and market in the domestic economy and greater management of relations with the international economy in pursuit of some conception of the national economic interest.

In addition to identifying these three broad paradigms, we have also found another, more precise intellectual triad useful in clarifying our thoughts about financial systems and financial reform. This is a distinction among three institutional models of a financial system made by Zysman (1983): first, a capital market–based system along Anglo-American lines which involves a competitive diversity of financial institutions and in which equity markets play an important role; second, a state-directed credit-based system along French, Japanese and Italian lines in which governments intervene directly to determine the prices of money and to direct credit in desired directions; third, an institution-directed credit-based system along German lines in which an oligopoly of large financial institutions, private or public (usually big banks), run the financial system without reliance on state support or subordination to state controls.

Though Zysman's classification is based on advanced capitalist economies, the clarification of these three models is salutary from the point of view of policy choice in the sense that it helps us to go beyond mere reliance on the conventional distinction between state and market in classifying economic systems. Leaving aside any putatively wide institutional difference between financial systems in a state-controlled 'socialist' and a market-based capitalist system, there exists a wide range of institutional possibilities within the framework of a basically private enterprise, market economy; in other words, there are several alternative institutional futures to which capitalist developing countries may evolve. Moreover, the institutional arrangements of these types of financial systems bear a correspondence with the broader paradigms outlined previously. The finance and development literature, with its emphasis on the diversification of financial assets and institutions and the development of financial markets, tends to suggest that the capital market–based financial system is most appropriate for developing countries; to the contrary, the NIC model of late development is consistent primarily with the state-directed credit-based system. The market socialist paradigm, though more vague, hypothetical and open-ended in nature, with a wide range of internal variation (more 'radical' and more 'conservative' variants), would seem to fall somewhere between these two.

Moving now to our 'power-theoretic' perspective, we wish to analyse China's financial reforms through a 'political economy' perspective which recognises the inextricability of politics and economics in the real world of policy and institutions and tries to identify and explain the specific ways in which they interact to promote or inhibit policy reform and institutional change. By *politics*, we do not refer solely to the actions or effects of governments, states or political systems. Rather the *political* element of *political economy* is defined in terms of the nature of, and interaction between, actors—individual, group or institutional—which are endowed with the power to affect social outcomes and which are situated in both the political and economic systems. From this perspective, an industrial enterprise or a bank is as much a 'political' actor as a government agency or a member of the Chinese Communist Party's Politburo, even though the exercise by each of its power and the pursuit of its institutional interests and objectives may take an 'economic' form.

Thus, the individual and institutional purveyors of 'politically neutral' policy analysis and advice, however strong their claim to objectivity and however technical their methods, figure as one element in the political equation, often with substantial influence and effect (Woolley [1984: p. 9] discusses this relationship between the realms of technical and "ordinary political discourse" in the arena of monetary politics in the context of the United States). While the discourse of econocrats commonly has its own implicit ideological character, political conflict between individuals and groups in the higher reaches of the Chinese Communist Party (CCP) carries a strongly explicit ideological tinge which cannot be reduced to a mere clash of interests or jockeying for power. This latter ideological dimension is all the more crucial because China is an 'ideocratic' polity in the sense that there is an official political orthodoxy, known as Marxism-Leninism-Mao Zedong thought, which, in theory at least, supplies the regime with its legitimacy and justifies the existing economic and political systems (for an analysis of the role of ideology in the Chinese reforms, see White 1993: ch. 5). Ideological differences between key sections of the top Communist leadership have played an important role in the process of financial reform in China. Thus the ideological factor, in both the previous senses, is an important element in our broad political economy approach.

From this general perspective, the financial reforms, like other areas of reform policy, involve complex processes of conflict, accommodation and pressure between ideas, interests and institutions in both polity and economy, which structure policy agendas, condition policy outcomes and push institutional changes in certain directions. We shall endeavour to demonstrate that this approach helps us to understand both the process of and the prospects for financial reform, combining an ability to explain with an ability to predict and prescribe. Without an explicit sensitivity to the political economy of the policy process (sadly lacking in much of the recent literature on central-eastern Europe and the former Soviet Union), policy prescriptions—however intellectually sound or technically proficient—may not be worth the paper they are written on.

We proceed as follows. In Chapter 2 we analyse the three paradigms and institutional models briefly outlined in this introduction and demonstrate their relevance to an understanding of China's financial reforms. In Chapter 3, we set the scene for our analysis of the Chinese reforms by providing an account of the structure and development of China's financial system during the pre-reform period 1949–1978. The chapter concludes with a brief discussion of the structure and performance of the economy during this period, which provides the background for the watershed decision of the Chinese Communist Party Central Committee's Third Plenum in 1978 to reform the previous economic system by introducing market mechanisms and opening more widely to the world outside. In Chapter 4 we analyse the reform of the Chinese financial system from 1979 to 1992. We see how the reforms passed through three major phases, from 1979 to 1984, 1985 to 1988 and 1988 to 1992. The first phase was guided by a moderate version of 'market socialism' and mainly involved structural changes in the state banking system. The second phase expanded the parameters of reform to countenance a move towards something approximating financial markets. Financial liberalisation moved rapidly in this second phase, including the introduction of bond and share markets, the beginnings of a money market, increasing competition between banks and a proliferation of non-bank financial institutions. The third phase involved a slowing down and partial reversion of the reform process, apparently ending with a new surge of reform stimulated by the dramatic intervention of Deng Xiaoping in early 1992. In Chapter 5 we focus our analysis more precisely on the macroeconomic and microeconomic effects of the reforms: first, by examining the causes of the alarming inflationary surge of 1988–1989 and second, by attempting to assess the impact of financial reforms on the behaviour of state enterprises. In Chapter 6, we focus on one particular component of financial reform with a detailed analysis of the introduction of bonds and shares.

The use of the political economy approach in Chapters 4–6 reveals the extent to which the dynamics of financial reform has been conditioned by a complex interplay of political and economic pressures. It also illustrates the wide range of issues generated by financial reform: technical issues—for example, just how do capital markets act as a disciplinary device on enterprises?; ideological issues concerning the nature of a 'socialist' financial system, such as the problem of unearned income from share ownership or the relationship between share issues and privatisation; issues of economic management concerning, for example, the way in which a central bank can control monetary aggregates by indirect rather than direct methods; political issues concerning the relationship between the financial system and the planning and fiscal agencies, or conflicts between central and local governments; and developmental issues concerning the respective roles of state and market regulation in the development process.

In 1992 China launched yet another leap forward in the overall economic reform process. Writing in late 1992, we are concerned to inquire into the likely future trajectory of financial reform and ask how one can assess the viability of hypothetical alternatives in policy reform and institutional change. In the concluding Chapter 7, we attempt some answers to these questions by assessing the experience of financial reform in China in the light of the three analytical paradigms of 'market socialism', 'finance and development' and 'the NIC model of late development'. At a very general level, we would argue that the future trajectory of policy choice between alternatives for financial reform will be determined not merely by the intellectual force of the arguments embodied in each paradigm but also by the political forces which benefit from, agree with and are willing to push each set of arguments. We believe that it is possible to construct a feasible—both politically and economically—course of financial reform which, by drawing on key elements of the 'market socialist' and 'late development' paradigms, could produce the type of economic performance which China, as a reforming socialist economy, is searching for. Such a solution requires significant institutional change in the financial sector as well as complementary reforms in other sectors. We discuss, in broad terms, what this might entail in Chapter 7.

In making proposals for reforming the financial system, we concentrate on elucidating the kinds of institutional arrangements which can tackle the two basic problems which face financial reform: inflation and the soft credit constraint. At the macro-level, the key issues involve the position of the central bank and the competitiveness of the financial system as a whole. On the first issue, we express reservations about the relevance of the conventional argument in favour of an "independent" central bank on both analytical and empirical grounds, drawing on both Chinese and comparative evidence. It is our view that whilst there is a strong case for increasing the range of decisional autonomy enjoyed by the central bank, the position of China as a late developer faced by mammoth socio-economic challenges and bent on achieving multiple national and sectoral priorities requires that the central government retain sufficient power over the central bank to ensure a financial system capable of implementing strategic developmental objectives. This arrangement, which bears comparison with other East Asian NICs such as South Korea and Taiwan, would rest on an agreed division of labour among, and institutionalised relationships between, the central bank and other major central agencies and would be mediated by the national political and governmental leadership. On the second macro-issue of competitiveness of the financial system, we conclude that although a move towards a more market-oriented financial system is clearly desirable in the Chinese context, China's character as a socialist late developer requires that this should be conditional upon retaining the predominance of some form of social ownership and preserving the capacity of the developmental state. These requirements suggest that the role of capital markets should be relatively limited and that non-competitively determined policy loans should continue, albeit on a different basis.

The issue of improving microeconomic performance relates to changes in the relationship between banks and enterprises, specifically the way in which the soft credit constraint can be hardened to improve enterprise productivity. In contrast to the common argument that this can only be achieved by privatisation (of both banks and enterprises), we argue that these goals can be achieved through ownership reform short of outright privatisation (on some form of joint-stock or "public share" basis). This alternative type of ownership reform will expose enterprises more directly to market pressures and, where subsidies continue to be offered, will restructure the relationship between the state and enterprises in such a way as to enable the former to set and enforce performance standards over recipient enterprises. This approach would also require a more autonomous and commercially oriented banking system, which can also be reached through some form of ownership reform (for example, a joint-stock or "public share" system for the state specialised banks and a truly—as opposed to nominally—cooperative system for current rural and urban credit cooperatives).

This possible future trajectory for China's financial reforms draws upon elements of the 'market socialist' and 'late development' paradigms and, together with complimentary reforms, might enable China to achieve the economic and developmental results which a socialist developing economy seeks.

However, we recognise that this scenario is only one of a number of possible outcomes. It is our assessment that over the past fifteen years, the political impetus behind distinctively 'socialist' economic institutions has waned, the power of 'finance and development'–type arguments has waxed and the adherence of Chinese governments, both central and local, to the political and institutional mechanisms of 'late development' has remained very strong. This suggests, therefore, that a contest between the latter two paradigms and the political forces which support them is also possible, indeed likely. This contest, which can also be detected in other East Asian contexts such as South Korea, is rooted in the fundamental issues of how market institutions and state action can be combined productively in the context of 'late development' and the extent to which the dictates of 'late development' in a country like China are consistent with the wholesale liberalisation envisaged by the 'finance and development' paradigm.

2

Market Socialism, Financial Liberalisation and Late Development

THE THREE ANALYTICAL PARADIGMS introduced in Chapter 1 are being used here because each tells us something distinctive about Chinese financial reform. The 'market socialist' framework implies that although the reforms are to involve a (contestable) degree of liberalisation, this is to be undertaken within some kind of socialist political and institutional shell. This means that to the extent that market institutions are introduced, they either carry a 'socialist' element within them (for example, the fact that enterprises operating in the market are publicly or socially owned in some sense) or are to be circumscribed by some form of 'socialist' control and regulation through the plan or through policy provisions such as the maintenance of full employment. This was the basic assumption underlying the post-Mao reform programme from the start, when reformers drew on the ideas and experience of market socialist theorists and experiments in east/central Europe. As of the early 1990s, there are clearly policy-makers in China, particularly towards the more conservative end of the reform spectrum, who hold that this is both desirable and feasible.

By contrast, the 'finance and development' paradigm, and its main programmatic message, financial liberalisation, while proclaimedly system-neutral and therefore applicable across the socialist-capitalist divide, carries within it the basic elements of an ultimately capitalist financial system based on competitive financial markets and private ownership of financial assets and institutions. This kind of thinking resonates among Chinese policy-makers and analysts in two very different ways. More conservative or centrist reformers adopt a traditional Chinese approach by arguing that the 'rational' aspects of foreign (predominantly Western) economic practices can be incorporated within the Chinese system without changing the system's basic institutional and political features; this is a contemporary version of the Qing dynasty's attempt in the late nineteenth century to incorporate foreign ideas and techniques for 'use' while retaining the Chinese 'essence'. There is a strong element of this in the economic thinking of Deng Xiaoping, and it is an important element of the conservative reformism of the post–June 4 incident leadership of Jiang Zemin and Li Peng. From this point of view, there is no incompatibility between market socialism and financial liberalisation. However, more radical reformers, particularly economists as opposed to officials and younger as opposed to older economists, have shown greater enthusiasm for the 'finance and development' message and greater willingness to follow its institutional implications through to their ultimate conclusion— a financial system based on fully fledged market competition and private ownership and fully integrated into the international financial system. In a nutshell, they are willing to sponsor a transition to capitalism, thereby moving outside the market socialist framework entirely.

The 'late development' paradigm has been both an implicit and explicit element of the thinking of Chinese elites, both official and non-official, since at least the late nineteenth century and continues to be highly influential today. It is connected with the widespread perception by the Chinese that their nation has been subjected to humiliations and oppression in the past and has still not fully recovered its deserved pride, that China is a potential great power that has still not gained its deserved position in the world, that it has been overtaken by otherwise unworthy competitors such as South Korea and Japan (not to mention the old enemy, the Kuomintang, in Taiwan) and that the constraints on national success lie in the country's economic and cultural backwardness and in the potentially negative impact of foreign powers and the international economy. These are the elements of the 'late development' paradigm, a combination of economic nationalism and the consequent desire to telescope the growth process to catch up with the more advanced nations. This combination is probably the most fundamental reason for the appeal of the Stalinist model of state socialism in the late 1940s. This deep-seated perception is a fundamental element of the Chinese situation and, as in the South Korean and Japanese cases, is not likely to dissipate in the short term. This perspective therefore has important implications for the concrete nature and trajectory of financial reform, particularly in relation to the issue of state control over the financial system.

Let us now begin the main task of this chapter—to analyse the paradigms in more depth and trace their implications for financial reform in China.

Market Socialism:
Towards a "Planned Commodity Economy"

Though the market-socialist paradigm first began to exert a widespread influence on policy in east/central Europe in the 1960s, it had intellectual antecedents in the 'socialist calculation debate' of the 1920s–1930s.[1] Since this debate was important for providing an intellectual precedent for later versions of market socialism, we will discuss it briefly here.

The Socialist Calculation Debate

The calculation debate is normally associated with the names of Lange, Lerner and Taylor on the socialist side and von Mises and Hayek on the opposing side, although numerous others also made contributions on both sides of the argument.[2] The central challenge to socialist economics came from von Mises in a 1920 essay which argued that socialism could not operate as an efficient economic system, since it had no markets, and hence no prices, on which to base decisions concerning the allocation of scarce resources. Of course, central planners could set prices, but such prices, in the absence of markets, were arbitrary in the sense that they did not reflect relative scarcities.

This challenge was met by Lange in his article "On the Economic Theory of Socialism".[3] Lange's model was based on state ownership of the means of production and contained markets for consumer goods and labour but not for means of production. Lange argued that when socialist central planners allocated non-traded capital goods, it was

---

1. See Swain (1992: p. 4). There has also been a substantial literature on the case for market socialism as applied to advanced capitalist economies. See, for example, Le Grand and Estrin (1989). We do not consider this literature here.

2. On the socialist side of the debate Dickinson, Enrico Barone, Eduard Heimann and Karl Polanyi all made contributions to the theory of market socialism. Other contributors were the philosopher Otto Neurath and the economists Maurice Dobb, Baran, Bettelheim and Paul Sweezy. See Blackburn (1991: p. 32). For a review of these and German and Soviet discussions on similar themes, see also Brus (1972: ch. 2). The critique of socialism came predominantly from von Mises, Hayek and Robbins. For detailed treatments of the debate, see Bergson (1949) and Lavoie (1985).

3. Originally printed in the *Review of Economic Studies* and reprinted in Lange and Taylor (1970).

possible for them to construct shadow prices, which enterprise managers would act upon to choose input combinations and the scale of output in ways which would be consistent with economic efficiency. Correct (i.e., equilibrium) shadow prices would be calculated by the Central Planning Board (CPB) by a trial and error process comparable to Walrasian *tatonnement,* the CPB playing a role analogous to the auctioneer in the Walrasian system. This meant that capitalism and socialism reached the same equilibrium by different means; why then would anyone prefer socialism? Lange's response was that socialism was superior to capitalism in several ways. First, the distribution of wealth and income was more equitable thanks to social ownership of the means of production and the fact that individuals would receive a share of the "social dividend" as a return from common ownership of the means of production, payable either as individual income or as collective goods such as education. Second, a socialist economy would be able to take account of *all* of the costs of production in determining the optimal allocation of output and would therefore take account of externalities and factors such as worker health and security. Third, a socialist economy could avoid the business cycle by being able to prevent the multiplier effects arising from unstable private investment decisions. Fourth, in comparing capitalism and socialism, Lange argued that actual capitalist systems were not perfectly competitive but were dominated by oligopoly and monopoly, with the result that markets would be far more competitive in a socialist economy.

The role of the financial system and financial markets is given little attention in this model and can only be inferred. Lange (1970: p. 84) does mention that a socialized banking sector would exist and that its functions would include lending to enterprises. However, it is clear that the banking system is subsumed under the state apparatus responsible to the CPB. The CPB sets the interest rate which ensures equilibrium between the demand and supply of capital; the responsibility of the banking system is to administer deposits and loans. Presumably, the latter are allocated to enterprises on the basis of their output decisions derived from certain behaviourial rules imposed by the CPB[4] and in response to prices set by the CPB.

Lange's model, even if it did not provide anything amounting to a comprehensive and practical blueprint for a market socialist economy, was important in creating an intellectual environment within

---

4. There are two basic rules: (i) that the choice of inputs must be used which minimises the costs of production and (ii) that marginal cost must be equal to price (Lange 1970: p. 75).

which the use of a market in a socialist economy could be contemplated.[5] It has also acted as a benchmark (for example, see Kornai 1986b) to assess the content of the reforms of those countries pursuing market socialism in the 1960s and 1970s, an experience to which we now turn.

Reform Experience in East/Central Europe in the 1960s and 1970s: The Blueprints

Market socialism as proposed by Lange was a purely theoretical construct. From the 1960s on, market socialism entered the policy agenda in east/central Europe, notably in Hungary. Unlike Czechoslovakia, where the reform experiment was squashed by Soviet intervention in 1968, Hungary was able to sustain the experiment until the late 1980s, albeit unevenly and with limited success. The Hungarian experience with market socialism is well known and will not detain us here (see Swain 1992). Rather we concentrate on the changes within the paradigm of market socialism, particularly as they relate to the financial system, in the east-central European context during the 1970s and 1980s. One can detect two distinct versions, sub-paradigms, and an accelerated transition between the two as the economic and political problems of state socialism in east/central Europe gathered pace in the mid-late 1980s.

The intellectual blueprints for the earlier, more moderate, version of market socialism—which we will call MSI—were provided by economists such as Brus in (and later outside) Poland and by those who designed the New Economic Mechanism (NEM) in Hungary. Brus's book *The Market in a Socialist Economy* (1972) was a pioneering attempt to justify and explain the use of the market mechanism in a socialist economy; however, his work was not heeded by policy-makers in his native Poland. Brus proposed the development of a "planned economy with a built-in market mechanism", in which the central plan would have 'primacy' and the market (rather than direct administrative orders) would be used as a way of fulfilling the plan. Central planners would continue to make the major macroeconomic decisions which would regulate the structure and growth of the economy (1972: p. 139). Enterprises would have some autonomy to operate within these general guidelines according to profit-maximising rules. Profit performance acts as a guide for the allocation of investment re-

---

5. Brus and Laski (1989: p. 59) argue that "the interwar debate certainly had the merit of advancing the idea of an alternative to the command system, as well as of showing how ill-founded was the traditional Marxist belief in the possibility of rational allocation without prices reflecting scarcities."

sources between enterprises in the same industry; the more profitable enterprises would expect to expand at the expense of the less profitable. The size of any particular industry and the industrial structure as a whole, however, would continue to be determined by the central plan. Thus, the role of the banks would be to lend to sectors in accordance with central planning priorities and to enterprises according to the principle of selectivity. Investment expenditures would be controlled hierarchically from the centre, and the model does not permit "free direct flow of capital between enterprises or branches" (1972: p. 142).

Such an economic system would be an improvement over the centrally planned model, Brus argued, because the market would provide competitive pressures for the production of those goods in the highest demand, would provide incentives for the lowering of costs and would lead to the full utilisation of inputs, rather than the concealment and stockpiling of inputs, which characterised enterprise behaviour under the centrally planned system. But the market element in this model is still subsidiary; in Brus's words, the market was not "a connection between independent capitalist enterprises, but a means for the realisation of the primary aims of the plan" (1972: p. 185). Markets are confined to the circulation of goods, not capital, and the basic actors in the system are enterprises under state ownership; in this respect, Brus's market socialist blueprint clearly reflected the influence of Lange's earlier theoretical work.

Brus's model was influential in the design of Hungary's "New Economic Mechanism". According to those who proposed the NEM, the aim was to create an economic system in which

> the national economic plan establishes the main objectives of the national economy . . . and determines the allocation of resources available for their realisation. In the new system of national economic control *this function of the plan is combined with the function of the socialist market.* This combination makes it possible to obtain a truer picture about the partial processes going on in the economy, about the perpetually changing needs of society and, especially, of the individual consumers, than we were able to obtain in the past. (Friss 1969: p. 12, emphasis in original)

While the central authorities were to retain control over the structure and growth of the economy, detailed plan targets would no longer be issued to enterprises; enterprises were to act as profit-maximising competitors within their particular industry. Thus there was an attempt to define a complementary division of labour between plan and market whereby the operation of the latter would enhance the efficiency of the former.

Whilst enterprises were given greater autonomy, the state still had considerable economic power, which could be exercised through six basic policies regulating prices, incomes, investment, credit, fiscal flows and foreign trade (Friss 1969: pp. 18–21). Credit and investment policies are of particular interest to us here. Credit policy was to be reformed so that the "hitherto essentially automatic granting of credits (up to the limits established by the plan)" (Sulyok 1969: p. 164) under the old system would be replaced with an allocation system more responsive to efficiency (profit) criteria. The banks were the key agents in this respect and their ability to exercise selectivity in the allocation of credit to enterprises was a crucial factor in determining the success of the reforms.

But bank credit was only one source of finance for enterprises; the others were retained profits and state budget allocations. The roles of these three sources of enterprise finance were defined as follows. Funds were divided into three parts: short term, medium term and long term. Short-term funds were for working capital, and it was considered desirable that enterprises should only finance 60–70 per cent of their working capital from their own sources and rely on bank credit for the remainder. This gave the banks some power to allocate credit selectively according to the relative performance of enterprises. Bank credit would thus play a double function—as an instrument to both attain plan objectives and stimulate enterprise efficiency in a market context (Sulyok 1969: p. 175).

With respect to medium-term (up to 3 years) and long-term (up to 6 years) investment funds, a complex system was envisaged. Nonproductive investment would be financed entirely by allocations from the state (or local government) budgets. Productive investment sponsored by the central or local authorities would be financed by state loans (subject to interest payments) or a combination of state loans and state budget allocations. Enterprise investment, which was to account for approximately 40 per cent of total investment, was to be decided by the enterprises themselves in response to market opportunities. However, only half of such investment was to be funded by the enterprise itself out of its development fund, with the rest being provided by bank credit. Here again, banks were to exercise selectivity based on the criterion of profitability.

The following picture thus emerges. Enterprises were to compete with each other in a market environment. Goods would compete with each other for purchasers, and enterprises would compete with each other for labour. Enterprises would find it necessary, however, to rely on bank credit to finance their day-to-day operations and the expansion of their activities over the longer term. In this way, the banks were theoretically placed in a powerful position to monitor and influence enterprise expansion and allocate resources on profitability criteria, given central direction over sectoral priorities. Other investment was undertaken directly by the state, and here the banks would operate under the old system of granting credits in accordance with central or local state plans. Thus, credit and investment policy were important areas where the state continued to exercise control over the economy.

Both Brus's model and the NEM are MSI models of partial financial reform. First, the monobank structure is retained by both and there is no role for competition in the banking system or in the development of other financial institutions. Second, while banks and enterprises have greater control over the allocation and use of financial resources, the state still maintains powerful controls over investment through budgetary allocation, control over bank lending policies and restrictions over the enterprise's use of its own retained funds or ability to raise funds outside of the banking system. In consequence, both banks and enterprises are heavily constrained by the priorities established by the central planners. The innovations of MSI in the financial sphere are first, that enterprises are now judged in part by their performance in the market rather than solely by their fulfilment of the plan and second, that the previous practice of extending credit indiscriminately is to be replaced by greater selectivity in credit allocation.

It is now generally acknowledged that the results of the market socialist experiments based upon this early model were disappointing. Whilst there has been much work evaluating the results of the Hungarian reform mechanism in all its aspects, we shall restrict our comments to those concerning the operation of the financial system. Perhaps the most persistent critic of the Hungarian reform process has been Kornai, who argues that the attempt to improve economic efficiency by integrating plan and market simply created a "dual dependence" for enterprises, dependence partly on the market and partly on the central authorities, with the latter dependence significantly outweighing the former (Kornai 1986b: p. 1725). Instead of operating according to a market logic, enterprises continued to operate according to the logic of a shortage economy, exhibiting an insatiable demand for inputs. The soft budget constraint, and all of its constituent elements, continued to exist (see also Brada and Dobozi 1989: p. 8). With respect to the financial system and the soft credit constraint, Kornai argued in 1986 that

> Hungary has a highly centralized monetary system. There is permanent excess demand for credit. The banking sector, except for new institutions . . . , acts as a credit-rationing administrative authority and not as a genuine bank following commercial principles. It is strongly connected with the planners' and the other authorities' supervision of state-owned

firms. Granting or denying credit is almost uncorrelated with the past or present profitability and credit worthiness of the firm. To some extent, the opposite relationship is true. The credit system is used frequently to bail out firms failing on the market. (1986b: p. 1696)

This assessment is also supported by Tardos, who argues that as of the early 1980s after further financial reforms had taken place, "the financial authorities (the Post Office, the National Bank of Hungary, the state budget) continued to help the low efficiency, loss-making firms or those struggling with liquidity problems. Thus, despite promises and pledges, money and the pressure of solvent demand have not become determinant in the life of enterprises" (Tardos 1989: p. 25). Similarly, Sokil argues that "under the NEM, the institutions of the capital market were changed, and enterprises' financial autonomy increased only to a very limited extent. . . . The untouched centralized monobank system remained as a safeguard for predominantly centralized investment decisions" (Sokil 1989: pp. 59–60).

In practice, the competitive pressures created by this first version of market socialism turned out to be weak. The state exercised considerable control over enterprises, and the financial system was one of the main channels through which state control was exercised. Reform of the financial system, therefore, became a focal point for renewed reform efforts in the 1980s and provided part of the impetus for a broadening of the original concept of market socialism to embrace a more comprehensive extension of the market mechanism into the financial sphere.

The Experience of Market Socialism in the 1980s and the Rise of MSII: Enter Financial Markets

The disappointing economic results of the market socialist experiments of the 1960s and 1970s led to demands in the 1980s that economic reform needed to be pushed much further by expanding enterprise autonomy and extending the operation of the market. While in part this reflected a recognition that markets in products had not been pushed far enough, the critique extended beyond product markets. It was now argued that one of the key prerequisites for genuine enterprise autonomy and real competition in product markets was reform of the financial system and the extension of the market to include capital, both physical and financial. This represented a significant departure from the previous market socialist blueprint. As Nuti stated in 1989, "The role of money and financial institutions under market socialism has been conspicuously neglected both in the classical literature on market socialism and—until very recently—in the blueprints for economic reform in Eastern Europe" (p. 433).

In the Hungarian context, the need for financial markets was advanced by Tardos. He argued that the development of financial markets was "a precondition of enterprise autonomy" (1989: p. 25), since it would be a major factor in forcing enterprises to use their autonomy in ways consistent with profit maximisation. Similarly Sokil (1989: p. 54) argued that a main task facing Hungarian reformers in the 1980s was to "create the institutional structures of the market system in factor markets. . . . [A] precondition for the operation of a free market mechanism in factor markets is that households as suppliers, and enterprises as final demanders of labour and capital resources, interact directly, with minimal central intervention."

The case for the introduction of financial markets into market socialist economies has perhaps been made most forcefully by Brus and Laski (1989).[6] Their starting point is that

> the experience of market-oriented economic reforms in some of the countries of 'real socialism', as well as of normative theories underlying these reforms, has shown that the half-way house of a product market alone, especially without a capital market, has failed to bring about the desired change from bureaucratic to market regulation and hence to provide the answer to the problems of inefficiency plaguing socialist economies. (1989: p. 105)

MSI attempted to encourage competition in the consumer goods industries by giving enterprises the right to make production decisions concerning input mix, marketing, the use of profits and so on. Meanwhile, the volume and direction of investment was still left under the control of the planners. Indeed, this accorded with one of the central claims of socialism, namely that planning could solve the instability of capitalist economies by guaranteeing the level of investment and hence guarantee full employment and crisis-free growth as well as lead to a more desirable structure of output tailored to meeting social needs.

Brus and Laski argued that a *sine qua non* of any market socialist economy is the operation of a "capital market", defined broadly as a "mechanism of horizontal reallocation of savings through transactions between the savers and the investors in productive assets" (1989: p. 106). This is necessary, they argued, in order to allow industry entry and exit, the expansion and contraction of existing firms and the restructuring of existing productive units, all without the influence of the planning authorities. If the state still controls the allocation of financial resources, product market competition can be effec-

---

6. The discussion of Brus and Laski draws upon Bowles, MacLean and Setterfield (1992).

tively undermined by a credit allocation system which protects enterprises from the consequences of poor performance in product markets. The state, through its control of the financial system, is able to subsidise whom it wishes, and the soft budget constraint continues despite a degree of product market competition. The task, therefore, was to reform the financial system and make it a market-oriented rather than a bureaucratic-oriented system.

It is clear that the introduction of the market mechanism into the financial sphere requires some major changes in the financial system. Reform of the banking system involves setting up a two-tier banking system to replace the monobank system (the latter will be discussed in detail in Chapter 3). That is to say, a system combining a central bank and branch banking is required in which the central bank has the responsibility for overseeing the overall development of the financial system and, among other objectives, for maintaining price stability. This, in turn, requires the establishment of reserve ratios and other measures of credit and liquidity control which will enable the central bank to control the branch-banking system. The central bank is responsible for money creation and has some autonomy from the government; in order to preserve price stability, it is desirable that the central bank be insulated from political pressures and the necessity of automatically financing government budget deficits through money creation. This restructuring of the socialist banking system is the reverse of the experience of the advanced capitalist economies. In the latter, central banks developed as a result of a perceived need to regulate an existing banking sector and act as a lender of last resort to provide stability and ensure public confidence in the banking and financial system; in the reforming socialist economies, the central bank must lead rather than follow the development of a banking system.

The idea behind the establishment of a competitive branch-banking system is that savers and borrowers will be more efficiently matched and that credit will be extended on profit criteria. This means that banks must develop a variety of deposits representing different terms and possibly different risks for savers and a correspondingly more varied loan structure. Thus banks must manage different term structures and spread risk. Since banks are themselves expected to be profit-seeking agents, they must distribute loans according to the profitability of enterprises. Thus, the old monobank system, whereby banks attract savings (with usually only a limited range of terms available) and where enterprise surpluses are transferred directly to the central budget and redistributed according to the plan, is replaced by a more decentralised and diversified system in which banks play an active role. Other non-bank financial institutions (NBFIs) such as insurance companies may also play a role in this process, as might joint venture and foreign banks, although the activities of the latter might be restricted to dealings with foreign-owned companies.

During the 1980s, even before the dramatic events of 1989–1990, some of the socialist countries embarked upon the reform of their financial systems. Banking reforms, and a two-tier banking system, were introduced in Bulgaria in 1987, Hungary in 1987, the Soviet Union in 1988 and Poland in 1989. (See Nuti 1990; Corbett and Mayer 1991.) In Bulgaria, 59 former branches of the National Bank of Bulgaria (now the central bank) were set up as commercial banks, in addition to the Bulgarian Foreign Trade Bank, the State Savings Bank and eight older commercial banks. In Hungary, the National Bank was made into a central bank in 1987 at the same time that five commercial banks were established. The latter were not allowed to attract deposits from households, a function which remained the responsibility of the National Savings Bank and the network of savings cooperatives (see Bacskai 1989: pp. 90–91). The National Bank of Poland (NBP) was made the central bank in 1989, and nine commercial banks were established to replace the former regional branches of the NBP. In Yugoslavia, a two-tier banking system already existed but was reformed with the intention of making the banks more profit-oriented, a necessary measure because it was estimated that "at least 35 to 40 percent of total banking assets are more or less nonperforming" (Gaspari 1990: p. 73).

In addition to supporting these reforms in the banking system, MSII also envisaged an increase in the use of other financial assets and the development of other financial markets. For example, government bonds would become more prominent as a device for the non-inflationary financing of government deficits. Enterprise bonds could be issued to allow for the direct flow of resources between the household and enterprise sectors and between enterprises. These instruments allow for a more flexible and efficient allocation of financial resources between sectors and enterprises. The existence of a competitive market for enterprise finance would, it was hoped, improve the efficiency with which enterprises allocated resources and stimulate technical and product innovation (provided, of course, that competitive products and labour markets also existed).

The possibility also existed for the issue of enterprise shares, raising the possibility of enterprise formation, mergers and takeovers based on market criteria rather than on bureaucratic initiative. This requires some form of share ownership system which may or may not involve individual share ownership. The use of bonds and shares may be limited to primary trading or may be extended to secondary markets.

Indeed, some socialist countries had begun experimenting with bond and share markets during the 1980s. Bond markets were introduced in Hungary, Poland and the USSR; share markets were introduced in Hungary (see Jarai 1989). The question of whether the financial system under reformed socialism should include a stock market was a matter for debate in the east/central European literature. The existence of shares obviously raises fundamental questions about the nature of social ownership and the class composition of the economy, yet it was envisaged that 'socialist shares' might have characteristics different from their capitalist counterparts: For example, the principle of social ownership might require a majority of shares to be owned by public bodies. Yet if individual minority-share ownership was permitted, the spread of 'unearned income' would mark a clear departure from the basic socialist principle of 'distribution according to work'. In addition to these political aspects of share-holding, there are also economic controversies regarding the case for stock markets. In part, this arises because capitalist economies vary considerably from the Japanese and German financial systems, which are dominated by bank finance, and the U.S. and British systems in which equity plays a more significant role. Even where stock markets do play a significant role in raising resources for firms, however, there is still serious doubt as to how far they act to enforce firm efficiency. We will return to some of these political and economic issues in our discussion of the Chinese reforms in Chapter 6.

These theoretical niceties aside, the dramatic political changes which occurred between 1989 and 1991 have changed the economic and political landscape of east/central Europe and the former Soviet Union. The project of 'market socialism' in any form has been abandoned, and post-socialist countries are engaged in various forms of 'transition to capitalism' guided by somewhat undigested, Polly-annaish notions of "the market", which is now regarded as synonymous with capitalism. The "naive reformers" of the past have been replaced by the "naive marketeers" of the present. Financial reform has gathered pace and has been linked to the new political and economic agenda. Financial liberalisation has continued with the formation of a three-tier banking system allowing private domestic and foreign-owned banks to operate. The reform of the financial system has also become tied up with the privatisation of the state-owned sector. Privatisation has been seen as necessary as an economic objective—on the assumption that markets do not work effectively without private ownership—and as a political objective, since the removal of state ownership is regarded as a critical symbol of the break with the past and a means to create a new capitalist class. Stock markets are a central part of this process, with most countries aiming initially at widely dispersed share ownership.[7] Stock exchanges are featured in the reform plans of Czechoslovakia, Poland, Hungary and Russia. The creation of a stock-based financial system has been criticised by some, even though they support the transition to a capitalist economy, for many of the economic reasons advanced by those opposing stock markets under market socialism (see, for example, Corbett and Mayer 1991, who argue for a bank-based financial system in the post-socialist countries).

Whilst the market socialism literature has lost its practical relevance in east/central Europe, it underwent substantial change during the 1980s with a clear general message: the need for much greater marketisation of the financial system, involving more competition between banks, a wider range of financial assets, a market-based allocation of credit and a radical reduction of direct state controls. Whether even these kinds of reforms could rescue socialism was however doubted by some, particularly if reforms were not accompanied by a radical change in the system of ownership. Chinese thought on the nature and feasibility of market socialism has passed through similar stages, partly in response to trends in Eastern Europe, partly under the influence of Western financial theory and institutional advice and partly in response to the evolution of Chinese financial reforms themselves during the 1980s, as we shall see in Chapter 4.[8]

Finance and Development: The Case for Liberalisation

While advocates of market socialism have moved towards an increasingly market-based approach to reforming socialist financial systems over the past twenty years, a liberal market approach has become the

---

7. The privatisation plans do in fact differ considerably between countries. Czechoslovakia is planning to use a widely dispersed voucher system for shares. Hungary is to use auction sales and the stock market for privatising enterprises. In Poland many enterprises will have the majority of their shares distributed freely to individuals, workers and financial institutions. See Corbett and Mayer (1991: p. 21). For an overview of current banking and capital market reforms and regulations in central/east Europe, see Lindsay (1992).

8. In the post-1979 era, China has developed an impressive coterie of financial analysts trained both at home and abroad. Certain figures stand out over the period, such as Zhao Haikuan, Liu Hongru and Li Maosheng. Key texts on the financial system and financial reform include Li Maosheng (1987), Zhao Haikuan (1985) and Wu Jiesi et al. (1985). Moreover, as we shall see when we discuss the Chinese experience in later chapters, some of the major Chinese theorists of economic reforms, such as Li Yining, Yu Guangyuan and Dong Fureng, have made specific interventions in the area of financial reform.

mainstream position among Western experts working on the relationship between finance and economic development. During the 1980s, this has been the predominant paradigm influencing the thought and action of international institutions in their relations with developing countries. The influential work of McKinnon (1973) and Shaw (1973) long ago challenged the practice, followed by many Third World governments in the post-colonial period, of keeping real interest rates low, and usually negative, in order to stimulate investment. McKinnon and Shaw both argued that direct government intervention in financial systems in the form of interest rate ceilings and selective credit programmes was misguided, since it resulted in 'financial repression', i.e., the limited development of financial markets, and that this hindered the growth of the real economy.[9] The initial policy advice focussed very much on the need for price liberalisation, in this case with respect to the interest rate; the neoclassical case for the market determination of prices was extended to financial markets. Government-controlled interest rates were seen as an obstacle rather than as a stimulus to economic development, and a strong case was made for market determined, positive, real interest rates.

The argument advanced in favour of positive real interest rates rests on two hypotheses. First, it was argued that positive real interest rates would encourage saving. Since developing countries were capital-scarce economies, raising the volume of savings for investment was crucial. Positive real interest rates offered incentives for savers and thereby increased the volume of savings. With a rise in savings, the process of financial deepening (i.e., the monetisation of the economy as measured by the ratio of monetary aggregates to GNP) would occur. Second, the allocation of investable resources would be improved and the efficiency of investment thereby raised. Negative real interest rates, it was argued, encouraged capital intensive investment inappropriate to the relative scarcities facing developing countries. Positive real interest rates, in contrast, ensured that those who borrowed funds were those with the highest prospective returns. Positive real interest rates therefore channelled credit to the most profitable borrowers. The developmental case for financial liberalisation was therefore considered to be a strong one, and Third World governments ignored it at their peril.

However, the strength of the case for market-determined interest rates depends on whether financial markets are competitive, since

---

9. This proposition has also been subject to empirical investigation. For a recent example see Roubini and Sala-i-Martin (1992). See also Fry (1982; 1988).

there is no particular welfare significance to a non-competitively determined market price. The argument has increasingly extended, therefore, from interest rate liberalisation to the liberalisation of the financial system as a whole: the need to promote competition among financial institutions in the determination of interest rates and the allocation of credit and to provide the greatest possible options for savers. In the context of developing countries, this position is articulated clearly in the World Bank's *World Development Report 1989.*

In the view of this *Report,* government-directed credit programmes suffer from a number of weaknesses. In particular, they alter the distribution of resources in favour of government clients who often do not use funds for intended purposes or who invest inefficiently. Furthermore, once in place such credit programmes "create a constituency of beneficiaries who do not want them stopped" (World Bank 1989: p. 59). Thus, if governments make mistakes in directing credit and wish to correct them, or wish to respond to changing circumstances, they find it difficult, politically, to do so. Such programmes have also had an adverse effect on the development and sustainability of the financial system:

> The ability to borrow at cheap rates encouraged less productive investment. Those who borrowed for projects with low financial returns could not repay their loans. . . . The distorted allocation of resources and the erosion of financial discipline have left intermediaries unprofitable and, in many cases, insolvent. . . . Moreover, by encouraging firms to borrow from banks, directed credit programs have impeded the development of capital markets. (1989: p. 60)

The direct involvement of governments in financial systems, in particular by using subsidised credit to pursue developmental objectives, is regarded as damaging not only to the financial system itself but also to the economy as a whole. The policies of governments in developing countries, therefore, should aim to "eliminate the difference between the subsidized [interest] rate and the market [interest] rate . . . since experience has shown that generous subsidies badly distort the allocation of resources" (1989: p. 129). Financial systems should be "less a tool for implementing interventionist development strategies and more a voluntary market process for mobilizing and allocating resources" (1989: p. 83). These policy recommendations concerning financial reform are based on a view of the links between the financial system and overall development policy; put simply, a market-based financial system is a requirement for a market-based development strategy. If governments continue to control and intervene in the financial system, this subverts or prevents the operation of the market system. Since the World Bank and liberal economists believe that the market is the best allocator of resources, and that an allocation of resources consistent with static efficiency will also enhance long-run growth, then it follows that financial liberalisation will be developmentally efficacious.

According to this paradigm, the thrust of financial reform in developing countries should be to restrict the role of the government as an active promoter of development and promote its role as the regulator of a market-led development process supported by a market-based financial system. As the *Report* states,

> To promote an efficient financial system there must be competition, but the system must also offer an array of services. Rather than restrict the growth and diversification of the main banking groups, governments in the larger economies would be wise to promote greater competition by encouraging money and capital markets, specialized credit institutions (such as leasing and factoring companies), and contractual savings and collective investment institutions. Economies too small to support such specialized institutions can spur competition by allowing economic agents to buy financial services abroad. (1989: p. 41).

Thus, the banking sector should be competitive in setting interest rates and in allocating credit. Competition can be stimulated not only by the deregulation of domestic financial institutions but also by permitting the operation of foreign banks. The pace of liberalisation may be debatable, but the end point of an open and competitive banking sector is not. Non-bank financial institutions (NBFIs) should also be allowed to operate freely, and there is also an important role for money and equity markets. The idea here is that savers may differ, for example, in their degrees of risk aversion, or in their preferences for the timing of the stream of returns, and that financial markets should cater to the variety of these needs to the extent possible, i.e., markets should be as complete and comprehensive as possible. Equity markets perform a role here in mediating "between the conflicting maturity preferences of lenders and borrowers" (1989: p. 109). They are held to be important because they share the risk of investment by making the returns to the equity holder dependent on the performance of the firm. In this respect equities differ from debt instruments (such as bonds), which stipulate a specified payment regardless of firm performance.[10] The secondary market is also believed, controversially, to promote a more efficient allocation of resources through the threat of takeover; enterprise managers are disciplined by

---

10. For an argument that equity-based finance is important in smoothing macroeconomic disturbances, see Stiglitz (1991a).

the equity market to behave in the interests of the ultimate owners of the firm, namely, the shareholders. The *Report* records with evident satisfaction that

> several developing countries have made great strides in recent years in establishing and invigorating equity markets. Such markets now exist in more than forty countries. Indeed, the market capitalization of stock exchanges (that is, the total value of listed shares) is a greater proportion of GNP in Jordan and Malaysia than in France and Germany, and India's stock exchanges list more companies than the stock markets of any other country except the United States. (1989: pp. 109–110).

The general policy prescription of financial liberalisation is relevant to economies wishing to reform the centrally planned system (or, indeed, to any other economy undergoing market-oriented reforms). As we will show in the next chapter, the financial system of the centrally planned system was rigidly hierarchical and subordinated to the dictates of the planning authorities. As a *direction* of change, therefore, financial liberalisation has policy relevance to reforming socialist economies. However, the finance and development paradigm goes beyond recommending a direction of change and advocates an end point, applicable to all economies, of a financial system based upon competition between financial institutions (both domestic and foreign) and of extensive equity markets based upon private ownership. The nature of this end state is heavily based on Anglo-American financial institutions and experience and, needless to say, is problematic for a country such as China.

Nevertheless, this general framework has formed the background for policy advice to China from international institutions (and academics) and became increasingly influential in the mid-1980s as the World Bank became, *nolens volens*, a participant in domestic Chinese policy debate. For example, following from the main principles of the argument for financial liberalisation, the Bank argues that in China's case

> the steps taken in the 1979–89 period helped the emergence of a broader financial market providing alternative financing sources for government, enterprises, households, and financial institutions. Taken together, the reforms helped to provide alternatives, first, to budgetary financing of enterprises and, second, to the reliance of enterprises on the specialized banking system. However ten years of reform and deepening have been less than fully successful in changing the bank-only structure of the financial system, in fostering price competition between financial institutions, and in allowing a meaningful role to the financial sector . . . in allocating credit. Additional fundamental reforms are needed in the financial sector for banks to become true intermediaries rather than

channelers of funds following government priorities. (World Bank 1990b: p. xi)[11]

The call for "fundamental reforms" contained in the last sentence has potentially critical implications for China's overall development strategy and institutional system. It raises a host of knotty questions both about the nature, degree and efficacy of financial liberalisation itself and about its compatibility with the issues raised in the two other paradigms we present here (i.e., the fact that China claims to be implementing a 'socialist' version of financial reform and that China, as a late developer, might rationally be disposed towards certain types of direct intervention in the financial system in pursuit of defensible developmental objectives).

The actual experience of financial liberalisation during the 1980s, as well as certain recent developments in economic theory, have led many to be more cautious in their claims for financial liberalisation. The practical record of financial liberalisation in the Southern Cone countries of Latin America in the early 1980s provided a lesson in the problems associated with such policies, with reforms ending in financial chaos and policy reversals (see Diaz-Alejandro 1985). The issue of proper sequencing has become topical with the need for macroeconomic stability, stressed as a prerequisite for financial liberalisation (see McKinnon 1991). The experience in the Southern Cone and the Savings and Loan debacle in the United States, have also led to a greater appreciation of the 'moral hazard' problem—unregulated or under-regulated banks with implicit or explicit insurance from government are under little pressure to behave efficiently (a capitalist version of Kornai's 'soft budget constraint', perhaps). The need for "prudential regulation" is now stressed. In the words of McKinnon, one of the pioneers of the finance and development literature, "Finance and trade liberalisation, with borrowing and lending at substantial real rates of interest made possible by a stable price level, is not easy and is full of potential pitfalls. . . . I am now more inclined to emphasize the pitfalls" (McKinnon 1989: p. 53).

Some of the key theoretical underpinnings of the financial liberalisation argument have also been brought into question. For example, the proposition that positive real interest rates raise savings rates has received considerable empirical investigation, resulting in no

---

11. See also Blejer et al. (1991: p. 11) for the view that "the establishment of securities markets is an integral element in the development of a more efficient financial sector." The finance and development paradigm has also been argued as relevant to China by Wang (1988).

clear support for the central hypothesis.[12] The importance of equity markets for developing countries has been questioned (see, for example, Mayer 1989), and, moreover, the allocative efficiency of financial markets has received attention in recent work on the economic impact of imperfect information.[13] This literature has pointed to the imperfections that are inherent in the operations of financial markets and has argued that these markets are not the perfect allocators of standard neoclassical theory. As Stiglitz states (1989a: p. 61),

> Allocating capital is . . . a much more complicated matter than the simple 'supply and demand' paradigm suggests. Unfortunately, much of the simplistic advice given by 'Chicago' economists is based on the hypotheses that markets for capital are just like markets for tables and chairs; that free markets—whether for chairs, tables, or capital—ensure Pareto efficient resource allocations; and that policies that move the economy closer to free market solutions are welfare enhancing. All three of these propositions are incorrect.

For Stiglitz, the essential feature of financial markets is imperfect information. This leads financial markets to behave quite differently from the predictions of standard models. For example, Stiglitz and Weiss (1981) argue that banks may choose to ration credit at lower than market-clearing rates of interest. This occurs because of the problem of 'adverse selection'—if interest rates are raised, then only riskier projects seek funding. Thus, the banking system may not act like an auction market but is likely to involve other forms of allocation.

The imperfect-information approach points out how financial markets may not operate as the advocates of free markets have suggested, but it does not thereby imply a significant role for government intervention. As Stiglitz states "In some instances, such as the imperfect capital market, I suspect that there may be little scope for government intervention" (1989b: p. 202). The reasons for this are that "governments face the same informational problems that the private sector does, and in addition faces some 'political economy' problems" (Stiglitz 1991b: p. 24) arising from the fact that

---

12. See, for example, Fry (1988), who supports the proposition, and Dornbusch and Reynoso (1989), who are more sceptical, arguing that "the financial repression paradigm in some ways seems like supply-side economics—a kernel of truth and a vast exaggeration" (p. 205).

13. We concentrate on the imperfect-information critique of the financial liberalisation position. However, there are other important critiques, notably from a post-Keynesian position. See, for example, Dutt (1991) and Studart (1991).

the government does not have the incentives to ensure that it (or its agents) does a good job in selecting and monitoring loans. The deep pocket of government means that any losses can easily be made up. Moreover, since economic criteria are often supplemented with other criteria (saving jobs, regional development), losses can be blamed not on an inability to make judgments about credit worthiness, but on the non-economic criteria which have been imposed. (1991b: p. 23)

The policy implications of the imperfect-information position are somewhat unclear, therefore, though some do point in the direction of financial market liberalisation. For example, the moral hazard problem may be partly overcome by relying on 'reputation effects'. That is to say, larger established banks are more likely to act prudently as a self-interested mechanism to protect their reputation; smaller, newer financial institutions may be more likely to engage in speculative activities. The policy implication is that developing countries undertaking financial reform *may* want to allow international banks to operate in their countries, as these are the banks with the most interest in preserving their reputations, rather than restricting new entrants to domestic financial firms only (Stiglitz 1989a: pp. 62-63).

The case for financial liberalisation, therefore, at least in its standard neoclassical form, has not gone unchallenged from within as well as outside of neoclassical economics for both its theoretical and empirical weaknesses. Given its problematic repercussions in real-world trials and the vulnerability of some of its key theoretical assumptions, the case for financial liberalisation should clearly be treated with a high degree of caution when embodied in policy advice. Of course, the argument can be demoted to 'second best' status: in other words, a view that even if the market does not work perfectly, it should be allowed to operate as the primary regulator of the economy because the alternative (government) is worse. Thus the argument about minimal direct government intervention in the financial system would still stand. But even in this form the argument is vulnerable to counter-evidence. Whilst the World Bank and other advocates of liberalisation can point to many instances of developing-country governments intervening in financial markets with adverse consequences, the evidence is not all in their favour. In fact, some of those countries which have grown most spectacularly over the past 25 years have followed financial policies which are vastly different from those proposed in the finance and development literature. As Cole and Wellons state (1989: p. 3), "some countries' economies performed very well despite the existence of a financial system that would be thought to impede good performance." In particular, the financial systems of the two major East Asian NICs, South Korea and Taiwan, have not resembled a liberalised financial system at all during the crucial period of their developmental breakthrough. It is to their experience that we turn in the next section.

The East Asian NIC Model of Late Development

Advocates of a market-based financial system in China, whether they be radical "market socialists" or advocates of financial liberalisation, face an awkward problem: The two East Asian NICs, South Korea and Taiwan, whose growth record has been the most impressive in the erstwhile developing world, have achieved this in a context of state-controlled financial systems. In both these countries, the role of the state has been substantial in owning financial institutions, administering interest rates and directing credit. .

The seeming paradox of rapid growth and state-controlled financial systems has therefore to be explained. Is it the case that the NICs were successful in spite of their financial systems and that their growth rates would have been even more impressive if they had established market-based financial systems early on? This is the implication of the finance and development paradigm. An alternative explanation suggests that control of the financial system played a crucial role in promoting the structural transformation of the economy and was a central component of a highly effective pattern of state-directed development. This alternative explanation is rooted in the theory of 'late development' and argues that developing countries need an active, interventionist state with control over the financial system to promote late industrialisation.

The theory of 'late development' has a long history, going back to debates about how Germany, France and Russia sought to overcome the disadvantages of economic backwardness in the nineteenth century to compete in a world dominated by Britain. Perhaps its most well known exponent is Gerschenkron (1962). This theory has recently received analytical and empirical support from comparative and ideographic studies of East Asian development (see, for example, White 1988 and Wade 1990) and has been further elaborated by Amsden (1989) in her study of South Korean industrialisation. For Amsden, the most significant feature of those economies which have successfully industrialised in the twentieth century is that they have done so by learning. This contrasts with the first industrial nation, Britain, which gained preeminence through invention, and the late industrialisers of the nineteenth century, which did so on the basis of innovation. Amsden argues that the large technological gap which has existed in the twentieth century between rich and poor countries can only be closed if the poor countries create institutions which enable them to learn. The state, always an important actor in the growth process, is a central institution for organising this process.

The conflicting demands placed on the economic system of late industrialisers (for example, the conflict between savers who want high interest rates and investors who want low ones) require that an active state intervene to partially reconcile these conflicts. Instead of exposing the economy to the full force of international market forces, the state mediates and tempers these forces and protects and fosters its own learning industries. Identifying which sectors to promote is a relatively manageable task for late industrialisers. As Wade writes with respect to Taiwan, "The fact that Taiwan has not been near any world technology frontier until very recently makes the selection of 'winners' easier than for more advanced countries" (1990: p. 189). A key element in the state's armoury to support such targeted industries has been the subsidy. Indeed, Amsden writes that

> the First Industrial Revolution was built on laisser-faire, the Second on infant industry protection. In late industrialization, the foundation is the subsidy—which includes both protection and financial incentives. The allocation of subsidies has rendered the government not merely a banker, as Gerschenkron (1962) conceived it, but an entrepreneur, using the subsidy to decide what, when, and how much to produce. The subsidy has also changed the process whereby relative prices are determined.
>
> Industrial expansion depends on savings and investment, but in 'backward' countries especially, savings and investment are in conflict over the ideal interest rate, high in one case, low in the other. In Korea and other late industrializing countries, this conflict has been mediated by the subsidy. Throughout most of the twenty-five years of Korean industrial expansion, long term credit has been allocated by the government to selected firms at negative real interest rates in order to stimulate specific industries. . . . The most critical price—that of long term credit— was wildly 'wrong' in a capital scarce country, its real price, due to inflation, being negative. (1989: p. 144)

Thus the state plays the crucial role of entrepreneur in late industrialisation, and control of the financial sector is critical to its ability to perform this role effectively. Let us now turn our attention to why this should be the case and how the financial system has been fashioned in the East Asian NICs to meet this function.

At this stage, it is useful to return to Zysman's threefold classification of financial systems, which we introduced briefly in Chapter 1: the capital market–based system, the credit–based system with administered prices and the credit system with oligopolistic banks. (See Zysman 1983: pp. 69–75.) This classification is helpful in that it highlights the different role that the state is able to play in the growth process in each of these systems. In the capital market–based system, shares and bonds are important sources of long-term industrial finance. A diversified and reasonably competitive financial sector exists and the market is responsible for determining financial prices and for allocating financial resources. The financial system has a high degree of autonomy from the state and the state acts predominantly as an economic regulator. The state can influence macroeconomic variables but does not intervene in the allocative workings of the financial system. Zysman regards the U.S. and British financial systems as fitting this model.

The second model, a state-directed credit-based system, permits, indeed requires, extensive direct state involvement in the economy. In this type of system, share and bond markets are largely inaccessible to firms, although bond markets might be used by governments. In these circumstances, firms rely heavily on bank credit for their external investment funds, and the banking system is thus central to the growth process. Governments intervene to set prices (interest rates) and to direct credit to particular priority sectors. Attention therefore focuses on how the government intervenes and what priorities it sets. This system is said to be characteristic of the financial systems in Japan, France and Italy. Note that although these financial systems involve a large role for the state—as an active player in the growth process rather than as mere regulator—the form which state intervention may take varies from country to country. Thus, according to Zysman (1983: p. 72), "The Italian financial system is more similar to the French than any other, but the discretion it affords is diffused among the warring factions in the Italian polity, whereas in the French system discretion is concentrated in the hands of the central executive."

In Japan, the most successful twentieth-century late industrialiser, it is argued that

> the credit based financial system served the government as a powerful instrument of policy. The political and policy strategies of the Japanese government would have been difficult to accomplish within the constraints of a capital market based financial system with freely moving prices and an elaborate securities market. . . . Access to credit was selectively manipulated to provide preference to favoured sectors and to push the Japanese economy slowly toward capital-intensive and knowledge-intensive production. (1983: p. 250)[14]

---

14. See also Eccleston, who argues with respect to Japan that "clearly the way the state has selectively promoted the development of leading companies through its role as a financial intermediary has been fundamentally important" (1986: p. 77).

The third system, an institution-directed credit-based system not subject to state direction, best describes the (West) German model. Here oligopolistic financial markets determine interest rates and the state is unable to intervene in the allocative decisions of banks. The financial institutions are, however, frequently negotiating with the government on macroeconomic policies and form part of a corporatist politico-economic structure.

Zysman also argues that each of these systems was constructed to meet particular developmental needs. In particular, he states that "both the second and third models are solutions to late development, whereas the first is tied to an earlier industrial transformation" (1983: p. 72). Thus, in late industrialising countries where the state plays a leading role in the growth process, a credit-based financial system is critical, since "selective credit allocation is the single discretion necessary to all state-led industrial strategies" (1983: p. 76). This framework helps to explain the seeming paradox between state-controlled financial systems and rapid growth. Contrary to the prescriptions of the finance and development literature and of more radical versions of MSII market socialism, credit-based systems with selective credit allocation are required to enable the state, a central institution of late development, to actively fulfil its developmental role.

The evidence provided by South Korea and Taiwan provides strong support for this argument. Governments in both countries have actively and directly intervened in their financial systems, though the degree of intervention has been higher in South Korea than in Taiwan. With respect to real interest rates, Taiwan and South Korea have followed different policies. In Taiwan (with the exception of several years in the 1970s), the government has implemented a policy of high real rates of interest on deposits since the early 1960s. In South Korea, real interest rates were only significantly positive in the period 1965–1971 following the implementation of a financial liberalisation plan supplied by U.S. advisors (John Gurley, Hugh Patrick and Edward Shaw). In the early 1960s the government kept real interest rates low or negative, a policy to which it reverted in 1972. (See Cho 1989: p. 91.) Both Taiwan and South Korea have had high investment rates in the range of 30 per cent of GDP. Taiwan has financed this almost exclusively from domestic savings, whereas South Korea has relied heavily on foreign borrowing to supplement domestic savings. It is in the allocation of credit, however, that we find the main similarities between the two countries and that the extent of direct government involvement becomes clear.

South Korea's financial history can be divided into four periods: 1961–1964, 1965–1971, 1971–1980 and 1980 onwards. We provide a very brief description of these periods before discussing the general features of the South Korean financial system.

If the South Korean industrialisation drive can be taken as starting from the military regime of General Chung Hee Park in the 1960s, then it is significant that in 1961 the banks were renationalised. This was important because South Korean leaders wished to create and foster the growth of large firms in an import-substituting strategy. According to Woo (1991: p. 52), this policy was chosen because following the dictates of a static comparative advantage would have meant linking South Korea's economy in a subordinate position to that of Japan. An alternative strategy of industrialisation was sought, therefore, which was embodied in five-year development plans and which required state control of the financial system. To this end, the banking system was strengthened and enlarged (Woo 1991: p. 84).

In 1965, under pressure from U.S. advisors, the government changed tack and adopted an outward-looking strategy which involved a massive devaluation of the *won* and a package of financial reforms centring on a rise in real interest rates on deposits. This led to an increase in domestic savings and financial deepening but not financial diversification or less state control, since the interest rate increase attracted savings out of the informal curb market into the state-owned banking system. Moreover, not all of the proposed financial reforms were implemented; in fact, subsidies through the directed-credit programme actually increased (Cho 1989: p. 92) and the raising of interest rates was deliberately selective (Woo 1991: p. 103). In Amsden's view, "interest rate 'liberalisation' (it lasted only seven years) did not do much to finance industrial expansion" (1989: p. 74). One result of the liberalisation, however, was a rapid increase in foreign borrowing, since borrowing on the international market was now cheaper than on the domestic market. South Korea's foreign debt, which stood at 6.8 per cent of GNP in 1965, rose to over 30 per cent of GNP in 1971 (Woo 1991: p. 105).

The economy hit a crisis in the early 1970s and the IMF had to be called in and a stabilisation package implemented. In 1971, banks had been unable to supply businesses with sufficient credit to meet their requirements; businesses therefore turned to the informal, and more expensive, curb market. When businesses found themselves unable to repay the curb loans, they went bankrupt. The government's response to this, in the Presidential Emergency Decree of August 1972, was to announce a moratorium on all corporate debt owed to the curb market (Amsden 1989: p. 96). The private lenders, who in the crisis years of the late 1960s and early 1970s had supplied around 30 per cent of corporate borrowing, were therefore sacrificed, and firms and foreign creditors were saved. Along with this bailout came a policy change and a return to negative real interest rates. In the 1970s the move towards heavy industry meant that state control over credit became tighter as the South Korean government targeted six key industries for rapid growth and channelled funds in their direction.

In the 1980s, pressures from the United States, upward movements in real interest rates, a decline in foreign credit and a desire to alleviate the banking system's burden of non-performing loans led to a degree of financial liberalisation. This involved a degree of privatisation and internationalisation of the banking system, a rapid growth in the equity market and an increasing role for NBFIs at the expense of the curb market. However, the state's role in the financial system continued to be very substantial, even though there was a move from formal to informal methods of regulation and control. Amsden and Euh (1990) provide a detailed account of the main areas of continuing state involvement, which include a continuation of policy loans channelled through the banks to strengthen target industries and to prevent 'sunrise industries' from failing. The role of the Ministry of Finance continued to be dominant and there was considerable continuity in its basic objectives: to push rapid industrialisation, maintain low real interest rates and protect the needs of production against any destabilising or speculative tendencies in the financial system. In the view of Amsden and Euh, the financial 'liberalisation' of the 1980s was very partial; though it did succeed in modernising the financial sector, this was achieved "by creating institutions or remodelling old ones, not by relying on market forces" (1990: p. 51).[15] This view is shared by Woo, who argues that the changes have been more apparent than real and that "a decade after the salvo of economic liberalisation and many pledges to carry it out, it still remains incomplete" (Woo 1991: p. 192).

It is also noteworthy that a good deal of the interactions between the state, the financial sector and the large corporations (*chaebol*) have been informal and that these informal links have become more important in the 1980s as a degree of formal liberalisation has taken place. In political economy terms, moreover, to the extent that the 1980s did see a reduction of direct state control over the financial system, this reflected the increasing countervailing power of the *chaebol*, the growth of which had been fostered by the state policies of the 1960s and 1970s. The partial liberalisation of the 1980s reflects the ambivalence of the *chaebol*, as Amsden and Euh (1990: pp. 49–50)

---

15. Wade (1985: p. 115) argues that "the post-denationalisation methods of bank control in Korea closely resemble those long used in Japan, where banks have been mostly privately owned. There too, the Government still fixes interest rates through the so-called 'overloan' provision".

point out: On the one hand, they wish to rid themselves of irksome state restrictions and extend their corporate influence into the financial sector; on the other, they still want to keep interest rates low and be able to rely on state support when in difficulties. The *chaebol* were in fact a major beneficiary of the bank privatisations of the early 1980s, since they were able to evade state attempts to limit their inroads into finance by taking a substantial share of bank equity; this resulted in a rise in economic concentration. (See Amsden 1989: p. 135.) This tendency towards a fusion between the productive and financial sectors in the context of an oligopolistic economic structure and the relationship between this increasingly powerful configuration of private economic power and the state will be a crucial determinant of future financial reform in South Korea, as will the increasing influence of external pressures. In general terms, this raises fascinating questions about the relationship between the interplay of these basic political variables and the specific institutional character of evolving financial systems in South Korea and elsewhere.

Having looked at the bare bones of recent South Korean financial history, we now look in more detail at how the financial system operated in the heyday of the South Korean breakthrough in the 1960s and 1970s. The model is best described as dualistic—a tightly controlled state-owned banking sector and an informal curb market.[16] The banks lent according to government priorities and favoured large firms; small firms and households relied on the curb market. In the formal sector, loans were subsidised, while interest rates were substantially higher on the curb market. The banking sector supplied in excess of 70 per cent of total credit to the economy and undoubtedly more than this to the major firms. There was an indeterminate amount of 'leakage' of subsidised credit to the curb market as firms used the opportunity to make easy profits from the interest rate differential.[17] Bank credit that was effectively used for intended purposes reflected the

---

16. The degree of dualism in the financial sector may be particularly high in South Korea and Taiwan, but a dualistic structure is common to many developing countries. The relationship between the formal and informal financial sectors has received a good deal of attention in the literature, particularly as it affects the outcome of financial liberalisation policies. This issue is not considered here. See Germidis et al. (1991) for an overview.

17. There is disagreement about the extent of leakage. Hong and Park (1986), for example, argue that there was a large amount of credit diversion, while Noland (1990: p. 98) states that "monitoring and supervision of industrial firms by banks was effectively managed, and this limited the diversion of directed credit for other uses". Lee (1992: p. 191) agrees with Noland and emphasises the influence of an ideology of an economy driven by exports, high penalties for transgressors and the effectiveness of monitoring institutions.

role of an entrepreneurial state which was using the banking system not only to subsidise credit but also to implement a strategic industrial policy. South Korea thus belongs to the family of East Asian capitalist economies (including Japan and Taiwan), which are all characterised by credit-based financial systems with banks being heavily dependent on the state. But as Woo argues (1991: p. 11), "The Korean banking system exhibits the most extreme case of dependence on the state". In this model, South Korean banks do not have any discretion over non-performing loans and do not have high collateral requirements.

The state's influence over the allocation of bank credit is not only through determination of interest rates but also through "policy loans" directed to specific sectors, industries or firms at interest rates lower than those of already subsidised bank loans. Banks had very little discretion over these loans, and bankers functioned as state bureaucrats rather than as commercially oriented businesspersons. Acting as long-term developers of industry rather than as independent short-term profit maximisers, the banks were agents of the state in, for example, bailing out large firms in times of economic crisis such as 1971.

The state was in a powerful position to direct credit, since with negative real interest rates, the demand for credit was high and the state was able to ration it in pursuit of its own economic objectives. These objectives were defined broadly in terms of supporting 'export activity', but especially during the 1970s, support was extended to particular firms within industries in an attempt to establish industrial leaders within specific sectors. By the end of 1981, there were 221 types of policy loans among a total of 298 types of bank loans (Woo 1991: p. 12).

Policy loans reached their zenith during the drive towards heavy industry in the 1970s. With private industry reluctant to invest in large, capital-intensive projects with long gestation periods and uncertain outcomes, the state used policy loans to the maximum effect to push firms into these industries. Noland (1990: p. 42) estimates that by the late 1970s, policy loans amounted to 60 per cent of total private domestic credit, and the annual interest subsidy had risen from about 3 per cent of GNP during 1962–1971 to about 10 per cent of GNP between 1972 and 1979. In the 1980s, with the end of the heavy industrialisation drive, the share of policy loans dropped to about 35 per cent of domestic credit, and in accordance with the new priorities laid down in the Fifth Five Year Plan (1982–1986), the commercial banks were now required to provide at least 35 per cent of their loans to small- and medium-sized firms (Noland 1990: p. 44).

The South Korean financial system can be summarised then as a dualistic one with a state-owned (state-controlled after the denationalisation of the early 1980s) banking system which extended subsidised credit and directed credit to specific sectors, industries and firms through policy loans. This system bears comparison with that of Taiwan, where the state-owned banking system has again been the major financier of industrial growth. As state-owned firms, the banks have been subject to government-controlled salary scales, and senior bank staff have been government appointees. NBFIs have been strictly controlled, and foreign banks have played only a minor role in the economy. Credit was available not only from the state-owned banking system but from the curb market, often in the form of suppliers' credit. The curb market provided a 'flexible edge', as Wade calls it, to the financial system and supplied about 20 to 30 per cent of total loans during the 1970s, primarily to small- and medium-sized firms (Wade 1985: p. 113).

The diversion of bank funds to the curb market is again an issue, but Wade concludes that this was kept down by the ability of banks to monitor enterprises' use of loans (1990: p. 171). This implies that government efforts to direct credit were largely effective and the state's role was considerable: In Wade's words, the state "sets the structure of interest rates and imposes tight limits on how much can be lent to any one borrower and on the purchase of company stocks. These controls are reinforced by stringent reporting requirements" (1990: p. 162). Subsidised credit was made available to exporters, and banks received lists of priority industries which were to be given preferential treatment. Specific subsidies were also made available to machinery importers. These policies have continued into the 1980s, and the Strategic Industry Fund, set up in 1982, provides subsidised credit for priority industries such as electronics (see Gee San 1990). All of these preferential schemes are administered by the banking system. However, in addition to these, government ministries also take direct control of some financial resources, including the important Development Fund (Wade 1990: p. 169).

There are, therefore, some basic similarities between the South Korean and Taiwanese financial systems. There are important differences as well, the high collateral required by Taiwanese banks being one example. Perhaps the most important difference, however, is in the extent to which the banking system has been used as an instrument of industrial policy. In South Korea it was used to a very large extent, whereas in Taiwan its role was more modest, with other complementary measures playing a more important role in guiding the economy in the state's chosen direction. As Wade writes with respect to Taiwan, "The high priority to economic stabilisation reinforced the position of the monetary authorities vis-à-vis the industrial authorities, limiting the use of selective credit as a primary instrument for steering the behaviour of private firms as compared to Korea. Hence the government's reliance on public enterprises, trade controls, and tax incentives" (1990: p. 196). One further contrast is that the pace of financial liberalisation in Taiwan has been even slower than in South Korea, with no rush to privatise the banks, as occurred in South Korea in the early 1980s.[18] The 'liberalisation' of interest rates, moreover, has been described by Wade as "simply substitut[ing] a banking cartel indirectly managed by the state for the old direct management by the central bank" (1990: p. 164).

Now that we know how the financial systems operated in these two East Asian NICs, we need to explore why such systems have apparently been so successful. Cho (1989) and Lee (1992) argue that this type of system has been beneficial because it overcomes some of the informational deficiencies of financial markets in developing countries. Lee draws on Williamson's notion of an 'internal organisation' to argue that the nexus of state-business relations involved in the South Korean financial system operates as a 'quasi-internal' capital market which can operate more efficiently than a 'free-market' financial system (1992: p. 194).

However, the role of the state-controlled financial system goes beyond solving problems of financial market 'imperfections'; rather it is an important part of the difference between a state-led and a market-led strategy of late industrialisation. As such, its importance extends beyond a compartmentalised view of the financial system. Control of the financial system enabled the state to mobilise resources for national developmental needs: for example, by strictly controlling the outflow of resources abroad and by channelling resources into productive uses. The Latin American elites may have been allowed to invest in luxury homes or financial assets overseas, but the South Korean and Taiwanese elites have not. This represents not merely a response to financial market imperfections but a refusal to allow markets to operate as the main mechanism of development.

The market-determined rate of interest was also not treated as sacrosanct. The rate which might be dictated by individual savers' rates

---

18. The process of financial liberalisation in Taiwan has so far been evidenced by the relatively modest policies of (i) allowing foreign institutional investors access to equity markets in December 1990; (ii) the licensing of 15 new private banks in June 1991; and (iii) a new public auction system for the sale of government bonds in November 1991. See Baum (1992: p. 46).

of time preference did not necessarily meet the needs of firms, and the state therefore interposed itself to subsidise the cost of capital. These subsidies were deemed necessary to enable domestic firms to compete with more advanced firms from developed countries. To this extent, the market was supplanted rather than merely supplemented; entry into the industry was strictly controlled and those firms which did enter particular industries were supported with subsidies until they were able to compete.

The initial weakness of firms and their particular reluctance to invest in capital-intensive projects meant that the state played the role of entrepreneur. It essentially intervened to socialise risk. Since the main source of credit was the banking system, firms became highly leveraged and therefore vulnerable to bankruptcy if demand decreased. Since the state viewed temporary fluctuations in demand as an insufficient reason to close enterprises, it had to either subsidise the firms' losses or provide additional financing to the banks to offset their non-performing loans. In such circumstances, extensive government financial controls are required to ensure the overall stability of the financial system (see Wade 1985: p. 122). Once the state enters into the role of risk-sharer, the non-financial targets set for firms and the ability of state agencies to enforce them take on more importance, since strict financial returns have less meaning.

Yet other developing countries have had similar state-controlled, credit-based financial systems and have not shared in the East Asian success. Why did it work so well in East Asia? The question becomes even more telling when we realise that public ownership, of both banks and enterprises, has been important in South Korea and Taiwan (see Wade 1990: pp. 176–78). Thus, we have a state-owned banking sector dispensing credit to an industrial sector which contains a significant portion of state-owned firms. Neoclassical economic theory would not predict rapid growth, so what explains the East Asian NICs' success? Any answer to this question is complex, since the NIC model in its entirety, not just its financial system, and the external environment in which it has flourished would need to be considered. While many other factors, both internal and external, are undoubtedly important ingredients of success, Woo (1991: pp. 6–7) also argues that in the case of South Korea, an understanding of the autonomy of the state and its control over finance is of critical importance in understanding the dynamics of success. This implies that the state is not only capable of defining the national economic interests and converting its objectives into strategic policy but is also able to rise above specific economic interests, both at home and abroad, in its effort to implement its programme of development. This requires a stable and committed political leadership and an administrative apparatus which is technically proficient and relatively uncorrupted.

These variables of state autonomy and capacity go a considerable way in explaining why a country such as South Korea was able to discipline firms in return for subsidies, thereby establishing a mutually productive reciprocity between the two parties. (See Amsden 1989: pp. 14, 146.) This means that the South Korean state was able to extract performance targets from firms in return for subsidised credit and intermittent financial support in difficult situations. The separation of finance from firms was crucial to the ability of the state to discipline them; if firms relied primarily on the state for financial resources, they were under heavy pressure to conform to the objectives set for them. Firms were disciplined by being rewarded when successful (for example, by meeting export targets) and penalised for poor performance. Poor performers were subject to rationalisation and some were allowed to go bankrupt if they proved to be poor performers in an otherwise healthy industry (for numerous examples from South Korea, see Amsden 1989: p. 15 and Woo 1991: pp. 165, 176).

It is the key variables of state developmental intelligence, state autonomy and state capacity which distinguish the experience of countries such as Taiwan and South Korea and constitute one major ingredient (out of several) in their success. To the extent that these features do not exist in other countries, the experience cannot be repeated even if other facilitating factors visible in the East Asian experience are present. However, it is our view that these characteristics are shared by their East Asian neighbour, China, which can also be situated within a historical context of 'late development'. Thus the NIC experience is highly relevant to the contemporary Chinese situation.

During the 1980s, however, there is evidence, particularly clear in the South Korean case but also more widely, that the particular constellation of political and economic forces which underpinned the East Asian breakthroughs are being eroded and transformed as domestic social, economic and political systems undergo changes and the pattern of external pressures also shifts. An exploration of this phenomenon, which one could refer to as 'the decline of the NIC model', is beyond the scope of this book; we would also argue that it is not as relevant to our topic as the earlier domestic experience of the East Asian NICs in the 1960s and 1970s, during which period the Taiwanese and South Korean economies were more comparable to the present Chinese economy. This said, however, the swirling political and economic currents of the 1980s and 1990s—such as the collapse of the Cold War, the possible emergence of trading blocs, internal and external pressures for economic and political liberalisation—cannot but affect the character and direction of contemporary Chinese development, just as they did the development of South Korea and Taiwan, and they must be kept firmly in mind.

Concluding Remarks

Table 2.1 provides a summary of the main "stylized features" of the three paradigms (with the 'market socialist' paradigm sub-divided into MSI and MSII) discussed in this chapter as they relate to some of the key features of the financial system and its relationship to the broader methods of economic control.

The three paradigms provide three different perspectives on our topic of Chinese financial reform. Though they share some common elements (particularly the first two paradigms), they reflect different historical experiences and different theoretical traditions, highlight different aspects of the issues involved, and result in different sets of policy prescriptions. Each paradigm has its analytical and empirical strengths and weaknesses, each has weaker and stronger versions and each has its proponents and detractors. Each provides a different estimate of what is desirable and feasible in the evolution of the Chinese financial system. Each appeals to different sets of beliefs and interests and thus has a particular constellation of political forces behind or against it.

It is our hope that the three paradigms will prove useful to the reader in making sense of the detailed exposition of the Chinese financial reforms which follows. In the next chapter we provide an account, by way of historical background, of the pre-reform financial system and then, in Chapters 4, 5 and 6, analyse the reforms to the Chinese financial system that have taken place since 1979. The reform of the financial system in China involves complex issues, both in themselves and in their connections with the wider political and economic systems within China and outside. They are also politically contested issues, a fact which means that the adoption of merely one analytical framework, while making the explicit task of analysis apparently easier, implicitly draws the analyst towards a particular overall perspective from the outset, an approach which may inhibit both understanding and judgment. We think it is more helpful at this stage to stand back and map out alternative conceptual terrains, even though (as may be apparent) we have our own standards of evaluation and views about the relevance of the three paradigms. In Chapter 7, we will spell these out explicitly and use them to develop an analysis of the future trajectory of the Chinese financial system in the 1990s.

TABLE 2.1   Three Paradigms of Financial Systems: Summary

Paradigm	Main Features				
	Banking System	Capital Markets	Foreign Participation	Means of Macro-economic Control	Determination of Composition of Output
Market socialism					
MSI	State-owned monobank	Limited use of government bonds	Limited	• Central planning	Central planning
MSII	Competitive state-owned banks NBFIs	Use of bonds and possibly of some form of shares	Permitted (but restricted)	• Planning (especially of rate of investment) • Monetary and fiscal policy	Market and some planning
Finance and development	Competitive private banks	Bonds and shares	Substantial	• Monetary and fiscal policy • Independent central bank	Market
NIC late development	State-controlled or state-owned banks Curb market	Limited use of bonds and shares	Restricted	• Monetary and fiscal policies • Limited planning	Market and sectoral planning

3

The Pre-Reform System: The Financial Institutions of Centrally Planned Socialism

THE CHINESE FINANCIAL SYSTEM on the eve of the reform era comprised the essential components of the "monobank" model inherited from the Soviet version of Marxist-Leninist socialism. As such, it functioned as an integral part of the centrally planned economy, an organisational form which embodied some of the key elements of Marx's original vision of a post-capitalist economy, such as a minimisation of market exchange and the use of money, of production for profit, and of private ownership of the means of production.[1] Unlike Marx's original conception of a socialist economy, however, the Soviet model of a planned economy was not a successor to developed capitalism; rather it offered a radical alternative to capitalism as a path to development. The state, rather than market-oriented private entrepreneurs, would be the allocator of resources and sponsor of accumulation. The development process required the transformation of the industrial structure, the creation of a whole new set of demands. This could be achieved more quickly and efficiently by the state than by allowing the existing pattern of consumer demand or the immediate profit prospects of private individuals to dictate resource allocations, particularly in the context of an international economy already dominated by the advanced capitalist powers. In transforming backward economies, moreover, socialist theorists argued that centralised directive planning would be a feasible proposition, since the planners

---

1. For Marx, money was an essential feature of the capitalist market, necessary for the operation of the law of value. Under communism, the abolition of scarcity would also mean the eventual abolition of the market and of money.

would not have to tackle the millions of decisions necessary to replace those made within complex markets. Rather they would have to make a relatively small number of key investment decisions concerning such things as electrification and coal and steel production, which were regarded as the crucial determinants of the speed and success of the industrialisation process.

In the centrally planned system, in its pure form at least, resources are allocated to enterprises in order for them to meet various targets (output, value-added and profitability, for example) set by the central planners. Producer goods are allocated by the planners to enterprises, and money plays only an accounting role as a 'shadow' representation of the circulation of physical resources. Money does, however, play a more active role in the market for consumption goods, which are sold to the public at prices fixed by the planners, and in the labour market, where differential wages in effect constitute the price of labour. In general though, in this pure system money and credit are not abolished but play a relatively peripheral role subordinate to the central planning mechanism.

However, in the historical practice of central planning, money and banks have played an important, if subsidiary, role in the economies of socialist states. This posed problems for theorists of socialist economics. As Garvy pointed out in the late 1970s, "Official Soviet economic theory has had considerable trouble in defending the very existence of money under socialism and in legitimizing the use of credit and interest charges. . . . A coherent theory underlying the management of money by the socialist state has yet to be formulated" (Garvy 1977: pp. 36–37). Moreover, many Western treatises on Soviet-style economies ignored the financial system and focussed almost exclusively on the central plan in its administrative and physical aspects. While such neglect was unwarranted in the context of east/central European state socialism, it is particularly so in the case of China where, as Byrd has argued, "Because of the country's relatively weak planning system and decentralized system of economic administration, financial resources may have been more important in affecting economic performance than in other centrally planned economies all along" (Byrd 1983: p. 2).

In the first section of this chapter, we outline the role of banking institutions in the general conception of a centrally planned economy. Since no complete theoretical model of the financial dimension of central planning exists, this section draws heavily upon the framework developed in the Soviet Union. The purpose of this section is simply to set out the institutional framework of the Soviet-type financial system and to illustrate the main theoretical principles behind its operation. We do not attempt to assess the operation of this system in the Soviet Union or the other countries of east/central Europe where it was adopted.[2] An assessment of the operation of this type of system is provided, however, in the second section of this chapter, where we move to the specific discussion of the Chinese case. In this section, we provide an overview of the framework of financial institutions in China from 1949 to 1978 and assess how it operated in practice. The third section provides a brief summary of the performance of the Chinese economy in the 1949–1978 period and points to why economic reforms in general, and financial reforms in particular, were thought to be necessary.

The Role of Banking Institutions
Under Central Planning

The ability of the banking system to regulate the structure of production in a capitalist economy was clearly recognised by the main architect of the Russian revolution, Lenin, who argued that socialism too needed to control a powerful banking system. A few days prior to the October Revolution he wrote that

> without big banks, socialism would be impossible. The big banks are the 'state apparatus' which we need to bring about socialism, and which we take ready-made from capitalism. . . . A single State Bank, the biggest of the big, with branches in every rural district, in every factory, will constitute as much as nine-tenths of the socialist apparatus. There will be country-wide bookkeeping, country-wide accounting of the production and distribution of goods; this will be, so to speak, something in the nature of the skeleton of socialist society. (Cited in Garvy 1977: p. 21)

Given this analysis, it is no surprise that "on the first day of the Bolshevik coup, October 25, 1917 (old calendar), an armed detachment of workers and soldiers, under direct orders from Lenin, occupied the main office of the State Bank in Petrograd"(Garvy 1977: p. 23).[3] In China, the first private enterprise to become socialised after the 1949 Revolution was a bank (Hsiao 1971: p. 27).

Lenin's idea of what is commonly referred to as a "monobank" system, the skeleton of the economy keeping track of the flow of finan-

---

2. For assessment see, for example, Brus and Laski (1989) and Nuti (1989).

3. Lenin's aim in taking over the state bank was not, however, realised immediately. As Garvy states, "As events turned out after the Bolshevik seizure of power, the monetary and banking system disintegrated under the impact of the civil war and the accompanying inflation. A state bank as envisaged by Lenin, complete with credit monopoly and complex control functions, did not materialise until almost fifteen years later with the first Five-Year plan well under way" (Garvy 1977: p. 22).

cial and physical resources, formed the basis for the development of the banking system in the centrally planned economy. Traditional central planning operated predominantly in terms of physical flows; targets for physical output were set and input requirements were assessed in physical terms through the input-output method of material balancing. In practice, these physical flows were matched by parallel financial flows. Brus, in his analysis of the "centralised model" of planning, noted that in relations between enterprises within the state sector, "movements of money generally follow movements of the material elements in the reproduction process which are carefully regulated from the centre" (1972: p. 78). This is partly because planners cannot know the details of all enterprises' production requirements. In addition, money is required to avoid the necessity of barter exchange on a large scale and for aggregation purposes.

It is these financial flows which are the concern of the banking system and the fiscal authorities (the Ministry of Finance); the system is more accurately described as a "monobank-monobudget" system. The Ministry of Finance is responsible for annual budgets and long-term financial plans. It collects budget revenues and makes budget dispersals, although it too keeps its account at the monobank, which administers certain of its functions on its behalf. Typically, the Ministry of Finance oversees tax setting and collection as well as inter-regional (or inter-provincial) fiscal transfers. The monobank and the Ministry of Finance are state institutions which work together to collect resources and to redistribute them to their desired uses. The bank is technically an enterprise in that it is responsible for its own profit and loss. However, it is not judged by its profit results and operates in effect like a government body.

The functions of the monobank are considerably more complex than those undertaken by Western banks and enable it to address its main tasks.[4] These are basically threefold: (1) developmental (2) microeconomic and (3) macroeconomic. We consider each briefly in turn.

Developmental Support

By controlling the flow of financial resources in the economy, the monobank is able to play a crucial role in supporting the strategic developmental objectives of the political leadership and economic planners. This involves, first, a concerted effort to change the sectoral structure of the economy. In the initial phases of communist regimes,

---

4. See Miyashita (1976: pp. 114–15) for a list of the specific functions of the monobank in Soviet-type economic systems.

this has meant supporting the socialised sector at the expense of the private sector, leading, with varying degrees of rapidity, to the dominance of the socialised (state or collective) sector. Once the socialisation of the economy has been achieved, the monobank acts to implement the sectoral priorities set by the central planners to achieve the structural transformation of the economy, normally through rapid industrialisation. At least in the initial phases, this has typically involved preferential support for heavy industry; in the Soviet, Chinese and North Korean cases, this was given impetus by the need to establish a credible military capability to counter external threats. Second, planners may have regional objectives, requiring the redistribution of resources along geographical lines. This may reflect a desire to limit inter-regional disparities of productive capacity and income or to involve strategic considerations such as the need to establish defence-related industries in militarily less vulnerable locations. Third, planners may have social objectives, such as the desire to keep industrial wages down in order to restrain rural-urban differentials, to limit income differentials within the urban/industrial sector, and to maintain full employment.

Microeconomic Supervision

The monobank is a unique organisation in the state socialist economic system in that it is a nationwide organisation penetrating every part of the economy and is the only organisation which can claim to be aware of the activities of all enterprises and units within the economy. It is the task of the monobank to supervise all units within the economy and ensure that they operate in accordance with the plan. This means that the microeconomic efficiency of the enterprise is a concern of the bank and also that macroeconomic control in the planning system has a strong microeconomic component. The relationship between banks and enterprises is therefore critical to the successful management of the economy.

The enterprise's need for resources to meet its output target is determined by various 'norms'. Fixed capital is strictly separated from working capital. Fixed capital requirements are funded from the central budget and are in grant form.[5] Working-capital requirements are both 'normal' (to finance work in progress and inventories, and to make wage payments, for example), and 'temporary' (caused by sea-

---

5. This was the Soviet system established in the early 1930s, although it was subsequently modified in 1965 when fixed-capital investment became the responsibility of the banking system and became credit rather than grants.

sonal factors, for example). The banking system has typically been responsible for providing the temporary component and some of the normal component of working capital in the form of short-term loans. This gives the bank a role in financing and monitoring each and every enterprise. From a theoretical point of view, it is not necessary to involve the banks in this way; normal working-capital requirements could simply be distributed as grants from the budget. In practice, however, socialist countries have found it desirable for the banks to be involved in the financing of normal as well as temporary working capital, since this allows greater control to be exercised over enterprises to enforce performance norms. As Podolski states with respect to the Soviet Union, the "authorities simply found credit to be a useful institution in the planning mechanism" (1973: p. 43).

The banking system was expected to play a key role in monitoring enterprise performance and ensuring compliance with plan targets. The banks and enterprises had virtually daily contact, enabling the banks to exercise more control than is possible by the more intermittent operations of the budgetary system. In theory, the monobank's role as the settlement bank enabled the bank to ensure that all enterprises settled their accounts promptly and could not increase their financial base by involuntary trade credit. The banks were responsible for ensuring that financial resources, once committed to an enterprise for a specific purpose, were in fact used for that purpose and not diverted to other uses. Both fixed capital and working capital funds were allotted for specific purposes, and separate accounts kept, and the monobank, or specialist banks under its supervision, were entrusted with the task of ensuring the correct use of funds by enterprises. The fact that all enterprise cash reserves had to be held at the bank also reduced enterprises' ability to behave in ways not sanctioned by the planners. Banks could also inspect enterprise accounts upon request and were to be consulted in the drafting of enterprise financial plans.

Furthermore, if enterprises did not comply with the rules governing the use of funds, did not repay credit, or failed to meet planned targets, it was the responsibility of the banks to change enterprise operations to rectify this. The way in which this was to be done and what precise responsibilities the banks actually had to intervene in enterprise management is not entirely clear. However, it is clear that the main instruments of control were the restriction or denial of credit to the enterprise, pressure to sell excessive inventories, and greater bank control over the use of funds. The ability to withhold credit was a potentially powerful instrument, since other sources of credit, including inter-enterprise credit, were prohibited. The monobank system was set up so that the bank was the only source of credit and the funds generated by the enterprise itself were relatively small; the bank was therefore in a powerful position. In this respect, Podolski argues that "banks in a socialist economy acted on behalf of the government to safeguard the efficient use of public property" (1973: p. 48).

Whilst this illustrates possible sanctions that the bank could use against enterprises, it is also true that if an enterprise could demonstrate a 'legitimate' need for credit, then the bank was obliged to grant it; the bank did not have discretionary power here. In this sense, credit was automatic in nature. Furthermore, enterprises were required to meet certain planned payments into the state budget from sales proceeds. However, if the enterprise did not have sufficient funds for this purpose, the balance would automatically be paid in the form of a bank loan. Thus, in spite of a potentially influential battery of control mechanisms, the existence of these kinds of automaticity, the pervasive presence of the 'soft budget constraint' and inevitable problems of imperfect information meant that the role of the banking system as a force for enforcing plan performance and enhancing microeconomic efficiency in practice was very circumscribed.

Macroeconomic Control

The monobank is also responsible for ensuring price stability and for preventing excessive inflationary pressures from emerging. In performing this task, the bank is of course dependent upon the central planners making internally consistent plans; if this is the case, then the volume of goods produced will be sufficient to satisfy demand at existing prices. The bank relies upon its position as the sole supplier of credit to the economy, its supervisory role over enterprise operations and the fact that all state units must hold accounts with the bank and all transactions within the state sector must go through it to ensure macroeconomic stability.

The bank is charged with ensuring that the volume of credit in the economy is consistent with the plan. This is done through administrative control over the quantity of credit, through the financial plan, rather than by varying the cost of credit (the interest rate). Whilst socialist economies often have differential interest rates, they have made little use of interest rate flexibility as a regulatory instrument. The financial plan is drawn up along with the physical plan; it is the monetary counterpart of the physical plan and is drawn up with bank input to ensure consistency between the two plans; it is the responsibility of the bank to ensure its adherence.

The financial plan has several components.[6] These are the financial

---

6. For the Chinese system, see Hsiao (1971: p. 10).

plans of enterprises; the state budget; and the cash and credit plans. There is then an additional plan which links all three of these categories together and ensures their consistency. Cash and credit plans are made separately to reflect the basic division of the economy into the household and enterprise sectors. Centrally planned systems operate on the principle of strictly separating these two sectors, the household sector and enterprise sectors, and preventing the leakage of resources from one to the other. Theoretically, the household sector receives cash payments and makes cash purchases; little opportunity exists for using credit. The enterprise sector, in contrast, primarily uses credit in settling accounts between its constituent parts with cash playing a minor role.

Each of these sectors is monitored to achieve macroeconomic balance. Thus, if planners set a target for the total wage bill, for example, then given a predictable velocity of circulation they can maintain price stability in the consumer goods sector by the appropriate production of consumer goods. For this reason, the bank is charged with ensuring that the wage fund for each enterprise is adhered to and that funds intended for other purposes are not diverted to this use. To assist the bank in this task, enterprises must deposit cash with the bank, and sources of unplanned demand are supposed to be strictly monitored. The centrally planned economy only works if planners have effective control over resources; sources of unplanned demand threaten the stability of the planning system. The bank is also responsible for collecting and regulating savings deposits from the public (the only legal form of asset holding typically permitted). Often these deposits are predominantly time deposits and, as such, are not regarded by the authorities as demand for commodities.[7] For the enterprise sector, the bank is responsible for ensuring that enterprise funds are used for intended purposes consistent with the plan. Financial balance is achieved when "budget resources available for investment plus retained enterprise profits earmarked for this purpose match planned investment requirements in excess of available depreciation reserves" (Garvy 1977: p. 158).

Thus, in theory, the monobank acts as an important complement to the physical planning system, plays an important role in maintaining macroeconomic stability, and is unique in its micro-financial supervisory role. Nevertheless, as Byrd states,

In the ideal model of the command economy the banking system plays no role in financing fixed investment, which is funded entirely by the

---

7. Obviously such a view is illegitimate if savings are not voluntary. For more on this, see Byrd (1983: p. 34).

state budget. It only finances a small part of investment in circulating capital: most of that is provided by the state budget as well. Private savings are absorbed in order to combat inflation rather than to increase investment. Therefore the banking system should not be viewed as a true financial intermediary. (1983: p. 35)

This gives a very brief introduction to the role designed for the monobank in a centrally planned socialist economic system and an indication of how it was intended that the monobank system should meet its objectives. The discussion has been at the level of theory, and, needless to say, theory and reality have often differed widely.[8] In turning to the specifics of the Chinese case, therefore, we will not only analyse how the Soviet-type financial institutions were adapted to China in the pre-reform period, 1949–1978, but we will also briefly assess their success in meeting the three objectives just outlined.

The Chinese Case

Institutional Structure

The vastness of the country has meant that physical planning in China has always been an incomplete method of organising the economy and that value planning, using monetary measures, has been important. The financial system in post-1949 China developed to act as a complement to physical planning and has undergone a number of changes in its history. The Ministry of Finance has had a fairly stable existence, but the banking system has had more fluctuating fortunes.

The People's Bank of China (PBC) was formed in 1948 and, unlike its Soviet equivalent, was regarded as a separate agency from the Ministry of Finance.[9] It expanded its organisation rapidly and by 1952 all banks were effectively under the supervision of the PBC. By 1957 it reportedly had 20,000 branches and sub-branches and controlled over 100,000 rural credit cooperatives (Miyashita 1976: p. 117). The PBC has assumed the major banking role in post-1949 China, being responsible for the issue and control of currency, management of government accounts and the administration and supervision of short-term loans for working capital. All enterprises, government units and coop-

---

8. It is beyond the scope of this book to assess the operations of the financial system, or the planning system in general, in the Soviet Union. For an introduction to the topic see Nove (1986), especially Chapter 9.

9. See Hsiao (1971: p. 10). The PBC's Soviet equivalent, Gosbank, was not separated from the Ministry of Finance until 1954. As Donnithorne points out (1967: p. 403), this feature of the Chinese system was a significant departure from the 'Soviet model', from which the CCP was borrowing extensively in the early years.

eratives had to keep their accounts with it and settle accounts between them through its agency; individuals also kept savings deposits
there (Donnithorne 1967: pp. 405–6).

The PBC was organised vertically in parallel with the state administrative structure, with each bank office responsible to the level immediately above it. Each bank operated under "dual leadership", that is,
control by the head office in Beijing and from the provincial party
committees (Byrd 1983: p. 10). For the organisational structure of the
PBC, see Figure 3.1.

The evolution of rural banking institutions has not been a smooth
one. Here, the vastness of the area to be covered, the underdeveloped
state of the economy and the size of the peasant population presented
particular problems in establishing rural financial institutions, necessary though they were both from the point of view of the central government in controlling and mobilising resources and from the point of
view of peasants wishing to escape the usurious practices of rural
moneylenders in the pre-1949 period. Two unsuccessful attempts
were made to form an Agricultural Bank (ABC) in the 1950s and another one in 1963 to undertake the specialist functions of lending and
supervision in the rural sector. However, all failed to take over adequately the functions of rural credit cooperatives the problem being to
ensure that the financial network reached down to the peasants but
did not interfere with the position of the PBC or create too high administrative costs.[10] Thus, rural credit cooperatives continued to operate under the supervision of the PBC and, according to Byrd, (1983:
p. 15) formed "a relatively complete rural financial network since the
late 1950s". These cooperatives played an important role in mobilising rural savings and making them available to state banks. The
present Agricultural Bank, established in 1979, now controls the rural
cooperatives.

Two other banks are worthy of mention. First is the Bank of China,
(BoC), originally founded in 1904, which is supervised by the PBC and
is responsible for foreign exchange transactions and overseas business.
The BoC played an important role during the 1950s but was of less
importance during the 1960s and early 1970s, when foreign trade
played a relatively minor role in the Chinese economy. The BoC
has contacts with and owns banks outside of China.[11] Second is the

---

10. Apparently the 1963 attempt was ended in 1965 because it was felt
that the ABC duplicated the functions of the PBC (see Byrd 1983: p. 17).

11. Byrd writes (1983: p. 20) that "China owns a considerable part of Hong
Kong's banking system", accounting for 17 per cent of total deposits and 10
per cent of total lending in the early 1970s.

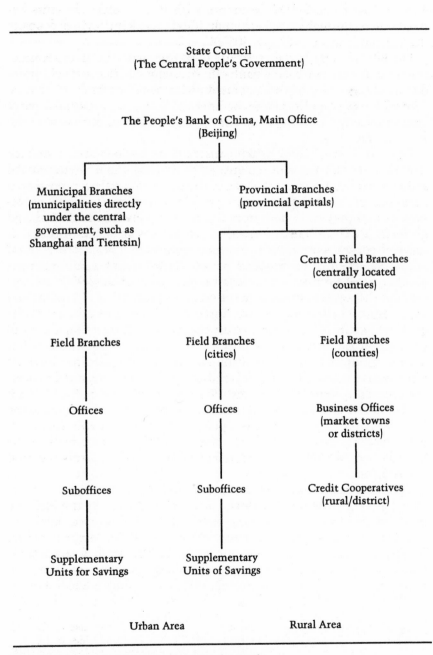

FIGURE 3.1 The Organization of the People's Bank
SOURCE: Hsiao 1971: p. 22.

People's Construction Bank of China (PCBC), founded in 1954 and formally supervised by the Ministry of Finance. The PCBC has a head office in Beijing and also has a network of branches and subbranches throughout China. It took over many of the functions of the Bank of Communications, which was one of the major banks operating in the Kuomintang period and which became a joint state-private bank after 1949 (Donnithorne 1967: p. 412). The PCBC has been a specialist bank concerned with investment and as such was responsible for administering fixed capital grants from the state budget in accordance with the plan and for settling business arising from funds allocated for fixed investment. The PCBC has really been a fiscal agent, therefore, despite being called a bank. In addition to supervising investment spending out of the state budget, local governments and enterprises were also supposed to deposit any investment funds which they had with the PCBC; this theoretically gave the PCBC control over the most important components of investment spending. It is the PCBC which has been primarily responsible, therefore, for guiding investment to those sectors and industries identified in the plan, for ensuring that the volume of investment is consistent with the plan, and for monitoring its efficiency. In this latter microeconomic role, the PCBC monitors fixed-capital expenditures in the same way that the PBC monitors working capital.

This organisational structure has not remained stable. In particular, the separation of banking and fiscal operations has not been continuous. In the period up to the Great Leap Forward in 1958, the PBC and the Ministry of Finance were formally separated and had equal authority. During the Great Leap Forward and the Cultural Revolution, however, the PBC was subordinated to the Ministry of Finance; in consequence, during the 1960s and much of the 1970s, the Ministry of Finance controlled the banking apparatus. The PBC did not regain its former status until 1976. The PBC did, however, maintain its nationwide banking network, and Byrd reports (1983: p. 10) that "as of the end of 1979, there were a total of over 15,000 different PBC sub-units throughout the country including 29 provincial-level branch banks, one for each province, autonomous region, and centrally administered municipality, 148 municipal-level subbranches (in cities directly subordinate to the provinces), 220 central subbranches in prefectures, 2,777 county-level subbranch banks, and 2,883 offices under the jurisdiction of county-level subbranches." Thus the PBC survived as the financial 'skeleton' of the socialist economy.

Having given a brief overview of the institutional structure of the banking system in this period, let us now consider its operational practices.

Banking Operations

We can consider the operation of the banking system by referring to the three main tasks identified previously, namely, developmental, microeconomic and macroeconomic.

Developmental Support. The People's Bank's first priority concerned establishing its position as the monobank. This was achieved by 1953 and the focus then changed to sectoral issues, notably the ownership structure of industry. Here the bank followed a policy of preferential treatment for the state sector, which received the major share of credit with loans to the private sector being negligible, and of providing inducements for enterprises to become joint private-public enterprises.[12] Both policies assisted in leading to the rapid 'socialist transformation' of private industry and commerce. The collectivisation of agriculture and the establishment of the commune system were also assisted by credit support from the People's Bank. Once the socialised sector was dominant, lending priorities were then defined mainly in terms of the central plans and the need to bring about the production structure set out therein. This involved, at various periods, preference for heavy industry, particularly during the First Five Year Plan (1953–1957), and for agriculture, especially during the 1960s. Other specific sectoral priorities included the experiment undertaken by the Shanghai branch of the PCBC to provide small loans for technical innovation to the light and textile industries during the 1960s and 1970s (Byrd 1983: p. 42). This experiment was expanded nationwide in 1975. Another specific sectoral objective was the support given to export industries to improve their quality, variety and packaging (Byrd 1983: p. 43). This programme also operated during the 1960s and 1970s with interruptions.

In regional terms, the central issues have concerned the relationship between the formerly more highly developed coastal regions and the more backward interior and the various attempts by the centre to redress imbalances not only through the fiscal system but also through the pattern of investment. Between 1953 and 1979, the initially less-industrialised provinces grew at a higher rate than the more industrialised ones (Riskin 1987: p. 227; see also Lardy 1978, Paine 1981, Lyons 1991). Perhaps the largest such programme during the Maoist period was the effort to create a vast 'Third Front' industrial base in the interior regions of the west and south-west between 1964

---

12. In this regard, Hsiao (1971: p. 129) notes that "the outstanding feature of the structure [of interest rates] was that the interest rate moved inversely with the degree of socialisation of the credit recipients".

and 1971 (Naughton 1988). In social terms, although the urban labour force was in many ways privileged, attempts were made to contain rural/urban differentials and to enforce a relatively egalitarian wage structure for industrial workers (see, for example, Paine 1976). The banking system was expected to play a role here through its monitoring of enterprise wage expenditures. Broader social goals included the provision of basic needs which, as will be shown, were goals which were successfully achieved.

Microeconomic Supervision. The banking system, and the PBC in particular, was responsible for overseeing the distribution of credit to each enterprise and for ensuring that the latter's operations were efficient and in conformity with planned targets. The PBC administered only working-capital loans with fixed capital being met out of the state budget and dispensed through the PCBC. Nevertheless, this placed the PBC in a potentially powerful role. In practice, however, this power has seldom been exercised.

In the early period, it was argued that in order to support production, the bank should not refuse any loans to enterprises. No effective restraints were placed on the granting of credit to enterprises; under the lending policy adopted in 1953, entitled the "balance of financial receipts and expenditures system", the PBC simply covered any losses necessary to balance an enterprise's account. Following the credit reform of 1955, however, the bank followed the 'real bills doctrine'. This doctrine stated that so long as credit was extended to match a flow of goods, such credit increases were not inflationary. Thus, while enterprises now had to provide a rationale for their uses of funds, as long as they could demonstrate that they needed funds to finance inventories and work in progress, credit was extended.[13] Attempts were made during the first Five Year Plan to place further limits on the conditions under which credit was granted. In 1955, for example, an attempt was made to reduce inter-enterprise credit by providing special loans to finance goods in transit and by enforcing payment obligations. However, in general, the PBC was in a difficult position, not least because of the inaccuracies of the planning mechanism. The PBC found it difficult to establish what should be the normal requirements of enterprises, and hence the responsibility of the budget, and what was temporary and therefore the bank's responsibility. Furthermore, what was legitimately temporary and what was due to enterprise inefficiency was also unclear. In such circumstances, credit was granted virtually upon request to enterprises.

---

13. The real bills doctrine has long been regarded by Western scholars as incorrect. For a defence of the doctrine in the context of a Soviet-type planned economy, see Podolski (1973: pp. 53–54).

In an attempt to reassert some bank control after the Great Leap Forward, planners stipulated in 1961 that enterprises would receive only 80 per cent of their required funds for working capital automatically through the budget and would have to justify to the PBC the need for the remaining 20 per cent, which was on loan terms (Miyashita 1976: pp. 192, 209). However, generally speaking, the PBC still granted loans when requested and had little independent authority. Loans were therefore made virtually upon request, but repayment was not strictly enforced. The overriding aim was to promote production as stipulated in the plan, and meeting this objective had the top priority; it was the banking system's job to ensure that this was done. Although the banks theoretically had the power to withhold credit to an enterprise, such a threat was non-enforceable if it implied bankruptcy for the enterprise. Usually, more credit was extended, and as a result, non-performing loans increased. To illustrate the scale of the non-repayment of loans, Byrd quotes sources which indicate that "at the end of 1979 the total value of agricultural loans which could not or would not be repaid when due exceeded 10 billion [yuan]. This was over half the total value of all loans to rural areas by banks and credit cooperatives outstanding at that time" (1983: p. 12).

Moreover, the banking system often became captive to local and provincial governments keen to promote production in their jurisdictions. As Byrd reports,

> From 1958 until 1979 local Party or revolutionary committees were in charge of appointment, dismissal, transfer, and promotion of bank personnel in places under their jurisdiction. This meant that political criteria often dominated the choice of bank cadres, specialised training and even elementary financial accounting were neglected, and bank employees making specific loan decisions were easily influenced by personal connections with those who had appointed them. Local party committees would often make direct requests for specific loan projects, which could not be refused. (1983: p. 12)

This institutional feature further weakened the ability of the banks to exercise discrimination in the apportionment of loans and exert disciplinary pressures on poorly performing enterprises.

This weakness was further reinforced during the Great Leap Forward and the Cultural Revolution, when financial concerns were downgraded (and even rejected as 'bourgeois'), when fiscal concerns dominated rather than banking principles and when the PBC was placed under the control of the Ministry of Finance. The PCBC was also brought under the control of the Ministry of Finance in 1958 but subsequently regained some independence. In these periods, the banking system was viewed as the financier, not the supervisor, of production, so that the promotion of the backyard steel mills during the Great Leap Forward, for example, was financed irrespective of their financial viability. Hsiao argues that during the Great Leap Forward period,

> the Bank [PBC] became a captive of the enterprises, local governments and rural communes; these units demanded loans not only for working capital but also for fixed capital, thereby undermining even the fundamental role of the Bank as a supplier solely of short-term credit. Quotas for working capital became meaningless; the distinction between budget funds and bank loans was blurred; and the Bank in fact served as an unlimited supplier of monetary capital. (1971: p. 77)

There was some recentralisation of bank control in the early 1960s, but this changed again during the Cultural Revolution, when financial accounting was the subject of attack in political campaigns. In Byrd's opinion, "In practice banks often have little ability to withhold loans. . . . Unplanned credit to finance inventory accumulation is common" (1983: p. 9). Indeed, he has gone so far as to argue that "local banks [were] little more than 'treasuries' for local governments" (1983: p. 37).

Inventory accumulation was automatically funded by bank credit. Given this, and the problems of ensuring a stable supply of material resources, inventory accumulation of inputs by enterprises could be expected to be high. Furthermore, unsold goods accumulated at the output end, again financed by credit. If the enterprise was unable to repay the loans, it would not be allowed to go bankrupt. Byrd attempts to measure the resulting inefficiency with which credit was utilised by pointing out that working-capital funds had grown faster than output between 1957 and 1975. The average value of circulating capital funds per 100 yuan of output value by state-owned industrial enterprises rose from 19.4 yuan in 1957 to 25.5 yuan in 1965 and 33.4 yuan in 1975. Byrd argues that these increases were "far greater than what reasonably could be attributed to changes in the sectoral composition of industrial output during the period" (1983: p. 46). Rather they reflect an increase in inventory accumulation. Byrd concludes that "bank loans to finance working capital did not promote economic efficiency. The way in which credit was extended encouraged excessive inventory accumulation as well as production and storage of defective goods. This caused a great amount of waste and to some extent inflated figures on China's economic performance" (1983: p. 48).[14]

---

14. This assessment is supported by an analysis of the 1950s by Hsiao, who argues that "the growth of outstanding loans was not entirely due to increased requirements for working capital resulting from economic growth. Instead, it was to a large extent caused by the accumulation of unmarketable inventories in industry and in commerce, by difficulties in the collection of agricultural loans, and by a lack of effective credit criteria in the early years. These phenomena were, in turn, symptoms of inefficient use of borrowed capital" (1971: p. 135).

In theory, the banks were in a powerful position to monitor enterprise efficiency; in practice, it seems that they were passive suppliers of credit. This can be attributed in part to policies followed during the period, especially during the Great Leap Forward and the Cultural Revolution. However, it has also been argued, most notably by Kornai, that this practice has systemic causes deriving from the institutional structures of state socialism.

Kornai's theoretical model of state socialism, based on the microeconomic-level phenomenon of the soft budget constraint and its macroeconomic manifestation as the shortage economy, has not been without its critics. (See, for example, Gomulka 1985, Davis and Charemza 1989, van Brabant 1990 and Szego 1991.) In our opinion the following are two of the most important weaknesses of the model. First, it tends to be too static and hence fails to adequately explain why socialist economies have performed well in their early periods, at least measured in conventional growth terms. Second, although a continuum of possible budget constraint "hardness" is theoretically possible (and empirically observable), with the key issue being the design of complementary institutional structures capable of achieving an acceptable degree of economic efficiency and social equity, the concept has often been used to implicitly assert that only "hard" budget constraints are consistent with (a crudely defined) economic efficiency; also, such budget constraints can only be realised under capitalist relations of production.[15] Despite these potential problems, however, the model does have merit in capturing an important institutional feature of state socialism. We believe that used judiciously, the model is useful for analysing centrally planned economies and, when the concept of budget constraint hardness is understood as a direction of change, has relevance for the discussion of the Chinese reform process.

Kornai's model is based on the empirical observation that the state's role as owner of the means of production in state socialist economies has meant that it does not allow enterprises to go bankrupt and ultimately guarantees their survival irrespective of performance. In such circumstances, enterprises operate under soft budget constraints. There are several sources of this softness, including soft subsidies, soft taxes, soft administered prices and soft credit (see Kornai 1986c: pp. 5–6). In each case, if the enterprise is in financial difficulties, it can always be rescued by administrative intervention in one of the forms previously identified. Of particular interest in our context is soft

---

15. Kornai's own position seems to have moved in this direction in the past decade. Compare, for example, the discussions in Kornai 1986c and 1990.

credit. This refers to credit granted without the full expectation of complete and timely repayment. In Kornai's words, "The firm is granted credit even if there is no guarantee of its ability to repay it according to schedule from its proceeds from sale. Credit is not strictly an 'advance payment'; the granting of it is not closely related to expected production and sales" (1986a: p. 42). Banks would loan funds to enterprises knowing that they might not be able to recover all of their loans and also knowing that they (the banks) would not be held responsible for such loans but that their losses would be similarly absorbed elsewhere in the system.

In such circumstances, the initial bargaining for resources within the planning framework could be intense. Ministries competed with each other for resources, and each unit attempted to minimise the claims on it by superiors and to maximise its claims over units lower in the hierarchy. Once resources have been claimed, however, there are no sanctions for their inefficient use, and the volume of resources claimed through the plan serves as a basis on which to claim more resources through the banking system.

Kornai describes the behaviourial characteristics of enterprises in this situation as an almost insatiable demand for inputs, both physical and financial. In his words, this demand for inputs "does not depend either on the purchasing price of input, or on the current and expected income of the firm. Sooner or later it can expect to be able to cover its costs on input and if its proceeds from sales of output are insufficient it will be able to cover costs from an external financial source" (1986a: p. 44). Other behaviourial characteristics of the enterprise include a low responsiveness to price changes (since if input prices change, the enterprise either can change its output prices on a cost-plus basis in response or, if it is unable to do this and suffers losses, can claim resources from various government bodies to cover such losses) and a low regard for efficiency (since the survival of the enterprise does not depend upon the ability to cover costs in the short run or even in the long run).

Analytically, the soft budget constraint "is unable to act as an effective behaviourial constraint and exists only as an accounting relationship" (Kornai 1986a: p. 44). The economy becomes one of "shortage" where enterprises are subject to "investment hunger". Each enterprise attempts to obtain inputs in order to overcome the vagaries of the supply system, to prevent other enterprises from obtaining them and to ensure plan fulfilment and increase output. The cost of such inputs can always be covered whilst there are rewards, both pecuniary and non-pecuniary, for plan fulfilment and output growth. Thus, enterprises stockpile inputs, but at the same time, they may also have excess inventories of finished goods, since there are no effective pressures to ensure that production is saleable; since production is to meet plan requirements, that is not their responsibility.

Thus, the soft budget constraint arises, it is argued, because the institutional arrangements of centrally planned socialism are particularly conducive to its existence. Part of the reform efforts of socialist economies has been aimed precisely at changing these institutional arrangements. The government-bank-enterprise nexus is clearly a central part of these institutional arrangements. The microeconomic impact of China's financial reforms in redefining this nexus is discussed in Chapters 4 and 5.

Macroeconomic Stability. Given the microlevel picture, with credit being freely extended to enterprises, it is perhaps surprising that at the macro-level, inflation was kept under control in the pre-reform era. Indeed, it is a major achievement that a high level of capital formation was possible whilst inflationary pressures were kept in check. With respect to the level of capital formation, the share of investment in GDP was approximately 23 per cent in 1957, rising to 31 per cent in 1979. Two things are remarkable about this. First, this represents a considerably higher share of investment in GDP than is typical in low-income countries. Second, this was financed entirely by domestic savings in China as foreign capital inflows have been absent. The monobank-monobudget system played an important role in mobilising this level of domestic savings.

High rates of growth and investment were accompanied by low rates of inflation. Apart from a couple of years, official figures show a high degree of price stability during the period, as shown in Table 3.1.[16]

The relatively high degree of price stability has been attributed to a number of factors not in fact connected with the banking system's control mechanisms. These factors include the insulation of the economy from world market price increases and the maintenance of balanced budgets. Given that the level of investment was determined by the central plan, the main task was to ensure a level of savings sufficient to meet this. The banking system was required, therefore, to mobilise a high level of savings. Whilst bank credit was passive, mobilising savings was the PBC's primary active function. This was done through savings drives and campaigns using interest rates and even

---

16. Chinese price statistics are of dubious reliability, particularly for parts of the pre-reform period (most notably during the Cultural Revolution). For a general discussion of the problems with Chinese price data, see chapter 5. The reasons for the inflation of 1961 are discussed in Peebles (1991).

TABLE 3.1   Inflation in China, 1951–1978

Year	Change in Retail Price Index (%)
1951	12.2
1952	−0.4
1953	3.4
1954	2.3
1955	1.0
1956	0.0
1957	1.5
1958	0.2
1959	0.9
1960	3.1
1961	16.2
1962	3.8
1963	−5.9
1964	−3.7
1965	−2.7
1966	−0.3
1967	−0.7
1968	0.1
1969	−1.1
1970	−0.2
1971	−0.7
1972	−0.2
1973	0.6
1974	0.5
1975	0.2
1976	0.3
1977	2.0
1978	0.7

SOURCE: SSB 1991: p. 198.

lotteries to attract savings, although not all methods used were voluntary. It has been suggested by Byrd (1983: p. 17) that one of the reasons the Agricultural Bank, set up in 1963, did not last very long was that it was "associated with semi-coercive methods of obtaining savings deposits." Rural savings mobilisation was often coercive in nature, and Hsiao writes that "the constant refrains of 'voluntary deposits, free withdrawals, confidential banking' and the equally frequent de facto violations of these principles persisted throughout the history of rural savings" (1971: p. 64).

In urban areas, inflation-proof time deposits were set up to induce saving in 1950–1952. Other tactics included political campaigns and social pressure exerted in the workplace and in neighbourhoods by unions and other community organisations. Time deposits were most actively promoted. In addition to savings deposits, government bonds were also issued during the 1950s. The People's Victory Bond was issued in 1950, and between 1954 and 1957, National Economic Construction Bonds were issued annually. All issues except for the 1950 issue were oversubscribed. Table 3.2 shows the amount of bonds issued in each year.

These sums represented approximately 2 per cent of budgetary revenues during the period. The People's Victory Bonds had a maturity of 5 years, whilst the National Economic Construction Bonds normally had a 10-year maturity period (the exception being the eight-year maturity of the 1954 issue). The latter carried a 4 per cent annual rate of interest payable once a year. Ecklund (1966: p. 89) reports that "it is probable that at least some of the 1950 bonds were purchased under duress." He does not say whether this was also the case for the 1954–1958 issues, although it is likely to have been the case. The 4 per cent interest on the bonds compared very unfavourably with savings deposit rates at the time. For example, in 1954 a one-year time deposit earned an interest rate of 14.4 per cent, whilst in 1958 it earned 7.92 per cent.[17] It is likely, therefore, that bond sales were semi-coercive in nature.[18] Central government bond issues stopped after 1958, but local governments were then permitted to issue bonds (see Ecklund 1966: p. 90).

Another important ingredient of financial stability was control over the wage fund. This was made possible in part by the drive for egalitarianism and against material incentives. Also of importance was the administrative control over labour allocation, which prevented wage increases in specific sectors from leading to increased wage pressures in other sectors. It is remarkable that average money wages in state-owned enterprises, for example, were roughly the same in 1957 and 1978, as shown in Table 3.3.

TABLE 3.2   Domestic Bond Issues, 1950–1958 (million yuan, current prices)

	1950	1954	1955	1956	1957	1958
Planned	n/a	600	600	600	600	790
Actual	260	836	619	607	650	n/a

SOURCE: Ecklund 1966: p. 87.

---

17. Calculated from Byrd (1983: p. 154).

18. This practice was also common in the Soviet Union. See, for example, Chapman (1963: p. 116), who argues that "throughout the period studied [from 1928 onwards], purchases of government bonds have been, to all intents and purposes, mainly compulsory."

TABLE 3.3   Average Nominal Wage in State-Owned Enterprises, 1952–1978 (yuan per annum)

1952	446
1957	637
1965	652
1970	609
1975	613
1977	602
1978	644

SOURCE: World Bank 1983: p. 396.

Whilst Chinese monetary policy was passive in the sense that the volume of credit tended to respond to enterprise demands, the major control device was qualitative, i.e., in regulating the uses to which credit could be put. As a part of this regulation, efforts were made to control the wage fund. Chinese policy seems to have aimed more at restricting the volume of currency than at controlling the quantity of credit. The implication of this is that the liquidity of the household sector was controlled more strictly, through savings drives, than the enterprise sector. These factors enabled inflationary pressures to be controlled even though credit expansion was often large. In general, however, one can agree with Byrd when he argues (1983: p. 41) that while China was very successful in controlling inflation between 1949 and 1976, the banking system had relatively little to do with this except in the early 1950s.

Economic Performance in the Pre-Reform Era

The overall performance of the Chinese financial system in the pre-reform period was mixed in terms of the three sets of objectives outlined earlier. It made a (relatively small) contribution to the maintenance of monetary stability and was an important instrument for implementing plans to change the sectoral and regional composition of output, but it was relatively unsuccessful in promoting efficiency at the enterprise level. This mixed performance of the financial system mirrors, not surprisingly, the performance of the economy as a whole during the pre-reform period.

Certainly, the Chinese economy from 1949–1979 underwent radical change. The means of production were socialised with dominant state ownership of industry and collective ownership of agriculture. The socialisation of industry was achieved rapidly. In 1949, private industry accounted for 63 per cent of the gross value of industrial output; but this had fallen to only 16 per cent in 1955, whilst the share contributed by socialist industry rose from 35 per cent to 68 per cent over the same period (Riskin 1987: p. 96). The collectivisation of agriculture took place rapidly in the mid-1950s. The structure of production also changed radically. In 1952, agriculture accounted for 58 per cent of national income and industry, 24 per cent. By 1979, however, agriculture contributed 37 per cent and industry, 50 per cent of national income.[19] In this structural transformation from a private, agriculturally based economy to a state socialist industrialising economy, control of the financial system was a critical element.

Economic growth was impressive. Net material product grew at an annual average rate of 5.8 per cent between 1952 and 1979. However, the growth rate of industry, at an annual average of 12.3 per cent, was considerably more impressive than that of agriculture at 2.7 per cent. Whilst growth rates were impressive, considerable gains were made in the quality of life. Average life expectancy, which was 36 years in 1950, increased to 64 by 1979. With regards to the provision of basic goods such as food, clothing, housing, medical care and schooling, the World Bank concluded in the early 1980s that "the poorest people in China are far better off than their counterparts in most other developing countries" (1983: p. 95).

However, whilst growth had been impressive and considerable gains had been made in raising the standard of living of the poor, the system also had clear problems. Most important, growth had been extensive rather than intensive, a common characteristic of centrally planned economies. The pace of technological change had been slow and product quality was low. Measuring productivity growth is a notoriously difficult task, with the need to make arbitrary assumptions about the weighting of capital and labour inputs. Nevertheless studies indicate that Chinese productivity growth had been low. For example, Dirksen (1983: p. 385) estimated that China's growth of labour productivity in industry was "on the lower boundary of the international mainstream (or below it, depending on what figure for industrial employment is used)." Similarly, Riskin has argued (1987: p. 265) that "it seems safe to conclude that most of China's industrial growth has come from increases in productive factors [and] very little of it was due to more efficient use of inputs."[20]

---

19. National income here refers to the Chinese measure of net material product. The figure given for 1979 is actually the average for 1977–1979 (World Bank 1983: p. 72).

20. For further evidence on the low rate of total factor productivity growth in China in the pre-reform era, and for a comparison with other developing countries, see World Bank (1986: p. 39).

The reasons for this failure to raise efficiency are complex and are, in part, due to policy choices. Many of the pressures for reform after the death of Mao Zedong in 1976 were political in character and origin (White 1993). However, there were also fundamental defects in the economic system, which fuelled the increasing demands for reform in the late 1970s. The reformers argued that the centrally planned economy, by severely limiting enterprise autonomy, had proven itself incapable of generating intensive growth. Of particular relevance for this study is the reformers' view that enterprises were not operating with effective sanctions for poor performance or incentives for good performance; the way in which the financial system had operated reflected this phenomenon and reinforced it. In the reformers' view, systemic problems needed systemic solutions, and the key was to change the relations of production and to introduce a fundamentally different operating mechanism into the planned economy, i.e., 'market regulation' (Bowles and Stone 1991). But what markets were to be introduced? In particular, should there be financial markets? What type of financial system should there be and how should financial resources be allocated? These are the questions we explore in the chapters which follow.

Concluding Remarks

The purpose of this chapter has been to describe the role of the financial system in centrally planned socialism. This description has been instructive for two main reasons. First and most obviously, it provides the background for an understanding of the tasks facing China's reformers as they sought to implement the reform of the financial system. The discussion presented in this chapter highlights the difficulty of the task of moving from a centralised financial system subsumed within the planning mechanism to a system in which financial resources are raised and allocated according to more market-oriented forces and in which financial institutions are required to play a more active and discretionary role.

Second, the discussion points to some important continuities between the pre- and post-reform financial systems; continuities which will become apparent in Chapters 4, 5 and 6. As a guide to the reader, these continuities relate to two important areas. First, as we have seen, banks were often viewed in the pre-reform period, to repeat Byrd's apt phrase, as "treasuries for local governments". As we shall see in the next two chapters, with the constraints of central planning removed, the pressures from local governments and other agents on the banking system have been a powerful feature of the reform period and remain an enduring problem for the central financial authorities and reform policy-makers. Second, the developmental objectives of the Chinese state have also been emphasized in this chapter, a developmentalism which has found expression since 1949 in the rapid industrialisation programme offered by Soviet-style central planning but which arises from the longer-term specificities of modern Chinese history as outlined in Chapter 2. Developmental objectives have remained strong during the reform period and have added a distinctive tinge to the evolution of the financial reforms, as we shall see in the chapters which follow. Whether this developmentalism, which manifested itself in the pre-reform period in classic Marxist-Leninist style, might evolve further to result in a financial system more akin to that found in the East Asian NICs is a topic which we consider in Chapter 7.

4

The Process of
Financial Reform

$\mathbf{F}$INANCIAL REFORMS have been a prominent part of China's overall programme of economic reform, which began in 1979. The basic principles of the reform programme were first, to change from administrative methods of regulation and control towards economic mechanisms and second, to decentralise the economic system by giving greater operational autonomy both to lower administrative levels within the state machine and, more important, to economic actors of all kinds, from large enterprises to households and individuals. The reforms involved the introduction of market mechanisms to the extent that economic actors were to gain greater freedom to make their own decisions in an increasingly competitive environment in which price signals and profit motivations were to become increasingly important determinants of economic behaviour. The market itself was to be regulated through the use of "economic levers" such as policies on taxation, interest rates, tariffs and prices. These basic principles were ultimately to be applied to all sectors of the economy, including the financial sector.

Reforms in the financial system were seen as an essential complement to the changes brought about by other components of the reform programme, most notably the decentralisation of financial resources into the hands of individuals and institutions, the *de facto* privatisation of agriculture, profit-retention schemes in state industry (see Lu and Qian 1984) and the "open policy" to the external world, which demanded greater compatibility between Chinese and international financial practices.

Our purpose in this chapter is not to provide a detailed, blow-by-blow account of the evolution of the financial reforms; such accounts already exist (for example, Byrd 1983, World Bank 1988 and 1990 and Donnithorne 1989). We shall describe the reforms with broad brush strokes, with two analytical aims in mind. First, we wish to understand how the overall policy paradigm of financial reform changed over time, passing from a more moderate phase from 1979 to 1984 to a phase far more radical than originally intended, which unfolded between 1985 and 1988. Second, we wish to understand why this transition took place, to situate the evolution of ideas and policy within a broader analysis of the political and economic dynamics of the reform process. Since the Chinese reforms seem on the brink of a third and more radical phase after a period of retrenchment prompted by the inflation of 1988–1989 and the political upheavals of 1989, an understanding of the deeper politico-economic dynamics of the policy process will help us to predict the problems which financial reform faces in the 1990s and its potential trajectory. In this chapter we focus primarily on the reform of the banking system and leave our analysis of the development of capital markets for Chapter 6.

Policy Process Phase I, 1979–1984: Financial Liberalisation Without Financial Markets

In this first phase, the scope of financial reforms was relatively circumscribed. Although there was a growth in new NBFIs (such as trust and investment companies and urban credit cooperatives), and though an insurance sector began to emerge and bonds began to be issued by governments and enterprises, the reforms focussed mainly on changes in the structure and operation of the state-owned banking system and reflected frustrations among the new leadership and their economic advisors with the deficiencies of the traditional state socialist mono-bank system outlined in Chapter 3.

At the macro-level, it was envisaged that bank credit would become an increasingly important source of investment finance as an alternative to budgetary funding and that banks and other financial institutions would become increasingly prominent in raising and aggregating savings and in allocating and regulating the use of credit. At the micro-level, it was envisaged that not only would banks themselves begin to operate more like profit-oriented commercial entities but they would act to increase the efficiency with which productive enterprises used investment funds by being more selective in making loans, varying the conditions on which loans were offered and monitoring the performance of recipient enterprises. By these means, the banks would contribute to the reduction in the degree of budget constraint softness facing enterprises.

The first major reform of the banking sector came in 1979 with the so-called Four Transformations and Eight Reforms, which set the agenda for the subsequent direction of the banking reforms (for a detailed discussion, see Byrd 1983: pp. 58–60). The main thrust of the reforms was towards changing the banks from administrative into economic entities operating more along commercial lines. Thus, the use of 'economic levers' such as the interest rate was introduced. In consequence, the People's Bank twice raised interest rates for urban and rural savings deposits in 1979 and 1980 and increased the range of rates on different types of deposit; in 1982, there was a comprehensive revision of the interest rates on savings deposits and industrial/commercial loans, the latter being divided into prime, floating and penalty rates to influence enterprise behaviour.

The banking system was to become more differentiated and banks were to operate with greater independence from other state bodies such as the Ministry of Finance and from their own head office. The Agricultural Bank was restored and resumed responsibility for raising and distributing funds for working capital in rural areas; a General Administration of Exchange Control (GAEC) was established to oversee foreign exchange transactions; and the China International Trust and Investment Company (CITIC) was established in October 1979 to facilitate foreign investment and joint ventures.

Bank branches were encouraged to explore new ways of attracting savings and were given more discretion in the allocation of credit. In relations between banks and enterprises, those enterprises which performed best in fulfilling the state plan were to be favoured in credit allocation, and banks were allowed more discretion to disburse credit "to fill in the gaps left by state plans". The practice of making interest-bearing loans to enterprises rather than non-repayable grants was gradually implemented with the aim of introducing a cost of capital for state enterprises. If banks did not act as an "economic lever" to improve enterprise performance, the unproductive vicious circle of the old system would be perpetuated. In the words of one colloquium of financial experts: "If the banks have no decision-making rights, then in pursuit of output value the enterprises will often report good news, commercial circles will report bad news, banks will settle accounts, fiscal departments will be in the red and the state will lose".[1]

These early reforms can be seen as operating within the conceptual framework of earlier market socialist experiments in Eastern Europe during the 1960s and 1970s, namely, MSI. The monobank system remained basically intact, but the banking system was expected to become more commercially oriented and discriminating in its loans to

---

1. *Guangming Ribao* (Glorious Daily), Beijing, 26 January 1980, in Foreign Broadcast Information Service (FBIS) 025.

enterprises. However, as part of the transition towards a more radical version of the market socialist paradigm (MSII), further reforms in the early 1980s pushed the financial system steadily towards the establishment of a two-tier banking system, which did not become a component of Eastern European reforms until the mid-late 1980s. In 1982, provision of funds for working capital was shifted wholly from the fiscal authorities to the banks, which also gained some limited role in providing investment funds. In January the following year, the Industrial and Commercial Bank (ICB) was set up. Its functions were to raise deposits and distribute credit for working capital and technical renovation to urban industrial and commercial enterprises. These functions had previously been undertaken by the People's Bank, but now the latter was freed to take up its role as China's central bank.[2] Henceforth, the People's Bank was to be responsible for managing the government's finances, for macro-financial control of the economy and for supervising the loan activities of the four 'specialised banks' (SBs), namely, the ABC, ICB, PCBC and BoC.[3] This organisational change separated the operation of loaning from that of the control of credit and issue of currency. The banks with whom enterprises dealt were no longer the ones which had the power to issue currency; thus the ability of the specialised banks to meet whatever demands enterprises placed upon them was, in theory at least, much less than under the previous system. The specialised banks were also permitted to expand their range of services into non-traditional areas such as housing loans, consumer credit, trust business and bond issuance.

In May 1984, the State Council formally established a branch-banking system under the supervision of the People's Bank. This still operated within the overall framework of the central plan. Once the plan had been formulated (a process in which the People's Bank, in consultation with the SBs, plays a role by formulating a credit plan), it was then left to the PBC to allocate funds to ensure that the plan was fulfilled. The PBC published credit targets which were mandatory (not to be exceeded) for fixed-asset loans and more flexible for working-capital loans. It also identified sectoral priorities and instructed the SBs what was required of them under the plan and allocated a portion of state funds to the SBs for these purposes. However, the accounts of the SBs at the People's Bank were not credited with sufficient funds to

---

2. For the new role of the People's Bank, see Lu and Qian (1984) and World Bank (1988: pp. 255–56). For a description of the original functions of the ICB, see *New China News Agency (NCNA)*, Beijing, 7 February 1984.

3. In controlling the activities of the SBs, the People's Bank was able to utilise an organisational structure which included branch offices at the provincial level.

cover planned expenditures, leaving the SBs with the need to raise funds from other sources (for example, urban enterprises and residents in the case of the ICB) in order to meet their loan targets. The SBs were required to keep 10 per cent of their deposits as reserves with the PBC and were permitted to make loans only on the basis of their deposits (the principle, to be introduced in 1985, was 'more deposits, more loans', *duocun duodai*).

Along with changes in the structure of the banking system came a rapid spread of other types of financial institutions, notably trust and investment companies (TICs). These were established by local governments or as trust divisions of local specialised banks. Of particular importance were the international TICs, which were set up in the localities on the model of CITIC to attract foreign investment for local enterprises and joint ventures (World Bank 1988: pp. 325–26). There was also a spread of rural and credit cooperatives servicing households and small-scale enterprises, operating under the supervision of the ABC and ICB, respectively.

By late 1984, when a decision was taken by the CCP leadership to accelerate the pace of overall reform in the urban-industrial sector, China's financial system had already undergone major changes. It was considerably more diversified and flexible than its predecessor, had introduced elements of commercial practice into its operations (notably more flexible use of interest rates, more systematic accounting procedures, and some limited competition for deposits, particularly in the non-bank sector). As a reform project, it had outpaced other areas of reform in the (urban/industrial) state sector; however, its scope was still very circumscribed. The financial system was still, directly or indirectly, a state monopoly and was still managed as an administrative system. Although interest rates were used more flexibly, they were still primarily set by central financial planners and not by some notional or real market process.[4] The autonomy of the banks was severely limited, whether this was the People's Bank in relation to the State Council and the Ministry of Finance, specialised banks in relation to the People's Bank, local bank branches in relation to local governments or individual bank branches in relation to their head offices. Though the number of banks had increased and they were increasingly encouraged to compete for deposits, there was little sanctioned

---

4. For a review of interest rate policies over this early period, see Jiang Weijun, "Forum on reforming bank interest", an account of a forum organised by the People's Bank, reported in *People's Daily*, Beijing, 13 August 1984, in *FBIS* 161.

competition between them in loans, since each specialised bank was supposed to operate within its own sectoral terrain (*hangye*). The banking system still acted as an arm of the economic planning system and was thus expected to implement sectoral plan objectives through policy loans at preferential rates (the same could be said of the mushrooming TICs set up by local governments). When macroeconomic problems emerged, therefore, such as the monetary over-expansions and inflationary surges of 1979–1980 and 1984–1985, the banking authorities responded by resorting primarily to traditional administrative methods of control.

As of late 1984, the central issue in financial reform was the extent to which it was to be extended to accompany the introduction of the economic reform programme into the urban-industrial sector after the resounding successes of agricultural reform in the early 1980s. At the top policy-making level, the reform consensus in the CCP leadership had been strengthened in the early 1980s as residual Maoists had been removed from positions of power; key reformers had taken their place, notably Zhao Ziyang as state premier in 1980 and Hu Yaobang as general secretary of the Communist Party in 1982. As far as they and other more radical reformists within the CCP leadership were concerned, a deepening of the reform process was necessary, and in this they received a good deal of supportive advice from economists in academic societies and research institutions, some of them acting as unofficial or official "brain-trusters" for individual leaders. The reformers advocated a decisive move beyond what they saw as relatively marginal changes in the structure and behaviour of the banking system towards something that could be called a "financial market" (*jinrong shichang*); this term is a broad one, encompassing a loan market in bank credit, a money market in short-term assets and a capital market in longer-term assets such as bonds and shares. For example, one young Turk attending a conference of the Chinese Finance and Banking Society in mid-1984 highlighted the lack of competition within the banking system:[5]

> [Financial reform so far] has been an endless game of administrative changes. The agricultural sector has been in and out of the People's Bank several times since 1949, but we are none the wiser. . . . There is no way a Central Bank can function properly without a financial market. . . . The four specialised banks each monopolise one corner of China's banking business and the flow of capital is blocked.

---

5. "Monopoly of banking by the state criticised", *China Daily*, Beijing, 9 June 1984.

Though proposals for the introduction of financial markets had been raised earlier,[6] they had been lone voices and had run into a lot of opposition on ideological grounds. Even in 1984, when the first phase of the overall reform programme had proven successful and the political context for deeper reform was more favourable, such proposals met with opposition along the lines, for example, that competition between banks would lead them to seek profit above all and neglect their social role, or that a capital market with private financial institutions and a share system would constitute incipient capitalism and was thus fundamentally incompatible with even a reformed "socialist" economy. This was evidence of the continuing importance of what one might call the *ideological imperative* in the policy process, the fact that different members of the political leadership and their expert advisors had different perceptions of the compatibility between financial reform and certain basic principles and institutions of state socialism inherited from the previous system. Ideological differences created a spectrum of political opinion from radical "reformers" at one end to diehard "conservatives" at the other.

But this was not the only axis of disagreement over financial policy. Underlying the economic reforms generally and the financial reforms in particular were two other imperatives which conditioned policy— the *control* and the *efficiency imperatives*. The former implied the desire to maintain strict macroeconomic control over the reform process for both economic and political reasons and was fuelled by the early experience with inflation during 1979–1980; the latter emphasised the need for systemic change to improve the performance of microeconomic actors. There was increasing disagreement among the leadership over the relationship between these two objectives and the relative priority to be accorded to them in overall reform strategy. This disagreement was to accelerate along with the reforms in the mid-1980s and coincides to an extent with the ideological distinction between 'reformers' and 'conservatives'. Conservatives such as Chen Yun were to lay increasing emphasis on the need for macro-financial stability and central control and argued that many microeconomic goals could be achieved within this framework, whereas reformers such as Zhao Ziyang and his advisors argued the over-riding need for systemic change as a precondition for improvements in allocative

---

6. For example, at a forum organised by a radically reformist newspaper in late 1981, a researcher from the Shanghai Academy of Social Sciences suggested a capital market which would exist outside the state financial system to collect surplus local funds beyond central control. See Pan Dehong (1981).

efficiency and enterprise performance and were willing to tolerate a looser or more unstable macroeconomic regime if it could facilitate these broader objectives.[7]

However, to understand the political dynamics of financial reform merely in terms of the views of central policy-makers would miss a crucial dimension of the policy process, the fact that in the short space of a few years, the real world of the Chinese economy had changed considerably and that official policies on financial reform were already being taken beyond their original intention. In terms of the "real" economy, the range of production governed by mandatory plans was decreasing, the commodity economy was emerging both within and outside the state sector, and the economy became increasingly 'monetised', as the figures in Table 4.1 indicate.

Moreover, the first five years of the reform programme had seen a massive dispersion of financial resources away from the direct control of the central planners and financial authorities into the hands of local governments, enterprises and households. State enterprises increased the resources at their disposal through new policies which allowed them to retain depreciation funds and a proportion of profits; increases in wages and in agricultural prices and productivity led to a

TABLE 4.1 Financial Deepening: Selected Ratios, 1979–1989 (per cent)

Year	M1/GDP	M2/GDP	Demand Deposits /GDP	Time Deposits /GDP
1979	30.0	37.5	23.0	7.6
1980	33.2	44.6	25.2	11.5
1981	36.1	49.9	27.5	13.8
1982	36.5	52.0	27.7	15.5
1983	42.2	55.7	32.7	13.5
1984	50.6	66.0	38.8	15.5
1985	45.1	62.6	38.2	17.6
1986	50.2	71.1	37.3	20.9
1987	51.7	75.5	38.3	23.8
1988	49.6	71.5	34.5	21.9
1989	38.4	59.8	26.6	21.4

SOURCE: World Bank 1990b: p. 145.

NOTE: M1 is defined as the sum of currency and demand deposits. M2 is equal to M1 plus time deposits and capital construction deposits. The data for 1989 are for the second quarter; all other figures are annual.

---

7. For a useful discussion of the differences between central leaders on economic issues, see Bachman (1986).

rapid increase in household savings, especially in urban areas (Naughton 1987); and the proportion of national income captured through central state revenue declined substantially from 37.2 per cent in 1978 to 26.6 per cent by 1985 (State Statistical Bureau [SSB] 1991: p. 20).[8] The central government's power to capture and control this revenue by fiscal means was declining, a trend which was also affecting local governments. However, although there were pressures on both central and local government budget revenues, the economic powers of local governments (and individual administrative departments at each level) were increasing dramatically, providing them with opportunities to increase their revenue base by other means. While local governments had been formally granted greater fiscal powers since 1980 (Oksenberg and Tong 1991), they had also greatly expanded their ability to capture a proportion of enterprise funds by various levies to create a rapidly increasing pool of "extra-budgetary funds" (*yusuanwai jijin*) which they could use for their own economic purposes.[9] At the local level, (formal and informal) fiscal decentralisation had led to a situation where different levels of government "eat from different kitchens", fostering an increasing fusion of interests between local governments and local state enterprises.[10] At the central level, the government was increasingly losing control over the overall level of investment as local governments, departments and enterprises used the burgeoning funds at their disposal to launch projects which were beyond the control of central planners, often made little economic sense and fuelled inflation.

Though these problems could be tackled by reforms across a wide front (involving changes in wage, price, interprovincial trade and fiscal policies), the banks were an obvious instrument to impose control. Banks were also required to play a more active role as financial intermediaries. The domestic savings rate remained high and indeed increased during the course of the 1980s, as shown in Table 4.2.

However, it is important to note that the composition of savings changed dramatically during this period. Specifically, rising real incomes together with the introduction of the responsibility system in the rural sector resulted in the share of household savings increasing rapidly whilst government budgetary savings (defined as the current account surplus of the state budget) correspondingly decreased as government revenues fell in response to the fiscal reforms which left en-

---

8. For a discussion of this perceived problem of financial dispersion, see Wang Jiye (1983).

9. See Table 6.4 for details of the increase in "extra-budgetary funds."

10. For an analysis of this fusion, see Song Tingming (1985).

TABLE 4.2   Domestic Savings as a Percentage of GDP, 1978–1988

Year	Saving Rate
1978	33.2
1979	34.6
1980	32.3
1981	30.0
1982	31.6
1983	31.5
1984	32.8
1985	34.5
1986	36.1
1987	39.0
1988	38.0

SOURCE: World Bank 1990c: p. 103.

terprises with greater control over enterprise profits.[11] The changing composition of savings is shown in Table 4.3.[12]

This shift in the composition of savings implied a parallel shift in the importance of the budgetary and financial systems as vehicles for the efficient functioning of the economy.[13] Thus, it became obvious early on in the reforms that the banking system would be required to be more active in raising, regulating and intermediating flows of financial resources and would also be required to play a more active role in ensuring that enterprises used their resources efficiently. However, these macro- and microeconomic objectives could not be

11. Whether the rise in household savings is voluntary or the result of "forced savings" is a controversial issue which we discuss further in Chapter 5.

12. The calculation of these figures requires some data manipulation because of the non-comparability of data prior to 1982. For the definitions of variables and the manner in which they have been calculated, see the note to Table 4.7 in World Bank, (1990c), p. 103. Whilst these data problems may reduce the reliability of the figures, the overall trends are nevertheless clear.

13. The rapid rise in the importance of household savings is particularly striking in the case of urban savings deposits. As the figures in Table 4.4 indicate, urban and rural savings held in the state banking sector were of equal importance at the beginning of the reform period. By the beginning of the 1990s, however, the volume of urban savings was over six times greater than the volume of rural savings. In part this was due to rising urban wages from the mid 1980s onwards and in part due to expansion of non-state financial institutions in rural areas (see Tam 1991 and Manoharan 1991) and the wider range of assets available to rural residents (especially housing). As the relative importance of urban savings rose, this further strengthened the general need to concentrate on the reform of the urban sector after the initial emphasis on the agricultural sector.

TABLE 4.3   Composition of Savings, 1978–1988 (per cent)

Year	Household Savings	Budgetary Savings	Enterprises and Other
1978	3.4	45.4	51.2
1979	9.0	29.0	62.0
1980	13.5	22.5	64.0
1981	11.4	22.0	66.6
1982	23.8	17.1	59.0
1983	31.5	18.1	50.4
1984	44.0	20.0	36.0
1985	39.0	20.4	40.6
1986	39.9	16.1	44.1
1987	41.6	11.4	47.0
1988	44.7	8.3	47.0

Source: World Bank 1990c: p. 103.

met unless the operational autonomy of the banking system was expanded. In the context of an economy which was more decentralised and less malleable, financial management at the central level needed coordination between the main agencies of macroeconomic regulation—the State Planning Commission (SPC), the Ministry of Finance, and the People's Bank.[14] This also implied a stable and agreed

TABLE 4.4   Urban and Rural Savings in National Banks, 1978–1990 (billion yuan)

Year	Urban Savings	Rural Savings	Ratio Urban/Rural
1978	15.49	15.44	1.0
1979	20.26	20.37	0.99
1980	28.25	23.98	1.18
1981	35.42	27.84	1.27
1982	44.73	32.99	1.36
1983	57.26	39.13	1.46
1984	77.66	37.24	2.09
1985	105.78	44.96	2.35
1986	147.15	55.96	2.63
1987	206.76	62.63	3.30
1988	265.92	66.96	3.97
1989	373.48	71.63	5.21
1990	519.26	85.03	6.11

Source: World Bank 1990b: p. 137; SSB 1991: p. 576.

---

14. A joint forum to achieve better coordination between the main central economic agencies in the effort to control extra-budgetary funds was held in mid-1983, in cooperation with the State Statistical Bureau. See Wu Renjian (1983).

division of labour (and powers) between the three agencies, each enjoying an area of relative autonomy from the others though subject to the overall authority of the State Council. The issue of bank autonomy was becoming crucial because one of the reasons for over-investment was the vulnerability of the SBs to external pressure—from local governments to provide credit for their favoured projects and from enterprises which (with the help of their "responsible departments" in the state economic bureaucracy) were able to maintain flows of credit regardless of poor loan or productive performance.[15] The banks also needed more autonomy to be able to vet "official" investment projects submitted within the plan in terms of their economic soundness. Relations between banks and the budgetary system also needed to be rationalised because there was an evolving conflict between them over financial claims on enterprises; the fiscal authorities resented the fact that priority was being given to the repayment of bank loans over the payment of taxes.

What seemed to be needed was a division of labour which would give banks in general, and the Central Bank (i.e., the PBC) in particular, a greater degree of autonomy to regulate the monetary system; but this did not mean outright independence, since the banks were still to act as a instrument of the plan. In this early stage, some progress was made in this direction by transferring to the banking system the prime responsibility for providing circulating funds to enterprises and going part-way in terms of the provision of funds for fixed asset investment; henceforth these were to be channelled through the ICB and PCBC, respectively.[16] There was also an understanding that the Ministry of Finance could decrease its pressure on the PBC to finance fiscal deficits by seeking alternative sources of revenue: partly by revising its fiscal relations with local governments and regularising the taxation system in general to provide a stable and adequate supply of revenue to the state budget; partly by increasing public debt through foreign loans and the sale of Treasury bonds; and partly by

---

15. For evidence of the pervasive phenomenon of local government intrusion in bank operations, see "Make full use of the role of banks in economic readjustment", *Shaanxi Ribao* (Shaanxi Daily), Xian, 27 April 1981, p. 2, in *FBIS* 104. For an early example of pressure from the fiscal authorities to finance government deficits through bank loans, see Huang Jubo (1981). The effects of these micro-level pressures on inflation are discussed further in Chapter 5.

16. Progress on the fixed-assets front was very limited, however, and the percentage provided by bank loans was estimated to be less than 10 per cent of total investment budgeted by the state. See the report on new measures introduced by the SPC and the PCBC in *NCNA*, 4 July 1984.

asserting the right to enforce certain special levies for important capital construction projects. But the question of bank autonomy was a thorny one, involving not only the basic logic of China as a developmental state but also powerful political forces at both the centre and in the localities, which had an interest in continuing to influence bank behaviour.

The central-local dimension was particularly important because the competing interests of the centre and the localities were also producing institutional changes which complicated the financial system and made any attempt to enforce financial policy from the centre increasingly difficult. One important new factor was the spread of NBFIs which were designed to further local politico-economic interests, providing the means whereby the localities could evade central controls exerted through the banking system (Liu Hongru 1982). The emergence of TICs was an early expression of an emergent dualism in the financial system, which reflected wider changes in the political and economic systems at large and was to become even more pronounced in the next phase of reform.

At the end of this first phase of reform in late 1984, therefore, there were powerful economic and political pressures operating to push the reforms on to a second, more radical phase. Partly these reflected the effects of the reform programme in general and the financial reforms in particular on China's economic structure and institutional system; partly they reflected the interplay of politico-economic forces at all levels which had benefitted from the reforms so far and had an interest in their continuance. Potentially powerful sceptics such as the Ministry of Finance could be accommodated to the new arrangements, and it was hoped that further reforms would weaken the power of influential CCP leaders who were worried about the financial reforms either because of their uncertain macroeconomic consequences or their threat to basic socialist values and institutions.

Policy Process Phase II, 1985–1988:
The Move Towards Financial Markets

The change in the paradigm of financial reform was a gradual process. It began with certain proposals by academics and other experts during 1982–1984, was given strength by the previously identified economic and political forces and was ushered in by further incremental changes along the lines of the initial reform paradigm during 1984 and 1985. This second stage marks a paradigm shift in the sense that it did not merely represent a continuation of earlier reforms but changed the framework of thinking about the nature of the desired financial system. It thereby challenged in a much more fundamental way the ideological assumptions and institutional character of the pre-reform system, in much the same way as the open-ended market socialist debate was doing elsewhere.

The new framework moved the notion of financial markets much closer to the centre of analysis and raised fundamental questions about enterprise autonomy, ownership and economic planning. It reflected (and reinforced) a "cosmopolitanising" of Chinese thinking on financial issues in the sense that Chinese policy-makers and officials became increasingly absorbed in an international discourse on financial systems and financial liberalisation among Western banking circles, financial experts and international institutions such as the World Bank and the International Monetary Fund, which became increasingly influential elements in the Chinese policy-making process in the mid-1980s (for a detailed discussion of this interaction, see Jacobson and Oksenberg 1990).

The new framework, however, represented a political rupture in the sense that it threatened still influential notions about the nature of a "socialist" economy, it infringed upon certain powerful political, economic and institutional interests wedded to the existing semi-reformed financial system and it promised to create new interests which would exert pressure to force the issue even at the cost of political conflict. In terms of the practicalities of policy implementation, moreover, the difficulties of engineering systemic transition had already led to serious problems of maintaining macro-control in a financial system which was on the one hand very responsive to reform initiatives but on the other hand responded in ways which reflected the characteristic tendencies of a semi-reformed shortage economy. In particular, new reform initiatives on the financial front threatened to uncage inflationary pressures, which brought political problems in their train by undermining popular consent for the reform programme and galvanising conservative forces who were eager to seize on problems to stop or slow down the reforms. In the light of all these political and economic constraints, therefore, the new paradigm of financial reform was not merely a logical extension of previous changes; it faced a political struggle to be born.

The debate over the way forward gathered intensity during 1984–1985 as the money supply rocketed, inflation increased, investment soared out of control and the balance of payments deteriorated drastically. This prompted a concerted effort during 1985 to reimpose control by traditional means and intensified the debate among politicians and specialists about how to proceed on the financial front. Conservative voices pointed to the dangers of destabilisation posed by further financial reform and the need to maintain strict administrative controls over the issue of currency and the allocation of credit.[17] Reformers argued to the contrary that the underlying problem was rooted in microeconomic distortions reflecting the incomplete state of economic reform in both the financial system and the economic system as a whole, and that problems of macroeconomic control could gradually be solved by switching from direct to indirect methods of regulation.[18]

Given the shift in the balance of power among the CCP leadership, analysed earlier, the reform position won through[19] but changes could not begin in earnest until the disequilibria which appeared in 1984 were brought under control—this was the major task of 1985, when a battery of direct and indirect controls were reimposed or tightened under the general heading of a policy of "killing first and resuscitating later" (*xiansi houhuo*). The new phase of reforms did not begin to accelerate until well into 1986, with five "experimental cities" (Chongqing, Guangzhou, Wuhan, Shenyang and Changzhou) leading the way by pioneering the development of NBFIs and opening up money/capital markets. By August of that year, official spokespeople were mapping out an optimistic strategy of the construction of a new "socialist monetary system" between 1986 and 1990.[20]

The new paradigm reflected the microeconomic concerns of the reformers and by now was drawing not merely on the MSII version of 'market socialism' but also on key ideas of the 'finance and development' paradigm drawn from external sources such as the World Bank. Its key propositions were as follows. First, there was increasing emphasis on the need to endow banks with far greater autonomy from the political and governmental leadership, at both central and local levels. Only then could the Central Bank act effectively as a kind of "supra-political" guarantor of financial stability; only then could individual banks be "turned into enterprises" (*qiyehua*) in order to operate as truly independent "economic entities" (*jingji shiti*) on a profit and loss basis. This move towards bank autonomy also implied greater autonomy for regional and local banks in relation to their head offices. Second, the financial authorities should move still further away from

17. For example, see Li Chengrui (1985).

18. See, for example, Wang Zhuo (1985) and Huang Yingfei and Xia Bin (1985).

19. By early to mid-1986, reformist analysis and policy prescriptions held undisputed sway. For example, see Shen Peijun (1986).

20. For example, see the address by Liu Hongru, vice governor of the PBC, to the annual meeting of the Chinese Monetary Society, reported by *NCNA* (English), 14 August 1986.

traditional administrative methods of direction and control over the banking system (notably credit ceilings and mandatory sectoral targets) towards the kind of indirect economic methods used in more "developed" financial systems (such as the use of reserve ratios, open market operations, variations in interest rates and the lending policy of the central bank). Third, not only should a greater diversity of financial institutions be encouraged, but this process should go beyond a mere differentiation of the state banking system to include the establishment of non-state banks and a much wider variety of non-bank financial entities, including cooperative and eventually private institutions.[21] Fourth, this in turn would produce a context more conducive to competition within the financial system, a *sine qua non* of a true financial market—competition between banks (including foreign banks), between banks and NBFIs and between different types of ownership. Fifth, new financial instruments should be popularised through the development of money and capital markets. The introduction of capital markets, especially the issue of shares, pushed to the limits the debate over how the ownership system of "reformed socialism" should be structured.[22]

These reforms in the domestic financial system were to be accompanied by an extension of the "open policy" to encourage a wider range of interaction with foreign sources of funding—whether private capital, governments or international institutions such as the World Bank, IMF and Asian Development Bank—and to develop a domestic market in foreign exchange. They were also to be underpinned by an acceleration of complementary reforms in other spheres, particularly in enterprise management, ownership, labour and employment policy, and the price system, in the recognition that if financial reforms ran ahead of the reform programme as a whole as they had in the first phase, they would lead to distorted results at both the macro-level (notably over-investment and inflation) and the micro-level (a perverse softening of the enterprise budget constraint), which would be self-defeating.

During 1986 and 1987, these reforms accelerated with remarkable speed (for example, the five experimental cities had already expanded to include 27 cities and the whole of Guangdong Province by the end of 1986). The role of the financial sector in the national economy continued to grow: The share of new bank deposits in national income continued to climb while the share of fiscal revenue continued to de-

---

21. See Tam (1992) for an account of the operations of the Hui Tong Urban Cooperative Bank, the first private bank to be opened during the reform era.
22. This is discussed in detail in Chapter 6.

cline (from 37.2 per cent in 1978 to 24.3 per cent in 1987 and 21.7 per cent by 1990)(SSB 1991: p. 55). The People's Bank's role as prime regulator of the financial system was consolidated. It began to acquire some limited degree of autonomy as a macroeconomic agent acting as the guardian of financial order against the overweening ambitions of economic planners and any temptation on the part of fiscal departments to fall back on the banking system to help them finance budget deficits. Its position within the central government was enhanced by the influence of its then governor, Chen Muhua, who was an alternate member of the CCP Politburo. However, for all this, it remained but one agency within an overall institutional system of economic planning, a fact which was reflected in the composition of the bank's council, where there are representatives of the Ministry of Finance, the State Planning Commission and the Economic System Reform Commission (World Bank 1990b: p. 5). At the same time, moreover, the power of the PBC's head office to control the national financial situation was reduced by moves to allow greater autonomy to provincial branches of the PBC (and their counterparts in the specialised banks).[23] For example, as part of the policy of 'loose control amid stability' (*wenzhong qiusong*) adopted in 1986, local PBCs, starting with Shanghai and Shenzhen SEZ, were allowed to increase their autonomy vis-à-vis their head office with the power to plan and regulate credit flows within their areas—this was hailed as a major change away from 'vertical' (*tiaotiao*) to 'horizontal' (*kuaikuai*) financial controls (see Rong Fenge 1986).[24]

The banking system in general diversified as the existing specialised banks established new branches and two new national banks were set up: The joint-stock Shanghai-based Communications Bank and a subsidiary of CITIC, the CITIC Industrial Bank, opened for business in 1987.[25] In the more "open areas" on the east coast, diversification went further as specialised banks and joint Chinese-foreign banks were set up to service foreign trade and investment in Guangdong Province, Shanghai and the southeastern Special Economic Zones of Xiamen, Zhuhai and Shenzhen.

---

23. For a detailed account of measures to expand the autonomy of local branches of the Agricultural Bank, for example, see Ma Yongwei (1987).

24. For a report on how the local PBC took on this role at the city level, see Huang Cunming (1989).

25. For a discussion of the significance of the establishment of the Communications Bank, see "A new product of the reform of our country's economic and financial system", *Zhongguo Jinrong* (Chinese Finance) (CH), March 1987, pp. 14–15. Fifty per cent of the initial shares were controlled by the PBC, and shares sold to the public were restricted to 20 per person (at 500 *yuan* per share).

Steps were also taken to accelerate the "enterprisation" of the banks. The specialised state banks increased their range of activities (for example, through the issue of bonds and the discounting of commercial paper), and the scope of interbank business expanded rapidly.[26] Banks were encouraged to move outside their own sectoral boundaries to compete for deposits and loans and allowed to expand their loan activities along with increases in their deposits. The link between loans and deposits established in 1985 (Liu Hongru 1986b) meant that a specialised bank might be able to make loans above planned targets on the basis of excess deposits. In 1986, for example, actual loans made by the ICB exceeded the plan by 30 per cent. SBs requiring extra deposits could obtain them in a number of ways. They could borrow from each other at the inter-bank loan rate, issue bonds with the permission of the People's Bank and borrow from the PBC at the discount rate. They faced penalties, in terms of higher interest rates, on the inter-bank market if they failed to repay loans on time.

Complementary measures were adopted to encourage the specialised banks to act more like commercial enterprises through the 'principle of differentiation', i.e., to allocate loan funds on the basis of enterprise profitability, thereby ensuring that no enterprises had an automatic right to credit. Auditing departments were set up in the People's Bank and the specialised banks, and in January 1986 the State Council issued an interim set of 'Regulations on Bank Management', which stressed the responsibility of banks to allocate credit efficiently.[27] Banks were increasingly required to use economic criteria in assessing loan applications: For example, in making loans to enterprises for technical upgrading, ICB branches were expected to evaluate loan applications according to the market demand for the product, the availability of raw materials, the profitability of the investment, and the prospect of repayment within three years. The People's Bank played an important supervisory role here, auditing the annual record of specialised banks in terms of scale of lending and loan performance both at the headquarters and branch levels. As another facet of "enterprisation", banks were increasingly able to keep a portion of their profits, like other state enterprises. According to the new system, in-

---

26. For a review of the development of money markets during 1986, see the report in *NCNA*, 30 December 1986, which, amongst other things, discusses the establishment of China's first post-revolutionary trans-regional financial networks.

27. For an English text of these regulations, see *NCNA*, domestic service, 16 Jan. 1986, in *FBIS* 018; for the Chinese text, see "Temporary Regulations for Bank Management in the PRC", *Zhongguo Jinrong* (Chinese Finance), Beijing, March 1986, pp. 11–17. The regulations are analysed by Liu Hongru (1986a).

stead of remitting all their profits to their 'superior' organ, banks paid an income tax of 55 per cent on profits, retained 35 per cent to add to their capital stock, and can then distributed the remaining 10 per cent for employee bonuses and welfare.

The PBC also moved to expand the range of indirect methods of financial regulation at its disposal. It was expected that the activities of the specialised banks could increasingly be regulated through variations in reserve deposits and in the terms and amounts of credit granted to them from the PBC. The PBC also moved to allow interest rates to be used more flexibly. The range of admissible rates was expanded and greater autonomy was granted to basic-level financial institutions: For example, bank managers in the 'experimental cities' were given increased powers to vary interest rates by up to 20 per cent and to reorganise and reward staff; in the case of rural and urban credit cooperatives, the range of variation was as high as 90 per cent above the PBC's base interest rate.

If the greater discretion granted to bank branches expanded the range of competition for loans and deposits, this was reinforced by a proliferation of NBFIs. Rural credit cooperatives (RCCs) expanded their business to absorb the rapid increase in rural household savings; per capita savings deposits by members of rural households rose from a pre-reform level of 7.1 yuan in 1978 to 84.8 yuan in 1985 and 253.5 yuan in 1989 (ZGJRNJ 1990: p. 62), and the value of deposits in the RCCs increased tenfold over the same period (ZGJRNJ 1990: p. 65). The RCCs loaned largely to township and village industries (54 per cent of loans in 1990) and households (37 per cent) (SSB 1991: p. 579). (For an overview, see Tam 1988.) Outside the RCCs emerged a new layer of formal and informal savings and credit institutions, some organised collectively under the auspices of village governments, some organised as cooperative funds by peasant households and others organised by private individuals and syndicates (Manoharan 1991).

In the urban areas, per capita savings deposits increased from 90.1 yuan in 1978 to 275.5 yuan in 1985 to 672.9 yuan in 1989, and urban credit cooperatives (UCCs) expanded rapidly from 1986 onwards to capture a share (ZGJRNJ 1990: p. 189); the bulk of UCC loans as of 1989 went to collective industrial and commercial enterprises (ZGJRNJ 1990: p. 66). Banks also joined with enterprises to establish joint-stock 'financial groups' to act as relatively independent financial agencies active in raising funds to supply the needs of component enterprises.[28] By 1989, moreover, there were 745 trust and investment

---

28. For an example, see the case of the Songjiang Financial Group, the first to be established in Jilin Province in the industrial north-east: *Jilin Radio*, 11 February 1987, in Summary of World Broadcasts (*SWB*) 8492.

companies (TICs) across the country, and they were increasingly joined by specialised entities such as leasing and finance companies. The number of insurance offices under the People's Insurance Company of China rose from 567 in 1981 to 2,861 in 1989, while the number of employees in insurance increased over tenfold (ZGJRNJ 1990: p. 189); between 1985 and 1990, the volume of insurance business tripled (SSB 1991: p. 582). Moreover, as we will discuss in detail in Chapter 6, there was a concomitant expansion in the issue and circulation of longer-term financial assets such as bonds and shares.

Clearly, from the vantage point of late 1987, the overall achievements of financial reform over the preceding three years had been impressive. At the same time the results were only partial. Indeed, the resulting financial system could be described as dualistic, proceeding in parallel with an increasing dualism in the economy as a whole. Branch banks could now get funds from their head office, but also from financial bonds, money market operations and borrowing from the People's Bank (at the same level). Enterprises could now get funds from the banks or could launch their own bond or share issues. Interest rates on bank loans were relatively stable, whereas those on the inter-bank call market varied constantly. The main state banks were now being joined by a plethora of non-bank financial institutions, many of them based on joint-stock or cooperative ownership. Overall, financial reform resulted in a system of relatively tight regulation (if not control over lending volumes) over the state banking sector and weaker controls over the burgeoning second financial sector. (For an analysis of this dualistic system, see Zhu Jicheng 1987.) There were thus elements of change and continuity. The continuities were fundamental and problematic, argued reform economists (for example Cao Xingren 1987): The state banks were still predominant; the central bank had insufficient independence on monetary matters both in relation to other central agencies, notably the SPC and the MOF, and in relation to the specialised banks.[29]

As the reforms accelerated during the heady years of 1986–1988, however, monetary aggregates spun out of control (ZGJRNJ 1991: p. 46) and the central authorities struggled to contain them beginning in the last quarter of 1987 by raising the reserve ratio from 10 to 12 per cent and the interest rate of loans from the PBC to the SBs. However, these and other measures introduced during the first half of 1988 to tighten credit and rein in the growth in the money supply met with very little success. By August 1988, official spokespeople were

29. For a critique along these lines, see Lu Mi (1989). For a specific discussion of the problematic relationship between the fiscal and banking authorities, see Jing Xiucheng (1988) and Wang Shaofei (1988).

describing the financial situation as "extremely grim". As inflation accelerated, the real value of bank deposits declined and people withdrew savings to purchase consumer goods, thereby adding to inflationary pressures; indeed there were three runs on the banks during the year.[30] As real interest rates became increasingly negative, the incentive increased for enterprises to buy and hoard scarce raw and processed materials financed by bank credit.[31] This was yet another more intense example of the first stage of a policy cycle of economic expansion and contraction which had been in evidence since the very early years of reform. Though earlier surges had been brought under control through a re-imposition of administrative controls, inflation began to reassert itself in 1985 and leapt to alarming proportions by 1988, in which year the retail price index rose by an officially recorded (and under-estimated) figure of 18.5 per cent (SSB 1991: p. 198).

Underlying this process, and the policy response to it, were the kinds of politico-economic pressures and ideological disagreements which had fuelled earlier periods of overheating. Local governments were still the major villains in the eyes of reform analysts because of their headlong rush to expand their industrial bases, particularly through a proliferation of quick-profit enterprises producing consumer items such as cigarettes, liquor and textiles.[32] Enterprise managers (and their superior government departments) still exhibited the "investment hunger" of a shortage economy, and managers were still willing (and able) to appease their workforces by issuing bonuses in advance of productivity gains, types of behaviour which we will examine further in Chapter 5. Reformist leaders and experts may have seen certain kinds of retrenchment as necessary to deal with inflation, but they argued that any programme of retrenchment should contain elements of both control and flexibility, that any control measures should be applied differentially to well and poorly performing enterprises, that economic rather than administrative methods should be used to control bank lending and that the priority for restraining inflation should not totally displace the needs of economic growth. They regarded any resort to administrative controls as only a temporary expedient in a situation which could ultimately, in their opinion, only

---

30. This was admitted by the governor of the People's Bank, Li Guixian, in early 1989. See *NCNA* (English), 12 January 1989.

31. See "Interest, the cost of capital", *NCNA* (domestic), 31 August 1988, in *FBIS* 173.

32. For a typical reform criticism of the role of local governments, see Nie Qingping (1988).

be resolved by deeper reforms.[33] Their more conservative counterparts were increasingly dismayed by the breakneck pace of an economic reform which was going further than they felt comfortable with because of their diminishing ability to control economic events and because of the mounting political costs of high inflation.

By the autumn of 1988, the situation was truly alarming, not merely because of the deteriorating macroeconomic situation but also because of the failure of earlier efforts to control the situation during 1988. This failure partially represents a clash in strategic intentions between a desire for both growth and stability. As one example of official sensitivity to the inflation/growth trade-off, "Chinese banking circles" were quoted in January 1988 as making the following argument: "China will not resort to depending on inflation to develop the economy. However, as a developing country, it cannot afford to operate such a credit squeeze [adopted in early 1988] for too long. This means the issue of currency should be appropriate to avoid inflation while meeting the needs of economic development".[34] The Delphic phrase "the needs of economic development" in fact reflects the kind of politico-economic interests and pressures which we have identified here, which had by 1988 evolved into a powerful constituency for both fast growth and further financial reform and which frustrated official efforts to regain macro-financial equilibrium. Reformist leaders within the leadership faced a particularly acute dilemma because this was "their" constituency; a radical and comprehensive financial retrenchment would go counter to its interests, undermine the progress of the economic reform programme as a whole and cede power to their conservative opponents within the Party leadership and the traditional system of administered economic planning. As Song Tingming, a spokesperson for the reformist State Economic Structural Reform Commission, pointed out in early 1988, "The reforms are in essence a readjustment of power and interests; therefore they will certainly meet with obstructions [such as] traditional concepts and customs, the old economic system ... and the ossified Leftist way of thinking".[35]

The difficulty for reformers in the area of financial reform (as opposed, say, to reforms in enterprise management or the labour/

33. For examples of this analysis of the situation, see Nie Qingping (1988) and the report on the suggestions put forward to the State Council by a group of economists from the Chinese Academy of Social Sciences, led by CASS vice-president Liu Guoguang in *NCNA*, 22 July 1988.

34. *China Daily*, Beijing, 16 January 1988.

35. *China Daily*, Beijing, 6 February 1988.

employment system, where opposition was powerful) was that, politically speaking, *both* the new, pro-reform elements in the politico-economic situation (in the rapidly expanding collective sector and in the more progressive provinces and SEZs) *and* the old, more conservative elements (notably unreformed large and medium state enterprises; their superior administrative departments, which feared the reform process as a matter of institutional life or death; and unreconstructed local governments still operating as a mini version of the traditional state-socialist developmental state) found they could benefit from financial liberalisation. One of the reasons for the difficulties encountered in trying to restrain monetary over-expansion in 1987–1988 reflects the massive yet contradictory power of this unholy coalition between "old" and "new" interests in the politico-economic system at large. This meant that in political terms, whichever group within the Party leadership threw its weight behind a comprehensive programme of financial retrenchment, it would face opposition not only from its opponent's constituency, but also from its own.

Retrenchment, Reversal and Renewal: The Financial Scene, 1988–1992

In terms of official policy, matters came to a head at the Third Plenum of the CCP Central Committee, held 26–30 September 1988. The official communiqué announced that the strategic emphasis over the next two years would be "to restore control over the economic environment and rectify economic order". This decision was seen as a setback for the reform wing of the leadership and Zhao Ziyang in particular and as a victory for more conservative figures such as Chen Yun, Premier Li Peng and Vice-Premier Yao Yilin. Other basic reforms, such as in the wage and price systems, were postponed until economic stability was re-established.

A series of measures were introduced to re-establish macro-financial equilibrium: Targets for monetary expansion and credit were made mandatory; the role of the head offices of the People's Bank and the SBs were strengthened and their branches were subjected to more rigorous scrutiny and control; reserve deposit requirements were raised (to 13 per cent); PBC branches at each level were ordered to cut back on their loans to specialised banks, and the interest rate for loans from the central bank was increased from 6 to 6.9 per cent p.a.; interest rates on deposits were indexed to keep pace with inflation; and attempts were made to restrict the proliferation of NBFIs on the grounds that an unviably large number had come into being and they were usually creatures of local governments and departments.[36]

These measures involved a concerted attempt to regain control over financial powers which had been ceded to the provinces. This phenomenon was seen as particularly serious in the case of branches of the PBC which had become "localised" (*difanghua*).[37] In the words of one provincial financial expert, "In the first phase before 1988, provincial branches of the People's Bank had more power [in relation to the PBC head office], but had weak control within the provinces; from 1988 onwards, the centre took back some power from the provinces".[38] These measures could not be seen as merely temporary, a case of *reculer pour mieux sauter*, since the inflation of 1988 had undermined the credibility of reform leaders (most notably Zhao Ziyang) as economic managers and had shifted power in favour of more conservative leaders, notably Chen Yun and Yao Yilin, whose vision of reform was less far-reaching than that of their radical counterparts. Indeed, the 1988–1989 inflation and the different responses to it by competing sections of the CCP leadership were important in setting the scene for the events leading up to the June 4 Incident in 1989. The social impact of rapidly rising prices created a rising tide of discontent in the cities, which expressed itself in a mounting antagonism to the Party leadership. Moreover, the events of 1988 had shattered the earlier consensus on reform within the CCP leadership, widened the political divisions between them and made any coherent response to the escalating crisis of mid-1989 more difficult. Members of the student and intellectual democratic movement were sensitive to these fissures in the Party and aware that the decision to impose economic retrenchment in late 1988 had weakened reformist leaders such as Zhao Ziyang; they therefore directed their political assaults against key conservative figures, intensifying divisions within the leadership still further and pushing conservatives towards a violent reaction.

In spite of the post-Tiananmen leadership's lack of political authority, the retrenchment package initiated in 1988 was highly effective as a programme of temporary economic stabilisation. The official inflation rate was brought down from 18.5 per cent in 1988 to 2.1 per cent in 1990; the total quantum of investment was kept below the

---

36. For example, see Ma Mingjia (1989).
37. For an example of this type of criticism, see Zhao Xiaomen and He Dexu (1990).
38. Interview with Sun Maolin, researcher in the Shandong Provincial People's Bank, Jilin, 8 April 1992.

1988 level for the next two years; and the expansion of the money supply was reduced. The success of this programme can be explained partly by the large amount of (dwindling) political resources which the central authorities put into the retrenchment programme and by the apparent fact that local governments were also willing to cooperate to a degree because they too had come under political pressures from the inflation of 1988–1989.[39]

Over the next few years, macroeconomic policy generally, and financial policy in particular, continued to reflect a tug of war between the central authorities and manifold interests—of enterprises, localities, institutions and social groups—pushing for a relaxation of controls over bank lending and a generalised increase in credit to keep enterprises in operation, meet official expenditure responsibilities and finance the continued ambitions of local governments. Rapidly expanding provinces such as Guangdong kept up pressure on Beijing to allow a faster growth rate and loosen controls over credit. This generalised pressure against Beijing reflected a desire not only for a loosening of controls but also for a continuation of the financial reforms of the previous few years, which had increased the financial power of these political and economic actors.

In enforcing a policy of financial stabilisation, Beijing's position was like that of someone trying to hold a ball under water. The next few years were characterised by policy fluctuations as the central authorities came under relentless pressure to relax the financial regime. They responded by relaxing controls on credit and then tried to re-establish control as credit volumes began to expand too rapidly again and the spectre of inflation loomed over the political horizon. Each attempt by the centre to re-impose controls provoked a counter-response which further weakened its capacity to control events. As a response to controls over financial flows through the state banking system, there was a continuing proliferation of non-bank financial institutions at all levels—sponsored by local governments, administrative departments, enterprises and individuals—intensifying the institutional dualism which had begun to emerge in the mid-1980s and increasing the volume of resources outside the reach of the central state.

Certain elements of the financial reform programme continued, albeit more slowly, such as the gradual expansion of markets in shares and bonds, particularly in the more dynamic cities and coastal provinces, where local governments saw share markets as useful channels

---

39. For this insight, we are indebted to Dr. Wang Shaoguang of Yale University.

to attract funds to their bailiwicks. These changes were outrunning central policies, which continued to see a continuation of the financial reforms of the mid-1980s as undesirable for reasons of ideological acceptability and macroeconomic stability. Some of the more radical aims of the pre-Tiananmen period were now officially out of favour: For example, the leadership did not view an out-and-out commercialisation of the state banking system as a desirable trend and continued to define the banks as an instrument of state planning.[40] In effect, there was a reversion to the MSI paradigm of "market socialist" reform.

However, events during the first half of 1992, and Deng Xiaoping's tour of the south-east in particular, promised to mark the beginning of a new era of renewed reform. If this is indeed the case, then our analysis of the process of financial reform in the 1980s suggests that the trajectory of financial reform in the 1990s will continue to be one determined by the complex interaction of key agents with vested interests and ideological commitments. Before speculating further on the future, however, we first examine in more detail the outcomes of the process of financial reform analysed in this chapter and then proceed to discuss the development of capital markets, an area of financial reform which lies outside of the banking system upon which we have concentrated in this chapter.

---

40. For a statement of the official position during this period, see Li Peng's speech at a meeting of the managers of banks and insurance companies, reported by *NCNA* on 19 January 1991; for a "conservative" analysis of the situation, see Wang Haifeng (1991).

5

Policy Outcomes: The Macroeconomic and Microeconomic Impact of Financial Reform

I̱ₙ THIS CHAPTER we focus more precisely on the macroeconomic and microeconomic impact of financial reform, particularly the outcomes of the period 1985 to 1988, when substantial progress was made in the directions desired by the reformers. The problems which emerged at both macro- and micro-levels during this phase seem to have been endemic to the process of financial reform; further elaborating how and why they occurred will be useful for our later analysis of the prospects for further financial reforms in the 1990s. We start by analysing the roots of the inflationary crisis of 1988-1989 and then assess the impact of financial reforms on the behaviour of enterprises.

Inflation

Our analysis of the process of financial reform has suggested that the second phase of the reforms from 1984-1985 onwards was initiated by the desire of the reformers to push further down the road to liberalisation, a desire given impetus by the key agents involved, who had interests in the creation of an increasingly decentralised financial system. This process, however, had as an unintended outcome the double-digit inflation of 1988 and 1989. We suggested in Chapter 4 that the pressures placed upon the reformed financial system, and on the banks in particular, by key agents in the economy was a major reason for the loss of macroeconomic control. We wish to examine this aspect further and to explore exactly how the dynamics of the process of financial reform contributed to inflation.

The acceleration in inflation is clear from official price data, even though measuring inflation is a problematic exercise in China. These problems arise from the fact that the same goods often have multiple prices (being sold at administered and free market prices) as a result of the "dual track" pricing system and that there is rationing of some goods. The notion of a general price index is further undermined by the existence of wide regional price variations. (See Hussain and Stern 1991: p. 146; World Bank 1990a: p. 38.) These factors mean that assigning weights in the construction of a price index becomes critical; the weights used in the official Chinese data are not publicly available and there is widespread belief that the official data underestimate the actual level of inflation.[1] Notwithstanding these measurement problems, it is clear from all sources that inflation increased substantially at the end of the 1980s, especially in 1988 and 1989, and that this requires an explanation. The official price data are given in Table 5.1.

In fact, the common experience of socialist economies undergoing reform has been that inflation has risen in the process. Part of the reason for this is attributed to "monetary overhang" (see Nuti 1986 for definitions). This means that individuals have excess money holdings (forced saving) which they would prefer to spend on goods or financial assets but are unable to do so because of the unavailability of such goods and/or assets. The existence of forced saving represents a failure of the planners to maintain a balance between consumers' incomes

TABLE 5.1   Inflation, 1978–1990 (per cent)

1978	0.7
1979	2.0
1980	6.0
1981	2.4
1982	1.9
1983	1.5
1984	2.8
1985	8.8
1986	6.0
1987	7.3
1988	18.5
1989	17.8
1990	2.1

1993   13% (handwritten)

SOURCE: SSB 1991: p. 198.

---

1. See Naughton (1990: p. 109, n. 1) for a good explanation of the problems with official price data.

and the supply of consumer goods and is a source of inflationary pressure (or repressed inflation). If price controls are relaxed, then this repressed inflation becomes open inflation. A common question in all socialist countries has been, therefore, whether forced savings exist and, if so, to what extent.

The existence of forced saving has been empirically examined in China using a number of different approaches. One approach has been the so-called disequilibrium approach, which has been applied to China by Portes and Santorum (1987) and which shows forced saving and excess demand present for the reform period studied, 1979–1983. Similar results are reported by Feltenstein and Farhadian (1987) and Feltenstein and Ha (1991), with the latter study covering the more extended period 1979–1988. Testing for forced saving is difficult given the existence of free markets which allow consumers to purchase goods in short supply at state prices on the free market, albeit at higher prices. The extent to which empirical tests of Chinese-repressed inflation explicitly incorporate this feature of the Chinese economy is one way of judging their reliability. More fundamental criticisms of the disequilibrium approach have come from the shortage school associated with Kornai. (See van Brabant 1990 and Davis and Charemza 1989 for discussions.) Given the problems of estimating forced savings by econometric means, other attempts have been made to ascertain their extent by survey interviews asking respondents whether their savings are voluntary. Certainly the fact that savings deposits in banks in China had risen to over one trillion yuan by 1992 (see Bei, Koontz and Lu 1992: p. 4) might suggest that some involuntary savings are occurring. Results from interviews indicate that forced saving may account for part of the savings of middle-income urban workers but is not as significant for other groups (see Dessi 1991).

At the present state of knowledge, therefore, it is uncertain whether forced saving has been a major factor in increasing inflationary pressures. For example, Blejer et al. (1991: p. 21) estimate that "the magnitude of repressed inflation in China may have been limited", although they suggest that this may be more true of goods sold at state prices but may not hold for high-quality imported goods. Furthermore, as Peebles (1992: pp. 24–25) notes, the World Bank has tried to test for the existence of forced savings but "comes to opposite conclusions in the space of two pages."

The rapid rise in household savings (see Table 4.4) may be explained by factors other than the accumulation of forced savings. Specifically, individuals and enterprises may build up money balances in response to the monetization of the economy. Prior to 1979, money was of relatively little significance for acquiring entitlement to goods, especially in rural areas. During the reforms, however, the economy has become increasingly monetized, with cash transactions playing a much larger role. The increase in the money supply could have reflected this increased demand for cash balances and could not, therefore, be regarded as inflationary. This is the explanation offered by Yi (1991) for the period 1979–1984, although he argues that this may not have been the case in the mid to late 1980s.

The existence of specific institutional factors, including the fact that the general price index is determined by both state-administered and free market prices and the fact that velocity has decreased substantially during the reform period (see Yi 1991: p. 79) due to monetisation and/or forced saving, has meant that those using the quantity theory of money to examine the direct relationship between changes in the money supply and changes in the price level have met with very limited success (for an example, see Chow 1987 and for criticism, Peebles 1992).[2]

In any case, what is required is an explanation of why monetary aggregates increased in the first place. This requires an analysis of the Chinese institutional setting and an understanding of the actors involved in the process.[3] It is this analysis which we wish to advance

---

2. The general retail price index is constructed on the basis of a weighted average of market and administered prices. The weight for free market prices is estimated to be about 12–15 per cent (see World Bank, 1990c, p. 35, n. 6). As a result, Peebles (1992: p. 25) argues that for the reform period considered (up to and including 1988), "the general retail price index mirrors changes in government list prices." The question is then, how are government list prices determined? Peebles, by stressing the continuity of the pre- and post-reform periods, implicitly argues that the state planners still have a significant role to play in setting prices and hence their behavioural responses to excess demand must be considered. (See also Peebles 1991: p. 199.) This is a controversial view, however, and others argue that there has been a much higher degree of price liberalisation. Naughton (1991, p. 211), for example, argues that over the reform period "substantial progress was made in liberalizing product prices." In this case, it is enterprises who are responsible for setting prices. In fact, many enterprises have taken the initiative in setting prices without central permission and there are cases of enterprises reselling their quota allocations of inputs at free market prices. It is certainly the case that there are various government controls on prices (in the form of fixed prices or ceiling prices, for example), although the extent to which these are effective is unclear.

3. Peebles's approach (1991, 1992) starts from a similar position. He argues that the monetary authorities cannot always control the total of money incomes paid out in any year and that if this causes excess demand, then planners will increase prices in an attempt to absorb the increased money supply. As Peebles (1992: p. 37) notes, his theory "argues that both monetary growth and price developments are a consequence of the same third factor; purchasing power imbalances."

here, although in so doing we should immediately state that the purpose of our discussion is not to present a history of Chinese monetary experience since 1979 or to offer any new empirical tests of the inflationary process. There have been many causes of inflation in China (see, for example, Peebles 1991 for an extended discussion), and that inflation should occur in the reform period is not surprising. The adjustment of relative prices such as that which occurred in China after 1979 is often accompanied by an upward movement of the general price level (see Naughton 1991; Peebles 1992). Furthermore, given China's very rapid growth rates during the 1980s, it is not surprising that bottlenecks in the production of key inputs would cause inflationary pressures (see Komiya 1989: p. 78 and Tsang 1990: pp. 227–29 for details of sectoral growth imbalances in the reform period). Our interest here is not in providing a comprehensive analysis of inflation but is much more limited in objective. Specifically, we will focus on the period since 1984, the period of the most significant reforms of the financial system, and trace the implications of these reforms for the inflationary process. In particular we wish to highlight the political nature of the inflationary process.

Inflation can be said to have come about because of a conflict over the distribution of resources between various agents. Conflict theories of inflation have been applied to advanced capitalist economies (see, for example, Rowthorn 1980). According to this argument, conflict between workers and capitalists over the distribution of income between wages and profits is seen as the main distributional conflict. Governments often respond to this, at least initially, by an accommodating monetary policy which allows firms to pass on cost increases and maintain profit rates; thus, governments resort to inflation as a way of enabling capital to maintain profit rates without dealing with the underlying distributional conflicts. This is possible in the short run, but eventually a crisis will be seen as the only way of disciplining labour and bringing down wage growth.

If we apply a conflict-type framework to China, the actors are different and the nature of the conflict is different. However, it is useful to think of the politico-economic system as composed of competing groups seeking to claim resources, with inflation as a possible by-product. This enables us to understand inflation as a political process and realise that changes to the institutional system which are designed to prevent the reemergence of inflation are not simply technical choices about methods of monetary management but political choices involving ways of redistributing claims over resources among competing agents, a topic which we pursue further in Chapter 7.

In the reformed banking system outlined in Chapter 4, the new institutional structure allowed pressures to be placed on the banking system, which led to high rates of growth of monetary aggregates, as illustrated in Table 5.2.

In understanding how the pressures on the banking system arose, it is necessary to identify the agents involved and the relationships between them. The key agents are as follows: (i) the central authorities represented by the CCP Politburo and the State Council; (ii) the banking system represented by the People's Bank and the specialised banks; (iii) local governments (provincial and below); and (iv) state-owned enterprises and their employees.[4] With the urban reforms which accelerated in 1984, the decentralisation of decision making to enterprises led them to exploit new ways of increasing the resources at their disposal. Part of their reason for doing this was to enable managers to pay increased wages and bonuses. Workers also benefitted from increased payments into the social fund (used, among other things, for housing). The strict central control of wages through the grade system gave way, in the reform period, to an emphasis on bonuses as an incentive device aimed at increasing labour productivity. See Table 5.3.

Bonuses were not under direct central control. Moreover, apart from

TABLE 5.2 Growth Rates of Monetary Aggregates, 1978–1991 (per cent p.a.)

Year	Net Domestic Assets	Currency	Broad Money (M3)
1978	11.7	8.5	9.5
1979	20.6	26.3	33.0
1980	37.3	29.1	32.9
1981	17.8	14.5	19.5
1982	7.9	10.9	13.1
1983	17.0	20.7	19.3
1984	31.1	49.4	42.4
1985	22.1	24.7	17.1
1986	33.9	23.3	29.3
1987	21.5	19.4	24.2
1988	20.7	46.6	21.0
1989	18.3	9.8	18.4
1990	–	–	28.0
1991	–	–	27.0

NOTE: Net domestic assets = loans to enterprises and individuals + net credit to the government + other items (net). Broad money (also referred to as money plus quasi-money) = currency + household demand deposits + enterprise deposits + official institutions' deposits + capital construction deposits + household term deposits. For more on the definitions used see Blejer et al. (1991: p. 15).

SOURCE: World Bank 1990c: p. 44; Blejer et al. 1991: p. 15; IMF, International Financial Statistics, August 1992, p. 152.

---

4. These distinctions are analytical rather than descriptive. Technically, the PBC is part of the (central) government.

TABLE 5.3 Composition of Nominal Wages for Workers in State-Owned Units, 1978–1990 (per cent)

Item	1978	1980	1985	1986	1987	1988	1989	1990
Total wage bill	100.0	100.0	100.0	100.0	100.0	100.0	100.0	100.0
Time wage	85.0	69.8	57.2	56.3	54.3	49.0	47.4	48.9
Piece rate wage	0.8	3.2	9.5	8.7	9.2	9.4	9.2	8.9
Above-quota payment	0.1	0.6	2.1	1.9	2.2	2.3	2.4	2.1
Bonuses	2.3	9.1	12.4	12.8	14.7	17.2	17.6	17.0
Subsidies	6.5	13.1	18.5	18.8	18.9	21.4	23.1	21.8
Overtime wage	2.0	1.6	1.6	1.8	1.9	1.9	1.7	1.6
Other	3.4	2.2	0.8	1.6	1.0	1.1	1.0	1.8

SOURCE: SSB 1991: p. 107.

the change in the proportions of income sources, there was also an increase in the overall level of incomes as urban workers sought to increase their share of national output and to keep pace with rising prices and rising rural incomes. The World Bank notes that "wages had been rising at low to moderate rates between 1978 and 1983, averaging just over 6 per cent p.a. with the fastest increase being at the very start of the reform movement in 1979/80" (1990a: p. 57). However, after 1983 nominal wages rose rapidly. See Table 5.4.

In part the wage and bonus explosion of 1984–1985 can be seen as a policy error in that, as Komiya (1989: p. 88) explains in the process of

TABLE 5.4 Annual Average Nominal Wage Levels, 1979–1990 (yuan)

				Annual Percentage Change		
	Total	State-Owned Units	Urban-Collective Units	Total	State-Owned Units	Urban-Collective Units
1979	668	705	542	8.6	9.5	7.1
1980	762	803	623	14.1	13.9	14.9
1981	772	812	642	1.3	1.1	3.0
1982	798	836	671	3.4	3.0	4.5
1983	826	865	698	3.5	3.5	4.0
1984	974	1,034	811	17.9	19.5	16.2
1985	1,148	1,213	967	17.9	17.3	19.2
1986	1,329	1,414	1,092	15.8	16.6	12.2
1987	1,459	1,546	1,207	9.8	9.3	10.5
1988	1,747	1,853	1,426	19.7	19.9	18.1
1989	1,935	2,055	1,557	10.8	10.9	9.2
1990	2,140	2,284	1,687	10.6	11.1	8.0

SOURCE: SSB 1991: p. 112.

introducing a new wage system attuned to the differential performance of both enterprises and individual workers, "It was announced in late 1984 that the total wage bills allowed to each enterprise in 1985 and later years would be assessed according to the level of actual payments in 1984. As a result at the end of 1984, various enterprises rushed to implement salary raises, promotions, and a variety of bonus payments, increasing greatly the overall amount of wages, allowances and bonuses." At the end of 1984, the total national wage bill was over 75 per cent higher than that of the previous year, and nominal wages continued to increase at a double-digit annual rate until the third quarter of 1985. The specialised banks responded to enterprise demand for more credit by extending more loans, as they too had been told that their lending for 1985 would be based on loans outstanding at the end of 1984. These policy errors may have contributed to the rate of wage growth, but the underlying cause was the decentralisation of decision making to enterprises which allowed workers to seek higher incomes, often with managers' support.[5] As Hussain and Stern argue, "In many cases enterprise managers collude with their labour force" (1991: p. 164) to increase the latter's real income in monetary and non-monetary terms. At the deepest level, this reflected the fact that enterprise reform lagged far behind the financial and wage reforms. Workers retained their rights to permanent jobs and exercised a good deal of implicit power within the enterprise; managers lacked a wide range of powers and complied with workers' demands in order to maintain production and morale.

The effects of decentralisation can also be seen in the expansion of enterprises' investment and in the increased demands placed upon the banking system as a result. Enterprises sought to increase supplies of inputs and extend production facilities in accordance with the behaviourial characteristics of enterprises continuing to operate under soft budget constraints (see Yenal 1990). The World Bank summarises that "the low cost of funds and soft budget constraints induced enterprises to borrow without restraint for investment purposes" (1990a: p. xv). Although interest rates did increase towards the end of the 1980s, this did little to constrain enterprise demand (Blejer et al. 1991: p. 14). National investment rose to over 39 per cent of GDP, as shown in Table 5.5.

Local governments were also in on the act, pressuring banks to finance enterprises and projects in their jurisdictions in order to promote local development. Local governments seek to maximise invest-

---

5. For an analysis of the welfare effects of decentralised wage setting in the context of a shortage economy, see Osband (1992).

TABLE 5.5   Gross Domestic Investment (GDI) as Percentage of GDP, 1970–1989 (current prices)

Year	GDI
1970–74	29.2
1975–77	29.9
1978–80	34.5
1981–83	29.3
1984	32.2
1985	38.8
1986	39.3
1987	39.2
1988	38.9
1989	36.5

SOURCE: World Bank 1990c: p. 86.

ment and growth locally, since their fiscal revenues and political authority depend upon the level of economic activity in their area (Wong 1992: p. 197). As the World Bank states, "The pressure that local governments feel to expand investment is naturally manifested in pressure on credit constraints which tend thereby to become somewhat too flexible" (1990a: p. 101). The pressure that local governments put on the local banks is quite effective, not least because the governments remain partly responsible for the selection of senior bank personnel at the local level.

All of these pressures, by enterprises and local government, are directed at the local branches of the specialised banks (or on the regional offices of the People's Bank). Thus, Yenal refers to the "expansion of credit by the regional branches of the specialized banks" (1990: p. 709) and Wiemer points to the "pressure on branch banks" (1992: p. 191) from local governments. (See also Oi 1992 for more evidence.) Part of the reason pressure is applied at this level and met with success prior to 1989 is undoubtedly because of a weakening of central control, particularly with the move towards 'horizontal' (kuai) regulation during 1986–1988.

If local banks do succumb to local pressures and extend excess loans, however, then this means that the loans of the local banks must be accommodated by the specialised banks' head offices, the provincial People's Banks, and ultimately by the People's Bank head office. The ability of the latter to resist this pressure and to impose financial discipline on the lower-level banks under its supervision, already weakened by the decentralisation of decision-making within the financial system outlined in Chapter 4, is constrained by two factors.[6] The first is the relative weakness of measures for fine-tuning the economy through interest rate policy, for example. Furthermore, the specialised banks depend on borrowing from the People's Bank to maintain financial balance, since their loans have typically exceeded their deposits by a large margin. In fact, borrowing from the People's Bank has often accounted for over 20 per cent of the specialised banks' total liabilities (Tsang 1990: p. 232). Given that the SBs have a very limited range of assets and few other sources of liquidity, any move to vary the funds available to them from the PBC would have a significant effect on the ability of the SBs to lend. This limits the ability of the PBC to intervene selectively without causing undue output fluctuations. The second, more fundamental point concerns the potential existence of a growth-versus-inflation trade-off. This type of trade-off is identified by Allsopp and Lin (1991); the clearly discernible cyclical pattern to monetary policy in China, with periods of monetary expansion being followed by periods of restraint and a subsequent loosening of monetary control as the real sector (particularly state-owned enterprises) was adversely affected, would lend credence to this.[7] Although the PBC has, therefore, sought to exercise monetary control at various points, as Tsang (1990: p. 234) argues, "In general [the PBC has] been rather reluctant in taking the initiative to implement monetary contraction" for fear that it would have large negative effects on the real economy.

Whilst the pressures on the banking system discussed previously have come from below, so to speak, and point to the need to develop an institutional framework capable of more effectively containing these pressures, another possible cause of excess money creation, and therefore potential inflationary pressure, comes from the central government. This arises if the government runs budget deficits and pressures the central bank into financing them through money creation. This monetization of budget deficits is widely viewed within monetarist circles as being a prime cause of inflation in advanced capitalist economies. In China, the reform period has been characterised by budget deficits in all years but 1978, so this mechanism would seem to be fertile ground for explaining Chinese inflation.

---

6. It should be noted that part of the People's Bank's inability to constrain lending by the specialised banks arises from the fact that the provincial-level People's Bank branches have only the same administrative status as provincial-level specialised banks.

7. Attempts to control the growth of monetary aggregates occurred in 1981–1983, mid-1985, the second half of 1987, late 1988 and again in 1989. For details see World Bank (1990c: p. 44). Fei (1988) argues that the growth-inflation trade-off is common to all developing countries.

Both central government expenditures and revenues have fallen during the reform period, although in each year after 1978 expenditures exceeded revenues, as shown in Table 5.6.[8]

Naughton (1991, 1992) argues that revenues have fallen because of the failure to broaden the tax base to reflect the changes that have taken place in the economic structure as a result of the reforms.[9] In the centrally planned system, Naughton argues, industrial sector profits are the primary source of tax revenue. For this reason, planners ensure that profits in this sector are high by restricting entry and setting monopoly prices. In the reform period, however, entry into the industrial sector has been significantly opened, and locally sponsored industries have sought to capture a share of the monopoly profits. As a result, the profits of state-owned industrial enterprises have fallen and the tax revenues accruing to the central government have been thereby reduced. The failure to reform the fiscal system and diversify the tax base has placed the central government in a position of running an almost continuous budget deficit. (See also Hussain and Stern 1991: pp. 171-3; Blejer et al. 1991: pp. 23–27.)

Has this budget deficit been financed by money creation through the central bank and therefore created inflationary pressures? Hussain and Stern argue that "the deficit was not of sufficient magnitude to play a role in accounting for the inflation" of the 1980s (1991: p. 165).

TABLE 5.6   Central Government Revenue, Expenditure and Budget Deficits, 1978–1989

Year	Government Revenue as a Percentage of GNP	Government Expenditure as a Percentage of GNP	Budget Deficit (Surplus) as a Percentage of GNP
1978	34.4	33.8	(0.6)
1979	31.6	37.3	5.7
1980	29.4	33.7	4.3
1981	29.0	31.2	2.2
1982	27.2	29.4	2.2
1983	27.4	30.0	2.6
1984	26.4	28.7	2.3
1985	26.3	28.0	1.7
1986	24.8	27.9	3.1
1987	22.2	25.8	3.6
1988	20.4	22.9	2.5
1989	19.8	20.8	1.0

SOURCE: World Bank 1990d: pp. 8, 13.

---

8. Chinese measures of the budget deficit do not correspond to international practice and understate the deficit as conventionally measured by including government bond sales as government revenue. See Komiya (1989: pp. 90–92) for details.

9. See also Hussain and Stern (1992).

They produce data (1991: p. 172) to illustrate that the proportion of the budget deficit financed by money creation fell steadily during the 1980s and was instead increasingly financed by bond sales and foreign borrowing. The data from Blejer et al. (1991: p. 26), although different for the later years, also confirms this trend. They do, however, reach a different conclusion on the significance of this, arguing that

> until 1986, government borrowing from the central bank had not significantly contributed to monetary expansion, but during 1986–88 such borrowing contributed importantly to reserve money growth. Seen against the increase in inflationary pressure during that period, the fiscal deficit and its financing became factors in the inflationary process, bringing the budget into the centre of macroeconomic management (1991: p. 25).

Peebles's figures (1992: p. 41) show that the role of the government deficit in increasing the money supply was modest (although it was more important in 1986 and 1987) compared to the explosion in bank lending to enterprises and local governments. This assessment is also supported by Yenal, who concludes that "budget deficits are usually the cause of monetary expansion in many other developing countries experiencing inflation, but in China this expansion was forced by the credit demands of large numbers of state and collective enterprises and the accommodation of this demand by the banking network" (1990: p. 709). Komiya (1989: p. 92), in discussing the 1984–1987 period, also concludes that the government deficit "was far less important as the primary cause of overheating than the increases in bank lending and in overall wage bills." The weight of the argument, therefore, seems to be on the side of those arguing that the financing of the budget deficit was not a major source of inflationary pressure (although arguably it may have been more important in some periods, notably 1986–1988, than in others).

However, even if the central government budget deficit did not contribute significantly to inflationary pressures, this does not mean that the central government was necessarily behaving in a fiscally conservative manner. As Naughton (1991: p. 210) argues, "If we take the central government investment plan as a measure of the real use of investment resources mandated by the central government, the total government borrowing requirements is equal to the sum of the budgetary deficit and the deficit in the central investment plan, amounting to a total of 7 percent of GNP in 1988." Thus, the budget deficit alone is not a reliable indicator of the central government's claim on resources. Hussain and Stern make a similar point when they argue that

> visible subsidies to loss-making enterprises are included in the budget. But bank lending to enterprises, at the behest of the government, which

is not justified by commercial criteria, constitute a potential financial liability for the government but is not included in the budget. As the volume of such lending appears to be substantial measured budget deficits may underestimate actual budget deficits by a significant margin. (1991: p. 172)

Thus, although the budget deficit may not itself be a leading factor, the central government may have been responsible for some of the pressure on banks to increase lending, identified by many as the major cause of excess demand. The relative importance of the pressure put on the banking system by claims for more resources by local governments, by enterprises acting autonomously and by the central government directly or through its ministries is difficult, if not impossible, to assess.

What does emerge clearly, however, is a picture of various agents in the economy pressuring the newly reformed and decentralised banking system to accommodate their claims for more resources. When the banking system responded, excess demand built up. The buildup of inflationary pressures, which led to the inflation in 1988 and 1989, could not be permitted to develop further. The situation had been allowed to get to this point because a consensus for controlling excess demand had not emerged and the central government was unwilling to move decisively, prior to late 1988, to limit its claims or those of other agents on resources. The non-state sector was growing rapidly and expanding employment and income for rural residents. Appeals were made to control excess investment, but the central government was unwilling to use the measures necessary to control it. Interest rates were raised but with little effect on enterprise borrowing. The costs of inflation, not simply in terms of the distortions that it created but, more important, in terms of the political costs of the social frustration that it was fostering, dictated that inflation had to be brought under control.[10] As indicated in Chapter 4, the political pressures arising from the inflation of 1988–1989 forced both central and local governments to accept the need for an effective counter-inflation policy. As we have seen, a credit squeeze and policy of retrenchment was therefore introduced in late 1988 which "involved the reintroduction of mandatory credit ceilings, as well as the use of indirect instruments including increases in interest rates, an increase in the reserve requirement, and firm control over the extension of PBC credit" (Blejer et al. 1991: p. 14). These policies successfully reduced inflation in 1990 but at the cost of slowing output growth significantly. See Table 5.7.

---

10. See also Hussain and Stern (1991: p. 152) for a discussion of the costs of inflation in China.

TABLE 5.7   Real Growth of Net National Income, 1978–1990 (per cent p.a.)

Year	Growth Rate
1978	12.3
1979	7.0
1980	6.4
1981	4.9
1982	8.2
1983	9.9
1984	13.6
1985	13.5
1986	7.7
1987	10.2
1988	11.3
1989	3.6
1990	4.6

SOURCE: Calculated from SSB 1991: p. 29.

The credit crunch, in effect, reduced the claims of some agents to the economy's resources by controlling agents' access to finance. In particular, there was a reduction in the ability of local governments to obtain credit and a consequent slowdown in the growth of rural industries which they sponsored; over 600,000 rural enterprises went bankrupt and 3 million workers lost their jobs.[11] State-owned enterprises were largely protected, but their losses mounted; wage growth was controlled by stricter regulation of the wage fund, forced bond sales and, in some cases, simply non-payment of a part of wages. Excess demand was therefore reduced by cutting state investment spending and by limiting the claims of local governments, enterprises and workers, but at the cost of reduced growth.[12] Concern with falling growth rates, rising enterprise losses and, as discussed in Chapter 4, continued pressures from provinces (especially the coastal ones) for a looser policy led to a partial relaxation of the credit controls in 1990; in early 1992 the State Council announced that inflation had been controlled, and the policy of retrenchment ended.[13] The question is, will the cycle now repeat itself? Initial indications suggest that it

---

11. *People's Daily*, March 2, 1991. See also Islam (1991) for a discussion of the growth of rural industries during the 1980s and the effects of the economic retrenchment of 1989.

12. The central government planned to reduce state investment spending in 1989 by 20 per cent; it actually fell by 9 per cent.

13. Industrial output grew at less than one per cent in the fourth quarter of 1989 and was stagnant in the first quarter of 1990. According to the Chinese press, one third of all state-owned enterprises were making losses at the end of 1990. See also Table 5.8.

might, with fixed-asset investment by state-owned enterprises increasing by 36.6 per cent in the third quarter of 1992 over the same period in 1991, for example, the largest rate of increase since 1986.[14] Inflation was brought under control by the central government—with the tacit consent of local governments—which resumed direct control over the economy and the banking system in particular. This is not, however, a long-term solution to inflation control. The types of institutional changes that might be required to permit a non-inflationary settlement of agents' competing claims are discussed further in Chapter 7.

The Relationship Between Banks and Enterprises in Practice

As will be clear from the previous discussion, inflation had microeconomic/political roots in the relationship between the banking system and other agents in the economy. In this section, we focus specifically on the relationship between banks and enterprises. As indicated in Chapter 4, one of the main goals which reformers identified for the financial reforms was the hardening of enterprise credit constraints, especially for state-owned enterprises. This was to be achieved to a significant degree by the reform of the banking system, making it considerably more market-oriented and more discriminating in its lending behaviour than had been the case in the pre-reform period (see Chapter 3 for details).

In assessing what has happened in practice, we are faced with a number of problems. One important issue concerns what has happened to enterprise productivity during the reforms. As stated in Chapter 3, low (or negative) rates of productivity growth were in many ways the Achilles heel of the centrally planned economic system. A major aim of the reforms was therefore to raise productivity growth, but establishing whether this has actually been achieved is fraught with problems. Conventional measures of productivity change are notoriously problematic and rely on assigning arbitrary weights to capital and labour in the production process. In the Chinese case, we have the added problems of limited data of dubious reliability (see Jefferson et al. 1992 for discussion). It is not surprising, therefore, that there has been considerable debate about whether productivity in state-owned enterprises has increased during the reform period, although a spate of recent studies all point to productivity rising significantly (see, for example, Chen et al. 1988; Dollar 1990; Lau and Brada 1990; Jefferson et

---

14. See *People's Daily*, overseas edition, 23 October 1992.

al. 1992; Prime 1992).[15] Indeed, the World Bank (1990c: p. 14) concludes its review of a number of studies of productivity growth by arguing that "evidence of rapid productivity increases since the inception of the reform program is unequivocal."

If it is accepted that enterprise productivity has increased during the reform period, then the reasons for this remain controversial. Dollar (1990: p. 90) suggests that "material incentives have been a source of [the] increase in allocative efficiency," whilst Lau and Brada (1990: p. 121) refer to the "normalization of the political situation" and, vaguely, the "reform in Chinese industry". Naughton (1992) regards increased competition in product markets as a possible explanatory factor, a view consistent with Jefferson, Rawski and Zheng's (1992: p. 240) statement that "Chinese reform may have begun to affect the efficiency of resource allocation despite the limited spread of factor markets." Which particular reforms are responsible for increased productivity growth, if such it be, are perhaps impossible to identify at present. Certainly, we do not suggest otherwise here. Rather, we will argue that the contribution of the financial reforms to increasing the efficiency of state-owned enterprises is unlikely to have been significant and, in fact, may have been negative. This point has been made, at least implicitly, in much of the previous discussion, but it may be useful to summarise and highlight the argument here, as it constitutes an enduring problem for the Chinese reformers and one to which we wish to return in Chapter 7.

As indicated in Chapter 4, the financial reforms created a two-tier banking system in which the SBs were intended to play a key role in ensuring that the allocation of credit reflected a more "rational" use of resources. The ways in which this was to be achieved may be summarised briefly as follows. First, the fact that the SBs now have to raise funds independently and are responsible for paying interest to depositors is an indication of the way in which the banking reforms are aimed at increasing the pressure on banks to administer loans according to the profit criterion. In theory, the only way the SBs can pay

---

15. Most of the studies cited consider only productivity growth in state-owned enterprises. Two exceptions are the studies by Jefferson et al. (1992) and Prime (1992), which consider productivity growth in both state-owned and collective industries. Jefferson et al. (1992) estimate, using gross output data, that productivity growth in collective industry outpaced that in the state-owned sector (although they still argue that "multifactor productivity in state industry has risen substantially during the reform period" [1992: pp. 239–40]). Prime (1992) finds similar results for Jaingsu province but, when net output data is used, finds that productivity growth in state-owned industry is higher than for collective industry.

their depositors is to ensure that the enterprises to whom they lend are capable of repaying their loans. If they are not, then the banks have the potential power, as the financiers of enterprises, to dictate which products they should produce, to reorganise management and to merge loss-making enterprises. In the last resort, enterprises can be declared bankrupt. Thus, there is no formal requirement for banks to continue lending to loss-making enterprises.

Second, as indicated previously, the banking system was to be more competitive. In the mid to late 1980s, the strict division of functions between the SBs was increasingly modified. According to the principle of "focus on one sector, but overlap where appropriate" (yiye wei zhu, shidang jiaocha), the SBs were encouraged to compete for deposits from individuals and enterprises. This meant that enterprises were increasingly able to borrow from any bank that they wished. Some SBs also began to experiment with leasing their smaller operational units to employees. This began in March 1987 in Shenyang, one of the cities chosen for experiments in urban reforms, with the leasing of two savings deposit offices under the ICB to employees.[16] As well as instituting these reforms in the state-owned banking sector, the government also planned to introduce competition by increasing the number of NBFIs (such as the TICs discussed in Chapter 4) as well as the number of joint-stock banks (such as the Communications Bank) and venture and foreign banks, which were increasingly allowed to operate (with restrictions) in the coastal provinces.

Third, there have been changes in the profit incentive system so that profit-related bonuses operate more at the branch bank level rather than at the level of the entire bank.

However, if the intention of the banking reforms has been to harden enterprise credit constraints by increasing the autonomy and commercial orientation of the banks, then the available evidence suggests that this was not realised during the period when reforms were forging forward. In fact, the credit constraint may have become softer. Quantitative estimates of "shortage" and budget constraint "softness" are difficult to derive because of both the difficulty of obtaining necessary data and the arbitrary nature of constructing any index based upon it.[17] Here we are interested not in total budget constraint "softness" but only in one element of it, namely, credit constraint softness. However, data limitations still effectively preclude the construction of any meaningful quantitative measure of such softness. Instead, we are left

---

16. See *China Daily*, March 21, 1987.
17. For two attempts at quantitative estimation see Naughton (1986) for China and Kraft and Vodopivec (1992) for Yugoslavia.

to draw on evidence from two sources: the banks themselves and their client enterprises.[18] This evidence is inevitably incomplete but is in our view sufficient to highlight the main point.

Clearly banks have used their new-found powers to expand the volume of credit, fuelled by the continuing demands of state enterprises and the ambitious spending plans of local government. Moreover, evidence on the lending practices of banks would support the view that they have not become significantly more discriminating in their granting of loans. For example, although the PCBC has had the power since 1983 to determine whether it should approve loan applications on the basis of expected profitability, of the 597 loan applications that it received in 1986, it rejected less than one per cent.[19]

Whilst in theory banks are empowered to restrict credit to loss-making enterprises and to require their restructuring, in practice this is rarely undertaken. The bankruptcy law, although passed by the National People's Congress, has only been implemented in a handful of cases and poses no serious threat to enterprise managers. China's first enterprise to be declared bankrupt was the Shenyang Explosion-Proof Apparatus Plant in August 1986. This received considerable publicity, but its importance should not be overestimated. It was a relatively small factory employing only 72 workers (all of whom have been given other jobs). Subsequently, four other enterprises in the same province were issued bankruptcy warnings. However, it is significant that all four were collective rather than state enterprises. As we shall see, it is the state-owned enterprises that are the major loss makers and employers, but they have been protected so far. Furthermore, the warnings were issued, and the bankruptcy declared, by the city government, not the banks. In such cases, banks do not act without the approval of higher authorities, in this case the city government. At any rate, bankruptcy is still a relatively infrequent occurrence and it only occurs on special terms, though its incidence was increasing in 1992. Even so, it is of strictly limited utility as a weapon in the armoury of the banks.[20]

The other, less dramatic, measures which banks have at their disposal, namely, the removal of managers and the merging of firms, have also been used in only a very limited number of cases. If enter-

---

18. In addition to consulting published sources, we obtained data through personal interviews in China between 1987 and 1992. Some of the material presented here is drawn from Bowles and White (1989).

19. Personal interview.

20. In any case, banks are typically accorded a low priority as creditors and hence it is not particularly beneficial to the banks to force bankruptcy upon enterprises.

prises are continually making losses, then the banks are empowered to audit them and make the necessary changes to restore profitability. However, even when banks do undertake such inspections, they are only able to make changes if it can be shown that the losses were caused by 'bad management'. If other 'objective' factors putatively outside management control are the cause of the losses, then the enterprise is not held responsible for them and lending continues without the need for internal changes. One such 'objective' factor might be price distortions caused by China's pricing policies. In particular, many enterprises have seen the prices of their raw materials increased without a corresponding increase in the prices of their outputs. Other 'objective' factors include problems in obtaining raw materials, poor quality of inputs, use of old technology, and unexpected decreases in demand.[21] In all these cases the enterprise is able to point the finger, often legitimately, at other ministries, departments or enterprises and hence shift the blame for any losses. The number of cases in which 'bad management' is therefore held responsible for poor enterprise performance is small.

Instead, banks usually continue to lend to loss-making enterprises and may try to help them restore profitability in other ways. Two examples of this are provided by the Hubei Provincial Branch of the ICB located in Wuhan, a major industrial city on the Yangtse River. In 1986, the Wuhan Truck Company, a large industrial enterprise and employer, incurred losses because of poor sales. To assist the company, the bank gave subsidies to its potential customers and increased sales in this way. In another case, a brick company, finding itself unable to sell its output, approached the bank for help. The bank again tried to find customers for the company and persuade them to purchase the surplus bricks (although no subsidy was involved in this case). The ICB's operations with respect to enterprises were described by its manager as being 'to praise the good and help the poor', an operating principle very redolent of the pre-reform era.[22]

The argument that we are making is that banks, although technically more autonomous, are not using that power to impose discipline on enterprises and thus the credit constraint continues to be soft. This analysis is also supported by many reform economists who argued

---

21. For example, the Ministry for Light Industry estimates that the amount of raw materials and energy consumed by backward factories is commonly 10 to 20 per cent, and occasionally 100 per cent, more than in the advanced factories. (See *China Daily*, March 9, 1987.) Losses due to these higher input requirements arising from the use of old technology are regarded as being outside of enterprise control.

22. Personal interview, 19 May 1987.

that despite the appearance of wide-ranging reforms, in practice the behaviour of banks had changed little; loans were still basically guaranteed to state enterprises and banks did not exercise efficiency-oriented pressures on managers with the result that "everyone was still eating from the same pot". Internal organisation within the banks still left much to be desired, and accounting methods remained rudimentary.

Given this, it is surprising to find that at least up until the 1988 retrenchment, although some banks had difficulties in securing loan repayments from enterprises, the general level of 'bad debts' was low. However, this reflects China's accounting conventions rather than the diligence of banks in recovering loans. First, 'bad debts' only refer to non-payment of interest, not to repayment of principal. Lin Senmu, head of the China Economic Research Institute on Urban and Rural Reconstruction, has estimated that of the 70 billion yuan that was issued as 'state allocation turned credit' between 1980 and 1986, only 3.2 billion yuan (4.6 per cent) has been repaid and that most enterprises default on their overdue repayment because their borrowing was not placed under any legal or contractual obligation.[23] Second, interest payments are included as part of enterprise costs so that enterprises' claims for funds in the next plan period automatically provide for the payment of bank interest. Thus, if enterprise performance is poor, then profits are reduced and the taxes paid to the Ministry of Finance are correspondingly reduced, but bank payments are already covered. Therefore, banks face little risk in lending—this has been shifted onto the Ministry of Finance in the form of reduced tax revenue. This has led to the observation that 'the bank hosts the banquet but the financial authorities pay the bill' and explains some of the reasons for the tension which arose between the Ministry of Finance and the banking institutions, which we discussed in Chapter 4.

Unpaid loans and a rapid rise in unofficial inter-enterprise credit did occur, however, after the 1988 retrenchment. The amount of bad debts to the SBs also grew alarmingly, yet branches found themselves under constant pressure to roll over poorly performing loans with fresh credit.[24] State enterprises found themselves falling into "triangular debts" (*san jiao zhai*) with other enterprises and found that the banks did not always have the funds to bail them out. While larger state enterprises could afford to ride out their financial crisis in the expectation of eventual salvation, smaller state and collective enterprises were

---

23. *China Daily*, Beijing, March 13, 1987.
24. For an example of these pressures on the ICB in Shandong province, see Song Xiuyi and Zhang Shiming (1989).

forced to turn to the expensive informal market to stay in business. The Agricultural Bank, which was charged with the responsibility of supplying funds to state procurement agencies to pay for agricultural produce, found its funds inadequate, and the procurement authorities were reduced to paying farmers in IOUs (so-called "white slips"), which increased rural discontent. The slowdown in growth caused major problems for enterprises, and credit was made much harder to obtain. However, the basic relationship between banks and state-owned enterprises remained unchanged, with mounting losses being covered by subsidies.[25] See Table 5.8.

State-owned enterprises were significantly hurt by the retrenchment program, with many curtailing output; but they were favoured in new allocations of credit and supplies of raw materials and fared considerably better than enterprises in the rural economy (see Zisner, 1991: p. 115). During this period, the recentralisation of control left banks acting strictly on orders from above and there was little discretion in loan advances beyond supporting the state sector as a whole.

From the enterprises' point of view, budget constraints may well have become softer rather than harder under the combined influence of both fiscal and financial reforms. As we have seen, in the pre-reform period, the enterprise budget constraint had a hard element to it in the form of the initial bargaining for budget allocations. Now, however, the proliferation of financial institutions and the introduc-

TABLE 5.8 Subsidies of Losses of State-Owned Enterprises, 1978–1991 (billion yuan)

	Subsidies	As Percentage of Government Fiscal Revenues
1978	12,490	11.1
1979	8,606	7.5
1985	24,523	13.6
1986	32,478	14.7
1987	37,643	18.5
1988	44,646	17.6
1989	59,976	21.5
1990	57,850	18.8
1991	55,672	16.2

SOURCE: Lardy 1992: p. 138.

---

25. It is estimated that around a third of state-owned enterprises are now operating at a loss. (See *Beijing Review*, no. 34, 1991, p. 5). The increase in the losses of state-owned enterprises during the reform period is consistent with the evidence on rising productivity if, as Naughton (1992: p. 34) states, "the reduction in profitability is caused by diminished barriers to entry and thus reductions in the level of monopoly profits."

tion of various profit retention schemes have relaxed this constraint. For example, the policy to encourage competition and overlapping between the specialised banks meant that enterprises were able to establish several accounts at different banks, thereby multiplying their sources of credit and enabling them to shift funds around to ward off pressures from any particular bank.[26] Moreover, an enterprise whose investment plan had been judged unsound by one bank might, and often did, find another bank willing to provide the funds. Ironically, this move towards competition made banks more reluctant to exert pressures on their client enterprises because "some fear that strengthening supervision may drive away clients".[27] To the extent that enterprises do face greater risk or pressure on financial matters, it is, as we have said, the smaller state and collective firms which are more vulnerable; the position of larger state-owned firms has been relatively unaffected.

The lack of control over enterprise finances shows up, for example, in the ways in which enterprises use their retained funds. In theory, these are to be used for four purposes: technical upgrading, general reserves, employee bonuses and employee welfare. The fiscal authorities regulate the ratios of expenditure; as a general rule, the employee bonus and welfare components are not to exceed 40 per cent of retained profits, and around 50 per cent is to be allocated to finance investment in new machinery. In practice, however, it has proved difficult to ensure that enterprises use funds in this way. The 40 per cent rule for the distribution of profits to workers' bonuses and welfare funds is commonly exceeded and was partly responsible for the wage and bonus explosion discussed previously. The decentralisation of power to enterprises as part of the reform process has enabled workers, who have guaranteed employment, to put pressure on enterprise managers for higher bonuses and welfare benefits. Depreciation allowances have also been rechannelled. In 1986 depreciation funds in industrial enterprises amounted to 100 million yuan. According to state regulations, these funds should be used primarily for technical upgrading. However, it is estimated that nearly half of this amount has been diverted to finance the construction of office buildings and workshops.[28]

Whilst this behaviour shows the extent to which enterprises are still operating in ways characteristic of firms in a shortage economy,

---

26. For an analysis of this phenomenon which argues that it became more difficult than before for banks to control enterprises as a consequence of the policy of "sectoral overlap"(*yewu jiaocha*), see Zheng Yan (1989: pp. 13ff).

27. For example, see the cases cited by Bo Daojiang (1988: pp. 20–21).

28. *Economic Daily*, Beijing, March 1, 1987.

the fact that funds for technical upgrading are being squeezed by rising labour costs and inventory expenses also reveals something about the enterprises' relationship with the banks. From the enterprises' point of view, if they are short of funds for technical upgrading, then they may expect the banks to extend more credit for this purpose and/or view the consequences of failing to upgrade as not being particularly serious.

Whilst much of this evidence has been fragmentary, it does seem reasonable to conclude that the banks have not become significantly more discriminating in their lending activities or more aggressive in the use of their power to reorganise and restructure ailing enterprises. From the point of view of the enterprises, the decentralisation of decision-making during the 1985–1988 period, together with the plethora of new financial institutions, may have actually further softened their credit constraints. If state-owned enterprises have indeed raised their productivity during the reform period, therefore, it is unlikely that the financial reforms, and the reforms introduced in the banking sector in particular, have played a significant role in this process.

Concluding Remarks

Chapter 4 outlined the process which guided the financial reforms and demonstrated how a more liberal financial system developed. However, some of the outcomes of this process were problematic, most notably the inflation of 1988–1989 and, relatedly, the essentially unchanged relationship between banks and enterprises. In this chapter we have focused on these problematic outcomes both because they require explanation and because their solutions pose difficult challenges to reformers. In the case of inflation, institutional mechanisms are required which will effectively determine the claims of competing agents in the economy. Hardening budget constraints also raises thorny issues. The commitment to socialist values, in particular to full employment and to job and wage security, as well as the strategic interests of ministries and local governments, has meant that state-owned enterprises have continued to be financed irrespective of performance. Any attempts to harden budget constraints must therefore address the issues of how workers can be protected and how ministries and local governments can be made less influential (or induced to change their behaviour). These questions are explored further in Chapter 7. Before this, however, we turn our attention to a further important aspect of the financial reforms, the introduction of bonds and shares and the move towards a socialist capital market.

6

Towards a
Socialist Capital Market?

THE REFORM of the financial system encompassed not only the reform of the banking sector, analysed in the previous chapters, but also the development of capital markets, i.e., markets in bonds and shares. It is the purpose of this chapter to analyse the operations of these new "markets".[1]

The development of capital markets initially proceeded at a slow pace followed by a rapid expansion in the number of agents issuing bonds and shares from 1985 onwards. The general path of the financial reforms sketched in Chapter 4 is also applicable to the specific case of the development of capital markets. That is, set against a continuing backdrop of concern with developmental objectives, capital market reforms proceeded initially in a manner consistent with MSI and then increasingly embodied the more market-oriented prescriptions of MSII; in some respects the reforms went even further than this and took on some of the characteristics of the finance and development paradigm.

Apart from illustrating this general point, our discussion in this chapter focusses upon three points. First, we are interested in examining the path of capital market reform, and in understanding how the use of financial assets can best be understood in a state socialist economy undergoing reform. In undertaking such a task we must of course take into account that the movement from a planned to a market economy is occurring in the context of other economic problems, most notably the structural readjustment of the economy away from the old (Stalinist) strategic priorities and the inflationary pressures outlined in Chapter 5. Thus, the introduction of capital markets in

---

1. This chapter combines revised and updated versions of Bowles and White (1992a) and (1992b).

China has taken place in a context of complex economic problems in which the control and efficiency imperatives have again sometimes appeared as competing agendas. Our second task, therefore, is to examine the diverse, and often competing, aims which have accompanied both the introduction of bonds and shares by the authorities and the attitudes of different economic agents towards these specific financial options. Third, we are also interested in identifying the political and ideological dimensions of the introduction of capital markets, particularly with respect to shares. Here the ideological imperatives, discussed in Chapter 4, have also been prominent and are specific to a process of financial liberalisation in a socialist context and have conditioned the specific path and character of financial reform in distinctive ways. Because of this, we will continue to employ a political economy approach in the sense that we are interested in elucidating the complex interplay between political and economic actors in a process of state-sponsored marketisation.

In this chapter, we first discuss the development of the bond market and provide an interpretation of the use which has been made of bonds in the Chinese context. Then, we consider the use of shares and the debate which has accompanied their introduction.

The Introduction of Bonds in the 1980s

It is useful in a discussion of the development of capital markets to distinguish between their impacts at three different levels. First, we can assess the impact of capital market development on the conduct and effectiveness of macroeconomic policy. Second, there is the effect on the inter-sectoral allocation of financial resources. Third, there is the impact on the microbehaviour of enterprises. Regarding bonds, it is the first two levels which are the most relevant.

Bonds are simply contracts between an issuer and a purchaser; in return for a specified sum of money advanced by the purchaser, the issuer agrees to make payments (usually of interest and principal) to the purchaser at specified dates. Beyond this, there is a considerable diversity in the terms of and types of bonds which are issued in advanced capitalist economies. They are issued by governments and firms to cover deficits and acquire assets; the different characteristics (in terms of risk, repayment conditions, etc.) of bonds are reflected in different prices determined by competitive markets. For governments, bond sales and purchases also form an important component of monetary policy through open market operations. For purchasers, bonds represent a vehicle for ensuring specified income flows in the future. However, purchasers do face the risk of default by the issuer, and when inflation is unpredictable, there is no guarantee of the purchasing power of the specified nominal income flow. Well-developed secondary markets usually exist which increase the liquidity of bond holding and also raise the possibility of the purchaser experiencing capital gains or losses as a result of interest rate changes. Thus, in capitalist economies, bonds enable governments to raise resources and provide them with a tool for monetary policy, whilst, in theory, the competitive issuing of bonds directs financial resources to their most profitable uses.

In China, policies towards bond issues have changed over time in response to changes in the overall economic and financial climate and in the relative strength of more conservative or reformist leaders within the CCP. However, policy-makers have had three basic objectives which underlie these fluctuations: first, the desire to provide a wider choice of financial assets in order to improve the flexibility of the financial system; second, to supplement the system of budgetary allocation and bank credit by allowing enterprises to raise their own funds for their own purposes; third, to provide a macroeconomic instrument for central government as a way to finance deficits in a non-inflationary way and to remove excess liquidity in the economy. In analysing Chinese practice, one can discern a basic tension between objectives here: between economic objectives aimed at improving the allocation of financial resources through the market mechanism and political objectives, achieved through administrative means, aimed at maintaining the fiscal viability of the state and the desire of political leaders to maintain control over the economy. These tensions are illustrated if we consider the evolution of policy towards bonds during the 1980s.

Whilst government bonds had been issued at points during the pre-reform period as shown in Chapter 3, their expanded use and regular issue has become a feature of the reform period. This has been true for both domestic bonds and bonds issued by Chinese institutions in foreign markets. With respect to the latter, foreign currency-denominated bonds have been issued since 1982 by the Bank of China; the Bank of Communications; the Ministry of Finance; CITIC; and the provincial or city-based TICs from Fujian, Guandong, Shanghai and Tianjin.[2] In keeping with the focus of this book, however, we concentrate on domestic bond issues.

---

2. Most of the bonds have been denominated in yen and issued in Tokyo. Others have been denominated in Deutschemarks, Hong Kong dollars and US dollars and have been issued in Frankfurt, Hong Kong, Singapore and London. For details of overseas bond issues, see *ZGJRNJ* (1990: pp. 135–36).

Official thinking about the role of bonds and policies towards their issue has fluctuated during the reform era. When bonds were first issued in 1981, in the form of state Treasury bonds under the auspices of the Ministry of Finance, they were seen as a useful macroeconomic instrument in the context of growing concern over fiscal and monetary disequilibria. The government budget deficits in 1979 and 1980 were the largest deficits (expressed as a percentage of national income) of the reform years and were financed predominantly by money creation.[3] Bonds were seen, therefore, as a means to finance the government deficit in a non-inflationary way and to reduce the money balances held by local governments and bureaucratic departments and enterprises, as well as by individuals. As shown in Table 6.1, Treasury bonds have been the dominant form of financial asset issued in China.

Whilst the total of bond and share issues of 166 billion yuan is not large, it does nevertheless represent an important development in the reform process.[4] Furthermore, as Table 6.2 shows, there was a rapid increase in bond and share issues after 1985.

With respect to Treasury bonds, except for 1981, all issues to individuals have been mandatory—issues to enterprises and other units have always been mandatory. The division of sales to individuals and units is shown in Table 6.3.

The procedure for mandatory issues is to assign purchase quotas to units (both for unit and individual purchases), and they are urged to

TABLE 6.1   Issues of Bonds and Shares, 1981–1989, by Category (billion yuan)

Type	Cumulative Total 1981–1989
State Treasury bonds	51.09
Special Treasury bonds	4.37
Value-proof Treasury bonds	12.52
Special state construction bonds	5.50
General state construction bonds	3.07
State capital construction bonds	9.46
Fiscal bonds	6.60
Financial bonds	22.07
Enterprise bonds	26.24
Transferable certificates of deposits	21.17
Shares	4.20
TOTAL	166.25

SOURCE: *ZGJRNJ* 1990: p. 71.

3. See Chapter 5 for a discussion of budget deficits and their financing.

4. The cumulative total of bond and share issues for the period 1981–1989 represents approximately 10 per cent of national income for 1989.

TABLE 6.2 Issues of Bonds and Shares, 1981–1989, by Year (billion yuan)

Year	Total
1981	4.86
1982	4.38
1983	4.16
1984	4.25
1985	6.56
1986	19.25
1987	24.79
1988	47.88
1989	50.12

SOURCE: *ZGJRNJ* 1990: p. 71.

meet or exceed the quota.[5] In the countryside, the household responsibility contract may include a provision for bond purchases. Mandatory purchases, however, simply represent a form of taxation and a continuation of traditional "directive" state controls. Moreover, that they are mandatory has led to resistance from "purchasers", and the terms of their issue have changed over the years to reflect both this and the

TABLE 6.3 State Treasury Bond Issues, 1981–1988 (billion yuan)

Year	Total	Units	Individuals	Percentage	
				Units	Individuals
1981	4.86	4.85	0.01	99.8	0.2
1982	4.38	2.41	1.97	55.0	45.0
1983	4.16	2.10	2.06	50.5	49.5
1984	4.25	2.04	2.21	48.1	51.9
1985	6.06	2.18	3.88	36.0	64.0
1986	6.25	2.29	3.96	36.6	63.4
1987	6.29	2.26	4.03	35.9	64.1
1988	9.22	3.49	5.73	37.8	62.2

SOURCE: *ZGJRNJ* 1990: p. 36.

---

5. For regulations on the bonds, see *New China News Agency* (*NCNA*), 8 March 1981; for a commentary on the issue, see "Subscribe to Treasury Bonds with enthusiasm", *People's Daily*, 9 March 1981, in *FBIS* 051. This first issue was of ten-year bonds carrying an interest of 4 per cent p.a.; they were repayable in five annual payments starting from the sixth year of issue. (*Agence France Presse*, 10 February 1981, in *FBIS* 028.) If individuals are reluctant to purchase bonds, they have been subject to "mobilization" to keep up the appearance of a "voluntary" transaction. See *People's Daily*, 2 February 1982.

changing financial climate. The bonds were unpopular in their early years, and when the fiscal constraints on the central government eased in 1983, questions were raised about whether they were still necessary. By this time, the central government had raised the possibility of extending their ambit to meet key investment priorities (particularly for projects in energy, transport, raw materials and infrastructure),[6] and bond issues by local governments were also proposed for the same purpose. From then on, Treasury bonds were partly defended in terms of "the need to concentrate resources for the modernisation programme", and financial spokespeople argued that they represented only a marginal levy on the balances held by agents in the economy.[7] In 1985, the terms of issue were improved: The interest rate for individuals and units was raised (to 9 per cent and 5 per cent p.a., respectively); the bonds were allowed to be discounted or used in mortgages at banks; and the repayment period was cut from ten to five years.[8] Even at an interest rate of 9 per cent, however, the bonds did not compare particularly well with a five-year bank savings deposit, which in 1985 was 8.28 per cent (up to July) and 9.36 per cent (from August on); and three-year deposits earned almost as much (7.92 per cent and 8.28 per cent, respectively).[9]

As we mentioned in Chapter 4, during 1984 and 1985 there was increased criticism of the reforms hitherto known as "an endless game of administrative changes". Reformist leaders and economists, with external advice and support, called for the introduction of a capital market with a diversity of financial institutions and assets to promote a more rational allocation of resources; these proposals included an argument that bond issues should be diversified.[10] As part of the ensuing liberalisation measures, moving the financial system more along the lines suggested by MSII, the People's Bank extended the power to issue bonds to other banks (notably the specialised banks) and enterprises. These reforms began in 1985 and spread initially to five cities (Guangzhou, Chongqing, Wuhan, Shenyang and Changzhou) in the spring of 1986. For example, the Agricultural Bank began bond issues in 1985; the capital raised was to be earmarked for specific categories

---

6. *Sichuan Radio*, 6 April 1983, in *SWB* 7305.

7. *NCNA*, 4 January 1984.

8. *NCNA*, 18 December 1984.

9. *NCNA*, 26 July 1985. The inflation rate in 1985 was 8.8 per cent, so the real rate of interest on bonds was only 0.2 per cent. For a complete list of interest rates on deposits during the reform period see World Bank (1990b: pp. 146, 149.

10. For example, see "Monopoly of banking by the state criticised", *China Daily*, Beijing, 9 June 1984.

of loans. The Industrial and Commercial Bank also launched a bond issue at the same time, with funds earmarked for loans to enterprises to be repaid at (a relatively high) 12–14 per cent interest rate.[11] The SBs' bonds were issued to individuals and, being for voluntary purchase, their terms were more attractive than those for Treasury bonds.[12]

Enterprises, both state and collective, were also allowed to issue bonds. In Guangzhou, for example, enterprise bonds were available either to the public or (in non-transferable form) to the enterprise's own workforce. The former were relatively liquid—they could be transferred, inherited, given away and used as security, but their interest rates were not allowed to be more than 20 per cent above bank interest rates on fixed savings deposits for the same repayment period. Enterprise bonds usually have a short maturity, and in theory at least, their purpose has been to allow enterprises with good market prospects to find resources for expansion more flexibly. Their issue nevertheless required the permission of the local branch of the People's Bank, which is charged with ensuring that the enterprise's proposed investment from the proceeds of bond issues is compatible with the state plan and with assessing the commercial/financial viability of the enterprise. Enterprise bond issues have not been restricted to urban centres but have also played an important role in rural areas where township and village corporations have been set up to attract savings to finance the growth of small-scale enterprises by issuing bonds to local residents (World Bank 1988, p. 140).

In this new phase of the financial reforms, bond transactions could take place both within and between the experimental cities and, together with similar measures to encourage share issues and to commercialise enterprise and bank behaviour, were seen as a "first step towards a monetary market".[13] This was to be followed by the establishment of a necessary regulatory framework, specifically a securities law and a securities transaction law as part of an overall framework of "indirect" financial regulation. In the short term, however, bond issues by banks and enterprises were to be regulated by the local branch of the People's Bank, which was charged with restricting their volume, regulating their terms and discriminating among their pur-

---

11. *NCNA*, 22 August 1985 and *NCNA*, 1 September 1985.

12. Although the interest rate on Treasury bonds increasingly matched that offered by the SBs' bonds, the shorter maturity of the latter was considered more attractive, especially when inflationary expectations took hold. For details of the terms on which various bonds were issued, see World Bank (1990b: pp. 170–72).

13. *NCNA*, 7 April 1986.

poses (for example, they were to contribute to priorities such as technical upgrading or the development of lagging sectors).

A further step towards the marketisation of bonds was taken in August 1986, when an experimental secondary market for negotiable securities was opened in the city of Shenyang in the north-east by the municipal trust and investment corporation. It could deal in enterprise bonds, but not those issued by governments or banks (and could not deal in enterprise shares).[14] This step towards a secondary market in bonds was hailed as a "breakthrough experiment in economy reform". But overall policy at the time was cautious: to allow secondary trading first in short-term assets (thus short-term bonds issued mainly by enterprises), while longer-term securities issued by governments and banks were to remain mainly non-tradeable (see Liu Hongru, 1986c). It was anticipated that the Shenyang securities market would gradually be extended to the other four experimental cities and to five more (Shanghai, Beijing, Tianjin, Harbin and Xian).[15] But in the short-term, localities were warned that "it would not be wise to copy it uncritically elsewhere".[16]

Notwithstanding this and other admonitions, 1986 saw a vigorous upsurge in bond issues as institutions and individuals saw advantages in this particular form of financial asset. At the end of the year, moreover, the process of marketisation took another step forward when the Shanghai branch of the Industrial and Commercial Bank began to sell transferable bonds. This was the first time that such financial bonds (as opposed to enterprise bonds) could be transferred, resold or used as collateral[17] and was a first step towards the marketisation of longer-term securities, which was part of the financial reform plan for 1987.

However, the increasing diversity of, and competition in, bond issuance and a gradual escalation of interest rates affected issues of Treasury bonds and caused the financial authorities concern. In response, they raised interest rates for the 1986 issue (from 5 per cent to 6 per cent for units and 9 per cent to 10 per cent for individuals), with the specific aim of improving the return in comparison with bank interest rates on fixed deposits and the rates offered by other bonds. Purchase of Treasury bonds was still mandatory, but incentives were clearly thought necessary to ease the political strain involved in enforcing allocation targets. There was also pressure to allow redemp-

---

14. See *NCNA*, 5 August 1986 for a description of the operations of the market.
15. *South China Morning Post*, Hong Kong, 8 September 1986.
16. *Jingji Ribao* (Economic Daily), 16 September 1986, in *SWB* 8368.
17. *NCNA*, 1 December 1986.

tion of earlier Treasury bond issues which had low rates of interest—this increased as inflationary pressures mounted in 1986–1987, as other more attractive assets became available, and as an illegal market in bonds began to spread. Since the earlier bonds had relatively long maturity periods (5 to 10 years), moreover, speculators were buying them at below their face value and cashing them at full value with the assistance of corrupt bank clerks. This illegal trade was recognised in the 1988 issue when terms were further improved by reducing the maturity date from five to three years, and limited trading in Treasury bonds was permitted in secondary markets in five experimental cities—they could be bought or sold or discounted at the bank from the second year after issue.[18]

Although Treasury bonds were still mandatory, Ministry of Finance officials continued to worry about their competitiveness. Issues by specialised banks tended to carry a rate of return greater than Treasury bonds and comparable bank deposits and they were therefore popular.[19] Enterprise bonds (mainly issued by state enterprises) were also a more attractive alternative to would-be purchasers.[20] Faced with this, the central government imposed an interest rate limit of 15 per cent on enterprise and bank bonds in 1986 in order to reduce the competition they offered to Treasury bonds.

In this increasingly complex and competitive context, central financial officials reacted to what they saw as the indiscriminate and unwise issue of bonds and the weakness of regulatory controls. They published a set of interim regulations controlling state enterprise bonds in March 1987.[21] These regulations set limits on the quantity of bonds issued and their rates of return and attempted to define priority uses. The central authorities clearly felt that they were losing too much control over both the volume and direction of investment. The regulations also reflected worries that many enterprise bond issues exceeded the financial capacities or business potential of the enter-

---

18. *NCNA,* 10 January 1988. For more details, see *China Daily* (Business Weekly), Beijing, 8 February 1988. Although maturity dates have been shortened to three years, the majority of Treasury bond issues still pay interest at the end of the term. Some bonds, picked by lottery, receive annual interest.

19. For example, about 1000 people started queuing at midnight to buy bonds issued by the Shanghai branch of the Construction Bank in late 1986 (*NCNA,* 26 November 1986).

20. These issues were often accompanied by prizes. On the Shenyang Securities Market, for example, bond holders had a 26 per cent chance of a prize, with the top prize being 8,000 *yuan (Beijing Review,* 1–7 February 1988).

21. *NCNA,* 4 April 1987.

prise or were used for excessive or unproductive investment. Some enterprises were also issuing bonds to cover debts (such as the huge Wuhan Iron and Steel Complex). Local specialised banks were also rushing into bond issues, partly as a way to avoid credit restrictions (particularly on investment funds) and expand their own loan portfolios in competition with other banks, and partly in response to pressure from local governments and client enterprises (Bo Daojiang, 1988).

In mid-1988, moreover, there was growing concern about the growth in national debt and the need to set up an effective system to manage it. The central financial authorities had built up a stock of domestic and foreign debt in the process of financing budget deficits.[22] The Ministry of Finance decided to set up a National Debt Management Department to oversee foreign and domestic debt and to supervise state bond issues. At the same time, however, reform economists were aware that state bond issues could play a valuable macroeconomic role if used judiciously, particularly as an alternative to money creation. It was also argued that there should be a greater variety in Treasury bonds (in terms of types, purchasers and maturities), that interest rates should be linked to controls over rates on bank and enterprise bonds and that the secondary market for state bonds should be expanded (Liu Baifu et al. 1988; Liu Xiuwen and Chen Ruqi 1988).

By early 1988, concern over "bond fever" increased as bonds became one of the scarcest "commodities" on the market; the inflation rate increased to 18.5 per cent in 1988, and households responded by reducing their bank deposits and buying goods and assets such as enterprise and bank bonds which offered some protection against inflation.[23] Financial officials were warned that enterprises' bond sales were getting out of control, even though they were supposed to be regulated by the People's Bank. Furthermore, some economists raised questions about the entire economic effectiveness of bond issues; it was argued that the issue of bonds did not induce higher savings but simply attracted funds from other sources.[24]

In the fight against inflation from late 1988 onwards, however,

---

22. *South China Morning Post*, Hong Kong, 30 March 1988; cf. the report of the vice-minister of Finance to the NPC Standing Committee on the 1987 state accounts, in *NCNA*, 26 June 1988.

23. For discussion of household behaviour see Hussain and Stern (1991: p. 148) and Blejer et al. (1991: p. 14, n. 50).

24. For example, in a survey of 245 residents of Beijing who purchased bonds, 1,367 m. out of 1,646 m. *yuan* was withdrawn from banks, including 1,121 m. *yuan* withdrawn from fixed deposits ahead of time. The debate over whether bond issues raise additional resources or simply redirect them away from the banking system has also been keenly debated in Hungary's financial reforms during the 1980s. See Jarai (1989).

bonds became both a weapon and a target. On the one hand, state bond issues for mandatory purchase became a tool for reducing enterprise discretionary funds and workers' discretionary income. New "value proofed" Treasury bonds, indexed to the inflation rate, were introduced, since long-term bonds with negative real interest rates were now very unattractive. On the other hand, greater controls were exerted over the issue of bank and enterprise bonds as a means to curb credit expansion and over-investment.[25] There were official complaints that "there have been mischievous dealings in the stock market. . . . Certain government departments and enterprises have, without the permission of the People's Bank of China, issued stocks or bonds, or run stock-exchange business, or set up security companies on their own, or even forced their workers and staff to buy shares or bonds during tight money periods."[26] A State Council circular was issued in early 1989 which forbade government departments and non-productive enterprises from issuing bonds and restricted issues of productive enterprises.[27] This slowing of the marketisation process in response to inflationary pressures was reinforced by the change of Party leadership after June 1989. The new leaders, though more "conservative", did not, however, renounce the basic aim of developing bonds as a distinct and eventually tradeable financial asset. Throughout the reform period there has been a tension between the central authorities' desire to use bonds as a way to forcibly collect resources from other agents and at the same time to promote a more competitive bond market as part of financial liberalisation measures. This tension is still

---

25. Whether such a concern was justified is open to some doubt. Enterprise bond issues at the end of 1988 represented approximately 1.5 per cent of money and quasi-money, and their importance in financing over-investment is therefore likely to have been minimal. The restrictions on bond issues were, in any case, only a minor part of the anti-inflationary policy, with credit control being the more important aspect. The control of bond issues does show, however, how seriously concerned the authorities were with inflation and the extent to which they felt they were losing control of the economy.

26. *China Economic News*, Hong Kong, X:3, 16 January 1989, p. 5. In fact, this situation seems to have a longer history, and examples of this type of behaviour were reported to us on our research visit in 1987 (for example, see White and Bowles 1987: p. 13). It is ironic that the central government should complain of forced bond sales, since this is precisely its own policy. Nevertheless, it does indicate the concern over the ability of the People's Bank to regulate enterprise bond issues. In fact, the relationship between state enterprises and their workers is a complex one. As indicated, there have been instances of enterprises forcing workers to purchase bonds. In other instances, however, bonds have been used by enterprises to make disguised payments to their workers (see Solinger 1989).

27. See *NCNA*, 25 March 1989, for details. Further restrictions have been introduced in 1990, see *FBIS* 051.

present and evident from the issue of government bonds in 1991. On the one hand, 2.5 billion yuan of Treasury bonds (out of a planned annual issue of 10 billion yuan) were underwritten by a syndicate of financial institutions and sold freely to individuals.[28] Whilst this represents a significant move towards the marketisation of primary Treasury bond issues, at the same time the Ministry of Finance also announced that it was to issue 2 billion yuan of Special National Bonds in 1991 by mandatory purchase.[29]

Clearly the introduction of bonds has been a complex, uneven and contradictory process. To understand it, we need to step back and look at certain basic factors: the nature of the political and economic agents issuing and purchasing bonds, their specific objectives, and the logic of the overall politico-economic system in which they are operating. We turn to these issues in the next section.

Bonds and the Politico-Economic Struggle for Resources

From an economic perspective, bonds are but one part of a broader process of establishing a capital market, which will, it is hoped, in turn lead to improvements in economic efficiency. Until this process was decelerated in response to the overheating of the economy in 1988–1989 and the advent of the more conservative post-Tiananmen leadership, one can argue that the goal of marketisation was being achieved incrementally (notwithstanding the continuing mandatory character of Treasury bond issues): There was a gradual diversification of the types and terms of bonds to provide increasing choice in initial purchase; there is evidence of the embryonic development of competition between bond issues (reflected in attempts to vary terms) and of market-type behaviour (both legal and illegal) on the part of purchasers; and there was limited progress towards a secondary market in securities (even though, by the end of 1989, 91 per cent of all trade in the new financial assets was in Treasury bonds).[30] This gradual move towards marketisation was partly the result of conscious policies and partly a reaction to the pressure of changing circumstances (for example, the legalisation of a market in Treasury bonds to forestall a growing black market).

As pointed out earlier, this appearance of gradual marketisation has not been a smooth one. At times, the emphasis has been on correcting

---

28. See *Far Eastern Economic Review*, 9 May 1991, pp. 42–43 for details.

29. See "Rules and Regulations for Special Bond Issue", *NCNA*, 21 April 1991 in *SWB*, FE/W0181/C2/1.

30. For data on bond and share sales in 1989 see *ZGJRNJ* (1990: p. 72).

macroeconomic disequilibria and financing the budget deficit. This emphasis has been reflected in the mandatory issue of Treasury bonds and by the attempts to limit the competitiveness of other assets. At other points, however, emphasis has been on developing mechanisms to promote a more efficient allocation of resources, reflected in policies designed to encourage a wider range of assets and horizontal financial linkages.

But has this gradual marketisation in fact led to a more efficient allocation of resources between enterprises? Ideally, bonds should channel funds to those enterprises able to make the most efficient use of them. As a general point, however, to be effective, capital market reforms depend upon complementary reforms to eliminate price irrationalities and increase competition in product markets. Even if we leave the question of complementary reforms aside, however, other problems can be identified. Although comprehensive data is difficult to obtain, Chinese analysts have argued that bond issues have in fact had little relation to enterprise profitability. Bond issues have not been restricted to the most profitable enterprises, hence it cannot be argued that the funds raised through these assets reflect a more rational allocation of resources. In fact, the influential (until June 1989) Economic System Reform Institute went so far as to suggest that there is an *inverse* relationship between enterprise profitability and bond issue. As one expert explained, "After all, good enterprises find it easy to get money from the bank and can repay it. It is the bad enterprises which are issuing bonds (and shares)."[31] Bonds represent, therefore, another avenue for poorly performing enterprises to acquire funds. There is indeed a logic to this given the relative unattractiveness (for enterprise managers) of raising funds through bond issues directly as compared to other sources such as an ordinary bank loan or a bank loan funded by a bank bond issue.[32] In the latter case, the loan to the enterprise carries a higher interest rate than does an ordinary bank loan. From the enterprise point of view this avenue is still preferable to a direct bond issue, since the bank has the task of repaying the loan

---

31. Personal interview, May 9, 1987.
32. A study carried out by the Economic Reform Research Institute found that bank loans were seen as the most popular form of borrowing by enterprises. See World Bank (1988: p. 138). An official of the Shanghai Industrial and Commercial Bank informed us that his bank had issued bonds and the proceeds had been used to finance enterprise working-capital funds. In his words, "We are actually helping to supply that part of an enterprise's working capital which the enterprise is supposed to find itself—according to the regulations. We will lend to them even if they have problems, however, because we are a state bank." Personal interview, 23 May 1987.

to the public; the enterprise then only has to deal with the bank, and enterprises (especially state ones) are, as argued in Chapters 4 and 5, in a strong position with respect to banks. Yet raising funds through direct issue is still preferable to no funds at all, and enterprises which cannot meet bond repayments are likely to be bailed out in some way (such as lower taxes or bank interest payments).[33]

This behaviour reflects a more fundamental problem, namely that the introduction of capital markets, such as they are, has taken place in the context of an attempt to transform a centrally planned economy. The use made of bonds by issuing agents must be interpreted within the logic of an only partly reformed socialist economy. Specifically, we must analyse *the way in which bonds have been used as an instrument in a complex politico-economic fight for resources* between central and local governments, banks, enterprises and individuals. Examining this more closely not only enables us to better understand the use made of bonds but also contributes to our understanding of the extent to which the economic reform process in general has succeeded in changing agents' behaviour.

The struggle for resources takes place within the context of an economy in which, as argued in Chapter 5, productive enterprises (and financial institutions like state banks) still operate under soft budget constraints. The impact of the financial reforms—in terms of decentralising control over financial resources and diversifying financial institutions and actors—has created a new arena for agents to fight for funds. It is within this context that the bond "market" must be understood. This arena is now more complex and comprises economic agents endowed with greater discretionary powers (whether legally sanctioned or not) as a result of the reform process.[34]

Thus, an important feature of bonds has been their use by agents to attempt to claim resources from other agents; the same distributional conflicts which, as was argued in Chapter 5, underlie the inflationary pressures in the reformed economy are also evident in the use which has been made of bond issues. To further examine this, let us briefly consider the identity and motivations of the main agents.

---

33. This argument was made by an expert at the Economic System Reform Institute. Personal interview, May 9, 1987.

34. To give two examples of other areas of conflict over resources (both of which are illegal): (i) the Ministry of Finance estimates that it lost over 12 billion yuan in 1988 from tax evasion and a survey showed that at least 50 per cent of state and collectively run enterprises had been involved in tax evasion (see *China Daily, Business Weekly,* 14 May 1989); (ii) there have been numerous reports of local governments appropriating the state advance payments to grain farmers in their areas for their own uses (such as the financing of township enterprises). See *China Daily,* 10 May 1989.

The Central Government

Quite apart from the wider developmental aims discussed earlier, the central government's underlying motives in issuing Treasury and other state bonds are that these bonds will serve to finance priority investment projects and as a method of financing budget deficits. In this latter aspect, they are a tool for financial centralisation in an era of decentralisation and for maintaining the share of state revenue in national income (see Jin Xiu 1983). Bonds are a useful device because the reform era has seen a dispersion of resources away from the state budgetary system and into the hands of individuals (personal savings increased about eighteenfold between 1978 and 1988)[35] and into the extra-budgetary funds of enterprises, government departments and local governments.[36] Table 6.4 shows the changing balance between

TABLE 6.4   Government Budgetary and Extra-Budgetary Revenues, 1979–1989 (million yuan)

		Extra-Budgetary Revenue				
Year	Government Budgetary Revenue	Total	As % of Budgetary Revenue	Local Govt. Finance Departments	Non-Profit Admin. Units	State-Owned Enterprises & Supervising Agencies
1979	106,796	45,285	42.4	3,994	6,866	34,425
1980	104,222	55,740	53.5	4,085	7,444	44,211
1981	101,638	60,107	59.1	4,130	8,490	47,487
1982	108,394	80,274	74.1	4,527	10,115	65,632
1983	121,116	96,768	79.9	4,979	11,388	80,401
1984	146,705	118,848	81.0	5,523	14,252	99,073
1985	183,716	153,003	83.3	4,408	23,322	125,273
1986	218,452	173,731	79.5	4,320	29,422	139,989
1987	226,242	202,880	89.7	4,461	35,841	162,578
1988	248,941	227,000	91.2	4,500	41,500	181,000
1989	280,381	265,883	94.8	5,436	50,066	210,381

SOURCE: SSB 1991: p. 196.

35. See Chapter 5 for details of the rise in individual savings.

36. Claiming back the funds accumulated by local governments was clearly a key aim of bond issues. A national symposium on financial theory in mid-1983 remarked on this: "There have been some advantages for the localities since the implementation of the new financial system. . . . But by providing loans for the localities and *selling them national Treasury Bonds* and by readjusting the percentage of profit for retention, the localities' benefits have been basically taken back by the state" (emphasis added) (Cai Xun, "Reforming and improving the socialist financial systems . . .", *Guangming Ribao* (Glorious Daily), 29 May 1983, in *FBIS* 116).

central budgetary revenue and the extra-budgetary funds held by other agents.[37]

Government reliance on debt financing has increased during the reform era: Table 6.5 shows the role of debt financing as a source of government revenue.

As we have seen, there have been some concerns raised about the steady growth in national debt, but most economists have been willing to admit its utility so long as it is subject to careful management. However, the mandatory nature of bond purchases (both Treasury bonds and special project bonds), particularly in times of inflation, has brought political costs which could be avoided if Treasury bonds came to be perceived as a valuable asset by willing purchasers. Since the central government clearly wishes to safeguard this source of revenue in an era when other avenues are closed and also wishes to restrict costs in terms of interest repayment, such a change towards a full market in state bonds is unlikely in the near future. Even so, the central authorities seem wary of provoking public discontent and have treated individual holders of Treasury bonds more favourably than other holders such as enterprises and non-productive units. As an example of this, of the 24.5 billion yuan worth of bonds due for repayment in 1990, the state repaid only the 12 billion yuan owed to indi-

TABLE 6.5   Government Debt Revenue, 1979–1990 (million yuan)

Year	Debt Revenues			Debt Revenue as a percentage of Total Govt. Revenue
	Total	Domestic	Foreign	
1979	3,531	–	3,531	3.2
1980	4,301	–	4,301	4.0
1981	7,308	–	7,308	6.7
1982	8,386	4,383	4,003	7.5
1983	7,941	4,158	3,783	6.4
1984	7,734	4,253	3,481	6.7
1985	8,985	6,061	2,924	4.8
1986	13,825	6,251	7,574	6.1
1987	16,955	6,307	10,648	7.2
1988	27,078	13,217	13,861	10.3
1989	28,297	13,891	14,406	9.6
1990	37,545	19,724	17,821	11.3

Source: SSB 1991: pp. 183, 194.

37. For discussion of the fall in central government revenues and the slower fall in central government expenditures, see Chapter 5.

viduals and rolled over redemptions on the 12.5 billion yuan worth of bonds held by enterprises.[38] In the complex struggle for resources, the central government exercises more power over its "own" enterprises than it does over individuals.

Local Governments

Local governments also find bonds useful and issue them through local branches of the People's Bank. They are important mainly as a source of investment finance, since local governments themselves are prone to "investment hunger", wishing to expand their bailiwicks in relation to other localities and to the central government. Though these bond issues depend more on voluntary purchases and tend therefore to have more attractive terms than Treasury bonds, local governments have in some areas emulated the example of the central government and resorted to forced sales, including arbitrarily deducting payments from workers' wages. More indirectly, moreover, since local governments have an interest in increasing the level of economic activity within their territories, they are motivated to "sponsor" bond issues by other economic agents such as local specialised banks and enterprises under local government jurisdiction.

Banks

Banks have issued bonds for a number of reasons. In some cases, they are acting under pressure from powerful clients—local governments and enterprises—who wish to acquire funds for investment projects which may be more difficult to finance through normal channels. But banks have important motives themselves. Since they too are subject to the same logic of the soft budget constraint, they too seek to expand their lending portfolios. This motive became greater as the banking system became more diversified and competition to attract savings increased (for example, among the specialized banks or between them and new financial institutions as discussed in Chapter 4). Banks may also resort to bonds to deal with cash-flow problems: For example, in 1986 the Bank of China branch in Beijing issued bonds to make up for losses arising from poor repayment from its client enterprises.

Enterprises

Enterprises have also found bond issues useful not merely as a way to obtain investment funds outside of normal channels. Enterprise bond issues were discussed earlier; now consider enterprise bond purchases.

---

38. *Far Eastern Economic Review*, 9 May 1991, p. 42.

These are of two types: the mandatory purchases of state Treasury bonds and voluntary purchases of other economic agents' bonds. Treasury bonds represent a form of taxation. In keeping with this, the quota assigned to units depends on their extra-budgetary funds and their after-tax profits. This type of additional profits tax ran into problems, however, when levied on loss-making enterprises. As a result, the approximately 20 per cent of large- and medium-sized state enterprises which were loss makers in 1989 were exempted from purchasing that year's Treasury bond issue. This therefore adds a further area for negotiation between enterprises and government: In addition to "soft credit" and "soft taxes", we now have "soft Treasury bond purchases" contributing to the soft budget constraint.

In relations between enterprises, bonds have served as a kind of shadow transaction in goods, reflecting a priority claim on the part of the purchaser (user) on the products of the issuer (producer). For example, the Zhujiang Cement Works in Guangzhou issued three-year bonds which could be redeemed at maturity either at an enhanced value or for a corresponding amount of cement. Similarly, the Shoudu Iron and Steel Corporation in Beijing paid interest on funds raised by bond issue by selling steel products to purchasers at below-market prices.[39] The Shanghai Volkswagen Company, the first joint venture to issue bonds on the domestic market in mid-1988, granted enterprise purchasers a priority in purchasing the Santana car, which was in short supply throughout China.[40] Whilst these transactions were aimed at correcting supply inadequacies within the planning system or rationing scarce goods by the use of a shadow market, they also shed light on the way in which financial assets are used within the context of a shortage economy. One of the arguments made in favour of bonds is that they provide inducements for enterprises to save in the form of financial assets rather than through inventories and hoarding; the use made of enterprise bonds in China indicates that rather than reducing an enterprise's demand for real resources, enterprise bond purchases are in some cases a new mechanism for obtaining such resources.

Individuals

Given that the reform period has witnessed a substantial rise in the volume of individual savings deposits and given that there are still

---

39. For Guangzhou, see *Zhongguo Xinwenshe* (China News Service), 25 June 1986, in *SWB* 8302; for Beijing, see *Liaowang*, no. 28, 14 July 1986, in *FBIS* 143.

40. *China Economic News*, vol. 21, 6 June 1988, p. 6.

few outlets for these savings, bonds provide a form of saving which is potentially attractive in that they may offer reasonable rates of return combined with security (of course, the mandatory issues of Treasury bonds have not been so appealing). Bonds issued by specialised banks and enterprises have been particularly attractive, and there have been numerous "runs" on banks to buy some popular issues. However, individuals have an interest in the availability of secondary markets, formal or informal, to increase the liquidity of their bond holdings.

This struggle for resources through bond issue can by no means be described as a real bond "market", meaning the free and voluntary sale and purchase of bonds. The politico-economic relationships involved are more complex, with at least three main aspects: First, *coercion* is embodied in a system of obligatory purchases and administrative decrees; thus the central government, through the People's Bank, has forced Treasury bond sales onto enterprises in an effort to capture enterprise funds for its own use. Enterprise workers have been subject to the same involuntary purchases. Moreover, some enterprises have forced their own bond issues onto their workers. Second, there is *collusion* between parties which see mutual interest in bond issues (between enterprises needing more investment funds and banks seeking to expand their portfolios; between enterprise managers seeking industrial peace and workers seeking higher wages or welfare; between enterprises seeking to raise funds and those wishing to ensure claims on supplies of key products). Third, a *market* exists in the sense of voluntary purchase and sale motivated by the material benefit derived from the transaction in a context of competitive alternatives.

Such a diversity of relationships falls short of anything that could be called a "market" and can be understood as reflecting the dynamics of a partly reformed and structurally ambiguous economy. The financial reforms were premised on the need to devise new methods of allocating resources and, specifically, of giving the market a greater role in the process. The bold initiatives after 1985 can be seen as an attempt to experiment with a decisive move in the direction of the market but as an attempt which resulted in complex, and often perverse, results because of the activities of powerful agents in the economy, agents which had no binding mechanisms to solve distributional conflicts. Part of the reason for this, it has been argued both inside and outside of China, has been the systemic features of the state socialist model. One of the basic foundations of these systemic factors is the institution of social (primarily state) ownership of the means of production, considered to be a cornerstone of the traditional form of state socialism. The emergence of "shares", however, as a new form of financial asset as part of the broad process of financial liberalisation called into question the meaning and utility of this institution and has allowed new forms of "social ownership" to emerge. Consequently, the emergence of shares has implications beyond the operations of the financial system and must also be placed in the wider ideological debate about the nature of a socialist economic system. It is to the relationship between shares and social ownership, and its economic implications, that we now turn.

The Introduction of Shares

Shares in advanced capitalist economies represent ownership—the purchaser owns a part of the productive assets of the issuing firm. As such, shares represent a vehicle for individuals to save indirectly in productive capital. Typically, shareholders are residual claimants, meaning that the firms' financial obligations to shareholders are only met after all other creditors are repaid. Thus, one attribute of shares is that they are relatively risky. Shareholders' returns consist of dividend payments and capital gains or losses. The price of shares is of interest not only to the holder of those shares but also to other firms who may wish to take over another firm if they think they can better utilise the latter's productive assets. The stock market, therefore, not only channels resources from savers to borrowers but also, it is hypothesised, acts as a constraint on firm behaviour (or, more strongly, ensures profit maximisation) for fear of take-over. Thus, it is argued that shares and stock markets channel savings to their most efficient users and act as a pressure for raising firm efficiency.

"Shares" in China differ in important respects from those in capitalist economies, although the Chinese reformers have argued that they might be capable of playing a similar economic role. Like bonds, shares were seen as a useful supplement to the financial system (Wu and Jin 1985; Rong 1986; Zuo 1986; Xu 1987). First, in the eyes of reformers, they facilitated the mobilization and redirection of savings in the context of an increasingly complex "capital market". Second, they established a mechanism to allow for a more rational allocation of investment resources, i.e., if share dividends indicated enterprise profitability, then investment funds would flow into the most efficient enterprises. Shares also offered the prospect of more efficient enterprises taking over less efficient ones if secondary markets were permitted.[41]

---

41. In this respect, as in many others, China's reformers have held an idealistic (or textbook) view of the operations of markets. In capitalist economies, it is in fact a matter of considerable dispute whether capital markets result in the takeover of the less efficient by the more efficient. This point is pursued further in the following pages.

Thus by allowing enterprises to purchase shares in other enterprises, reformers hoped to develop a genuine capital market in which the responsibility for assets, and industry entry and exit, is removed from the state to the enterprises themselves.

As discussed in Chapter 5, as part of the reform process the specialised banks, as the financiers of enterprises, have been given the power to reorganise, merge or close down loss-making enterprises. However, as also argued, this arrangement has not as yet led to a significant rationalisation of productive assets, and it was argued that a secondary market in shares would provide a much more effective mechanism. Third, it was argued that if shares are purchased by members of the workforce, then this provides incentives for workers to respect enterprise property and to increase productivity, since workers would now receive a part of the profits in the form of dividend payments. It was hoped that share ownership would lead to the same increases in "enthusiasm" that were displayed by the peasants as a result of the reform of the system of land management in the rural sector. Fourth, share-issuing enterprises have potentially more financial autonomy than other enterprises and can respond in a more dynamic way to market opportunities. They also have greater ability to cut through the regional and departmental ties which characterise the rest of China's economy.[42]

Not all of these arguments are in fact consistent, and again conflicting objectives are evident. For some, shares represent a way of channelling individual saving into investment and hence provide a way of increasing and absorbing individual saving. For others, however, shares represent the mechanism whereby enterprises are forced to act more efficiently for fear of takeover. In a capitalist economy these two objectives need not be in conflict; in a socialist economy, however, if at least some shares are owned by individuals, then there is a concern to limit capital gains and unearned income. In such circumstances, restrictions placed upon share price movements reduce the ability of shares to act as a device for raising enterprise efficiency. However, if individuals are barred from share ownership, then the role of shares as a potential asset for savers is obviously lost. This illustrates the possible contradictions between the economic rationale for shares and the

---

42. The China Tourism Souvenirs Enterprise provides a case in point (Rong 1986). This enterprise was formed with contributions from 80 shareholders and has now invested in 43 factories nationwide producing handicrafts for the tourist industry. The noteworthy point about the enterprise is that the shareholders were from different regions, departments and types of ownership systems and, as such, it was the first enterprise of its kind in China.

political prerequisites of a socialist economy. We now turn our attention to how the Chinese have attempted to address these possible contradictions in practice.

The quantitative importance of share issues has been minor compared to bonds; by the end of 1989 only 4.2 billion yuan of shares had been issued compared to a total value for bonds of over 162 billion yuan. This figure for shares underestimates the extent of actual shareholding in China, since it refers to officially sanctioned issues from the socialist sector, by state or collective enterprises; whereas there has been a proliferation of different forms of joint-stock enterprise *outside* the existing socialist sector during the reform era as part of a general process of diversification of the ownership system.[43] New joint-stock enterprises have included joint ventures with foreign firms, joint-stock financial institutions (many of which were former urban credit cooperatives), new enterprises formed by joint investment of state or collective enterprises, agglomerations of private capital (often called "cooperative" or "associative") and various hybrid forms. In this joint-stock form, shares are issued to investors or cooperatives who then become the owners of the institution, entitled to a share of profits and responsible for the risks. While the development of these ownership forms has been dynamic during the 1980s, especially in the countryside and in certain regions (most obviously in the Special Economic Zones on the East Coast), the public (state and collective) sector has remained dominant in the non-agricultural economy as a whole[44] (Table 6.6 provides figures on forms of ownership in the industrial sector) and will be the main focus of our attention here.

If we look at the evolution of policy and practice on shares, at least until 1986–1987, it takes a similar trajectory to that of bonds and illustrates similar kinds of conflicting objectives and impulsions. There

---

43. For a discussion of share issues outside of the state sector see Tam (1991). Figures provided by Tam suggest that by the end of 1988 a total of 6 billion yuan of shares had been issued by all categories of enterprises.

44. Outside the Special Economic Zones, in the domestic economy proper, foreign participation in share ventures was not encouraged until 1988, when, for example, the Shenyang Automobile Industry Corporation set up a financial institution, the Jinbei Automobile Co. Ltd., which was the first enterprise in China to issue shares to foreigners with the purchase price and dividends being payable in foreign exchange (*China Economic News*, vol. 17, 9 May 1988, p. 14). Indeed, in the late 1980s the fiscal crisis of the Chinese state has led to foreign companies being encouraged to purchase entire Chinese enterprises for technical upgrading, especially in the Special Economic Zones.

TABLE 6.6   Shares in Gross Industrial Output Value by Form of Ownership, 1979–1990

Year	Total (billion yuan)	State %	Collective %	Individual %	Other %
1979	468.13	78.5	21.5	–	–
1980	515.43	76	23.5	0.02	0.48
1981	539.98	74.8	24.6	0.04	0.58
1982	581.12	74.4	24.8	0.06	0.68
1983	646.04	73.4	25.7	0.12	0.78
1984	761.73	69.1	29.7	0.19	1.01
1985	971.65	64.9	32.1	1.85	1.2
1986	1,119.43	62.3	33.5	2.8	1.5
1987	1,381.30	59.7	34.6	3.6	2.0
1988	1,822.46	56.8	36.2	4.3	1.7
1989	2,201.71	56.1	35.7	4.8	3.4
1990	2,392.44	54.6	35.6	5.4	4.4

SOURCE: Calculated from SSB 1991: p. 353.

were debates and experiments quite early in the reform process; indeed, as early as 1980 positive statements about the possible virtues of joint stock companies started to appear in the press. There were also cases of primary share issues: For example, the Wuhan city government issued shares in 1980 to finance the establishment of a trade centre building, shares mostly sold to state and collective enterprises; in Shandong province, a thermal power station was financed in 1981 by shares sold to local state/collective enterprises and agricultural cooperatives.[45] At this stage, however, such initiatives were seen as quite bold, and opposition was strong. For example, when the Shanghai No. 17 Textile Mill issued shares to its workers in 1980, it was forced to retract in the face of criticism.[46] This was early evidence of the fact that shares, unlike bonds, raised certain basic political-ideological issues concerning the nature of ownership in a "socialist" economy.

However, when the reform of the urban-industrial economy became the focus of the reformers' attention in 1984, the question of introducing financial markets came more squarely onto the policy agenda, and the rate of share issues accelerated. Share issues were featured in

---

45. The social scientist Sun Gua advocated joint-stock companies in a letter to the *Workers' Daily* (reported by *Agence France Presse*, Hong Kong, 25 September 1980; the Wuhan share issue was reported in *Ta Kung Pao*, Hong Kong, 30 November 1980, in *FBIS* 233; for the Shandong power station, see *NCNA*, 19 November 1981, in *SWB* W1161.

46. Personal interview, 27 May 1987.

certain reform-oriented cities in mid-1984[47] and the expansion of experiments was sanctioned by the central authorities in late 1984, in the first instance to include five cities (Chongqing, Guangzhou, Wuhan, Shenyang and Changzhou), with an eventual aim of spreading beyond them.

Some state enterprises were allowed to issue shares to their own workers, and a number of enterprises were allowed to experiment with public share issues in designated cities (either to other units or to the general public). The bulk of officially sanctioned share issues outside the enterprise has apparently been purchased by state or collective institutions—this again represents sensitivity to the relationship between the economic rationale for shares (as one financial asset among many) and social ownership as an institutional foundation of a "socialist" economy.[48]

Small-scale secondary markets began in several cities (but most trading was in bonds, not shares), but more ambitious plans for a nation-wide network of stock markets were shelved in 1988–1989 in response to mounting inflation and perceived financial disorder. More recently, however, secondary trading has been developed in the Special Economic Zone of Shenzhen. However, there were initially only five enterprises whose shares were being traded, although there are plans to expand this number.[49] Individuals who purchase shares must register them, and they can only legally be traded in the official market; a black market does exist, but technically the purchasers, since they are not registered, are not the legal share owners. Because of concern over potentially destabilising speculation and the desire to limit capital gains income, share price movements were controlled. Changes in share prices were constrained to a maximum daily increase of 1 per cent and a maximum daily decrease of 5 per cent.[50]

---

47. For example, the Municipal Financial Trust Company in Wuhan expanded its share base with a public issue of 12 million yuan in July (*Hubei Daily*, 7 July 1984, in *FBIS* 142); in Beijing, a new department store, the Tianqiao, was launched through a public issue of 100,000 shares at 100 yuan each (*China Daily*, 28 July 1984); in Shanghai, collective enterprises were authorised to issue shares (*NCNA*, 21 August 1984).

48. For a quasi-official discussion of this issue, see the article by Xu Shuxing, a researcher in the People's Bank of China, "Selling shares can help the nation to raise investment capital", *China Daily*, 23 April 1985.

49. The five enterprises (all state-owned) included the Shenzhen Development Bank, an electronics trading company and a land and real estate company. None of the five enterprises were manufacturing enterprises.

50. See *Far Eastern Economic Review*, 26 July 1990, p. 55. A maximum decrease was set because it was feared that if money from Hong Kong, which played a large role in financing the stock market boom, suddenly left, then share prices would fall, leaving Shenzhen residents with large capital losses. Whilst the authorities sought to limit capital gains, they did not want the experiment to fail because of individuals suffering significant capital losses.

Nevertheless, share prices rose rapidly during 1989 and 1990.[51] Allegations were made that local government officials were taking advantage of their position and making large profits as a result. This prompted the Chinese central government to set up its first "insider trading" investigation in April 1990. The investigating commission recommended that (i) there should be regulations governing the purchase of shares by officials; (ii) the People's Bank should exercise a greater supervisory role, and (iii) more state enterprises should be permitted to issue shares so that the demand for existing shares would be reduced and hence lessen price movements. "Adjustment" of the Shenzhen exchange was decided upon by the State Council in 1989, including a prohibition on Party and government officials buying or selling shares.[52]

In the aftermath of the Tiananmen incident, it is clear that stock markets have became a testing ground for rival political ideologies. While negative reports of the Shenzhen stock market were sent to Beijing, positive reports were also sent, and the Shenzhen authorities sent officials to Beijing to lobby the State Council. This reflects differences among policy-makers over the advisability of stock markets and the performance of the Shenzhen Special Economic Zone. By early 1990, the political tide was turning in favour of stock markets. The Shenzhen stock market has been encouraged (it was officially opened on July 3, 1991) and indeed is expanding its listings, although the rioting which accompanied the scramble to obtain share purchase application forms in August 1992 has done nothing to reduce controversy.[53] The central leadership has also established a stock market (for both bonds and shares) in Shanghai as a counterweight to Shenzhen.[54] Shanghai's recently reopened stock exchange now lists a dozen or so

---

51. Share prices rose between 700 and 900 per cent. This was despite the fact that only the Shenzhen Development Bank was making high profits. In early 1992, the authorities abandoned their efforts to control share price movements, and the daily limits were abolished.

52. *Wen Wei Po*, Hong Kong, 21 Nov. 1990, in *SWB* 0934.

53. Although not as dramatic as scenes in Shenzhen, a "share euphoria" occurred in Xiamen in June 1992 when there was a huge demand for shares in four local companies. See *International Herald Tribune*, June 23, 1992.

54. There is no common set of regulations for the two exchanges, and China's regulations for stock exchanges are, in fact, still in the process of being written with the assistance of outside agencies such as the Asian Development Bank. For a discussion of the differences between the regulations of the Shenzhen and Shanghai exchanges, see Potter (1991). For a discussion of the development of the Shanghai stock exchange, see Zhu (1992).

shares and plans to float a further 34 by early 1993.[55] Included in Shanghai's current listings is the Shanghai Vacuum Electron Device enterprise, which became the first Chinese enterprise to issue shares to foreigners (termed 'B shares'). B share issues are viewed positively by enterprises, since if at least 25 per cent of shares are sold to foreigners, then the enterprise is classified as a joint venture with all the tax and other benefits that come with it. Issues of B shares expanded rapidly in 1992 to attract overseas investors: Shanghai Vacuum was allowed to issue US $100 million, and ten newly listed enterprises, US $300 million.[56] The central government's policy has been to encourage enterprises from all regions to seek listings on the Shanghai and Shenzhen exchanges. However, this policy of turning the Shanghai and Shenzhen exchanges into national exchanges has met with resistance from other localities who have wanted to set up their own exchanges in order to ensure that local savings are invested in their own areas, a motive reinforced by the reluctance of the Shanghai and Shenzhen authorities to list enterprises from other areas on their exchanges.[57] Whatever the intentions of the centre, cities and localities have been pressing to establish their own stock markets (especially in the southeastern provinces of Guangdong and Fujian) and have taken steps to do so without waiting for Beijing's permission.[58] By early 1992, the centre responded by announcing its intention to establish another stock market in the north.[59] Development of stock exchanges

---

55. See Kaye (1992b). An expanded role for the Shanghai stock exchange is also envisaged in order to assist in the financing of the ambitious Pudong New Development Area. For examples of arguments by Chinese economists for the need for an expanded role for share issues in this context, see Ma and Chen (1992).

56. At present, B shares represent the only way foreign investors can purchase equity in Chinese state-owned enterprises. However, there are plans for one such enterprise, Brilliance China Automative Holdings, to list on the New York stock exchange (see Sender 1992), and approval has been given for 9 Chinese companies to list on the Hong Kong stock exchange (see *Far Eastern Economic Review*, 15 October 1992, p.74). See also Bei, Koontz and Lu (1992).

57. The Shanghai exchange lists only one non-Shanghai-based enterprise. All of the planned listings for 1992 are for Shanghai-based enterprises. Shenzhen lists only Shenzhen-based enterprises. See Kaye (1992a).

58. For example, the Shenzhen exchange switched from over-the-counter to open transactions in December 1990 without the approval of Beijing. See *Far Eastern Economic Review*, Hong Kong, 4 April 1991, p. 29. Hainan set up its own stock exchange in March 1992 only to see it ordered closed by Beijing one month later. Share trading does occur, however, without central approval, in Guangzhou, Xiamen, Fuzhou and Chengdu. See Kaye (1992a).

59. See *People's Daily*, overseas edition, 13 March 1992.

appears to be not only an expression of autonomy from Beijing but also a way of reinforcing that autonomy by enabling local economic agents to obtain resources independently of the centre.[60]

The issue of shares, although of relatively minor importance economically, has become an important political issue. We will discuss the impact of shares under two headings: first, the actual economic effects of share issues and official and expert reactions to them and, second, the broader political-ideological issues sparked by the tentative experiments in new forms of shareholding in the state sector, which led to a wide-ranging debate about ownership reform in a socialist economy. This gathered momentum in the mid-1980s and represented a critical point in the reform process—whether to replace traditional state ownership with new forms of social ownership in an effort to break the pervasiveness of "state paternalism".

Debate on the Economic Impact of Shares

Even though share issues lagged behind the bond issues of state enterprises, they came in for serious criticism from certain Chinese financial analysts as a contributing factor to over-investment and inflationary pressure from 1986 on. The State Council responded in 1987 by issuing an edict which forbade state enterprises to issue shares to the public.[61] In many ways, enterprises were using shares in the way they used bonds. First, share issues tend to have a guaranteed return, equal to the bank deposit rate plus an additional payment based upon enterprise profitability. In practice, all shares pay the maximum allowable return and there is no relationship between dividends and profitability. Thus they do not present any risk to their purchasers, which defeated part of their purpose[62] (this may not be the case for shares in *collective* enterprises, many of which, especially in rural areas, went

---

60. In some sense, informal stock markets already exist in that enterprises which purchase shares in other enterprises often do so at the behest of, and on behalf of, their own workers. The enterprise, as a "legal person", acts as the umbrella for individual purchasers. The regulations for share transactions involving legal persons are less strict than those applicable to individuals, and Beijing has less control over such purchases. We are grateful to Professor Yun-win Sung of the Chinese University of Hong Kong for bringing our attention to this point.

61. *NCNA*, 6 April 1987. The Chinese text is reprinted in *Zhongguo Jinrong*, (Chinese Finance), May 1987, p. 16.

62. For discussion of this problem, see *NCNA* 16 November 1988 and 3 April 1989; and the comments by Zhang Yanning, vice-minister of the State Commission for Economic System Reform on *Beijing Radio*, 20 February 1988, in *SWB* 0392.

bankrupt in the retrenchment from late 1988 on). Second, share issues were sometimes used by unprofitable enterprises to cover losses, and in some cases sums paid out in interest and dividends exceeded the enterprises' total net profits. They economised, moreover, by paying differential return rates to state and non-state purchasers, with state shareholders receiving lower returns. However, the fact that shares are similar to bonds in guaranteeing high dividend payments has deterred many profitable firms from issuing them.[63] Third, share issues were also being used, in much the same way as bonds, to distribute bonuses to enterprise workforces and to distribute scarce goods between enterprises.[64]

While these facets of actual share issues are predictable in the context of a socialist economy undergoing reform, they tended to obstruct any contribution which they might have made to increasing the productivity of financial resources. They also gave cause for concern in terms of their contribution to the macroeconomic problems of 1987–1988; it was in this context that more conservative financial analysts criticised shares for many of the same reasons that they also criticised bonds (see, for example, Wu and Cheng 1990). First, they argued, the banking system can operate as an effective channel for turning savings into investment, and there is no need for share issues on those grounds. Indeed, share issues are hard to control and tend to disperse funds with the result that they evade or obstruct state efforts at financial regulation and also exert claims on scarce raw materials and energy supplies, which may subvert planned production and investment. Second, since dividend payments are in fact irrationally high and in many cases nothing but a disguised bonus payment, they contribute to inflationary pressures. Rates of return on shares issued by collective enterprises during 1985–1986, for example, were such that annual dividend and other payments on shares were as high as 20–40 per cent, which was substantially higher than bank interest rates and

---

63. The Communications Bank in Shanghai provides a good case in point. This was set up as a shareholding bank but has so far refused to issue new shares on the local capital market on the grounds that they are too much like bonds and therefore represent an expensive way of borrowing money. It is pointed out by Communications Bank officials that dividend payments are not the main way in which shareholders receive their returns in other countries, that returns rather are realised through capital gains resulting from the increased value of the shares (reflecting investment by the enterprise). Since shares do not operate in this way in China, the Bank has not issued any (*China Economic News*, vol. X, no. 2, 9 January 1989).

64. For the former, see *China Daily*, 30 November 1988, p. 1, and Xu (1987: p. 510; for the latter, see the case of the Shandong power station, which supplied electricity to shareholders in proportion to investment (*NCNA* 19 November 1981).

higher than state bonds. In spite of state efforts to limit dividends, in 1988 some enterprises were issuing shares to their workforce with returns of 50–100 per cent, evading the official 15 per cent ceiling on share dividends through "creative" accounting. Third, it is argued that share issues are "unhealthy" in social terms, leading to a situation where certain people derive unearned income from the surplus produced by others, which in turn may bring increasing and unjustified material inequality, even to the point of class polarisation. Hence, returns on shares have been treated officially as interest-type payments and do not include capital gains or "speculative" returns in general. Thus, "shares" in practice have been debt instruments rather than equity instruments, as in capitalist economies. This third argument points to the wider ideological debates concerning ownership in a socialist economy, debates to which we return further on.

These criticisms all related to a concern that the centre was "losing control" as a result of share issues. At one level, this is clearly a weak argument. The contribution of shares to financing investment is minimal compared to other sources of funds, such as bank credit and retained profits, available to enterprises, notwithstanding the legitimate point that the economic consequences of share issues have been problematic.[65] However, beyond this immediate concern with "overinvestment" is the argument that the development of new financial assets, often propelled from below and without official sanction, poses a threat to the state's role in the economy. Of course, the move towards a more market-based allocation of resources is precisely what the reforms were intended to achieve; what has concerned critics, even at this embryonic stage, is whether this will undermine the state's ability to pursue its developmental objectives. In the complex process of moving to a new financial system, therefore, underlying many policy debates were more fundamental debates about the nature of the reformed financial system and the reformed economic system in general.

Nowhere are these fundamental debates clearer than in the discussion of ownership reform which emerged during the 1986–1988 period, when the economic reforms in general, as well as the financial reforms in particular, were being implemented at a rapid pace. The ownership debate brought to the fore the question of the ultimate aim of the reforms and the type of economic system to which China wished to move. There was a wide range of positions advanced, all of which had implications both for the nature of the economy as a whole

---

65. For example, Tam estimated in 1985 that the value enterprise shares issued in that year "would only account for about 2 per cent of the year's total fixed capital investment" (1991: p. 519).

and for the nature of the financial system within it. As we show in more detail next, some reform advocates clearly had in mind the transition to a capitalist economy with a financial system premised on the 'finance and development' paradigm to serve it. Others sought to explore the limits of a market socialist economy, whilst concerns about retaining the developmental capacity of the state in any reformed economy were also evident.

Ownership Reform in a "Socialist" Economy

Before discussing the various positions advanced in this debate, let us first step back a little and put the issue in context. Social ownership of the means of production is, for state socialist societies, not an end in itself but a means to an end. In the Marxian canon, social ownership of the means of production is desirable as an alternative to private ownership because the latter is exploitative, and therefore unjust, since it entails the private appropriation of surplus labour. Furthermore, social ownership, managed through some kind of planning system, allows in theory for the rational organisation of society's productive forces and avoids the contradictions inherent in capitalist economies, namely, the existence of excess capital, excess labour and unsatisfied wants. At a deeper level, social ownership is a means to achieve human liberation: Workers are not alienated from the products of their labour (characteristic of private ownership in capitalist economies) because "associated producers" are allowed control over the means of production.[66] Thus, the existence of social ownership of the means of production is a definitive characteristic of socialism. It is in this light that the debate over shares and ownership in China must be understood.

Reformist leaders and economists argued that shares are a natural component of a commoditised economy and therefore are consistent with both a capitalist and a socialist commodity economy.[67] The in-

---

66. Social ownership is a necessary but not sufficient condition for this process of human liberation and self-realisation. A further condition is the abolition of scarcity. For further discussion, see Cohen (1988). Furthermore, social ownership in itself leaves unresolved the question of social relations in the workplace.

67. This view was spelled out in Zhao Ziyang's address to the 13th National Congress of the Communist Party in 1987. Here Zhao argued that "some of the things we have introduced in the process of reforms, such as expanded markets for the means of production, funds, technology and labour service and the issuance of stocks and bonds, are phenomena which are not peculiar to capitalism but are bound to appear in the work of large-scale socialised production and development of a commodity economy. Socialism can and should make use of them, trying at the same time to minimize their negative effects in practice" (Zhao Ziyang 1987: p. 33).

troduction of shares in China, therefore, is viewed as being compatible with social ownership of the means of production; shares are not viewed as being *necessarily* a rejection of socialism. The question arises, therefore, of defining the conditions under which share-issuing enterprises can be considered socialist.

This question in turn is incapable of resolution until the meaning of "ownership" is defined. The World Bank, in its discussion of the question of ownership in China (1988: p. 93), has defined ownership in terms of a bundle of property rights consisting of (a) the right to determine how enterprise assets are used; (b) the right to receive the surplus produced by the enterprise; and (c) the right to sell, trade, or transfer the assets to another party. Chinese scholars Ma and Hong have used a similar approach and have defined ownership as "the power to occupy, use and deploy the means of production" (1987: p. 505). At present, it is the state (its policy-making, planning and administrative agencies) which acts on behalf of the whole people and exercises these rights; this is more precisely *public* ownership, which is but one possible form of social ownership.

During 1987–1988, a debate developed among reform economists who were concerned to carry reforms further but disagreed about how best to do this.[68] The topic was subject to impressive mental gymnastics, complete with the obligatory quotations from Marx et al. to justify various points of view. One central focus of debate was whether the decisive breakthrough thought necessary in the overall reform process could be achieved by comprehensive price reforms or by ownership reform of state enterprises. Some economists, such as Wu Jinglian for example, argued that, since the price mechanism was the key pivot of a commodity economy, establishing a rational system of market prices was a precondition for all reforms. If prices were irrational, profits were arbitrary; so share dividends did not represent rational distribution. Professor Li Yining of Beijing University argued that, on the contrary, since the ownership system defined the basic interests, responsibilities and incentives of enterprises, ownership reform was the key to the whole economic reform and should be pursued first (Li 1986).

Whether or not other reform economists aligned themselves with either side of this debate, most of them shared, to various degrees, certain misgivings about the economic advisability of traditional state ownership. Since the actual location of ownership of state assets was vague and confused, they argued, enterprises were not responsible for the management of the assets or their disposal, with predictable eco-

---

68. In addition to the writings surveyed here, Hsu (1991: pp. 53–91) provides an overview of the Chinese debates over ownership.

nomic consequences. In the words of Liu Guoguang (Liu 1986: p. 5), ownership reform "can make the system of ownership more specific and thus put an end to the previous situation whereby everybody is the owner of the assets of an enterprise owned by the whole people, but nobody is responsible for its assets". In other words, traditional state ownership was seen as leading to the situation where the economy was characterised as being one of "agents without principals." Ownership reform would, it was thought, contribute decisively to severing the previously umbilical relationship between particular sectors of the state apparatus and "their" enterprises, granting enterprises greater autonomy to operate in a market environment.

There was a high degree of consensus on the need for some reform of the traditional system of state ownership, in part fuelled by the size of state-owned enterprise losses. Whether these losses reflected low enterprise efficiency, however, is a controversial issue, as the evidence on productivity growth surveyed in the previous chapter illustrates. In any case, despite consensus on the need for enterprise reform, there was wide disagreement about how to go about this task. Four basic positions (each with their internal variants), moving from more conservative to more radical, can be discerned:

1. A familiar conservative position has been to admit the need for diversification of the concrete forms of social ownership but not take the step towards a basic transformation of the ownership of large and medium state enterprises through some kind of shareholding system. Rather, these analysts maintained that the problems of the old system could be corrected by *separating the rights of ownership* (still vested in the state) *and the functions of management*. This could be achieved by expanding enterprise autonomy and working out new relationships between state and enterprises (based, for instance, on profit or production contracts) which created a mutually beneficial system of rewards and penalties to direct enterprise behaviour in desired directions. This view was articulated, for example, by certain economists linked with the State Planning Commission (Fan et al. 1986) who argued for a system of "restraint on benefits" through which enterprises and their employees would be motivated "in accordance with the principle of income commensurate with contribution". They buttressed their argument about the irrelevance of shareholding to large state enterprises by references to trends in large-scale production in the West and in Japan, where the decision-making power in enterprises was passing from the hands of property owners to specialised managers. Theorists argued that what was required was not an increase in the power of new enterprise owners but rather a

reduction in the power of state owners and a separation of ownership from management. Economic efficiency, it was argued, could be increased in the state sector by a 'managerial' or 'entrepreneurial revolution', not by an 'ownership revolution'. Advocates of this position were willing to admit more radical changes of ownership outside the medium/large-scale state sector: the leasing or sale of small state enterprises, the conversion of state into collective enterprises, the formation of joint-stock companies and other kinds of "semi-socialist" forms of ownership, and toleration of limited share issues within the state sector proper.[69] However, the state sector was to be predominant in the non-agricultural economy as a whole and was to remain basically unreformed in terms of ownership.

2. Another approach to ownership reform was based on the notion of *joint-stock enterprises.* The most visible proponent of this was Li Yining (1986, 1987), but it also received support from influential economists such as Liu Guoguang, (1986, 1988), vice-president of the Chinese Academy of Social Sciences. Though the joint stock idea could take a variety of forms (for example, with shares held largely by individuals or by groups of enterprises), the form that has found favour, particularly since it meets the political priority of maintaining the dominance of "socialist" ownership, is for enterprise shares to be owned by state agencies of various kinds, often operating through some form of holding company.[70] Li Yining's (1986) version of the joint stock idea is more flexible in that he allows for differential state ownership in different types of enterprises—in smaller, less important ones, shares may be owned predominantly by the enterprise itself or by other enterprises. The result would be a dual economy dominated by large joint-stock firms (Li Yining 1986):

> On the one hand, several hundred of the larger enterprises will form a system consisting of parent companies, branch companies and affiliated small companies, and form enterprise consortia by controlling shares at various levels. The larger enterprises will determine the orientation of

---

69. The term *semi-socialist* is used, for example, by Dong Fureng in "More on the forms of socialist ownership", *Jingji Yanjiu* (Economic Research), no. 4, 20 April 1985, in *FBIS* 114.

70. In Shenyang, for example, which has been a leading city in experimenting with capital market reform, it was reported in 1987 that 130 enterprises had become shareholding enterprises. However, it was also reported that "private ownership . . . is limited. It can amount to no more than 10 per cent of the stock issued. This means that government and collectively owned shares form the bulk of such investment. In other words, *public ownership remains dominant, thus ensuring the socialist nature of the economy.*" *China Reconstructs*, vol. XXXVI, No. 3, March 1987, p. 42 (emphasis added).

the development of our country's industrialisation and technological progress. . . . On the other hand, tens of thousands or even millions of small enterprises, including cooperative enterprises, individually-owned enterprises and small enterprises under combined ownership, will form a closely linked cooperative network and compete among themselves.

This type of reform, its advocates argue, can improve enterprise performance by separating the state's role as governor from its role as owner of economic assets, with a clear responsibility for ownership vested in boards of directors which represent the interests of different shareholders; it would also allow a more effective supervision of the performance of enterprise managers and allow more flexible and better-directed flows of investment resources. The joint stock company proposal, with the majority (if not all) shares owned by state agents, is an attempt to introduce into a socialist economy the functions which private ownership is perceived as performing in a capitalist economy.

Conservative critics of this position argued that it is management, not ownership, which is the key and that, in any case, having a predominance of state agencies among shareholders is not conceptually different from the existing situation of direct state control over enterprises. Furthermore, a variety of state agencies as co-owners of state enterprises would import inter-governmental and inter-departmental rivalries into the running of enterprises (Fan et al. 1986). More radical critics argued that if the aim of share issue is to establish clear responsibility for such assets, then this is only partly achieved if shareholders are other state agents. The basic problem of removing the state from its paternalistic relationship with enterprises is not solved.

3. *"Enterprise ownership"*, the least worked-out alternative, with various versions, involved a transfer of ownership rights from the state to the enterprise itself. The shares would be owned predominantly by the enterprise's own workforce, but minority ownership by external agencies or individuals would also be possible. This would come about after a transitional process which starts with a separation of state assets and enterprise assets and deepens as the enterprise repays the state for its investment and gains control over, and responsibility for, its own assets (Han 1986). From then on, the enterprise would be responsible for its own operating profits and losses, and the role of the state would merely be "parametric", i.e., regulation by macroeconomic policies, or "economic levers", as they are called in China.

4. The most radical form of ownership reform is the *"privatisation"* of state enterprises through the sale of shares to the public.[71] However,

---

71. See, for example, the proposal for a "universal share system" by Li Dawei (*NCNA*, 7 Sept. 1988) and the experiment at the Qiqihar No. 1 Machine Tool Plant (reported by Wu et al. 1988).

given political constraints, this option has not been given much public airing (the outspoken pro-reform Shanghai-based *World Economic Herald* was an exception; see Chen 1988, Huang and Yang 1989 and Li Yunqi et al. 1989). However, reports on economic symposia suggest that it has had its open adherents,[72] and private conversations with Chinese economists reveal that it has a good deal of covert support. While this solution is aimed at providing full enterprise autonomy, it clearly constitutes a transition to a private, capitalist economy (despite some of the peculiar assertions to the contrary by some of its proponents).[73] Privatisation of state assets has now become a central plank of economic policy in the countries of the former Soviet bloc which, as a result of the political revolutions in 1989–1991, have now renounced social ownership of the means of production and sought to construct (capitalist) social market, rather than market socialist, economies. In China, this option is no longer openly discussed because the "Declaration of Private Ownership—China's Hope" was made public in April 1989 as part of the events leading up to June 4 (see Jin Jian 1989), and the post-Tiananmen leadership has tended to view privatisation as one of the planks of an "anti-socialist" opposition. After 4 June 1989, therefore, the issue of ownership reform became politically sensitive and was put further down on the list of reform priorities. Since the dramatic intervention of Deng Xiaoping in early 1992, however, the issue is back on the agenda; indeed, a formal list of 'Experimental Methods for Share-System Enterprises' was promulgated in June that year.[74] We return to the possible options for ownership reform in Chapter 7.

Clearly the debate about ownership in 1986–1988 went far beyond any discussion of the merits or demerits of shares as a financial asset; it concerned the essential nature of a state socialist economy. The more conservative position (1) discussed above, views managerial reform as the most important factor in increasing the productivity of state-owned enterprises. As such, it minimises the extent to which financial reforms are needed. Positions (2) and (3), however, both advocate redefining social ownership; position (2) by the introduction of

---

72. For example, see Jiang Xuemo, "China faces a big debate over socialist economic theories", *Qunyan*, no. 1, 7 January 1987, in *FBIS* 039.

73. Some have used Zhao Ziyang's general statement that "whatever is conducive to the growth [of the productive forces] is in keeping with the fundamental interests of the people and is therefore needed by socialism and allowed to exist" (1987: p. 48) to argue that widespread private ownership is needed by socialism. See, for example, Huang and Yang (1989).

74. See *People's Daily*, overseas edition, 19 June 1991, p. 2.

joint-stock enterprises with the majority of shares owned by other public bodies and position (3) by shares being distributed to enterprise workers. Both of these positions would therefore require some further evolution of the financial system broadly consistent with the main features of MSII. The privatisation position (4), by contrast, calls for widespread individual share ownership and implies a financial system closer to that described by the finance and development paradigm. In this way, the evolution of the financial system is intimately connected with the wider debate over ownership.

Despite the breadth of the debate in 1986–1988, there has been only limited progress in systematically examining the ownership question and in resolving the basic theoretical issue of the circumstances under which shares are consistent with socialism. If it is true that if shares are owned by public agents then the issuing enterprise is still "socialist", there can be no theoretical objection to state enterprises issuing shares under these circumstances. Certainly there are practical economic difficulties in terms of asset valuation, what to do about the different enterprise pension costs which affect profitability, and, not least, the distorted price structure. All of these difficulties are real and would mean that some enterprises would be considerably more profitable than others for reasons not connected with their own efficiency. More important in the current context are the political objections of those who see even marginal ownership changes as creeping privatisation en route to capitalism. The compromise that seems to have been reached is that existing state enterprises should not issue shares but that new joint stock companies can be formed (in which state enterprises can participate) and that collectives can be permitted to issue shares. It should be noted, however, that this represents a pragmatic solution rather than a theoretical resolution to the question of "socialist" share issues.

In large part, therefore, a pragmatic solution was dictated by the political environment operative during 1988–1992. However, it would be a mistake to view this solely as an outcome dictated by the specificities of internal CCP politics; the push for further reforms in the future will still face important theoretical challenges irrespective of the political climate. First, the importance of ownership reform for economic efficiency has yet to be decisively established; the relationships between markets, managers, entrepreneurship and ownership structures have still yet to be fully understood in either socialist or capitalist economies. Even in dealing with capitalist economies, there is a wide diffusion of views on the importance of the role played by private ownership in exerting pressures, through the capital market, on managers to act efficiently. There are several plausible hypotheses here, but despite a plethora of empirical studies, they remain just that—hypotheses.[75] Second, it is useful to return to our earlier point that social ownership is a means to certain ends: In economic terms, these are both macro- and microeconomic rationality (in both static and dynamic terms); in socio-political terms, these are an avoidance of excessive income inequalities (including the avoidance of unearned income as an important distributional factor), the removal of exploitation in the production process and a corresponding increase in the control of workers over the means of production. However, despite the hopes of socialist practitioners in China and elsewhere, it would seem that no single model of ownership could meet all of these objectives. The absence of clear guidelines on these two crucial issues—the economic effects of ownership relationships and the ability to reconcile the competing aims of social ownership—provide socialist reformers with many difficult theoretical problems as they attempt to construct a reformed socialist economy.

Concluding Remarks

The analysis presented in this chapter has shown the complexity of the process of introducing capital markets at a number of levels. This complexity is evident at the levels of both economics and politics. Economically, bonds and shares have not led unambiguously to improving the efficiency with which financial resources are used. On the basis of our analysis, it might be tempting to conclude that the economic effects of these new financial assets, in terms of allocative efficiency, have even been negative. At this stage, however, it is impossible to make a quantitative evaluation given the absence of systematic data and the unreliability of available data; also given the facts that share and bond issues are relatively recent phenomena and it is difficult to separate their effects from a plethora of other economic reforms, financial and otherwise. Nevertheless, it is possible to conclude, along the same lines as we did for the banking reforms analysed in Chapter 5, by saying that the use made of bonds and shares is certainly unlikely to have led to any significant increases in

---

75. For discussion of some of the empirical evidence see, for example, Cosh et al. (1989) and Cowling et al. (1980). See also Komiya (1987a, 1987b), who argues that if Chinese enterprises were reorganised along Japanese lines and if price competition was promoted, then ownership reform is not necessary in China. Recent theoretical work in "agency theory" has also demonstrated the problems which shareholders in capitalist economies face in devising incentive-compatible rules for firms' managers to follow.

enterprise efficiency in the state sector; if, as studies indicate, state-owned enterprise efficiency has increased, then the role played by the introduction of capital markets in achieving this has been minimal. Nevertheless, there continues to be substantial pressure from a number of sources for the greater use of capital markets. These pressures, emanating from individuals, local governments, and outside actors (including Hong Kong), as well as from a growing stratum of financial dealers, may lead to a "spontaneous" mushrooming of share issues and stock markets which Beijing can do little to control. The economic consequences of this are discussed further in Chapter 7.

Politically, the issue of bonds and shares has demonstrated once more the conflicting interests of agents in the economy, particularly between different levels of government. The central government and local governments have generally viewed the financial system as one in which "crowding out" occurs, i.e., financial flows to one agent correspondingly reduce the financial resources available to other agents. This would occur if the development of new financial assets simply redistributed but did not increase the volume of savings.[76] Thus, local governments have often sponsored enterprise bond issues and supported the development of stock markets in their jurisdictions without central approval. For its part, the central government has sought to use mandatory bond issues as a mechanism to obtain resources and has placed restrictions on the competitiveness of assets issued by other agents.

The political issues concern not only the conflicting objectives of different agents but also the nature of social ownership. The emergence of shares is intimately connected with the debate on social ownership, and this debate has raised the most fundamental questions about the evolution of the reformed economy.

Underlying all of these processes and events is the simple point that the shape of the reformed economy has yet to be determined at the theoretical level. The term *transition* is often used in discussions of the economic status of the countries of the former Soviet bloc, a term which is defensible in the sense that the transition has an identifiable end point, namely, a capitalist economy. In China, however, no such identifiable end point as yet exists. The reform process is, by contrast, open-ended, and a number of different outcomes are still possible.

---

76. We are grateful to Dr. R. Heunemann for drawing our attention to the "crowding out" analogy. Singh (1990) argues that given China's high savings rate, new financial assets are in fact unlikely to lead to a significant increase in the savings rate. The implications of this are discussed further in Chapter 7.

In terms of the financial reforms, the analysis of this chapter and Chapter 4 have shown that all three paradigms for financial reform have their supporters. Certainly, the developmental objectives of the Chinese state (both central and local) remain strong. It is possible, therefore, that the financial system could evolve in a manner consistent with the main tenets of the late-development model outlined in Chapter 2. It is also evident that the market socialist and finance and development paradigms have also been influential in shaping the way in which the market mechanism has been introduced in the mobilisation and allocation of credit and in promoting the emergence of capital markets. As a general trend, we have argued that up until the mid-1980s, MSI was the most influential paradigm. However, from the mid-1980s onwards the financial reforms became more radical, with both MSII and elements of the finance and development paradigm becoming influential, especially in the context of debates about ownership. The further evolution of the financial system is therefore still capable of exhibiting considerable variation as the proponents of our three paradigms vie for influence in the context of shifting political alignments in Beijing. How the financial reforms might evolve in the 1990s is the topic of our concluding chapter.

7

Conclusion:
Future Trajectories

THE ECONOMIC RETRENCHMENT in the face of inflation in 1988 and 1989 together with the political fallout from the June 4th incident led to a suspension and then gradual revival of the reform process. In mid-1992, however, China embarked upon another phase of accelerated reform. The financial system by this time had changed significantly from the monobank system which the reformers had inherited in 1978. There had been major changes in the structure of the financial system with the creation of a branch-banking system, the proliferation of financial institutions inside and outside of the state sector and the emergence of capital markets; and all this in the context of a rapidly monetised economy in which the flow of financial resources controlled by the central state budgetary system fell dramatically. Moreover, as we have shown in previous chapters, there were strong forces operating to push the reforms considerably further still. And yet while the structure of the financial system had changed considerably and had become more decentralised and more prominent in its role as a genuine intermediary, it still encountered some old problems as well as some new ones. In particular, the relationship between banks and enterprises, especially in the state sector, continued to be problematic, with the banks still acting ineffectively as monitors of enterprise efficiency. In addition, a new problem, that of persistent inflationary pressure which culminated in the inflation of 1988 and 1989 had arisen, a pressure to which the reformed financial system seemed particularly prone. In embarking on a new round of reforms, therefore, one central question facing the reformers is how to proceed with the reform of the financial system and how to avoid a repetition of the problems encountered in the mid to late 1980s, problems which indeed appeared to be reasserting themselves in the latter part of 1992.

Our intention in this chapter is to relate the insights realised, the problems identified and the issues generated by our analysis of the Chinese financial reforms so far to a discussion of the future trajectory of the financial reforms. We will focus on two sets of related problems which face the reformers as they seek to establish a more flexible and productive financial system. These two problems were just identified and were discussed in Chapter 5, namely the inflationary pressures which culminated in the inflation of 1988 and 1989 and the relationship between banks and enterprises. Our focus, therefore, will be upon exploring new institutional arrangements which will redistribute the claims of participating agents within the financial system in ways which can mitigate or restrain inflationary pressures, and upon new ways of reorganising bank-enterprise relations to improve microeconomic performance.

In undertaking this analysis we are keenly aware of the need to be both choice-theoretic and power-theoretic, i.e., the need to make judgments about what is feasible as well as about what is desirable. Analysis of the future course of financial reform needs to pay close attention to the ideological disputes and clashes of interests which have characterised the reform process to date and are likely to continue to shape its future trajectory. The interests and objectives of the various political actors which we have identified in Chapters 4, 5 and 6 (the CCP leadership, the central planning and regulatory authorities, the banking system, local governments, enterprises, individuals and external agencies) all need to be taken into account.

It is our position that a financial system and a set of financial institutions could be developed that would respond to the three specific characteristics of the Chinese situation, i.e., China as a large country, as a socialist system undergoing reform, and as a late developer.

In making these arguments, we will use the three paradigms of financial systems to guide our analysis and prescription. The market socialist paradigm is of relevance given that the stated intention of the Chinese reformers is to construct a reformed socialism; the late-development paradigm is also useful because China is a classic case of a late developer. We will argue that a selective combination of features from these two paradigms presents a plausible and possible future direction for the Chinese financial reforms. Such a fusion of the two paradigms is possible provided that the market socialist paradigm is used flexibly and not reduced to a "free market plus social ownership" position, which some of the more radical market socialist literature supports (in almost latter-day Langean fashion) and which precludes any role for the state beyond ownership. While certain specific aspects of the finance and development approach are valuable in understanding and designing the mechanics of institutional change, we find it less relevant as an overarching framework of reform because (a) some of its central arguments are already available in the market socialist literature; (b) it is premised on the operations of a capitalist economic system, i.e., its end point is incompatible with a socialist economy; and (c) its end point is also incompatible with a late-development model because it ends up advocating virtually exclusive reliance on financial markets and a minor role for the state. In our view, a forging of elements from the market socialist and late-development paradigms represents a possible way forward for China's financial reforms. Our intention here is not, to repeat, to produce a blueprint and timetable for reform but rather to sketch the parameters governing the future course of the financial reforms, analyse the actors involved and assess the implications of reforms for these actors and for the Chinese economy.

However, whether the financial system will actually evolve in this way is an open question and depends a great deal on the evolution of power relations among the Chinese leadership. Indeed, our analysis of current political trends in China suggests that such an outcome is doubtful in the long run and that an alternative systemic solution which further relegates or abandons any commitment to "socialism" is increasingly likely. If that were the case, one would look for a solution which reflected elements of the finance and development and late-development paradigms. Either way, the finance and development paradigm by itself is an inadequate guide to the future of China's financial system.

Desirable and Feasible Reform: A Scenario

The reimposition of central controls over the financial system and the reintroduction of tight credit ceilings in 1988 were seen by most observers as a necessary but regrettable step; necessary because it was the only way to control inflation given China's existing institutional framework and regrettable as it halted the further reform of that framework. Now that the period of retrenchment has officially been declared successful and therefore ended, the task is to continue the reform process and develop the institutions capable of sustaining a reformed "socialist market economy". In discussing what types of institutional reform are necessary to meet China's current needs, we pay particular attention to ways in which new institutional frameworks address the two key problems highlighted earlier, namely, control of inflation and the soft credit constraint.

Institutional Reform:
The Position of the Central Bank

Whilst most observers agreed with the need for the short-term recentralisation of monetary control in 1988, a common prescription advanced by international agencies is that this should be followed, after stability has been restored, by further decisive financial liberalisation together with a strengthened central bank. (See, for example, World Bank 1990a and Blejer et al. 1991: 19. The latter are particularly keen on advocating an expanded role for capital markets.) The argument here runs that recentralisation may enable inflationary pressures to be constrained in the short run but that in the long run this will only continue resource misallocation. Therefore, it is argued, there is a need to create a competitive market for finance which, it is hoped, will discipline financial institutions in their lending behaviour and lead to greater allocative efficiency. How one moves from short-run recentralisation to long-run liberalisation is, of course, a moot point (see World Bank 1990b).

Two key elements which must be addressed, therefore, by any proposed new institutional frameworks are the position of the central bank and the competitiveness of the financial system. Let us consider these issues. To counter inflationary pressures in both developed and developing countries, a conventional prescription has been to make the central bank "independent", thereby insulating it from the "political" process and the influence of vested interests (the arguments for central bank independence are summarised in Cargill 1989; Castello-Branco and Swinburne 1992; and Cukierman, Webb and Neyapti, 1992). The case for central bank independence has also been applied specifically to the Chinese case (notably Allsopp and Lin 1991). Let us state our position clearly. As our analysis in the preceding chapters has already shown, in the Chinese case, the need for greater central control over the banking system, improved methods of monetary management, and a weakening of the ability of local governments and enterprises to pressure the local branches of the specialised banks to extend credit on demand are all evident. However, acceptance of this does not automatically lead us to support the call for an "independent" central bank and, in fact, the terms in which the conventional case is presented is open to serious criticism.

Those supporting the case for an independent central bank in China argue that this would not only be a recentralisation of power (and thereby reduce the influence of local governments and enterprises) but would also be a policy initiative capable of reducing the influence of the central government over the banking system. This is deemed desirable on both specific and general grounds, namely that (i) central government expenditures have been important in generating inflationary pressures; and/or (ii) the central government's developmental objectives are inconsistent with price stability.

Perhaps the most forceful exponents of the case for an independent central bank in China have been Allsopp and Lin (1991). They argue that the central bank should have only one objective: price stability.[1] If it has multiple objectives, it is argued, such as price stability and developmental objectives, then central banks are faced with difficult choices and often err on the side of development at the cost of price stability. If the central bank has a responsibility only for price stability, then it can be relieved of these dilemmas and a constituency will have been created which has as its *raison d'être* price stability.

In assessing the relevance of this for China, a number of points need to be made. First, as is generally recognised, measuring central bank independence is a problematic exercise, since "independence" is a slippery concept and embodies a wide range of formal and informal relationships between the central bank and other political/institutional forces. As Allsopp and Lin point out (1991: p. 18), the word *independence* can carry with it certain connotations of total political insulation and a corresponding lack of political (and social) accountability, a situation which would be extremely difficult to achieve in political terms and, even if achievable, would be undesirable (particularly in the context of a democratic society). Following other authors, we would prefer to use the term *autonomy* or *discretionary autonomy*, which describe a more politically viable (and empirically common) situation in which the central bank is subject to certain continuing pressures for accountability, acts in coordination with other government agencies according to an agreed-upon division of regulatory labour and exercises a degree of discretion in a specific range of decisions guaranteed by a variety of formal and informal mechanisms which may vary across countries and over time. Even in the case of the relatively autonomous Federal Reserve System in the United States, one of its former chairmen, W. M. Martin, described it as "independent within the government not of the government" (quoted in Kaufman 1992: p. 495).

Second, the empirical case for greater central bank independence

---

1. Only two countries—Germany and the Philippines—mandate their central banks to maintain price stability to the exclusion of all other objectives. See Cukierman, Webb and Neyapti (1992: p. 357).

leading to lower inflation is weak. As Castello-Branco and Swinburne (1992: p. 20) note, "Although some empirical studies support the view that central bank independence promotes improved inflation performance, the evidence is not conclusive. Furthermore, there are some important 'anomalous' cases where inflation performance has been superior, despite the absence of a central bank with substantial statutory independence. Japan and France are important examples." Most of the empirical studies are also deficient in that they are usually only concerned with developed countries and they measure the independence of the central bank by its legal status, a measure which, as we pointed out, does not take account of other possible channels of influence.[2] Some of these problems are addressed by Cukierman, Webb and Neyapti (1992). They conclude that laws determining the degree of central bank independence are statistically insignificant in explaining variations in inflation across time or between developing countries (although they are significant for developed countries). However, they do find evidence to suggest that informal measures of central bank independence (in particular, the rate of turnover of central bank governors) do have some explanatory power in developing countries. Overall, however, the results are not strong, and the authors point out, for example, that "Korea and Japan have lower inflation than their indicators of central bank independence predict, probably because the governments, to which their central banks are subservient, have their own commitment to price stability. These examples demonstrate that high central bank independence is not necessary for price stability." (Cukierman, Webb and Neyapti 1992: p. 382). This suggests the need to examine the specificities of country experience and institutions before rushing to embrace central bank "independence" as the cure for inflation. We discuss this point below with respect to China.

Third, it is misleading to think of a putatively "independent" central bank as being "apolitical". A central bank which is independent of other political and institutional interests is still a political actor pursuing its own interests and arguing for its own preferences. As Goodman points out in his study of "monetary sovereignty" in Western Europe (1992: p. 8), by creating an independent central bank, "governments add a new actor to the political system, one that surely seeks to preserve its own autonomy". To the extent that such an institution's primary goal is price stability, moreover, as opposed to growth or employment creation, its decisions inevitably have specific polit-

---

2. These studies also employ cross-section data and regress inflation on various measures of (legal) central bank independence. For a critique of such testing procedures see Cargill (1989: pp. 19–20).

ical consequences which, in the words of Woolley in his analysis of the U.S. Federal Reserve System (1984: p. 2), "involves the central bank inescapably in favouring certain financial interests over others". As Woolley points out (1984: p. 12), the proclaimed "independent" role of a central bank involves a fundamental political contradiction: "It is asked to be politically neutral while regulating an economic system that is not politically neutral in its results".

Moreover, to the extent that the central bank does enjoy some degree of autonomy, we need to inquire into the nature of the constellation of political forces that created this situation in the first place and continue to guarantee it. In the case of the United States, for example, the act of legislation which created the Federal Reserve System in 1913 and is responsible for its decentralised structure reflected, in Kaufman's words (1992: p. 490), "a compromise among diverse and, at times, conflicting forces. The urban business community favoured a highly centralised organization, independent of the federal government and dedicated to stabilizing the purchasing power of the dollar. Rural agricultural interests favoured a decentralized, government-owned system oriented towards providing credit on liberal terms". In the case of the German Bundesbank, the role of external agents (the allied occupation authorities) and of domestic regional interests, the Länder, was crucial in establishing its particular political status. Comparative work on the political character of central banks also emphasises their links with, and reliance on, the domestic financial community as well as their actions to mobilise support for their preferred policies (see, for example, Goodman 1992: p. 8 and Epstein 1992: p. 11). Looked at from this perspective, central bank autonomy represents not so much an insulation from political forces but an institutional crystallisation of those forces. This perspective is a necessary corrective to a common underlying strain of utopian technocracy in some of the literature on central bank independence, which tends to pose the issue in terms of a sensible/sound central bank operating in rational economic terms and in terms of unwise/unsound forces operating in irrational political terms. (Compare the analysis by Grindle 1991 of the econocratic tendency to counterpose "positive economics" and "negative politics".) As Woolley points out in his study of monetary politics in the United States, "apparently technical debates often turn out to be non-technical debates carried on by other means" (1984: p. 6).

Fourth, and following on from the above, when we consider the political forces which create and condition the nature and extent of central bank autonomy, we need to consider external influences. The reality facing developing countries in the 1990s is that international agencies are increasingly involved in their domestic policy debates. China is no exception to this, although the degree of influence is certainly less than in many other smaller and more vulnerable countries. The central bank is a particularly important institution in the economy, and a greater independence from the government is likely to result in a closer alignment between the central bank and, to borrow Hirschman's apt phraseology, the "international money doctors" because of both common concerns and ideological outlooks.[3] For example, in many developing countries the central bank is a key ally for the World Bank and part of the internal "coalition" supporting structural adjustment programmes (see Mosley, Harrigan and Toye, 1991: vol. 1, p. 79). Comparably, advocates of central bank autonomy in China in the mid to late 1980s cited the World Bank in support of their argument. This highlights the problem of a combined process of domestic political deracination and international alignment in the context of a growing corporate culture of financial institutions. This phenomenon is also visible in the industrialised countries, as, for example, Goodman (1992) points out when documenting the general decline of "monetary sovereignty" and the increasing inability of countries to insulate their economies in the face of global financial integration. Paradoxically, as Epstein (1992: p. 2) notes, these trends have tended to increase the domestic political power of central banks and have led to pressures to increase their independence as a way of establishing their credibility in increasingly speculative global financial markets. This raises particularly important issues for developing countries whose central banks are becoming increasingly powerful domestic political actors but also are being incorporated into the evolving global financial order in dependent positions with respect to both more powerful national central banks (especially those of Germany, Japan and the U.S.) and international financial institutions. This is an important area for further analysis and points to a range of potentially serious political issues which fall beyond the range of this study.

Fifth, the specific features of Chinese political economy mean that the central government does in fact have a strong aversion towards inflation. This arises partly because of the horrendous experience of hyper-inflation in the late 1940s and the role this played in the CCP's rise to power, partly because the CCP's political legitimacy since 1949 has been based to a degree on its ability to maintain economic stability, and partly because the political costs of inflation, in terms of social unrest and popular protest, have been all too apparent in the

---

3. Hirschman quoted in Woo (1991: p. 178).

reform era, most notably during 1988–1989. There is reason to believe, as suggested in Chapter 4, that this concern was also shared by local governments for similar reasons, particularly after the upheavals of 1988–89. Furthermore, a social constituency already exists which has a strong interest in price stability, namely, workers on fixed incomes and individuals with savings deposits and other assets. These are groups which the Chinese government worries about, and in the inflationary period of 1988 and 1989 the government sought to protect them by imposing price freezes and index-linking savings deposits and bond yields. Furthermore, as the discussion in Chapter 5 highlighted, the central government's budget deficit does not appear to have been a major source of inflationary pressure during the reform period, and domestic bond sales and foreign borrowing were used extensively to finance deficits rather than pure money creation through the central bank. This is important; as Cukierman, Webb and Neyapti (1992: p. 378) argue, "providing credit to the government would seem to be the most important channel through which the lack of central bank independence leads to inflation because the issue of how to finance its budget deficit is immediately relevant to the government." To the extent that this has not occurred in China, and we must bear in mind that the central government influences central bank lending in ways other than through the budget deficit, the specificities of the Chinese case suggest that the inflationary bias of the central government may be weaker than in some other developing countries and the case for central bank independence correspondingly weaker.[4]

At present, it is the State Council which sets monetary targets and policies rather than the People's Bank. To the extent that pressures from ministries and local governments are effective in influencing the State Council, it is desirable to reorganise the responsibilities of the State Council and the PBC to give the latter greater say in both setting and implementing monetary policy with a view to maintaining financial equilibrium.[5] A reorganisation of powers along these lines would certainly be welcomed by the People's Bank, and the Ministry of Finance would probably support it, since it has a track record of supporting macro-financial stability (see Solinger 1980 and Bachman 1989). Moreover, both agencies have a common cause in

---

4. In fact, there is only a weak relationship between deficit financing and central bank independence in all countries, as Cukierman, Webb and Neyapti (1992: p. 379) acknowledge.

5. The PBC has, in fact, gained more autonomy recently as evidenced by the fact that the new head of the PBC, Li Guixian, abolished the PBC council on which representatives from the Ministry of Finance and SPC were present.

defending central powers against the rising influence of local governments. This said, however, there was friction between the two agencies in the 1980s, and it is likely that the Ministry of Finance, like its French or Japanese equivalent (for France, see Green 1986; for Japan, see Tatewaki 1991: ch. 12) would still like to retain some considerable degree of influence, formal or informal, over financial policy generally and over the People's Bank in particular.

From the point of view of China as a late developer with multiple macroeconomic priorities, the task of the central authorities in reforming the role of the central bank should be seen as the need to find a balance between two imperatives: the need to strengthen the power of the central bank, particularly over the specialised banks, in order to counter the influence exerted on them by local governments, branch departments and enterprises, and at the same time the need to retain sufficient political control over the central bank to ensure a financial system capable of implementing key developmental objectives such as regional/sectoral redistribution, rapid growth and employment creation. As we have argued, it is therefore more realistic to view the issue of the central bank's role in terms of discretionary autonomy within, rather than independence of, the central government. This would rest on an agreed division of labour between the PBC and the other key central agencies (notably the Ministry of Finance and the State Planning Commission) and on institutionalised methods of consultation, coordination and conflict resolution among them, mediated by the State Council and the political leadership in the CCP. This is certainly the case in the NICs, where the central bank has some autonomy but is also subordinated to the demands of the development process and does not exist independently "outside" of that process.[6]

In the Chinese context, reducing inflationary pressures in the economy requires in particular control over the activities of enterprises, administrative departments and local governments. With respect to the first of these, controlling enterprise wage costs is an important element in reducing inflationary pressures. This has long been a feature of the Chinese economic system, and despite the current unfashionability of income policies in Western academic and policy-making circles, they have and can continue to have an important part to play in maintaining price stability in China. Exclusive reliance on central bank "independence" as an anti-inflation policy is therefore misguided. Controlling enterprise wage growth does, however, require

---

6. For example, Wade points out in the case of Taiwan (1990: pp. 208–9) that while the central bank has considerable power and autonomy, it is also integrated within the wider policy-making process.

monitoring, a role to which the banks are particularly suited. The banks' effectiveness in this role depends upon their relationship with enterprises, a topic to which we turn in the next section.

As regards local governments, their influence on the specialised banks has been well documented in many studies, as indicated in Chapter 5. To counter the activities of local governments, it is tempting to argue that local governments need to be cut down to size.[7] Whilst we have also suggested that the influence of local governments should be reduced, it is important that any policy proposals advanced in the Chinese context recognise that the reforms of the past 15 years have given local governments substantially more powers, which they are unwilling to give up and which the central government is now no longer strong enough to take back. The central government has tried to play some regions against each other (recently by developing the Shanghai-Wuhan-Yangtse region to counter the power of Guangdong, for example), but the distribution of political power inside China now prevents any wholesale stripping of local government power even assuming that this is desirable.

More relevant to the Chinese context for financial reform, and in keeping with the current institutional structure, is a strengthening of the provincial offices of the People's Bank. As noted in Chapter 4, the People's Bank is unlike central banks in many countries in that it has branches in each of the provinces which supervise the activities of the provincial SBs. In a large diversified country such as China, this arrangement makes good sense and can be compared with the regional/ state offices of the Federal Reserve and the Bundesbank. The task of strengthening the institution of the central bank thus needs to focus on the powers of the PBC head office and its provincial offices in relation to the SBs at both levels.[8] Central power was enhanced in 1988 when the PBC head office gained the sole power to appoint the managers of provincial branches and sub-branches (World Bank 1990b: p. 5). This move was intended to reduce the influence of local governments over the PBC, a move which might be further enhanced by another proposal under active consideration, namely, having the sub-national branches of the PBC operate at the level of an economic region based on one or more big cities rather than on a province. This reform could be complemented by measures to lower inter-provincial trade barriers and by a more cogent national industrial policy to prevent local dupli-

---

7. This policy prescription is common in many areas. For example, in discussing inter-provincial trade barriers, Wong (1992: p. 223) refers to the need to "strip local governments of their power."

8. See also Letiche (1991: pp. 24–25) on this point.

cation. Moreover, the provincial/regional banks could be granted some form of representation in the decision-making structure of the central PBC according to a principle comparable to that stipulating the representation of regional banks on the Federal Open Market Committee in the United States (Kaufman 1992: p. 491) or the representation of state central banks on the Central Bank Council of the Bundesbank (Schneider et al. 1986: p. 51). These kinds of approaches, which seek to redefine the structure of the PBC system and incorporate the power of local interests, seem potentially more fruitful than mere calls for central bank "independence" or a blanket stripping of local governments of their power.

Those proposing that the central bank should have independence in order to pursue a single objective of monetary control and price stability logically conclude that the central bank should not therefore be concerned with allocative decisions. Thus, it is argued that the allocative function should be devolved to a diversified and competitive financial system including capital markets (see, for example, Wang 1988; Blejer et al. 1991; Allsopp and Lin 1991). This prescription, drawing upon the finance and development paradigm, is inappropriate to China as a late developer, and a financial system which represents a fusion of certain elements of the market socialist and NIC late-development model is more appropriate. In this context, though a move *towards* a more market-oriented financial system in China is certainly desirable, it should be conditioned upon maintaining the predominance of some form of social ownership and preserving the capacity of the developmental state. Both of these requirements suggest, at most, a limited role for capital (especially share) markets and the continuance of non-competitively determined policy loans.

These requirements stem from the socialist argument concerning both the socio-political objectives of 'socialism' and the efficiency objectives of 'market socialism' and from the developmental argument about the role of the state and its ability to achieve developmental objectives through a certain relationship with the financial system. If a basic requirement for socialism is the principle of economic distribution according to work, individual share ownership should remain of marginal importance in China and secondary markets should be limited. There is also an economic case to support these political/ ideological considerations. First, as the discussion in Chapter 6 indicated, the role of capital markets in promoting enterprise efficiency through the takeover mechanism or stockholder pressure is far from proven. Second, as the experience of both developed and developing countries has demonstrated of late, stock markets have in general not played a major role in industrial finance (Mayer 1989) and are prone to instability, corruption and speculative pressures which limit (or negate) any positive impact on the real economy. Third, as Singh (1990: pp. 169–71) has argued, since China has a high savings rate already, it is unlikely that the development of new assets would significantly increase savings. Fourth, from the perspective of the late-development paradigm, a credit-based financial system has the advantage that it is capable of being used as an allocating device to support industries capable of competing in markets currently dominated by early industrialisers. The symbol of such a financial system is, of course, the policy loan.

It could be objected that such a system would favour the large-scale (less dynamic) state sector over the (more dynamic) small-scale non-state sectors. However, the NIC model is in fact that of a dualistic financial structure with a state-controlled banking system coexisting with a "flexible fringe" (the curb market). The latter has been particularly important for small- and medium-sized enterprises in Taiwan and South Korea. Given the growth of the rural enterprise sector in China and its contribution to employment generation, it may be the case that the flexible fringe should be wider in China's case than it has been in the NICs. Recent evidence of the rapid expansion of formal and informal non-bank institutions in both cities and countryside suggests that this financial dualism is a growing reality, regardless of the intentions of central policy-makers. Given the political importance of small-scale industries in providing employment, supplying consumer demands and generating exports, moreover, there are good reasons for extending policy loans outside the state sector.

Another common objection against limiting competition between the banks and maintaining policy loans is that such policies create and perpetuate inequalities. Specifically, it is often argued that such policies favour the well-connected urban/industrial elites at the expense of the poor, both urban and rural. This is undoubtedly a legitimate concern, and we would respond to this in the following ways. First, while it is quite true that government control over the financial system does benefit particular groups, the key questions are, Which groups are benefitting? and What are the developmental consequences thereof? If the beneficiaries are groups of corrupt officials and their parasitic capitalist cronies, for example, then such an arrangement would be developmentally indefensible. What is crucial here, therefore, is an assessment of the precise socio-political character of the state and its relations with specific social groups. In the Chinese case, this would in essence amount to an overall evaluation of the developmental performance of the post-Maoist reformist regime, i.e., the extent to which it has acted to further a broad conception of the national developmental interest as opposed to its own interests or those of its officials, and the extent to which the developmental programme it has designed and implemented has benefitted the wider society more generally (including the vast rural population) or merely its own officials. While opinions vary, there is a great deal of evidence to suggest that on each of the previous two points, the development and equity interests have largely dominated, notwithstanding a continuing investment bias towards heavy industry and a growing level of official corruption.

Furthermore, in China's case, an argument can be made for continuing state control of the financial system on equity grounds. While the current system contains numerous inequalities, the Chinese reform experience has been distinctive in the extent to which it has been able to achieve a widespread introduction of market relations while restraining the resulting growth of inequalities by institutional guarantees and redistributive policies. (For discussions of these issues, see Sen 1992 and Nolan and Sender 1992.) Rapid marketisation of the financial system might well bring consequences which are problematic from an equity perspective. If, for example, an inter-bank market was operating freely, then the probable outcome would be a large net flow of resources to the coastal provinces. As a socialist country, China has placed emphasis on regional equality with some apparent success (see Hussain, Lanjouw and Stern 1991; Lyons 1991). However, a "free" national capital market is likely to increase regional inequalities, a trend which could not be countered simply by placing central government investment projects in the inland provinces. Some control of the flow of resources is therefore desirable on the grounds of regional equity. The essential point here is that the distributive outcomes of markets are not necessarily more "just" than non-market outcomes. The calculus of neoclassical welfare economics may suggest that market-determined outcomes increase everyone's welfare by theorising that the gainers from market processes could more than compensate the losers but misses the point that in practice such compensation depends upon the ability of the losers to claim such payments from the winners; whether losers are powerful enough to do this is an empirical question, and there is plenty of evidence from all societies to suggest that those who lose from market processes are seldom groups who have maintained a powerful voice over distributional issues. Furthermore, as noted in Chapter 2, the financial system of the late-development NIC model essentially socializes risk. By so doing, it encourages investment and enterprise growth. Such a system can be considerably more equitable in an economy with social ownership where the benefits can be redistributed than in a privately owned economy where risk is socialized but profits are private property.

The case that we have sketched supports a credit-based financial system adaptable to China's position as a reforming socialist late developer. One major topic remains, namely, the relationship between banks and enterprises and, in particular, how the soft credit constraint can be hardened in order to contribute to increasing enterprise productivity.

Institutional Reform:
Bank-Enterprise Relations and the Soft Budget Constraint

Some commentators, both inside and outside China, have argued that the constraints on enterprises can only be hardened by enterprise privatisation (for example, Wiemer 1992; Yenal 1990), a prescription which would of course transform the Chinese economy into some form of capitalism. But this is not the only way in which soft credit constraints could be hardened. In addition to the institutional changes suggested previously, which are aimed at reducing the influence of local government over the specialised banks and increasing the control of the People's Bank, again, a selection of some of the elements of the market socialist and late-development models may prove useful.

The task is to develop a banking system that is capable of allocating non-policy loans according to market criteria and of administering policy loans in such a way that the reciprocity that explains much of the NICs' success with policy loans can be repeated in China. As we have argued, the logic of late industrialisation reveals that subsidies and policy loans are a necessary component of an over-arching neo-Listian state-led development strategy in a global economic system in which early industrialisers hold distinct advantages. The task, therefore, is not to eliminate subsidies and place all faith in market prices but rather to change the basis on which subsidies are allocated.[9]

As the NIC experience suggests, subsidies should not be extended unidirectionally and used to cover whatever level of losses may occur, as in current Chinese practice, but should rather be given in conditions of reciprocity. That is to say, in return for subsidies, enterprises should meet certain performance standards in terms of, for example, exports or profits.

This requires that the state have the political will to discipline enterprises in this way. We would argue that it will be easier to change

---

9. For details of the differential interest rates applied to various sectors of the Chinese economy, see World Bank 1990b, Annex Tables 1.11b and 1.14.

the basis on which subsidies are granted than to abolish subsidies altogether, as the finance and development literature ultimately prescribes (as indeed does some of the more radical market socialist literature). This will mean that enterprises that do not meet certain performance criteria will be merged, restructured or ultimately bankrupted. This does not mean that the state would expose enterprises to the dictates of the market in situations of short-run decreases in demand, for example, but it does mean that poorly performing enterprises in otherwise profitable industries will face sanctions. This requires a reorientation of the state, not its dissolution, and as such is likely to be more appealing to state interests (both central and local) than a free market route.

It is clear that in such a system the banks will play a critical role. In restructuring and reorganising enterprises and industries, the banks may play a leading role. Certainly, the specialised banks have this notional role in China now, although as we argued in Chapter 5, they seldom play it in practice. A strengthened banking system might be capable of exercising these powers more aggressively than before, particularly if combined with price reform and enterprise ownership reform.

In order to enable the banks to play this role more effectively, it is clear that they require autonomy from the enterprises to whom they lend. What is required therefore is the development of an *autonomous banking system* (not simply an independent central bank), an autonomy which is required for the banking system to fulfil its monitoring and disciplinary role as well as its role in controlling inflation. The existing structure of the Chinese banking system may permit such an outcome, since banks have a long history of monitoring enterprises, a situation similar to the banks in the NICs which, by such close supervision, appear to have prevented the diversion of policy loans to other uses from occurring on a significant scale.[10]

Enabling the banks to perform these functions depends upon the relationship between the banks and the enterprises, which in turn depends on how enterprises are run. The evolving consensus among Chinese reformers in the early 1990s is that some form of ownership reform is necessary in order to reduce the power of the central branch ministries and local industrial departments, which now control the

---

10. See Chapter 2 for a discussion of the role of the banks in ensuring the non-diversion of policy loans in the NICs. It is true, however, that the degree to which banks in the NICs have played a larger supervisory role over enterprises has varied with banks playing a relatively minor role in this respect in Taiwan. See Wade (1990: pp. 262–64).

enterprises directly in a "unitary" fashion. As of mid to late 1992, the officially preferred option is a form of joint-stock system, discussed in Chapter 6, which seeks to change the nature of state enterprise ownership while still preserving social ownership, and which would dilute the bureaucratic forces operating on enterprises and replace them with market forces. In this system, shares in enterprises would be held by a variety of agents, including the workers and staff of the enterprise itself and other public enterprises and institutions, possibly including banks.[11] (For early proposals along these lines, see Nuti 1988 and Wood 1991; for a Chinese discussion of the emergence of the share system in the early 1980s, see Han and Liu 1991.)[12]

The enterprise would then be accountable to a group of other agents, probably dominated by other public agencies including banks, who would be responsible for exerting pressures on the enterprise to operate efficiently. Such an "insider" system of control has operated successfully in the Japanese and German economies and provides, as Corbett and Mayer have argued, "both commitment to long-term policies and a mechanism for penalizing poor management" (1991: p. ii). To the extent that banks play a role as owners in such a system, in Mayer's words, (1989: p. 23), "finance can be seen as a layer of management. Firms determine the allocation of resources across projects; banks allocate resources between firms; and central banks allocate resources between banks and industries". While this principle of financial control could operate throughout the industrial economy, it could also be realised in the form of enterprise groups along the lines of the Japanese *keiretsu*, which often have a "main bank" at their centre.[13] (For a proposal for a "bank-centric" system of "insider monitoring" along these lines, see Bardhan and Roemer 1991: pp. 19–24.)

---

11. For an analysis of the function and nature of the proposed joint-stock system, see the comments by the noted Chinese economist Ma Hong, reported by the *NCNA*, 14 October 1992.

12. See Nuti (1988) and Wood (1991) for a discussion of how such shares could be valued and the conditions under which they might be traded. We do not enter into this technical discussion here except to point out that such proposals do not involve the development of a "capital market" in the conventional sense and certainly not in the sense envisaged by the finance and development paradigm.

13. The role of the banks in monitoring enterprise behaviour in Japan is supported by recent evidence presented by Lichtenberg and Pushner (1992). They find that in a sample of 1,241 large Japanese manufacturing firms, those firms whose equity is owned mainly by financial institutions performed better than similar firms whose shares are owned by individuals or nonfinancial companies.

This raises the further question of who monitors the banks. In the NICs the banks were state-owned for much of the period and under state control even after the South Korean privatisation of 1983. The ability of state-owned banks in the NICs to perform their disciplinary role effectively undoubtedly owed much to the state's relation with capital in general. That is, the high degree of state autonomy within the NICs enabled state agencies to impose disciplinary measures on private capital. It is also important to note, however, that the state played a disciplining role with respect to the public sector, which, as we showed in Chapter 2, has played a significant role in the NICs. This suggests that political will and the state's position relative to private capital have been important factors in explaining the reciprocity that has characterised state-enterprise relations in the NICs. The position of the state in China is, of course, different; the state is the dominant owner of the means of production. Whilst ownership reform of enterprises may be necessary, as indicated previously, it is possible that the banks might also have to be reorganised if they are to have sufficient autonomy from enterprises to impose disciplinary measures effectively. Thus, the banks themselves might become owned by several other public agencies; China has already experimented with joint stock banks (such as the Bank of Communications, the Shenzhen Development Bank, the Fujian Industrial Bank and the Guangdong Development Bank; see Dipchand n.d.), but they play only a minor role at present. Whether or not it is feasible to extend this principle, it is of key importance that policy-makers make a commitment—in terms of policy, law and institutions—to permit the disciplining of enterprises, without which banks, whether state-owned or joint stock, are unlikely to be effective monitors.

In addition to this commitment from policy-makers, a disciplining device to regulate bank behaviour may be possible, as Bardhan and Roemer (1991) point out: "The reputational concerns of the main bank managers may act as an antidote to easy susceptibility to political pressures. In Japan even though the banks have been closely regulated by the Ministry of Finance, there is some keenness on the part of the bank managers to preserve their reputation as good monitors, and there is competition among banks in seeking the position of main bank for well-run firms. ... The managerial labour market may not 'forget' if a bank manager 'forgives' bad loans or non-performing firms on his (her) watch too often" (pp. 26–27). Increasing competition between banks for enterprise deposits has already occurred during the course of the Chinese reforms, and further moves in this direction may enable banks to compete on the basis of their ability as "delegated monitors". A managerial labour market for bank managers, as well as for enterprise managers, might also be possible.

A complementary reform to the financial reforms just outlined is price reform. Part of the soft credit constraint can be seen as the result of information problems. That is, in the context of financial relations, the banks do not know whether enterprises should be held responsible for losses or whether other factors, beyond enterprise control, are the cause of poor performance. This situation is common in China; examples of the problems facing banks in this respect were given in Chapter 5. However, this informational problem could be reduced by greater competition within product markets and greater exposure to international prices.[14] With complementary price reforms, and the continuation of the open door policy, the task of identifying poorly managed firms might be made easier for the banks as monitors in the future.

A further essential complementary reform is welfare reform. A reformed financial and enterprise system such as suggested previously might lead to less secure employment. For socialist economies, even the task of moving from a system of job security (meaning a secure claim on a particular job, the "iron rice-bowl") like the one that operates in China at present to a system of employment security (meaning the right to a job but not to a particular one) is politically and socially problematic, as the difficulties encountered by labour reforms over the past decade have demonstrated. Organised labour in the state sector retains a powerful capacity to obstruct, if not deter, serious efforts to reform the employment system. In order to reduce this opposition by mitigating the effects on workers of the restructuring of state-owned enterprises, a new social security policy will be required, especially since enterprises are currently providers not simply of employment but also of housing and other benefits.[15] Whilst this issue has entered the policy agenda of the early 1990s, it has not been accorded the political priority and resources that it merits. The political logic of these policy linkages continues the problem of the relationship between "easy" and "hard" reforms, which we identified in the experience of the 1980s. The success of the financial reforms depends on the success of a chain of related reforms throughout the industrial

---

14. As well as pricing, more information could be made available to enterprise monitors by reforming China's accounting procedures. For a discussion of this point see Gordon (1991).

15. For a discussion of China's social security system see Ahmad and Hussain (1991).

economy, without which the financial reforms themselves, however impressive their short-term effects, will ultimately be self-defeating.

To conclude, the sort of financial system that we have sketched here, combining elements of the market socialist and late-development paradigms, together with complementary reforms, might be capable of achieving the economic and social results which a reformed socialist economy seeks.

An Alternative Scenario

We have attempted to incorporate the issue of feasibility into our analysis by taking systematic account of the main actors and interests involved in any of the proposed reforms. We have sketched a possible future direction for the financial reforms which we think addresses China's needs as a reforming socialist late developer. However, to repeat, the overall viability of the direction that we have suggested depends, from our perspective, on the *relative political power behind each paradigm of reform*. While we believe that the direction we have outlined above is both desirable and feasible, we do harbour significant doubts about whether it will be the course actually followed.

It is our judgment that the political weight behind a late development model will continue to be strong given the fact that both central and local governments are keen on active intervention in the economy to promote the national and local economic interests. These forms of state involvement, which at the local level often take on highly entrepreneurial forms, reinforced by strong nationalist and localist ideologies, suggest that China will retain the political impetus for an active, interventionist developmental state for the foreseeable future.

Where we have real doubts, however, is whether there exists strong enough support for the type of progressive and innovative form of market socialism in the financial sphere that we have indicted above. The Party conservatives, it seems, can't get much beyond the old methods and institutions. The centrist reformist leaders have been relatively silent since the June 4 Incident and the young radical reformers, found amongst the ranks of economists and in other research institutes are, in reality, intent on establishing a fully fledged capitalist economy. There is a danger that the moderate, incremental and still residually socialist section of the political leadership are marginalised and that policy alternatives polarise between the conservatives and the radicals.

Besides these ideological factors, the fiscal crisis of the state as well as local governments' desires to explore any and all methods of raising resources locally may build up a momentum for a fully marketised financial system, including private banks and capital markets, that may prove difficult to stop.[16]

Furthermore, the market socialist position has been weakened by the events of 1989–1991 in Eastern Europe, and those supporting a transition to capitalism have been strengthened as China has become more ideologically and systemically isolated and the force of external pressures has become more homogeneous and uni-directional. These external forces, particularly pressure from the United States, will influence the political weight behind the late-development model, but they are undoubtedly more serious for the socialist cause.[17] Moreover, the strength of external opposition to the late-development model may also be tempered by the possibility of disagreement and conflict between the Washington Consensus/Bretton Woods institutions on the one side and mounting Tokyo/East Asian bloc pressures on the other side.[18]

Given this analysis, it is quite possible that the direction of the financial reforms will not be a fusion of the market socialist and late-development models but rather a moving tension between the late-development and finance and development models. Given the different underlying theoretical premises of these two views and their different evaluations of the efficacy of market and state-led strategies, supporters of these two paradigms are unlikely to find much common ground. The financial reforms will be a scene of competing agendas regarding such issues as central bank independence, the extension of capital markets, the extent of policy loans, the determination of interest rates and the role of foreign banks in the economy, all of which are likely in practice to lead to increased dualism both regionally and in terms of financial and industrial structures. We might expect to see

---

16. It is interesting to note that in the Eighth Five-Year Plan the generally conservative reforms envisaged for the financial system nevertheless includes the continued experimentation with stock markets in major cities.

17. International agencies and neoliberal economists have consistently sought to downplay or deny the importance of the role of the state in the NICs. For comment see Wade (1992). The World Bank has also sought to downplay the significance of the NIC financial system for China by arguing that Japan and South Korea's directed credit programmes were both "temporary" and "narrowly focused" (World Bank 1990a: p. 43, emphasis in original), an assessment which is contradicted by the evidence provided in Chapter 2.

18. For evidence of this see, for example, Far Eastern Economic Review, 12 March 1992, p. 49.

increasingly speculative and unregulated financial markets (especially in the coastal provinces) co-existing with a significant proportion of the banking sector remaining unreformed and weighed down by bad debts.

In broader terms, under this scenario it is still possible that a polarisation between conservatives and radicals could lead to some kind of showdown, a breakdown of the previous order and a spasmodic lurch towards a full market economy, with an Eastern European-style morass presenting itself.[19] Such an outcome is not inevitable, however, and it is more likely that the policy terrain of Chinese financial reforms, and the character of Chinese political economy more generally, would increasingly resemble those of their East Asian state-capitalist counterparts and would contribute dramatically to the eastward shift in the global balance of power within international capitalism.

---

19. The economic crisis in Eastern Europe has prompted even Western apostles of the free market, such as the London-based Adam Smith Institute (1992), to deplore the plunge into privatisation and markets and to direct attention to the "Eastern promise" of the East Asian NIC model.

Bibliography

Adam Smith Institute, (1992), *Eastern Promise*, London.

Ahmad, E., and Hussain, A., (1991), "Social Security in China: A Historical Perspective," in Ahmad, E., Dreze, J., Hills, J., and Sen, A., (eds.), *Social Security in Developing Countries*, pp. 247–304, Oxford: Clarendon Press.

Allsopp, C., and Lin, C., (1991), "Strengthening Monetary Policy and Financial Market Development in China", paper prepared for World Bank/UNDP/SCRES International Seminar on "Financial Sector Reform in China", Hainan, 16–20 December.

Amsden, A., (1989), *Asia's Next Giant: South Korea and Late Industrialisation*, Oxford University Press.

Amsden, A., and Euh, Y–D (1990), "Republic of Korea's Financial Reform: What are the lessons?", *UNCTAD Discussion Papers*, no. 30.

Bachman, D., (1986), "Differing Visions of China's Post-Mao Economy: The Ideas of Chen Yun, Deng Xiaoping and Zhao Ziyang," *Asian Survey*, vol. XXVI, no. 3 (March), pp. 292–321.

——, (1989), "The Ministry of Finance and Chinese Politics", *Pacific Affairs*, vol. 62, no. 2, (Summer).

Bacskai, T., (1989), "The reorganisation of the banking system in Hungary", *Eastern European Economics*, 28, 1.

Bardhan, P., and Roemer, J., (1991), "Market Socialism: A Case for Rejuvenation", University of California at Berkeley, Department of Economics, *Working Paper no. 91–175*.

Baum, J., (1992), "The new kids on the block", *Far Eastern Economic Review*, 24 September.

Bei, D., Koontz, A., and Lu, L.X., (1992), "Emerging Securities Markets in the PRC", *mimeo*.

Bergson, A., (1949), "Socialist Economics", in Ellis, H.S., (ed.)., *A Survey of Contemporary Economics*, vol. 1, Homeward, Ill.: Irwin.

Blackburn, R., (1991), "Fin de Siècle: Socialism After the Crash", *New Left Review*, 185, January-February.

Blejer, M., Burton, D., Dunaway, S., and Szapary, G., (1991), *China: Economic Reform and Macroeconomic Management*, IMF Occasional Paper, no. 76, Washington, D.C.

Bo Daojiang, (1988), "Step up guidance over competition within the financial industry", *Jingji Guanli* (Economic Management) (CH), no. 5, in FBIS 149.

Bowles, P., and Stone, T., (1991), "China's Reforms: A Study in the Application of Historical Materialism", *Science and Society*, vol. 55, no. 3, Fall, pp. 261–90.

Bowles, P., and White, G., (1989), "Contradictions in China's Financial Reforms: The Relationship between Banks and Enterprises", *Cambridge Journal of Economics*, 13, 4, pp. 481–95.

———, (1992a), "The dilemmas of Market Socialism: Capital Market Reform in China—Part I: Bonds", *Journal of Development Studies*, 28, 3, (April).

———, (1992b), "The dilemmas of Market Socialism: Capital Market Reform in China—Part II: Shares", *Journal of Development Studies*, 28, 4, (July).

Bowles, P., MacLean, B., and Setterfield, M., (1992), "Socialist Economics: Which Way Now?", *Review of Radical Political Economics*, vol. 24, nos. 3/4.

Brada, J., and Dobozi, I., (1989), "Economic Reform in Hungary: An Overview and Assessment", *Eastern European Economics*, vol. 28, no. 1, (Fall).

Brus, W., (1972), *The Market in a Socialist Economy*, Routledge and Kegan Paul, London.

Brus, W., and Laski, K., (1989), *From Marx to the Market: Socialism in Search of an Economic System*, Oxford: Oxford University Press.

Byrd, W., (1983), *China's Financial System: The Changing Role of Banks*, Westview Press, Boulder, Colorado.

Cao Xingren, (1987), "Achievements and problems in China's financial system reform," *Jingji Guanli* (Economic Management) (CH), no. 11 (November), pp. 25–6, in FBIS 008.

Cargill, T., (1989), *Central Bank Independence and Regulatory Responsibilities: The Bank of Japan and the Federal Reserve*, Monograph Series in Finance and Economics, no. 1989-2, New York: Solomon Brothers Centre for the Study of Financial Institutions.

Castello-Branco, M., and Swinburne, M., (1992), "Central Bank Independence", *Finance and Development*, March.

Chapman, J., (1963), *Real wages in Soviet Russia Since 1928*, Cambridge (Mass.): Harvard University Press.

Chen, K., Jefferson, G., Rawksi, T., Honchang Wang, and Yuxin Zheng, (1988), "Productivity Change in Chinese Industry: 1953–1985", *Journal of Comparative Economics*, 12, pp. 570–91.

Chen Shenshen, (1988), "Clarifying Property Rights Relationship is a Necessary Premise", *Shijie Jingji Daobao* (World Economic Herald), no. 401, (25 July 1988) as reprinted in *Chinese Economic Studies*, 23, no. 1, Fall 1989.

Cho, Y.J., (1989), "Finance and Development: The Korean Approach", *Oxford Review of Economic Policy*, vol. 5, no. 4, pp. 88–102.

Chow, G., (1987), "Money and Price Level Determination in China", *Journal of Comparative Econmics*, 11, 3.

Cohen, G., (1988), "The Dialectic of Labour in Marx" in *History, Labour and Freedom*, London: Oxford University Press.

Cole, D., and Wellons, P., (1989), "The Financial System, Financial Reform and Economic Development", Harvard Institute for International Development, *Discussion Paper no. 312*, September.

Corbett, J., and Mayer, C., (1991), "Financial Reform in Eastern Europe:

Progress with the wrong model", Centre for Economic Policy Research, *Discussion Paper No. 603*.

Cosh, A., Hughes, A., Lee, K., and Singh, A., (1989), "Institutional investment, mergers and the market for corporate control", *International Journal of Industrial Organisation*, 7, pp. 73–100.

Cowling, K., et al., (1980), *Mergers and Economic Performance*, Cambridge: Cambridge University Press.

Cukierman, A., Webb, S., and Neyapti, B., (1992), "Measuring the Independence of Central Banks and Its Effect on Policy Outcomes", *World Bank Economic Review*, vol. 6, no. 3.

Davis, C., and Charemza, W., (1989), *Models of Disequilibrium and Shortage in Centrally Planned Economies*, London: Chapman–Hall.

Dessi, R., (1991), "Household Saving and Wealth in China: Some Evidence from Survey Data", Department of Applied Economics, University of Cambridge, *Working Paper*, no. 9112.

Diaz-Alejandro, (1985), "Good-bye Financial Repression, Hello Financial Crash", *Journal of Development Economics*, vol. 19.

Dipchand, C., (n.d.), "The Ownership Structure of China's Banks", *mimeo*, Dalhousie University.

Dirksen, E., (1983), "Chinese Industrial Productivity in an International Context", *World Development*, vol. 11, no. 4.

Dollar, D., (1990) "Economic Reform and Allocative Efficiency in China's State-owned Industry", *Economic Development and Cultural Change*, 39, 1, (October), pp. 89–105.

Donnithorne, A., (1967), *China's Economic System*, London: George Allen and Unwin.

———, (1989), "Reform of the fiscal and banking systems in China" in Cheng, J.Y.S. (ed.), *China: Modernization in the 1980s*, Hong Kong: Chinese University Press.

Dornbusch, R., and Reynoso, A., (1989), "Financial Factors in Economic Development", *American Economic Review*, Papers and Proceedings, vol. 79, no. 2.

Dutt, A., (1991), "Interest Rate Policies in LDCs: A Post-Keynesian View", *Journal of Post-Keynesian Economics*, 13, 2, Winter 1990–91.

Eccleston, B., (1986), "The State, Finance and Industry in Japan", in Cox, A., (ed.), *State, Finance and Industry: A Comparative analysis of Post-war trends in Six Advanced Industrial Economies*, New York: St. Martin's Press.

Ecklund, G., (1966), *Financing the Chinese Government Budget: Mainland China, 1950–59*, Chicago: Aldine.

Epstein, G., (1992), "Political Economy and Comparative Central Banking", *Review of Radical Political Economics*, vol. 24, no. 1.

Fan, Maofa, Xun Dazhi, and Liu Xiaoping, (1986), "The Joint Stock System is not the Direction for Enterprises Owned by the Whole People", *Jingji Yanjiu* (Economic Research), no. 1, (10 January) in *FBIS* 055.

Fei, J., (1988), "A Theoretical Framework for the Analysis of Inflation in the PRC", Economic Growth Centre, Yale University, Discussion Paper, no. 563.

Feltenstein, A., and Farhadian, Z., (1987), "Fiscal Policy, Monetary Targets and the Price Level in a Centrally Planned Economy: An Application to the Case of China", *Journal of Money, Credit and Banking*, 19, 2.

Feltenstein, A., and Ha, J., (1991), "Measurement of Repressed Inflation in China: The lack of Coordination between Monetary Policy and Price Controls", *Journal of Development Economics*, 36, 2, pp. 279–94.

Friss, I., (1969), "Principle Features of the New System of Planning, Economic Control and Management in Hungary", in I. Friss (ed.), *Reform of the Economic Mechanism in Hungary*, Akademiai Kiado: Budapest.

Fry, M., (1982), "Models of Financially Repressed Developing Economies", *World Development*, 10, 9.

———, (1988), *Money, Interest and Banking in Economic Development*, Johns Hopkins University Press: Baltimore, MD.

Garvy, G., (1977), *Money, Financial Flows, and Credit in the Soviet Union*, Cambridge, Mass.: National Bureau of Economic Research.

Gaspari, M., (1990), "Recent Developments in Yugoslavia" in Federal Reserve Bank of Kansas City, *Central Banking Issues in Emerging Market-oriented Economies*.

Gee San (1990), *The Status and Evaluation of the Electronics Industry in Taiwan*, OECD Development Centre, Technical Paper no. 29.

Germidis, D., Kessler, D., and Meghir, R., (1991), *Financial Systems and Development: What Role for the Formal and Informal Financial Sectors?*, Development Studies Centre, OECD.

Gerschenkron, A., (1962), *Economic Backwardness in Historical Perspective*, London: Harvard University Press.

Gomulka, S., (1985), "Kornai's Soft budget constraint and the shortage phenomenon: A criticism and restatement", *Economic Planning*, vol. 19, no. 1.

Goodman, J.B. (1992), *Monetary Sovereignty: The Politics of Central Banking in Western Europe*, Cornell University Press, Ithaca, London.

Gordon, M.J., (1991), "Market Socialism in China", *mimeo*, University of Toronto.

Green, D. (1986), "The state, finance and industry in France", in Cox, A., (ed.), *State, Finance and Industry: A Comparative Analysis of Post-War Trends in Six Advanced Industrial Economies*, New York: St. Martin's Press.

Grindle, M.S. (1991), "The new political economy: Positive economics and negative politics", in Meier, G., (ed.), *Politics and Policy Making in Developing Countries: Perspectives on the New Political Economy*, ICS Press, San Francisco, pp. 41–67.

Han Zhiguo, (1986), "Useful exploration into the operational mechanism of the socialist commodity economic", *Renmin Ribao*, (People's Daily), 3 October, in *SWB* 8389.

Han Zhiguo and Liu Jipeng (1991), "The emergence and development of a share system: An investigation report on China's share economy", *Social Sciences in China*, (November), pp. 10–31.

Hong, W., and Park, Y.C., (1986), "The Financing of export-oriented growth in Korea", in Tan, A., and Kapur, B., (eds.), *Pacific Growth and Financial Interdependence*, Sydney: Allen and Unwin.

Hsiao, K.H.Y. Huang, (1971), *Money and Monetary Policy in Communist China*, New York: Columbia University Press.

Hsu, R., (1991), *Economic Theories in China, 1978–1988*, Cambridge: Cambridge University Press.

Huang Cunming, (1989), "The initial form of a regulatory system with a regional central bank", *Zhongguo Jinrong* (Chinese Finance) (CH), no. 2, (February), pp. 47–8.

Huang Jubo, (1981), "A problem in seeking a unified balance between state revenue and credit supply", *People's Daily*, Beijing, 17 February, p. 5, in FBIS 039.

Huang Yingfei and Xia Bin, (1985), "Rudiments of a capital market have existed in our country in the past and there may be a two-level market in the future", *Jingji Ribao* (Economic Daily), Beijing, 14 December, in SWB 8145.

Huang Yuoguang and Yang Xiaokai, (1989), "Why should China implement the policy of converting enterprises to management by the people in one single leap across the river?", *Shijie Jingji Daobao*, (World Economic Herald), no. 429 (6 February 1989) and no. 430 (20 February 1989), as reprinted in *Chinese Economic Studies*, Fall 1989.

Hussain, A., and Stern, N., (1991), "Effective Demand, Enterprise Reforms and Public Finance in China", *Economic Policy*, 12, pp. 141–86.

———, (1992), "Economic Reforms and Public Finance in China", Development Economics Research Programme, *Working Paper CP no. 23*, London School of Economics.

Hussain, A., Lanjouw, P., and Stern, N., (1991), "Income Inequalities in China: Evidence from Household Survey Data", Development Economics Research Programme, Working Paper CP no. 18, London School of Economics.

Islam, R., (1991), "Growth of Rural Industries in Post-Reform China: Patterns, Determinants and Consequences", *Development and Change*, 22, pp. 687–724.

Jacobson, H., and Oksenberg, M., (1990), *China's Participation in the IMF, the World Bank, and GATT; Toward a Global Economic Order*, Ann Arbor, University of Michigan Press.

Jarai, Z., (1989), "Goals and Conditions for setting up a stock market in Hungary, 1988", *European Economic Review*, vol. 33, no. 2/3.

Jefferson, G., Rawski, T., and Yuxin Zheng, (1992), "Growth, Efficiency, and Convergence in China's State and Collective Industry", *Economic Development and Cultural Change*, 40, 2, (January), pp. 239–66.

Jing Xiucheng, (1988), "Some ideas about rationalising the relationship between the banks and the fiscal authorities", *Caimao Jingji* (Finance and Trade Economics) (CH), no. 1, pp. 51–53.

Jin Jian, (1989), "Comments on 'Declaration on Private Ownership'". *Renmin Ribao* (People's Daily), 2 December 1989, in *SWB* 0633.

Jin Xiu (1983), "Appropriately increase the ratio of state revenue to national income", *Renmin Ribao* (People's Daily), 15 July 1983, in *FBIS* 141.

Kaufman, George G., (1992), *The U.S. Financial System: Money, Markets, and Institutions*, Prentice-Hall, Englewood Cliffs, New Jersey.

Kaye, L., (1992a), "Out of the loop: Provincial bourses are on hold for the time being", *Far Eastern Economic Review*, 16 July, pp. 52–53.

——, (1992b), "Waiting for Godot: Shanghai holds Key to China's stock experiment", *Far Eastern Economic Review*, 16 July, pp. 50–51.

Komiya, R., (1987a), "Japanese firms, Chinese firms: Problems for economic reform in China. Part I", *The Journal of the Japanese and International Economies*, vol. 1, no. 1, pp. 31–61.

—— (1987b), "Japanese firms, Chinese firms: Problems for economic reform in China. Part II", *The Journal of the Japanese and International Economies*, vol. 1, no. 2, pp. 229–247.

—— (1989), "Macroeconomic Development of China: 'Overheating' in 1984–1987 and Problems for Reform", *Journal of Japanese and International Economies*, 3, 1, pp. 64–121.

Kornai, J., (1986a), *Contradictions and dilemmas: Studies on the Socialist economy and Society*, Cambridge (Mass.): MIT Press.

——, (1986b), "The Hungarian Reform Process: Visions, Hopes and Reality", *Journal of Economic Literature*, XXIV, December.

——, (1986c), "The Soft Budget Constraint", *Kyklos*, 39, no. 1, pp. 3–30.

——, (1990), "The Affinity between Ownership forms and coordination mechanisms; The common experience of reform in socialist countries", *Journal of Economic Perspectives*, vol. 4, no. 3, pp. 131–48.

Kraft, E., and Vodopivec, M., (1992), "How Soft is the Budget Constraint for Yugoslav Firms?", *Journal of Comparative Economics*, 16, 3, pp. 432–55.

Lange, O., and Taylor, F., (1970), *On the Economic Theory of Socialism*, New York: Augustus Kelley.

Lardy, N., (1978), *Economic Growth and Distribution in China*, Cambridge: Cambridge University Press.

Lau, Kam-Tim, and Brada, J. (1990), "Technological Progress and Technical Efficiency in Chinese Industrial Growth: A Frontier Production Function Approach", *China Economic Review*, 1, 2, pp. 113–24.

Lavoie, D., (1985), *Rivalry and Central Planning: The Socialist Calculation Debate Reconsidered*, Cambridge: Cambridge University Press.

Le Grand, J., and Estrin, S., (1989), *Market Socialism*, Oxford: Oxford University Press.

Lee, C.H., (1992), "The Government, Financial System, and Large Private Enterprises in the Economic Development of South Korea", *World Development*, vol. 20, no. 2, pp. 187–198.

Letiche, J., (1991), "Restructuring Centrally-Planned Economies: The Case of China in the Long Term", *Journal of Asian Economics*, vol. 2, no. 2.

Li Chengrui, (1985), "An important question in macro-economic management—strict control of the issue of currency by the state", *People's Daily*, Beijing, 26 April, p. 5, in FBIS 087.

Lichtenberg, F., and Pushner, G., (1992), "Ownership Structure and Corporate Performance in Japan", *NBER Working Paper*, no. 4092.

Li Maosheng (1987), *Zhongguo Jinrong Jiegou Yanjiu* (Research on the Chinese Financial System), Shanxi People's Publishing House.

Lindsay, M., (1992), *Developing Capital Markets in Eastern Europe: A Business Reference*, London: Pinter.

List, F., (1885), *The National System of Political Economy*, New York: Augustus Kelley.

Liu Baifu et al., (1988), "A brief discussion on flexible issues of Treasury Bonds", *Renmin Ribao* (People's Daily), 26 September 1988, in *FBIS* 191.

Liu Guoguang (1986), "Certain problems concerning the reform of the system of ownership", *Jingji Ribao* (Economic Daily), 4 January 1986, in *SWB* 8159.

———, (1988), "Deepen Reform by Taking Caution Steps", *Renmin Ribao* (People's Daily), 8 March 1988 in *FBIS* 047.

Liu Hongru, (1982), "Enhance the role of banks and develop domestic capital", *Hong Qi* (Red Flag), 1 June, in *SWB* FE W1192.

———, (1986a), "On the establishment of a socialist financial system with a central bank as its nucleus", *Zhongguo Jinrong* (Chinese Finance) (CH), Beijing, March, pp. 7–10.

———, (1986b), "Improve macro control by the central bank and perfect methods for managing credit capital", *Zhongguo Jinrong* (Chinese Finance) (CH), November, p. 12.

———, (1986c), "Systematically open up and build the capital market", *Renmin Ribao* (People's Daily), 22 August 1986, in *SWB* 8353.

Liu Xiuwen and Chen Ruqi, (1988), "Establish and perfect a financial supervisory system", *Guangming Ribao* (Glorious Daily), 1 October 1988, in *FBIS* 201.

Li Yining, (1986), "A conception of reform of the ownership system in our country", *Renmin Ribao* (People's Daily), 26 September 1986, in *SWB* 838.

———, (1987), "Whither the economic reforms?", *Jingji Ribao*, (Economic Daily), 15 August 1987, in FBIS 170.

Li Yunqi, et al., (1989), "The Individualisation of Ownership of State Owned Property", *Shijie Jingji Daobao* (World Economic Herald), no. 431 (27 February 1989) as reprinted in *Chinese Economic Studies*, 23, no. 1, Fall 1989.

Lu Baifu and Qian Zhongtao, (1984), "Establish a new socialist banking system in our country", *People's Daily*, 1 February, in *FBIS* 033.

Lu Mi, (1989), "The present situation in measures for banking regulation and proposals for improvement", *Zhongguo Jinrong* (Chinese Finance) (CH), no. 4, 1989, pp. 34–35.

Lyons, T., (1991), "Interprovincial Disparities in China: Output and Consumption, 1952–87", *Economic Development and Cultural Change*, 39, 3 (April), pp. 471–506.

Ma Bin and Hong Zhunyan, (1987), "Enlivening large state enterprises: Where is the motive force?", *Journal of Comparative Economics*, 11, pp. 503–508.

Ma Mingjia, (1989), "Opinions about the current situation and rectification of our country's financial organisions", *Zhongguo Jinrong*, (Chinese Finance) (CH), no. 3, pp. 50–51.

Manoharan, T., (1991), "Credit and financial institutions at the rural level in China—between plan and market," in Vermeer, E., (ed.), *From Peasant to Entrepreneur: Growth and Change in Rural China*, Wageningen: Pudoc, pp. 183–216.

Mayer, C., (1989), "Myths of the West: Lessons from Developed Countries for Development Finance", *PPR Working Paper Series*, WPS 301, World Bank.

Ma Yongwei, (1987), "The enterprisation of the Agricultural Bank: A New Step in Reform", *Zhongguo Jinrong* (Chinese Finance) (CH), March.

Ma Zhizhou and Chen Weishu, (1992), "The Prospects for the Development of Shanghai as a Financial Centre", paper presented at the University of Sussex-Fudan University Workshop on Pudong and China's Coastal Development Strategy, Shanghai, September 22–25.

McKinnon, R., (1973), *Money and Capital in Economic Development*, Washington, D.C.: Brookings Institute.

——, (1989), "Financial Liberalisation and Economic Development: A Reassessment of Interest Rate policies in Asia and Latin America", *Oxford Review of Economic Policy*, vol. 5, no. 4.

——, (1991), *The Order of Economic Liberalisation: Financial Control in the Transition to a Market Economy*, Baltimore: Johns Hopkins University Press.

Miyashita, T., (1976), *The Currency and Financial System of Mainland China*, New York: Da Capo Press.

Mosley, P., Harrigan, J., and Toye, J., (1991), *Aid and Power: The World Bank and Policy-based Lending*, 2 vols., London: Routledge.

Naughton, B., (1986), *Saving and Investment in China: A Macroeconomic Analysis*, unpublished Ph.D. dissertation, Yale University.

——, (1987), "Macroeconomic policy and response in the Chinese Economy: The Impact of the Reform Process", *Journal of Comparative Economics*, 11, pp. 334–53.

——, (1988), "The Third Front: Defence Industrialization in the Chinese Interior", *China Quarterly*, 115, pp. 351–86.

——, (1990), "Monetary Implications of Balanced Economic Growth and the Current Macroeconomic Disturbance in China", in Cassel, D. and Heiduk, G., (eds.), *China's Contemporary Economic Reforms as a Development Strategy*, Nomos-Verlagsgeseillschaft: Baden-Baden.

——, (1991), "Why has Economic Reform led to Inflation?", *American Economic Review*, Papers and Proceedings, 81, 2, pp. 207–211.

——, (1992), "Implications of the State Monopoly over Industry and its Relaxation", *Modern China*, 18, 1, pp. 14–41.

Nie Qingping, (1988), "To control currency, relax control on interest rates and develop markets—a few suggestions on the present macroscopic financial policy", *Shijie Jingji Daobao* (World Economic Herald), Shanghai, 19 September, in FBIS 198.

Noland, M., (1990), *Pacific Basin Developing Countries: Prospects for the Future*, Washington, D.C.: Institute for International Economics.

Nolan, P. and Sender, J., (1992), "Death rates, life expectancy and China's economic reform: A critique of A.K. Sen", *World Development*, 20:9 (September), pp. 1279–1304.

Nove, A., (1986), *The Soviet Economic System*, 3rd edition, London: Unwin Hyman.

Nuti, D.M., (1986), "Hidden and Repressed Inflation in Soviet-type economies: Definitions, Measurements and Stabilization", *Contributions to Political Economy*, 5, pp. 37–82.

——, (1988), "Feasible financial innovation under market socialism" in Kessides, C., King, T., Nuti, M. and Sokil, C., (eds.), *Financial Reform in Socialist Economies*, World Bank: Washington, D.C.

————, (1989), "Remonetisation and Capital Markets in the Reform of Centrally Planned Economics", *European Economic Review*, vol. 33, no. 2/3, pp. 427–38.

————, (1990), "The Pace of Change in Central and Eastern Europe", paper delivered to the conference on "An East European Recovery Programme" held at the European University Institute, Florence, 19–20 February.

Oi, J., (1992), "Fiscal reform and the economic foundations of local state corporatism in China", *World Politics*, vol. 45, no. 1, October, pp. 99–126.

Oksenberg, M., and Tong, J., (1991), "The evolution of central-provincial fiscal relations in China 1971–84: The formal system", *China Quarterly*, no. 125, (March), pp. 1–32.

Osband, K., (1992), "Economic Crisis in a Shortage Economy", *Journal of Political Economy*, 100, 4, pp. 673–90.

Paine, S., (1976), "Balanced development: Maoist conception and Chinese practice", *World Development*, vol. 4, pp. 277–304.

————, (1981), "Spatial Aspects of Chinese Development: Issues, Outcomes, and Policies, 1949–1979", *Journal of Development Studies*, 17, (January), pp. 132–95.

Pan Dehong, (1981), "Economists and financial experts put forwards proposals", *Shijie Jingji Daobao* (World Economic Herald), Shanghai, 7 December 1981, in FBIS 011.

Peebles, G., (1991), *Money in the People's Republic of China: A Comparative Perspective*, Sydney: Allen and Unwin.

————, (1992), "Why the Quantity Theory of Money is not applicable to China, together with a tested theory that is", *Cambridge Journal of Economics*, 16, 1, pp. 23–42.

Podolski, T., (1973), *Socialist banking and monetary control: The experience of Poland*, Cambridge University Press.

Portes, R., and Santorum, A., (1987), "Money and Consumption Goods Market in China", *Journal of Comparative Economics*, 13, 3.

Potter, P., (1991), "Securities Regulation in China: The Potential for Foreign Participation", paper presented at the Canadian East Asian Studies Conference, Brock University, Canada, October 4–6.

Prime, P., (1992), "Industry's response to market liberalisation in China: Evidence from Jiangsu Province", *Economic Development and Cultural Change*, vol. 41, no. 1.

Riskin, C., (1987), *China's Political Economy*, Oxford: Oxford University Press.

Rong Fenge, (1986), "A major reform in the system for managing loan capital", *Zhongguo Jinrong* (Chinese Finance) (CH), September, pp. 19–21.

Rong Wenzuo, (1986), "Establishing socialist joint stock companies", *Jingji Yanjiu* (Economic Research), January 1986, pp. 11–16, in *Chinese Economic Studies*, 20, no. 3, Spring 1987.

Roubini, N., and Sala-i-Martin, X., (1992), "Financial Repression and Economic Growth", *Journal of Development Economics*, vol. 39, no. 1.

Rowthorn, R., (1980), *Capitalism, Conflict and Inflation*, London: Lawrence and Wishart.

Schneider, H., Hellwig, H-J, and Kingsman, D.J. (1986), *The German Banking System*, Fritz Knapp Verlag, Frankfurt.

Sen, A.K. (1992), "Life and death in China: A reply", World Development, 20:9 (September), pp. 1305–1312.

Sender, H., (1992), "In Capitalist Clothes: China makes its Wall Street debut", Far Eastern Economic Review, 1 October, pp. 90–91.

Shaw, E., (1973), Financial Deepening in Economic Development, New York: Oxford University Press.

Shen Peijun, (1986), "The 33rd Symposium on the strategy for China's economic and social development held in Beijing", Jingjixue Zhoubao (Economics Weekly), Beijing, June, in SWB 8300.

Singh, A., (1990), "The Stock Market in a Socialist Economy" in Nolan, P., and Dong Fureng (eds.), Economic Reform in Post-Mao China, Cambridge: Policy Press.

Sokil, C., (1989), "Hungarian Financial and Labour Market Reforms: Developing Conditions for the Market Mechanism?", Eastern European Economics, 28, 1.

Solinger, D., (1980), "The 1980 Inflation and the Politics of Price Control in the PRC", in Lampton, D., (ed.), The Implementation Problem in Post-Mao China.

——, (1989), "Capitalist measures with Chinese Characteristics", Problems of Communism, XXXVIII:1 (Jan.-Feb.), pp. 19–33.

Song Tingming, (1985), "A key to solving the problem of investment expansion", Jingji Ribao (Economic Daily), Beijing, 24 August, in FBIS 169.

Song Xiuyi and Zhang Shiming (1989), "Difficulties and measures in readjusting the loan structure", Zhongguo Jinrong (Chinese Finance) (CH), no. 11, pp. 30–31.

State Statistical Bureau, Statistical Yearbook of China, various.

Stiglitz, J., (1989a), "Financial Markets and Development", Oxford Review of Economic Policy, vol. 5, no. 4.

——, (1989b), "Markets, Market Failures and Development", American Economic Review, Papers and Proceedings, vol. 79, no. 2, May.

——, (1991a), "Capital Markets and Economic Fluctuations in Capitalist Economies", Marshall Lecture delivered to the European Economics Association Meetings, August, Cambridge, U.K.

——, (1991b), "Government, Financial Markets and Economic Development", NBER Working Paper, no. 3669.

Stiglitz, J., and Weiss, A., (1981), "Credit rationing in markets with imperfect information", American Economic Review, vol. 71.

Studart, R., (1991), "Financial repression and Economic development: A Post-Keynesian Response", University College London, Discussion Papers in Economics no. 91-19.

Sulyok, B., (1969), "Major Financial Regulators in the New System of Economic Control and Management", in Friss (ed.)., Reform of the Economic Mechanism in Hungary, Akademiai Kiado: Budapest.

Swain, N., (1992), Hungary: The Rise and Fall of Feasible Socialism, London: Verso.

Szego, A., (1991), "The logic of a shortage economy: a critique of Kornai from a Kaleckian macroeconomic perspective", Journal of Post-Keynesian Economics, vol. 13, no. 3, pp. 328–36.

Tam, On-kit, (1988), "Rural Finance in China", *China Quarterly*, no. 113, (March).

———, (1991), "Capital market development in China", *World Development*, 19, 5, pp. 511–532.

———, (1992), "A Private Bank in China: Hui Tong Urban Co-operative Bank", *China Quarterly*, September, 131, pp. 766–77.

Tardos, M., (1989), "Economic Organizations and Ownership", *Acta Oeconomica*, vol. 40, no. 1/2.

Tatewaki, Kazuo (1991), *Banking and Finance in Japan: An Introduction to the Tokyo Market*, Routledge, London.

Tsang Shu-ki, (1990), "Controlling Money During Socialist Economic Reform: The Chinese Experience", *Economy and Society*, 19, 2.

van Brabant, J., (1990), "Socialist economics: The Disequilibrium School and the Shortage Economy", *Journal of Economic Perspectives*, 4, 2, pp. 157–75.

Wade, R., (1985), "East Asian Financial Systems as a Challenge to Economics: Lessons from Taiwan", *California Management Review*, vol. XXVII, no. 4, pp. 106–127.

———, (1990), *Governing the Market: Economic Theory and the Role of Government in East Asian Industrialization*, Princeton University Press.

———, (1992), "East Asia's Economic Success: Conflicting Perspectives, Partial Insights, Scanty Evidence", *World Politics*, 44, 2.

Wang Haifeng, (1991), "A brief discussion on China's monetary policy and financial system", *Jingji Ribao* (Economic Daily), Beijing, 2 February 1991, p. 3, in FBIS 044.

Wang Jiye, (1983), "Appropriately strengthen the degree of centralising financial work", *People's Daily*, Beijing, 26 August, in FBIS 170.

Wang Shaofei, (1988), "Opinions about coordinating and reforming the fiscal and banking systems", *Caimao Jingji* (Finance and Trade Economics) (CH), no. 3, pp. 17–22.

Wang, Y., (1988), "Financial Reform: Decentralization and Liberalisation", in Lyons, T., and Wang, Y., *Planning and Finance in China's Economic Reforms*, Cornell University East Asia Papers, no. 46.

Wang Zhuo, (1985), "'Damming' is not a good method for tightening the money market", *Guangming Ribao* (Glorious Daily), Beijing, 31 August, in FBIS 178.

White, G., (ed.), (1988), *Developmental States in East Asia*, Macmillan, London.

White, G., (1993), *Riding the Tiger: The Politics of Economic Reform in China*, New York: Macmillan.

White, G., and P. Bowles, (1987), *Towards a Capital Market? Reforms in the Chinese Banking System*, China Research Report no. 6, IDS, Unviersity of Sussex.

Wiemer, C., (1992), "Price Reform and Structural Change: Distributional Impediments to Allocative Gains", *Modern China*, 18, 2, pp. 171–96.

Wong, C., (1992), "Fiscal Reform and Local Industrialization: The Problematic Sequencing of Reform in Post-Mao China", *Modern China*, 18, 2, pp. 197–227.

Woo, J-E., (1991), *Race to the Swift: State and Finance in Korean Industrialization*, New York: Columbia University Press.

Wood, A., (1991), "Joint Stock Companies with Rearranged Public Ownership: Invigoration of China's State Enterprises Further Considered", Development Economics Research Programme, *Working Paper CP no. 11*, London School of Economics.

Woolley, J.T. (1984), *Monetary Politics: The Federal Reserve and the Politics of Monetary Policy*, Cambridge University Press.

World Bank, (1983), *China: Socialist Economic Development*, World Bank: Washington, D.C.

———, (1986), *China: Long-term Development Issues and Options*, Annex 5: *China: Economic Structure in International Perspective*, Washington, D.C.

———, (1988), *China: Finance and Investment*, Washington, D.C.

———, (1989), *World Development Report 1989*, Oxford University Press.

———, (1990a), *China: Between Plan and Market*, Washington, D.C.

———, (1990b), *China: Financial Sector Policies and Institutional Development*, Washington, D.C.

———, (1990c), *China: Macroeconomic Stability and Industrial Growth under Decentralised Socialism*, Washington, D.C.

———, (1990d), *China: Revenue Mobilization and Tax Policy*, Washington, D.C.

Wu Fumin and Cheng Wanquan, (1990), "While letting the tiger return to the hill, we must prevent it from hurting people", *Jingji Cankao* (Economic Reference), 1 Feb., in *SWB* 0390.

Wu Jianxing, (1987), "Some views on the choice of a strategy for reform", *Jingji Yanjiu* (Economic Research), no. 2, 20 February, in *FBIS* 077.

Wu Jianxing and Jin Lizuo (1985), "Establishing a stockholding system for enterprise", *Jingji fazhan yu tizhi gaige* (Economic Growth and Structural Reform), no. 12, in *Chinese Economic Studies*, 23, no. 1, Fall 1989.

Wu Jiesi et al., (1985), *Woguo Jinrong Tizhi Gaigede Tansuo* (An Investigation of Our Country's Financial System Reform), Beijing, Chinese Economics Publishing House.

Wu Peizhen, et al., (1988), "Qiqihar No. 1 Machine Tool Plant reforms the enterprise property right system", *Renmin Ribao*, 10 October, p. 1.

Wu Renjian, (1983), "National forum to discuss comprehensive planning of finance and credit", *People's Daily*, Beijing, 20 May, in *SWB* 7344.

Xu Jin'an, (1987), "The Stock-share system: A new avenue for China's economic reform", *Journal of Comparative Economics*, 11, pp. 509–514.

Yenal, O., (1990), "Chinese Reforms, Inflation and the Allocation of Investment in a Socialist Economy", *World Development*, 18, 5, pp. 707–721.

Yi, G., (1991), "The Monetization Process in China during the Economic Reform", *China Economic Review*, 2, 1, pp. 75–95.

Zhao Haikuan (1985), *Huobi Yinghang Gailun* (An Overview of Currency and Banking), Beijing, Economic Science Press.

Zhao Xiaomen and He Dexu, (1990), "Some reflections on financial reforms in the last decade of this century", *Caijing Jingji* (Financial Economics) (CH), no. 6, 1990, pp. 22–26.

Zhao Ziyang, (1987), "Advance along the road of socialism with Chinese characteristics", Report to the 13th National Congress of the CCP, reprinted (in part) in *Beijing Review*, 30, no. 45, November 9–15, pp. 23–49.

Zheng Yan, (1989), "From an analysis of the pros and cons of financial sectoral overlap, we can see the necessity for rationalising and rectifying sectoral overlap", *Zhongguo Jinrong* (Chinese Finance) (CH), December.

Zhongguo Jinrong Nianjian (ZGJRNJ—Chinese Financial Yearbook), (1990) edited by the Chinese Financial Study Association, Beijing.

Zhu Jicheng, (1987), "The dual financial system and reform of the financial system", *Jingji Guanli* (Economic Management), no. 11, (November), pp. 27–28, in FBIS 008.

Zhu Zhongdi, (1992), "Shanghai Securities Market and International Finance", paper presented at the University of Sussex-Fudan University Workshop on Pudong and China's Coastal Development Strategy, Shanghai, September 22–25.

Zisner, L., (1991), "The Performance of China's Economy" in *China's Economic Dilemmas in the 1990s: The Problems of Reforms, Modernization and Interdependence*, study papers submitted to the Joint Economic Committee, Congress of the United States, April.

Zuo Mu, (1986), "An exploration into several problems created in the restructuring of the system of ownership", *Jingji Yanjiu* (Economic Research) January 1986, pp. 6–10, in *Chinese Economic Studies*, 20, no. 3, Spring 1987.

Zysman, J., (1983), *Governments, Markets and Growth: Financial Systems and the Politics of Industrial Change*, Cornell University Press.

About the Book and Authors

$\mathbf{T}$HIS PATHBREAKING WORK analyzes the evolution of China's financial reforms since 1979. China's reformers have stressed the construction of a more diverse, flexible, and competitive financial system as a crucial element of China's economic reform program.

The authors assess the theory and practice of financial reform in light of China's specific characteristics as a large, developing country that still claims to be pursuing the goal of establishing a new form of "socialist" market economy. The authors utilize two approaches. First, they place the overall design and trajectory of financial reform since 1979 within a broad comparative framework of alternative strategies of financial reform and financial systems. Second, they use a political economy perspective to explore the complex interactions among the political and economic actors— individual, group, or institutional—that affect reform outcomes. Integrating these two approaches, the authors conclude by assessing future directions for feasible and desirable financial reform in China.

Paul Bowles is professor of economics at the University of Northern British Columbia. **Gordon White** is a professorial fellow at the Institute of Development Studies at the University of Sussex.

Index

ABC. *See* Agricultural Bank of China
Agricultural Bank of China (ABC), 56, 66, 74, 75, 76, 118, 126
Agriculture, collectivisation of, 69
Allsopp, C., 107, 164
Amsden, A., 33, 37, 38

Bad debts, 117, 181
Bank-enterprise relations, 10–11, 112–120, 160, 174–179. *See also* Credit allocation, to enterprises
Banking system, 2, 9, 55–63
  autonomy of, 83–84, 86, 175, 177
  bond market and, 137
  central bank and. *See* Central bank
  centrally planned economy and, 15, 17, 19, 49–55
  competition in, 22, 23, 25, 28, 29, 76–77, 78, 114, 119, 177–178
  credit allocation by. *See* Credit allocation
  decentralisation and, 105
  diversification of, 88
  enterprisation of, 89–90
  financial liberalisation and, 38
  industrialisation and, 37
  inflation and, 102–112, 175
  microeconomic supervision by, 51–53, 60–65
  monitoring of, 177
  oligopolistic, 6, 34, 36
  operational practices of, 59–68
  privatisation of, 38, 39
  reform of, 22, 23, 29–30, 73–77, 80–84, 102–103, 112, 114, 163–179

  in rural sector, 56, 66
  share market and, 148
  specialised banks and. *See* Specialised banks
  structure of, 55–58
  three-tier, 24
  two-tier, 22, 23, 75, 113
  See also under individual countries
Bank of China (BoC), 56, 75, 123
Bank of Communications, 58, 114, 123, 177
Bankruptcy, 61, 62, 63, 111, 114, 115
Baran, Paul, 14(n2)
Bardhan, P., 177
Barone, Enrico, 14(n2)
Bettelheim, Charles, 14(n2)
Blejer, M., 109
BoC. *See* Bank of China
Bolshevik coup, 49
Bonds, 24, 35, 96, 157–158
  categories of, 124(table)
  central government and, 135–137
  defined, 122
  enterprise profitability and, 133
  evaluation of, 135, 138
  financial liberalisation and, 126–127, 131
  inflation and, 123, 129, 130–131, 134, 136
  introduction of, 122–140
  marketisation of, 128, 131, 132–133
  purchased by individuals, 138–140
  vs. shares, 142

See also Enterprise bonds;
  Government bonds
Bonuses, 103, 104, 105
Brada, J., 113
Branch-banking system, 22, 160
Britain, financial system in, 6, 35
Brus, W., 16–17, 19, 21, 50
Budget deficit(s), 107, 108–110, 130,
  133, 168
Bulgaria, banking reforms in, 23
Bundesbank, 166, 170
Byrd, W., 2, 54–55, 56, 61, 62, 66

Capitalism, 2, 13, 24, 174
  vs. socialism, 15, 21, 47, 141, 150
  transition to, 13, 180, 181
Capital market(s)
  defined, 21
  enterprise efficiency and, 171
  financial reform and, 77, 78, 86, 87,
    121, 173, 180
  financial system based on, 6, 34, 35
  introduction of, 157, 158
  share market and, 140, 141
Castello-Branco, M., 165
CCP. *See* Chinese Communist Party
Central Bank, 83, 86. *See also*
  People's Bank of China
Central bank
  "independence" of, 10, 163–166,
    168, 171, 180
  international agencies and, 167
  role of, in future reforms, 169
Central government
  bond market and, 67, 135–137, 139,
    158
  central bank and, 164
  inflation and, 109–110, 167–168
  national income and, 80
  share market and, 145, 146
Centrally planned economy
  banking system and, 15, 17, 19, 49–
    55
  decentralisation of, 79–80
  financial liberalisation and, 29
  resource allocation in, 48

role of money in, 48, 50
tax revenue and, 108
Chaebol (large corporations), 38–39
Chen Muhua, 88
Chen Yun, 78, 94, 95
China
  banking system in, 55–63, 73–77,
    80–84, 86–91, 94, 97, 102–103,
    105–107, 110, 112–120, 137, 160,
    165–171, 172, 174–178
  bond market in, 123–132
  domestic savings in, 65–66
  economic stabilisation in, 95–96
  financial liberalisation in (1979–
    1984), 73–84
  financial markets in (1985–1988),
    84–94
  gross domestic product of, 65
  industrialisation in, 69
  inflation in, 65, 66(table), 98–112,
    169
  institutional structure of, 55–58,
    170
  late development and, 11, 13, 44
  macroeconomic stability in, 65–68
  monetary policy in, 68
  move toward financial markets in,
    84–94
  in pre-reform era, 47, 49, 55–70
  retrenchment programme in (1988–
    1992), 94–97
  share market in, 140–147
  state-enterprise relations in, 177
China International Trust and
  Investment Company (CITIC),
  74, 76, 88, 123
Chinese Communist Party (CCP), 8,
  55(n9), 76, 77, 84, 86, 95, 103,
  123, 169
Chinese Finance and Banking
  Society, 77
Cho, Y. J., 42
Choice-theoretic orientation, 4–7,
  161
Chung Hee Park, 37
CITIC. *See* China International Trust
  and Investment Company

Cole, D., 32
Command economy, 54
Communism, 47(n1)
Competition
  in banking system, 22, 23, 25, 28,
    29, 76–77, 78, 114, 119, 177–178
  in bond market, 129, 132
  in consumer goods industry, 21
  in enterprise sector, 18
Corbett, J., 176
Credit allocation
  by bank branches, 74
  to enterprises, 15, 18–20, 51–53, 54,
    60–65, 74, 118
  by monobank system, 52–53
  by People's Bank of China, 59, 60–
    61, 62
  by specialised banks, 113–114
  state control of, 35, 36, 39–40
Credit-based financial systems
  advantages of, 172
  as future orientation, 174
  institution-directed, 36
  state-controlled, 6, 27, 35, 36, 38,
    40
Cukierman, A., 165
Cultural Revolution, 58, 61, 62, 63
Curb market, 37, 38, 39, 172
Currency, issuance of, 75, 93
Czechoslovakia, privatisation in,
  25(n7)

Debt, national, 136
Decentralisation, 79–80, 105, 106,
  119, 134, 135
"Declaration of Private Ownership—
  China's Hope," 155
Deficits, budget. *See* Budget deficits
Deng Xiaoping, 9, 13, 97, 155
Depreciation funds, 119
Deregulation, 28
Development Fund, 41
Dickinson, H., 14(n2)
Difanghua (localized bank branches),
  95
Differentiation, principle of, 89
Dirksen, E., 69

Disequilibrium approach, 100
Dobb, Maurice, 14(n2)
Dollar, D., 113
Domestic savings, 65–66, 80,
  81(table)
Donnithorne, A., 55
Duocun duodai, principle of, 76

Eccleston, B., 35
Ecklund, G., 67
Economic reform, 2, 8–9, 72, 77, 134,
  149. *See also* Financial reform
Economic System Reform
  Commission, 88
Economic System Reform Institute,
  133
England. *See* Britain
Enterprisation of banks, 89–90
Enterprise-bank relations. *See* Bank-
  enterprise relations
Enterprise bonds, 23, 124(table), 127,
  128, 129–130, 131, 137, 138
Enterprise ownership, 154
Enterprise reform, 105
Enterprise sector
  banking reforms and, 112–120
  bond market and, 23, 124(table),
    127, 128, 129–130, 131, 133, 137–
    138
  competition in, 18
  credit allocation to, 15, 18–20, 51–
    53, 54, 60–65, 74, 118
  decentralisation of decision
    making to, 105, 119, 120
  fund use by, 119–120
  household sector and, 54
  local governments and, 105–106
  losses incurred by, 111, 115–116,
    118, 137, 152
  monitoring of, by banks, 18–19,
    176, 178
  productivity of, 112–113
  profitability of, 113–114, 115, 116,
    133
  recentralisation and, 163
  share market and, 141, 142–150
  subsidies granted to, 174–175

Enterprise shares, 23
Epstein, G., 167
Equity market, 28, 29, 31, 38
Euh, Y.-D., 38
"Experimental Methods for Share-
System Enterprises," 155
Extra-budgetary funds, 80, 82(n14)

Federal Open Market Committee
(U.S.), 171
Federal Reserve System (U.S.), 164,
166, 170
Finance and development paradigm,
5, 6, 11, 86, 159, 171
evaluation of, 162
financial liberalisation and, 12, 25–
33
as future orientation, 180
main features of, 46(table)
ownership reform and, 150, 156
Financial bonds, 124(table), 128
Financial deepening, 79(table)
Financial groups, joint-stock, 90
Financial liberalisation, 5, 9, 24, 30,
32–33, 94
capital markets and, 122
central planning and, 29
development and, 28
as future orientation, 163
without financial markets, 73–84
*See also under individual
countries*
Financial markets, 9, 21
elements of, 77–78
move towards, 84–94
Financial plan, components of, 53–54
Financial reform, 7–11
approaches to, 4–6, 9
decentralisation and, 105, 106, 119,
134
financial liberalisation and, 73–84
financial markets and, 84–94
future orientation of, 160–181
inflation as a consequence of, 2, 9,
10, 85, 92, 98–112, 120, 160
key propositions of, 86–87
ownership reform and, 149

policy choices and, 9–10, 27, 78
See also Finance and development
paradigm; Late development
paradigm; Market socialism
paradigm
Financial repression, 5, 26, 31(n12)
Financial system(s)
classification of, 6–7, 34–36
credit-based, 6, 27, 35, 36, 40, 174
development process and, 3
market-based, 6, 7, 22, 25, 27
oligopolistic, 6, 34, 36
Soviet-type, 47, 48–49
state-controlled. *See* State-
controlled financial system(s)
stock-based, 25
*See also under individual
countries*
Fiscal bonds, 124(table)
Five Year Plans, 40, 59, 60, 180(n16)
Fixed capital, 51
"Flexible fringe," 172
Forced savings, 81(n11), 99–100
Four Transformations and Eight
Reforms, 73–74
France, financial system in, 6, 35, 165
Free markets, 31, 100, 181(n19)
Fujian, 1

GAEC. *See* General Administration
of Exchange Control
Garvy, G., 48, 49(3)
GDI. *See* Gross domestic investment
GDP. *See* Gross domestic product
General Administration of Exchange
Control (GAEC), 74
Germany, financial system in, 6, 36,
166, 176
Gerschenkron, A., 5, 33, 34
Goodman, J. B., 165, 167
Gosbank, 55(n9)
Government bonds, 23, 66–67, 123,
124, 132
Government intervention. *See* State-
controlled financial system(s)
Great Leap Forward, 58, 61–62, 63

Gross domestic investment (GDI), 106(table)
Gross domestic product (GDP), investment as percentage of, 65, 105, 106(table)
Guangdong, 1, 96
Gurley, John, 36

Hard budget constraints, 63, 118, 120
Hayek, F. A. von, 14(n2)
Heimann, Eduard, 14(n2)
Heunemann, R., 158(n76)
Hong Kong, banking system in, 56(n11)
Hong Zhunyan, 151
Horizontal financial controls (*kuai*), 88
Horizontal regulation (*kuaikuai*), 106
Household responsibility contract, 125
Household savings, 80, 81(nn 11, 13), 90, 100
Household sector, 54
Hsiao, K.H.Y., 59, 62
Hungary, 16
    banking reforms in, 23
    bond market in, 24, 130(n24)
    credit allocation in, 19–20
    financial markets and, 21
    market socialism and, 16
    privatisation in, 25(n7)
    share markets in, 24
Hussain, A., 105, 108, 109
Hu Yaobang, 77

ICB. *See* Industrial and Commercial Bank
IMF. *See* International Monetary Fund
Imperfect-information approach, 31, 32
India, stock exchanges in, 29
Industrial and Commercial Bank (ICB), 75, 76, 83, 89, 114, 116, 127, 128
Industrialisation, late, 33–34, 42, 174
Industry, socialisation of, 68–69

Inflation
    banking system and, 102–112, 175
    bond market and, 123, 129, 130–131, 134, 136
    budget deficits and, 107
    central bank "independence" and, 163–165
    conflict theories of, 102
    as consequence of reform, 2, 9, 10, 85, 92, 98–112, 120, 160
    forced savings and, 99–100
    vs. growth, 107, 110
    indexed interest rates and, 94
    monobank and, 53
    as political process, 102
    in pre-reform era, 65, 66(table)
    temporary decline in, 95
"Insider monitoring," of enterprises, 176
"Insider trading" investigation, 145
Insurance companies, 22–23, 91
Interest rates, 26, 30, 36, 180
    on bonds, 126, 127, 128, 129(n18)
    credit recipients and, 59(n12)
    inflation and, 94, 110
    liberalisation of, 27, 37
    market-determined, 42–43
International banks, 32
International economy, 6
International Monetary Fund (IMF), 37, 85
Inventory accumulation, 62
Investment spending, 58, 65, 111(n12)
"Iron rice-bowl," 178
Italy, financial system in, 6, 35

Japan, financial system in, 6, 13, 35, 38(15), 165, 167, 176, 177, 180(n17)
Jefferson, G., 113
Jiang Zemin, 13
Jinrong shichang (financial market), 77
Joint-stock banks, 177
Joint-stock enterprises, 142, 153–154, 155, 156, 176

Jordan, equity markets in, 29
June 4 Incident, 95, 179. *See also*
   Tiananmen

Kaufman, George C., 166
Keiretsu (enterprise groups), 176
Komiya, R., 104, 109
Korea. *See* North Korea; South Korea
Kornai, J., 19, 63–64, 100
Kuomintang, 13, 58

Lange, O., 14–16, 17
Laski, K., 21
Late development paradigm, 5–6, 11,
   13, 44
   credit-based financial system and,
   36, 172
   as future orientation, 159, 161, 169,
   173–174, 179, 180
   main features of, 46(table)
   See also NIC model of late
   development
Late industrialisation, 33–34, 42, 174
Latin America, financial
   liberalisation in, 30
Lau, K.-T., 113
Lee, C. H., 42
Lenin, V. I., 49
Leninism, 8, 47
Lerner, Abba, 14
Liberalisation. *See* Financial
   liberalisation; Interest rate
   liberalisation; Price liberalisation
Li Guixian, 168(n5)
Li Maosheng, 25(n8)
Lin Senmu, 107, 117, 164
Li Peng, 13, 94
List, Friedrich, 5
Liu Guoguang, 152, 153
Liu Hongru, 25(n8)
Li Yining, 25(n8), 151, 153
Loan market, 77
Loans
   to enterprises, 60–61, 74–75, 109–
   110, 117, 133–134
   interest rate for, 94

profit performance and, 22, 113–
   114, 115
by specialised banks, 89
unpaid, 61, 62(n14), 64, 117
See also Credit allocation
Local governments, 79, 103, 180
   bond market and, 67, 135(n36),
   137, 158
   enterprise sector and, 105–106
   national income and, 80
   specialised banks and, 170, 174
   stock market and, 158

Ma Bin, 151
Malaysia, equity markets in, 29
Mao Zedong, 8, 70
Market-based financial systems, 6, 7,
   22, 25, 27
Market in a Socialist Economy, The
   (Brus), 16
Marketisation, of bond market, 128,
   131, 132–133
Market regulation, 1, 32, 70
Market socialism paradigm
   banking system and, 8–9
   financial liberalisation and, 5, 12,
   13
   financial markets and, 21
   first version of (MSI), 16–20, 21,
   46(table), 74, 97, 121
   as future orientation, 161–162, 171,
   174, 179
   investment policy and, 18, 19, 21
   late development paradigm and, 6,
   10, 11
   main features of, 4, 46(table)
   second version of (MSII), 20–25,
   46(table), 75, 86, 121, 126, 156,
   159
Martin, W. M., 164
Marx, Karl, 47(n1)
Marxism, 8, 47
Mayer, C., 176
McKinnon, R., 26, 30
Ministry for Light Industry, 116(n21)
Ministry of Finance (MOF), 55, 82,
   84, 91

banking system and, 50, 58, 61, 74, 83, 88, 117, 168–169
bond issuance and, 123, 124, 129, 130, 132
MOF. *See* Ministry of Finance
Monetary aggregates, 103(table), 107(n7)
Monetary overhang, 99
Monetary policy, 68, 107
Monetisation, of economy, 79(table), 100–101, 160
Money market, 9, 77, 86, 87
Money supply, 101, 109
Monobank-monobudget system, 50, 65
Monobank system, 2, 19, 20, 22, 47, 49, 74
    credit allocation by, 52–53
    developmental support by, 50–51
    macroeconomic control by, 53–55
    microeconomic supervision by, 51–53
Moral hazard problem, 30, 32
MSI. *See* Market socialism paradigm, first version of
MSII. *See* Market socialism paradigm, second version of

National Bank of Poland (NPB), 23
National Debt Management Department, 130
National Economic Construction Bonds, 67
National People's Congress, 115
Naughton, B., 108, 109, 113, 118(n25)
NBFIs. *See* Non-bank financial institutions
NBP. *See* National Bank of Poland
NEM. *See* New Economic Mechanism
Neurath, O., 14(n2)
New Economic Mechanism (NEM), 1, 16, 17, 19, 20
Newly industrialising countries (NICs), 6, 169, 174, 175, 177, 180(n17)
Neyapti, B., 165

NIC model of late development, 4, 5–6, 7
    decline of, 44
    as future orientation, 171, 172, 173–174
    industrialisation and, 33–34
    main features of, 46(table)
    See also Late development paradigm
NICs. *See* Newly industrialising countries
Noland, M., 40
Non-bank financial institutions (NBFIs), 22–23, 28, 38, 73, 84, 86, 87, 90, 94–95, 96, 114
North Korea, 51
Nuti, D. M., 20

Open-door policy, 178
Oligopolistic financial system, 6, 34, 36
"Overloan" provision, 38(n15)
Ownership
    defined, 151
    enterprise, 154
    private, 150, 153(n70), 155(n73)
    share, 23, 24, 25, 141
    social, 139, 140, 150, 155, 158
Ownership reform, 11, 87, 149, 150–157, 175–176, 177

Patrick, Hugh, 36
PBC. *See* People's Bank of China
PCBC. *See* People's Construction Bank of China
Peebles, G., 101(nn 2, 3), 109
People's Bank of China (PBC), 74, 82, 83, 110, 174
    bond issuance and, 126, 127–128
    formation of, 55
    Ministry of Finance and, 168–169
    operational practices of, 59–61
    organisation of, 56, 57(table), 58
    primary active function of, 65
    provincial branches of, 95
    specialised banks and, 75–76, 88, 89, 90, 94, 103, 106, 107, 170

People's Construction Bank of China (PCBC), 58–61, 75, 83, 115
People's Insurance Company of China, 91
People's Victory Bonds, 67
Planned commodity economy, 14
Podolski, T., 52, 53
Poland, 16
  banking reforms in, 23
  bond market in, 24
  privatisation in, 25(n7)
Polanyi, Karl, 14(n2)
Policy loans, 40, 172, 174, 180
Politburo, 103
Political economy, defined, 7
Power-theoretic orientation, 4, 7–8, 161
Pre-reform era, 47–71
  banking system in, 49–55
  China's experience in, 47, 49, 55–70
  economic performance in, 68–70
  enterprise budget constraint in, 118
Presidential Emergency Decree, 37
Price liberalisation, 26, 101(n2)
Price reform, 175, 178
Price stability, 53, 54, 65, 164, 165, 168
Private banks, 180
Private ownership, 150, 153(n70), 155(n73), 156
Privatisation, 10–11, 24, 181(n19)
  of banking system, 39
  of enterprises, 154–155, 156, 174
Profit performance, 16–17, 18, 113–114, 115, 116

Qing dynasty, 13

Rawski, T., 113
Real bills doctrine, 60
Recentralisation, 163
Reformed socialism, 87, 179
Reforms. *See* Banking system, reform of; Economic reform; Enterprise reform; Financial reform;

Ownership reform; Price reform; Urban reforms; Welfare reform
"Regulations on Bank Management," 89
Reputation effects, 32
Retrenchment policy, 73, 110, 117, 118, 148, 160, 162
Riskin, C., 69
Robbins, Lionel, 14(n2)
Roemer, J., 177
Rural credit cooperatives (RCCs), 56, 90
Russia, 25

Savings, 26, 30, 36, 38
  composition of, 80–82
  domestic, 65–66, 80, 81(table)
  forced, 81(n11), 99–100
  government budgetary, 80
  household, 80, 81(nn 11, 13), 90, 100
  individual, 138, 141
  rural, 82(table)
  urban, 81(n13), 82(table)
SBs. *See* Specialised banks
Sectoral overlap, 119(n26)
Sectoral terrain (*hangye*), 77
SEZs. *See* Special Economic Zones
Shadow prices, 15
Share ownership, 23, 24, 25, 141, 155
Shares, 9, 24, 35, 96–97, 157–158
  vs. bonds, 142
  economic impact of, 147–150
  evaluation of, 148–149
  introduction of, 140–147, 151
  issuance of, 124(table), 142, 143–144, 146–149
  ownership reform and, 153, 176
  prices of, 144–145
  social ownership and, 140
  See also Share ownership
Shaw, Edward, 26, 36
Shortage economy, 63, 64, 85, 92–93, 119, 138
Singh, A., 172
Socialism
  banking system and, 49, 52, 58

vs. capitalism, 15, 21, 47, 141, 150
centrally planned, 47–48
reformed, 87, 179
state, 13, 16, 48, 63, 139
Socialist calculation debate, 14–16
Socialist commodity economy, 4
Socialist market economy, 162
Socialist monetary system, 86
Social ownership, 139, 140, 150, 155, 157, 158, 171, 176
Social security policy, 178
Soft administered prices, 63
Soft budget constraint, 19, 30, 53, 63, 64–65, 105, 114, 138
Soft credit constraint, 10, 19, 114, 116, 163, 174, 178
Soft subsidies, 63
Soft taxes, 63
Sokil, C., 20, 21
Song Tingming, 93
South Korea, 10, 11, 13, 32
    credit allocation in, 36, 39, 44
    curb market in, 172
    financial history of, 36–39
    financial liberalisation in, 42
    financial reform in, 39
    financial system in, 32–33, 36–39, 41, 180(n17)
    industrialisation in, 33, 37
    privatisation in, 177
    public ownership in, 43
Soviet-type financial system, 47, 48–49
Soviet Union
    banking reforms in, 23
    bond sales in, 67(n18)
    centrally planned economy in, 47, 48–49, 51(n5), 52
SPC. *See* State Planning Commission
Special Economic Zones (SEZs), 88, 94, 142(n44), 145
Specialised banks (SBs)
    bad debts to, 117
    bond issuance and, 126, 127, 130, 139
    competition among, 114
    loans to enterprises by, 113–114

local governments and, 170, 174
loss-making enterprises and, 141
People's Bank of China and, 75–76, 88, 89, 90, 94, 103, 106, 107, 170
Special National Bonds, 132
State-controlled financial system(s), 6, 19, 20, 21–22
    credit allocation and, 22, 35, 36, 39, 42, 44
    financial risk and, 43
    late industrialisation and, 33–34, 36, 42
    policy loans and, 40
State Council, 103, 145, 147, 168
State Economic Structural Reform Commission, 93
State paternalism, 147
State Planning Commission (SPC), 82, 88, 91, 152
State socialism, 13, 16, 48, 63, 139
Stern, N., 105, 108, 109
Stiglitz, J., 31
Stock-based financial system, 25
Stock markets, 24–25, 140, 146–147, 171–172, 180(n16)
Strategic Industry Fund, 41
Sunrise industries, 38
Sweezey, Paul, 14(n2)
Swinburne, M., 165

Taiwan
    credit allocation in, 36, 42
    curb market in, 172
    financial liberalisation in, 42(18)
    financial system in, 10, 36, 41, 169(n6)
    industrialisation in, 34
    late development and, 6
    public ownership in, 43
Tam, On-kit, 142(n43)
Tardos, M., 20, 21
Tatonnement, 15
Taylor, F., 14
"Third Front" industrial base, 59–60
Third Plenum, of CCP Central Committee, 8, 94
Three-tier banking system, 24

Tiananmen, 145. *See also* June 4
  Incident
TICs. *See* Trust and investment
  companies
Transferable bonds, 124(table), 128
Treasury bonds, 124, 125(table), 130,
  136
  inflation rate and, 131
  issuance of, 126, 127, 128, 132, 139
  purchase of, 128
  redemption of, 128–129
Triangualar debts (*san jiao zhai*), 117
Trust and investment companies
  (TICs), 76, 77, 84, 90–91, 114, 123
Tsang Shu-ki, 107
Two-tier banking system, 22, 23, 75,
  113

United Kingdom. *See* Britain
United States, financial system in, 6,
  35, 164, 166, 167
Urban credit cooperatives (UCCs), 90
Urban reforms, 103
Urban savings, 81(n13)
USSR. *See* Soviet Union

Vertical financial controls (*tiaotiao*),
  88
Vietnam, 1
von Mises, Ludwig, 14

Wade, R., 34, 41–42

Wage fund, 67, 111
Wage system, 103–105, 111
Walrasian system, 15
Webb, S., 165
Weiss, A., 31
Welfare reform, 178
Wellons, P., 32
Wenzhong quisong, policy of, 88
White slips (IOUs), 118
Wiemer, C., 106
Williamson, Oliver, 42
Woo, J.-E., 37, 38, 43
Woolley, J. T., 166
Working capital, 51–52
World Bank, 3, 27, 29, 85, 104, 105,
  106, 113, 167, 180(n17)
World Development Report 1989, 27,
  28, 29
Wu Jiesi, 25(n8)
Wu Jinglian, 151

Xiansi houhuo, policy of, 86

Yao Yilin, 94, 95
Yenal, O., 106, 109
Yugoslavia, banking reforms in, 23
Yu Guangyuan, 25(n8)

Zhao Haikuan, 25(n8)
Zhao Ziyang, 77, 78, 94, 95, 150(n67)
Zheng, Yuxin, 113
Zysman, J., 6, 34, 35, 36

The United States and Global Capital Shortages
The Problem and Possible Solutions

SARA L. GORDON

Q

QUORUM BOOKS
Westport, Connecticut • London

Library of Congress Cataloging-in-Publication Data

Gordon, Sara L.
　　The United States and global capital shortages : the problem and possible
solutions / Sara L. Gordon.
　　　p.　cm.
　　Includes bibliographical references and index.
　　ISBN 0-89930-772-8
　　1. Capital movements. 2. Capital movements—United States.
3. Saving and investment—United States. 4. Balance of payments—
United States. 5. Investments, Foreign—United States.　I. Title.
II. Title: The United States and global capital shortages.
HG3891.G67　　1995
332'.041'0973—dc20　　　　　　95-3264

British Library Cataloguing in Publication Data is available.

Library of Congress Catalog Card Number: 95-3264
ISBN: 0-89930-772-8

First published in 1995

Quorum Books, 88 Post Road West, Westport, CT 06881
An imprint of Greenwood Publishing Group, Inc.

Printed in the United States of America

The paper used in this book complies with the
Permanent Paper Standard issued by the National
Information Standards Organization (Z39.48-1984).

10 9 8 7 6 5 4 3 2 1

Contents

Tables and Figures   vii

Preface   ix

Chapter 1   U.S. Capital Flows   1

Chapter 2   Changes in Global Capital Markets During the 1980s   13

Chapter 3   Foreign Direct Investment in the United States   33

Chapter 4   The Saving Deficiency in the United States   61

Chapter 5   Policies Designed to Raise the U.S. Saving Rate   99

Chapter 6   Capital Flows and Balance-of-Payments Adjustment   125

Chapter 7   Global Capital Requirements   159

Chapter 8   Summary and Conclusion   181

Bibliography   215

Index   223

Tables and Figures

TABLES

2.1 Gross Capital Flows of Fourteen Industrial Countries, 1975–89   14

2.2 United States: Summary Balance of Payments, 1985–91   15

2.3 U.S. Portfolio Transactions, 1975–89   16

2.4 U.S. International Transactions, 1975–93   20

2.5 U.S. Balance of Payments, 1988–93   22

2.6 Germany, Japan, and the United States: Indicators of Relative Importance of Banks in Financial Activities of Corporations and Households, 1980, 1985, and 1990   27

3.1 U.S. Foreign Direct Investment Flows, 1973–93   35

3.2 Alternative Measures of the Role of Foreign-Owned Affiliates in the U.S. Economy, 1977–90   36

3.3 Merchandise Trade of U.S. Affiliates of Foreign-Owned Firms, 1977–91   39

3.4 Foreign Direct Investment Position: Historical Cost, 1973–91   52

3.5 Foreign Direct Investment Position: Market Value and Current Cost, 1982–91   54

4.1   Summary of Sources and Uses of Saving in the Industrial
      Countries, 1977–95   63

4.2   Saving Rates for Major Industrial Countries, 1976–95   66

4.3   The Budget Outlook Through 2004   71

4.4   Gross Saving and Investment, 1965–92   77

4.5   Private Net Saving and Investment, 1965–90   82

4.6   Personal Saving Rate, Wealth-to-Income Ratio, and
      Debt-to-Wealth Ratio, 1960–89   84

5.1   Federal Spending as a Percent of GDP, 1994, 2000, and
      2004   105

5.2   Deficit Projections, Fiscal Years 1992–99   109

7.1   Balance of Payments on Current Account, 1986–95   161

7.2   Industrial Country Current Account Balances, 1992–2000   164

7.3   Developing Countries: Capital Flows, 1971–92   167

7.4   Capital Flows to Asia, 1986–91   174

FIGURES

3.1   U.S. Foreign Direct Investment Position, 1973–91   53

4.1   Lifetime Income, Consumption, Savings, and Wealth in the
      Life-cycle Model   79

6.1   Fiscal Expansion and Exchange Rate Appreciation   130

6.2   Fiscal and Monetary Expansion in the Mundell-Fleming
      Model   138

Preface

By 1982 the United States had become a net importer of capital. Low personal saving rates and large federal budget deficits were responsible for the drop in the U.S. national saving rate, which fell from 20.8 percent of gross domestic product in 1977–81 to 14.6 percent in 1993. Although it declined continuously, the domestic investment rate exceeded the saving rate, and foreign capital supplied the difference. Large internal imbalances between saving and investment were reflected in external imbalances between exports and imports, and it has been projected that the current account deficit in the U.S. balance of payments will remain at about 2.4 percent of gross domestic product for the remainder of the decade. This means that the United States will continue to import foreign capital and increase its external indebtedness, resulting in ever increasing outflows of resources to service the foreign debt.

The United States remains the largest net importer of capital, contributing to a shortage of global capital. Such a shortage foreshadows severe economic consequences in the form of high real interest rates, stagnant levels of investment and economic growth, and reduced standards of living for the industrial nations. The developing nations and the emerging market economies of Central and Eastern Europe and the countries of the former Soviet Union will also suffer greatly from inadequate levels of trade and investment.

The motivation to write this book resulted from recognition of the fact that the large saving-investment imbalances and the need of the United States for substantial amounts of foreign capital would continue unless measures were taken to raise the national saving rate sufficiently so that national savings equalled or exceeded domestic investment. The problem will continue until public saving is raised by lowering and, ultimately, eliminating the federal deficit, and the rate of personal saving is increased. The book addresses the problem of the large capital inflows into the United States during the 1980s and 1990s, explains the relationship between the low level of national savings and current account deficits, and examines solutions to the problem.

Just as the book went to press, the U.S. Senate rejected the proposed balanced budget amendment to the Constitution. Not only would such an amendment have been detrimental to the U.S. economy when future recessions occur, but it could also have adversely impacted the stability and growth of the global economy. Even if the budget was balanced during a period when the economy was operating with actual output close to potential, during a recession decreases in revenue and increases in outlays such as food stamps and unemployment insurance would automatically produce a deficit. Given the large role of federal government spending in the economy, to cut expenditures to balance the budget during a recession would be contractionary, contributing to a further drop in the value of output. A better way to achieve budget balance would be for Congress to reduce outlays and raise revenues. Given the growth of entitlement spending in the federal budget, it is unlikely that budget balance can be achieved without finding ways to reduce the growing percentage of federal spending going for entitlements.

A program of deficit reduction would have to be broad-ranging and courageous. The 1993 Omnibus Budget Reconciliation Act must be credited with having made substantial progress toward deficit reduction, but additional steps are necessary. The book makes a number of recommendations to help achieve further deficit reduction.

Because a large drop in the personal saving rate contributed to the lowering of the national saving rate, the book discusses motivations for saving and recommends some measures that might help to raise the personal saving rate. One big question is whether the aging of the baby boom generation will help raise the personal saving rate during the late 1990s and the first decade of the twenty-first century.

A continuation of increased U.S. external indebtedness ultimately results in a transfer of resources abroad and reduced living standards at home. Also, because so much foreign capital goes to finance U.S. external deficits, world real interest rates remain high, thereby reducing investment at home and abroad.

I would like to make a number of acknowledgments. First, I would like to thank Marshall Pomer, Director of the Macroeconomic Policy Institute, for insightful comments when the book was in its initial stages, and Evelyn Katz who carefully read most of the manuscript and made many thought-provoking suggestions. I would also like to thank Anne Egan-Cunningham for doing the graphic work; Anna Maria Tuttalmondo, my graduate assistant at St. John's University; St. John's University's Word Processing Center; and Katie Chase, copy editor for the Greenwood Publishing Group, for helping to make the manuscript more clear and readable. Finally, I owe a great debt of gratitude to St. John's University for giving me a research leave from my academic responsibilities to work on the manuscript.

CHAPTER 1

U.S. Capital Flows

Since 1982 the United States has had current account deficits that have been financed by inflows of capital from abroad. This is in marked contrast to the earlier postwar period, when the United States generally functioned as a major supplier of international capital to the rest of the world. By the 1980s, Japan had assumed the role of the major supplier of international capital to the global economy.

It is suggested that the 1980s pattern of capital flowing from Japan, which had been growing rapidly, to the United States, which had a slower growth rate, was an outgrowth of the stages of economic development that the two countries had reached. Economists have shown that stages can be detected in the balance of payments of a country throughout the course of its economic development. It can be assumed that Japan moved out of the stage where it was a debtor to the stage of a young creditor when its assets exceeded its liabilities and it had net claims on the rest of the world. By way of contrast, the United States has become a mature creditor, which is defined as one living off the interest and dividends on its net claims and may even be consuming some of its capital.[1] The two countries have reached structural and developmental stages where Japan's rate of saving is high and that of the United States has fallen to very low levels. In Japan the domestic savings rate exceeds the rate of domestic investment, while in the United States the rate of domestic investment, which has declined significantly during the past decade, still exceeds the rate of savings. The United States makes up the difference between domestic investment and domestic saving by borrowing foreign capital.

It has been hypothesized frequently that the existence of flexible exchange rates has been a key factor in enabling the United States to sustain current account deficits over a large number of years. Under a fixed exchange rate system, a country must conduct monetary policy designed to keep its rate of interest in line with the level prevailing in the rest of the world. However, a country with a flexible exchange rate system has more discretion in its conduct of monetary policy. Large federal government deficits in combination with a tight monetary policy during the 1980s contributed to real interest rates in the United States that were greater than those in the rest of the world, and this attracted foreign capital. It was the existence of a flexible exchange rate system that permitted the United States to continue to run current account deficits that averaged 3 percent of gross domestic product (GDP) in 1985–89 without necessitating policy measures to reduce aggregate demand. Without the existence of flexible exchange rates, it would have been impossible for the United States to have sustained such large current account deficits over a number of years.

After averaging over $125 billion for 1985–90, the current account deficit declined to $8 billion in 1991, largely as a consequence of transfer payments from U.S. allies in the Gulf War and reduction of imports during the 1990–91 recession. However, the current account deficit began to climb again, rising to $67 billion in 1992 and $104 billion in 1993. The deficit is projected to remain in excess of $100 billion for the remainder of the decade.

During the 1980s the current account and budget deficits both rose as proportions of GDP. With large budget deficits and a falling personal saving rate, the rate of domestic saving was lower than domestic investment, and the difference was made up by an inflow of foreign capital. Large federal government borrowing together with a tight monetary policy helped keep interest rates high. In turn, high interest rates attracted foreign lenders and, by increasing the demand for dollar-denominated assets, had caused an appreciation of 58 percent in the value of the dollar. An expensive dollar led to a reduction in the growth of U.S. exports compared to imports. By 1987, two years after the value of the dollar had peaked, the current account deficit had increased to $167 billion. The large real appreciation of the dollar had reduced the international competitiveness of many segments of American industry, and it is taking years for manufacturing to recover from such a shock. The real value of the dollar has fallen sharply since its 1985 peak, and it is now close to its 1980 level. Because of the depreciation of the dollar and decline in relative unit labor costs in manufacturing, U.S. firms have become very competitive in world markets. However, the recovery of U.S. export markets was delayed until the economies of Japan and Europe had begun to recover.[2] The fact that the United States continues to run large current account deficits means that it will continue to absorb large amounts of international capital.

POLICY MEASURES AND THE U.S. IMPORT OF
GLOBAL CAPITAL

U.S. economic policy played a major role in the growth of capital movements into the United States during the 1980s. Three areas of economic
policy were particularly important: a tight monetary policy during much of
the 1980s that was aimed at controlling inflation; the efforts of the Reagan
administration to reduce the size of the federal government by cutting taxes;
and, until 1985, an exchange rate policy that precluded all but a minimal
amount of intervention in foreign exchange markets. It was the interaction
of these three policies that contributed to the very large budget and current
account deficits, loss of U.S. international competitiveness in manufacturing,
drop in the national saving rate, and large inflows of foreign capital to the
United States.

Throughout the 1980s the Federal Reserve pursued a monetary policy
geared toward preventing the recurrence of accelerating inflation. Because
the loose fiscal policy followed by the Reagan administration provided a
powerful stimulus to the economy, the tight monetary policy pursued by
the Federal Reserve helped counter such a stimulus. This fiscal policy led to
an explosion of federal government debt, which contributed to high real
(long-term) interest rates throughout the 1980s.

The large federal tax cuts of the early 1980s produced budget deficits that
averaged more than 5 percent of GDP over the period 1982–86. Although
deficits of such magnitude did help the economy recover from the deep
recession of 1981–82, they had impacts on the economy that would be
problematic for years to come.

The Reagan administration believed that the size of the federal government had to be reduced, and it perceived that cutting revenues from taxes
would reduce the size of the public sector because less revenue would be
available to spend. The administration also believed that cutting taxes would
raise savings in the economy. Within the context of such a philosophy, the
Economic Recovery Tax Act of 1981 was passed. The act reduced tax rates
and introduced reforms in the structure of the tax system. At the same time,
the administration focused on raising national defense outlays and attempted
to reverse the growth of federal spending on domestic programs. Large
actual and structural budget deficits persisted as a consequence of increased
defense outlays and large tax reductions. As a result, the gross federal debt
as a share of GDP rose from 33.5 percent in 1981 to 55.4 percent in 1989
and 69.1 percent in 1993.

The large budget deficits of the 1980s proved to have been very trouble-
some because the American personal saving rate, which is among the lowest
in the world, actually declined in the 1980s. Because of rising budget deficits
and declining personal saving, national saving as a share of GDP fell dramatically during the 1980s. The gap between national saving and national

investment was large, and the United States imported enormous amounts of foreign capital. In conjunction with the savings-investment imbalance and large foreign borrowings, the current account balance changed from small surpluses in 1980–81 to large deficits. Although the ability to import large amounts of foreign capital limited the rise in real U.S. interest rates, which shielded investment from the consequences of large federal deficits, the United States became the largest debtor nation in the world.[3] Had the foreign borrowing gone into increasing the nation's investment rate, future generations would have benefitted from this borrowing, but the borrowing only helped to maintain the rate of investment and much of it went for consumption activities.

A third area of policy concerns the exchange rate—the price of foreign currencies in relation to the dollar. The dollar began to reverse a downward trend in 1980 in response to monetary tightening by the Federal Reserve and large federal budget deficits, and the dollar began its long period of appreciation, which was to last until 1985. Between 1980 and 1984 the dollar appreciated by 46 percent in nominal terms and 42 percent in real terms in response to the large interest rate differentials in favor of the United States arising from the very tight monetary policy. The appreciation continued until February 1985. Throughout the period 1981–84, the Reagan administration followed a policy of laissez-faire to the foreign exchange market and was firmly opposed to any attempts to depress the value of the dollar by intervening in international currency markets. The upward movement of the dollar was not viewed as being problematic by the administration, and, generally, the authorities refrained from intervening in the foreign exchange market. The dollar continued rising and peaked in February 1985. By the time the Group of Five (G-5: the United States, West Germany, the United Kingdom, Japan, and France) met at the Plaza Hotel in New York in September 1985 and agreed to bring down the value of the dollar, the dollar had depreciated by 13 percent. This 13 percent decline can be attributed partly to policy changes in the second term of the Reagan administration.[4] Since 1985 the U.S. authorities have followed a policy of intervention in foreign exchange markets, although recent interventions have been very limited.

The unprecedented appreciation of the dollar between 1981 and 1985 was the result of large inflows of foreign capital purchasing dollar-denominated assets. An expensive dollar had serious medium-term impacts on the economy. American exporters lost competitiveness on world markets and import-competing firms contracted; also the expansion in the growth in imports and reduction in the growth of exports caused the current account balance to deteriorate sharply. The contraction of domestic firms and expansion of foreign competitors who gained market share in the United States had effects that persisted for years after the exchange rate depreciated.

The policy measures of the 1980s are still having serious macroeconomic repercussions on the economy. The national saving rate fell from over 17 percent of GDP in 1980 to 12 percent in 1992 as a consequence of large federal deficits and a drop in the personal saving rate. Implementation of the Economic Recovery Tax Act of 1981 reduced total federal revenues as a percentage of GDP from an average of 19.9 percent in 1980–81 to an average of 18.6 percent for 1983–93. Throughout the decade, actual and structural federal deficits as a share of GDP remained higher than at any time since the end of World War II. With the increase in public-sector debt, the amount going to interest on the debt steadily increased, rising to over 14 percent of total outlays, or 3.4 percent of GDP by the early 1990s. The deficit problem was creating insurmountable difficulties, and in August 1993 the Omnibus Budget Reconciliation Act (OBRA) of 1993, a major package of tax increases and spending cuts, was enacted. The legislation makes major improvements in the size of federal deficits for the remainder of the 1990s, but increases in spending for Medicare and Medicaid are the dominant factors that push projected deficits up beginning in 1999. Even without the enactment of further legislation, OBRA 1993 should help to raise the national saving rate. The personal saving rate, which averaged over 8 percent of disposable income in 1980–81 and declined to over 4 percent in 1993, is a major factor reducing the national saving rate. It is possible that over the next few years the personal saving rate may gradually rise because of the demographic makeup of the population and the ratio of wealth to income, which is relatively low.[5]

By affecting the macroeconomic fundamentals, the policies of the early 1980s adversely impacted the current account. The federal budget deficits reduced the national saving rate and helped to create saving-investment imbalances, since the level of domestic investment was greater than the level of domestic saving. A tight monetary policy coupled with significantly increased borrowings by the U.S. Treasury contributed to high interest rates in the United States. Interest rates that were higher than those prevailing abroad helped attract foreign investors during the 1980s. The increased demand for dollar-denominated assets significantly increased the demand for dollars to purchase these assets. With flexible exchange rates and minimal intervention in foreign exchange markets by the U.S. authorities during the first term of the Reagan administration, the dollar appreciated by over 50 percent. Such an unprecedented appreciation of the dollar, by raising the prices of U.S. exports and reducing prices of imports, led to a current account deficit of $125 billion in 1985, the year the value of the dollar peaked. After February 1985 the depreciation of the dollar began, and by 1986 interest rates had declined significantly. Because of the J-curve effect, the growth in imports continued to exceed the growth in exports, and the current account deficit continued rising until it reached $167 billion in 1987. It was not until 1988, after the value of the dollar had declined by 50 percent in nominal terms and 44 percent in real terms, that the size of the current account deficit began to fall.

The United States was able to sustain large current account deficits for so many years because of flexible exchange rates and increased international capital mobility. Instead of being forced to adopt measures to correct the saving-investment imbalances, current account deficits were financed by inflows of capital from abroad. Accordingly, for over a decade the United States has functioned as the principal borrower on international capital markets, and this situation has prompted concern that U.S. budget deficits were contributing to a shortage of global capital.[6]

POLICY MEASURES TO RAISE SAVINGS RATES AND REDUCE THE IMPORTATION OF GLOBAL CAPITAL

There has been a growing recognition of the fact that policy measures must be implemented to raise the national saving rate and reduce the importation of foreign capital. The most significant effort was legislation that passed OBRA 1993. Although in earlier years legislation had been passed to reduce the growth of expenditures, OBRA 1993 took a major step forward in reducing the share of the nation's saving that federal budget deficits will be absorbing, and, ultimately, will help to keep real interest rates low. The design of the 1993 deficit reduction plan was guided by several principals. First, deficit reduction had to be large, genuine, and credible, and to these ends the administration proposed hundreds of revenue increases and spending cuts. Second, it was necessary that the package be balanced between spending cuts and tax increases. For instance, in fiscal 1998 the projected deficit reduction will be divided between $87 billion in net spending cuts (including $25 billion in debt service reduction) and $59 billion in additional revenue. Third, the tax increases were highly progressive and were heavily skewed toward the people who had benefitted the most from the tax cuts of the early 1980s and who had the greatest ability to pay. Income taxes were raised for only the top 1.2 percent of taxpayers.[7] It has been projected that by fiscal 1998 the policy changes from the legislation will reduce the projected deficit by 1.75 percent of GDP, representing a 1.75 percent increase in the saving rate if offsetting changes do not occur.[8] The saving from deficit reduction could be offset if private savings were to decrease or if the current account balance were to improve.

Because the experiences of the 1980s provide strong evidence that private savers did not respond to ballooning federal deficits by increasing private saving, there is no reason to suggest that they would respond to deficit reductions by reducing savings.[9] However, deficit reduction is expected to be partially offset by decreases in the current account deficit. In the 1980s, a large part of reductions in national saving resulting from the federal deficits was offset by increases in the current account deficits, which were financed by capital inflows (foreign lending). In conjunction with deficit reduction, the current account balance is expected to improve. An expansion in net exports stimulates the economy and partially offsets the contractionary impact on aggregate demand of increased taxes and spending cuts occasioned by deficit reduction. Studies have suggested that net exports will increase by about 40 percent of the value of initial deficit reduction.

Deficit reduction is also expected to increase the rate of national investment. Taking into account the expectations that a drop in the private saving rate probably will not occur and net exports will increase as a result of deficit reduction, it has been estimated that after three years the 1993 deficit reduction legislation should increase the share of national investment in GDP by 1 percentage point, increasing the capital stock as productive capital is substituted for government debt in private portfolios.[10]

OBJECTIVES OF THIS BOOK

One objective of this book is to explain the development of the U.S. economy from a net international creditor to the largest net debtor in the world, which for the past decade has been gobbling up most of the supply of international capital. The book explains the reasons for the United States progressing from the status of a net creditor in the early 1980s to that of a net debtor nation within less than a decade. Economic policies pursued during the early 1980s were instrumental in causing the emergence of the United States as the world's largest international debtor within such a short period of time. Large federal budget deficits and a large drop in the personal saving rate caused a large decline in the national saving rate. A relatively tight monetary policy during much of the 1980s kept real interest rates several percentage points above levels during earlier periods of economic expansion. Real interest rates that exceeded those prevailing in the rest of the world caused the dollar to appreciate by over 50 percent, and U.S. price competitiveness in international markets deteriorated. The fact that the Reagan administration followed a policy of not intervening in international currency markets during its first term contributed to the appreciation of the dollar and the loss of U.S. competitiveness in international markets.

A second key objective of the book is to attempt to assess the extent to which the United States will continue to absorb a major proportion of the supply of international capital during the remainder of the 1990s. During the 1980s, the United States ran large current account deficits, which were predominantly a consequence of large saving-investment imbalances brought about by its macroeconomic policies. During the 1980s, two major industrial countries—Germany and Japan—as well as several of the newly industrializing Asian economies, including Korea, had current account surpluses. The U.S. trade deficit was the major imbalance in the mid- and late 1980s. In the 1990s, Japan's global trade surplus stands out as the only major one that is significant for international comparisons. This is partly related to the fact that by the late 1980s the real exchange rate of the yen was undervalued against all major currencies and, given a two-year lag resulting from the J-curve effect, the impact on Japan's trade surplus appeared in the early 1990s.[11] Substantial appreciation of the yen occurred in 1993 and 1994, and Japan's trade balances should show some deterioration by the mid-1990s as Japan succeeds in recovering from recession. It has been projected that the surplus will decline from an estimated $135 billion in 1994 to $129 billion in 1995.

As noted above, the United States has made policy changes that in the long-term should lower the current account deficit in relation to GDP. Most important is budget deficit reduction legislation passed in 1993, which, by lowering the federal deficit, will also reduce the current account deficit. Since 1985, exchange rate policy has involved limited active intervention, which should help to keep the exchange rate below levels of the early 1980s. In the early 1990s this was aided by a monetary policy that lowered interest rates to stimulate the economy. However, a somewhat tighter monetary policy and an increased demand for capital to invest raised both long-term and short-term interest rates in 1994. In addition, the Clinton administration has been pursuing a policy based on long-run investments, which will improve America's international competitiveness. Measures in the administration's economic plan that are geared toward improving competitiveness include creating the requisite opportunities to improve education and training of the labor force to augment the stock of human resources and building public infrastructure, including highways, bridges, and water and sewer systems, as well as repairing structures. Because it is known that over time rising productivity depends on improvements in technology, the administration requested that Congress extend the research and expenditure tax credit that was done in OBRA 1993, and is also increasing funding for research partnerships with industry.[12]

The nonsynchronous nature of cyclical patterns among industrial countries during the 1990s affected current account developments, driving import demand higher in countries recovering from recession and lower in countries that were still in recession. The United States, which has been recovering from recession, experienced increases in the volume of imports averaging almost 12 percent in 1992–93. At the same time, growth in the volume of exports slowed, falling from an average of 7.3 percent in 1991–92 to 5.2 percent in 1993, leading to a widening in the current account deficit to $104 billion. The International Monetary Fund projected that this deficit would widen to $149 billion in 1994 and $168 billion in 1995. In the longer term, deficits should narrow to a more sustainable equilibrium as industrial countries recover from recession and U.S. export demand picks up. It has been suggested that a feasible international equilibrium in the world economy can be maintained with the United States running current account deficits equal to 1 percent of GDP (currently about $60 billion).[13]

Whereas both Germany and Japan had large current account surpluses in the 1980s, Japan is now the only major industrialized country with surpluses, and these surpluses rose to record levels of $118 billion in 1992 and $131 billion in 1993. As noted above, Japan's current account surplus is projected to decline in 1995. Japan's practices appear to have contributed to current account deficits in the United States and the other Group of Seven (G-7): the United States, West Germany, the United Kingdom, Japan, France, Canada, and Italy. Although Japan's bilateral current account balance with the United States has risen more slowly than its overall current account balance, it is still problematic to the United States, and in negotiations with Japan, the United States has repeatedly requested that Japan change its trading practices and that it also increase its use of fiscal policy to stimulate aggregate demand, thereby raising its purchases of imported goods.

Although important, the balance-of-payments problem caused by Japan is only one of several affecting the current account. The problem of the low U.S. national saving rate still remains serious, even though the policy changes in OBRA 1993 are projected to reduce the federal deficit from 4.2 percent of GDP to 2.3 percent in 1995, before beginning to climb if additional deficit reduction legislation is not passed. The projected budget deficits as percents of GDP are much smaller than projected in early 1993, which showed the deficit averaging 4.2 percent of GDP prior to the passage of OBRA 1993. Effectively, the legislation, by reducing the deficit as a share of GDP, raises the national saving rate by almost 2 percent of GDP. Domestic savings are the sum of government savings (Sg) and private savings (Sp), and private savings are the sum of business saving and personal savings. Although the relative share of business savings has remained fairly constant over the past decade, the share of personal saving is about 60 percent of its 1980 level—since 1980 the rate of personal saving has fallen from about 8 percent of disposable income to less than 5 percent. This means that even with substantial federal budget deficit reduction, the national saving rate will remain low.

Comparisons for personal savings rates for the G-7 countries show that the United States has a personal saving rate that is much lower than that for any of the other countries. Some of the differences could be caused by differences in international accounting conventions. For instance, Japanese accounts treat capital depreciation differently while the U.S. accounts do not distinguish between public consumption and public investment, treating all government expenditures as current consumption. Furthermore, there are conceptual inadequacies in the national accounts of both countries that could overstate the actual difference between Japanese and U.S. saving behavior. However, despite the problems with the total, Japan does save considerably more than the United States.[14]

The size of the U.S. personal saving rate is also a matter with which policymakers should be concerned, and it is necessary that consideration be given to implementing measures to raise the personal saving rate. Raising the national saving rate by federal deficit reduction at the same time that efforts are made to raise the personal saving rate would go a long way toward making the United States less dependent on the import of foreign capital. In addition, a large supply of savings would be accompanied by lower rates of interest, and if aggregate demand is maintained, the rate of domestic investment would increase.

Raising the national saving rate will have positive impacts on the standard of living in the United States. As already shown above, higher rates of domestic saving would ultimately lead to lower U.S. current account deficits. The alternative would be a continuous depreciation of the dollar that could work to adjust the current account toward equilibrium. Adjustment to deficits through depreciation of the currency reduces wealth and income by depressing consumption and investment (domestic absorption) as changes in the trade balance work to transfer resources (cheaper imports) abroad. Without depreciation, growing current account deficits (the value of imports growing faster than the value of exports) increases American unemployment if domestic demand does not rise by an offsetting amount. Thus, a trade balance deficit implies the existence of a transfer of resources to the rest of the world, and adjustment to growing deficits by depreciation of the real exchange rate means that a country continues to lower the world price of its exports at the same time that it pays more for imported goods. In addition, a further transfer of resources abroad is required because of the necessity of financing the accumulated foreign debt.[15]

PLAN OF THIS BOOK

This book addresses the problems created by the large capital inflows into the United States during the 1980s and early 1990s and discusses the outlook for the future. Chapter 2 addresses the growth of international capital mobility in the 1980s. After looking at the growth in gross capital flows for the industrial countries, the chapter examines data for the growth in U.S. capital flows. The chapter then looks at some of the major changes that have taken place in the world financing system in the postwar period, including liberalization of exchange rates and capital controls, securitization, and technological advances in financial markets.

Chapter 3 focuses on foreign direct investment in the United States during the 1980s. First, the role of foreign direct investment in the U.S. economy is addressed. The chapter then examines alternative theories explaining foreign direct investment, including cost of capital theories, theory of the firm explanations, the eclectic paradigm, and models of the strategic behavior of firms toward their foreign operations. Sources of growth of foreign direct investment in the United States are then addressed.

Chapter 4 assesses the role of the United States in producing global capital shortages. The chapter first examines global savings and investment imbalances; it then assesses prospects for reducing the U.S. saving-investment imbalance by raising public-sector savings and the personal saving rate.

Chapter 5 addresses policies that have been suggested to raise the national saving rate. These include proposals to reduce the federal budget deficit beyond the reductions that are projected from OBRA 1993 and policies that could be implemented to raise the personal saving rate.

Chapter 6 focuses on the process whereby under the prevailing flexible exchange rate system, large domestic savings-investment imbalances led to large current account imbalances and capital flows in the United States in the 1980s. The relationship between the level of interest rates and the value of exchange rates is then examined. Subsequently, the balance-of-payments adjustment that occurred from 1985 to 1991 is analyzed in terms of the Mundell-Fleming model. The chapter next looks at several empirical studies of flexible exchange rates and the balance-of-payments adjustment mechanism during the 1985–91 years. Finally, projections for the U.S. current account balance during the mid-1990s are examined.

Chapter 7 assesses global capital requirements in the mid-1990s. In particular, it examines current account projections for industrial countries, developing countries, and countries in transition to market economies. It then examines the recent growth in capital inflows to developing countries and countries in transition to market economies.

Chapter 8 provides a summary and conclusion to the topics covered in the first seven chapters of this book.

NOTES

1. Charles P. Kindleberger, *International Capital Movements* (Cambridge: Cambridge University Press, 1987), p. 36.

2. United States, Council of Economic Advisors, *Economic Report of the President* (Washington, D.C.; Government Printing Office, 1994), p. 241.

3. Ibid., p. 27.

4. C. Fred Bergsten and Marcus Noland, *Reconcilable Differences: United States-Japan Economic Conflict* (Washington, D.C.: Institute for International Economics, 1993), pp. 5–15.

5. Congress of the United States, Congressional Budget Office, *The Economic and Budget Outlook: Fiscal Years 1995–99* (Washington, D.C.: Government Printing Office, January 1994), p. 8.

6. Madis Senner, "The Grim Shortage of Global Capital," *New York Times,* July 6, 1991, p. D10.

7. *Economic Report of the President,* pp. 32–33.

8. Ibid., p. 82.

9. Ibid., pp. 82–83.

10. Ibid., p. 83.

11. Bergsten and Noland, *Reconcilable Differences*, p. 27.

12. *Economic Report of the President*, pp. 39–45.

13. Bergsten and Noland, *Reconcilable Differences*, p. 35.

14. Ibid., pp. 36–38.

15. Robert Z. Lawrence, "The International Dimension," in *American Living Standards: Threats and Challenges*, ed. Robert E. Litan, Robert Z. Lawrence, and Charles Schultze (Washington, D.C.: Brookings Institution, 1988), pp. 23–56.

CHAPTER 2

Changes in Global Capital Markets During the 1980s

Several factors characterize the structure of capital flows in the 1980s, including the rapid growth of direct investment, especially within industrial countries; capital inflows being substituted for declining domestic saving in capital-importing countries instead of being used to increase investment; a sharp growth in aggregate "two-way" capital movements as international assets become more liquid and diversified; and declining capital flows to developing countries in contrast to developed countries.[1] The rapid growth in direct investment in the 1980s will be discussed in Chapter 3. In addition to focusing on the growth in portfolio capital flows in the United States, this chapter will also discuss liberalization of institutions governing capital flows and financial innovations occurring in conjunction with the international movement of capital.

The 1980s was a period of growing current account imbalances and associated capital flows. Not since before World War I had worldwide current account imbalances as a share of gross national product (GNP) been as large.[2] Unlike in earlier years, capital movements increasingly began to take the form of transactions among developed countries, with the proportion going to the developing countries declining. In 1975–79, 34 percent of the total capital flows going to industrial countries and developing countries went to the developing countries as contrasted with 19 percent in 1985–89. This pattern of inflows was brought about by lower savings rates in capital-importing industrial countries.

Table 2.1 shows gross capital flows of fourteen industrial countries as a share of GNP for 1975–89. For all categories of the capital account, out-

Table 2.1
Gross Capital Flows of Fourteen Industrial Countries, 1975–89 (percent of GNP[1])

	1975-84	1985	1986	1987	1988	1989
Outflows (Resident ownership)						
Direct investment	0.6	0.7	0.9	1.2	1.1	1.3
Investment in bonds	0.5	1.3	1.5	0.9	1.3	1.3
Investment in equities	0.1	0.2	0.3	0.2	0.2	0.6
Public-sector investment	0.5	0.4	0.7	1.2	0.6	0.6
Long-term bank lending	0.8	0.5	0.7	0.8	0.8	1.0
Inflows (Nonresident ownership)						
Direct investment	0.4	0.4	0.6	0.8	0.9	1.1
Investment in bonds[2]	0.2	0.9	0.8	0.6	0.8	1.1
Investment in equities	0.1	0.2	0.3	0.0	0.1	0.4
Public-sector borrowing[3]	0.8	0.9	1.2	0.9	0.9	1.1
Long-term bank lending	0.5	0.5	0.7	0.8	0.9	1.1
Short-term bank lending net	0.3	0.5	0.8	1.0	0.6	0.4
Other, net	-0.1	-0.1	-0.5	0.2	0.0	0.1
Net capital flow	-0.6	0.3	-0.2	0.1	0.2	0.5
Current account	-0.2	-0.6	-0.1	-0.2	-0.3	-0.5
Errors and omissions[4]	0.4	0.3	0.3	0.2	0.0	0.1

Source: Philip Turner, *Capital Flows in the 1980's: A Survey of Major Trends.* BIS Economic Papers, No. 30, Basle: Bank for International Settlements, April 1991.

1.   GDP was used for France.
2.   Excludes investment in public-sector bonds.
3.   Includes investment in public-sector bonds.
4.   Equals current account minus net identified capital flows.

flows as well as inflows were a rising share of GNP. Excluding short-term lending, in 1989 inflows for the fourteen industrial countries averaged 4.8 percent of GNP as contrasted with an average of 2 percent for 1975–84. Although a number of industrial countries incurred large government deficits during the 1980s and had to import capital from abroad, because of its economic size, the United States had a much greater impact on world capital markets than other economies.

The current account deficits for all industrial countries and for the United States alone for 1985–91 are given in Table 2.2. For most years, the United States accounted for a large share of the combined current account deficits of industrial countries, this share ranging from 82 percent in 1985 to 7 percent in 1991, an exceptional year because of the weakness in the U.S. economy and the large transfer payments received by the United States for its role in the Gulf War.

During the second half of the 1980s, foreign direct investment comprised a substantial part of U.S. net capital inflows, but net inflows of portfolio

Table 2.2
United States: Summary Balance of Payments, 1985–91 (in billions of U.S. dollars)

	1985	1986	1987	1988	1989	1990	1991
Current Account Balance	-122.2	-143.4	-160.2	-126.4	-106.4	-92.2	-8.7
Net Direct Investment	5.9	15.4	27.1	41.5	37.2	3.8	-7.3
Portfolio Investment							
Bonds	63.8	55.6	13.4	41.7	53.5	-9.7	26.4
Equities	0.6	16.0	17.7	-1.4	-10.3	-21.5	-21.0
Bank Flows	33.3	22.1	46.5	16.1	11.7	16.9	-5.4
Other	4.6	-13.3	5.4	1.3	12.9	10.5	-5.6
Changes in Reserves[1]	-5.8	33.8	56.8	36.3	-17.0	28.5	24.8
Errors and Omissions	19.9	15.9	-6.7	-9.1	18.4	63.6	-3.2
Total Current Account Deficits of Industrial Co.[2]	145.8	177.5	201.7	202.8	215.8	211.1	128.1[3]
Percent U.S.	82.3	81.9	79.4	62.3	49.3	43.7	6.8

Source: International Monetary Fund, World Economic and Financial Surveys, *International Capital Markets: Developments, Prospects and Policy Issues* (Washington, D.C.: International Monetary Fund, September 1992), pp. 26 and 56.

1.   Includes acquisition of liabilities by foreign monetary authorities (- increase).
2.   Sum of all current account deficits, including official transfers.
3.   Estimate

investment (bonds and equities) contributed an even larger proportion. Variations in net portfolio inflows were wide. With the exception of 1987, net bond inflows were substantial over the period 1985–89. Following the stock market crash of 1987, net equity inflows became negative. In some years changes in reserves, including U.S. government liabilities of foreign central banks, made substantial contributions to payments balances.

AGGREGATE CAPITAL ACCOUNT TRANSACTIONS IN THE 1980s

Aggregate capital account transactions of the United States underwent enormous growth during the 1980s.[3] The value of total international securities transactions rose from about $250 billion to almost $5,500 billion between 1980 and 1989 (see Table 2.3). This huge increment was concen-

Table 2.3
U.S. Portfolio Transactions, 1975–89 (in billions of U.S. dollars)

	1975	1980	1985	1987	1989
Total international					
transactions	66.3	251.2	1,497.3	3,911.4	5,473.3
of which					
Bonds	37.0	158.1	1,292.6	3,239.6	4,826.6
Equities	29.3	90.1	204.7	671.8	646.7
U.S. transactions in					
foreign securities					
Bonds					
Purchases	8.7	18.1	85.2	207.0	240.0
Sales	2.4	17.1	81.2	199.1	234.1
Equities					
Purchases	1.7	10.0	24.8	94.4	121.4
Sales	1.6	7.9	20.9	95.5	108.9
Foreign transactions in					
U.S. securities					
Bonds					
Purchases	14.3	66.6	585.2	1,443.3	2,220.7
Sales	11.5	56.3	541.0	1,390.2	2,131.8
Equities					
Purchases	15.4	40.3	82.0	249.1	213.0
Sales	10.7	34.9	77.1	232.8	203.4

Source: Philip Turner, *Capital Flows in the 1980's: A Survey of Major Trends*, BIS Economic
Papers, No. 3 (Basle: Bank for International Settlements), April 1991, p. 29.

Notes: (i)   Data cover transactions between a resident and a nonresident; transactions between
              two foreign residents in a U.S. security and transactions between two U.S.
              residents in a foreign security are excluded.
        (ii) Under U.S. transactions, purchases refer to purchases by U.S. residents (shown as
              foreign sales in the *Treasury Bulletin*).

trated largely in bonds rather than equities, with bonds rising thirtyfold
compared with a sevenfold rise in the value of equity transactions. Given
that U.S. equity prices tripled over the period, the growth in foreign activity
in U.S. securities occurred mainly in bonds.

Several interesting observations emerge from a comparison of U.S. residents' transactions in foreign securities with foreigners' transactions in U.S.
securities. First, the growth in aggregate U.S. transactions in foreign bonds
and equities was much smaller than the growth in foreign transactions in
U.S. securities: aggregate U.S. transactions in foreign securities rose from
$53 billion in 1980 to $664 billion in 1989, whereas foreign transactions
in U.S. securities rose from almost $200 billion to over $4,700 billion.
Second, the increased activity in U.S. securities markets was concentrated
predominantly in bonds.

The growth in the magnitude of purchases and sales in relation to net
capital movements suggests that many of the transactions were actually short

term and relative positions of different countries could have been rapidly reversed. Such transactions are a part of the widening and deepening of international capital markets that occurred during the 1980s. Financial instruments were becoming more diversified, and new financial instruments were developed to better service the needs of borrowers and investors.[4]

The preceding summary has focused on the growth in aggregate portfolio capital flows over the 1980s. Aggregate capital flows include all transactions between residents and nonresidents and, hence, correspond to "turnover" in financial assets. These do not correspond to gross outflows (or inflows), which include purchases by residents (nonresidents) of foreign (domestic) assets minus their sales of these assets. Annual balance-of-payment figures for gross capital flows correspond to these consolidated figures for gross outflows or inflows. Net outflows in the balance of payments are found by subtracting out gross outflows from gross inflows. For instance, the balance on goods and services would be the value of exports minus the value of imports.

BALANCE-OF-PAYMENTS DATA ON CAPITAL FLOWS

Prior to 1976, the U.S. Department of Commerce distinguished between short- and long-term capital flows. Long-term capital transactions included foreign direct investment and portfolio capital (bonds and equities), and short-term transactions consisted of all those embodied in instruments of less than one year's maturity. Using James Meade's terminology developed in 1951, long-term capital transactions were considered "autonomous," whereas short-term capital transactions were considered to be "accommodating."[5] Autonomous transactions are capital flows that take place regardless of the size of other balance-of-payments items. Accommodating capital flows occur because autonomous capital flows alone do not completely add up to the value of current account deficits or surpluses. Foreign direct investment and investment in securities would be considered autonomous. Temporary short-term capital movements and movements in international reserves would be considered accommodating.

Within this context, the concept of the "basic balance"—the balance on current account and long-term capital account—was used to determine the size of the balance that must be financed or accommodated, either by short-term private capital flows or by official reserve transactions. With the concept of the basic balance, the balance on current account and long-term capital account were considered above the line, and transactions on short-term capital account and official reserve transactions were considered below the line and had the role of financing or accommodating transactions above the line.

It has been contended that the concept of the basic balance was applicable as long as exchange rates were fixed; with floating exchange rates, the current account, capital flows, and exchange rate movements were to occur simultaneously, and it would not be possible to distinguish between autonomous and accommodating transactions.

Beginning with 1976 data, the U.S. Department of Commerce focused on the current account balance and no longer distinguished between long-term and short-term capital movements, because with the advent of floating rates, official settlements flows would not necessarily measure official accommodation of balance-of-payments imbalances. In theory, if exchange rates were free to float up and down according to the demand and supply of foreign exchange, official settlements balances would equal zero.

There are at least two other reasons why the distinction is not made between the basic balance and other capital movements. First, long-term investment instruments (equities and bonds) were becoming increasingly liquid so that temporary capital movements could take place in long-term financial instruments. Second, autonomous, short-term capital flows that had little or no relation to balance-of-payments financing increased in importance.[6]

A central concern of this volume is the switch of the United States to an importer of capital. The net inflow of capital on the balance of payments represents the import of savings from abroad, and these savings make up the deficiency between total domestic investment and domestic savings.

U.S. balance-of-payments data are shown in Table 2.4. The current account is made up of the net balance on imports and exports of goods and services plus unilateral transfers. Although current account deficits had occurred during earlier years, the period of large current account deficits commenced in 1983. In that year, the economy was recovering from the 1981–82 recession, and the deficit rose to $44.5 billion. It increased continuously to $167.1 billion by 1987 before declining to $91.7 billion in 1990 and $6.9 billion in 1991. In part, the fall in the size of the deficit resulted from the 50 percent depreciation of the dollar between 1985 and 1991. Because the response of exports to changes in the value of a currency is lagged, it was not until 1987 that merchandise exports of the United States increased significantly. It is noteworthy that despite the depreciation of the dollar between 1985 and 1989, the value of merchandise imports continued to grow, increasing from $338 billion to $477 billion, but with the delayed impact of the weak dollar and the slow growth in national income caused by the recession of 1990–91, the value of imports remained fairly stable between 1989 and 1991. Since the overall balance of payments must balance, large capital imports occurred, and in 1987 the United States became a net debtor instead of a net creditor. Unilateral transfer payments from U.S. allies in the Gulf War amounting to $17.0 billion in 1990 and $42.5 billion in 1991 also contributed to reduction in the current account deficits.

In Table 2.4, U.S. exports of capital are represented in U.S. assets abroad (line 33), and U.S. imports of capital are represented by foreign assets in the United States. The sums of the current account U.S. assets abroad and foreign assets in the United States do not sum to zero because of statistical discrepancies (line 63). The net capital inflow into the United States is the difference between the export of capital (U.S. assets abroad) and imports of capital (foreign assets in the United States). With the exception of a category called "other U.S. government liabilities" (line 53), foreign official assets in the United States represent changes in foreign holdings of reserves in the form of U.S. dollars. Excluding 1989, large foreign purchases of U.S. dollars occurred over the periods 1986–90 and 1992–93.

The category called "other foreign assets" (line 56) shows changes in private capital inflows by foreigners. These include foreign direct investment and long-term and short-term portfolio capital inflows. The large inflows of foreign direct investment (line 57) during the 1980s will be discussed elsewhere. Line 58 represents the changes in foreign private holdings of U.S. government securities. Changes in U.S. securities other than U.S. government securities (line 59) represent net foreign purchases of stocks plus corporate and other bonds. Another large item is U.S. liabilities reported by U.S. banks, not included elsewhere (line 61). These bank-related flows include changes in both long-term and short-term liabilities.

By definition, the current account (CA) equals the sum of the capital account (KA) plus official reserve transactions (ORT): CA = KA + ORT. Because every debit has an offsetting credit somewhere, CA − (KA + ORT) = 0. A current account surplus can be offset when claims on foreigners are accumulated and/or when the central bank acquires foreign assets by adding to its foreign exchange reserves. A current account deficit can be offset when its residents borrow from abroad and/or when the central bank is selling foreign exchange reserves in exchange for domestic currency that private agents want to sell. During the 1980s, U.S. current account deficits were matched by capital inflows as well as Federal Reserve sales of foreign exchange reserves (line 34). These sales were especially large in 1989.

An examination of the U.S. balance of payments for the 1980s indicates the extent to which the United States relied upon the net inflow of private foreign capital during those years. But in a number of years, private net capital inflows were insufficient and foreign central banks made up the difference; inflows of capital that brought about balance-of-payments equilibrium were provided by both private and public sources. Between 1983 and 1985, private capital flows were sufficient to finance the current account deficits. But between 1986 and 1988, private capital inflows were insufficient and foreign central banks made up the difference.

The large falloff in private capital flows continued into the early 1990s (see Table 2.5). For 1990, the current account deficit amounted to $91.9 billion, but net private capital inflows fell to only $27 billion, and $34 billion was supplied by foreign central banks. It was also a year when statistical discrepancies were exceptionally large. In 1991, a year when the current

Table 2.4
U.S. International Transactions, 1975–93 (millions of dollars)

(Credits +; debits −)[1]	1975	1976	1977	1978	1979	1980	1981	1982	1983	1984	1985	1986	1987	1988	1989	1990	1991	1992	1993	Line
Exports of goods, services, and income																				1
Merchandise, adjusted, excluding military[2]																				2
Services[3]																				3
Transfers under U.S. military agency sales contracts[4]																				4
Travel																				5
Passenger fees																				6
Other transportation																				7
Royalties and license fees[5]																				8
Other private services[6]																				9
U.S. Government miscellaneous services																				10
Income receipts on U.S. assets abroad																				11
Direct investment receipts																				12
Other private receipts																				13
U.S. Government receipts																				14
Imports of goods, services, and income																				15
Merchandise, adjusted, excluding military[2]																				16
Services[3]																				17
Direct defense expenditures																				18
Travel																				19
Passenger fees																				20
Other transportation																				21
Royalties and license fees[5]																				22
Other private services[6]																				23
U.S. Government miscellaneous services																				24
Income payments on foreign assets in the United States																				25
Direct investment payments																				26
Other private payments																				27
U.S. Government payments																				28
Unilateral transfers, net																				29
U.S. Government grants[4]																				30
U.S. Government pensions and other transfers																				31
Private remittances and other transfers[4]																				32
U.S. assets abroad, net (increase/capital outflow (−))																				33
U.S. official reserve assets, net[5]																				34
Gold																				35
Special drawing rights																				36
Reserve position in the International Monetary Fund																				37
Foreign currencies																				38
U.S. Government assets, other than official reserve assets, net																				39
U.S. credits and other long-term assets																				40
Repayments on U.S. credits and other long-term assets[5]																				41
U.S. foreign currency holdings and U.S. short-term assets, net																				42
U.S. private assets, net																				43
Direct investment																				44
Foreign securities																				45
U.S. claims on unaffiliated foreigners reported by U.S. nonbanking concerns																				46
U.S. claims reported by U.S. banks, not included elsewhere																				47
Foreign assets in the United States, net (increase/capital inflow (+))																				48
Foreign official assets in the United States, net																				49
U.S. Government securities																				50
U.S. Treasury securities[9]																				51
Other[10]																				52
Other U.S. Government liabilities[11]																				53
U.S. liabilities reported by U.S. banks, not included elsewhere																				54
Other foreign official assets[12]																				55
Other foreign assets in the United States, net																				56
Direct investment																				57
U.S. Treasury securities																				58

20

U.S. securities other than U.S. Treasury securities — rows 59–70

Line		Line
59	U.S. securities other than U.S. Treasury securities	59
60	U.S. liabilities to unaffiliated foreigners reported by U.S. nonbanking concerns	60
61	U.S. liabilities reported by U.S. banks, not included elsewhere	61
62	Allocations of special drawing rights	62
63	Statistical discrepancy (sum of above items with sign reversed)	63
	Memoranda:	
64	Balance on merchandise trade (lines 2 and 16)	64
65	Balance on services (lines 3 and 17)	65
66	Balance on goods and services (lines 64 and 65)	66
67	Balance on investment income (lines 11 and 25)	67
68	Balance on goods, services, and income (lines 1 and 15 or lines 66 and 67)	68
69	Unilateral transfers, net (line 29)	69
70	Balance on current account (lines 1, 15, and 29 or lines 68 and 69)	70

Source: U.S. Department of Commerce, Economics and Statistics Administration, Bureau of Economic Analysis, *Survey of Current Business*, 79, no. 6 (June 1994). **1.** Credits, +: Exports of goods, services, and income; unilateral transfers to United States; capital inflows (increase in foreign assets (U.S. liabilities) or decrease in U.S. assets); decrease in U.S. official reserve assets; increase in foreign official assets in the United States. Debits, −: Imports of goods, services, and income; unilateral transfers to foreigners; capital outflows (decrease in foreign assets (U.S. liabilities) or increase in U.S. assets); increase in U.S. official reserve assets; decrease in foreign official assets in the United States. **2.** Excludes exports of goods under U.S. military agency sales contracts identified in Census import documents, and reflects various other adjustments (for valuation, coverage, and timing) of Census statistics to balance of payments basis; see table 2. **3.** Includes some goods: Mainly military equipment in line 4; major equipment, other materials, supplies, and petroleum products purchased abroad by U.S. military agencies in line 18; and fuels purchased by airline and steamship operators in lines 7 and 21. **4.** Includes transfers of goods and services under U.S. military grant programs. **5.** Beginning in 1982, these lines are presented on a gross basis. The definition of exports is revised to exclude U.S. parents' payments to foreign affiliates and to include U.S. affiliates' receipts from foreign parents. The definition of imports is revised to include U.S. parents' payments to foreign affiliates and to exclude U.S. affiliates' receipts from foreign parents. **6.** Beginning in 1982, the "other transfers" component includes taxes paid by U.S. private residents to foreign governments and taxes paid by private nonresidents to the U.S. Government. **7.** For all areas, amounts outstanding March 31, 1994, were as follows in millions of dollars: Line 34, 76,810; line 35, 11,052; line 36, 9,383; line 37, 12,135; line 38, 44,239. Data are preliminary. **8.** Includes sales of foreign obligations to foreigners. **9.** Consists of bills, certificates, marketable bonds and notes, and nonmarketable convertible and nonconvertible bonds and notes. **10.** Consists of U.S. Treasury and Export-Import Bank obligations, not included elsewhere, and of debt securities of U.S. Government corporations and agencies. **11.** Includes, primarily, U.S. Government liabilities associated with military agency sales contracts and other transactions arranged with or through foreign official agencies; see table 4. **12.** Consists of investments in U.S. corporate stocks and in debt securities of private corporations and state and local governments. **13.** Conceptually, the sum of lines 70 and 62 is equal to "net foreign investment" in the national income and product accounts (NIPA's). However, the foreign transactions account in the NIPA's (a) includes adjustments to the international transactions accounts for the treatment of gold, (b) includes adjustments for the different geographical treatment of transactions with U.S. territories and Puerto Rico, and (c) includes services furnished without payment by financial pension plans except life insurance carriers and private noninsured pension plans. A reconciliation of the balance on goods and services from the international accounts and the NIPA net exports appears in the "Reconciliation and Other Special Tables" section in this issue of the *Survey of Current Business*. A reconciliation of the other foreign transactions in the two sets of accounts appears in table 4.5 of the full set of NIPA tables (published annually in the July issue of the *Survey*). Additional footnotes for historical data in June issues of the *Survey*. **14.** For 1974, includes extraordinary U.S. Government transactions with India. See "Special U.S. Government Transactions," June 1974 *Survey*, p. 27. **15.** For 1978–83, includes foreign currency-denominated notes sold to private residents abroad. **16.** Break in series. See Technical Notes in the June 1989, June 1990, June 1992, and June 1993 *Survey* issues.

Table 2.5
U.S. Balance of Payments, 1988–93 (billions of dollars)

Item	1988	1989	1990	1991	1992	1993	Changes 1992-93
U.S. Current Account							
Goods and services, net	-114.9	-90.3	-78.3	-27.9	-39.7	-76.7	-37.0
Trade balance	-127.0	-115.2	-109.0	-73.8	-96.2	-132.4	-36.2
Services, net	12.1	24.9	30.7	45.9	56.4	55.7	-.7
Investment income, net	12.6	14.9	20.3	13.1	6.2	.1	-62
Direct investment, net	38.7	48.9	56.2	52.8	48.3	46.0	-23
Portfolio invesstment, net	-26.1	-34.0	-35.9	-39.7	-42.0	-45.9	-39
Unilateral transfers, net	-25.0	-26.1	-33.8	6.6	-32.9	-32.5	.4
Foreign cash grants to the U.S.	*	*	17.0	42.5	1.3	*	-1.3
Other transfers	-25.0	-26.1	-50.8	-35.9	-34.2	-32.5	1.7
Current account balance	-127.2	-101.6	-91.9	-8.3	-66.4	-109.2	-42.8
Memo							
Current account balance excluding foreign cash grants	-127.2	-101.6	-108.9	-50.8	-67.7	-109.2	-41.5
Composition of U.S. Capital Flows							
Official capital, net	39	-16	34	26	43	70	27
Foreign official assets in the U.S.	40	9	34	18	41	71	30
U.S. official reserve assets	-4	-25	-2	6	4	-1	-5
Other U.S. government assets	3	1	2	3	-2	-0	2
Private capital, net	88	100	27	-3	36	13	-23
Net inflows reported by U.S. banking offices.	14	5	32	-8	44	47	3
Securities transactions, net	35	43	-34	10	15	-21	-36
Private foreign net purchases of							
U.S. Treasury securities	20	30	-3	19	37	24	-13
U.S. corporate bonds[1]	23	28	12	27	31	61	30
U.S. corporate stocks	-1	7	-15	10	-4	18	22
U.S. net purchases of foreign securities	-8	-22	-29	-45	-48	-125	-77
Direct investment, net	45	35	25	-6	-28	-19	9
Foreign direct investment in U.S.	57	68	48	24	2	32	30
U.S. direct investment abroad[1]	-12	-33	-23	-30	-31	-50	-19
Other	-7	17	3	1	5	6	1
Statistical discrepancy	0	17	31	-15	-12	27	39

Source: William Helkie, "U.S. International Transactions in 1992," *Federal Reserve Bulletin*, May 1993, p. 387, and Catherine L. Mann, "U.S. International Transactions in 1993," *Federal Reserve Bulletin*, May 1994, pp. 365-78. Data taken from U.S. Department of Commerce, Bureau of Economic Analysis, U.S. International transactions accounts.

*Less than 0.05.

1. Transactions with finance affiliates in the Netherlands Antilles have been excluded from direct investment outflows and added to foreign purchases of U.S. securities through 1992. This adjustment was discontinued in 1993 because of the assumption that virtually all the Eurobonds issued by the Netherlands Antilles affiliates before mid-1994 have already come due.

account deficit had declined to only $8.3 billion, the United States experienced a net outflow of private capital of $3 billion. Unilateral transfers from U.S. allies after the Gulf War helped reduce the current account deficit.

The current account deficit widened to $66.4 billion in 1992 and $109.2 billion in 1993. The growth in the deficit in 1992 can largely be attributed to a return of unilateral transfers to a more normal level and an expansion in economic activity in the United States. The continued worsening of the deficit in 1993 occurred largely because growth in most major U.S. markets abroad remained slow while domestic economic activity rebounded. Deterioration in net goods and services and investment income caused the deficit to increase by almost $43 billion.[7]

In both 1992 and 1993, net official capital inflows offset more than 60 percent of current account deficits. In 1993 the net inflow of private capital into the United States totalled only $13 billion, even though private capital inflows had totalled $186 billion because private capital outflows in the form of securities transactions and foreign direct investment were much greater than in earlier years. On net, U.S. private purchases of foreign securities increased from $48 billion in 1992 to $125 billion in 1993, and it has been argued that the increase in deregulation of foreign financial markets, higher returns in foreign markets than in the United States, and a desire to diversify portfolios have raised U.S. investors' demand for foreign stocks and bonds. In 1993, over 80 percent of net purchases of foreign securities were from industrial countries.[8]

U.S. foreign direct investment abroad rose to a record level of $50 billion in 1993. Foreign direct investment in the United States rose to $32 billion in 1993, but remained substantially below levels reached in 1986–90.

STRUCTURAL CHANGES IN THE WORLD FINANCING SYSTEM

In order to analyze the change in U.S. capital flows during the 1980s and early 1990s, it is necessary to comprehend some of the structural changes that have taken place in the world financing system in the postwar period. These changes occurred simultaneously with the growing integration of the global economy.

Liberalization of restrictions on the movement of foreign exchange and capital across national borders and cost-reducing technological innovations in financial markets, which greatly reduced transactions costs, have helped to produce intense competition in the financial systems of major industrial countries. By the early 1990s, domestic financial markets had become more adaptive and international, and segmented financial structures were becoming broader based and integrated. It is contended that competition has led to disintermediation from banking systems, especially from wholesale banking, into securitized money and capital markets.[9] These three factors—liberalization, technological advances in financial markets, and securitization—are structural changes that occurred simultaneously with changes in movements in the U.S. capital account.

LIBERALIZATION OF EXCHANGE AND CAPITAL CONTROLS

In a world in which international trade occurs, foreign exchange is used to pay for commodities and services. In the immediate postwar period, trade restrictions were high as many countries imposed exchange restrictions and capital controls. A primary goal of the International Monetary Fund (IMF) in the postwar period was to have exchange restrictions on payments for current transactions lowered[10] and to oversee a reduction in barriers to trade. However, because it was widely believed that during the 1920s and 1930s capital flows had been disequilibriating and had been a primary cause of the economic crisis during the interwar period, the original Articles of Agreement of the IMF allowed countries to impose such controls as were necessary to restrict international capital movements.[11] Except for use in current external payments, most other types of capital movements were assumed to be disruptive. It was not until after 1973, with the change to a system of floating exchange rates, that the major industrial countries removed or lowered remaining capital controls.

The U.S. dollar functioned as the key currency during the Bretton Woods era of fixed exchange rates (1946–73). Because of its role as a key currency, the dollar could not be devalued even if the demand for the dollar was weak. In the 1960s, when many countries holding overseas dollar balances began increasingly to convert these dollar balances into gold, the United States imposed controls to prevent further capital outflows.

During the 1960s, capital outflows from the United States were occurring because the current account was generally in surplus. Yet foreign countries were becoming less willing to absorb further dollar balances and were converting dollars for gold. As the U.S. gold stock was being diminished, the United States adopted more stringent capital controls to prevent a further outflow of capital. One such control came in the form of an "interest equalization tax" that reduced the rate of return on foreign assets, thereby reducing the attractiveness of U.S. investment abroad. Another action to control capital outflow was the program implemented to limit foreign lending by U.S. banks.

After March 1973, when the Bretton Woods system of fixed exchange rates was abandoned, capital controls that had been implemented by the United States and other major industrial countries during the 1960s and 1970s were no longer deemed necessary, and these controls were either eliminated entirely or relaxed.

The history of capital controls is more complex for many of the European countries that restored convertibility for current account transactions only in 1958 following the postwar reconstruction period. One of the outcomes of these actions was to "undermine the distinction made between current account payments which were welcome and capital account transactions that were not, which in turn lessened governmental restraints on capital accounts generally."[12] Despite the trend toward reducing such controls, some European countries that, like the United States, had been concerned about the balance of payments and pressure on exchange rates, imposed capital controls in the 1960s and 1970s.

Some controls on capital outflows still remained in place in the United Kingdom until 1979, and even though London was home to the largest

Euromarket, legal restrictions prevented British banks from merging their "offshore" and domestic accounts.[13] The separateness of these two types of accounts was reflected in substantial differentials between the Europound interest rate and the U.K. interbank rate. For instance, the three-month Europound rate exceeded the U.K. interbank rate by an average of 1.43 percent per annum.[14] Yet beginning in 1979, when the remaining controls were abolished, the differential was already close to zero.[15]

France and Italy maintained effective capital controls into the 1980s. After 1986, in order to meet the 1990 deadline for liberalization imposed upon them by the twelve-member European Community, capital controls were dismantled in both countries.

Germany and Japan were two of the countries that maintained capital controls to prevent the inflow of capital that would have put upward pressure on exchange rates and lessened their ability to maintain monetary independence.

In Germany, controls put into place in the early 1970s were designed to prevent foreigners from acquiring German assets. The German government imposed three types of controls: (1) a prohibition on payments of interest to nonresidents on large bank accounts; (2) taxation of any new credits by nonresidents to German banks; and (3) prohibition of the purchase of German bonds by nonresidents. These controls were effective in restricting capital inflows, and for the period 1970–74, the mark interest rate in Frankfurt remained in excess of the Euromark interest rate. In 1981 Germany removed restrictions on the purchase of domestic bonds and money market instruments by nonresidents. After the removal of German capital controls, the interest differential declined sharply.[16]

Unlike many other industrial countries that reduced capital controls after the advent of floating exchange rates in 1973, Japan maintained strict controls on capital inflows until 1980. The controls prohibited foreign residents from holding assets in Japan. The long-term upward trend in the yen against the dollar was reversed in 1979, increasing the competitiveness of Japanese imports. Because the Japanese were more confident of their exporters' ability to compete on world markets, foreigners were exerting political pressure to buy Japanese assets, and the government did not consider a sharp depreciation of the yen desirable. The Ministry of Finance removed prohibitions on foreign investment in 1980. Subsequently, further liberalization measures were undertaken, especially in 1984, as a consequence of pressure from the U.S. government.[17] In conjunction with liberalization, between 1979 and 1983 the interest differential between the three-month interest rate in Tokyo and the European rate fell sharply to a negative 0.26 percent in November 1983. The plan to remove Japan's remaining capital controls in May 1984 accelerated the yen depreciation and capital outflow from Japan.

By the early 1980s, capital controls in all the major industrial countries and in most smaller industrial countries had been almost abolished. The removal of capital controls in conjunction with a system of managed floating of exchange rates was instrumental in developing an environment conducive to the growth of international capital markets.

SECURITIZATION

Within the past few decades, a number of changes occurred in international banking. These include the development of the Eurodollar market in the 1960s and large-scale lending by commercial banks to developing countries during the 1970s. After the less-developed country debt problem emerged during the early 1980s, banks retrenched their lending operations to developing countries, and international bank lending declined. In the United States, the public became concerned about the stability of the banking system, and the Federal Reserve and other regulatory agencies pressured the banks to raise their capital-to-loan ratio. Consequently, banks began to rely less on lending to earn income and more on fees for other services. During the early 1980s, a process of financial disintermediation occurred whereby the ultimate borrowers and lenders bypassed financial intermediaries.

This process of international financial disintermediation, referred to as "securitization," was a competition-driven disintermediation from the banking system into securitized capital and money markets. Creditworthy corporate borrowers in major industrial countries could satisfy their financing, liquidity, and risk management requirements by participating directly in liquid securities markets.[18] Instead of engaging in financial intermediation with ultimate savers lending to financial institutions, which then lent to the ultimate borrowers, deposit liabilities were leaving the banking system as funds flowed into liquid securities such as bonds.

With such a pattern, some of the risk that would have been borne by the financial intermediary would be shifted forward to the purchasers and backward to issuers of securities. This process has been called the "unbundling" of risk.

For the early 1980s, securitization coincided with a reduction in the dominance of bank-intermediated international financial flows as flows through capital markets became increasingly more important. It has been shown that for the period 1981–85, of the new lending facilities arranged in international financial markets, the securities market facilities (international bond issues plus note issuance facilities) as a share of total new facilities rose from 25.5 percent to 91 percent.[19]

The International Monetary Fund refers to securitization as a key feature in the new financial environment in which relationship banking was being replaced by transactions-driven securities finance.[20] Aggregate portfolio data show the declining importance of the banking sector in the United States, Germany, and Japan (see Table 2.6). In both Germany and Japan, the share

Table 2.6
Germany, Japan, and the United States: Indicators of Relative Importance of
Banks in Financial Activities of Corporations and Households, 1980, 1985,
and 1990 (in percent)

	Bank Deposits as a Proportion of Corporate Financial Assets	Bank Deposits as a Proportion of Household Financial Assets	Bank Loans as a Proportion of Corporate Liabilities
Germany			
1980	57.7	60.5	63.3
1985	51.1	54.5	60.9
1990	43.8	48.9	61.3
Japan			
1980	78.9	64.4	67.4
1985	77.8	58.5	67.4
1990	46.5	53.2	58.8
United States			
1980	17.8	23.1	33.0
1985	21.5	23.4	29.2
1990	18.8	21.3	25.4

Source: International Monetary Fund, World Economic and Financial Surveys, *International Capital Markets: Developments, Prospects, and Policy Issues* (Washington, D.C.: International Monetary Fund, September 1992), p. 3.

of corporate and household deposits in financial assets declined significantly over the 1980s. (A similar trend took place in the United States in the early 1980s.) At the same time, bank loans as a share of corporate liabilities declined steadily for all three countries.

The assumption of a continued trend away from international bank financing has been questioned. A study by the Bank for International Settlements (BIS) looked at estimated net lending in international markets. Included in total financing were bank lending and bond financing. It showed that after the abnormally high level of bank lending reached a peak of over 80 percent of total net international financing in 1981 (mainly as a consequence of bank lending to developing countries), it declined and by the mid-1980s bank lending and bond financing each represented about one-half of total international financing. However, BIS data indicate that after 1985 this process of securitization appears to have been reversed as bank lending resumed, particularly among industrial countries. By 1989, bank lending represented three-fourths of all international financing recorded by the BIS, and bond financing represented the remainder. However, foreign holdings of domestic bonds are not included in these statistics of international lending, and during the 1980s there was a large growth in foreign holdings of domestic bonds.[21]

TECHNOLOGICAL INNOVATIONS
IN FINANCIAL MARKETS

Following the demise of the system of fixed exchange rates and the lib-eralization of capital flows, the need for a whole spectrum of innovations arose. One group of innovations stemmed from the necessity of avoiding currency risk associated with floating exchange rates. Any entity that en-counters the necessity of making future foreign-currency-denominated pay-ments or receiving payment in a foreign currency at some future date is exposed to the risk of future exchange rate changes.

With the growth of world trade and increasing globalization of the world economy by multinationals, the need for hedging and arbitraging facilities increased. Further needs for innovation arose from the growth of foreign currency trading and the growing diversification into international portfo-lios, involving both short-term and long-term securities transactions. These activities dramatically increased the lending and borrowing of multiple cur-rencies across national boundaries and the relative importance of banking assets having a cross-border or cross-currency characteristic. For instance, in December 1982 banking offices in fifteen industrial countries and eight off-shore banking centers reported banking assets of nearly $2.7 trillion having some international characteristics. By the spring of 1986 this figure had increased by at least $800 billion.

Eurocurrency banking and international banking in general are interbank phenomena and less than one-third of banking claims having international characteristics represent claims on nonbanking economic units. Conse-quently, international banking has been regarded as largely a phenomenon whereby funds are channelled among financial institutions themselves. It is less involved in providing direct financial intermediation and maturity trans-formation between ultimate savers and ultimate borrowers.[22]

Note issuance facilities and Eurocommercial paper facilities are medium-term arrangements that let a borrower issue a series of short-term debt ob-ligations backed by bank underwriting commitments (usually referred to as Euronotes). A further development in the market for Euronotes was the emergence in the mid-1980s of the Eurocommercial paper market. How-ever, although Eurocommercial paper facilities allow a borrower to issue short-term Euronotes, they are not backed by guarantees or commitments from banks. The Eurocommercial paper market has almost displaced the market for other Euronotes in recent years because of a wider range of maturities and a greater flexibility of issuance procedures.[23]

Fluctuating exchange rates and interest rate differentials between different countries introduce elements of risk into day-to-day transactions. As a con-sequence of such risk, markets for derivative securities have developed; and in recent years the most significant development has been the expansion of trading in these derivative securities,[24] which include forward rate agreements, foreign exchange futures, currency swaps, and currency options.

The forward exchange market evolved after the advent of floating exchange rates. Participants can protect themselves against the risk of changes in the exchange rate after they commit themselves to a transaction but before they get paid. For instance, French exporters who invoice exports to the United States in dollars would risk a loss if the value of the dollar in terms of the French franc were to fall before the dollars are converted to francs. The exporter can be protected by "hedging" or selling the dollar forward for future delivery at a certain rate on a given date. Importers and investors in short-term overseas securities such as U.S. Treasury bills also can hedge currency risk in the forward exchange market. Speculators participate in the forward exchange market by taking an exposed (or open) position.

In addition to hedgers and speculators, a third set of participants in the forward exchange market are "covered interest arbitragers." Covered interest arbitrage would occur were an investor to invest in a foreign security instead of a domestic security. For instance, if a one-year U.S. Treasury note pays one percentage point less than a one-year U.K. Treasury note, an American investor may invest in the U.K. asset if the risk that the pound/dollar exchange rate might change can be eliminated. The investor uses the forward market to be certain the risk is eliminated and the U.K. asset is covered.

An active market exists in foreign exchange futures. A futures contract usually calls for delivery of a specific amount of a given financial instrument at a fixed date in the future. The contracts are standardized, and buyers and sellers need only agree on the price and number of contracts traded. The International Financial Futures Exchange places minimum margin requirements on contracts to prevent against default.

Whereas a forward foreign exchange contract occurs between a bank and an individual, a futures foreign exchange transaction occurs within an organized exchange dealing in standardized contracts. The futures market is more liquid than the forward market. Also, unlike the forward foreign exchange markets, there are only a limited number of days on which futures markets mature. This results from the smallness of the market compared to commercial banks' forward markets. Finally, foreign exchange futures are traded on centralized exchanges whereas the banking system arranges for forward transactions.

Forward agreements exist only for time horizons of up to one year. Investors in overseas bonds would thus be exposed to exchange rate risk. With currency swap instruments, two counterparties in different countries issue bonds denominated in the other's currency and agree to exchange streams of interest payment obligations over time. Even more popular than currency swaps are interest rate swaps—one way of managing risk if variable interest rates are used.

Another set of innovations is currency and interest rate options. Unlike the holder of a forward contract, the holder of an option has the right but not the obligation to exercise the option on the underlying security at a fixed price (strike price) before or at a given future date. Call and put options exist. For instance, the holder of a call option has the right to buy deutsche marks (DMs) in the future while the holder of a put option has the right to sell DMs. Options are frequently used for speculative purposes.[25]

The introduction of financial innovations in the 1980s encouraged securitization by separating and shifting risks. Instead of transactions involving direct intermediation by banks or other financial intermediaries, a whole range of marketable securities was created that bypassed intermediation by banks.[26]

NOTES

1. Philip Turner, *Capital Flows in the 1980s: A Survey of Major Trends,* BIS Economic Papers, No. 30 (Basle: Bank for International Settlements, April 1991), pp. 21–28.

2. Ibid., pp. 13–20.

3. Ibid., p. 31. Aggregate transactions include the value of all transactions between residents and nonresidents (the turnover in financial assets).

4. Ibid., pp. 28–29.

5. James E. Meade, *The Theory of International Economic Policy,* Vol. 1: *The Balance of Payments* (Oxford: Oxford University Press, 1951).

6. Turner, *Capital Flows in the 1980s,* pp. 84–85.

7. Catherine Mann, "U.S. International Transactions in 1993," *Federal Reserve Bulletin,* May 1994:366–68. The principal determinants of changes in U.S. trade flows and the current account balance are changes in relative prices of exports and imports and rates of economic activity in the United States and its trading partners abroad. Since 1989, relative prices have remained fairly constant, and differences between rates of economic growth in the United States and its major trading partners have been the major factor affecting the external balance. Econometric analyses have estimated that the responsiveness of U.S. imports to changes in U.S. economic activity is 1.25 to 1.67 times greater than the responsiveness of U.S. exports to similar changes in economic activity abroad. Because relative prices are projected to remain fairly constant in the near term, the size of the current account deficit in the near future will be dependent on the growth in economic activity of U.S. trading partners.

8. Ibid., pp. 376–78.

9. International Monetary Fund, World Economic and Financial Surveys, *International Capital Markets: Developments, Prospects, and Policy Issues* (Washington, D.C.: International Monetary Fund, September 1992), pp. 2–3.

10. International Monetary Fund. *Articles of Agreement* (Washington, D.C.: International Monetary Fund, 1968), pp. 2–3.

11. Ibid.

12. Ralph Bryant, *International Financial Intermediation* (Washington, D.C.: Brookings Institution, 1987), p. 70.

13. Michael Artis and Mark Taylor, "Abolishing Exchange Control: The U.S. Experience," in *Policy Issues for Interdependent Economies,* ed. A. Courtis and M. Taylor (London: Macmillan, 1990).

14. Richard Caves, Jeffrey A. Frankel, and Ronald W. Jones, *World Trade and Payments: An Introduction,* 5th ed. (Glenview, Ill.: Scott, Foresman Little, Brown Higher Education, 1990), p. 530.

15. Jacob Frenkel and Richard Levich, "Transactions Costs and Interest Arbitrage: Tranquil Versus Turbulent Periods," *Journal of Political Economy,* 85, no. 6 (1977): 1209–26; and Jacob Frenkel and Richard Levich, "Covered Interest Arbitrage in the 1970s," *Economic Letters,* 8, no. 3 (1981):267–74.

16. Michael Dooley and Peter Isard, "Capital Controls, Political Risk and Deviations from Interest Rate Parity," *Journal of Political Economy,* 88, no. 2 (April 1980):370–84.

17. Jeffrey Frankel, *The Yen-Dollar Agreement: Liberalizing Japanese Capital Markets* (Washington, D.C.: Institute for International Economics, 1984).

18. IMF, *International Capital Markets,* p. 2.

19. Bryant, *International Financial Intermediation,* p. 56.

20. IMF, *International Capital Markets,* pp. 2–5.

21. Turner, *Capital Flows in the 1980s,* pp. 33–34.

22. Bryant, *International Financial Intermediation,* pp. 28–30.

23. Ibid., pp. 51–53.

24. International Monetary Fund, World Economic and Financial Surveys, *International Capital Markets: Part I, Exchange Rate Management and International Capital Flows* (Washington, D.C.: International Monetary Fund, April 1993), p. 4.

25. Caves, Frankel, and Jones, *World Trade and Payments,* pp. 546–48; and IMF, *International Capital Markets: Part I,* pp. 24–39.

26. Bryant, *International Financial Intermediation,* p. 54.

CHAPTER 3

Foreign Direct Investment in the United States

CHARACTERISTICS OF FOREIGN DIRECT INVESTMENT IN THE UNITED STATES

During the 1980s, the pattern of foreign direct investment inflows into the United States differed markedly from the pattern of the preceding period. Balance-of-payments data indicate that it was only by the early 1980s that capital inflows of foreign direct investment (FDI) exceeded outflows. During the 1980s, foreign-owned affiliates of U.S. businesses produced an increasing, though still small, share of U.S. GDP and accounted for a growing proportion of U.S. nonbank employment, indicating that the effect of FDI on the U.S. economy had become more important.

Although the role of FDI in the U.S. economy grew substantially during the 1980s, in comparison to the size of the U.S. economy, U.S. affiliates of foreign-owned firms still play a relatively small role. For instance in 1990, affiliates accounted for 5.0 percent of all nonbank employment, and 4.4 percent of GDP. Even in manufacturing, which accounted for a substantial share of FDI by 1990, affiliates employed only 10.5 percent of manufacturing employees and accounted for 14.5 percent of sales in manufacturing. U.S. affiliates' share of the book value of total assets of all U.S. manufacturing business amounted to 18.6 percent.

Concern about the growing role of FDI in the United States has been increasing, but as indicated above, foreign-owned firms still play a minor role in the U.S. economy. The relative increase in the role mirrored the changing nature of the international economy. The net outflows of U.S.

foreign direct investment abroad from the 1950s through the 1970s reflected the dominant role of the United States in the international economy. By the 1960s and 1970s, many European and Japanese firms were reaching maturity and beginning to compete internationally with older, more established firms. It was a natural outcome that FDI inflows into the United States would increase in conjunction with the changing nature of international competition.

THE ROLE OF FOREIGN DIRECT INVESTMENT IN THE U.S. ECONOMY

This section examines alternative measures of the role of FDI by foreign-owned affiliates in the U.S. economy. These indicators include the shares of nonbank gross product and employment accounted for by U.S. affiliates; comparisons of productivity growth, compensation per worker, and research and development expenditures; and the shares of manufacturing assets and sales accounted for by U.S. affiliates.

The flows of FDI into the United States as measured in the capital account of the balance of payments is a commonly used measure of changes in foreign control of the U.S. economy. Although FDI inflows into the United States were increasing during the 1970s, it was only by 1981 that the U.S. became a net importer of direct investment capital (see Table 3.1). From 1981 to 1986 net direct investment inflows averaged $11 billion. Between 1987 and 1989 these inflows accelerated and averaged $37.2 billion over the period, but since the U.S. recession that commenced in 1990 the reduction in net direct investment inflows was exceptionally large. These net inflows fell to $12.4 billion in 1990. Beginning in 1991, FDI outflows exceeded inflows, and net outflows averaged $23.9 billion during 1991–93.

The growth of the role of FDI in the United States during the 1980s can be illustrated by examining a number of different measures. Table 3.2 sets forth a number of indexes of the FDI role in the U.S. economy. One indicator of the contribution of U.S. affiliates to the U.S. economy is their share of nonbank gross product. Between 1977 and 1980, U.S. affiliates increased their share of gross product from 2.3 to 3.3 percent.[1] By 1990 this share had increased to 4.4 percent. Over the period, U.S. affiliates' contribution to U.S. output was concentrated largely in manufacturing and wholesale trade. In 1977, manufacturing contributed 47.3 percent and wholesale trade contributed 14.3 percent to affiliates' gross product. Whereas the manufacturing share remained fairly constant, wholesale trade declined to 12.4 percent in 1987 and 10.4 percent in 1990 as other activities—including finance (excluding banking), insurance, and other services—were becoming a little more significant.[2] U.S. affiliate output has been much more heavily concentrated in manufacturing and wholesaling than were all U.S. nonbank businesses. For instance, in 1987 manufacturing and whole-

Table 3.1
U.S. Foreign Direct Investment Flows, 1973–93 (millions of dollars)

Year	Capital Outflow	Capital Inflow	Net Inflow
1973	-11,353	2,800	- 8,553
1974	- 9,052	4,760	- 4,292
1975	-14,244	2.603	-11,641
1976	-11,949	4,347	- 7,602
1977	-11,890	3,728	- 8,162
1978	-16,056	7,897	- 8,159
1979	-25,222	11,877	-13,345
1980	-19,222	16,918	- 2,304
1981	- 9,624	25,195	-15,571
1982	991	12,464	13,455
1983	- 4,889	10,457	5,568
1984	-10,948	24,748	13,800
1985	-13,401	20,010	6,609
1986	-17,090	35,623	18,533
1987	-27,181	58,219	31,038
1988	-15,448	57,278	41,830
1989	-28,995	67,872	38,877
1990	-32,694	45,137	12,443
1991	-27,135	11,497	-15,638
1992	-34,791	2,378	-32,413
1993	-50,244	31,519	-19,625

Source: U.S. Department of Commerce, Bureau of Economic Analysis, "International Investment Position of the United States in 1991," *Survey of Current Business*, June 1992, Table 1, pp. 78-79, and "U.S. International Transactions, Fourth Quarter and Year 1993," *Survey of Current Business*, March 1994, Table L, p. 59.

saling comprised only 24 percent and 9 percent, respectively, of U.S. gross product.

U.S. affiliates were an important contributor to the growth of output in manufacturing. Between 1977 and 1987 their share in the gross product of all manufacturing rose from 3.7 to 8.6 percent.[3] This share rose to 11.5 percent in 1990.

Another way to evaluate the role of U.S. affiliates is to examine employment. Here, the quantity of U.S. affiliates' employment is compared with that for all U.S. business nonbank employment as well as for manufacturing alone. Nonbank U.S. affiliates increased their employment from 1.2 to 4.7 million workers between 1977 and 1990. Their employment more than tripled at the same time that employment by all nonbank U.S. business rose by a little over one-fourth. Between 1977 and 1987, the share of all nonbank employment by U.S. affiliates increased from 1.8 to 4.1 percent, and then rose to 5 percent by 1990. This large growth largely reflected acquisitions of U.S. companies by foreign investors.

Classified by industry of sales, manufacturing accounts for a little over four-tenths of total U.S. affiliate employment, accounting for 2 million out

Table 3.2

Alternative Measures of the Role of Foreign-Owned Affiliates in the U.S. Economy, 1977–90 (percent of U.S. totals)

	1977	1980	1987	1989	1990
All Nonbank Private Affiliates					
Gross Product	2.3	3.3	3.5	4.3	4.4
Employment	1.8	2.7	4.1	4.8	5.0
Manufacturing Affiliates					
Gross Product	3.7	3.5	8.6	10.9	11.5
Employment	3.6	8.2	9.3	10.6	
Assets	6.3	8.3	14.7	17.6	18.6
Sales	5.0	7.1	12.7	14.9	14.5
R&D Expenditures	4.1	5.7	10.9		
Merchandise Trade					
Exports	20.2	23.1	18.9	23.7	23.5
Imports	29.0	31.5	35.3	36.3	36.9

Sources: U.S. Department of Commerce, Bureau of Economic Analysis, *Survey of Current Business*, various issues, and U.S. Department of Commerce, Economics and Statistics Administration, *Foreign Direct Investment in the United States: Review and Analysis of Current Developments* (Washington, D.C.: Government Printing Office, August 1991), pp. 20 and 30, and Table 5-2, Table 5-4, Table 5-5, Table 5-7, Table 5-9, and Table 5-18.

of 4.7 million workers in 1990. Retailing plus wholesaling accounted for another one-fourth.

A comparison of productivity growth and average compensation per employee can also help assess the role of U.S. affiliates in the economy. Proponents of FDI often argue that foreign firms are a source of technological change, and hence contribute to productivity growth. Growth in productivity can be assessed by looking at output per person employed. A Department of Commerce study has shown that in both 1980 and 1987, average gross product per employee grew more rapidly in U.S. manufacturing affiliates than in the manufacturing sector as a whole. The same study also found that in conjunction with higher productivity growth, the average earnings of workers employed by foreign-owned firms were about 20 percent higher than the average amount received by all U.S. workers—$30,517 as contrasted with $25,489 per worker for all U.S. workers in 1988.[4]

Although data for all industries indicate that compensation paid by U.S. affiliates is greater than for all U.S. firms, it has been shown that the difference is caused by variations in industrial composition. Heavy concentration of foreign ownership in capital-intensive industries such as petroleum refining and mining raise the average compensation per employee of U.S. affiliates. However, for manufacturing as a whole and for industries within manufacturing, no systematic difference is evident between foreign and all U.S. firms.[5]

Assuming that higher capital intensity tends to increase wages paid to workers because they would be more productive with more and better tools, the Department of Commerce study compared capital intensity in manufacturing firms of U.S. affiliates to all U.S. manufacturing. Although data were not available to measure capital intensity directly, an indirect comparison was made by comparing annual plant and equipment data per employee. The data suggest that on the average, U.S. affiliates have greater capital intensity than all U.S. manufacturing. For instance, in 1988, new plant and equipment expenditures by U.S. affiliates exceeded by 45 percent outlays for all other manufacturing businesses—$12,200 versus $8,400 per employee, respectively.[6] For the economy as a whole, foreign-owned firms as a group invest more in plant and equipment than the average for all U.S. firms—$11,184 versus $4,284 per worker for all U.S. businesses in 1988.[7]

Foreign affiliates can contribute to the domestic economy through their expenditures on research and development (R&D). Research and development outlays can create externalities when the technologies so developed are transferred to the rest of the economy. U.S. affiliates contribute to the technology base of U.S. industry through the inward transfer of technology from foreign parents and from in-house technology improvements.[8] Although U.S. affiliates have been active in making R&D expenditures, there has been much concern that the parents of U.S. affiliates will prefer to undertake their R&D spending at their headquarters abroad. However, available evidence does not substantiate these concerns.

One factor indicating a rapid rise in technology inflow is outward payments for royalties and license fees that have doubled from $899 million in 1986 to $1.7 billion in 1989. Another frequently used indicator of technology inflow is the ratio of R&D expenditures to gross output, often referred to as the technology intensity of output. In manufacturing, U.S. affiliates increased the technology intensity of their gross product by two-thirds between 1977 and 1987, with the ratio rising from 4.5 percent in 1977 to 7.5 percent in 1987. The technology intensity rose because R&D spending grew more rapidly than did gross output. Compared with all U.S. manufacturing in 1987, the technology intensity of U.S. affiliates in manufacturing in 1987 at 7.5 percent exceeded the technology intensity for all U.S. manufacturing, which stood at 6.5 percent.

Another measure is R&D per worker. When broken down into different industries within manufacturing, average R&D expenditures per worker for U.S. affiliates in chemicals and machinery greatly exceeded outlays in other manufacturing industries for the period 1977–87. When comparing R&D per worker in U.S. affiliates in manufacturing with R&D in U.S. manufacturing firms in 1988, it has been shown that outlays for U.S. firms at $4,640 per worker exceeded the average outlay of $3,630 per worker in U.S. affiliates. But when federally funded expenditures in U.S. manufacturing are excluded, the average outlay of U.S. firms for company-funded R&D drops to $3,110 per worker, indicating that R&D spending by U.S. affiliates is fairly comparable to U.S. firms.[9]

The data appear to indicate that foreign firms do not behave differently from U.S. firms and that there is no sign of a "headquarters effect," whereby foreign firms undertake a disproportionately large share of their research spending in the home country.

A comparison of assets owned by U.S. affiliates with all U.S. businesses can be made only for manufacturing because comparable data for assets in other sectors are not available. In manufacturing, U.S. affiliates accounted for 6.3 percent of the book value of all assets in 1977 and for 8.3 percent in 1980. By 1990 this share had more than doubled, accounting for 18.6 percent. An exceedingly large amount of takeover activity during the period 1987–89 accounted for a large part of this increase.

For two reasons, U.S. affiliates' share of manufacturing assets exceeded their share of employment. First, affiliates are more heavily concentrated in capital-intensive activity such as chemicals and allied products than are all U.S. businesses. Second, much of the growth in foreign direct investment has been through acquisitions. When a company is acquired, its assets are revalued to reflect the value implied by the acquisition price. Since the major share of foreign investment by foreign-owned companies has taken the format of acquisitions as opposed to new establishments, the portion of assets revalued recently would undoubtedly be higher for U.S. affiliates than for all U.S. businesses.[10]

Total sales of U.S. manufacturing affiliates can also be compared with sales of all U.S. manufacturing firms. Sales of U.S. affiliates as a share of all U.S. manufacturing business rose from 5.0 percent in 1977 to 7.1 percent in 1980 and then to 14.5 percent in 1990. These shares were somewhat below the U.S. affiliates' shares of U.S. manufacturing assets, probably reflecting the fact that sales would not be distorted by the differences in valuation noted above.[11] For instance, in 1990, U.S. affiliates accounted for 16.4 percent of sales by all U.S. businesses compared with 18.6 percent of all assets. As such, sales probably provide a superior indication of the role of U.S. affiliates than do assets.

THE ROLE OF U.S. AFFILIATES
IN MERCHANDISE TRADE

To a certain extent, FDI is a substitute for international trade because multinationals frequently produce merchandise in the host country that previously had been produced at home. Whereas it would be assumed that such

Table 3.3
Merchandise Trade of U.S. Affiliates of Foreign-Owned Firms, 1977–91

Year	Mdse. Exports as a % of Affil. Sales	Mdse. Imports as a % of Affil. Sales	Affiliate Exports as a % of Total U.S. Mdse. Exports	Affiliate Imports as a % of Total U.S. Mdse. Imports	Mdse. Imports as a % of Total Purchases
1977	12.8	22.6	20.2	29.0	27.2
1978	13.3	23.4	22.1	32.1	28.0
1979	13.5	19.2	23.8	30.0	22.5
1980	12.6	18.4	23.1	30.9	21.9
1981	12.6	16.1	26.8	31.5	19.5
1982	11.6	16.3	27.8	34.6	20.2
1983	10.0	15.2	26.2	31.6	19.2
1984	9.8	16.9	26.0	30.4	21.3
1985	8.9	17.9	25.8	33.7	22.5
1986	7.4	18.7	21.8	34.4	23.5
1987	6.0	18.0	18.9	35.3	24.2
1988	9.7	19.4	21.6	35.3	22.0
1989	8.7	17.3	23.7	36.3	20.4
1990	8.4	15.4	23.5	36.9	19.4
1991	8.5	15.4	23.3	36.9	19.6

Source: U.S. Department of Commerce, Economics and Statistics Administration, *Foreign Direct Investment in the United States: Review and Analysis of Current Developments*, August 1991, Tables 5-20 and 5-21; U.S. Department of Commerce, Bureau of Economic Analysis, *Survey of Current Business*, October 1993, pp. 52-66.

import substitution of foreign-owned operations has a low local content and would contribute to a growth in imports, as production expands, foreign affiliates also export merchandise from the host country and can contribute to export earnings of the host country. Because forces pull in opposite directions, it is difficult to assess the net impact of foreign production on the merchandise trade balance of the host country.

Data for merchandise trade of U.S. affiliates are given in Table 3.3. The data show a declining role of exports and imports when compared to sales of foreign affiliates. By 1990, exports represented a much smaller share of affiliates' sales, declining from almost 13 percent in 1977 to an average of 8 percent for 1989 and 1990. Imports as a share of sales also declined, falling from almost 23 percent in 1977 to an average of about 16 percent for 1989 and 1990. Some of the decline in the export share during the first half of the 1980s could probably be attributed to the appreciation of the dollar, but even with the large fall in the value of the dollar after 1985, the share in total sales of affiliates did not increase significantly. The increased cost of imports associated with a depreciated dollar could have contributed to the fall in imports as a percent of sales in 1989 and 1990.

However, when a comparison of affiliates' merchandise trade is made with total U.S. merchandise exports and imports, the role of affiliates' imports becomes increasingly significant. U.S. affiliates' role in U.S. merchandise trade is more significant than their role in other aspects of U.S. economic activity. This stems from the fact that U.S. affiliates are active participants in the international market and are integrated with their parent company in an international global web.

From an average of 32 percent of total merchandise imports in the first half of the 1980s, the affiliates' share rose to an average of almost 36 percent in 1989–91. After averaging about 26 percent in the first half of the 1980s, affiliates' exports declined to an average of 20 percent in 1987 and 1988 before rising to an average of over 23 percent in 1989–91. Whereas a lagged response to the fall in the value of the dollar after 1985 may explain the recent rise in affiliates' export share (the J-curve effect), the increased role in imports in recent years cannot be explained in terms of relative exchange rate changes.

It is to be noted that U.S. affiliates engaged in distribution accounted for the dominant shares of imports and exports. Wholesale trade accounted for about 70 percent of affiliates' imports during the 1980s and early 1990s. For instance, in 1991, of the $179.7 billion in imported merchandise shipped to affiliates, $112.1 billion, or almost two-thirds, were accounted for by wholesale trade. Manufacturing affiliates were much less dependent on imports than affiliates engaged in trade, and in 1991, manufacturing affiliates accounted for 26 percent of total imports of U.S. affiliates. Wholesaling, which also dominated exports, accounted for 53 percent of U.S. affiliates' exports compared to 40 percent for manufacturing in 1991.

Edward Graham and Paul Krugman have tried to determine whether the allegation that the high propensity to import of foreign-controlled firms is due to a preference for foreign supplies is an adequate description of their behavior with respect to foreign trade.[12] Imports per worker in domestic manufacturing were compared with imports in foreign affiliate manufacturing. It was found that imports per worker were approximately $7,000 for domestically owned firms as contrasted with $18,000 for U.S. affiliates. Given that in 1988 there were some 1.8 million U.S. residents employed by foreign-owned manufacturers, had these firms been domestically owned, total U.S. merchandise imports would have been about $20 billion less (about 4 percent of total merchandise imports).

The extent to which U.S. affiliates were dependent on imports also varies widely depending on country of ownership, particularly in manufacturing. In 1987, Japanese manufacturing firms imported $48,270 per worker as contrasted with $15,910 for U.S. affiliates from all countries taken together.[13] There are several possible explanations for this phenomenon. One explanation could result from measurement bias, whereby some Japanese marketing firms may be misclassified as manufacturing firms. Also Japanese firms are newer to the American market than are affiliates from other nations, many of which have been in the States for decades. Generally, U.S. affiliates purchase an increasing share of domestic inputs as they mature. A similar pattern has been evident in the behavior of U.S. multinationals in Europe.[14] Furthermore, until recently, Japanese firms have engaged in "greenfield" investments (new establishments, including automobile producers), which initially commence production using a large share of imported content. By contrast, other countries have engaged largely in the acquisition of existing firms.

The import propensity of foreign-owned U.S. affiliates can be assessed by looking at the import content of purchased inputs. In 1991 the import content for all U.S. affiliates was 20 percent, and domestic content was 80 percent. For manufacturing affiliates, 17 percent was imported. U.S. affiliates' import content was compared to the share of imports in total purchased imports of U.S. parent companies. Data for U.S. parent companies were used because industry-level data on imported inputs by all U.S. businesses are not available. In 1989, the year for which data are available, the share of imports for U.S. affiliates was about twice as large as the share for U.S. parent companies. The import share for U.S. affiliates in wholesale trade was 35 percent compared to 17 percent for U.S. parents. The comparable shares for petroleum were 20 and 11 percent; and for manufacturing, 16 and 11 percent. For all manufacturing sectors, import shares for U.S. affiliates were greater than for U.S. parents.[15]

The major question concerns the impact of this higher import propensity on the current account. To answer that question, it is necessary to revert to a macroeconomic explanation to be developed in the following chapters, where it will be shown that the overall level of the current account is determined by an underlying trend regarding national savings and investment. If, as Graham and Krugman have suggested, imports would have been $20 billion lower without foreign direct investment in 1988, the somewhat lower trade balance would have meant that the equilibrium value of the dollar would have been at most 4 percent higher than was actually the case. Given the large swings in exchange rate behavior, a 4 percent depreciation of the dollar is insufficient to indicate significant harm to the U.S. economy.

THEORIES OF FOREIGN DIRECT INVESTMENT

The preceding section has shown that, until the 1980s, U.S. foreign direct investment abroad greatly exceeded the inflow of direct investment into the United States. As already shown, it was not until the late 1970s that the United States was to become the recipient of large direct investment inflows. While it may be tempting to relate these FDI inflows to factors causing balance-of-payments problems and the reversal of the U.S. capital account during the 1980s, it can be hypothesized that the causes of the large FDI inflows during the 1980s were to a significant extent independent of the factors that gave rise to balance-of-payments difficulties. It is possible that factors related to the growth and maturity of foreign-controlled firms, increased integration of the global economy, and the relative decline of U.S. technological and managerial leadership can better explain this phenomenon.

Theories that seek to explain FDI have been classified into "cost of capital" and "theory of the firm" explanations. According to cost of capital explanations, FDI occurs because any given cash flow is valued more highly by the foreign firm because it has a lower cost of capital than domestic firms. Theory of the firm explanations say FDI occurs because the factory is more profitable when owned by a foreign firm that is able to offset any advantage that domestic firms might have when producing in their home country.[16]

In a book concerned with capital flows it is important that sources of FDI growth in the United States during the 1980s be explained. If FDI is explained by cost of capital theories and is linked to capital flows resulting from current account imbalances, then the future of FDI flows could be inextricably interwoven with factors causing current account imbalances. But should FDI in the United States be motivated by theory of the firm motivations as well as increasing integration of the world economy, then the long-term trend in FDI inflows may be expected to move independently from imbalances in the current account.

COST OF CAPITAL EXPLANATIONS

Although the majority of economists studying FDI have tended to focus on theory of the firm explanations, the experience of the United States during the 1980s caused renewed interest in cost of capital explanations, especially in the popular press. The plunge of the United States into net debtor status during the 1980s coincided with the growth of total foreign claims on the United States, including FDI. Popular discussion of motives of foreign investors also stressed the high price of foreign (especially Japanese) stocks and high values of foreign currencies relative to the dollar, which from a foreign perspective would have made U.S. assets appear cheap.

Cost of capital explanations of FDI focus on market imperfections in capital and foreign exchange markets. Robert Z. Aliber emphasized imperfections in both foreign exchange and capital markets.[17] John Makin has explained FDI in terms of changes in the levels of exchange rates, associating overvaluation of a currency with the outflow of FDI and undervaluation with an inflow.[18] The desire to engage in portfolio diversification offers another explanation of FDI. For instance, T. B. Agmon and D. F. Lessard used portfolio theory to explain the relation of FDI to the needs of multinationals to diversify and stabilize earnings. They observed that at the corporate level, FDI rather than portfolio capital movements offered the multinational corporation an opportunity to diversify that would not otherwise be available.[19]

Aliber explains FDI as an outcome of the existence of different currency areas. All firms based in a particular currency area are given the same advantage, and multinational firms can have an advantage over host country firms in the international capital markets. FDI occurs when source country firms can capitalize the same stream of earnings at a higher rate than host country firms because the market is able to give different capitalization rates to future streams of income that are denominated in different currencies. These capitalization rates differ because, according to the market mechanism, a premium must be attached for bearing uncertainty over exchange rate risk. Accordingly, a difference in the yields on equities from two different countries may reflect an expectation of depreciation of the weaker currency and a premium for bearing the uncertainty of the future price of the weaker currency in terms of the stronger currency.[20] Thus, firms from countries with currencies that command a premium have an advantage in investing abroad because the market capitalizes the host country stream of earnings at a higher rate if it is earned by a firm from a source country with a currency commanding a premium. Aliber suggests that this exchange risk theory of FDI explains the geographic and industrial patterns of FDI. The geographic pattern of FDI reflects capitalization rates for equities denominated in different currencies. According to the theory, FDI will tend to concentrate in the more capital-intensive industries because the larger is the contribution of capital to production, the greater is the advantage of the foreign-owned firm. Aliber also explains that these differences in capitalization rates explain FDI through mergers and acquisitions.

Other researchers have attempted to explain FDI as being caused by misalignments in the level of exchange rates, an overvaluation of a currency being associated with an outflow of FDI and an undervaluation with an inflow. An overvalued currency represents a tax on exports and a subsidy on imports. Hence, overvaluation of the currency reduces the size of a firm's export and domestic markets and makes some of the firm's capacity redundant. If some of the redundant capital were to be used to undertake FDI abroad, unit costs of production would be lowered.[21]

Stephen Kolhagen has examined the effects of devaluations in the United Kingdom, France, and West Germany during the 1960s on FDI inflows.[22] A model of relative profitability in alternative production locations—the source country and the host country—was developed. Whereas the net result depends on the effect of a devaluation on costs and prices in the two locations, the devaluation probably increases relative profitability in a country with a devalued currency. Kolhagen showed that the major devaluations in the United Kingdom, West Germany, and France during the 1960s increased the profitability of investment in the devaluing countries and induced inflows of FDI into those countries. However, production in the devaluing country would become relatively less profitable if the devaluing country has a very open economy and the domestic demand and supply for tradeable goods are relatively inelastic.

Dennis Logue and Thomas Willet have analyzed the impact of exchange rate changes for the United States from 1967 to 1973 and found that exchange rate changes encourage inflows of FDI.[23]

Aliber revised the exchange risk theory in 1993.[24] This revised theory explains the country-specific component of foreign direct investment and highlights the distinction between the location decision and the ownership decision. The revised exchange risk theory also explains changes in the distributional pattern of foreign direct investment as reflecting changes in the distribution of ownership and locational advantages of a given country. For instance, if the U.S. dollar was undervalued compared to its equilibrium (purchasing power parity) value, the United States would have a locational advantage as a host country because the undervalued dollar would increase anticipated profit of investing in plant and equipment in the United States.

The changes in the distribution of ownership advantages between U.S. and foreign firms can be measured by changes in the relationships of the market value of firms headquartered in the United States with that of other countries. This relationship can be measured by changes in the Q ratios of the source and host country, the Q ratio being defined as the market value of a firm divided by its book value. The Q ratio for a firm increases if the interest rate used to discount anticipated profits declines and also if its anticipated profits increase. A firm in a country with a relatively low interest rate has an ownership advantage. Furthermore, according to this theory, changes in real exchange rates can bring about changes in the international pattern of foreign direct investment, because funds flow toward countries that have undervalued currencies.

Finally, it is a necessary condition of the exchange risk theory of foreign direct investment that national markets for securities denominated in different currencies be partially segmented because portfolio investors demand a premium when they bear exchange rate risk. The greater the premium demanded by portfolio investors for bearing risk related to the international flow of funds, the greater is the difference in interest rates and Q ratios between countries and the greater will be the ownership advantages of firms headquartered in particular countries.

ALTERNATIVE THEORIES OF FOREIGN DIRECT INVESTMENT

The industrial organization theory was the leading theoretical explanation of FDI by the early 1970s. Even though production abroad entails disadvantages (including additional costs and risks), large oligopolistic firms engage in production abroad because they have firm-specific (ownership) advantages enabling them to obtain larger profits than domestic firms. These firm-specific advantages make it more profitable to produce abroad instead of licensing or producing at home and exporting. These advantages stem from imperfections in the goods market, economies of scale internal and external to the firm, and government-imposed market imperfections.

According to Stephen Hymer, FDI belongs to the theory of imperfect competition because multinational corporations (MNCs) are usually large firms operating in imperfectly competitive markets. For firms to invest in imperfect markets abroad they must have certain net advantages over firms in the host country.[25]

Richard Caves stressed the industrial organization theory of FDI and noted that the critical advantage of multinationals was the ability to differentiate a product. Firm-specific advantages of multinationals could include a number of intangible assets, such as product and process technologies and organizational and marketing skills. Caves also investigated whether the MNC could help promote allocative efficiency in the host country. On the one hand, because MNCs could overcome high entry barriers and upset local, entrenched oligopolistic firms, they produce more active rivalry and improve market performance, thereby enhancing allocative efficiency. However, the entry of MNCs also has a negative aspect, for entry may raise seller concentration in the market of the host country, especially if the presence of the new rival were to induce mergers among domestic firms. In such instances, the entry of foreign firms could even raise domestic prices.[26]

According to Charles Kindleberger, who also focused on the role of firm-specific advantages, the investing firm can not only earn more abroad than at home, but it can also earn a higher return in the market where it is investing than existing or potentially competitive firms in that country, because of the possession of monopolistic advantages. These firm-specific advantages were classified under several headings: departures from competition in goods markets (product differentiation, marketing skills, administered prices, and so on) and factor markets (priority knowledge, discrimination in access to capital, and managerial skills); external and internal economies of scale, including those arising from vertical integration; and government-imposed intervention to facilitate import substitution, which contributes to "defensive investment" undertaken by the MNC to defend market share in the host country. These advantages enable the foreign firm to overcome its lack of knowledge of local conditions and compensate for the foreign firm's cost of operating at a distance.[27]

Currently, internalization theory is a widely accepted theoretical explanation of multinationals. According to the industrial organization theory, there are many ownership-specific advantages. Instead of selling or leasing these advantages to other firms, multinational firms internalize these advantages across national boundaries within their own organizations, thereby either replacing the market or alternatively augmenting it. The idea that firms can bypass the market and internalize their ownership advantages draws upon developments in the theory of the firm that are generally attributed to Ronald Coase in his writings on market imperfections and their impact on transactions costs.[28] Peter Buckley and Mark Casson attributed the creation of the multinational to the internalization by firms across national boundaries. Internalization takes place because of transactions costs resulting from exogenous market imperfections. Transactions costs result from the existence of natural market imperfections or from governments imposing costs to international trade when trade barriers are created.[29]

Internalization involves the analysis of the costs and benefits to the firm of internalizing markets, especially markets in intermediate goods. The benefits from internalization come from avoiding imperfections in the external market. Buckley and Casson list the advantages of internalization (control by the firm as opposed to a market situation) as (1) increasing the ability to plan and control production and to coordinate flows of crucial inputs; (2) exploiting market power by discriminatory pricing; (3) avoiding bilateral market power; (4) avoiding uncertainties in the transfer of knowledge between parties; and (5) avoiding potential government intervention by mechanisms such as transfer pricing.[30]

However, there are costs of internalizing a market. These consist of increased costs of communication within the internalized market; the resource cost of fragmentation of the market; the cost of political discrimination against foreign owned firms; and the administrative cost of the internal market.

Markets can be internalized across national boundaries in a number of ways. Vertical integration of production can give rise to multinational enterprises. Also, because of the profitability of R&D, a high degree of multinationality can be generated by internalization of the knowledge market.[31] Here the public goods nature of knowledge in conjunction with the lack of internationally accepted property rights (such as patents) give rise to the multinational.[32] Also, human skills can be internalized, especially in areas such as marketing and finance where there can be high returns to team cooperation.[33]

A number of writers studied the role of MNCs in reducing coordinating costs. For instance, John McManus theorized that MNCs will emerge in industries characterized by a substantial amount of interdependence among producers in different countries and substantial costs of coordinating their activities through licensing or the market mechanism.[34]

Stephen Magee's appropriability theory of direct investment parallels the explanation that multinational firms internalize ownership-specific advantages. According to Magee, the need to appropriate the private returns from investment in information becomes an explanation of FDI. Multinationals, he states, specialize in producing information that is less efficient to transmit through markets than through firms. Because the appropriability of the social value of new ideas is higher for sophisticated technology than for simple technologies, MNCs produce sophisticated technologies, and the appropriability of the returns from and complimentaries among different types of information dictate large, optimum plant size.[35]

The eclectic theory was proposed by John H. Dunning. It is a general theory that integrates much of the existing body of knowledge concerning the reasons for FDI.[36] Earlier, in a paper written in 1973, he had hypothesized that trade and foreign production were alternative forms of international production that could be explained in terms of ownership and locational advantages.[37] In a 1981 paper, entitled "Trade, Location of Economic Activity and Multinational Enterprises: A Search for an Eclectic Approach," Dunning offered a theory that combined the different strands of thought with respect to FDI theory.[38] His theory, which explained the willingness and ability of firms to exploit markets as well as the reasons they seek to exploit markets through foreign production, drew on three areas of economics: industrial organization theory, the Coaseian theory of the firm, and international trade theory. The combination of ownership, internalization, and locational advantages made it possible for firms to engage in international production. To serve particular markets, the investing firm, in contrast with firms of other nationalities, must possess net ownership-specific assets that are exclusive or specific to the investing firm. Most of these advantages can be explained by industrial organization theory of FDI as discussed above. These advantages include firm size, established position, access to raw materials, and exclusive possession of intangible assets such as patents, trademarks, management and organizational skills, and marketing channels. Other advantages such as accrued knowledge and more favorable access to foreign markets arise from the multinationality of the firm.

In his 1983 writing, Dunning distinguishes three types of ownership advantages (sometimes called competitive or monopolistic advantages): (1) those stemming from exclusive possession of or access to particular income-generating assets; (2) those generally enjoyed by a branch plant as opposed to a separately established firm; and (3) those that result from geographical diversification or multinationality. Dunning later distinguished between asset and transaction advantages of multinationals. Asset advantages arise from multinationals' ownership of specific assets, whereas transaction advantages reflect the ability of multinational hierarchies vis-à-vis external markets to capture transactional benefits or lessen transactional costs arising from governance of a network of these assets that are located in different countries.[39] It is also seen as important to distinguish between structural and market imperfections in determining the ownership advantages of multinationals.

However, it may be more beneficial for the firm itself to bypass the market and internalize its ownership advantages rather than to sell or lease them to other firms. Extending its activities through FDI allows the firm to internalize its ownership advantages.[40]

According to Dunning, the three main types of transactional market failure that lead to internalization are usually identified as: (1) those arising from risk and uncertainty; (2) those stemming from the ability of firms to exploit the economies of large-scale production, but only in a situation of imperfect competition; (3) those occurring when the transaction of a particular good or service yields costs and benefits external to the transaction, but not reflected in the terms agreed to by the transacting parties. The presence of one (or more) of these forms of transactional market failure gives rise to the desire by firms to integrate the different stages of the value added chain, to engage in product diversification, or to capture the economies of the use of complementary assets. The greater the multinational's perception of the costs of transactional market failure, the more likely that the multinational will exploit a competitive advantage through international production rather than through contractual arrangements with foreign firms.[41]

In addition to market imperfections, Dunning points out that enterprises may internalize activities as a result of government intervention in the allocation of resources. One example of such intervention occurs when the government encourages internalization of production and/or sale of technology. Governments have facilitated internalization by subsidizing R&D activities, continuing the patent system, and permitting a milieu in which firms internalize their knowledge-producing and knowledge-consuming activities. The second example of public intervention arises when the government's different economic policies lead to distortions in the allocation of economic resources.[42] Other reasons to internalize operations across borders include cushioning the adverse effects of government legislation, minimizing exposure from fluctuating exchange rates, and taking advantage of interest rate differentials.

Ownership and internalization advantages are firm-specific. Research has shown that location-specific advantages are important determinants of FDI. During the 1950s and 1960s, a number of researchers used theories of location and international trade to explain why MNCs chose to produce in one country rather than in another. Location-specific advantages include price, quality, and productivity of inputs; government intervention in the form of tariff and nontariff barriers, tax rates, foreign investment incentives, and political stability; the available infrastructure; transport and communications costs; foreign exchange effects from locating in one country as opposed to another; the large size of markets in the host country; and the psychic closeness of cultures in the home and host countries.

Dunning categorizes locational advantages as the third strand in the eclectic paradigm. He states that firms will choose to engage in international production if they perceive that it is to their advantage to combine spatially transferable intermediate products produced in the source country with some immobile factor endowments or other intermediate products in the host country. He also distinguished between the different kinds of market imperfections that can influence the locational decisions of multinationals. Structural market distortions such as those arising from some form of government intervention that affects the costs of producing in different locations may affect inward direct investment. But even if such distortions were not to occur, multinational investment could still take place if there were transaction gains resulting from the governance of activities in different locations. Examples of such advantages are enhanced leverage and arbitrage opportunities, reduction of exchange risks, improved coordination of financial decision making, the possibility of gaining by transfer pricing, and protection offered by a hedged marketing or multiple sourcing strategy.[43]

The eclectic paradigm of international production depends on the coming together of three factors—ownership-specific advantages, the propensity to internalize these advantages across international borders, and the relative attractiveness of a foreign location for production. Dunning goes on to explain that the specific ownership, internalization, and location parameters that will influence individual multinationals will vary according to motivations underlying such production in any given instance.[44]

The product cycle and oligopolistic reaction theories are two attempts to model the way decision makers within multinationals respond to a set of economic and other variables, as well as the way the idiosyncratic behavior of firms might influence and respond to cross-border market failure. The product cycle model developed by Raymond Vernon and Frederick Knickerbocker's theory of oligopolistic reaction regards much of foreign production as an attempt to gain an ownership advantage over one's rivals.

Vernon, in his description of the product cycle theory, explains why innovative and oligopolistic U.S. firms undertake FDI. The innovating firm begins by producing the technologically sophisticated product for its home market because of the availability of a demand for the product and the need to coordinate R&D with production units. Because of economies of scale, as demand increases in the home market, per unit costs of production fall. As a market for the product arises in other advanced countries, the firm begins to export the product to other industrial countries. As foreign demand grows and technology of producing the product stabilizes, production takes place in other advanced countries, often by U.S. subsidiaries who invest abroad as part of "defensive investment." The shift to production outside the United States coincides with an erosion of America's technological advantage. Finally, as technology in producing this product line becomes standardized, the product is sold on the basis of price competitiveness. That is, in the final stage the product line matures, and the rest of the world becomes a net exporter as the advanced country (the United States in Vernon's initial writings) becomes a net importer. The MNC may undertake production in less developed countries (LDCs) because with standardization of technologies, low wages give the LDCs a comparative advantage.[45]

Although the product cycle theory was originally useful in explaining U.S. FDI in other advanced countries as well as the eventual production by MNCs in low-labor-cost countries, the theory has become outdated. First, the United States is no longer the only dominant foreign investor. European and Japanese investors have been contributing an increasing share to global FDI. Second, the MNCs are now able to develop, mature, and standardize products almost simultaneously and can differentiate their product without incurring significant time lags.[46] The product cycle theory was developed to explain U.S. FDI in Europe in the 1950s and 1960s and cannot explain all types of FDI. Recent changes involve deterioration of U.S. technological leadership and leveling of income differentials that once existed between the United States and other developed economies. It is within this context that Vernon himself has recognized that the power of the product cycle theory to explain trade and investment has become weaker. U.S. firms are no longer the only firms enjoying firm specific advantages.[47]

Rivalry can occur among oligopolistic firms operating in the same industry but not necessarily in the same country. Knickerbocker, in his theory of oligopolistic reaction, has argued that firms in concentrated industries may engage in FDI to match the investment patterns of rivals.[48] Oligopolistic reaction is applicable after a leading oligopolistic competitor makes the first FDI in an industry. This investment induces a clustering of investment by other leading oligopolistic competitors because firms in a given industry perceive this mutual interdependence and follow the behavior of rival firms undertaking FDI. He constructed an entry concentration index (ECI) for 187 American manufacturing MNCs, which showed that entry of American firms into foreign markets are bunched in time. He also found a positive correlation between the ECI and U.S. industrial concentration ratios, which indicated that, except at very high concentration ratios, a high level of industrial concentration produced reactions by rivals in undertaking FDI.

Edward B. Flowers investigated the growth in FDI in the United States by European and Canadian firms during the period 1945–75. This approach is a variation of Knickerbocker's hypothesis of oligopolistic reaction. Flowers showed that in relatively concentrated industries, competitive interactions by the leading firm led to their undertaking FDI at roughly the same time. The study regressed a measure of FDI entry concentration on a measure of industrial concentration for each investing country. The ECI was computed to measure the strength of the FDI entry. The results showed that in highly concentrated European and Canadian industries, the FDI of the leading firms in each country had a tendency to come into the United States in clusters of subsidiaries in response to the activities of the firms investing in the industry, with the clustering of oligopolistically reactive FDI occurring within three years of the first investment by a leading firm. Industrial concentration of the investing industries was able to explain almost one-half of the European and Canadian FDI coming into the United States during the three decades.[49]

ASSESSING THE GROWTH OF FOREIGN DIRECT INVESTMENT IN THE UNITED STATES

The problem of assessing the growth of FDI in the United States is made more difficult by the fact that it coincided with the shift of the United States to a net debtor position during the 1980s. At the same time that portfolio capital flows increased, inward FDI expanded.

There are reasons to believe that it was not the movement of the United States into a net debtor position, but rather the growing preeminence of other major industrial nations in the world economy that propelled FDI growth in the United States during the 1980s. That is, foreign firms reached maturity and developed firm-specific ownership advantages over rival firms, and when they matured they found it more profitable to internalize their ownership advantages, including their accumulation of technological and managerial skills, and invest in the large U.S. market. Whereas other industrial nations (excluding Japan) had been large recipients of FDI during the 1960s and 1970s, during the 1980s the United States began to catch up as a recipient of these inflows. Such an argument would conform less to cost of capital explanations than to industrial organization explanations.

The growth of FDI in the United States was part of the surge in FDI in the major industrial countries during the past decade. For the 1980s, DeAnne Julius examined outward and inward FDI flows for the Group of Five (G-5). During the decade, companies from these five industrial countries spent $650 billion on direct investment in other countries, of which 75 percent stayed within the G-5. This $650 billion represented about 70 percent of the total stock of overseas direct investment owned by companies from these five countries. The rate of growth of FDI during the 1980s was greatly in excess of what might have been expected from GNP growth. For instance, during the period 1983–89, GNP growth in the G-5 averaged 3.6 percent per annum. A simple regression analysis relating real FDI growth during the past 25 years to real GNP growth produced a regression coefficient of 3.44, indicating that one would have expected FDI to grow by more than 12 percent a year; in reality it grew by 27 percent a year during the decade. Julius explains this phenomenon as having been caused by two factors: liberalization of service industries (especially banking, insurance, and telecommunications), and the emergence of Japan as a major investor together with the United States and Great Britain.[50] What makes the United States unique is the fact that FDI flows into the States accelerated much more rapidly than for other countries.

There is widespread belief that the rise of foreign direct investment in the United States in the 1980s was related to the shift of the United States into

Table 3.4

Foreign Direct Investment Position: Historical Cost, 1973–91 (millions of dollars)

Year	FDIUS	FDIA	Net FDI Position	FDIUS FDIA	FDIUS GDP
1973	20,556	101,313	-80,757	0.203	1.523
1974	25,144	110,078	-84,934	0.228	1.723
1975	27,772	124,050	-96,388	0.224	1.751
1976	30,770	138,809	-100,039	0.222	1.740
1977	34,595	145,990	-111,395	0.237	1.752
1978	42,471	162,727	-120,256	0.261	1.902
1979	54,462	187,858	-133,396	0.290	2.188
1980	83,046	215,375	-132,329	0.386	3.067
1981	108,714	228,348	-119,634	0.476	3.587
1982	124,672	207,752	-83,075	0.600	3.958
1983	137,061	207,203	-70,142	0.662	4.025
1984	164,583	211,480	-46,897	0.778	4.357
1985	184,615	230,250	-45,635	0.802	4.571
1986	220,414	259,800	-39,386	0.848	5.164
1987	263,394	314,307	-43,913	0.838	5.802
1988	314,754	335,893	-21,039	0.937	6.423
1989	368,924	372,419	-3,495	0.991	7.026
1990	396,702	424,086	-27,384	0.935	7.153
1991	407,577	450,196	- 42,619	0.905	7.123

Sources: U.S. Department of Commerce, Bureau of Economic Analysis, *Survey of Current Business*, various issues.

a net debtor status. This belief is based upon the fact that the growth of large direct investment inflows during the 1980s coincided with the shift of the current account position into one of continuous deficits commencing in 1982. However, it is possible to argue that the growth of direct investment inflows was an independent phenomenon. First, although smaller than in the 1980s, FDI increased significantly during the 1970s, a period during which the U.S. current account balance was not persistently in deficit. As a consequence of the growth of FDI inflows during the 1970s, the FDI stock in the United States was continuously expanding. When FDI stock in the United States is taken as a share of GDP, the result is an almost continuous increase in the share, which rises from over 1.52 percent of GDP in 1973 to 7.12 percent in 1991 (see Table 3.4).

Second, the U.S. net FDI position has undergone significant change since the 1970s. Figure 3.1 shows changes in the ratio of the stock of direct investment in the United States to the stock of U.S. direct investment abroad. It is shown that until 1989 the net direct investment position of the United States was continuously growing as the United States was increasingly becoming a host country for multinational enterprises. The ratio

Figure 3.1
U.S. Foreign Direct Investment Position, 1973–91 (historical, market, and current costs)

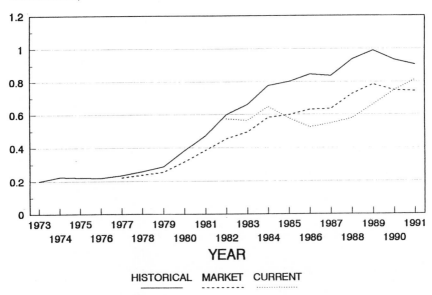

showing the U.S. net investment position at historical cost rises from 20.3 percent in 1973 to 99.1 percent in 1989 before falling somewhat to 90.5 percent in 1991. It is again evident that the trend toward the United States increasingly becoming a host country for direct investment had begun prior to the chronic current account deficits of the 1980s.

The ratio of FDI in the United States to U.S. FDI abroad depends on the techniques used to measure foreign direct investment, and different measurement techniques will change the measured significance of FDI in the United States. In the "historical cost" or "book value" approach, the value is calculated using the initial cost of the investment and ignores subsequent changes in the value of the investment. The current value of the investment is substantially understated, and currency fluctuations can distort the value.[51] To eliminate these distortions, two other measures for valuing direct investment were introduced: the current cost (replacement cost) basis and the current stock market value of investments.[52] Using data from Table 3.5, Figure 3.1 shows that the ratio of FDI in the United States to FDI abroad (FDI position) is higher when FDI is measured at historical cost rather than at either market value or current cost, because the average age of FDIs abroad exceeds that of such investments in the United States.

Third, further insight can be gained by comparing foreign direct investment stock with total foreign claims (foreign assets in the United States).

Table 3.5
Foreign Direct Investment Position: Market Value and Current Cost,
1982-91 (millions of dollars)

A. Market Value[1]

Year	FDIUS	FDIA	Net	FDIUS FDIA	FDIUS[3]. FAUS
1982	130,428	226,638	- 96,210	0.575	0.188
1983	153,318	270,768	-117,450	0.566	0.192
1984	172,377	265,822	- 93,455	0.648	0.190
1985	219,996	379,108	-159,022	0.580	0.200
1986	272,966	518,711	-245,745	0.526	0.195
1987	316,200	576,960	-260,760	0.548	0.198
1988	391,530	678,614	-287,084	0.577	0.211
1989	534,734	807,896	-272,662	0.662	0.242
1990	536,560	716,441	-179,881	0.749	0.237
1991	654,094	802,000	-147,906	0.816	0.263

B. Current Cost[2]

Year	FDIUS	FDIA	Net	FDIUS FDIA	FDIUS[4] FAUS
1977	56,715	252,832	-196,117	0.224	0.174
1978	69,581	291,039	-221,458	0.239	0.174
1979	88,335	343,940	-255,605	0.257	0.196
1980	125,944	396,249	-270,305	0.318	0.232
1981	159,926	412,418	-252,492	0.388	0.254
1982	176,870	387,239	-210,369	0.457	0.239
1983	184,394	371,667	-187,273	0.496	0.222
1984	211,201	361,588	-150,387	0.584	0.224
1985	231,326	387,183	-155,857	0.598	0.208
1986	265,833	421,167	-155,334	0.631	0.191
1987	313,451	493,341	-179,890	0.635	0.197
1988	374,345	515,702	-141,357	0.726	0.197
1989	433,164	552,822	-119,658	0.784	0.206
1990	466,515	623,587	-157,072	0.748	0.214
1991	487,022	655,260	-168,238	0.743	0.210

Source: Russell B. Scholl, Raymond J. Mataloni, Jr., and Steven D. Bezirganian, "The International Investment Position of the United States in 1991," *Survey of Current Business*, June 1992, pp. 46-59.
1. Direct investment position valued at the current stock-market value of owner's equity.
2. Direct investment position when the reinvested earnings component of direct investment capital is measured on a current-cost (replacement-cost) basis after adjusting for reported depreciation, depletion, and expensed exploration and development costs.
3. Foreign direct investment in the United States divided by foreign assets in the United States with foreign direct investment at market value.
4. Foreign direct investment in the United States divided by foreign assets in the United States with foreign direct investment at current cost.

Table 3.5 shows FDI stock as a share of total foreign claims on the United States. When FDI is calculated at market value, this share remains fairly constant between 1982 and 1987, but then rises from 19.8 per unit in 1987 to 26.3 percent in 1991. When foreign direct investment is valued at current cost, this share increases from 17.4 percent in 1977 to 25.4 percent in 1981 but subsequently falls continuously, reaching 19.1 percent in 1986 before it begins to rise again, rising to 21.0 percent in 1991. When foreign direct investment is measured at current cost, foreign claims appear to have shifted in favor of direct investment until 1981, and it was only with the surge in foreign portfolio investment after 1981 and the recessionary period of the early 1980s that the composition of foreign claims shifted toward portfolio investment. Only with the surge in foreign direct investment in the second half of the 1980s did foreign claims again shift in favor of FDI. It must be assumed that had FDI been closely related to the same factors that caused portfolio capital flows, neither the shift in claims in favor of direct investment during the 1970s nor the large shift toward foreign portfolio investment in the early 1980s would have occurred. Rather, the long-term trend in direct investment appears to have been related to the change in the international position of the U.S. in the global economy.

Evidence from balance-of-payments inflows confirms that FDI inflows during the 1980s were not a principal factor in the shift of the United States to a net borrower. Even during 1989 when direct investment inflows reached a peak of almost $68 billion, FDI inflows represented less than one-third of total capital inflows.

CONCLUSION

Although many have perceived the rise in net borrowing during the 1980s as an outcome of macroeconomic forces, the theory of FDI and much of the evidence of FDI in the United States support the contention that the growth in direct investment inflows into the United States during the 1980s represented a microeconomic phenomenon.

Foreign direct investment is part of a firm's strategy for production and sales.[53] Foreign firms reached maturity and developed firm-specific owner-ship advantages. It was most profitable to internalize these advantages through managerial control over foreign operations. The enhanced global competitiveness of foreign-owned corporations over their U.S. rivals was reflected in their increased exports to the United States and direct invest-ment. Direct investment can be a substitute for trade, and with increasing U.S. sentiment for protectionism during the mid-1980s foreign firms, es-pecially Japanese firms, made the long-term decision to shift production facilities to the United States.

But setting up operations abroad can be a costly and risky option as com-pared with exporting. These disadvantages must be counterbalanced by lo-cational advantages in the host country. For instance, during the 1980s, production in the United States offered several advantages, including the potential for increased protectionism in the United States and a decline in the relative cost of U.S. labor, both of which helped encourage Japanese auto producers to undertake assembly operations in the United States. The U.S.-Canada Free Trade Agreement concluded in 1989 and the 1993 North American Free Trade Agreement have also given further impetus to the United States as a production location. Another advantage is the enhanced opportunities to avoid taxes through advantageous transfer pricing of imported inputs, which increases a multinational's after-tax profits by allowing it to shift reported profits between tax jurisdictions. In fact, the Clinton administration has claimed that by engaging in transfer pricing, foreign companies are thereby avoiding paying their fair share of U.S. taxes.[54]

It is also claimed that the large decline in the value of the dollar against its major trading partners beginning in 1985 and the collapse of the U.S. stock market in October 1987 contributed to a surge in direct investment activity. For instance, Norman Glickman and Douglas Woodward suggest that exchange rate movements during the latter part of 1985 increased the attractiveness of purchasing real U.S. assets. As the dollar exchange rate plummeted during the late 1980s, foreign investors shifted from portfolio investment to foreign direct investment and they refer to this phenomenon as the "debt-for-equity" swap, with the weak dollar giving investors, especially the Japanese, the opportunity to turn the liquid assets that they had built up during the years of trade surpluses with the United States into an equity stake in America.[55] They also point out that the stock market crash in October 1987 intensified the search for undervalued assets. Although the authors do appear to imply that the cost of capital may have impacted the large surge of foreign direct investment into the United States during the late 1980s, they nevertheless indicated that exchange rate movements mainly influence short-term investment decisions.[56] Because foreign direct investment can be a substitute for trade, with increasing protectionism during the 1980s, foreign firms, especially Japanese firms, made the long-term decision to shift production facilities to the United States.

NOTES

1. U.S. Department of Commerce, Economics and Statistics Administration, *Foreign Direct Investment in the United States: Review and Analysis of Current Developments* (Washington, D.C.: Government Printing Office, August 1991), p. 31.

2. U.S. Department of Commerce, *Survey of Current Business*, November 1992, p. 47.

3. U.S. Department of Commerce, *Foreign Direct Investment in the United States*, p. 32.

4. Ibid., pp. 34–35.

5. Edward M. Graham and Paul L. Krugman, *Foreign Direct Investment in the United States*, 2d ed. (Washington, D.C.: Institute for International Economics, 1991), p. 70.

6. U.S. Department of Commerce, *Foreign Direct Investment in the United States*, p. 35.

7. Ibid., p. 18.

8. Ibid., p. 35.

9. Graham and Krugman, *Foreign Direct Investment in the United States*, pp. 72–73.

10. U.S. Department of Commerce, *Survey of Current Business*, May 1992, p. 55.

11. Ibid., pp. 55–56.

12. Graham and Krugman, *Foreign Direct Investment in the United States*, pp. 67–70.

13. Ibid., p. 70.

14. U.S. Council of Economic Advisors, *Economic Report of the President* (Washington, D.C.: Government Printing Office, January 1991), p. 261; and U.S. Department of Commerce, *Foreign Direct Investment in the United States*, p. 33.

15. Graham and Krugman, *Foreign Direct Investment in the United States*, pp. 69–70.

16. Ibid., pp. 35–38.

17. Robert Z. Aliber: "The Theory of Foreign Direct Investment," in *The International Corporation*, ed. Charles P. Kindleberger (Cambridge, Mass.: M.I.T. Press, 1970); and *The Multinational Paradigm* (Cambridge, Mass.: M.I.T. Press, 1993), pp. 169–207.

18. John Makin, "Capital Flows and Exchange Rate Flexibility in the Post Bretton Woods Era," Essays in International Finance, No. 103 (Princeton, N.J.: Princeton University Press, 1974).

19. T. B. Agmon and D. F. Lessard, "Investor Recognition of Corporate International Diversification," *Journal of Finance*, 33, no. 4 (1977), pp. 1049–55.

20. Aliber, "A Theory of Foreign Direct Investment," pp. 28–29.

21. Makin, "Capital Flows and Exchange Rate Flexibility," pp. 7–10.

22. Stephen Kolhagen, "Exchange Rate Changes, Profitability, and Direct Foreign Investment," *Southern Economic Journal*, 44 (1977), pp. 43–52.

23. Dennis Logue and Thomas Willet, "The Effects of Exchange Rate Adjustment on International Investment," in *The Effects of Exchange Rate Adjustments*, ed. Peter B. Clark, Dennis E. Logue, and Richard Sweeney (Washington, D.C.: Department of the Treasury, 1977).

24. Aliber, *The Multinational Paradigm*, pp. 169–207.

25. Stephen A. Hymer, *The International Operations of National Firms: A Study of Foreign Direct Investment* (Cambridge, Mass.: M.I.T. Press, 1976).

26. Richard E. Caves, "International Corporations: The Industrial Economics of Foreign Direct Investment," *Economica*, 38 (February 1971), pp. 1–27.

27. Charles P. Kindleberger, *American Business Abroad: Six Essays on Direct Investment* (New Haven, Conn.: Yale University Press, 1969).

28. Ronald Coase, "The Nature of the Firm," *Economica*, 4 (November 1937), pp. 1–40.

29. Peter Buckley and Mark Casson, *The Future of the Multinational Enterprise* (New York: Holmes and Meier, 1976), pp. 35–65.

30. Peter Buckley and Mark Casson: *The Economic Theory of the Multinational Enterprise* (New York: St. Martin's Press, 1985), pp. 9–11; and ibid., Chapter 2.

31. Buckley and Casson, *The Economic Theory of the Multinational Enterprise*, p. 10.

32. Alan M. Rugman, "New Theories of Multinational Enterprises: An Assessment of Internalization Theory," *Bulletin of Economic Research*, 38 no. 2 (May 1986), p. 105.

33. Buckley and Casson, *The Economic Theory of the Multinational Enterprise*, p. 10.

34. John McManus, "The Theory of the International Firm," in *The Multi-*

national Firm and the Nation State, ed. Giles Paquet (Toronto: Collier-Macmillan, 1975), pp. 66–93.

35. Stephen P. Magee, "Information and the International Corporation: An Appropriability Theory of Foreign Direct Investment," in *The New International Economic Order*, ed. Jagdish Bhagwati (Cambridge, Mass.: M.I.T. Press, 1977), pp. 317–40.

36. John H. Dunning, "Trade, Location of Economic Activity and Multinational Enterprises: A Search for an Eclectic Approach," in *International Production and the Multinational Enterprise*, ed. John H. Dunning (London: George Allen and Unwin, 1981), pp. 21–45.

37. John H. Dunning, "The Determinants of Multinational Production," *Oxford Economic Papers*, 25 (January 1973), pp. 289–336.

38. Dunning, "Trade, Location of Economic Activity, and Multinational Enterprises."

39. John H. Dunning: "Changes in the Structure of International Production in the Last 100 Years," in *The Growth of International Business*, ed. Mark Casson (London: Allen and Unwin, 1983); and "Market Power of the Firm and International Transfer of Technology," *International Journal of Industrial Organization*, 1 (1983), pp. 333–51.

40. Dunning, "Trade, Location of Economic Activity, and Multinational Enterprises," p. 30.

41. John H. Dunning, "The Eclectic Paradigm of International Production: A Restatement and Some Possible Extensions," *Journal of International Business Studies*, Spring 1988, p. 3.

42. Dunning, "Trade, Location of Economic Activity, and Multinational Enterprises," pp. 30–31.

43. Dunning, "The Eclectic Paradigm of International Production," p. 4.

44. Ibid., p. 15.

45. Raymond Vernon, "International Investment and International Trade in the Product Cycle," *Quarterly Journal of Economics*, 80 (May 1966), pp. 190–207.

46. Peter Buckley, "A Critical Review of Theories of the Multinational Enterprise," *Assenwirtschaft*, 36, no. I (1981), pp. 70–87.

47. Raymond Vernon, "The Product Cycle Hypothesis in a New International Environment," *Oxford Bulletin of Economics and Statistics*, 40 (1979), pp. 255–67.

48. Frederick Knickerbocker, *Oligopolistic Reaction and Multinational Enterprises* (Cambridge, Mass.: Harvard Business School, Division of Research, 1973).

49. Edward B. Flowers, "Oligopolistic Reactions in European and Canadian Direct Investment in the United States," *Journal of International Business Studies*, 7 (Fall/Winter 1976), pp. 43–55.

50. DeAnne Julius, *Foreign Direct Investment: The Neglected Twin of Trade*, Occasional Papers 33 (Washington, D.C.: Group of Thirty, 1991).

51. Congress of the United States, Office of Technology Assessment, *Multinationals and the National Interest: Playing by Different Rules*, OTA-ITE-569 (Washington, D.C.: Government Printing Office, September 1993), p. 53.

52. The current cost (replacement cost) basis technique to measure direct investment capital flows was introduced in 1992. Direct investment capital flows are now measured on a current cost basis after adjustments to reported depreciation, depletion, and expensed exploration and development costs. These three items make up

the current cost adjustment, which is classified as a valuation adjustment. Capital gains and losses are also removed from the capital flow data and are classified as a valuation adjustment. U.S. Department of Commerce, Bureau of Economic Analysis, *Survey of Current Business,* June 1992, pp. 46–59.

53. Rachel McCulloch, "Foreign Direct Investment in the United States," *Finance and Development,* 30, no. 1 (March 1993), p. 14.

54. Ibid.

55. Norman Glickman and Douglas Woodward, *The New Competitors: How Foreign Investors Are Changing the U.S. Economy* (New York: Basic Books, 1989), pp. 115–16.

56. Ibid., pp. 116–17.

CHAPTER 4

The Saving Deficiency in the United States

It is generally believed that the world is facing an acute shortage of capital. Such a shortage foreshadows severe economic consequences in the form of high real interest rates, stagnant levels of investment and economic growth, and reduced standards of living for the industrial nations. The developing nations and the emerging market economies of Eastern Europe and the countries of the former Soviet Union will also suffer greatly from inadequate levels of trade and investment.

Throughout much of the 1980s, the United States absorbed large amounts of internal and external savings to help finance its large budgetary deficits. At present, budget deficits in the United States, as well as in some other industrial countries, continue to create a demand for external savings, and these movements are mirrored in international capital flows.

For the United States, net international capital flows were large during the 1980s, mainly reflecting financing requirements for large government deficits. At the same time, the United States experienced large net inflows of foreign direct investment as foreign-owned multinationals established subsidiaries in the United States and also acquired establishments. By the mid-1980s the United States was on the verge of becoming a net debtor instead of a net creditor.

Before the problem of future world capital shortages is resolved, the United States, which bears a large responsibility for the creation of this dilemma, must take steps to solve its economic problems and regain its ability to once more become a net exporter of capital. In addition to large budget deficits and a low rate of national savings, the problems of fragility in the financial sector that restricted credit availability was another problem. By resolving its own domestic problems, the United States should be able to play a pivotal role in shaping the nature of the world economy for generations to come.

A country's national savings consists of private savings plus government savings. In a closed economy, national savings would equal gross domestic investment, but in an open economy the national savings must equal the sum of domestic investment plus foreign investment (net international lending, which is the value of the current account balance). When domestic investment is subtracted from national savings the remainder becomes foreign investment, which can be positive or negative.

Throughout, we will make the assumption made by many economists that domestic factors that affect national savings (private savings plus public savings) and domestic investment affect the current account and the amount of capital inflow or outflow (net international lending). Furthermore, it is assumed that domestic macroeconomic policy becomes the deciding factor affecting the current account. And net capital inflows (or outflows) become the difference between private savings and domestic investment. Changes in international capital flows are determined by changes in private savings minus domestic investment.

To comprehend the role of the United States in exacerbating global capital shortages, it is necessary to look at the different components of savings—private savings, government savings, and savings from the rest of the world. This chapter will examine historical data on savings and investment for the period 1977–81 to 1993 to show the changes that took place as the United States became a large user of global capital.

GLOBAL SAVING AND INVESTMENT IMBALANCES

The decline in private savings as a fraction of gross domestic product is a phenomenon that is not unique to the United States. Most industrial countries have experienced a large decline in private savings since the 1973 oil shock. Data for savings and investment as a percentage of GDP for the industrial countries are given in Table 4.1. Between 1977–81 and 1993, the national savings rates for the group fell by 3.7 percent and is expected to start increasing for 1994 and 1995.

The principal reason for the trend decline in national savings has been the widespread increase in budgetary imbalances. Although there was some improvement in national savings in 1987–89 as a result of increases in government savings, national savings rates fell again in 1990–93 as a consequence of a further decline in government saving.[1]

Although the private savings rate rose by 0.4 percent in 1993, for the period as a whole it fell by 1.3 percent of GDP and is projected to fall by an additional 0.2 percent of GDP by 1995. Government savings, which fell

Table 4.1
Summary of Sources and Uses of Saving in the Industrial Countries,
1977–95 (in percent of GDP)

	Averages 1977-81	Averages 1982-86	1987	1988	1989	1990	1991	1992	1993	1994[a]	1995[a]
Industrial countries											
Saving	22.9	20.7	20.5	21.2	21.4	20.7	20.1	19.4	19.4	19.8	20.2
Private	21.5	21.0	19.6	19.8	19.3	19.2	19.6	19.8	20.2	20.3	20.0
Public	1.4	-0.3	0.9	1.5	2.2	1.5	0.5	-0.5	-0.7	-0.5	0.2
Investment	23.2	21.0	21.0	21.7	22.1	21.6	20.6	20.0	19.6	20.0	20.5
Private	19.4	17.3	17.5	18.2	18.6	17.9	17.0	16.4	15.8	16.3	16.8
Public	3.7	3.7	3.5	3.5	3.6	3.8	3.6	3.6	3.7	3.7	3.7
Net lending	-0.2	-0.3	-0.6	-0.5	-0.7	-0.9	-0.4	-0.7	-0.1	-0.2	-0.2
United States											
Saving	20.8	17.5	16.0	16.6	16.4	15.2	14.6	13.9	14.9	15.6	16.0
Private	18.8	18.6	16.1	16.4	15.6	15.4	15.8	16.0	16.1	16.0	15.9
Public	1.9	-1.2	-0.1	0.2	0.8	-0.2	-1.1	-2.2	-1.3	-0.5	0.1
Investment	21.0	19.4	18.9	18.4	18.2	16.9	15.2	15.5	16.2	17.4	18.0
Private	18.5	17.1	16.5	16.2	15.8	14.6	12.9	13.2	14.0	15.2	15.9
Public	2.5	2.2	2.4	2.2	2.3	2.3	2.3	2.3	2.2	2.2	2.1
Net lending	-0.2	-1.9	-2.9	-1.8	-1.7	-1.7	-0.6	-1.6	-1.3	-1.8	-2.0
European Union											
Saving	21.7	20.0	20.3	21.1	21.6	21.1	19.9	19.0	18.7	19.4	20.0
Private	21.5	20.9	20.7	21.0	21.0	21.5	21.1	21.3	21.9	22.2	22.2
Public	0.2	-1.0	-0.4	0.1	0.5	-0.4	-1.2	-2.3	-3.2	-2.9	-2.2
Investment	22.2	19.7	19.8	21.0	21.7	21.6	20.9	20.0	18.6	19.0	19.5
Private	19.0	16.2	16.5	17.6	18.2	17.6	17.5	16.7	15.4	15.8	16.2
Public	3.2	3.5	3.3	3.4	3.5	4.0	3.4	3.3	3.2	3.2	3.3
Net lending	-0.5	0.3	0.5	0.1	-0.2	-0.5	-1.0	-1.0	--	0.3	0.5
Japan											
Saving	31.9	31.0	32.3	33.4	33.8	34.0	34.7	34.4	33.5	32.6	32.0
Private	28.2	26.7	25.8	25.5	24.2	23.6	25.0	25.1	25.4	26.0	24.4
Public	3.7	4.3	6.5	7.9	9.6	10.4	9.7	9.3	8.1	6.6	7.6
Investment	31.5	28.4	28.7	30.6	31.8	32.8	32.5	31.2	30.4	29.6	29.3
Private	21.8	20.6	21.8	23.7	25.0	26.0	25.6	23.5	21.7	20.6	20.7
Public	9.7	7.8	6.9	6.9	6.7	6.8	6.9	7.6	8.7	9.0	8.6
Net lending	0.4	2.6	3.6	2.7	2.0	1.2	2.2	3.2	3.1	3.0	2.7

Source: International Monetary Fund, World Economic and Financial Surveys, *World Economic Outlook, May 1994* (Washington DC: International Monetary Fund, 1994), p. 173.

[a] Projections

from 1.4 percent of GDP in 1977–81 to −0.7 percent in 1993, were projected to rise to 0.2 percent of GDP by 1995. With the exception of Japan, which has had general government surpluses since 1987, the six other major industrial countries generally experienced deficits in their general government financial balances. Although most of the seven major industrial countries had initiated programs of deficit reduction, the fiscal situation deteriorated for most because of weak economic performance in the early 1990s.[2] But even if cyclical influences were to be removed, it was forecast that structural deficits would continue into the medium term for all of the major industrial countries except Japan. Structural deficits for 1994 and 1995 were estimated to be in the range of 2 to 7 percent of GDP.[3]

Table 4.1 also shows investment rates for the industrial countries. Over the period, the domestic investment rate generally exceeded the national saving rate by 0.1 to 0.9 percent of GDP. However, the saving rate and the investment rate each fell by more than 3 percent of GDP. A large part of the decline in the national saving rate was caused by the deterioration of budgetary performance in the public sector, as public saving declined from 1.4 percent of GDP to −0.7 percent. In addition, a reduction in the rate of private saving also contributed substantially to a decline in the national saving rate.

Table 4.1 also shows savings and investment for the European Union, the United States, and Japan. Over the period 1977–81 to 1993, private savings for the European Union rose by 0.4 percent of GDP compared with a 3.6 percent of GDP decline in private investment. National saving declined by 3 percent of GDP largely because of budgetary deficits incurred during most of the 1980s as governments struggled to maintain domestic demand. Increased government outlays associated with reunification of East and West Germany led to a widening of these deficits in the early 1990s. For most years, the European Union was a net importer of capital, but in 1983–88 the Union was a net exporter of small amounts of capital. In 1991–93, Germany's current account was in deficit after years of running large current account surpluses, and this caused the European Union to become a substantial borrower of international capital in 1991–92.

For the United States, the trend in the rate of investment for the period 1977–81 to 1986–90 differs from the longer period 1977–81 to 1993. Between 1977–81 and 1987–90, the private savings rate fell by slightly more than the private investment rate—a decline of 2.9 percent of GDP for private saving compared with 2.7 percent for private investment. But when 1977–81 is compared with the average of 1991 to 1993, private savings fell by 2.8 percent of GDP compared with 4.9 percent of GDP for private investment. The recession of the early 1990s had a very severe impact upon private investment in the United States. As in the European Union, the national savings rate fell by more than the private savings rate because of large government deficits. Throughout the 1980s and early 1990s, the United States was a net borrower of international capital, and this borrowing peaked in the mid-1980s when the United States experienced very large current account deficits and large budgetary deficits (the so-called twin deficits problem).

In Japan, the national saving rate increased by about 1.6 percent of GDP over the period 1977–81 to 1993. This occurred despite the fact that the private saving rate declined by 2.8 percent of GDP because the public sector rate of saving steadily increased. Also, from 1977–81 to 1990, private investment increased as a percent of GDP while public investment fell. But in 1991–93, private investment declined while public investment rose. National savings were sufficiently high that during the 1980s and early 1990s, national savings exceeded domestic investment and Japan's net international lending rose.

Because of high national savings, Japan increased its foreign lending. From 0.4 percent of GDP in 1977–81, Japan's net lending rate soared to 3.1 percent of GDP in 1993, making Japan the major supplier of international capital. Although Germany had substantial surpluses during the 1980s, by 1991 Germany became a borrower of foreign capital because of problems associated with the reunification and rebuilding of the former East Germany.

Of the seven major industrial countries—the United States, Japan, Germany, the United Kingdom, Italy, France, and Canada—only the United Kingdom has a lower national savings rate than the United States. Also, of these seven countries, the United States has the lowest rate of household savings (see Table 4.2).

Household savings have been one factor affecting national savings rates. Data for net household savings out of disposable income show divergent trends over the period 1976–93 for the major industrial countries. For the United States, Japan, Italy, France, and Canada, the trend was clearly downward. For the United Kingdom, however, the overall trend in this rate was downward for 1976–85 to 1986–90 but then rose to its earlier level. No clear-cut trend was evident for Germany.

Japan saves a much larger share of personal disposable income than most of the six other major industrial countries, but its household saving rate underwent a large drop: from 20.4 percent of disposable income in 1977–81 to 14.7 percent in 1991–93. The U.S. share also declined significantly over the period, from an average of 7.6 percent of disposable income to 4.7 percent in 1990–93. It is noteworthy that not all of the major industrial countries experienced a large drop in net household savings as a percentage of disposable income. For instance, Germany's saving rate remained fairly constant over the entire period, ranging from 11 to 14 percent of disposable income.

Three areas—the United States, the European Community, and Japan—account for the major share of international capital movements, and the savings-investment balances of these three areas have been reflected in current account imbalances. This has occurred in a climate where exchange rates float up and down in response to the supply and demand for foreign exchange and capital can move freely between different countries. For instance, in a country in which national saving was less than domestic investment, real interest rates would rise because of the imbalance between national savings and domestic investment. When interest rates rise, because of the imbalance between savings and investment, capital would in theory flow into a country, and that country's exchange rate would appreciate until

Table 4.2

Saving Rates for Major Industrial Countries, 1976–95

	1976-80	1981-85	1986-90	1991	1992
United States	20.1	18.6	16.2	15.4	14.5
Japan	31.9	30.9	33.5	35.1	33.9
Germany[1]	22.4	21.1	24.5	23.1	22.7
France	24.3	19.6	20.9	20.7	19.7
Italy	25.8	22.1	20.4	18.6	17.2
United Kingdom	17.8	17.0	15.5	13.5	12.8
Canada	21.2	20.1	18.7	14.4	13.6

B. Household Saving as a Percentage of Disposable Income

	1976-80	1981-85	1986-90	1991	1992	1993	1994[2]	1995[2]
United States	7.3	8.0	4.7	4.9	5.0	4.6	4.3	4.4
Japan	20.4	16.5	14.8	15.1	14.3	14.6	14.8	14.2
Germany[1]	12.6	12.0	12.8	12.8	12.9	12.1	11.3	11.1
France[3]	18.7	15.9	11.8	13.1	13.9	14.1	13.6	13.1
Italy[3]	25.1	20.2	17.5	18.2	18.8	18.9	18.0	16.7
United Kingdom[3]	11.3	11.1	7.5	10.1	12.3	11.5	9.9	8.8
Canada	12.5	15.3	10.0	10.3	10.8	10.6	10.4	10.0

Source: Organization for Economic Cooperation and Development, *OECD Economic Outlook, June 1994* (Paris: OECD, 1994), pp. A27-A28.

1. West Germany
2. Projections
3. Gross saving

real interest parity is achieved. Real interest parity occurs when the expected returns on deposits of any two currencies are equal if measured in either of the two currencies. When the higher real interest rate in the country in which appreciation occurs plus the expected rate of depreciation of that currency equals the real interest return in the other country, deposit returns in the two countries are equalized and real interest parity is achieved. Capital moves into the country with the higher return until real interest parity is achieved.

Throughout 1993, monetary policy remained expansionary. But in February 1994 the Federal Reserve pushed up the federal funds rate by one-quarter of one percentage point because it wanted to forestall fears of inflation and to raise short-term interest rates. Subsequently, on several other occasions, the Federal Reserve raised the federal funds rate as well as the discount rate, the latest increase coming in February 1995. By the beginning of September, the actions of the Federal Reserve, combined with an increased demand for credit as economic expansion continued, raised interest rates back up to the level prevailing at the end of 1991. Despite the increase in U.S. interest rates in 1994, there has not yet been a tendency for the dollar to appreciate against the currencies of the major industrial countries. This could have happened because of increasing expectations that the U.S. rate of inflation would rise with the continuation of economic expansion. Higher expected inflation could keep the U.S. real rate of interest from rising above world levels even if nominal interest rates were to rise. Also, rising U.S. trade balance deficits, caused because other industrial countries' econonomies were slower to emerge from recession, led to the depreciation of the dollar against the currencies of the major industrial countries.

In the country in which the appreciation has occurred, the price of imports decreases and the price of that country's exports increases. Depending on the elasticities of demand for exports and imports, following a time lag, the current account should worsen and the change in the current account balance would equate the value of capital imports. Thus, the saving-investment imbalance, by affecting the rate of interest and the exchange rate, drives the changes in the current account, which is ultimately reflected in the value of capital imports.

In the early 1980s, as a consequence of the 1981 tax reductions in the United States, large budget deficits appeared. Because of large federal government borrowing needs, interest rates in the United States were in excess of those in many other countries and capital moved into the United States. The dollar exchange rate appreciated, which made U.S. exports expensive while imports became cheaper and the current account deteriorated. Although the appreciation of the dollar peaked in 1985, the current account continued to deteriorate until 1987, mainly because it takes time for a currency depreciation to affect the balance of trade. From 1988 to 1991 the current account improved and was almost in balance. But as the U.S. economy slowly began to improve from the 1990–91 recession at the same time that many of the industrial countries were mired in recession, the current account deteriorated again.

At the same time that the U.S. current account was deteriorating, Germany and Japan ran large surpluses. From $20.8 billion in 1983, Japan's current account surplus rose to $49.2 billion in 1985, and, despite the large appreciation of the yen against the dollar, rose to $87.0 billion in 1987. Although it declined to $35.8 billion in 1990, it rose again, reaching $117.6 billion in 1992 and $131.4 billion in 1993 and is forecast to decline a little in 1995. In the 1980s and early 1990s, Japan has functioned as a major supplier of capital to industrial countries with current account deficits as well as to developing countries.

Like Japan, West Germany experienced growing current account surpluses that rose steadily from $5.4 billion in 1983 to $57.4 billion in 1989. Because of large outlays associated with the rebuilding of East Germany after reunification occurred in June 1990, in 1991–93, Germany incurred substantial deficits.

It is noteworthy that during the period, U.S. deficits were almost as large as, and at times exceeded, the combined surpluses of Germany and Japan. With the United States absorbing so much of the world's savings, less was left to finance other economies' requirements, including those of the developing countries and countries in transition. Although 1991 and 1992 were years of lower U.S. deficits, it has been estimated that in 1994 and 1995 U.S. current account deficits will exceed Japan's current account surpluses of over $130 billion. Such an imbalance in the U.S. current account position can only be resolved within the context of correcting the country's imbalance between savings and investment.

REDUCING THE U.S. SAVING DEFICIENCY

Prospects for Public-Sector Saving

The large savings-investment imbalances of the United States in the 1980s coincided with large capital inflows into the country. Large federal budget deficits were very instrumental in bringing about these inflows. Because of large budgetary deficits, government borrowing added excessively to the demand for capital, and for much of the period real interest rates remained high by historical standards. High interest rates contributed to an appreciated dollar, which raised prices for U.S. exports and reduced prices for imports, and for much of the period current account deficits were very large. High real interest rates adversely affected domestic investment and capital formation, and this will contribute toward a reduced rate of growth in future U.S. living standards.

It is noteworthy that whereas the growth rate of U.S. fixed capital formation during the period 1983–85 was significantly greater than in Japan and the European countries of the Organization for Economic Cooperation and Development (OECD), in the late 1980s, the U.S. rate of growth of fixed capital formation was much lower than in either Japan or Europe. Over the period 1986–89, the annual growth rate for fixed capital formation in the United States averaged 1.0 percent compared with 8.9 percent for Japan and 6.4 percent for the European countries of the OECD.[4]

The American public became increasingly aware of the problem of large budget deficits during the presidential election of 1992, and in August 1993 the Clinton administration oversaw the passage of the Omnibus Budget Reconciliation Act of 1993 (OBRA 1993)—a major package of revenue increases and spending reductions—that the Congressional Budget Office (CBO) of the United States initially estimated will reduce cumulative federal government budget deficits between fiscal year 1994 through 1998 by $433 billion compared with baseline projections produced in the winter of 1993.[5] Estimates for yearly deficits that were made in January 1994 reduce the cumulative five-year total by an additional $115 billion. Of these additional savings, $60 billion will result from revised projections of economic growth and a lower overall inflation rate in 1993 than was originally forecast. The remainder will come from technical reestimates, of which $21 billion are related to saving on federal deposit insurance.

Tax increases are expected to contribute $280 billion to the five-year savings; direct spending cuts, $77 billion; debt service savings, $81 billion; and new discretionary spending limits for 1996, 1997, and 1998, $69 billion.

It has been estimated that more than one-half of the deficit reduction will come from changes in tax policy that increase revenues. As a consequence of the 1981 tax reduction package, taxes on high income earners had been significantly reduced. OBRA 1993 restores some of the progressivity to the U.S. personal income tax by including new tax brackets of 36.0 percent and 39.6 percent; increasing the alternative minimum tax; phasing out personal exemptions on high income earners; and limiting the amount of deductions.

In September 1993 it was estimated by the CBO that these measures will contribute $115 billion over a five-year period. Another $31 billion in saving would be raised by higher taxes on the sale of gasoline; $29 billion would come from repealing the cap ($135,000) on earnings subject to the Medicare payroll tax; $25 billion from taxing income up to 85 percent of an individual's Social Security benefits if the recipient is a single filer earning in excess of $34,000 or a joint filer with a combined income in excess of $44,000; $16 billion from raising the corporate tax rate from 34 percent to 35 percent; and $15 billion from reducing the deductible part of business entertainment and meals from 80 percent to 50 percent.[6]

The CBO has estimated that over 80 percent of the net increases in tax revenue would be paid by families having incomes of at least $200,000 and over 90 percent by families having incomes of at least $100,000, and that the effective rate on the 1 percent of families with the highest income would be at its highest level since 1979. In addition to enhancing the progressivity of the system, the tax package will reduce the taxes paid by an average family with income under $36,000 when, in 1996, the expansion of the earned income tax credit will be fully phased in.[7] This will reduce the effective tax rate on the 20 percent of families in the lowest income quintile to less than one-half its 1985 level and lower than it had been for sixteen years.

Although an ideological debate occurred in the Congress of the United States between those who wanted much of the deficit reduction to come from increased taxes levied on those most able to pay and other members of Congress who focused attention on spending reductions, it is estimated that in the final version of the legislation less than half of the deficit reduction comes from expenditure reductions. It was estimated that the $193 in spending cuts would be distributed as follows: $76.9 billion from mandatory spending categories, including $56 billion from Medicare; $68 billion from limitations on discretionary spending; and $47 billion from savings on servicing of the public debt.

The 1993 budget agreement reduces significantly the projected size of the federal deficit by fiscal year 1998. Whereas the CBO had estimated in the winter of 1993 that the deficit would grow from $290 billion in 1992 to $360 billion in 1998, and that debt held by the public would grow from 51 percent to 62 percent of GDP, in a recently revised estimate the deficit falls to $197 billion by 1998, or from 4.9 percent to 2.4 percent of GDP, and debt held by the public rises to only 51.7 percent of GDP (see Table 4.3).

For a number of reasons, the 1993 budget agreement can only be regarded as a first step in efforts to bring down the size of the deficit. For instance, the CBO takes note of two possible threats:

But two threats cloud the budget outlook. First, experience teaches that budget projections can go quickly awry. Shortly after the 1990 budget agreement was enacted into law, CBO projected that the deficit would virtually disappear by 1995. But in actuality, slower-than-expected economic growth, unanticipated increases in Medicare and Medicaid spending, and other factors beyond the direct control of the President and the Congress swelled the deficit and necessitated another round of deficit reduction. Second, even if they hold up, the new projections suggest that rising health care costs will cause the deficit to grow again after 1998. By 2003, if current policies are maintained, the deficit would reach $359 billion.[8]

It is possible to list several factors that could retard the amount of deficit reduction that could occur by 1998. Most important is the rate of growth in real GDP, which was projected to grow by 3.9 percent in fiscal year 1994, 3.0 percent in 1995, and average 2.2 percent a year between 1996–99. If growth were to be slower or another recession were to occur, the average growth rate for the period would be lower. Because tax revenue collections depend largely on income, revenue would be lower than projected. Outlays could also be higher than anticipated. In a recession, outlays on programs such as unemployment insurance and food stamps would increase. Because economic growth in 1994 was higher than expected, the Federal Reserve undertook monetary tightening measures, which could precipitate a recession by 1996. Unexpected events in the international economic and political environments could affect U.S. economic growth through changes in net exports and global capital markets.

One other outlay that could easily change is the amount expended to service the public debt. Net interest on the debt is now expected to grow from 3.0 percent of GDP in fiscal year 1994 to 3.3 percent by 2004. In the winter of 1993 it had been estimated that net interest would grow to 4.5 percent of GDP by 2003. The decline in the projection of net interest on the public debt is largely a result of policy measures to reduce the deficit. The projection that net interest outlays would amount to 3.3 percent of GDP by 2004 is based on a number of highly specific assumptions, which

Table 4.3

The Budget Outlook Through 2004 (by fiscal year)

	1994	1995	1996	1997	1998	1999	2000	2001	2002	2003	2004
					In Billions of Dollars						
Revenues	1,265	1,363	1,433	1,492	1,562	1,632	1,713	1,799	1,891	1,988	2,091
Outlays											
Discretionary	545	546	550	547	547	566	585	605	626	647	669
Mandatory											
Social Security	317	333	350	368	388	408	430	452	476	501	528
Medicare	158	177	195	216	238	263	290	320	354	391	434
Medicaid	84	96	108	121	135	151	168	186	206	227	250
Federal Pensions	63	65	68	71	74	79	83	87	91	95	100
Other	172	175	176	189	197	205	213	220	227	235	243
Subtotal	794	847	898	965	1,032	1,107	1,183	1,265	1,354	1,451	1,555
Deposit insurance -5	-17	-14	-5	-5	-4	-2	-2	-2	-2	-2	
Net Interest	202	226	245	253	264	277	290	307	325	346	368
Offsetting receipts	-68	-77	-72	-75	-80	-83	-86	-90	-94	-98	-103
Total	1.467	1,525	1,609	1,664	1,758	1,863	1,970	2,086	2,209	2,343	2,488
Deficit	202	162	176	193	197	231	257	287	319	355	397
Deficit Excluding Deposit Insurance	207	180	188	198	202	235	260	288	320	357	399
Debt Held by the Public	3,440	3,611	3,801	4,011	4,226	4,476	4,753	5,059	5,397	5,771	6,188
					As a Percentage of GDP						
Revenues	19.0	19.3	19.3	19.1	19.1	19.0	19.0	19.0	19.0	19.0	18.9
Outlays											
Discretionary	8.2	7.7	7.4	7.0	6.7	6.6	6.5	6.4	6.3	6.2	6.1
Mandatory											
Social Security	4.7	4.7	4.7	4.7	4.7	4.8	4.8	4.8	4.8	4.8	4.8
Medicare	2.4	2.5	2.6	2.8	2.9	3.1	3.2	3.4	3.5	3.7	3.9
Medicaid	1.3	1.4	1.5	1.6	1.7	1.8	1.9	2.0	2.1	2.2	2.3
Federal Pensions	0.9	0.9	0.9	0.9	0.9	0.9	0.9	0.9	0.9	0.9	0.9
Other	2.6	2.5	2.4	2.4	2.4	2.3	2.4	2.3	2.3	2.2	2.1
Subtotal	11.9	12.0	12.1	12.4	12.6	12.9	13.1	13.4	13.6	13.8	14.1
Deposit insurance	-0.1	-0.2	-0.2	-0.1	-0.1	a	a	a	a	a	a
Net interest	3.0	3.2	3.3	3.2	3.2	3.2	3.2	3.2	3.3	3.3	3.3
Offsetting receipts	-1.0	-1.1	-1.0	-1.0	-1.0	-1.0	-1.0	-1.0	-0.9	-0.9	-0.9
Total	22.0	21.6	21.6	21.6	21.5	21.7	21.8	22.0	22.2	22.3	22.5
Deficit	3.0	2.3	2.4	2.5	2.4	2.7	2.9	3.0	3.2	3.4	3.6
Deficit Excluding Deposit Insurance	3.1	2.5	2.5	2.5	2.5	2.7	2.9	3.0	3.2	3.4	3.6
Debt Held by the Public	51.5	51.1	51.2	51.4	51.7	52.2	52.7	53.4	54.1	55.0	56.1

SOURCE: Congress of the United States, Congressional Budget Office, *The Economic and Budget Outlook: Fiscal Years 1995-1999* (Washington, D.C.: Government Printing Office, August 1994), p. 31.

include an inflation rate of a little over 3 percent in 1996–2004; real GDP growing at 4.0 percent in 1994, 3.0 percent in 1995, and averaging 2.2 percent in 1995–2004; short-term interest rates of 4.1 percent in 1994, 5.5 percent in 1995, and an average of 4.9 percent in 1996–2004; and ten-year Treasury note rates of 6.4 percent in 1994, 6.9 percent in 1995, and an average of 6.5 percent in 1996–2004.[9] Were economic growth to be less than projected, annual deficits would be larger, and if the inflation rate accelerated, nominal interest rates would go up accordingly and net interest outlays would rise. Interest payments on the federal debt amounted to 14.13 percent of total outlays in fiscal year 1993. These outlays are expected to rise to 15.22 percent by 1996 and then decline to 14.79 percent by 2004. Without the 1993 budget agreement, net interest outlays were projected to rise to 15.88 percent of total outlays in 1998 and 17.78 percent in 2003.

The 1993 budget agreement was only a first step in efforts to reduce the size of the federal deficit. As already noted, it is currently projected that the deficit will start to rise again if no further steps are taken. In order to bring the size of the structural deficit (the deficit that removes the effect of the business cycle on federal revenues and spending) down to zero, further tax increases and expenditure reductions can be proposed. Given current projections for federal revenues and spending, the structural deficit in 1998 is estimated at $164 billion.

During the debate over the 1993 budget agreement, the administration had proposed a 10 cents a gallon increase in the federal excise tax on motor fuels, but the legislation passed by the Congress reduced the increase in the tax to 4.3 cents a gallon. Over the five-year period 1994–98, had an excise tax increase of 10 cents a gallon been implemented, an estimated $30 billion in revenues would have been raised, furthering deficit reduction.[10]

The fastest growing part of federal outlays in the next decade is in mandatory expenditures as opposed to discretionary expenditures. Over the period 1994 to 2004, discretionary expenditures have been projected to rise by 22.8 percent to $658 billion, and as a share of GDP they fall from 8.2 percent to 6.1 percent. At the same time, mandatory expenditures (the entitlements) would grow by 95.9 percent to $1,555 billion, or from 11.9 percent of GDP to 14.1 percent. Of the $1,555 billion, Social Security, Medicare, and Medicaid will contribute 77.9 percent. These three outlays will comprise 48.7 percent of total outlays in fiscal year 2004, an increase from 38 percent in 1993. If measures are not taken to reverse the growth in these three entitlements, by the year 2020, when many of the baby boom generation will have reached retirement age, very little will be left for discretionary outlays.

Efforts will be necessary to rein in the growth of mandatory outlays. It is possible to reduce the growth in Social Security outlays without abandoning the original mandate of the 1935 Social Security Act. Originally, Social Security was intended to resemble private insurance, with funds being paid into a trust fund by workers and employers, interest was to be credited to the trust fund balances, and a worker's previous earnings would determine benefits upon retirement. But as the system evolved it no longer resembled an insurance scheme. Benefits received have been greater than what would have been justified by payroll taxes paid in plus a reasonable rate of return. Trust fund balances now finance only a small part of a beneficiary's benefit payment, and the remainder is financed by current workers.[11] Because of revenue requirements, in 1984 Congress began taxing 50 percent of the benefits of higher income recipients having income earnings from other sources, and in the 1993 budget agreement, the proportion of benefits from higher income recipients that was taxable was raised to 85 percent.

Based on a law passed by Congress in 1983, benefits were reduced and payments accelerated in order to make the Social Security system solvent. It was anticipated that because there would be few retirees born in the 1920s and 1930s when birth rates were low, current workers would contribute sufficient amounts to make the system solvent, and that contributions would be sufficient to pay benefits until at least 2025.[12]

Because current law taxes only 85 percent of the benefits of these higher income earners, it still leaves higher income recipients with benefits for which they made no contributions. Such benefits are paid to individuals even if they have incomes of $100,000, $1 million, or $10 million from other sources. At present, a substantial number of retirees have very comfortable incomes. Yet under present law they receive Social Security and Medicare benefits.

National savings include both private savings (personal plus business savings) and government savings, and reductions in the federal government deficit raises national savings. But one cannot anticipate that national savings will increase by the full amount of the reduction in the deficit because reductions in private savings stemming from higher taxes will offset some of the improvement associated with the new policies. Deficit reductions in the 1993 budget agreement depend heavily on higher taxes, and based on a number of statistical studies, the CBO projections assume that a reduction in private savings will offset about 30 percent of the estimated reduction in the deficit. Furthermore, some of the savings from deficit reduction would come from reducing the federal government's net borrowing from abroad and would not be available for domestic investment.[13]

In the autumn of 1993 the Congressional Budget Office estimated the impact of deficit reduction on the national saving rate. It was projected that the federal government deficit would fall from an estimated $360 billion to $200 billion and that nominal GDP would equal $8,078 billion in 1998. Assuming 30 percent of the $160 billion in savings was to be offset by higher taxes leaves $112 billion or an increment in the national saving rate of 1.4 percent of GDP.

A decline in a government's deficit as a share of GDP would raise the national saving rate and increase the supply of capital available to the domestic economy. Because of a falloff in the government's demand for credit, interest rates should fall. The Clinton administration's intention to reduce the budget deficit was made public in early 1993, and in the first three months of the year, long-term interest rates declined by 0.6 percentage points, and further reductions occurred thereafter. For instance, between

October 27, 1992, and October 27, 1993, the 30-year Treasury bond rate fell by 1.60 percentage points to 6.00 percent. (Assuming a 3 percent rate of inflation the real rate of interest fell to 3 percent.)

On a number of occasions in 1994 and once in February 1995, the Federal Reserve raised short-term interest rates in order to guard against inflation in an expanding economy. Between early 1994 and early 1995, short-term interest rates increased by over 2 percentage points and long-term rates increased by 1.5 percentage points. Although the Federal Reserve intended only to raise short-term interest rates, long-term rates also increased because of the expansion of the economy and higher demand for capital to invest in plant and equipment as well as a deterioration in inflationary expectations. However, real long-term interest rates are still at least 3 percentage points below real long-term interest rates after the 1981–82 recession. Because real long-term interest rates affect investment decisions, lower long-term rates can create a more favorable climate for investment than occurred following the 1981–82 recession. An increased rate of investment in plant and equipment raises the overall level of an economy's economic growth.

It has been argued that an important reason for high real long-term interest rates in the 1980s was a fear of a worldwide shortage of capital. As long as the United States did not take determined steps to reduce the federal deficit, it was feared that U.S. borrowing needs would continue to contribute to a shortage of global capital.

The Congressional Budget Office argues that some of the decrease in government borrowing would go toward reducing federal government borrowing from abroad, and would not be available for investment. The CBO has estimated that between 32 and 47 percent of deficit reduction would go toward the reduction of net capital inflows. Taking the 30 percent decline in private savings that would occur with deficit reduction as a consequence of higher taxes, only about 30 percent of the decline in government borrowing would be available for private investment.[14]

Deficit reduction has implications for the international availability of capital. It is estimated that of a $160 billion reduction in the deficit by 1998, 40 percent or almost 1 percent of U.S. GDP would go toward reducing foreign borrowing by the U.S. government, capital availability on global markets would increase, and lower U.S. demands for foreign capital would reduce interest rates on international capital markets.

Thus, consequently, reducing the federal government's budget deficits would make capital more readily available on international capital markets and would raise the national saving rate. This rate declined by 4.5 percent of GDP during the 1980s compared with the 1970s. About one-half of this decline was caused by the large federal government deficits, but a lower rate of personal saving was also a major factor. Although it has been difficult for economists to account for the decline in the personal saving rate, the following section will examine some of the reasons for this decline. It also must be noted that major revisions in savings data have frequently occurred ex post facto, and that some of the data for savings may be revised upward or downward.

Deficit reduction could also be achieved if the economy were to grow more rapidly during the 1990s than projected. The Congressional Budget Office has projected that real GDP growth would average less than 2.7 percent a year during the remainder of the 1990s, which by historical standards is fairly low. Were the real rate of growth to average between 3 and 4 percent during the remainder of the 1990s, the revenue base would be larger than estimated at present, annual revenues would be higher than projected, and transfer payments such as unemployment compensation would be lower.

Raising the level of economic growth beyond the projected average of less than 2.7 percent for the remainder of the 1990s would contribute toward the reduction of the federal deficit. In March 1992, a group of 100 leading economists, including six Nobel laureates, proposed a plan to stimulate the economy, which was still in a prolonged period of slow economic growth, and to foster long-run economic growth and increased productivity. The economists focused on increasing investment, and proposed $50 billion a year in grants-in-aid for state and local governments to invest in education and physical infrastructure; the restoration of the Investment Tax Credit, which they believed had served the economy well between 1962 and 1986; and an effort by the Federal Reserve to cut interest rates still further than they had already been reduced. Although contributing an additional $50 billion a year to the deficit, by stimulating investment and economic growth, the stimulus package would ultimately have led to a narrowing of the deficit as more rapidly rising GDP produced higher tax revenues and lower transfer payments. With only slow growth anticipated for the remainder of the decade, the 100 economists focused on a stimulus package designed to propel the economy toward higher rates of economic growth.

Slow growth adversely affects revenue prospects because 90 percent of federal revenues are derived from the personal income tax, the payroll tax, and the corporate income tax, all of which are dependent on the level of income. Because the overall burden of this tax structure is moderately progressive, were economic growth to average 4 percent rather than the 2.7 percent assumed by the staff of the CBO, federal revenues could rise by an additional $100 billion by 1998, leaving the deficit at an estimated $80 billion instead of $180 billion. Furthermore, smaller deficits would reduce interest payments on the public debt, which increased from 10 percent of total federal outlays in 1980 to 14 percent in 1993, and at the same time help lower interest rates in the global economy.

If the budget were brought into balance, the net public savings rate would rise from an estimated minus 3 percent of GDP to zero, thereby raising the national saving rate by 3 percent. The other part of the problem is to raise the private saving rate.

Prospects for Raising the Personal Saving Rate

The gross private saving rate is calculated by dividing the sum of personal saving and gross business saving by gross domestic product. In the United States, personal saving represented 4.9 percent of GDP in 1965–69—the personal saving rate being obtained by dividing personal saving by GDP (see Table 4.4). Over the first half of the 1970s, this rate rose to 5.8 percent. However, in the late 1970s, after the 1974–75 recession (the largest recession since the Great Depression) the saving rate dropped to 5.1 percent of GDP. During the years 1980–84, the rate rose again and averaged 5.8 percent, but in the late 1980s and early 1990s, the personal saving rate plummeted to very low levels, averaging 3.7 percent of GDP in 1985–89, and 3.4 percent in 1990–91. It rose to 4.0 percent in 1992, and then fell again in 1993. The explanation that is usually given for this pattern is the fact that between 1985 and 1990 consumers took on unprecedented amounts of debt, and repayment burdens (scheduled principal and interest payments on home mortgages and consumer debt as a percentage of disposable income) rose from an average of 15–16 percent over the period 1965–85 to more than 18 percent in 1989–91. Because of the large buildup of personal debt, consumers needed to restructure their balance sheets, which made it harder for consumption to contribute to recovery from the 1990–91 recession. Although increased demand for consumer loans had been important in increasing consumer spending during earlier recessions, consumers did not increase their consumption sufficiently after the 1990–91 recession to help spur large increases in economic growth, and the economy was slow to recover.

However, gross business saving behaved differently from personal saving over the period, and no significant upward or downward trend emerged. Gross business saving rose from 12 percent of GDP in 1965–69 to an average of 13 percent over the period 1985–90, and then declined to an average of 12.4 percent in 1991–92.[15]

The gross private saving rate combines personal saving and gross business saving. Between 1965 and 1992, fluctuations in this rate, largely as a consequence of changes in personal saving, were substantial. Between 1965 and 1969, gross private saving fell from 17.6 to 15.6 percent of GDP. This rate then increased to 19.3 percent in 1975, the trough of the 1974–75 recession, but then fell to a little over 18 percent throughout the late 1970s. During the years 1980–84, the rate increased again, averaging 19.2 percent of GDP. Like the personal saving rate, this rate declined precipitously during the late 1980s, falling to 16.4 percent of GDP by 1990 and 15.9 percent by 1991. In 1992, as consumers were still retrenching after the 1990–91

Table 4.4
Gross Saving and Investment, 1965-92 (percentage of GDP)

	1965-69	1970-74	1975-79	1980-84	1985-89	1990	1991	1992
Gross Saving	16.5	16.7	17.2	16.7	14.1	13.7	12.5	11.9
Gross Private Saving	16.9	17.2	18.4	19.2	16.7	16.4	15.9	16.4
Personal Saving	4.9	5.8	5.1	5.8	3.7	3.4	3.5	4.0
Gross Business Saving	12.0	11.4	13.3	13.4	13.0	13.0	12.4	12.4
Government Saving	-0.3	-0.6	-1.3	-2.8	-2.5	-2.6	-3.5	-4.5
Gross Investment	16.7	16.8	17.7	16.9	13.9	13.8	12.9	12.3
Gross Private Domestic	16.3	16.5	17.5	17.4	16.6	15.3	12.7	13.2
Net Foreign	0.4	0.2	0.2	-0.4	-2.7	-1.5	0.2	-0.9

Source: Council of Economic Advisors, *Economic Report of the President*. (Washington, D.C.: Government Printing Office, 1994), pp. 268 and 302.

recession and the buildup of consumer debt during the late 1980s, this rate rose to 16.4 percent of GDP. It is evident that the large reduction in the personal saving rate made a significant contribution to the reduction in the national saving rate.

Factors That Could Have Caused a Decline in the U.S. Personal Saving Rate

To comprehend some of the possible causes of the decline in the personal saving rate, the forward looking theory of saving is first summarized.

John Maynard Keynes in *The General Theory* assumed that the ratio of saving to income, the savings rate, increases as the society becomes richer; as people get richer, they save a larger portion of their disposable income.[16] This theory of the consumption function fits empirical observations when savings behavior is observed for a given time period. People with low income do not save and may even dissave, and the saving ratio rises for groups that are richer. But historical time series data for the period since 1900 indicate that, when averaged over major business cycles, the savings rate for the United States has remained remarkably stable.

During the 1950s, Milton Friedman's permanent income hypothesis and Franco Modigliani's life-cycle hypothesis were developed to explain the apparent inconsistency in the movement of the savings ratio when measured by time series and cross-section data.[17] These two hypotheses are forward looking. The consuming unit is seen as having a current income from work and wealth as well as plans and expectations about its future income. The more the consuming unit chooses to save today, the greater will be its future income, including earnings from wealth and labor. Given its vision of future needs, the consuming unit's decision on current consumption and saving reflects its attempt to achieve an optimum pattern of total consumption over its lifetime.[18] According to Modigliani, consumers aim to maximize their utility, and consumption depends only on lifetime resources—the present value of income from labor plus any bequests received—and not on current income. The representative consumer chooses to consume at a stable rate over time, and short-run deviations in income that depart from average lifetime resources will go into saving.[19]

Friedman's hypothesis makes the simplifying assumption that life is indefinitely long and that consumers base their expenditures on their perceptions of expected or "permanent" income. A constant fraction of permanent income is consumed. The difference between actual and permanent income is called "transitory" income. Aggregate permanent income is based on a moving average of actual aggregate income over a number of years. The marginal propensity to consume out of permanent income is high; but the marginal propensity to consume out of transitory income is low and very little is consumed.

Modigliani in the life-cycle hypothesis assumes that the household has a

Figure 4.1
Lifetime Income, Consumption, Savings, and Wealth in the Life-cycle Model

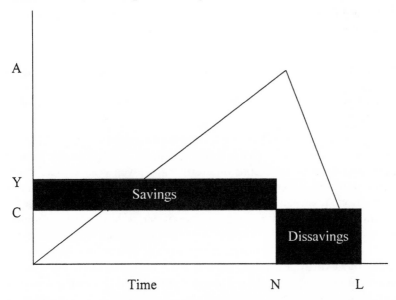

finite lifetime. As in Friedman's permanent income hypothesis, individuals prefer to maintain a stable consumption pattern but, unlike Friedman, individuals try to stabilize consumption over their lifetimes. Modigliani adds the concept of a "lifetime budget constraint," whereby the household's consumption over a lifetime equals income from work plus income from asset holdings from other sources such as gifts and bequests. The life-cycle hypothesis focuses on the household's needs occurring over a lifetime due to changes in family size, reaching maturity, and retiring.[20]

The life-cycle path of saving and wealth is described in Figure 4.1. In the graph, Y, C, and A on the vertical axis equal income, consumption, and assets, respectively. On the horizontal axis, L and N refer to lifetime and age of retirement. The individual saves over a lifetime, acquiring assets (wealth or humped saving) and then uses up assets (or dissaves) during retirement.

In the basic life-cycle hypothesis, these implications follow:

1. The saving rate of a country is entirely independent of its per capita income.

2. Differing national saving rates are consistent with an individual's life cycle.

3. Between countries with identical individual behavior, the aggregate saving rate will be higher the higher the long-run growth rate of the economy.

4. The wealth-income ratio is a decreasing function of the growth rate thus being largest at zero growth.

5. An economy can accumulate a very substantial stock of wealth relative to income even if no wealth is passed on by bequests.

6. The major parameter that controls the wealth-income ratio and the saving rate for given growth is the prevailing rate of retirement.[21]

In the model, short-run behavior of aggregate consumption is described by an aggregate consumption function that is linear in aggregate labor income and in wealth:

$$C = \alpha YL + \delta W$$

where C is consumption, Y is aggregate income, L is length of a working lifetime, and W is wealth. Consumption in any given year is some fraction (perhaps 0.70) of income from work during the household's lifetime plus some fraction (less than 0.07) of wealth.

A controversy that exists about the role of bequests affects the usefulness of the life-cycle hypothesis. The life-cycle hypothesis makes the assumptions that the contribution of bequests is not a major source of existing wealth, and that most of the existing wealth is accumulated because labor income tapers off after retirement. Modigliani has found that the proportion of existing wealth that has been inherited is not greater than 25 percent,[22] that the remainder is accumulated by the humped saving during the individual's working lifetime, and that bequests play an important role only for those in the very highest income brackets. For individuals in the lower income brackets, he assumes that the precautionary motive is responsible for bequests. Uncertainty over the length of life often brings about saving in excess of an amount necessary for retirement, implying that households on the average leave substantial bequests relative to peak wealth. Bequests arising from other than the precautionary motive can be attributed to a genuine bequest motive. This observation differs from other studies that find that intergenerational transfers play a very important role in savings and in the accumulation of wealth in the United States,[23] but it appears that much of the difference between the results of different studies can be explained by differences in data defining income and wealth.

It was shown earlier in this chapter that the United States has one of the lowest personal saving rates for any of the major industrial countries, and that a large decline in this rate occurred in the late 1980s. This follows directly from the third assumption of the life-cycle hypothesis, which states that for countries with identical individual behavior, the saving rate will be higher the higher the long-run growth rate of the economy. The long-run growth rate of disposable income for the United States has fallen below earlier levels and is lower than for a number of major industrial countries.

A number of factors could have caused the large drop in the personal saving rate in the United States. A very important assumption of the life-cycle hypothesis is that for countries with identical individual behavior, the saving rate will be higher the higher is the long-run growth rate for the economy.

Barry Bosworth has compared saving rates with long-term output growth rates for fifteen industrial countries (see table 4.5). Because household saving rates are not truly comparable across countries, overall private saving (household plus business savings) were taken as a percentage of net domestic product to obtain the rate of private saving. Unlike U.S. saving data, which are measured on a gross basis, the data were measured on a net basis by deducting capital consumption allowances. For the first time period examined, saving rates over 1965–72 were compared with output growth rates for 1960–73, and for the later time period, saving rates over 1984–90 were compared with output growth rates for 1973–90. It is noteworthy that total savings for the fifteen industrial countries fell from an average of 12.6 percent of net domestic product in 1965–73 to 9.6 percent in 1984–90. Between the period 1960–73 and 1973–90, output growth for the group of fifteen industrial countries fell from 4.8 percent to 2.7 percent a year. High saving rates for individual countries coincided with high growth rates for the period prior to the 1973 oil shock, and when growth rates for all of the fifteen countries slowed after 1973, saving rates declined for all of the countries except for Canada, Austria, Belgium, and the Netherlands.[24]

Saving rates and output growth rates for the seven major industrial countries plus Australia can be compared during the pre-1973 period and the later period. For the earlier period, for all of the countries except Canada, high saving rates were associated with high rates of output growth. During the later period, long-term growth throughout the industrial world had slowed considerably, and the dispersion of growth rates was much narrower, ranging from 1.9 to 3.9 percent a year, making it somewhat more difficult to easily compare saving rates with growth rates, yet for seven of the eight countries, higher saving rates were associated with higher growth rates.

Demographics and productivity changes are two sources of economic growth. Productivity measures the average amount of output produced per employee. Within the context of the life-cycle hypothesis, it is possible to assess the impact of productivity growth upon savings.[25] With productivity growth, the younger (unretired) age cohorts of the population will have larger lifetime resources than did the retired cohorts, which would make the savings of the younger cohorts larger than for the retired group if people planned their consumption as if they were not anticipating a future growth in income. If consumers did fully anticipate future income growth, they would consume more in the present and thus reduce their accumulation of wealth.[26] This implies that saving rates would rise with productivity growth if consumers failed to anticipate future changes in income.

For the industrial countries, productivity slowed markedly following the 1973 oil shock. For the United States, between 1947 and 1973, productiv-

Table 4.5

Private Net Saving and Investment, 1965–90 (as a percentage of net domestic product)

Country	1965-72 Private Saving	1965-72 Private Investment	1984-90 Private Saving	1984-90 Private Investment	Output Growth Rate 1960-73	Output Growth Rate 1973-90
United States	10.5	8.7	7.4	5.6	4.0	2.6
Canada	8.9	11.3	12.2	9.8	5.4	3.3
Japan	20.0	20.7	12.0	9.9	9.6	3.9
Australia	10.9	13.9	4.4	10.3	5.6	3.0
France	15.4	15.8	9.3	7.2	5.4	2.4
Germany	13.4	13.7	11.6	7.4	4.4	2.1
Italy	20.3	12.7	17.7	7.1	5.3	2.9
United Kingdom	6.9	7.9	5.2	7.2	3.2	1.9
Austria	11.5	14.4	12.1	10.9	4.9	2.5
Belgium	15.0	11.2	15.6	6.9	4.9	2.2
Denmark	9.7	15.4	6.5	9.5	4.3	1.8
Finland	7.6	13.0	6.6	9.9	5.0	3.0
Netherlands	15.8	15.6	16.1	8.7	4.8	2.1
Norway	7.0	13.3	4.0	9.8	4.3	3.4
Sweden	4.4	10.2	4.1	6.7	4.1	1.8
Total (15 countries)	12.6	12.1	9.6	7.3	4.8	2.7

Source: Barry P. Bosworth, *Saving and Investment in a Global Economy* (Washington, D.C.: Brookings Institution, 1993), p. 58.

ity growth averaged 3 percent a year compared with 1.0 percent after 1973.[27] The Council of Economic Advisors is optimistic about future growth in productivity in the nonfarm sector. Labor productivity growth, which had been slipping in recent decades, is expected to increase over the experience of the last two decades because the average age of the workforce continues to increase and a move toward a more experienced workforce is usually associated with higher productivity; the oil shocks of the 1970s diverted spending into energy-saving equipment, making the economy less vulnerable to energy shocks; and interest rates are expected to remain low, thereby promoting increased capital investment and labor productivity.[28]

Capital deepening is likely to occur as businesses respond to real long-term interest rates that are lower than in the 1980s, and this will increase capital intensity. And it is believed that the Clinton administration's policy of promoting public investment, including an improved communications and transportation infrastructure, and human capital formation should raise private-sector productivity. If this optimistic assumption is correct, it is plausible that private saving rates in the United States will rise to levels of the 1970s.

In addition to productivity changes, demographic changes can affect economic growth and consumption. Two types of demographic changes—the rising percentages of people between the ages of 45 and 64, and those in their retirement years—are expected to affect the saving rate. Members of the first group are considered to be the high savers because they are the closest to retirement, at which time they will become dependent upon accumulated savings to maintain their living standards. Between 1960 and 1985, the proportion of high savers had dropped from 39 to 31 percent of the adult population, but by 1992 it had risen to almost 34 percent. The proportion of retirees had increased steadily, rising from 13.5 percent to over 16 percent of the adult population. A large increase in the percentage of retirees is expected to occur after the first decade of the twenty-first century.

By the late 1980s, most of the baby boom generation had entered the labor force. This generation is comprised of individuals born between 1945 and 1965, and it represents a large group compared to the older generation. By the 1970s and 1980s, this group represented a growing share of the working population and became a larger group of workers compared with those born during the 1920s and 1930s, the high saving group. It is possible that the increased entry of baby boomers into the labor force and the formation of young households could have contributed to a drop in the saving rate. By the late 1990s, many of the workers born in the 1920s and 1930s will become retired dissavers, while many of the large group in the baby boom generation will have begun to worry about retirement.

Although one might expect that the increase in the number of retirees as a share of the population and the fall in the proportion of high savers would

Table 4.6
Personal Saving Rate, Wealth-to-Income Ratio, and Debt-to-Wealth Ratio,
1960–89 (percent)

	1960-69	1970-79	1980-89	1980-84	1985-89
NIPA Personal Saving Rate[2]	6.7	7.7	6.5	8.0	5.0
Wealth-to-Income Ratio	502	460	483	479	488
Debt-to-Wealth Ratio	13.4	14.9	16.8	15.4	18.2

Source: Congress of the United States, Congressional Budget Office, *Assessing the Decline in the National Saving Rate* (Washington, D.C.: Government Printing Office, April 1993), p. 32.

1. Congressional Budget Office calculations based on data from the Department of Commerce and the Federal Reserve Board of Governors.
2. NIPA = national income and product accounts.

have been factors that contributed to the decline in the saving rate in the late 1980s, empirical research has shown conflicting evidence that the impact of these changes was significant. Some studies found that the difference in savings between the two age groups is insufficient to account for the decline. Also, it has been suggested that the demographic changes started occurring in the late 1960s and early 1970s, much sooner than the large decline in the saving rate, and the demographic shifts were too small to affect the decline in the saving rate significantly.[29]

It has also been hypothesized that personal saving rates can be affected by changes in the ratio of wealth-to-disposable income, the ratio of debt-to-wealth, the real (after-tax) rate of return on wealth, and the rate of inflation. Furthermore, financial liberalization and deregulation in the 1980s may also have affected the rate of personal saving.

The standard theories of saving imply that individuals plan for a given amount of wealth for their retirement. Thus when the ratio of wealth to disposable income rises, individuals would tend to reduce their saving. During the 1970s and 1980s, existing assets were revalued upward with the rise in real estate values in the 1970s and the stock market boom of the 1980s. Revaluations of assets contributed about three-fifths of the growth of wealth in the 1980s. The wealth-to-disposable-income ratio rose from 460 percent during the 1970s to 483 percent during the 1980s (see Table 4.6). For the period 1985–89 this ratio rose to 488 percent, compared with 479 percent in 1980–84. The growth in the wealth-to-income ratio appeared to accompany the drop in the personal saving rate, which averaged 8.0 percent of disposable income in 1980–84 and 5.0 percent in 1985–89. It has been estimated that the rise in the wealth-to-income ratio could explain about nine-tenths of the decline in the personal saving rate during the entire 1980s but could only explain one-sixth of the drop in the saving rate that occurred in 1985–89.[30]

Another phenomenon that occurred during the 1980s was a surge in the debt-to-wealth ratio that accompanied the decline in the saving rate in 1985–89. Also, whereas the ratio of household interest payments had remained between 14 and 16 percent of disposable income from 1960 to 1983, it had risen to 18 percent by the end of the decade.[31] Consumers were increasing debt relative to their wealth and disposable income. The growth in debt may have represented increased confidence in the economy as it continued its prolonged expansion during the 1980s. Consumer confidence surged in 1984 and 1985, and confidence in the economy remained high until the end of the decade.

With the economy in recession in 1990–91 and with the slow growth thereafter, consumer confidence fell and the saving rate slowly increased. Households reduced spending and borrowing in an effort to strengthen balance sheets, and by 1992 the ratio of household debt to interest payments had fallen to about 16.5 percent.

The real rate of return on wealth has the potential to affect the saving rate, but both the theory of saving and empirical evidence have been ambiguous about the direction in which the increased returns affect the personal saving rate. Two possible effects on savings are possible—the negative income effect and the positive substitution effect. A negative income effect could occur because higher real returns permit higher consumption and lower savings without diminishing an individual's wealth. But higher real returns on saving could also have a positive substitution effect on savings because each dollar that is not consumed in the present allows the individual to enjoy greater consumption in the future. Only if the substitution effect dominates over the income effect will higher real returns raise the saving rate. Empirical studies have been performed to determine the effect of higher real returns on saving, but most studies have found the effect to be small.

During the 1980s, as a consequence of a fairly tight monetary policy, the real rate of interest was higher than during the 1970s. Also, the tax cuts of the Reagan administration raised the fraction of after-tax income that savers could keep. But even though after-tax rates of return were higher, the saving rate fell.[32]

Bosworth has confirmed that although the personal rate of saving did not rise in response to higher after-tax real rates of return, inflation did have a positive impact on the rate of saving.[33]

For much of the period 1965–92, personal saving rates appeared to be positively related to inflation. For instance, between 1965 and 1969, when inflation rates were relatively low, savings averaged 6.6 percent of disposable income. But between 1970 and 1974, when the rate of inflation was rising rapidly, the saving rate rose to an average of 8.2 percent of disposable income. In the years 1973 and 1974, when rising inflation was becoming a central concern, the saving rate averaged 9.0 percent. As inflation subsided and leveled off, the saving rate declined to an average of 7.3 percent during 1975–79. However, double-digit inflation following the second oil shock of the late 1970s produced much uncertainty, and the personal saving rate averaged 8.3 percent between 1980 and 1984. Even though inflation had subsided by 1982, savings remained high. From 1983 the inflation rate was low, and over the eight years between 1985 and 1992, the personal saving rate averaged only 5.0 percent.

Several reasons may account for the positive relationship between savings and inflation. The first reason concerns expectations. During inflation, people expect that the Federal Reserve might react by tightening monetary policy, which would cause a recession, and people cut back on consumption because they expect rising unemployment. Inflation might also have caused people to lose confidence concerning the adequacy of their savings for retirement as they saw the purchasing power of their savings and pensions being eroded by the inflation of the 1970s and early 1980s.[34]

Another way at looking at the positive relationship between saving and inflation relates to the fact that the inflation component of interest rates is actually a return to principal that compensates for inflation's effect on the purchasing power of funds loaned out.[35] Although in the conventional measure of saving, the inflation component of interest is regarded as income, savers may save it to compensate for reduced purchasing power of their savings deposits.

Financial liberalization and deregulation in the 1980s may also have contributed to the reduced rate of saving by giving households greater access to credit. The availability of adjustable rate mortgages, home equity lines of credit, longer repayment periods, and easing of qualifications needed for credit could all have reduced savings. As noted above, consumers accumulated large amounts of debt in the 1980s, and debt burdens were high. During the early 1990s, a period of recession followed by a slow recovery of employment, people tried to pay off some of their debt to reduce debt burdens, and the saving rate slowly began to creep upward. Debt burdens would also have been lowered because of a "credit crunch" with lenders being more reluctant to extend credit.

Two policy measures—wage and price controls imposed during 1971–74 and credit controls imposed for a relatively short period by the Federal Reserve in March 1980—could have contributed to the increase in personal saving rates during those periods. Wage and price controls did coincide with a period of increased personal saving rates, and the 1980 credit controls also coincided with a period of rising saving rates. In fact, when measured in real terms, consumption expenditures fell by 0.5 percent in 1980.

Economists have theorized about reasons for personal saving. This section has focused primarily on the life-cycle hypothesis, which assumes that the household's consumption remains steady over its lifetime, and that saving is done to take care of its retirement needs. Consumption depends on income from labor and wealth. Changes in income and wealth can affect the level of saving. It has also been theorized that demographic factors, real returns on existing wealth, inflation, financial liberalization and deregulation, the desire to leave bequests, and government tax and credit policies can affect savings.

The standard theories of saving have suggested three motives for personal saving. The life-cycle motive focuses on the desire of the household to maintain a stable consumption path during its lifetime and the hypothesis that consumption is motivated by the desire to save for retirement. The precautionary motive deals with the desire to save for unforeseen events, such as uncertainty about the length of a lifetime that will be spent in retirement, health-related emergencies during the later years of life, and the possibility of unemployment and inflation. The precautionary motive can easily fit in with the life-cycle motive. The bequest motive deals with that part of savings that is accumulated to leave bequests for future generations. Whereas bequests can occur with the precautionary motive because of uncertainties about the length of a lifetime and other uncertainties, the bequest motive provides a motive for saving that is apart from the life-cycle motive and also suggests that saving will extend into the retirement years.

Many empirical studies have been undertaken during the past fifty years to determine reasons for savings and consumption. In an effort to cast some light on the decline in the personal saving rate in the United States, the results of several recent studies will be discussed in the following section.

Several Empirical Studies of Saving Behavior

It has already been suggested that in the medium term one of the factors that might have positive impacts on the personal saving rate in the United States would be the aging of the large baby boom generation born between 1945 and 1965. Because more and more members of this generation are reaching their forties, they are now falling into the mature worker group that begins to save for retirement. It will not be until the second decade of the twenty-first century that large numbers of them will be retiring. Whereas the aging of a large share of the population is expected to become a more important factor in Japan and in the European countries in the 1990s, it is not expected to become an important factor in North America until the next century.[36]

Some have predicted that demographic factors will exert a positive impact on the personal saving rate in the United States. Robert Mundell, basing his argument on the life-cycle assumption that each family uses its intertemporal budget constraint to maintain constant consumption over its lifetime, has hypothesized that generational differences in the age structure of the population can alter net national lending and, hence, the balance of trade. A four-generational model is used to describe the trade balance effects of "generational blips." The model includes two working generations, plus a very young and very old group of dependent generations. The focus is on the relative numbers in each of the working generations. It is assumed that the two working generations have similar earning and saving potentials, but the junior working generation invests more largely in consumer durables than it saves and the senior working generation saves more than it invests and lends the difference. Were the junior generation to be larger than the senior generation, investment would be larger than saving, and if the senior generation were larger than the junior generation, saving would exceed investment. For Mundell, not only the personal savings rate but also the balance of trade depend on the relative size of the two working generations. The greater the proportion of junior members to senior members of the working generation, the smaller will be the personal saving rate and the trade balance.[37]

In the United States, births were low in the 1930s and early 1940s, and the generation was small; by contrast the baby boom generation was large. By the late 1990s, many of the baby boom generation will have become members of the senior working generation and, as a group, will have become net lenders instead of net borrowers. When the baby boom generation matures to become net savers, the ratio of senior working generation borrowers will be reversed and savings will rise. Using such a model, Mundell extends the life-cycle hypothesis and suggests that because savings in the United States will rise substantially by the late 1990s until after the first decade of the twenty-first century when baby boomers retire, there will be excess savings, substantial capital outflows, and a direct reversal in the current account.[38]

This optimistic outlook for the future current account balance stems from the argument that the rate of personal saving will rise substantially in the United States by the late 1990s. This argument gains support in the work of Michael Boskin and Lawrence J. Lau.[39]

One of the focal points of several studies by Boskin and Lau is "the critical dependence of U.S. aggregate consumption and saving on the age and vintage distribution of resources."[40] The authors focused on behavior of those born before and after 1939 (the Depression and post-Depression households). They argue that, over time, changes in the age and vintage distribution of household wealth in the U.S. economy caused systematic variations in patterns of aggregate consumption and saving.

Boskin and Lau assessed the impact of a number of independent variables, including the age composition and vintage composition of the population on aggregate consumption, as well as other independent variables on aggregate consumption. The authors divided the post-Depression period studied into two subperiods—1950–62 and 1963–80. It was in the later subperiod that growth in aggregate consumption expenditures accelerated. In the 1950–62 subperiod, aggregate consumption expenditures grew at an annual rate of 2.89 percent a year, but accelerated to an annual growth of

3.27 percent a year in 1963–80. During the first subperiod, 38 percent of the growth in real consumption per household was due to a time trend, and the real wage rate accounted for an additional one-third. Of the remainder, 14 percent was accounted for by the share of wealth held by the Depression-vintage households and 13 percent by the age distribution of real wealth.

During the second subperiod, the most important source of growth of real consumption per household was the fall in the share of wealth held by the Depression-vintage households, which accounted for 117 percent of the rate of growth in real consumption per household. The age distribution of wealth, the time trend, and the real wage rate accounted for −61 percent, 52 percent, and 29 percent, respectively. Age and vintage distribution of wealth combined were the most important sources of growth in real consumption per household, accounting for 56 percent. The huge reduction in the share of wealth held by Depression-vintage households is an important factor in explaining the growth in real consumption per household during the second subperiod. And, as the baby boomers came of age in the second subperiod, growth in the share of wealth held by households headed by persons born after 1939 accelerated.

Lau concluded that demographic factors—changes in the rate of household formation and the distribution of wealth by age and vintage of households—are the most important factors explaining the growth in aggregate real consumption for the period 1950–80. Large changes in the distribution of income and wealth in the United States over the period 1950–80 had important effects on aggregate consumption and saving. Consumption and saving patterns differed according to vintage, and the movement of the Depression generation into ages where their savings propensities increased was being offset by the post-Depression generation, which had higher propensities to consume at young ages. Personal saving would have been higher and aggregate consumption would have been lower if the post-Depression cohorts' consumption and saving patterns were similar to those of the Depression vintage. Boskin and Lau demonstrated that had the saving rates of the post-Depression vintage been similar to those of the Depression vintage, the personal saving rate would have been more than twice its actual 1980 level. In the 1980s, the saving rate continued to decline as the relative shares of aggregate income received and total wealth belonging to the post-Depression vintage increased.

The study indicates that in the future demographic factors could contribute to an increase in the personal saving rate. Because the share of wealth held by the Depression-vintage households has already declined significantly, it is not expected that this decline will contribute much to a future drop in the aggregate personal saving rate. Furthermore, it is expected that as post-Depression-vintage households age and start planning for retirement, their saving rate will increase. The younger age cohorts, those who are not members of the baby boom generation, are demographically a relatively small group compared to the baby boom generation. The younger group, an age group that typically does not save much, will have a relatively lower saving rate than the baby boomers. With current consumption patterns, it is only after the end of the first decade of the twenty-first century, after the baby boomers start reaching retirement age and the younger cohorts start to save for retirement, that the personal saving rate should fall again.

A study by the Brookings Institution that used microeconomic data instead of national accounts data is not so optimistic about future increases in the rate of personal saving.[41] Using two different household budget surveys, the study attempts to explain the decline in the U.S. saving rate. Using the life-cycle hypothesis as a base of reference, they examined the extent to which changes in the age structure of the population could have contributed to the fall in the saving ratio. The life-cycle hypothesis posits that heads of households accumulate savings during much of their working years and dissave during retirement, but the younger heads of household do not save much and frequently go into debt. If younger workers had become a large proportion of all workers, as had happened in the 1970s and 1980s with the entry of baby boomers into the labor force, one would anticipate that the aggregate saving rate would have declined.

The authors used two different household surveys and divided the samples into five different age groups—25–34, 35–44, 45–54, 55–64, and 65 and over. For the Survey of Consumer Finances (SCF) they compared saving rates in 1963 with 1983–85; and for the Consumer Expenditure Survey (CES) they compared saving rates in 1972–73 with 1982–85. Both surveys showed the decline in the personal saving rates that occurred in the 1980s. Particularly interesting is the fact that the saving rates declined for almost all age groups and the evidence did not corroborate the belief that the decline in savings was concentrated in the baby boom generation. For the periods covered, the SCF reported that saving rates fell by only 1 percent for the 25–44 year olds, and the CES reported a decline of only 1.7 percent for households headed by someone aged 25–44. Much larger was the decline in saving rates for households headed by someone over 45, which declined by 7 percent using the SCF survey and 6 percent with the CES survey.

Not only did the study find that saving rates dropped for all age groups, but when they used population projections from the Social Security Administration to forecast the future course of the aggregate rate of personal saving, the forecasts indicated that the demographic shift of baby boomers into older age groups will have only a small impact on future rates of saving. The aggregate saving rate is forecast to rise only slightly until the year 2000 and to decline by 1 percent between 2000 and 2020. The study concludes that changes in the age structure of the population will continue to have only small impacts on the rate of personal saving. The study found that instead of the entry of the large baby boom generation into the labor force, it was the sharp reductions in savings by middle-aged and older consumers that were responsible for the fall in the personal saving rate.

The study notes several other factors that may have contributed to the decline in the saving rate. For households headed by someone 45 years or older, a group that by the beginning of the 1980s had a substantial amount of assets, the wealth effect of higher returns on assets may have affected saving rates. But an examination of the data showed that in the SCF the decline in saving for those households that were stock and bond holders was actually smaller than for householders with no financial assets between 1963 and 1983–85. The authors found no support for the idea that reduced saving in the United States in the early 1980s was concentrated among consumers who were owners of financial assets.

However, the large rise in home prices during the 1970s may have helped cause the drop in savings. In both the SCF and CES surveys, saving rates for nonhomeowners fell by much less than for homeowners. Also, the decline in savings for homeownership is most pronounced in the middle-aged group.

The 1993 study by Bosworth cited above uses data for the seven major industrial countries plus Australia, Belgium, Denmark, Finland, and Sweden. Bosworth has attempted to measure the impact of a number of factors on the rate of private savings (private savings as a fraction of disposable income). Time series analysis covering a twenty-five-year period (1965–90) were used.

In the first method of analysis, regressions were estimated for each of the countries in the sample to determine the extent to which the structure of the saving relationship was uniform across countries and to identify variables having statistical significance in a majority of countries. As indicated above, the most uniform finding was a positive relationship between savings rates and income growth, but results for other variables varied widely across countries. Demographics were statistically significant in five countries, but the coefficients were particularly large for only Denmark and Japan. For interest rates, positive coefficients that were statistically significant were obtained for only two countries. However, inflation had a consistently positive effect on savings, perhaps implying that inflation created uncertainty and encouraged people to save for the future. For six of the countries, there was evidence of a small but negative correlation between variations in government and private saving rates, indicating some trade-off between government and private saving. The equations for almost all countries had a highly significant coefficient on a simple time trend, indicating the presence of some unspecified influence upon private saving rates.

In the second method, the data were pooled into a single regression. Again, the coefficients for income growth were positive and highly significant. However, demographic changes still continued to have only a small but positive impact on savings. Though statistically significant, the coefficient for interest rates was negative instead of positive as it was in the equations for individual countries. Again, there was a small but highly significant negative correlation between government and private savings. Both the individual equations and the pooled regressions suggest that 20–30 percent of any change in public-sector savings will affect private saving, giving limited credence to the Barro-Ricardo equivalence theory.[42] The regressions also showed that the terms of trade (the price of a country's exports in terms of imports) had a positive and significant coefficient—in this case, a 10 percent increase in the terms of trade in favor of the exporting country raised the private saving rate by 0.4 percentage point.

Bosworth's general conclusion is that empirical results suggest that lower rates of income growth are primarily responsible for reduced private saving rates. The precise role that income growth has on saving rates remains unclear.[43]

Although the use of different methodologies might produce different results, the two studies discussed above did not offer much hope that demographic changes over the next one or two decades will significantly raise personal saving rates in the United States. However, even if the maturing of the baby boom generation cannot, by itself, be a significant factor in restoring the personal saving rate to earlier levels, it may be expected that as the baby boom generation begins to save for retirement, it will play some role in raising saving rates.

Another factor that might affect the savings rate is consumer pessimism about unemployment. Christopher Carroll shows that the "buffer-stock"[44] model of saving implies a central role for unemployment expectations. He argues the following:

In the buffer-stock model, consumers hold assets mainly so that they can shield their consumption against unpredictable fluctuations in income; unemployment expectations are therefore important because typically the most drastic fluctuations in a household's income are those associated with spells of unemployment.

Buffer-stock saving behavior can emerge from the standard dynamic optimization framework when consumers facing important income uncertainty are both impatient, in a sense that if income were certain, they would like to borrow against future income to finance current consumption, and prudent, in Miles Kimball's sense that they have a precautionary saving motive. The buffer-stock behavior arises because impatience makes consumers want to spend down their assets, while prudence makes them reluctant to draw down assets too far.[45]

According to Carroll, the tension between impatience and prudence can, under plausible circumstances, imply the existence of a target wealth stock. In the model, unemployment expectations are key. When consumers become more pessimistic about unemployment, their target buffer-stock increases because uncertainty about future income increases, and they increase saving to build up additional wealth to meet the new target wealth stock.

Even if expectations about the average level of future wealth do not change, simulations of the model showed that changes in the expected probability of "bad events" (e.g., unemployment) have a major impact on current levels of consumption and saving. Clearly, very bad events (unemployment) do have a direct effect on increasing the saving rate.

Given the existence of the precautionary saving motive, with increased uncertainty about unemployment, consumers neither increase borrowing nor decrease saving during recession. Furthermore, the evidence shows that consumers save more when they expect that the unemployment rate will be rising or when the unemployment rate is already high. According to Carroll, the fundamental message of his results is that precautionary saving is important for an understanding of the cyclical behavior of consumption and saving.[46]

Carroll then applies the results to explain the secular decline in the personal saving rate over the past fifteen–twenty years and to explain why saving was so low recently. Many economists, including Carroll, perceive the secular decline in the personal saving rate as having commenced in the mid-1970s, despite the fact that during the 1981–82 recession the saving rate reached high levels similar to those reached during the 1974–75 recession. It was not until after 1985 that the saving rate fell below the lowest levels reached in almost forty years. In his paper, Carroll showed that the personal saving rate at the target net wealth-to-income ratio in the buffer-stock model tended toward $s^* = gw^*$, where s^* equaled the personal saving rate, g the growth rate of permanent income, and w^* the target net wealth-to-disposable-income ratio. In the buffer-stock model, either a fall in g or a fall in w^* can explain the long-term decline in the saving rate.

From 1960 to 1980 the annual growth rate of per capita personal income was 2.5 percent, but it fell to 1.3 percent from 1980 to 1991. Over the same two periods, the average personal saving rate fell from 7.3 to 6.0 percent. Using the buffer-stock model, Carroll shows that the drop in the income growth rate can account for no more than one-half of the drop in the saving rate.[47]

Carroll tells us that the model cannot explain all of the fall in the saving rate because the target wealth ratio, w^*, is not large enough. Two factors—declining income uncertainty and relaxation of liquidity constraints—may have acted to reduce the target wealth ratio in the past twenty years.

One factor that may have reduced income uncertainty and, hence, the target wealth ratio, over the past twenty years, is a large increase in labor force participation by married women, from 40.8 percent in 1970 to 57.8 percent in 1989. The existence of more two-earner families would reduce uncertainty over a total loss in income from unemployment. Carroll then speculates that the long expansion in the 1980s combined with a continuous drop in the unemployment rate could have caused consumers to revise downward their estimated probability of unemployment and variance of income shocks. Because of the depth and long duration of the latest recession, it is possible that consumers will have more pessimism concerning the possibilities of unemployment, leading to a growth in the personal saving rate. Indeed, the rate of personal saving out of disposable income had increased from a low of 4.1 percent in 1989 to 5.0 percent in 1992 before declining to 4.6 percent in 1993.

Relaxation of borrowing constraints in the 1980s is also considered. Carroll argues that part of the decline in the personal saving rate was caused by a relaxation of borrowing constraints and growth in debt. As was noted above, the consumer debt burden (the share of personal disposable income devoted to servicing debt) increased over the 1980s and was in the process of being reduced during the early 1990s. And whereas the ratio of total liabilities to income rose by about 0.3 percentage points a year, or from 68 percent of disposable income to 73 percent between 1961–65 and 1976–80, from 1976–80 to 1986–90 this ratio grew by 1.5 percentage points a year, or from 73 to 89 percent of disposable income. This rapid growth in debt and debt burden took place within a context of liberalization and deregulation of financial markets. Credit became more readily available and repayment terms were more lenient; from the mid- to late 1980s debt repayment problems rose substantially. Carroll goes on to suggest that "easier credit may be the most plausible explanation of the low saving rate of the 1980s."[48] It is also suggested that the saving rate would have partially recovered when credit stopped loosening, and in fact this had occurred.

Reduced consumption accompanies a rise in the saving rate, and following the 1990–91 recession, consumption was slow to recover. A commonly given explanation for this phenomenon was the existence of a "debt overhang." Carroll then asks why is it that a level of debt that was acceptable in 1989 should suddenly become unacceptable? Within the "buffer-stock" framework, the recession would have caused the target level of wealth to increase, making consumers less readily able to accept a target wealth-to-income ratio that was acceptable a few years before. His analysis suggests that the low income growth rate and high unemployment rate would increase the target ratio of wealth to income. An index of expected unemployment was calculated, which showed that consumers' expectations concerning unemployment after the 1990–91 recession differed from periods immediately following earlier recessions. Although this index behaved the same as in earlier recessions until the 1990–91 recession reached the trough of the cycle, it did not recover at the same rate as it had following earlier recessions. Consumers' expectations of prolonged unemployment placed a damper on the recovery of spending on consumption.

The Future of the Personal Saving Rate in the United States.

Several factors could interact to raise the personal saving rate during the remainder of the 1990s. Although it is possible that demographic factors associated with the maturing of the baby boom generation will have some role in raising the saving rate, the consensus is mixed. Even if demographic factors were to increase the saving rate by only 1 percentage point for the remainder of the decade, the impact on personal saving and capital flows would not be insignificant. For instance, in 1991 disposable income amounted to $4.2 trillion. Had the personal saving rate been 1 percentage point higher, an additional $42 billion in savings would have been available to the economy.

Another factor that might raise the saving rate is a reduction in consumers' borrowing. Beginning in 1990, consumers became more reluctant to assume additional debt, and they were reducing their debt burdens. Combined with a reluctance by consumers to borrow was the tightening of loan eligibility by financial institutions. Carroll has argued that part of the decline in the personal saving rate was caused by a relaxation of borrowing constraints and the growth in debt. The lax lending standards of the late 1980s contributed to serious insolvencies, bankruptcies, and foreclosures. If the commercial banks and the savings and loan associations refrain from engaging in a lending spree similar to that of the late 1980s, reduced consumer borrowing will be another factor raising the personal saving rate.

Because employment was slow to recover following the 1990–91 recession, people may continue to have higher expectations of unemployment than would be normal following a recession. Economic forecasters predict that for much of the 1990s the average rate of economic growth will not exceed an average of 2.2 percent a year. Because employment was so slow to recover following the 1990–91 recession, consumers may be wary of unemployment. If consumers continue to expect unemployment, the precautionary motive could operate to raise saving.

As a consequence of demographic factors, the tightening of credit by financial institutions, and a continuance of unemployment expectations, it is possible that the personal saving rate will undergo a small increase by the second half of the decade. Even a small increment can have an important impact on domestic investment, the current account, and the amount of the inflow of foreign capital.

NOTES

1. International Monetary Fund, World Economic and Financial Surveys, *World Economic Outlook, May 1993* and *May 1994* (Washington, D.C.: International Monetary Fund, 1993 and 1994), pp. 30 and 41–45.

2. IMF, *World Economic Outlook, May 1993*, pp. 28–35.

3. IMF, *World Economic Outlook, May 1994*, p. 43.

4. Organization for Economic Cooperation and Development, *OECD Economic Outlook*, June 1994 (Paris: OECD, 1994), p. A8.

5. Congress of the United States, Congressional Budget Office, *The Economic*

and Budget Outlook: An Update (Washington, D.C.: Government Printing Office, September 1993), pp. 33–43.

6. Ibid., p. 28.

7. Ibid., p. 31.

8. *The Economic and Budget Outlook: An Update,* September 1993, p. xii.

9. Congress of the United States, Congressional Budget Office, *The Economic and Budget Outlook: An Update* (Washington, D.C.: Government Printing Office, August 1994), pp. 18–19.

10. This assumes that the elasticity of demand for gasoline is zero. Were the elasticity of demand to be greater than -1.00 and no other changes were to occur, since the tax raises the price of gasoline, the quantity demanded would decline sufficiently that the revenue collected by the tax increase would be less than the additional \$30 billion.

11. Joseph A. Pechman, *Federal Tax Policy* (Washington, D.C.: Brookings Institution, 1983), pp. 210–11.

12. Ibid., p. 218.

13. *The Economic and Budget Outlook: An Update,* September 1993, p. 18.

14. Congress of the United States, Congressional Budget Office, *The Economic and Budget Outlook: Fiscal Years 1994–1998* (Washington, D.C.: Government Printing Office, January 1993), p. 76.

15. These calculations are based on gross savings, which includes capital consumption allowances.

16. John M. Keynes, *The General Theory of Employment, Interest, and Money* (London: Harcourt Brace, 1936), Chapters 8 and 9.

17. Milton Friedman, *A Theory of the Consumption Function* (Princeton, N.J.: Princeton University Press, 1957); Franco Modigliani and R. E. Brumberg, "Utility Analysis and the Consumption Function," in *Post-Keynesian Economics,* ed. K. K. Kurihara (New Brunswick, N.J.: Rutgers University Press, 1954); and A. Ando and Franco Modigliani, "The Life Cycle Hypothesis of Saving: Aggregate Implications and Tests," *American Economic Review,* 53 (March 1963), pp. 55–84.

18. Gardner Ackley, *Macroeconomics: Theory and Policy* (New York: Macmillan, 1978), p. 540.

19. Franco Modigliani, "Life Cycle, Individual Thrift, and the Wealth of Nations," *American Economic Review,* 76, no. 3 (June 1986).

20. Ibid., p. 300.

21. Ibid., pp. 300–1.

22. Franco Modigliani, "The Role of Intergenerational Transfers and Life Cycle Saving in the Accumulation of Wealth," *Journal of Economic Perspectives,* 2, no. 2 (Spring 1988), pp. 15–40.

23. Laurence J. Kotlikoff, "Intergenerational Transfers and Savings," *Journal of Economic Perspectives,* 2, no. 2 (Spring 1988), pp. 41–58; Laurence J. Kotlikoff and Lawrence H. Summers, "The Role of Intergenerational Transfers in Aggregate Capital Accumulation," *Journal of Political Economy,* 89 (August 1981), pp. 706–32; and Laurence T. Kotlikoff and Lawrence H. Summers, "The Contribution of Intergenerational Transfers to Total Wealth: A Reply," National Bureau of Economic Research Working Paper No. 1827 (1986).

24. Barry P. Bosworth, *Saving and Investment in a Global Economy* (Washington, D.C.: Brookings Institution, 1993), pp. 55–61.

25. Modigliani, "Life Cycle, Individual Thrift, and the Wealth of Nations," p. 306.

26. James Tobin, "Life Cycle Saving and Balanced Growth," *Ten Economic Studies in the Tradition of Irving Fisher*, ed. W. Fellner (New York: John Wiley, 1967).

27. United States, Council of Economic Advisors, *Economic Report of the President* (Washington, D.C.: Government Printing Office, 1992), p. 91.

28. United States, Council of Economic Advisors, *Economic Report of the President* (Washington, D.C.: Government Printing Office, 1994), pp. 94–95.

29. Congress of the United States, Congressional Budget Office, *Assessing the Decline in the National Saving Rate* (Washington, D.C.: Government Printing Office, April 1993), p. 35.

30. Ibid., p. 32.

31. United States, Council of Economic Advisors, *Economic Report of the President* (Washington, D.C.: Government Printing Office, 1993), p. 88.

32. *Assessing the Decline in the National Saving Rate*, p. 33.

33. Barry Bosworth, "Institutional Changes and the Efficacy of Monetary Policy," *Brookings Papers on Economic Activity*, No. 1 (1989), pp. 77–124.

34. It took a number of years for inflationary expectations to subside. For a number of years after inflation subsided, real interest rates remained high.

35. *Assessing the Decline in the National Saving Rate*, p. 33.

36. International Monetary Fund, World Economic and Financial Surveys, *World Economic Outlook, May 1991* (Washington, D.C.: International Monetary Fund, 1991), p. 47.

37. Robert Mundell, "The Great Exchange Rate Controversy: Trade Balances and the Current Account," in *International Adjustment and Financing: The Lessons of 1985–91*, ed. C. Fred Bergsten (Washington, D.C.: Institute for International Economics, 1991), pp. 189–238.

38. Ibid., pp. 208–11.

39. Michael J. Boskin and Lawrence J. Lau, "An Analysis of Post-War U.S. Consumption and Saving," National Bureau of Economic Research Working Papers Nos. 2605 and 2606 (1988); and Lawrence J. Lau, "U.S. Saving Behavior in the Post-War Period," in *World Savings: An International Survey*, ed. Arnold Heertje (Cambridge: Blackwell, 1993), pp. 141–77.

40. Lau, "U.S. Saving Behavior in the Post-War Period," p. 170.

41. Barry Bosworth, Gary Burtless, and John Sabelhous, "The Decline of Saving: Some Microeconomic Evidence," *Brookings Papers on Economic Activity*, No. 1 (1991), pp. 183–256.

42. Robert J. Barro, "Are Government Bonds New Wealth?" *Journal of Political Economy*, 82 (November/December 1974), pp. 1095–1117. The Barro-Ricardo equivalence theorem assumes that tax cuts would be balanced by increases in savings. According to the theory, when people see tax cuts, they anticipate that these cuts will be met by tax increases in the future when the government is required to pay interest on the mounting debt. According to the theorem, people increase their saving to neutralize the effects of public dissaving and the burden that the debt imposes upon future generations. However, this theory is not substantiated by evidence of the 1980s when large tax cuts were implemented in the United States.

43. Bosworth, *Saving and Investment in the Global Economy*, pp. 62–80.

44. Christopher D. Carroll, "The Buffer-Stock Theory of Saving: Some Macro-

economic Evidence," *Brookings Papers on Economic Activity*, No. 29 (1992), pp. 61–156.

45. Ibid., pp. 61–62.

46. Ibid., pp. 110–11.

47. Ibid., p. 112. In the buffer-stock model, slow growth can cause low saving, whereas the causality often goes from low saving to low growth. This goes against the permanent income hypothesis and the life-cycle hypothesis, where lower income growth leads to lower lifetime resources, lower consumption, and therefore, higher saving rates.

48. Ibid., p. 120.

CHAPTER 5

Policies Designed to Raise the U.S. Saving Rate

The previous chapter focused on the low rate of saving in the United States and showed that both the public sector and the private sector have contributed to the large decline in savings that occurred during the 1980s. The rate of private saving underwent a large drop in the second half of the 1980s at the same time that the public-sector deficits were absorbing a large share of private saving. Also, the federal government relied heavily on foreign capital to finance its deficits. Because of large foreign borrowing, by the middle of the decade the United States had become a net debtor nation. To raise national saving, it is necessary that the federal government implement a variety of policy measures. These include additional measures to reduce the federal government's budget deficit, measures to raise the private saving rate, and efforts to reduce current account imbalances.

Federal government deficit reduction beyond the amounts that it is estimated will result from the 1993 Omnibus Budget Reconciliation Act and measures to raise the private saving rate can have contractionary impacts on the economy unless it becomes a policy goal to stimulate the growth of income and productivity. Accordingly, the measures that should be undertaken include policy measures that are designed to reduce the federal deficit, raise the private saving rate, bring about balance in the current account, and stimulate income and productivity growth.

POLICY MEASURES TO RAISE PUBLIC SAVING

Chapter 4 showed that largely as an outcome of OBRA 1993 the cumulative federal deficit is estimated to fall by over $500 billion over a five-year period. It is estimated that the deficit will decline from $290 billion in 1992 to $162 billion in 1995 and then rise to about $231 billion in 1999. In that year the deficit is estimated to equal 2.7 percent of GDP compared with 4.9 percent in 1992. However, if no further efforts are made to reduce the growth of the deficit, it then rises continuously to $257 billion or 2.9 percent of GDP by the year 2000 and $397 billion or 3.6 percent of GDP by 2004, to a large extent a consequence of the growth in Medicare, Medicaid, and interest on the public debt. Although it is expected that the share of GDP spent on net interest on the debt remains fairly constant between 1998 and 2004, the share of GDP going for Medicare and Medicaid combined rises from 4.6 to 6.2 percent of GDP. Were expenditures on Medicare and Medicaid to grow only as fast as GDP, the overall deficit would decline to 1.4 percent of GDP by 2004.

A PLAN FOR DEFICIT REDUCTION

Because of a strong concern over the projected growth of the deficit, Peter G. Peterson decided to write a book recommending a number of changes in spending and taxation.[1] Several of these recommended measures were already incorporated into OBRA 1993. Peterson has twenty-four proposals to balance the budget, organized into eight major budget categories: one for defense, one for domestic discretionary spending, four for entitlements, and two for general revenues. A ninth category for interest costs is also included.[2]

Under Peterson's plan, total discretionary expenditures would fall from 8.3 percent of GDP in fiscal year 1994 to 6.8 percent in fiscal year 2004. Included in discretionary expenditures is $100 billion (or 1 percent of GDP) for new investment spending. Substantial cuts would be made in defense outlays.[3]

Up to 1998, the recommendations for defense cuts are similar to President Clinton's recommendations. After that, defense spending rises at the rate of inflation. Reductions in defense spending would be achieved by eliminating the Armed Forces' duplication of services and weapons systems, requiring our allies to assume a larger share of the peacemaking burden, and by realistically assessing the new threats America is likely to face.

It is recommended that current budget discretionary outlays be cut by 10 percent. But because of the large numbers of unmet public investment needs facing the nation, Peterson recommends spending an additional 1 percent of GDP to meet these needs. This investment spending will cost $85 billion in 2000 and will rise to $101 billion in 2004. This money is to be earmarked for R&D and investment in physical and human capital formation programs that can demonstrate high rates of return, and each proposal for new spending would have to be accompanied by a productivity impact statement. In the event that cyclical economic conditions provided a need for fiscal stimulus, Congress would be able to move up projects.

The major cuts necessary to balance the budget would come from entitlement spending. The pivotal point of Peterson's plan to balance the budget is to significantly reduce outlays for entitlements. A comprehensive "affluence test" for wealthier-than-average beneficiaries and expansion of the taxability of most benefits are expected to result in large budget savings. The affluence test, or "graduated entitlement benefit reduction," would cover all federal benefits, and only households with incomes above the median would be affected. Because much of entitlement spending goes to households with annual cash incomes in excess of $50,000, it is believed that large savings in outlays can result from implementing the affluence test. Implementation of this proposal is expected to result in savings of at least $47 billion in 1998, $71 billion in 2000, and $93 billion in 2004. These savings come from Social Security, Medicare, railroad retirement, unemployment compensation, veteran's pensions, all means-tested cash and tax-credit benefits, and all federal pensions. Because much of what is now spent on these benefits is unearned by prior contributions, people would not be denied the return of funds they had contributed.

The key to the proposal is a single comprehensive means test for all benefits programs. It is important that under the plan no family having an income below the U.S. median would have benefits reduced. Furthermore, the rates applied to earnings above the median are sharply progressive, and it is only on earnings over $75,000 to $100,000 that a substantial share of benefits would be withheld. The use of the affluence test for federal benefits is a major element of Peterson's plan, and he believes it can help to achieve large budget savings.

It is estimated that a further saving of $25 billion by 2000 and $22 billion by 2004 could be achieved by expanding the taxability of some federal benefits, including Social Security and Medicare. An additional $16 billion in savings by 2000 and $36 billion in 2004 could come from raising the Social Security retirement age from sixty-five to sixty-eight. Whereas it was legislated that the Social Security retirement age will be raised in stages to sixty-seven between 2000 and 2020, Peterson's plan would raise the Social Security full-benefit retirement age beginning in 1995 and then proceed by three months a year until 2006. Eligibility for early retirement would rise in tandem until age sixty-five. Federal government pensioners now have retirement benefits that are much more generous than those offered by private industry. Cutting back some of the benefit package for federal pensioners could save $4 billion in 2000 and $6 billion in 2004.

In order to encourage more productive people to remain in the labor force, a complete elimination of the Social Security "earnings test" is proposed. Currently, Social Security checks for persons aged sixty-two to sixty-nine are reduced according to a formula for each dollar earned over a relatively low threshold. The cost of this reform is estimated at $5 billion in 2000 and $4 billion in 2004.

Peterson recommends a package of health care reforms to help reduce federal government outlays, slow the growth in U.S. health care spending, and extend health care insurance to a large majority of Americans who have no health care insurance. It is projected that large savings can come from tightening up on the fastest growing component of Medicare, the Supplementary Medical Insurance Program (SMI), which pays for physician services for the elderly and disabled. The first reform proposal suggests that savings on health care can come from three measures aimed at controlling the SMI cost problem. First, the annual deductible that beneficiaries must pay is raised from $100 to $150. Second, 20 percent copayments would be extended to the use of clinical laboratory services and home health and skilled nursing facilities. Finally, the SMI premium would be raised so that it covers 30 percent of the program's cost instead of 25 percent at present.

The second major reform would focus on employer-paid health care insurance. Because our tax code is progressive, the largest tax break from the current open-ended tax exclusion for employer-paid health care goes to the upper-middle and upper-income Americans. Peterson's plan would limit the tax exclusion for employer-paid health care to $170 a month for individual coverage and $410 per month for family coverage. Any cost of employer-paid health care above these caps would be treated as taxable income accruing to individual households. This should raise federal revenues equal to $40 billion in 2000 and $56 billion by 2004. Indirectly, savings on health care outlays would result from employers who reduce insurance premiums when they switch to lower cost and more cost effective plans.

The third health care reform would extend health insurance to the uninsured. The proposed change would extend coverage by combining an employer mandate with an expansion of Medicaid. All employers with at least 25 employees would be required to offer health insurance coverage to their workers, and employers would be required to cover at least 75 percent of premium costs with the remainder being borne by employees. Furthermore, the plan raises the Medicaid eligibility threshold to 100 percent of the poverty level in each state, and households having incomes from 100 to 200 percent of the poverty level could "buy in" on a sliding scale to Medicaid. The additional cost of this reform is expected to raise costs by $37 billion in 2000 and $53 billion in 2004.

The fourth health care reform would entail the enactment of a comprehensive health care cost control act that is expected to generate savings of $22 billion in 2000 and $82 billion in 2004.

Altogether, it is projected that the combined savings from the four health care reforms will total $53.4 billion in 2000 and $126.3 billion in 2004, of which the health care cost control program would generate 41 percent in 2000 and 65 percent in 2004.

It is also proposed that because of the magnitudes involved, several entitlements going to special groups should be reduced. One tax expenditure that would be reduced is the home mortgage deduction, which would be capped at $12,000 a year for an individual and $20,000 for a couple. Revenue savings would amount to $6 billion in 2000 and $10 billion in 2004. Additional savings from benefits going to special groups are reduced aid to farming and increased user fees on those either directly benefiting from a special federal service or using a resource owned or managed by the federal government.

Because it is difficult to make further reductions in spending to balance the budget, it is proposed that higher taxes be imposed to raise revenues. These revenue measures include levying a 5 percent consumption tax, raising the federal motor fuel tax by 50 cents a gallon, and raising federal "sin" taxes.

Of all the industrial countries, the United States relies the least on consumption taxes. At the same time, the saving rate is higher in most of the other industrial countries. In order to raise additional revenue and make our system more prosaving, Peterson proposes a 5 percent national retail sales tax. Because sales taxes are regressive, certain types of household expenditures—namely, food, housing, and education—would be exempted. These exemptions would reduce to 2.5 percent the tax rate on total consumption that would be paid by lower income households. It is estimated that revenues from the 5 percent consumption tax would amount to $105 billion in 2000 and $125 billion in 2004.

OBRA 1993 raised the federal motor gasoline tax by 4.3 cents a gallon, and Peterson suggests increasing the amount by an additional 45.7 cents a gallon. He suggests that in addition to raising revenue, such an increase would encourage energy conservation, reduce pollution, and reduce our dependence on foreign oil. Although we are the world's richest nation, we pay much less in gasoline taxes than do other industrial countries. This tax increase raises an additional $42 billion in 2000 and $53 billion in 2004.

To reduce consumption of alcohol and tobacco and raise revenues, it is proposed that by 2000 the federal excise tax on cigarettes be raised to $1 a pack and that on alcoholic beverages to $16 per proof gallon, and that, thereafter, both taxes be indexed to 1994 prices. These tax increases are expected to raise $22 billion in 2000 and $25 billion in 2004.

Finally, several investment incentives are proposed, the purpose of which is to direct national savings into those domestic investment projects having the highest rates of return. These include enacting a permanent tax credit for business research and development, indexing capital gains, and setting worker training incentives.

Since 1981 the federal government has provided temporary incentives for R&D efforts that were likely to lead to inventions and innovations that had public benefits. The legislation provided for a 20 percent tax credit for corporate spending on incremental basic research and development. It is proposed that the legislation be made permanent so firms know the credit will continue and that all eligible R&D spending be included instead of spending for only basic research and incremental expenditures. The tax credit would be set at 10 percent of all eligible R&D outlays.

Because a worker can no longer expect to be continuously employed in one line of work, it is proposed that a permanent 10 percent tax credit be introduced for all employer training and education. Individuals would also be permitted to deduct from their income taxes costs of undertaking formal education and training programs to qualify for a new job.

Finally, in order to focus on incentives that enhance productivity, the plan proposes indexing the prices of newly purchased productive assets to the rate of inflation in order to reduce taxation of capital gains on sales of these assets. Excluded would be investments in art, real estate, and collectibles.

It has been estimated that implementing these three investment incentives would cost a total of $14 billion in the year 2000 and $18 billion in 2004, which is not a high cost if productivity were enhanced.

The last category of the plan is concerned with reduction in the interest cost of servicing the public debt, because required borrowing would be lowered if the budget were balanced by 2004. In the Peterson Action Plan, net interest savings of $69.5 billion would occur in 1998, $132 billion in 2000, and $281.5 billion in 2004. Under the Action Plan, it is estimated that the net interest cost of servicing the debt falls to 2.0 percent of GDP by 2004 compared with 3.3 percent recently estimated by the Congressional Budget Office.

DISCUSSION OF THE PETERSON ACTION PLAN

The Peterson Action Plan is a proposal to balance the budget over a ten-year period. The Plan relies heavily on reductions in entitlement spending and increases in general revenue. In addition, it would provide additional benefits to the working poor, legislate additional investment incentives, and provide for public investment. Using a projection for slow economic growth, the Congressional Budget Office has estimated that under current legislation, the budget would still be left with a deficit of over $197 billion by 1998, assuming that the economy would be operating at close to the non-inflationary rate of full employment. At that time, the deficit is projected to be 2.4 percent of GDP and, assuming no increase in the rate of unemployment, would rise to 3.6 percent of GDP by 2004. Even with discretionary expenditures declining by 2.1 percent of GDP between 1994 and 2004, increases of 1.5 percent of GDP for Medicare and 1.0 percent for Medicaid

Table 5.1

Federal Spending as a Percent of GDP, 1994, 2000, and 2004 (fiscal year estimates)

	CBO	Action Plan	CBO	Action Plan	CBO	Action Plan
	1994		2000		2004	
Total Outlays	22.2	22.9	21.8	21.4	22.5	21.3
Discretionary[1]	8.2	8.2	6.5	7.2	6.1	6.8
Mandatory	11.9	12.5	13.1	12.9	14.1	13.6
Social Security	4.7	4.9	4.8	4.5	4.8	4.4
Medicare	2.4	2.6	3.2	2.8	3.9	3.3
Medicaid	1.3	1.4	1.9	2.4	2.3	2.7
Federal Pensions	0.9	1.1	0.9	1.0	0.9	1.0
Other	2.6	2.5	2.4	2.2	2.2	2.1
Net Interest	3.0	3.2	3.2	2.4	3.3	2.0
All Other	-1.1	-1.0	-1.0	-1.1	-0.9	-1.1
Total Revenue	19.0	18.7	19.0	21.8	18.9	21.8
Deficit (Surplus)	-3.4	-4.3	-2.9	-0.3	3.6	0.5
Debt Held By Public	51.5	55.4	52.7	46.9	56.1	38.1

Source: Peter G. Peterson, *Facing Up* (New York: Simon and Schuster, 1993), p. 390.; and Congress of the United States, Congressional Budget Office, *The Economic and Budget Outlook: Fiscal Years 1995-1999: An Update*, August 1994 (Washington, D.C.: Government Printing Office), p. 31.

1. The Action Plan projections include 1 percent of GDP in new investment spending.

raise the deficit to 3.6 percent of GDP. It has been estimated that the deficit would rise to $397 billion by 2004 if no further spending cuts and revenue increases are legislated; by contrast the Action Plan achieves a small surplus by 2004.

Projected outlays and revenues for the Action Plan are compared with the CBO baseline projections, which incorporate OBRA 1993 (see Table 5.1). The decline in total outlays as a percentage of GDP is substantially greater under the Action Plan than for the CBO baseline. Because the Action Plan includes a projection equal to 1 percent of GDP for new investment spending, discretionary spending is higher than in the revised CBO baseline. However, whereas mandatory expenditures rise in both the CBO baseline and the Action Plan, the growth in total outlays is less in the Action Plan, despite the fact that it eliminates the Social Security "earnings test," extends health insurance coverage to the working poor, expands Supplemental Social Insurance (SSI) to those at or somewhat above the poverty line, and provides for public investment spending. Slower growth in Social Security and Medicare outlays reduces mandatory expenditures in the Action Plan in comparison with the CBO baseline. Lower deficits under the Action Plan imply lower costs of servicing the public debt. By the year 2000, interest outlays are 0.8 percent of GDP less for the Action Plan than projected by the CBO, and by 2004 the difference is 1.3 percent of GDP. The combined total for all outlays in the last year in which the comparison is made is greater in the CBO estimate than in the Peterson Action Plan—22.5 percent of GDP compared with 21.3 percent of GDP. At the same time the deficit has been turned into a small surplus in the Action Plan, whereas the CBO estimates show deficits rising from 2.9 percent of GDP in 2000 to 3.6 percent of GDP in 2004. The Action Plan shows a surplus in 2004 because it relies upon a large growth in revenues to close the budget gap. Also, less borrowing during earlier years lowers the interest cost of servicing the public debt.

For the CBO baseline, revenues remain at about 19.0 percent of GDP over the period. But for the Action Plan, general revenues rise to 21.8 percent of GDP by 2000 and remain at that level in 2004, the difference between the projections for the CBO baseline and the Action Plan being almost 3.0 percent of GDP.

To raise the share of federal revenues to almost 22 percent of GDP would represent a reversal of tax policy that has ensued for much of the postwar period. Since 1960, the average share of federal revenue was 18.6 percent of GDP. In the late 1960s, it surpassed 20 percent due to the income tax surcharge levied during the Vietnam War; and the share rose again to 20 percent in 1981 after several years of rapid inflation pushed the income of taxpayers into higher tax brackets. By 1984 the share was brought down to 18 percent because of large tax cuts enacted in the Economic Recovery Act of 1981 (ERTA) combined with the effect of the 1980 and 1980–82 recessions.[4]

Raising additional federal revenues to achieve budget balance turns out to be a matter of limited alternatives. Given the growth in entitlements, it would be difficult to sharply reduce these outlays without breaking the social contract this nation has made with its citizens. To cut discretionary outlays any further leaves very little to pay for the international obligations that a superpower such as the United States assumes, plus to meet the many other domestic obligations such as education and transportation facilities that our nation requires. One is thus left with the option of focusing on revenue increases as a way to achieve budgetary balance and to remove some of the burden that enormous deficits will impose on succeeding generations of Americans.

Deficit reduction can affect the rate of economic growth. If it is planned that the process of balancing the budget will take ten years, an average of at least $30 billion a year will have to be cut every year from the deficit and the impact on the growth of the economy would be small. For instance, the CBO has done simulations that show that eliminating the deficit over the five years between 1994 and 1998 would, on the average, reduce the short-term growth of the economy by an average of 0.5 percent a year without an accommodating monetary policy, and that if the deficit were to be eliminated in a ten-year period, the short-term impact on growth would be less. In the winter of 1993, when the simulations were done, it was forecast that the economy would grow at a little less than 3 percent a year for the ten-year period 1994–2003 and that deficit reduction by itself would not push the economy into a recession. The CBO argued that in the absence of an accommodating monetary policy, slower growth resulting from deficit reduction may adversely affect labor market conditions. However, at the time, a rate of economic growth that was 0.5 percent less than the baseline projection did not appear sufficient to raise the rate of unemployment.[5]

After the enactment of the 1993 OBRA, it was predicted that economic growth would average 2.6 percent a year until 1998 and 2.1 percent a year until 2003 and that it would take until 1998 for the unemployment rate to fall to 5.7 percent. However, when these forecasts were made, the unemployment rate for 1993 was forecast at 6.9 percent, but because the economic climate improved considerably by the end of the year, economic growth rose to 3.1 percent and the unemployment rate averaged 6.8 percent for the year. Because of a pickup in economic growth in 1994, it fell to an average of 6.1 percent. The problem is the rate of unemployment at the nonaccelerating inflation rate of unemployment (NAIRU), a rate that is considered the rate at which inflation does not accelerate, is now estimated at 6 percent. Although in February 1995 the Federal Reserve continued its actions to raise short-term interest rates because of its fear of inflation, keeping the unemployment rate as low as 6 percent might be difficult in an economy undergoing conversion to peacetime and where downsizing and restructuring are continuously occurring.

Because deficit reduction can exert a contractionary impact on the economy, further deficit reduction would have to be handled carefully, and the Federal Reserve should work to be certain that its monetary policies help to maintain economic growth and prevent the tighter fiscal policy associated with additional deficit reduction from exerting a drag on the economy. An accommodating monetary policy by the Federal Reserve would be required to offset any dampening effect that reducing the deficit would have on the demand for goods and services. Keeping money growth sufficiently high to prevent interest rates from rising by very much would prevent investment spending and net exports from falling and would help offset any short-term weakening of the economy that would occur as deficit reduction proceeded.[6]

It would be difficult to maintain an accommodating monetary policy over the time period that would be required to balance the federal budget, especially if the process were to proceed slowly over a ten-year period. First, monetary actions operate on the economy with an uncertain lag. According to some economists, easing of monetary policy increases the level of prices in a relatively short period and has little impact on real output, but according to other economists, prices are determined by the interaction of aggregate demand with aggregate supply and a substantial time period can elapse before monetary policy might affect prices.[7] Even though it may be problematic to maintain an accommodating monetary policy over the period of time required to balance the budget, if further deficit reduction measures are taken, coordination with the Federal Reserve is necessary.

In addition to pursuing an accommodating monetary policy when engaged in fiscal tightening, it may be feasible to combine some elements of a stimulatory fiscal policy in conjunction with cutbacks in expenditures and transfer payments and increases in revenues that will be required to significantly reduce the deficit.

Because of large federal deficits, little use was made of fiscal policy measures beyond the automatic stabilizers[8] to stimulate the economy during the 1990–91 recession, and economic recovery was very slow. Economists use the concept of the structural deficit (also called the standardized or full-employment deficit) to analyze the impact of a recession on the economy. During a period when actual output is below potential, the cyclical deficit is the difference between the actual deficit and the structural deficit. In Table 5.2 actual structural deficits (standardized-employment deficits) for 1992 and 1993 and projections for the structural deficit for 1994–99 are shown. Removal of the cyclical component lowers the deficit considerably, especially during the early years while employment and output were recovering from the recession. These figures calculated in August 1994 assume the unemployment rate falls to 5.8 percent in 1996 and then rises to 6.1 percent in 1998 and 1999. For much of the period the difference between actual and potential output is assumed to be minimal. Whereas in 1992 the actual deficit as a percentage of GDP differed from the structural deficit by 1.6 percent of GDP, by 1994 the difference was assumed to be minimal.[9] Because real economic growth averaged 3.1 percent for 1993 and was estimated to have grown by 4 percent in 1994, the size of the actual deficit was not significantly larger than the structural deficit.

Much of the discussion about the deficit focuses on the size of the actual deficit. Because part of the deficit (about one-fourth in 1992) was caused by the economy operating below its potential, the deficit problem has been magnified. The CBO calculated that about one-half of potential budget reduction in 1994–98 would come from the recovery of the economy. Because of the recovery, even if tax rates and spending remain the same as projected, the deficit falls as revenues automatically rise and transfer payments such as unemployment compensation and welfare payments fall. With increased economic growth in 1994, additional deficit reduction was automatically occurring.

Table 5.2
Deficit Projections, Fiscal Years 1992–99

	Actual 1992	Actual 1993	1994	1995	1996	1997	1998	1999
In Billions of Dollars								
Total Deficit	290	255	209	162	176	193	197	231
Standardized-Employment[1] Deficit	206	221	184	183	195	200	196	223
As a Percentage of GDP								
Total Deficit	4.9	4.0	3.0	2.3	2.4	2.5	2.4	2.7
Standardized-Employment Deficit[2]	3.3	3.4	2.7	2.6	2.6	2.6	2.4	2.6

Source: Congress of the United States, Congressional Budget Office, *The Economic and Budget Outlook: Fiscal Years 1995-1999: An Update,* August 1994 (Washington, D.C.: Government Printing Office), p. xiii.

1. Excludes the cyclical deficit, spending for deposit insurance, and contributions from allied nations for Operation Desert Storm. The last of these contributions was received in 1992.

2. Shown as a percent of potential GDP.

With respect to pursuing a stimulatory fiscal policy in conjunction with serious attempts to reduce the deficit, it is important to focus on one part of the Peterson Action Plan. Reference has already been made to the proposal to dedicate 1 percent of GDP toward a group of public investment projects. These projects would be directed toward R&D and physical and human capital formation projects that have high rates of return; and it would be necessary that each spending proposal be accompanied by a "productivity impact statement," no funds be allocated for projects for which a private market exists, and that the nation's investment priorities be ranked in advance of their funding. With such a list of investment projects, were economic stimulus to be necessary at any time, it was suggested that Congress could move up projects according to a rational criterion. It is suggested that one-half of these funds be used to support basic infrastructure projects such as high-speed railroads and deepwater ports; one-quarter be directed to basic R&D efforts targeting cutting-edge technologies; and the remaining one-quarter be used to finance a comprehensive health, education, and neighborhood care program for all low-income preschool children.[10]

It was proposed that new public investment spending be phased-in over time until it becomes 1 percent of GDP by the year 2000. With the cutback in federal outlays and substantial increases in taxation that would occur under the Action Plan, it would be advisable that if the economy begins to show weakness, new public investment spending should rise to 1 percent of GDP prior to the year 2000. It is very important that the large growth in revenues as a share of GDP projected under the Action Plan not be permitted to have a contractionary impact on the economy.

The Action Plan provides for three investment incentives: enacting a permanent tax credit for business R&D, establishing worker training tax incentives, and indexing capital gains to encourage productive investments. The combined cost of these three investment incentives is estimated at $13.4 billion in 1998, $14 billion in 2000, and $17.6 billion in 2004.

In 1981 the federal government legislated a 20 percent tax credit for incremental R&D expenditures. Only R&D outlays above previous amounts qualified for the credit. Because the tax credit has always been temporary, it was difficult for firms to engage in long-range planning. The Action Plan would make the credit permanent and allow all R&D outlays to qualify for the credit. All R&D expenditures that qualified would get a 10 percent tax credit. Worker training incentives in the form of a 10 percent credit for all employer outlays on employees' training and education as well as employees' deductions for costs of formal education and training programs to help qualify for a new job would be established. Finally, the prices of newly purchased productive assets would be indexed for inflation. Although the first two investment incentives do not appear to be controversial, indexing capital gains on productive assets could be.

One measure that could aid the growth of the economy—the restoration of the Investment Tax Credit (ITC) that provided a substantial investment incentive and served the economy well between 1962 and 1986—should be seriously considered.[11] Credits were allowed for the purchase of new equipment (although new buildings were not entitled to the credit, special credits were made available for the rehabilitation of structures). This credit was originally set at 7 percent of investment and was raised to 10 percent in 1975.[12] Firms were permitted to deduct as a credit against their taxes 10 percent of the amount of new qualifying investment with a recovery period of at least three years. Because the credit effectively reduced the cost of the asset, it increased the rate of return.[13] Although the revenue cost of restoring the ITC would exceed the combined cost of the three investment incentives recommended in the Action Plan, it would be able to provide a substantial investment incentive.

Although reenactment of the investment tax credit would raise the cost of investment incentives, it would focus sharply on new investments. The new investment spending would help to stimulate economic activity by raising investment, and the new equipment would raise future productivity. Because it focuses on new investment, it might be more effective than indexing capital gains on productive assets. It has been proposed that the reenacted ITC should be given for incremental investment above a recent base period.[14]

The Action Plan includes a number of measures to raise revenues: gradually raising the gasoline tax by an additional 45.7 cents a gallon, a 5 percent national retail sales tax, increased excise taxes on cigarettes and alcoholic beverages, and limits on the amount of interest on home mortgages that is deductible.

The Action Plan relies heavily on indirect taxes or consumption taxes to raise revenues. The excise tax on a particular commodity or group of commodities is a common form of consumption tax. The immediate effect of imposing or raising an excise tax is to raise the price of the commodity. If the demand for the commodity is relatively inelastic, most of the burden of the tax falls on the consumer, and generally most excise tax revenues come from goods having a relatively inelastic demand. Selective excise taxes have the drawback of being regressive and discriminating among different items of consumption. However, other reasons may exist to recommend higher excise taxes on cigarettes, alcoholic beverages, and gasoline.

Excises on goods or services that are considered morally or socially undesirable such as alcoholic beverages and tobacco products are called sumptuary taxes. Such taxes are imposed because the consumption of these goods creates "external costs," which are additional costs to society that are not borne by producers and not reflected in the prices they charge. Consumption of liquor creates costs to society in the form of lost labor time, increased healthcare costs, serious accidents, broken homes, and increased criminality. Cigarette consumption has been associated with a wide range of illnesses. Raising excise taxes increases prices so that they more closely reflect social costs as well as private costs and discourage consumption of these goods.[15]

In the United States, excise taxes have represented a declining share of GDP because they are generally levied on quantity and not the value of the goods, and excise taxes have not been raised to keep up with inflation. Increasing excise taxes on alcoholic beverages and cigarettes could raise a substantial amount of revenue. For instance, the CBO has estimated that by 1999, increasing alcoholic beverage taxes to $16 per proof gallon and the cigarette tax to 99 cents a pack would add $4.6 billion and $9.6 billion, respectively, to revenues.[16]

In addition to raising revenue, raising the federal excise tax on gasoline by 10 cents a gallon in each year for five years can be incorporated into an overall energy policy. At present the United States is dependent on foreign sources for 45 percent of its petroleum, and such a heavy dependence on overseas suppliers makes the nation vulnerable to volatile oil prices and political conflicts in energy-producing areas, such as was experienced during the Gulf War. Significantly higher energy taxes, by reducing consumption, would promote resource conservation and reduce pollution. This would also promote the further development of transportation sources that are alternatives to the automobile and, therefore, reduce road congestion. Although different ways to tax energy could be considered, increasing the federal excise tax by 10 cents a gallon each year for five years might be the easiest to impose. Even with a significantly higher excise tax, gasoline prices would remain much below prices in other OECD countries. Because higher gasoline taxes would impose additional burdens on those who commute long distances to work by car and on the trucking industry, it has been suggested that the excise tax increase should be phased-in over a five-year period. It is also easy to ease the burden on certain groups by providing tax credits against their income taxes. For instance, low-income people who qualify for an earned income credit might be given a credit against their income taxes if they can provide documentation that they need to drive more than a certain number of miles to get to work.

It has been estimated that each additional penny of tax would generate almost $1 billion in revenues a year. Raising the federal excise tax by 10 cents a gallon for each of five years would generate an additional $42 billion in revenue by 1999. Because the price of gasoline is currently near the peak of $1.39 a gallon in 1981, even an increase of 50 cents a gallon would leave the price in real terms below what has already been experienced.[17]

The Action Plan also proposes a 5 percent national retail sales tax on most consumption expenditures. To prevent the consumption tax from being regressive, expenditures on food, housing, and education would be excluded. After these three items are excluded, the tax would be effectively 2.5 percent on lower income households. Increasing the earned income tax credit for low-income households would be another way of providing compensation. Because it is believed that it is easier to administer a sales tax than a value added tax (VAT), the sales tax was selected even though Peterson believes that in the future a redesigned federal tax system should be focused entirely on taxing consumption.[18] It is estimated that the revenue from the consumption tax would be high. For instance, by 1998 it could contribute $97.2 billion in revenue and by 2004, $124.5 billion. By 1998, about two-thirds of the deficit reduction in the Action Plan would come from the consumption tax, but this share declines in later years.

During the past two or three decades, much has been written concerning the relative merits of a consumption tax or VAT, and many countries have moved toward a system of value added taxes. The argument for some type of consumption tax is that it is the only kind of tax that is neutral with respect to the saving rate. It has been argued that for the aggregate household sector, the effects of a tax on wages and salaries are similar to a tax on consumption from the household's point of view because both reduce the real purchasing power of lifetime resources and, thus, the level of real consumption and savings streams. According to this argument, substituting a consumption tax for a progressive income tax would affect the after-tax income distributions across households. If the marginal propensity to save increases as the level of income rises, a consumption tax would raise aggregate savings.

It has also been argued that a tax on wages and salaries affects household savings by influencing the choice between work and leisure. If the income effect of a tax increase on wages and salaries predominates, workers will substitute labor for leisure, but if the substitution effect predominates, workers will substitute additional leisure for work time because leisure has become cheaper. Because for a saver the income effect and substitution effect from an income tax increase work in opposite directions, the net effect is inconclusive. Results of empirical studies still show responsiveness of savings to after-tax rates of return to be uncertain.[19]

Because a broad-based tax on consumption, such as a retail sales tax or a VAT is regressive, it is more burdensome on the lower income classes than the upper income classes. The burden on the low-income households can be reduced if they are granted a credit against income taxes paid and certain consumption expenditures are exempted. Also, substituting a consumption tax for an income tax greatly reduces the built-in flexibility of the income tax. With a taxation system based largely on income taxes, during a recession, revenues drop by more than the fall in the level of income, and during an upswing taxes rise by more than the level of income. However, if the retail sales tax or VAT were to remain at a low level such as 5 percent, taxes on households would still accrue largely from income taxes.

The Peterson Action Plan limits the deductibility of home mortgages. Under current law, taxpayers may deduct interest outlays on total mortgage debt of $1 million for primary and secondary residences and up to $100,000 in home equity loans. This means that investment in very expensive homes is subsidized, and that persons with sufficient equity in their homes can qualify for loans to be used for consumer purchases such as automobiles and vacations. The Action Plan would cap mortgage interest deductions at $12,000 for an individual and at $20,000 for a joint filing couple. Limiting deductibility should raise $7.6 billion in revenues in 1999 and about $10 billion in 2004.

Interest deductibility on owner-occupied homes encourages saving in the form of housing and discriminates against renters, because owner occupants are not taxed on the imputed rental value of owner-occupied homes. Limits proposed might free some funds for business investment, thereby improving the allocation of resources. Also, because homeowners with considerable equity in their homes can deduct interest on $100,000 of home equity loans, they use some of that amount for consumer purchases, thereby lowering their saving propensity.

The Action Plan also proposes to limit the tax exclusion of employer-paid health insurance at $170 per month for individual and $470 a month for family coverage. In addition to raising more revenue, such a cap would reduce the demand for high-priced health care. Because employer-paid insurance premiums are not now included in gross income, these caps would increase revenues from both income tax and payroll tax (Social Security tax). Using caps of $175 per individual and $375 per family, the CBO has calculated that by 1999, $17.8 billion in income tax revenues and $12.1 billion in payroll tax revenues would be raised.[20]

RECOMMENDATIONS FOR ECONOMIC GROWTH AND ADDITIONAL DEFICIT REDUCTIONS

The 1993 Omnibus Budget Reconciliation Act has made some inroads toward deficit reduction. But even by 1995, when the federal deficit is projected to fall to 2.3 percent of GDP, the negative savings of the public sector will still substantially reduce the net national saving rate.

One important reason for eliminating the federal budget deficit is to raise the national saving rate. Even with the deficit reductions that are expected to occur during the next several years, the federal deficit contributes to a low national saving rate. Because public-sector savings are negative and personal saving is low, domestic investment exceeds domestic saving and the United States remains dependent on foreign capital.

Policies aimed at achieving further deficit reduction are necessary. With the economy recovering from recession and economic growth expected to remain close to 3 percent over the next year or two, the rapid implementation of additional deficit reduction measures would be advisable. A program for further budget reduction measures must reduce expenditures and raise revenues.

It is doubtful that sizable reductions can come from discretionary expenditures. Large reductions have already been made in these outlays, including defense spending, and between fiscal years 1993 and 2004, discretionary outlays are projected to fall from 8.8 percent of GDP to 6.1 percent. Over the same period, mandatory outlays will rise from 12.3 to 14.1 percent of GDP as a consequence of increases in Medicare and Medicaid.

Before commenting on the policies that should be implemented in a budget reduction plan, it is necessary to discuss current estimates of the size of the deficit over the next few years.

Because growth of the economy during the second half of 1993 and the first half of 1994 was significantly higher than anticipated, deficits in fiscal year 1994 and 1995 are forecast to be smaller than previously estimated. GDP growth in 1993 was 3 percent and it was originally estimated that in 1994 it would be a little over 3 percent.[21] However, the economy grew at an estimated rate of 4.1 percent in 1994. These rates are almost 1.0 percent higher than earlier estimates. Estimates for federal budget deficits were revised downward. For fiscal year 1993, the budget deficit was $255 billion. In August 1994 the Congressional Budget Office estimated the 1994 deficit at $202 billion and the 1995 deficit at $165 billion. But because of growth in mandatory outlays (entitlements) the deficit is estimated to rise to \$397 billion in 2004 if no further deficit reduction occurs. A number of proposals in the Peterson Action Plan could be incorporated into a deficit reduction plan that is recommended below.

The phasing in of new investment spending to equal 1 percent of GDP is a very important proposal. This provides public investment for research and development and investment in physical and human capital formation activities that the private sector cannot provide—basic infrastructure; basic R&D efforts targeting cutting-edge technologies; and health, education, and neighborhood care programs for low-income preschool children. Whereas the Action Plan recommends spending one-quarter of this new investment spending on low-income, preschool children, it is recommended that a much larger share of the new investment spending be allocated for education, both on the preschool level as well as on primary, secondary, and higher education. Until the 1980s, Americans were willing to spend money to educate future generations, but more recently many communities have continuously voted down bills to raise money for schools by floating bonds. In a society that is becoming increasingly technologically advanced, living standards and productivity cannot rise unless educational standards rise.

The Action Plan calls for a phasing in of the new public investment spending over a six-year period until it reaches 1 percent of GDP in the year 2000, and it was suggested that Congress should be able to move up spending on public investment projects if fiscal stimulus was required. Because budget deficit estimates for 1994 and 1995 are lower than estimated in September 1993, it should be feasible to push up spending so that this new public investment spending on the projects that America desperately needs commences in fiscal year 1995 and becomes fully phased in by 1996 or 1997. Projects could still be advanced if an economic downturn occurs and economic stimuli are required. Because increases in taxation that must be implemented to achieve budget balance could have a contractionary impact on the economy, raising public investment spending would help to maintain a steady state of economic growth of about 3 percent a year. It is well known that the expansionary impact of a \$1 increase in spending is greater than the contractionary impact of a \$1 increase in taxation. Increasing investment spending at the same time that taxation is rising could help to mitigate a slowing down of economic growth as deficit reduction proceeds. It is strongly recommended that the proposal to spend 1 percent of GDP on public investment projects be implemented.

Spending 1 percent of GDP on investment projects would raise the rate of economic growth by 0.75 to 1.00 percentage point.[22] Since the economy is now projected to grow by 3 percent in 1995 and an average of about 2.2 percent per year for 1996–99, increasing spending by 1 percent of GDP should raise economic growth to between 2.95 and 3.2 percent between 1996 and 1999.

Even though it has been estimated that federal revenue for the period 1994–95 will average about 19.1 percent of GDP, which is slightly above the average level of 18.6 percent of GDP for the period 1960–93, it will be necessary for this share to rise to between 21 and 22 percent of GDP for the United States to achieve budget balance without a severe reduction in expenditures. Although the long-term revenue share of GDP has remained fairly stable, important shifts in major sources of revenue have occurred. Since 1960, the GDP share of social insurance taxes (mainly Social Security taxes) has increased continuously from 3 percent of GDP to almost 7 percent because payroll tax rates, the share of wages subject to taxation, and coverage have increased. Over the same period the GDP shares claimed by corporate income taxes and excises have declined. The corporate income tax share fell from about 4 percent of GDP in 1960 to almost 2 percent in the 1990s as a result of legislated reductions in tax liability and a decline in corporate profits as a share of GDP. Excise taxes declined steadily from a little over 2 percent of GDP to less than 1 percent. This decline was a consequence of the fact that excise taxes are levied largely on quantity rather than the value of goods, and Congress has not raised tax rates to keep up with inflation. Income taxes have averaged over 8 percent of GDP, even though the share has fluctuated considerably over this period.

Examining movements in the major sources of federal revenues leaves one with the impression that had social insurance tax revenues not increased over the period, Americans would be paying a smaller share of GDP in the form of federal tax revenues. At the heart of the matter is the fact that, as a society, we have chosen to buy more Social Security coverage for those who previously were uncovered, to protect the Social Security earnings of beneficiaries by offering cost of living allowances (COLAs), and to provide needed health care coverage to the elderly. Related to this concern with the well-being of society was the creation of Medicaid, which provides health services and nursing home care to the poor. However, unlike Social Security benefits and Medicare, which have been funded by social insurance taxes, Medicaid comes out of other revenues, leaving less to pay for the many outlays that a society requires, such as physical and social infrastructure.

If a society has decided that its welfare is enhanced by covering more recipients with Social Security benefits and providing health care benefits to the poor and elderly, it would be advisable to pay for these outlays by raising the share of revenues out of GDP and not by running large budget deficits or reducing expenditures on other goods that we as a society require.

For several reasons, higher excise taxes on alcoholic beverages and cigarettes are a good source of revenue. First, excise taxes have represented a declining share of GDP because they are generally levied on quantity and not quality of goods, and excise tax rates have not been raised to keep up with inflation. Second, the external costs, including higher health insurance costs from smoking cigarettes and excessive consumption of alcoholic beverages, are high. If excise taxes of $1 per pack of cigarettes and $16 per proof gallon could reduce consumption of these products, external costs to society would be reduced.

Higher federal excise taxes on motor fuel should be part of an overall energy policy that would be focused on making the United States less dependent on foreign sources of petroleum and reducing pollution. A high excise tax on gasoline would raise the price to the ultimate consumer, and some of the external cost imposed on society by pollution and road congestion would be included in the price of gasoline, less gasoline would be consumed, and a more optimum allocation of resources would occur.

Deficit reduction in the Action Plan depends heavily on enactment of a 5 percent national sales tax, which would raise a large amount of revenue and help balance the budget. Although regressive, the tax would be effectively 2.5 percent for lower income households after exemptions for food, education, and housing are subtracted out. Low-income households could receive further compensation if the earned income tax credit were increased. A 5 percent sales tax would be in addition to the present federal income tax, and raising revenue would be its primary function.

Even though a 5 percent sales tax can raise the large amounts of revenue required for deficit reduction, such a tax raises too many questions to be recommended for inclusion in a deficit reduction plan. First, the national sales tax is regressive and would be more burdensome on the lower income classes than on the upper classes, even if exemptions for food, education, and housing are included. Second, the states and localities are heavily dependent on sales taxes to finance necessary expenditures, and a national sales tax will impinge on their ability to finance needed expenditures. Finally, substituting a consumption tax for an income tax reduces the built-in flexibility of the present progressive income tax structure. Because of the enactment of the 1981 Economic Recovery Tax Act and the Tax Reform Act of 1986, some of the progressiveness of the federal income tax was lost, and the ability of the income tax to stabilize the economy against the fluctuations in the business cycle was diminished. OBRA 1993 raised the progressiveness of the federal personal income tax back to its 1977 level. By 1990, most taxpaying income groups were paying the same share of their income in federal income taxes as in 1977, but the top 1 percent of the income distribution paid a lower share. The 1990 Omnibus Budget Reconciliation Act increased the maximum marginal income tax rate to 31 percent and limited benefits from itemized deductions and personal exemptions for these families. The 1993 Omnibus Budget Reconciliation Act added new income tax rates of 36 percent and 39.6 percent and made all earnings subject to the Medicare payroll tax. As a result of these changes, the total share of income that the highest income families pay in taxes is the same as that which had existed for such families in 1977. Expansion of the earned income tax credit has reduced the share of income taxes paid by the lowest quintile below that group's 1977 level.

The income tax is the only tax source over which policymakers can control the distributional burden, and this burden on different quintiles of the population is now similar to 1977. But, for the past two decades the distribution of family incomes has become increasingly unequal, and family income growth has stagnated. Real incomes of the bottom 60 percent of American families were lower in the 1990s than in the late 1970s. Whereas family incomes grew fairly evenly for all income quintiles between 1947 and 1973, for 1973–92 real incomes for the top income quintile increased substantially, real incomes for the middle quintile have stagnated, and real incomes for the bottom quintile fell. The 1960s trend toward greater equality was reversed in the 1970s and 1980s. Factors contributing to the widening inequality are increasing returns to education and experience, the decline of unions, and the erosion of the minimum wage by inflation.[23]

Within the context of widening income inequality, it seems reasonable to suggest that marginal income tax rates for the higher income brackets be raised to help balance the budget and at the same time slightly reduce income disparities. It is recommended that the 15 and 28 percent marginal rate brackets remain the same and that the higher rates be raised to a minimum of 30 percent, 33 percent, 38 percent, and 42 percent and that the alternative minimum tax be raised to 30 percent. Although a significantly larger amount of revenue could be raised by the 5 percent national sales tax, a tax increment that is based on the ability to pay and improving the income distribution is recommended.

A number of other revenue measures not included in the Peterson Action Plan are also strongly recommended. Indexing of the personal exemption, the minimum and maximum dollar amounts for each tax bracket, the standard deduction, and the threshold for the phaseout of personal exemptions and the earned income credit were introduced in the 1980s. Indexing for inflation was introduced when prices were rising at an unsatisfactorily high rate. The CBO has estimated that if inflation averages 3 percent, repealing indexing (except for the earned income credit) would raise large amounts of revenue—$51 billion by 1999. Because serious efforts need to be made to achieve budget balance, repealing indexing must be seriously considered.

Arguments can be made for and against indexing the income tax. It is argued that without indexing, increases in effective income tax rates take place with inflation (the effective rate being the amount of tax divided by income). With a progressive tax system, without indexing, total tax payments rise faster than inflation.

But an important argument that can be made against indexing is that during periods of cyclical expansion and inflation, it reduces the built-in stabilizing effect of the income tax. With inflation, tax revenues rise automatically and growth in demand is reduced, which contributes toward stabilization of the economy. Furthermore, when inflation rates are low, some of the growth in fixed-base price indexes really reflects changes in buying patterns and quality of goods, such as improved quality in consumer electronics. It has been suggested that because of the difficulty of distinguishing quality improvements, if a system of indexing income taxes were used, it should only be made operational when the inflation rate had risen to 5 percent.[24]

Currently, with an inflation rate of about 3 percent, taxpayers are not burdened with a large inflation factor when paying income taxes, and large amounts of revenue have been lost each year because of indexing of the income tax. The idea of indexing the income tax achieved prominence after annual inflation rates had risen to over 10 percent. But with inflation almost as low as in the 1960s, indexing is not necessary. An immediate repeal of indexing would have a significant impact on achieving a balanced budget.

Other recommendations include limiting the deductibility of home mortgage interest and eliminating the deductibility of interest on home equity loans unless the borrower can document that the borrowed funds were used for capital improvements on the home. Limiting the tax exemption of employer-paid health plan premiums above a certain minimum and taxing other nonretirement fringe benefits such as life insurance, taxing investment income from life insurance products, and taxing capital gains held until death are also recommended.

A central thesis of the Peterson Action Plan is its focus on the continuing growth in entitlements, which has created a windfall for current retirees and burdened younger generations of taxpayers. A windfall for retirees is believed to have occurred because many of them are receiving more in benefits than was ever believed possible. Indexing of Social Security benefits with generous COLAs has caused large increases in payments to retirees and many have received much more than the amounts they contributed plus a reasonable rate of return on their contributions. The introduction of Medicare in the 1960s also provided large benefits. Peterson recommended an affluence test or graduated entitlement benefit reduction for wealthier-than-average beneficiaries because a substantial amount of entitlement spending goes to individuals with incomes in excess of $50,000. Large savings would result if this proposal was implemented, but the proposal should be carefully examined before recommendations are made to adopt it. Raising the Social Security retirement age could also save considerable amounts of revenue. Whereas current law mandates that the retirement age is to be raised in stages to sixty-seven in 2020, Peterson recommends phasing in an increase in the retirement age until it reaches sixty-eight in 2006. It is recommended that this be implemented.

Recommendations will not be made for changes in health care spending. The Clinton administration and the U.S. Congress had been planning a major revision of our health care system in order to provide universal health care coverage to all Americans, but passage of such legislation appears unlikely given the Republican domination of Congress. However, some type of health care legislation is still envisaged.

POLICY CHANGES TO RAISE HOUSEHOLD SAVING

Studies on household savings suggest that governments might implement three policy options to increase the level of savings. However, the savings response to these changes is largely unknown. These three measures are, according to Jeffrey Owens,

a shift from direct to indirect taxes may increase household saving ratios. Given the higher propensity of corporations than households to save, shifting part of the tax burden from corporations to households may marginally increase overall private savings. Limiting the deductibility of interest for consumer credit and housing may also increase household saving.[25]

When commenting upon Owens' paper, Modigliani discusses the manner in which taxation affects saving in the following:

Jeffrey Owens' assignment is to deal with the effect of taxation on saving. He reminds us of the fact that taxation affects saving basically by changing the after-tax rate of return. This means that while there are many ways of impinging on the rate of return, such as taxing labor income and property income at different rates, or taxing consumption rather than income, the effectiveness of any approach must finally depend upon the response of consumers to the rate of return. This point is important because the response to the rate of return is basically uncertain, as noted earlier. One can therefore not be sure that a tax measure raising returns will have [a] favorable effect, especially if in detaxing interest the government loses revenue. Proposed measures have to be scrutinized very carefully and designed to minimize the income effect. The substitution of an income tax with an equal revenue consumption tax (say through indirect taxation) may on balance not have a very marked net income effect and thus succeed in raising saving. Still opponents point to the unfavorable distributional aspect, as between income classes and age classes, resulting from the substitution, though it must be remembered that a sales tax can easily be made progressive through variation in rates by type of goods and through a rebate offered to all.[26]

The impact of a tax is to change the after-tax rate of return. The response to a tax is dependent upon savers' responses to changes in the rate of return, but empirical studies have shown this response to be uncertain.

The response to a change in the after-tax rate of return is dependent on the interest elasticity of saving, which depends on the strength of the income effect and the substitution effect of a change in the rate. The income effect and the substitution effect work against each other, and the outcome is ambiguous. An increase in the interest rate (or rate of return) makes current consumption more expensive and the household is induced to postpone consumption (the substitution effect). If the substitution effect were the only effect from the increase in the rate of return, it would be possible to state categorically that increases in the after-tax rate of return would increase saving. But the income effect of an increase in the rate of return works in the direction of raising consumption now as well as in the future and lowering current saving because creditors and other owners of wealth will be more well-off. It is an empirical question whether the income effect outweighs the substitution effect, and because the results of numerous tests have been contradictory, it is not possible to say that the interest elasticity is significantly positive or different from zero and that tax incentives geared toward raising saving would actually increase the level of saving.[27]

One policy option that studies suggest might raise household saving ratios is to shift from direct to indirect taxes. It is frequently assumed that a consumption tax affects saving less than an income tax. Many economists have recommended that the United States should go toward a value added system of taxation. Although both the value added tax and the income tax reduce the aggregate household sector's lifetime resources, and thereby its consumption and income streams, if the marginal propensity to save of households were to rise with income, substituting the progressive income tax with an equal value consumption tax should raise aggregate saving. Such a change in the system of taxation would have an unfavorable distributional aspect unless, as suggested above, it is accompanied by rebates or tax credits and exemptions (or lower rates) for certain types of purchases. However, as indicated above, a consumption tax as opposed to a progressive income tax would reduce the built-in flexibility of the present system of taxation in the United States.

Because balancing the budget will require large revenue increases, many have suggested that we supplement our progressive income tax system with a consumption tax that includes a number of exemptions. This would mean that our tax system would become somewhat more dependent on indirect taxation.

The proposal to shift some of the tax burden from corporations to households is difficult to assess, and it has been frequently suggested that household and business sector savings move in opposite directions, resulting in a relatively stable savings ratio, and that if investors were completely rational, it makes little difference if the profit were taxed at the corporate level or shifted back to the consumer who is the owner of equity in the corporation.

The third suggestion for policy action to affect the level of saving is to limit the deductibility of interest for consumer credit and for housing. Although tax deductions for consumer interest payments have been eliminated in the United States, households are still permitted to deduct interest on up to $100,000 of home equity borrowing. To the extent that households use the proceeds from these borrowings to purchase consumer goods and services, saving is discouraged. Also, deductibility of interest payments on mortgages of up to $1 million is now permitted. This results in a subsidization of the purchase of expensive homes and an allocation of resources into housing instead of business investment. As discussed above, it is recommended that interest on home equity borrowing should be deductible only if the funds are used to renovate a home. Also, it was recommended that caps be placed on the amounts of mortgage interest that could be deductible.

Many countries provide tax benefits related to retirement pensions. These tax benefits provide households with financial incentives to save by placing their savings in pensions. The incentives to save for retirement differ in various countries. In some cases, premiums paid are deducted from taxable income at the marginal rate existing in the year that they are paid into the plan. In other instances, the accrued earnings from these contributions are tax exempt until they are paid out during retirement. In the United States both of these incentives are applicable. If the marginal rate at which premiums have been deducted is higher than the rate at which marginal benefits are taxed, subsidization of savings in the form of pension contributions occurs, which means that these pension contributions receive favorable treatment over other investment opportunities.[28]

In addition to private pension contributions, self-employed individuals may establish Keogh plans having tax-deductible premiums, and in which accrued earnings are nontaxable until they are paid out. Contributions of up to $2,000 a year for a single person and $2,250 for a married couple can be paid into an individual retirement account (IRA), and, again, the contribution is tax exempt during the year in which it is paid in and the accrued earnings are not taxable until they are paid out. The question that concerns Keogh plans and IRAs is whether they actually encourage saving or merely substitute for other forms of saving (the displacement effect).

Some evidence exists showing that incentives to save provided by plans such as IRAs and Keoghs do have a positive effect on saving. Christopher Carroll and Lawrence Summers examined differences in saving rates in the United States and Canada, and found that saving rates in the two countries were similar until the early 1970s, when they started to diverge.[29] The treatment of retirement saving, which had become increasingly more generous in Canada than in the United States, was one of the factors that was identified as contributing to this divergence. Canada increased ceilings on tax-sheltered employer-sponsored pension plans and individual Registered Retirement Savings Plans. Although the United States introduced Keogh plans and IRAs providing tax incentives for retirement savings, these plans were much more limited than the Canadian plans.

A recent study has shown that the growth of 401k employer-sponsored retirement plans and IRAs has not been displacing other savings but is helping to increase wealth in the United States.[30] For the elderly, 401k plans and IRAs have been the principal factor increasing wealth in the form of personal financial assets. Comparing contributors to 401k plans and IRAs having incomes of $40,000–$60,000 with noncontributors with similar incomes, it was found that whereas total personal financial assets for contributors increased between 1984 and 1991, no evidence of changes in personal financial assets was evident for noncontributors. It was concluded that as more workers reach retirement, contributions to IRAs and 401k plans will become a more important source of retirement wealth.

It is recommended that additional tax incentives be provided for retirement plans such as IRAs and 401k plans. First, some evidence exists showing that such plans contribute to an increase in saving. Second, it is possible that the Social Security system as it now exists will be unable to continue in its present "pay-as-you-go" form when large numbers of baby boomers reach retirement age, and it is quite possible that a larger share of retirement benefits will have to come from private sources. At present the ceilings on IRAs are very low and many people are excluded from investing in them because their incomes are too high and/or they are covered by retirement plans. The ceilings on IRAs should be raised substantially, giving more people the opportunity to invest in them. Ceilings on employee contributions to 401k plans should also be raised to encourage employees to increase their contributions.

The preceding discussion has focused on tax incentives to raise saving. However, the slowdown in the rate of growth of income has consistently been shown to be the principal contributing factor in the decline of household saving rates. If income in the United States as well as in other industrial countries were to grow at rates experienced in the 1950s and 1960s, it appears likely that saving rates would increase. Growth rates that are substantially higher than those at present being forecast for the remainder of the 1990s would help to raise private saving and would also help to reduce budgetary deficits because tax revenues would increase automatically. Using policy measures to raise the rate of economic growth would raise savings and help make the United States less dependent on foreign capital.

NOTES

1. Peter G. Peterson, *Facing Up* (New York: Simon and Schuster, 1993).

2. Ibid., pp. 260–312.

3. Ibid., pp. 267–71.

4. Congress of the United States, Congressional Budget Office, *The Economic and Budget Outlook: Fiscal Years 1994–1998* (Washington, D.C.: Government Printing Office, January 1993), pp. 63–64.

5. Ibid., pp. 79–80.

6. Ibid., pp. 76–78.

7. Another problem is fear of inflation. Some economists see an expansion of the money supply beyond a certain target rate of increase as inflationary. However, until early 1994, the view that inflation was not yet a major factor had substantial support.

With overseas demand weak, unit labor costs rising at only about 2 percent a year, and oil prices relatively low when measured in real terms, it appeared unlikely that inflation would accelerate significantly in the near future. By the second half of 1994, with plant utilization near capacity and unemployment at 6.1 percent, inflation fears increased.

8. Automatic stabilizers are the taxes and transfer payments that are built in to the system. When GDP rises during an economic expansion, the surplus rises (deficit falls) automatically. More tax revenues are generated and transfer payments fall. The extra tax revenues and lower transfer payments resulting as income rises help to restrain the boom. In a recession, the opposite occurs. Tax revenues fall and transfer payments rise, reducing leakages from the income stream and helping to dampen the recession.

9. Congress of the United States, Congressional Budget Office, *The Economic and Budget Outlook: Fiscal Years 1995–1999, An Update* (Washington, D.C.: Government Printing Office, August 1994), p 28.

10. Peterson, *Facing Up*, pp. 270–71.

11. "Fixing the U.S. Economy," Statement by 100 economists given at the National Press Club, Washington, D.C., March 30, 1992.

12. Joseph A. Pechman, *Federal Tax Policy* (Washington, D.C.: Brookings Institution, 1983), pp. 153–54.

13. Ibid., p. 154.

14. "Fixing the U.S. Economy."

15. Pechman, *Federal Tax Policy*, pp. 190–91 and 204–5.

16. Congress of the United States, Congressional Budget Office, *Reducing the Deficit: Spending and Revenue Options* (Washington, D.C.: Government Printing Office, March 1994), pp. 341–43.

17. Ibid., p. 344.

18. Peterson, *Facing Up*, pp. 292–94.

19. Jeffrey Owens, "Taxation and Savings," in *World Saving: An International Survey*, ed. Arnold Heertje (Cambridge: Blackwell, 1993), pp. 116–18.

20. *Reducing the Deficit*, pp. 311–12.

21. Lawrence Klein, "The New Administration: First Year Appraisal," Roundtable, Allied Social Science Association, Boston, January 1994.

22. James Tobin, "Thinking Straight About Fiscal Stimulus and Deficit Reduction," *Challenge*, March 1993, p. 16.

23. United States, Council of Economic Advisors, *Economic Report of the President* (Washington, D.C.: Government Printing Office, February 1994), pp. 114–21.

24. Pechman, *Federal Tax Policy*, pp. 107–9.

25. Owens, "Taxation and Savings," p. 119.

26. Franco Modigliani, "Introduction," in *World Saving*, p. 20.

27. Ibid., pp. 6–7.

28. W. F. Duisenberg and A.H.I.M. Wellink, "Toward an International Saving Policy," in *World Saving*, p. 330.

29. Christopher Carroll and Lawrence Summers, "Why Have Private Savings Rates in the United States and Canada Diverged?" *Journal of Monetary Economics*, 20 (1987), pp. 249–70.

30. James Poterba, Steven Venti, and David A. Wise, "Targeted Retirement Saving and Net Worth of Elderly Americans," *American Economic Review*, 84, no. 2 (1994), pp. 180–85.

CHAPTER 6

Capital Flows and Balance-of-Payments Adjustment

During the decade of the 1980s, international capital flows between industrial countries underwent a large expansion. To a certain extent, such flows were a consequence of the further development of international capital markets and institutions, but these increased flows also stemmed from the balance-of-payments adjustment process. During the 1980s, a number of industrial countries experienced domestic imbalances that, through the interplay of the balance-of-payments adjustment process, produced large external imbalances. In several major industrial countries, including the United States, Canada, and Italy, budgetary deficits were large in relation to GDP, and savings-investment imbalances led to large external imbalances.

This chapter will first focus on the process whereby domestic macroeconomic imbalances in the present system of flexible exchange rates cause external imbalances that result in capital movements. The chapter will also examine projections that have been made of U.S. external imbalances for the 1990s, because such projections can help assess the future role of the United States in absorbing international capital. Ultimately, the size of the U.S. current account deficits helps determine the availability of international capital for financing economies in transition to capitalism and the developing economies. Under the flexible exchange rate system in the post-Bretton Woods era, fluctuations in currency values reflect divergent macroeconomic policies and performance as well as international economic shocks.

During the late 1970s, the value of the dollar was low because the dollar had depreciated substantially in response to an expansionary monetary policy that had increased inflation and lowered real interest rates relative to foreign rates and led to large capital outflows. But commencing in 1980, the dollar decline was reversed in response to major changes in U.S. macroeconomic policies and differences in economic performance between the United States and its trading partners. In efforts to restrain double-digit rates of inflation, in 1979 the Federal Reserve implemented an extremely tight monetary policy, which produced significant increases in U.S. interest rates and contributed to the severity of the 1981–82 recession. Tax reductions in 1981–83 and large increases in military expenditures greatly expanded the size of the federal deficit, contributing to the rise in U.S. interest rates. High real interest rates and an improved environment for business resulting from very large tax reductions and an expanding economy encouraged foreign investment into the United States and prompted large capital inflows. These large capital inflows pushed up the value of the dollar in international capital markets.

The unprecedented rise in the value of the dollar, in conjunction with the savings-investment imbalances resulting from large federal government deficits and a fall in the personal saving rate, contributed to an increase of the U.S. trade deficit and growth in large surpluses in Germany and Japan. By 1985 there was growing concern that the dollar was overvalued, and in early 1985 the dollar began to decline. Also, monetary policy had begun to ease in 1984, and by 1985 real interest rates declined substantially at the same time that attempts were made to reduce inflation abroad. The gap between U.S. and foreign interest rates narrowed.

During the latter part of 1985, the Reagan administration, which had been following a policy of nonintervention in foreign currency markets, decided to change directions, which involved intervention in foreign currency markets to lower the value of the dollar and attempts to coordinate macroeconomic policies with other industrial countries. In September 1985 the G-5 countries (the United States, Germany, France, Japan, and the United Kingdom) reached the Plaza Accord, agreeing to more closely coordinate macroeconomic policies to lower the dollar further. The dollar fell continuously and by 1987 it had declined by almost 60 percent in nominal terms from its 1985 high. In February 1987, six major industrial countries, the G-5 plus Canada, reached an agreement, the Louvre Accord, to strengthen their policy coordination and stabilize the dollar. However, the dollar continued to decline until the end of the year. Because of the large fall of the dollar at the same time that the economies of the other major industrial countries were strengthening, the U.S. trade gap narrowed from its peak of $159.6 billion in 1987 to $74.1 billion in 1991.

Much has been written about the relationship between variations in exchange rates to trade balances and the current account during the 1980s. It is necessary to bear in mind that under the present system of flexible exchange rates, the exchange rate itself is an endogenous variable.

Exchange rate changes offer another possible explanation of the trade deficit. It is widely believed that dollar depreciation can affect the trade balance, and that depreciation since 1985 has started an adjustment process that is gradually reducing the trade deficit.

At the outset, however, a difficulty sets in. Under the present flexible exchange rate system, the exchange rate is an endogenous variable. Variations in the exchange rate represent the outcome of a solution of a system of general-equilibrium equations. The effect of a change in the exchange rate on the trade deficit can only be determined in the context of changes in the exogenous variables that brought about changes in the exchange rates.[1]

This chapter focuses on the process whereby domestic imbalances caused external imbalances that brought about international capital flows. Chapter 4 focused on the decline in the national saving rate in the United States, which led to a gap in the saving-investment balance, which contributed to the large current account imbalances and capital inflows under a system of flexible exchange rates.

In a flexible exchange rate system, the equilibrium exchange rate is that rate which clears the foreign-exchange market. If there is no official intervention in the foreign-exchange market—as in the case of a freely floating rate—the exchange rate will equilibrate the current account and the capital account. Any reduction in the trade deficit must be exactly matched by an equal reduction in capital imports; similarly, any worsening of the trade deficit must be accompanied by an increase in capital imports. It is possible, therefore, to determine the direction of change in the trade balance by predicting the direction of change in capital imports.[2]

EXCHANGE RATES AND BALANCE-OF-PAYMENTS ADJUSTMENTS

The balance of a country's international payments can be explained in terms of the national income account identity of the savings-investment imbalance to its export-import gap. Within the context of the national income accounting framework, it can be shown that current account deficits are equal to capital flows. Throughout the discussion, it is assumed that a system of flexible exchange rates exists.

In the national income identity, output (Y) can be decomposed into the sectors to which the output is sold ($C + I + G + X - M$) or it can be decomposed from the viewpoint of those who earn it ($C + S_p + T$).

$$C + I + G + X - M = Y = C + S_p + T$$

where C is household consumption, I is domestic investment, G is government spending on goods and services, X is exports, and M is imports. S_p is private savings and T is taxes (net of government transfer payments such as welfare and social security). Subtracting C from both sides and rearranging gives

$$S_p + S_g - I = X - M \text{ or } I - S_p - S_g = M - X$$

where $(T - G)$ is government saving, S_g. Foreign investment is the difference between domestic saving $(S_p + S_g)$ and domestic investment, and is represented as the difference between imports and exports (the current account balance). If imports exceed exports, the country has a current account deficit, foreign investment is positive, and the rest of the world accumulates net financial claims on this country. When exports exceed imports, the country has a current account surplus, foreign investment is negative, and the country accumulates claims against the rest of the world.

In international trade models, exports and imports are not autonomous but are determined by real exchange rates and measures of economic activity.

$$M = a + b\bar{E} + cY_h$$
$$X = d - e\bar{E} + fY_f$$

where M is imports, X is exports, $\bar{E}$ is the real exchange rate (price adjusted nominal exchange rate), Y_h is GDP in the home country and Y_f is GDP in the foreign market. In the import function, imports are positively related to the level of the exchange rate and the level of income in the home country. A rise in the home country's exchange rate (an appreciation of the currency) and growth in income would cause an increase in imports. In the export function, the level of exports is negatively related to the value of the exchange rate. A decrease in the exchange rate would increase the price of the home country's exports and, therefore, reduce the value of exports, but a growth in income abroad would raise the value of exports.

The trade deficit can be defined as follows:

$$M - X = (a - d) - (b + e)\bar{E} + cY_h - fY_f$$

where the trade deficit depends on the real exchange rate and the levels of economic activity in the home country and foreign market.[3]

It is assumed that the country operates under a system of flexible exchange rates and that international capital is highly mobile between that country and the rest of the world. The exchange rate, $\bar{E}$, is dependent on the interest differential between the domestic interest rate and the foreign interest rate.

$$\bar{E} = E_0 + (i - i_f)$$

where E_0 is the real exchange rate that would exist in the long run under conditions of purchasing power parity,[4] i is the domestic interest rate, and i_f is the foreign interest rate.

A familiar line of causation is that changes in the levels of saving and investment can influence the trade balance and, ultimately, the exchange rate. Events of the 1980s are commonly described using this chain of causation. Large federal budget deficits caused S_g to decline at the same time that S_p was falling. Because investors and the government were in competition for a smaller pool of domestic savings $(S_p + S_g)$, real interest rates remained high. A fairly tight U.S. monetary policy during the early 1980s also contributed to high real interest rates. These rates attracted large inflows of capital from abroad, and the U.S. exchange rate continued to appreciate until 1985. The high exchange rate and rapid growth of income produced a large deterioration in the current account balance. When exchange rates rose, exports became more expensive, contributing to a loss in U.S. international competitiveness. Also the large rate of growth in GDP relative to slower growth rates in much of the industrial world during the early 1980s led to a large growth in imports at the same time that the demands for U.S. exports were undergoing little expansion. As a consequence, there was much discussion among economists of the "twin deficits" problem during the 1980s.

The chain of causation could also originate with a strengthening of the exchange rate. Exchange rate changes can result from an outside event such as political uncertainty or upheaval in various parts of the world that promote capital flight, or oil price shocks that raise worldwide prices when dollar prices are used.[5] In these cases, an exogenous strengthening of the dollar would lead to a deterioration in the trade balance, which would reduce GDP, consumption, and private savings S_p. Because automatic stabilizers increase government outlays and reduce revenues as GDP falls, government savings, S_g, would also decline.

The following shows the process of external adjustment as being jointly determined by the equation giving the identity of the saving-investment balance and trade balance and the equation defining the trade balance as being driven by activity variables (Y_h and Y_f) and the real exchange rate. The solutions can be shown using Figure 6.1. The level of the home country's GDP (Y) is given on the horizontal axis. The vertical axis shows either the value of the trade balance $(X\text{-}M)$ or the excess of saving over investment $(S\text{-}I)$. According to the Keynesian formulation, the level of savings increases with GDP. Although investment does rise as GDP increases, it does not rise as fast as savings and the upward sloping line shows the excess of saving over investment for each level of GDP. The downward sloping line represents the trade balance, the difference between exports and imports, for a given level of GDP. Imports of goods and services rise as income rises. Equilibrium in the economy is determined at point E_0 where the two lines intersect. In this example, equilibrium occurs at a point where the trade balance equals zero, and savings equal investment. However, the choice of this location for the equilibrium point is arbitrary, because equilibrium could have occurred either above or below the horizontal axis.

The events of the early 1980s in the U.S. economy related to the large

Figure 6.1
Fiscal Expansion and Exchange Rate Appreciation

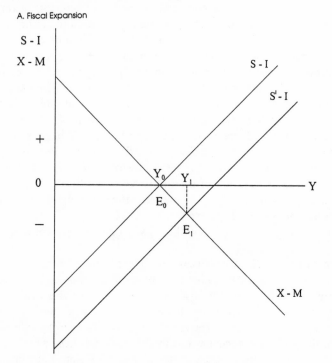

A. Fiscal Expansion

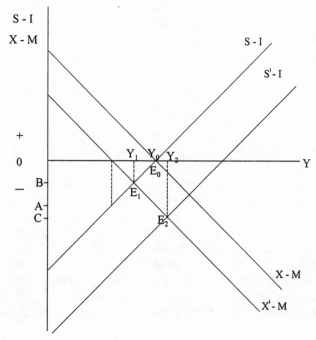

B. Fiscal Expansion and Exchange Rate Appreciation

fiscal expansion and large external deficits can be represented in Figure 6.1A. In 1983, as a result of tax cuts and increased military spending, fiscal expansion produced large budget deficits and reduced national savings. A fiscal expansion shifts the S-I curve down by the amount of the excess of government expenditures over revenues (T-G), and E_1 occurs where the difference of savings and investment equals the deterioration in the trade balance. GDP now rises to Y_1. For a closed economy, equilibrium would have occurred where the S'-I line crossed the zero axis line. In an open economy, because of a leakage into imports as GDP expands, the multiplier from a fiscal expansion is smaller than in a closed economy, and equilibrium income at Y_1 is to the left and therefore is less than in a closed economy. Because higher income leads to more imports, the fiscal expansion produces a deterioration in the trade balance.

Because of the excess of investment over savings that accompanied the fiscal expansion and tight monetary policy followed by the Federal Reserve in the early 1980s, real interest rates rose and large inflows of foreign capital occurred. The increased demand for dollars led to a large appreciation of the dollar.

The effect of an appreciation of the exchange rate can be shown in Figure 6.1B. Again, it is arbitrarily assumed that E_0 represents the initial equilibrium. Because a real appreciation of the currency raises imports and reduces exports, the X-M curve is shifted downward, and equilibrium is now at E_1. If the decline in income could be ignored, the trade balance would deteriorate from zero to OA. But the decline in income resulting from the drop in exports as prices of U.S. exports increase abroad reduces imports, and the trade balance deteriorates to OB.

From 1980 to 1985, interest rates were high, the real value of the U.S. dollar appreciated by over 50 percent, and the trade balance deteriorated. However, because of the large fiscal expansion, represented by the downward shift of the S-I line, GDP did not decline but rose over the period. In Figure 6.1B fiscal expansion is again represented by a downward shift of the S-I line, and the intersection of the S'-I line and X'-I line shows the equilibrium level of GDP (represented by Y_2) and the trade balance, which deteriorates to OC.[6]

FLOATING EXCHANGE RATES
AND CAPITAL MOBILITY

Under the Bretton Woods system of fixed exchanged rates, countries could not run current account deficits over a prolonged period of time. Except for the United States, which had the key reserve currency, the duration of a country's current account deficit was limited by its holdings of foreign exchange reserves. With the exception of countries such as Japan and West Germany, which had been running large current account surpluses since the 1960s and were accumulating large holdings of foreign exchange reserves, and the United States, which held the reserve currency, the ability of countries to run current account deficits was generally limited by holdings of reserves equal to several months' imports. Limited reserve holdings forced countries to pursue policies to bring about a balancing of their current account disequilibrium.

In the 1960s and early 1970s, many economists contended that by equating demand and supply for a currency, flexible exchange rates would automatically remove current account imbalances and eliminate the need to hold foreign exchange reserves. In retrospect, there is no evidence that the system of flexible exchange rates eliminated current account imbalances and the need for holdings of foreign exchange reserves.

With the relaxation and elimination of capital controls in the industrial countries, capital could move freely between them. Countries with current account deficits could finance these deficits by borrowing from countries having current account surpluses. Because of the increased mobility of international capital, countries were under less pressure to pursue contractionary domestic macroeconomic policies that could have eliminated current account deficits. Savings-investment imbalances could be financed by an inflow of foreign savings. Within this climate of flexible exchange rates and enhanced capital mobility, in the early 1980s the United States undertook large tax reductions and increased defense outlays, resulting in growing fiscal deficits. Until 1985, the Federal Reserve pursued a tight monetary policy that kept interest rates high. The large federal government demand for credit also contributed to high interest rates. High real interest rates made investment in the United States attractive, and foreign investors financed a substantial part of the fiscal imbalances.

The expansionary fiscal policy and high interest rates contributed to large trade deficits in two ways. First, in conjunction with the large fiscal expansion, GDP in the United States grew at a much higher rate than for most of its trading partners during the first half of the 1980s. Because imports depend on the level of income, U.S. import growth exceeded the growth of its exports. But a second factor was operating to increase the size of the trade deficit. High interest rates caused by the tight monetary policy of the Federal Reserve and the federal government's large demand for capital encouraged an inflow of foreign capital and increased the demand for dollars. By early 1985, the dollar had appreciated by about 50 percent when measured in real terms, raising prices of U.S. exports on world markets at the same time that import prices declined because foreign currencies were then cheaper for Americans. The large dollar appreciation adversely affected the competitiveness of American goods.

A comprehension of the nature of U.S. capital flows since the beginning of the 1980s requires an explanation of the relationship that exists between interest rates and exchange rates in an environment where capital controls have been eliminated as is now the case in most of the industrial countries.[7]

As presented above, real exchange rates are dependent on the difference of the domestic and foreign interest rates.

$$\bar{E} = E_0 + (i - i_f)$$

The following shows the derivation of this equation,[8] and can be useful in explaining the movement of international capital in a situation of perfect capital mobility. Throughout, it is assumed that a determinant of a country's capital account is the difference between its interest rate and foreign interest rates. Investors' decisions concerning the decision to invest internationally depend on real interest differentials as well as expectations about future changes in exchange rates.

It is assumed that expected returns on assets are equalized across countries when they are expressed in common units. Barriers that slow down portfolio adjustment do not exist, and investors treat foreign bonds and domestic bonds as perfectly substitutable in their portfolios. In such a situation the condition is one of uncovered interest parity.

$$i - i_f = \Delta s^e \tag{1}$$

where s^e is the expected rate of depreciation of the domestic currency. In equilibrium, were a Japanese investor to find that the interest rate on a U.S. bond exceeded the interest rate on a Japanese bond of similar maturity by $i - i_f$, the dollar would be expected to lose value in the future against the yen by Δs^e, and the Japanese investor would have to subtract the future fall in the value of the dollar when contemplating the purchase of the U.S. bond. However, investors consider real, not nominal, rates of return when purchasing financial assets.

In order to convert the uncovered parity condition to real terms, the expected inflation differential, $\Delta p^e - \Delta p_f^e$, between the domestic and foreign country must be subtracted from both sides of the equation in order to express the interest differential in real terms.

$$(i - \Delta p^e) - (i_f - \Delta p_f^e) = s_e - \Delta p_e + \Delta p_f^e \tag{2}$$
$$\text{or } r - r_f = (\Delta s_{real})^e$$

where Δp^e and Δp_f^e are expected changes in the rates of domestic and foreign inflation, r and r_f are the domestic and foreign real interest rates, and $(\Delta s_{real})^e$ becomes the expected rate of change in the real exchange rate between the two countries, which is equal to the differential in the real interest rates. When a country's real interest rate exceeds foreign real interest rates, investors expect that the country's currency will depreciate in the future. For example, in 1984, when the U.S. dollar had appreciated substantially, investors expected the dollar to depreciate in real terms in the future, and in 1985 a large depreciation occurred.

It is assumed that purchasing power parity represents the long-run equilibrium of the exchange rate and that when the exchange rate deviates from the long-run equilibrium value, investors expect that over time, the exchange rate will move back in the direction of the long-run equilibrium. After a disturbance, the exchange rate has a tendency to slowly return to the long-run equilibrium until another disturbance comes along. It has been shown that there is a tendency for the exchange rate to eliminate 15 to 30 percent of the gap between the actual and long-run exchange rate in a year.[9]

$$\Delta s^e_{real} = -\Theta(S - \bar{S})/\bar{S} \qquad (3)$$

In the equation S represents the level of the exchange rate, and $\bar{S}$ the long-run equilibrium value. If the current exchange rate is overvalued, investors will expect it to depreciate toward equilibrium by a fraction equal to Θ, and if it is undervalued, it is expected to appreciate toward equilibrium, the parameter Θ being the rate at which the real exchange rate is expected to regress towards purchasing power parity.

Combining equations (2) and (3) gives the following:

$$r - r_f = -\Theta(S - \bar{S})/\bar{S}$$

It is now possible to solve for the exchange rate as a function of the real interest differential.

$$(S - \bar{S})/\bar{S} = -(1/\Theta)(r - r_f) \qquad (4)$$

Given the value of the exchange rate at purchasing power parity and the real interest rate differential, the value of the exchange rate depends upon Θ, the speed of adjustment. The value of the currency will be greater than its long-run equilibrium value if the domestic real interest rate exceeds the foreign real interest rate. If the Japanese real interest rate exceeds the U.S. rate, the U.S. currency depreciates because international investors increase their demand for Japanese assets. Given an appreciation of the Japanese currency above its long-run equilibrium value, it is expected that it will have to depreciate in the future because it is overvalued. The Japanese currency appreciates until the expectation of its future depreciation is sufficiently large to offset the differential in the real interest rate. At that point, U.S. investors become indifferent between holding U.S. or Japanese assets, and they are happy to hold U.S. assets.

The U.S. exchange rate followed such a pattern during the early 1980s. Because of the buildup of strong inflationary forces, in October 1979 the Federal Reserve shifted toward a contractionary monetary policy. U.S. real interest rates, which had been below zero in the period 1976–79, had risen sharply, and by 1981–82 the real interest rate differential between the United States and its trading partners had increased to 3 percent. Largely because of reduced expectations of U.S. inflation, the real interest rate differential continued until mid-1984. By then, the U.S. real long-term rate of interest on ten-year bonds exceeded that of its trading partners by over 3 percent, increasing the attractiveness of investing in U.S. assets. If one considers ten years to be the appropriate time period required for the real exchange rate to return to its long-run equilibrium level, which was calculated to have been 30 percent below the prevailing exchange rate in 1984, and if the real interest rate differential on ten-year bonds was over 3 percent, the expectation would have been that investors expected the real exchange rate to depreciate in real terms by at least 3 percent over the next ten years until it had depreciated by 30 percent and reached its long-run equilibrium. At this point the real interest differential would have been zero. Here, the speed of adjustment each year, the value of Θ, would have equalled .10, and $1/\Theta$ in equation (4) would have equalled 10.[10]

The tendency for an exchange rate to appreciate (or depreciate) beyond its long-run level is explained in the "overshooting" model. The phenomenon of overshooting occurs because the speed of adjustment to a shock that brings about a disequilibrium is much faster in the money market than in the market for goods and services. When authorities follow an expansionary policy that expands the money supply, the domestic real interest rate declines, and the interest differential between the domestic and foreign interest rate declines, producing a decline in the domestic currency. At the time that the money supply expands, because prices have not had time to adjust due to rigidities of the price level, the real money supply, M/P, increases. As a condition of money market equilibrium, the monetary expansion drives down the real interest rate. Because international investors now reduce their purchase of domestic assets, the currency depreciates.

The size of the depreciation can be determined using equation (4). According to the equation, a positive deviation of the exchange rate from its long-run level occurs in conjunction with an interest differential favoring the purchase of foreign assets, and a negative deviation of the exchange rate from its long-run level occurs in conjunction with an interest differential favoring domestic assets.

In the long run, the exchange rate rises in the same proportion as the increase in the money supply, and domestic and foreign real interest rates are equal. Until the long-run equilibrium occurs, the foreign interest rate exceeds the domestic rate. When the domestic currency depreciates by $(1/\Theta)$ times the fall in the real interest rate, investors will expect the currency to appreciate back to the (new) long-run equilibrium value. These expectations are referred to as regressive expectations. Because investors expect the exchange rate to appreciate to its new long-run equilibrium, they are willing to hold domestic assets even though these assets now pay a lower rate of interest than foreign assets. This phenomenon whereby in the short run exchange rates exceed their (new) long-run equilibrium is known as "overshooting."

In the long-run equilibrium, because of an excess demand for goods and services, prices rise in proportion to the increase in the money supply. Although the nominal money supply is larger, the real money supply, the real interest rate, and the real exchange rate are all back to their original level. However, the nominal magnitudes have changed proportionately, and in the new long-run equilibrium, the exchange rate has depreciated from its old equilibrium value, and the nominal rate of interest has declined.

The appreciation of the dollar until 1984 represented a classic case of exchange rate overshooting in response to monetary tightening by the Federal Reserve. Based on economic fundamentals, it would have appeared that the real appreciation of the dollar should have peaked by July 1984. But the real exchange rate appreciated by another 20 percent before it peaked in February 1985. The final increase of 20 percent has frequently been characterized as a speculative bubble where investors lost sight of economic fundamentals and extrapolated past trends.

The exchange rate started to decline in February 1985. Because of U.S. concern over the impact of the price of the dollar on U.S. competitiveness, the G-5 countries met in New York in September 1985, and drafted the Plaza Accord in which the five industrial nations agreed to officially intervene in order to bring the exchange rate down. Previously, the Reagan administration, with a few exceptions, had not actively intervened in foreign exchange markets.

The balance-of-payments adjustment that occurred in 1985–91 can be analyzed in terms of the model developed by Robert A. Mundell and Marcus J. Fleming in the early 1960's.[11] More recently this model has been revised to adjust for expectations of inflation as well as depreciation of the currency. Balance-of-payments adjustment involves interest rate differentials and capital mobility.[12]

The first relationship is a Keynesian-type assumption that at any moment of time output is demand determined. Aggregate demand for domestic output equals the sum of domestic spending ($C + I + G$) plus net exports ($X - M$). Domestic spending is dependent on income and the real rate of interest. As discussed in the beginning of this chapter, net exports depend (at minimum) upon domestic income, foreign income, and the real exchange rate.

Another relationship concerns equilibrium in the monetary sector in which the supply of money is determined by the central bank and must equal the demand for money ($M_s = M_d$). The demand for money depends on the price level (P), the level of income (Y), and interest rates (i).

$$M_d/P = L(Y, i)$$

The next relationship is given in an equation that shows how exchange rates are determined. Such an equation was given above.

$$(S - \bar{S}/\bar{S}) = -(1/\Theta)(r - r_f)$$

This equation encompasses the idea that investors require expected returns on foreign assets to equal expected returns on domestic assets. When the domestic real interest rate exceeds the foreign real interest rate, the spot value of the real exchange rate exceeds the expected long-run equilibrium value. Investors then see the real exchange rate as reverting gradually to some long-run equilibrium.

The final element is a relationship for the rate of inflation. It can be assumed that the price level is predetermined at any moment in time. The inflation rate is then determined by an expectations-adjusted Phillips curve, where inflation depends on the level of output relative to trend as well as expected or core inflation.[13] Core inflation is adaptive because it adjusts slowly in response to actual inflation.

The revised Mundell-Fleming model presented above is an updated IS-LM model where markets for goods and services are in equilibrium with markets for money and financial assets. When estimating empirical models, it is common to view equilibrium in the medium term, a time frame that is sufficiently long for trade to have completely adjusted to the exchange rate and in which the adjustment of prices and inflationary expectations can be ignored.[14] This leaves three relationships—the Keynesian income identity, the equation for money market equilibrium, and the equation for the determination of the exchange rate—to simultaneously determine equilibrium in the markets for goods, money, and financial assets.

The revised Mundell-Fleming model can be useful when describing the effects of monetary and fiscal policy on the external balance in the 1980s. During much of that period, fiscal policy was highly expansionary. It is assumed that monetary policy is given, the money supply is constant, and all points of equilibrium in the money market for different combinations of income and interest rates are represented by the LM curve. With a given money supply, as income rises, people would only be willing to hold a given amount of money if interest rates were higher. The IS curve represents all combinations of income and interest rates where the goods market would be in equilibrium. The intersection of the IS and LM curves gives a unique equilibrium—a rate of interest and level of income—where the money market and the goods markets are in equilibrium. FX shows combinations of real interest rates and the real exchange rates associated with these interest rates (see Figure 6.2A).[15]

An expansionary fiscal policy is represented by a shift of the IS curve to the right, and output expands. An expansion in output raises the demand for money at given interest rates, and, with a given money supply, interest rates rise. Because domestic investment is negatively related to the rate of interest, with little or no capital mobility, higher interest rates crowd out some domestic investment. With perfect capital mobility, the increased rate of interest in the United States causes a large inflow of capital, and if no expectations of future exchange rate changes exist, the world real interest

Figure 6.2
Fiscal and Monetary Expansion in the Mundell-Fleming Model

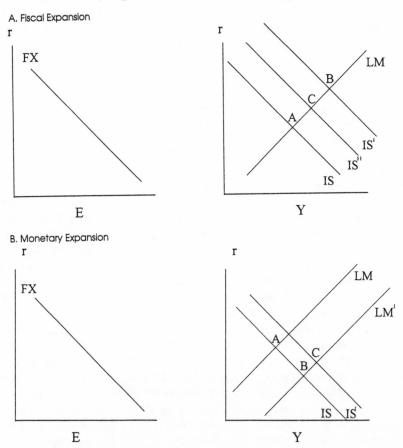

A. Fiscal Expansion

B. Monetary Expansion

rate would rise until it equals the domestic rate. Because of the availability of international capital, the domestic interest rate does not rise as high as it would without capital mobility. With an interest rate higher than the original interest rate, the exchange rate appreciates and the trade balance worsens. Accordingly, the *IS* curve shifts down to the left, and equilibrium occurs at *C*. The exchange rate has appreciated and interest rates are higher than at *A* but lower than at *B*. Net exports fall because exports are now more expensive and imports are cheaper. The fall in net exports resulting from the fiscal expansion is transmitted to the rest of the world because of an increased U.S. demand for foreign output.

In 1983 and 1984, fiscal expansion in the United States, in conjunction with a tight monetary policy, produced a scenario similar to the above. The fiscal expansion generated economic recovery in the United States. Interest rates rose, attracting capital from abroad, and the dollar appreciated against the Japanese yen and European currencies. The U.S. trade deficit rose sharply, and trade balances in much of the rest of the world improved. The fiscal expansion, by improving trade balances for the rest of the world, helped pull the rest of the world out of recession.

The impact of monetary expansion can also be shown using the revised Mundell-Fleming model (see Figure 6.2B). Again, it is assumed that capital is perfectly mobile. A monetary expansion, if there were no change in the exchange rate, would push the *LM* curve downward and to the right, and equilibrium would occur at *B*. The interest rate would fall and income would rise. But, in an open economy with perfect capital mobility, the fall in the interest rate in relation to that of the rest of the world causes an outflow of capital. The domestic currency depreciates, and, because foreign interest rates are now greater than domestic interest rates, the currency of the rest of the world appreciates. The domestic trade balance improves at the same time that the foreign trade balance worsens. The improvement in the domestic trade balance is reflected in increased spending on domestic output, and the *IS* curve shifts upward and to the right. Equilibrium now occurs at *C*. Because of the trade balance improvement, income and the rate of interest are now higher than at *B*. Output has expanded because lower interest rates encouraged higher investment. It should be noted that the depreciation produces an improvement in the trade balance and raises output only if the sum of the elasticities of demand for domestic imports and domestic exports are greater than one (the Marshall-Lerner condition holds).[16]

In the early 1980s, especially in 1983 and 1984, an expansionary fiscal policy was combined with a tight monetary policy, but beginning with 1985, as part of a serious attempt to bring down the value of the dollar and reduce the trade deficit, monetary policy became expansionary. Because of the J-curve effect, a substantial improvement in the external account position did not occur until 1988.[17] As a share of GDP, the current account deficit fell from a peak of 3.6 percent of GDP in 1987 to 2.6 percent in 1988. As an outcome of the 1990–91 recession in the United States and the receipt of payments from U.S. allies in the Gulf War, by 1991 the current account was almost in balance, but by 1993, as the U.S. economy improved and the Japanese and European economies remained in recession, the current account deficit rose to 1.7 percent of GDP.[18]

As indicated above, the expansionary monetary policy that was followed in the latter part of the 1980s and early 1990s can be represented by a shift to the right of the *LM* curve. The improvement in the external position that resulted from the depreciation of the dollar between 1985 and 1990 can be represented by a shift in the *IS* curve. This means that income was higher than if there had been no improvement in the external account position, and interest rates at *C* were higher than at *B*.

The preceding discussion implies a large mobility of international capital

to finance current account imbalances. In such a world, capital is highly
mobile and foreign investment flows to wherever the investors' net returns
can be maximized. But, in a controversial article, Martin Feldstein and
Charles Horioka argued that international capital markets are not well integrated because countries' domestic investment rates did not diverge widely
from their savings rates, and that incremental additions to the domestic
supply of capital did not seem to move to where the net of tax return would
be maximized. It is assumed that if perfect world capital mobility existed,
there would be no relation between domestic saving and domestic investment. To determine the relation between savings rates and investment rates,
the average ratio of gross domestic investment to gross domestic product
over the period 1960–74 for each OECD country was regressed on the
average ratio of gross saving to gross domestic product. Cross-section data
were used to remove cyclical effects on the data. It was assumed that a
regression coefficient close to one would show that domestic investment
rates were heavily dependent on savings rates, and that a regression coefficient close to zero would imply little relation of domestic investment rates
with domestic saving rates, and, hence, high capital mobility. Regressions
for the period 1960–74 and for several subperiods gave correlation coefficients that were not significantly different from one, and provided evidence
of low capital mobility.[19]

The initial findings were published by Feldstein and Horioka in 1980.
During the 1980s, there were large changes in international capital markets,
and the enormous inflows of international capital to the United States were
unprecedented. During the decade, government barriers to international
capital flows in Europe and Japan were either lowered or eliminated, and
many financial innovations were introduced. In order to determine whether
the empirical regularity observed for the industrial countries during the
1960s and 1970s between long-term saving rates and investment rates continued into the 1980s, Feldstein and Philippe Bacchetta compared the experience for the period 1980–86 to results for the 1960s and 1970s.[20]

The empirical analysis used the following regression equation:

$$I_t/Y_t = a_o + a_1 S_t/Y_t$$

where I_t represents gross investment (as defined by the OECD and includes
inventory investment), Y_t represents gross domestic product, and S_t, gross
saving. Data for 23 OECD countries (excluding Luxembourg) were used.
Gross and net savings and investment relations were estimated. Each country
represents a unit of observation and the data for that country's observation
has been averaged over given groups of years (e.g., 1960–73). The coefficient a_1 represents the "savings retention coefficient" and gives the proportion of domestic saving that is invested domestically.

Estimates for the savings retention coefficient were made using gross investment and gross saving. During the decade of the 1960s, each dollar of incremental gross saving increased investment by 91.4 cents, and in 1970–79 this declined to 80.5 cents, a difference of 10.9 cents. For the period 1980–86, the fall in the savings retention ratio was larger, falling by 19.8 cents to 60.7 cents. When the fixed exchange rate period (represented here by 1960–73) is compared to the period of floating rates (1974–86), during the latter period, the savings retention coefficient falls from 91.1 cents to 66.9 cents, a difference of 24.2 cents. For the entire period, 1960–86, the savings retention coefficient was 79.1 cents. When the regressions are done using net savings and net investment, the fall in the net saving retention coefficients over the time period is much smaller than for the gross saving retention coefficients.

Although the coefficients using gross investment and gross saving drop significantly over time when the sample of 23 OECD countries is used, results differ when estimates are calculated for smaller samples of countries; one subsample is comprised of 9 European Community (EC) countries and the other is comprised of the remaining OECD countries. The gross savings retention coefficients are lower for the 9 EC countries than for the entire OECD, and these coefficients decline more rapidly from the 1970s to the 1980s, falling from 0.742 in the 1960s to 0.653 in the 1970s to 0.356 in 1980–86. For the remaining OECD countries, the gross saving investment coefficients were much larger—the coefficient was 0.962 in the 1960s, 0.810 in the 1970s, and 0.578 in the 1980s. To Feldstein and Bacchetta, the results appear to indicate that capital outflows from the individual EC countries exceeded those of the non-EC countries. The existence of strong institutional links among EC capital markets is used to explain the low values of the savings retention coefficients.

The Feldstein-Horioka hypothesis has been subjected to numerous econometric critiques, and many of these studies have tended to confirm the existence of high correlations between investment rates and saving rates. There is also much evidence showing lower savings retention coefficients for the 1980s than for earlier years.

One focal point for researchers has been the interpretation of these results, which shows that domestic saving and investment rates have been highly correlated even though financial capital is highly mobile. These interpretations have been classified into several types, including the "policy endogeneity" view and the "endogenous saving" or "common factor" view.[21] The policy endogeneity view makes the argument that countries adapt their macroeconomic policies in order to prevent continuation of current account imbalances (saving-investment gaps).

James Tobin and several others have suggested a policy endogeneity argument to explain the Feldstein-Horioka results. Tobin refers to it in the following:

Anyway the cross-section results may be influenced by government policies with respect to . . . the current account balance. If policies have tried to balance the current account on average, the Feldstein results would be easy to understand. Of course, if these policies continued when saving was increased, and if full employment were maintained, the extra saving would raise domestic investment.[22]

As was explained earlier, the value of the current account balance must equal the saving-investment gap, and if the policy objective was to keep the current account balance close to zero, savings would be approximately equal to investment.

Lawrence Summers tested the hypothesis that the high correlation between saving and investment reflected policy responses of government to differences between private saving and private investment. He averaged budget deficit to GDP ratios for 1973–80 for a cross-section of fourteen industrial countries, and then regressed these averages on the saving-investment gaps averaged over the same period.[23]

Summers obtained a regression coefficient of 0.72, implying that each dollar of a country's private saving-investment gap results in the government increasing its budget deficit by 72 cents. Summers concluded that the endogeneity of fiscal policy was able to explain a major part of the correlation between saving and investment.

Tamin Bayoumi also tested the endogeneity hypothesis.[24] One test used cross-section data for ten industrial countries. Regressions were run for the period 1965–86 and for several subperiods. For each country the dependent variable was the average gross investment to nominal GNP ratio, and the independent variable was the average domestic saving to nominal GNP ratio. The results were similar to the Feldstein-Horioka conclusions. However, when private saving as a ratio of GNP was regressed on private fixed investment as a ratio of GNP, the value of the coefficient declined, indicating that private capital was highly mobile, especially after the mid-1970s. And for the periods 1976–86 and 1980–86, the coefficients were much lower, possibly as a result of increased capital mobility in the latter period.

Another test used data for the gold standard period, 1880–1913, a period characterized by little government intervention, few capital controls, and substantial international capital movements. Regressions of total investment as a share of GNP against total savings as a share of GNP shows little correlation between savings and investment. These results seem to imply that the observed postwar correlations reflected government policy and do not indicate structurally low capital mobility. During the earlier part of the postwar period, government policy frequently involved the use of controls on the mobility of international capital, whereas in the more recent period many of these controls have been abandoned.

Jeffrey Frankel sees that a basic problem lies with the definition of capital mobility that one uses:

By the second half of the 1970s, international economists had come to speak of the world financial system as characterized by perfect capital mobility. . . . Even among the five major countries without capital controls, capital was not perfectly mobile by some definitions.

There are at least four distinct definitions of perfect capital mobility that are in widespread use. (1) *The Feldstein-Horioka definition:* exogenous changes in national saving . . . can be easily financed by borrowing from abroad at the going real interest rate, and thus need not crowd out investment in the originating country (except to the extent that the country is large in world financial markets). (2) *Real interest parity:* International capital flows equalize real interest rates across countries. (3) *Uncovered interest parity:* Capital flows equalize expected rates of return on countries' bonds, despite exposure to exchange risk. (4) *Closed interest parity:* Capital flows equalize interest rates across countries when contracted in a common currency. The four possible definitions are in ascending order of specificity. Only the last condition is an unalloyed criterion for capital mobility in the sense of the degree of financial market integration across national boundaries.

As we will see, each of the first three conditions, if it is to hold, requires an auxiliary condition in addition to the condition that follows it. Uncovered interest parity requires not only closed (or covered) interest parity, but also the condition that the exchange risk premium is zero. Real interest parity requires not only uncovered interest parity, but also the condition that expected real depreciation is zero. The Feldstein-Horioka condition requires not only real interest parity, but also a certain condition on the determinants of investment. But even though the relevance to the degree of integration of financial markets decreases as auxiliary conditions are added, the relevance to questions regarding the origin of international payments imbalances increases.[25]

According to Frankel's system of classification, the Feldstein-Horioka definition of perfect capital mobility requires that the country's real (inflation-adjusted) interest rate is tied to the world real interest rate by the criterion that real interest parity holds because in theory saving and investment depend on the real interest rate and not the nominal rate. Here, for the Feldstein-Horioka criterion of capital mobility to hold, the real interest parity condition must hold, and for real interest parity to hold, not only must the uncovered interest parity condition hold, but ex ante purchasing power parity must exist.

According to Frankel, the broadest measure of barriers to international capital mobility is the existence of differentials in real interest rates. With real interest parity, the difference between the domestic real interest rate and the foreign real interest rate would equal zero:

$$r - r_f = 0.$$

As noted above, a differential in real interest rates would be defined as:

$$r - r_f = (i - \Delta p^e) - (i - \Delta p_f^e)$$

The terms Δp^e and Δp_f^e represent the expected changes in the domestic and foreign price levels, respectively.

Subsequently, the real interest differential is decomposed into a part due to "political" or country factors (the covered interest differential) and a part due to currency factors:

$$r - r_f = (i - i_f - f_d) - (f_d - \Delta p^e - \Delta p_f^e)$$

where f_d is the forward discount on the domestic currency, the forward discount (or premium) being defined as $F - S/S$ (the difference between the forward exchange rate and the spot exchange rate divided by the spot rate). The forward discount can be either positive or negative. The term ($i - i_f - f_d$) is the covered interest differential that captures the barriers to integration of financial markets across national boundaries. It is called the political or country premium. The second term ($f_d - \Delta p^e - \Delta p_f^e$) is the real forward discount. This is called the currency premium because it captures differences in assets in terms of the currencies in which they are denominated and not in terms of the political jurisdictions in which they are issued.[26] The currency premium is made up of an exchange risk plus an expected real currency depreciation.

Because the covered interest differential encompasses those factors related to the political jurisdiction where the asset is issued, the most narrow definition of international capital mobility would be measured by its size and variability. Frankel uses a sample of 25 countries, large and small, developing and industrialized. The data for the "country premium" or covered interest differentials for the period September 1982 to April 1988 show that the variability for covered interest differentials is much smaller for open economies that have low barriers to international capital than for economies that have significant barriers. The results also show that capital mobility has increased since the 1970s and supports the criterion of the covered interest differential as being a proper test of financial market integration.[27]

Frankel then attempts to explain why the covered differential criterion gives different results from the Feldstein-Horioka hypothesis, which shows that the degree of savings retention in industrialized countries is high. The explanation centers on the size of the currency premium that is measured by the "real forward discount":

$$f_d - (p^e - \Delta p_f^e)$$

which says that the currency premium is the forward discount minus the differential between the domestic and foreign expected price levels. A number of countries, including Germany, Switzerland, the Netherlands, Austria, and Japan, which exhibited no substantial country premium, had substantial currency premiums (real forward discounts) that produced large real interest rate differentials. In fact, the real forward discount (the currency premium) was more variable than the covered interest rate differential for all but three of the 25 countries, and in most countries remained the major obstacle to real interest parity.

The results show that as a result of increased capital mobility, covered interest rate differentials are small. Because real and nominal exchange rate variability is large, a currency premium exists in a number of industrialized countries. Thus, even if covered interest rates are equalized, the differentials in real interest rates are still large, and the criterion of real interest rate parity is not achieved. The existence of real interest parity is a condition for the Feldstein-Horioka hypothesis, and without the attainment of real interest parity, the Feldstein-Horioka definition of capital mobility cannot be achieved.

EMPIRICAL STUDIES OF FLEXIBLE EXCHANGE RATES AND THE BALANCE-OF-PAYMENTS ADJUSTMENT MECHANISM DURING 1985–91

The U.S. economy began the decade of the 1980's with a small trade deficit of $25.5 billion. By 1985 the deficit had increased to $122.4 billion, and by 1987 it peaked at $159.6 billion. Between 1980 and 1985, the growth in the trade deficit coincided with a large appreciation in the real exchange rate for the dollar, which had increased by about 45 percent over the period. By 1986 the real value of the dollar had already fallen by almost 30 percent, and by 1988 it fell another 15 percent. But because of a lagged response to the decline in the exchange rate, the trade deficit continued to increase until 1987. It was not until 1988 that it began to fall, and the decline continued until 1991, when the trade deficit fell to $74.1 billion. In that year, the current account was almost in balance because of payments for U.S. activities during the Gulf War by its allies.

Between 1985 and 1987, the continuous growth in the trade deficit was a source of great concern because it did not react to the large dollar depreciation. It took more than three years for the balance-of-payments adjustment process to begin to work in the direction that conventional economic theory had predicted.

During the late 1980s and early 1990s a number of empirical studies were done to evaluate the balance-of-payments adjustment process. A study by Peter Hooper and Catherine Mann examines the causes of the large U.S. current account deficits in the early 1980s and also gives reasons for the deficits' persistence and growth through 1987.[28] Two of these studies that analyzed the balance-of-payments adjustment to the large exchange rate changes between 1985 and 1991 were those by William Cline for the Institute of International Economics and Robert Lawrence for the Brookings Institution.[29]

The study by Hooper and Mann provides an excellent review of the initial causes of the U.S. current account deficit during the early 1980s. It also gives reasons for the deficit's persistence and growth through 1987, even though the value of the dollar had declined sharply by late 1987. One type of analysis sees the rise in the current account as having been a consequence of the decline in U.S. price competitiveness (resulting from the large dollar appreciation in the early 1980s), higher domestic economic growth in the United States relative to other industrial countries, and the international debt problem of developing countries. An alternative type of analysis focuses on more fundamental factors associated with shifts in U.S. fiscal and monetary policy that reduced the national saving rate and produced increases in real interest rates, domestic growth, and the value of the dollar compared with other countries.[30]

Hooper and Mann showed that partial-equilibrium macroeconomic factors could fully account for the widening of the trade deficit from 1980 to 1986. The principal cause of the widening of the deficit was the change in relative prices of exports and nonoil imports associated with the dollar appreciation. The relatively higher rates of GNP growth and domestic expenditures $(C + I + G)$ compared with those abroad also increased the deficit, contributing about 40 percent to the total decline in net exports of goods and services.

A conventional macroeconomic trade model that reflected the experience of the two preceding decades performed fairly well in predicting the persistence of the nominal trade deficit through 1987 as an outcome of normal lag effects as trade flows adjusted to exchange rate changes. The normal macroeconomic relationships used in the model were less able to explain the persistence of the deficit measured in real terms (constant dollars) than the nominal deficit. Trade volumes adjusted more slowly in response to the fall in the dollar than the model predicted, in part a consequence of the fact that the model overpredicted a rise in import prices in 1986 and 1987. The sluggishness of prices reflected a squeezing of profit margins, a reduction in foreign production costs that were not adequately picked up by the model employed, and the continuation of a sharp decline in the pricing of business machines.

Shifts in monetary and fiscal policies reduced the national saving rate and raised real interest rates, exchange rates, and the value of the dollar relative to other countries, all of which contributed significantly to the widening current account deficit from 1980 to 1986. Hooper and Mann assessed the extent to which shifts in monetary and fiscal policies in the United States and abroad affected real interest rates, the dollar exchange rate, and the current account balance.

To quantify the effects of shifts in the domestic and foreign policy mix on the current account deficit, Hooper and Mann used a group of twelve multicountry macroeconomic models to do simulations for the effects of sustained exogenous shifts in government spending and an exogenous increase in the U.S. money supply. The reported results were averages of a wide range of results.

Between 1980 and 1985, U.S. fiscal policy expanded the structural deficit by about 3.5 percent of GNP at the same time that contractionary fiscal changes in other industrial countries decreased foreign structural budget deficits by about 2.5 percent of GNP. Macroeconomic models estimated that each increase in government spending equal to 1 percent of GNP caused U.S. GNP to increase, producing a 0.5 percent increase in U.S. real interest rates relative to foreign interest rates, a 2 to 2.5 percent real appreciation of the dollar against an average of OECD currencies, and a $14–20 billion decline in the nominal current account balance. In addition, the foreign fiscal contraction also led to an appreciation of the dollar and a fall in the nominal current account balance.

In the early 1980s, the U.S. fiscal expansion was accompanied by a monetary tightening, which raised the real interest rate differential and exchange rate at the same time that it reduced real U.S. income. The U.S. monetary contraction had a negligible impact on the current account balance because the fall in income resulting from higher interest rates reduced imports, but this was offset by an appreciated dollar, which depressed net exports.

It was calculated that the U.S. fiscal expansion combined with a fiscal contraction abroad could have contributed two-thirds to the $140 billion increase in the current account deficit from 1980 to 1986. At the same time, these shifts in fiscal policy were able to explain only one-third of the increase in real interest rates and even less of the rise in the dollar.

In late 1979 the U.S. shifted to a relative tightening of monetary policy compared with monetary policy abroad, and the remaining two-thirds of the rise in the long-term real interest rate differential can be attributed to the monetary tightening. It was concluded that monetary tightening caused the dollar to rise by about 32 percent (one-half of its total increase). It was assumed that the reduction in income and, hence, imports, resulting from a very tight monetary policy, offset the increase in the current account deficit resulting from the higher value of the dollar.

Together, monetary and fiscal policy explained two-thirds of the increases in both the current account deficit and the value of the dollar. It was suggested that one-third was accounted for by exchange market bubbles, the debt crisis, and other exogenous factors including the fall in the U.S. private saving rate.

The macroeconomic evidence accounted for the widening of the nominal deficit and its persistence until 1987. However, Hooper and Mann concluded that the evidence was not able to entirely explain the persistence of the deficit in real terms. Microeconomic evidence suggested that pricing behavior changes of foreign exporters plus worldwide protectionism slowed the adjustment of trade volumes to the decline in the dollar.

It was suggested that passage of multilateral trade negotiations under the Uruguay Round and increased productivity of U.S. workers would be helpful in reducing the trade deficit. Hooper and Mann, writing in 1989, suspected that the trade deficit would continue to be large even after prices and trade volumes adjusted fully to the level of exchange rates prevailing in 1987. They assumed that the external deficit would persist until the U.S. budget deficit is either reduced significantly or eliminated and the U.S. private saving rate relative to investment rises significantly.[31]

Lawrence used a partial equilibrium model to predict the current account deficit. Equations estimated over the 1976–84 period were used to track the performance of U.S. exports and imports over the second half of the 1980s. Because the behavior of petroleum imports and agricultural exports can be shown to be idiosyncratic, the study concentrated on trade in goods and services excluding petroleum imports and agricultural exports. Also, because of the serious measurement problems associated with computer prices over the decade, the decision was made to omit computers from the regression analysis.

Export and import data for 1976–84 were used to forecast the behavior of the U.S. nonoil, nonagricultural, noncomputer trade deficit over the remainder of the decade. For those years, the equations forecasted the sizes of the trade deficits fairly accurately, and the results indicated that neither hysteresis[32] nor other structural factors inhibited the adjustment.

Working with several widely used measures of the real effective exchange rate, Lawrence showed that by the first half of 1990 the dollar had almost returned to its 1980 level. In such a case, if the trade balance response to rises and falls in the exchange rate had been symmetrical, import and export prices should have returned to their 1980 levels in relation to domestic prices. With computers excluded from the price calculations that Lawrence constructed, over the decade the constructed export and import price indexes grew by 30 percent and 31 percent, respectively. The growth in U.S. export prices matched the growth in the U.S. domestic price level and the OECD's manufactured price index of U.S. competitors, and the rise in U.S. import prices was similar to the rise in domestic prices, foreign unit labor costs, and foreign export prices. As a consequence, by the end of the 1980s, foreigners competing in the U.S. market had lost the relative advantage they had had earlier in the decade when the dollar was stronger.[33]

Regression equations were used to explain how import and export volumes responded to the exchange rate changes. Then the results of the regressions were used to show that the behavior of the U.S. trade and current account balances up to the first half of 1990 could be fairly well explained by conventional models.

The export price equations explained U.S. nonagricultural, noncomputer export prices as a function of both the U.S. producer price index excluding foods and foreign export prices. Over time, if foreign prices are given, each 1 percent appreciation (depreciation) of the dollar exchange rate raises (lowers) U.S. export prices measured in dollars by 0.24 percent.

For the import price equations, U.S. nonoil, noncomputer import prices were explained as a function of foreign export prices and U.S. domestic prices. The results suggested that after a year, 70 percent of the change in foreign prices had been passed through into U.S. import prices.

The results indicated that relative export and import prices have responded in a symmetrical fashion to the appreciation and subsequent depreciation of the dollar. In line with the real effective exchange rate, by the first half of 1990, relative prices had returned to their 1980 levels.

Lawrence then used regression analysis to explain trade flows, both by estimating equations for trade volumes and, alternatively, for trade values. When estimating the quantity of nonoil, noncomputer imports, it was found that over the long run when actual and potential output grew at the same rate, each 1 percent increase in output was associated with a 2.5 percent increase in imports. In the short-run, price effects generated a J-curve. In the first year, a 1 percent increase in relative import prices reduced volume by 0.8 percent, but over 18 months, the volume reductions outweighed the price effects, and in the long run (two and one-half years) import volumes fell by 1.5 percent. When estimating equations for export volumes, it was found that each 1 percent increase in foreign demand raised U.S. nonagricultural, noncomputer exports by 1.6 percent. The long-run price elasticity of U.S. exports was 1.1 percent.

In the equation for import volume, it was estimated that a 1 percent growth in output coincided with a 2.5 percent increase in imports. The equation for export volume found that a 1 percent growth in foreign demand coincided with a 1.6 percent growth in exports. These results are in conformity with the "Houthakker-Magee effect," stating that similar rates of growth in the United States and the rest of the world are associated with a declining trade balance or continuous real dollar depreciation. "Over the long-run, my regression equations suggest that the activity elasticity for U.S. exports is 1.6 while the activity elasticity for U.S. imports is 2.5 percent. Thus, with unchanged relative prices, rates of growth in the United States that are 60 percent of those abroad are required to keep exports and imports growing at similar rates."[34]

Although during the first half of the 1980s, U.S. economic growth exceeded foreign economic growth, for the entire decade of the 1980s, GNP growth in the United States was lower than GDP growth abroad—30.4 percent in the United States compared with 34.9 percent abroad. Also, at the end of the decade, Lawrence found that U.S. export and import prices were at about the same levels as in 1980. With relative prices the same as in 1980 and with slightly slower growth in domestic output than abroad, the trade balance still had deteriorated by $80.0 billion over the decade. Lawrence indicated that the decline in the nonoil, nonagricultural trade balance measured the decline in U.S. competitiveness over the decade. Restoring the trade balance in goods and services to its 1980 level would have required a devaluation of about 8 percent between 1980 and 1990, or roughly 1 percent a year.

The study indicates that if relative prices for exports and imports were to remain unchanged and the U.S. economy were to grow by 2.5 percent a year, growth in nonagricultural exports will match the growth of nonoil imports if the rest of the OECD were to grow by 4.1 percent. To keep exports and imports growing at the same rate, for each percentage point that foreign growth falls short of 4.1 percent, the real exchange rate would have to fall by 1 percent a year.[35]

Lawrence has looked at the problem of the widening of the trade deficit during the 1980s from the perspective of a partial equilibrium framework and explained the problem by referring to the Houthakker-Magee effect. One discussant of his paper looked at the problem within a general-equilibrium framework in which exogenous shifts in domestic savings and investment become transmitted to trade flows by changes in income (domestic demand) and relative prices. It was argued that although U.S. GNP grew at almost the same rate as foreign GNP over the decade, U.S. domestic demand $(C + I + G)$, which increased at about 4 percentage points more than foreign demand over the decade, can explain the widening of the deficit.[36]

William Cline studied the adjustment record of the United States to the large imbalances of the 1980s within the context of a general-equilibrium framework. The study assessed the causes of the deficits emerging in the middle of the 1980s, explained how these deficits were reduced toward the end of the decade, and used the adjustment models to examine the prospects for the trade balance and current account during the period 1990–95.

Cline used two alternative models for projections of the U.S. current account.[37] The EAG (External Adjustment with Growth) model is a multi-country model that divides the world into 17 major countries and regions. He estimated equations for the trade of each country (or region) with each other country (or region). "U.S. exports to a given trading partner depended on the price of the U.S. export (unit value) relative to the price of the partner's competing domestic good (wholesale price index); the U.S. export price relative to that of competing third countries (export unit value); and the real growth rate in the importing country (activity variable)."[38] Similar estimates were done for U.S. imports, but the estimates were made from the standpoint of each trading partner's exports to the U.S. market. Special treatment was provided in the model for oil trade. The trade projections were translated into current account estimates by taking proportionate relationships of nonfactor services to merchandise trade and assuming a simple 7 percent rate of return applied to cumulative current account deficits after 1988.

The HHC (Helkie-Hooper-Cline) model was adopted from the Helkie-Hooper model of the U.S. current account that was developed at the Federal Reserve Board. In his adoption, Cline simplified the agricultural and oil equations of the model and imposed an adjustment to trade prices, setting them halfway between the observed and predicted levels for the fourth quarters.

When comparing actual outcomes for the external accounts for 1988–90 with projections for the external accounts using the EAG and HHC models, Cline found that conventional models were able to explain what had happened over the three-year period, especially if they avoided or corrected for the computer pricing problem. The key finding was that the behavior of the current account confirmed the expectations of the modelers and policymakers who stressed the impact of the dollar depreciation on current account adjustment in the late 1980s.

The EAC model and a revised HHC model were used to forecast the future outlook for the U.S. external accounts. As of October 1990, the five-year outlook showed the current account stabilizing in the $100 billion range during the 1990s and trending downward to 1.5 percent of GNP by 1995.

For Cline, the plateauing of the current account imbalances at about $100 billion raised two questions. The first arose from the Houthakker-Magee asymmetry.[39] If this asymmetry truly held, the current account deficit should have been shown as rising over the period. However, in the EAG model, the modest asymmetry in the elasticities for the period was offset by the projection that economic growth in the remainder of the OECD would be greater than U.S. growth for the period 1990–95, and the revised HHC model had symetrical export and import income elastisities. The second question referred to the "gap factor," which should have shown an eventual rise in the deficit. The gap factor refers to the fact that by 1987, despite a large reversal in export and import growth rates, imports had risen to a level 64 percent above exports, whereas the gap had been only 11 percent in 1980. Had the dollar depreciation not occurred, the trade balance deficit would have been much larger. In the projections for 1990–95, during the first two or three years, there were to be lagged benefits stemming from the further decline of the dollar in 1990 and the slowdown in U.S. economic growth. In later years, the steady state growth of export earnings (11 percent) was to be higher than that of imports (10 percent) and would permit a declining trade deficit to offset a rising factor service deficit.

There are several conclusions regarding the adjustment of the balance of payments to movements in the dollar. The projected current account deficit of $100 billion for 1990 (the actual deficit was $92 billion) conformed well to predictions in other models, but it did not represent a complete return to 1980 levels. Cline explains this by referring to the IMF's real exchange rate, which is calculated by deflating export unit values. According to this exchange rate index, in 1989 the dollar was 15 percent above its real level at the beginning of the decade. In this exchange rate index, the dollar is shown as having fallen less than was normally believed. Another conclusion is that the Houthakker-Magee income elasticity asymmetry is given less credence than in other studies of the adjustment process for the same period.

CURRENT ACCOUNT PROJECTIONS

To be able to assess if the United States will remain a large user of international capital during the second half of the 1990s, it is necessary to look further at projections for the U.S. current account.

The OECD in its December 1994 *OECD Economic Outlook* has short-term current account forecasts through 1995, and the IMF in its *World Economic Outlook October 1994* has short-term forecasts for the current account for 1994 and 1995.[40] Medium-term projections are also available.

The IMF has projected movements in the U.S. external accounts. The U.S. current account went from being almost in balance in 1980 to a deficit of $167.1 billion in 1987. Although the large depreciation of the dollar commenced in 1985, because of lag effects associated with the J-curve effect, it was not until 1988 that the current account began to improve. From $167.3 billion or 3.7 percent of GDP in 1987, by 1990 the current account deficit declined to $91.7 billion or 1.7 percent of GDP as the trade balance responded to the large depreciation of the dollar and the recession in the United States that commenced in 1990. In 1991 the current account deficit fell to 0.1 percent of GDP, reflecting cyclical factors associated with the 1990–91 U.S. recession and the large inflow of transfer payments from other countries associated with the financing of the regional conflict in the Middle East. However, in 1992 the current account deficit widened to $67.9 billion or 1.1 percent of GDP. Because of growing cyclical disparities between economic growth in the United States and other industrial countries that were only beginning to emerge from the trough of recession, the U.S. current account widened to $103.9 billion or 1.7 percent of GDP in 1993. It is estimated that the deficit rose to $149.4 billion in 1994 and will rise to $167.5 billion in 1995, representing 2.2 percent of GDP in 1994 and 2.4 percent in 1995.[41]

In the *World Economic Outlook* for October 1993, the IMF projected that the U.S. current account deficit will average about 1.9 percent of GDP for the period 1994–98. These medium-term projections were conditional upon several assumptions being met, including an unchanged fiscal policy except for measures announced and likely to be implemented, an unchanged monetary policy, constant real effective exchange rates, and stable real commodity and oil prices.[42]

However, forecasts for the current account deficit were revised upward for 1994–95, and, assuming constant real exchange rates and little change in the fiscal deficit, the average current account deficit for 1994–98 is projected to average about 2.4 percent of GDP. The nonsynchronous nature of the business cycle among industrial countries is reflected in the movement of current account balances. Import demand is increasing more in those countries recovering rapidly from recession than in those that are recovering more slowly. Real effective exchange rates are also an important determinant of current account developments. The fairly rapid pace of economic recovery in the United States combined with a small increase in the real effective exchange rate have contributed substantially to a widening of the current account deficit.[43]

Over the next five years, real GDP growth in the industrial countries as a group is expected to recover. Real GDP growth in the United States is projected to fall to a yearly average of 2.5 percent of GDP in 1995–99, and inflation is expected to stabilize at 3 percent. For all other industrial countries as a group, growth is projected to rise from 2.25 percent in 1994 to over 3 percent a year in 1996–99. In general, medium-term growth is expected to be subdued, resulting in excess capacity in output and labor markets in most countries. As a consequence, significant inflationary pressures are not expected to reemerge. Because of the recovery in output, over the medium term, fiscal deficits for the industrial country group (excluding the United States) are projected to decline significantly. However, for the industrial countries as a group, little change is expected in current account deficits for 1994 and 1995. Even though the U.S. current account deficit is expected to widen, the current account for the European Union shows an increasing surplus, which is projected to rise from $8.3 billion in 1993 to $45.2 billion in 1995; and Japan's current account surplus, which was $131.4 billion in 1993, is now forecast to fall slightly to $128.8 billion in 1995.

Assuming that countries maintain current policies, medium-term projections suggest that current account deficits are not expected to narrow significantly in 1996–99 for most industrial countries. Given the assumptions of constant real exchange rates and little change in the fiscal deficit, the U.S. current account deficit is expected to remain at about 2.5 percent of GDP. Assuming that in real effective terms the yen does not change, it is projected that with the recovery of economic activity in Japan, the current account surplus will fall from 3.1 percent of GDP in 1993 to 2.4 percent in 1996–99.

The December 1994 *OECD Economic Outlook* gives current account projections through 1995 that are based on the organization's independent assessment of the world economy. The OECD's world macroeconomic model was used in the projections to insure national and international consistency. For the United States, OECD projections for 1995 show slightly more deterioration in the current account deficit (to $173 billion) than the IMF's forecasts (to $167.5 billion). The OECD data emphasize that part of the deterioration in the current account deficit will come from a worsening of the investment income balance.

The multicountry EAG model discussed above has also been used to project current account balances for Japan and the United States for the period 1993–97.[44] The model incorporated the effects of exchange rate changes already in the pipeline, including the 26 percent appreciation of the yen from 1991 to mid-1993. Using equations estimated for the period 1973–87, the EAG model estimated bilateral trade flows between seventeen countries or regions. For each set of bilateral trade flows, the change in exports was dependent on the GDP growth rate of the importing country, the export price in relation to wholesale prices in the importing country, and the exporting country's price relative to prices of third countries competing in the same market. It was assumed that trade responds to prices with a distributed lag over eight quarters. Nonfactor services were assumed to be proportional to the merchandise trade base. The initial net asset position plus the change in net assets caused by cumulative current account surpluses or deficits were used to determine capital services. To project external balances, it was assumed that worldwide price inflation would amount to 2 percent a year and the real exchange rate for the yen was frozen at the June 30, 1993, level of 107 yen to the dollar. It was assumed that the U.S. economy would grow at 2.7 percent in 1993 and 2.5 percent in 1994–97. (The actual U.S. growth rate was 3.1 percent in 1993 and was about 4 percent in 1994.) For Japan, growth rates of 1.7 percent for 1993 and 4.0 percent in 1994–97 were forecast. Because the Japanese economy is now recovering very slowly from its recession, its growth rates are much lower than previously forecast.[45] (For 1993, Japanese economic growth actually measured only 0.1 percent and is expected to grow at 1.0 percent in 1994 and 2.5 percent in 1995.)

The projections show a large U.S. current account deficit through 1997. According to the projections, the trade balance deficit for the United States was estimated at $94 billion in 1993 and $118 billion in 1994, and was projected to deteriorate to $125 billion in 1995–97. (However, the actual 1993 trade balance deficit was worse than forecasted, declining to $132 billion.) Over the period the current account deficit was projected to rise from 1.1 percent of GDP in 1992 to 1.8 percent in 1994 and 1995 and then decrease to 1.6 percent in 1997. These projections, which were more optimistic than IMF projections in its October 1994 *World Economic Outlook,* are not reassuring. To avoid the accumulation of an excessive amount of foreign debt, to keep the external sector from becoming a drag on external growth, and to avoid the escalation of pressure for protectionism, it is believed that the current account deficit should be held down to 1 percent of GDP.[46]

The most current projections point to U.S. current account deficits of almost 2.5 percent of GDP during the mid- and late 1990s. The tendency has been to place much of the blame for the large trade imbalances on Japanese trade policies. In 1993 the U.S. bilateral trade deficit with Japan amounted to $60 billion out of a $116 billion trade deficit. The EAG model projected that as Japan emerges from recession, the U.S. trade deficit with

Japan will fall and then remain fairly constant in a range of $40 billion to $50 billion between 1994 and 1997.

In the United States, politicians argue that Japan's trade is insensitive to macroeconomic adjustment, and attempts are made to get Japan to remove trade barriers and open its markets to exporters. Whereas the U.S. trade deficit with the European Union (EU) went from a deficit in 1987 to a surplus in 1992, the U.S. bilateral deficit with Japan remains large. But a statistical illusion obscures the fact that like the trade balance with the EU, Japan's trade balance has adjusted to the large depreciation of the U.S. dollar. Cline considers the percentage change in the underlying trade flows to be the appropriate criterion for assessing adjustment to exchange rate changes. From 1986–87 to 1991–92, U.S. exports to the EU rose by 82 percent and to Japan by 74 percent. Over the same period, U.S. imports from the EU rose by 17 percent and from Japan by 15 percent. The problem was not the difference in the response of U.S.-Japan trade to relative prices, but the much larger initial imbalance between exports and imports with Japan than with Europe. From an average deficit of $26 billion in 1985–86, the U.S. bilateral trade balance with the EU was reversed to a surplus of $7 billion by 1991–92, but the U.S. bilateral deficit with Japan fell only from an average of $59 billion to $51 billion. The apparent disparity results from the difference in the trade base. For U.S. trade with Europe, in 1986–87, U.S. exports started from a base of 70 percent of imports, whereas U.S. exports with Japan started from a base of only 32 percent of exports.[47]

As indicated above, it is expected that the U.S.-Japan bilateral balance will decline to $40 to $50 billion between 1994–97. Furthermore, even if Japan were to completely remove its barriers against trade, its trade surplus with the United States would fall by only between $9 billion and $18 billion,[48] and over the next three to five years, only half of this potential effect of liberalization would occur.

The prospect is that for the next few years large trade imbalances with Japan will persist, even if Japan removes its trade barriers, and reduction of the U.S. current account deficit as a share of GDP does not appear likely given the large savings-investment imbalances. A large dollar depreciation has taken place, and even after the European Union and Japan fully emerge from recession, the prospect is one of current account imbalances that are going to become increasingly difficult to sustain. The solution to reducing these imbalances to a level where they become sustainable (e.g., 1 percent of GDP) is more a matter of removing the large U.S. savings-investment imbalances.

NOTES

1. Robert A. Mundell, "The Great Exchange Rate Controversy: Trade Balances and the International Monetary System," in *International Adjustment and Financ-*

ing: The Lessons of 1985–91, ed. C. Fred Bergsten (Washington, D.C.: Institute for International Economics, 1991), p. 213.

2. Ibid., p. 214.

3. William R. Cline, "U.S. External Adjustment: Progress, Prognosis, and Interpretation," in *International Adjustment and Financing,* p. 36.

4. Purchasing power parity is achieved with an exchange rate between the two countries that equals the ratio of the price levels of the two currencies ($P = EP^f$ or $E = P/P^f$) where E is the exchange rate and P and P^f are the domestic and foreign price levels, respectively.

5. Cline, "U.S. External Adjustment," p. 37.

6. In the absence of capital mobility, the trade deficit would decline automatically, the X-M curve would shift back to E_0 and the X-M curve becomes irrelevant. Also, because foreign capital would not help finance imbalances, the S-I curve would shift up until it crossed the X axis at Y_0, and as a result, GDP returns to its old equilibrium.

7. Some readers may prefer to skip the few technical pages that explain the relationship between floating exchange rates and capital mobility.

8. This derivation follows that presented in Richard E. Caves, Jeffrey A. Frankel, and Ronald W. Jones, *World Trade and Payments: An Introduction,* 5th ed. (Glenview, Ill.: Scott, Foresman/Little, Brown Higher Education, 1990), pp. 665–78.

9. Ibid., p. 669.

10. Ibid., pp. 670–71.

11. Robert Mundell: "The Appropriate Use of Fiscal and Monetary Policy Under Fixed Exchange Rates," *IMF Staff Papers,* 9 (March 1962), pp. 70–77; and "Capital Mobility and Stabilization Policy Under Fixed and Flexible Exchange Rates," *Canadian Journal of Economics and Political Science,* November 1962, pp. 475–85; and J. M. Fleming, "Domestic Financial Policies Under Fixed and Under Floating Exchange Rates," *IMF Staff Papers,* 9, no. 3 (1962), pp. 369–79.

12. An example of this revision is provided in Paul R. Krugman, *Has the Adjustment Process Worked?* Policy Analysis in International Economics, No. 34 (Washington, D.C.: Institute for International Economics), October 1991, pp. 6–11 and 51–53.

13. The Phillips curve shows the trade-off between the rate of change in the price level (or wage rate) with the level of unemployment in the economy.

14. Krugman, *Has the Adjustment Process Worked?* p. 7.

15. Ibid., p. 52. *FX* represents the determination of the real exchange rate.

16. The Marshall-Lerner condition states that a depreciation or devaluation will improve the trade balance (and current account) if the sum of the price elasticities of domestic demand for imports and foreign demand for the domestic country's exports is equal to or greater than unity ($\Sigma_m + \Sigma_x \geq 1$), where Σ_m is the elasticity of demand for domestic imports and Σ_x is the elasticity of demand for domestic exports.

17. Frequently, a worsening of the trade balance immediately follows a depreciation (or devaluation) of the currency, even though after a lagged period of time an improvement in the trade balance does come about. The pattern of response in the trade balance with the passage of time resembles a J-curve.

18. International Monetary Fund, World Economic and Financial Surveys, *World Economic Outlook, May 1994* (Washington, D.C.: International Monetary Fund, 1994), p. 142.

19. Martin Feldstein and Charles Horioka, "Domestic Saving and International Capital Flows," *Economic Journal,* 90 (June 1980), pp. 314–29.

20. Martin Feldstein and Philippe Bacchetta, "National Saving and International Investment," in *National Saving and Economic Performance,* ed. B. Douglas Bernheim and John B. Shoven (Chicago: University of Chicago Press, 1991), pp. 201–26.

21. Robert A. Blecker, "Policy Implications of the International Saving-Investment Correlation," paper presented at the Economic Policy Institute Conference on Saving and Investment, Washington, D.C., April 21–22, 1994, p. 17.

22. James Tobin, "Comments: 'Domestic Saving and International Capital Movements in the Long-Run and the Short Run' by M. Feldstein," *European Economic Review,* 21 (1983), pp. 153–56.

23. Lawrence H. Summers, "Tax Policy and International Competitiveness," in *International Aspects of Fiscal Policy,* ed. Jacob A. Frenkel (Chicago: University of Chicago Press, 1988).

24. Tamin Bayoumi, "Saving-Investment Correlations: Immobile Capital, Government Policy, or Endogenous Behavior?" *IMF Staff Papers,* 37, no. 2 (June 1990), pp. 360–87.

25. Jeffrey A. Frankel, "Quantifying International Capital Mobility in the 1980s," in *National Saving and Economic Performance,* pp. 228–29.

26. Ibid., p. 240.

27. Ibid., p. 245.

28. Peter Hooper and Catherine L. Mann, *The Emergence and Persistence of the U.S. External Imbalance, 1980–87,* Princeton Studies in International Finance, No. 65 (Princeton: Princeton University Press, 1989).

29. Cline, "U.S. External Adjustment," pp. 13–55; and Robert Z. Lawrence, "U.S. Current Account Adjustment: An Appraisal," *Brookings Papers on Economic Activity,* no. 2 (1990), pp. 343–92.

30. Hooper and Mann, *The Emergence and Persistence of the U.S. External Imbalance,* p. 7.

31. Ibid., pp. 92–93.

32. Hysteresis is a term describing a phenomenon in which it is alleged that it is hard to regain market shares that were lost to competitors during a period of overvaluation of a domestic currency. Between 1985 and 1987, when the U.S. trade balance failed to respond to the large depreciation of the dollar, hysteresis was blamed for the lack of trade balance response.

33. Lawrence, "U.S. Current Account Adjustment," pp. 353–54.

34. Ibid., p. 366.

35. Ibid., p. 381.

36. Ibid., pp. 385–386.

37. Cline: "U.S. External Adjustment," pp. 25–29, and *United States External Adjustment and the World Economy* (Washington, D.C.: Institute for International Economics, 1989).

38. Cline, "U.S. External Adjustment," p. 25.

39. Ibid., p. 34.

40. Organization for Economic Co-operation and Development, *OECD Economic Outlook,* December 1994 (Paris: OECD, 1994), pp. A52–A53; and IMF, *World Economic Outlook, October 1994,* pp. 151–53.

41. IMF, *World Economic Outlook, October 1994*, pp. 151–53.

42. IMF, *World Economic Outlook, October 1993*, p. 23.

43. IMF, *World Economic Outlook, October 1994*, pp. 42–44.

44. William R. Cline, "Japan's Current Account Surplus," Institute for International Economics, Mimeographed Paper, July 1993.

45. *OECD Economic Outlook*, December 1994, p. A1.

46. Cline, "Japan's Current Account Surplus," p. 14.

47. William R. Cline, "Macroeconomics and the US-Japan Trade Imbalance," *International Economic Insights*, 4, no. 4, (July/August 1993), pp. 5–8.

48. C. Fred Bergsten and Marcus Noland, *Reconcilable Differences: United States Economic Conflict* (Washington, D.C.: Institute for International Economics, 1993), p. 189.

CHAPTER 7

Global Capital Requirements

One of the central roles of this volume is to determine the extent to which future U.S. international borrowing will affect the global supply and demand for capital. Since the early 1980s, the United States has been a net borrower of international capital, and by the mid-1980s the status of the country changed from that of an adult creditor to that of a mature creditor. According to Charles Kindleberger, Japan, which has been exporting capital to the United States, had entered the stage of a young creditor at the same time that the United States had become a mature creditor. Kindleberger defines a country as having passed into its young creditor stage when assets exceed its liabilities and it accumulates net claims on the rest of the world. The country finally becomes a mature creditor that lives off the interest and dividends on its net claims, and it may even consume some of its capital. Japan, with its high rate of domestic saving is in the young creditor stage, while the United States, with a large governmental deficit and very low rate of personal saving, is in the mature creditor stage.[1] Kindleberger predicted that it would be difficult to reduce the large saving-investment imbalances of the United States.

My intuition tells me, however, that the task of eliminating the governmental deficit and stimulating personal savings in the United States is a formidable one, not readily responsive to readily achieved changes in policy. Similarly while Japanese savings may decline as the immediate postwar generation gets older, the process of reducing personal and corporate savings in Japan will meet forces that are deeply resistant. If so, the flow of long-term capital to the United States from the Pacific area will not be readily reversed.[2]

Earlier chapters in this book have examined the underlying forces behind the large U.S. capital inflows and whether there are prospects for change during the remainder of the 1990s. Raising savings rates will involve substantial efforts to reduce federal deficits and increase the rate of personal savings. Raising the national savings rate reduces the need for capital inflows and, ultimately, in conjunction with real exchange rate changes, reduces current account imbalances. Because the United States has been such a large user of international capital, reducing the need for capital should help to keep world interest rates low.

Current account deficits measure the size of net capital inflows that are required to bring about balance-of-payments equilibrium. Countries with current account surpluses finance the current account imbalances of deficit countries. The role of the United States in absorbing international capital can be assessed by comparing U.S. capital inflows to the capital inflows and outflows of the rest of the world. The following section will examine the role of the United States in absorbing global savings since the 1980s. It will also look at how the capital needs of developing areas in Latin America and Asia as well as countries in transition from centrally planned economies affect global savings needs.

CURRENT ACCOUNT BALANCES IN THE 1990s

The relative magnitude of capital inflows that have accompanied the progression of the United States to the status of a mature creditor can be shown by comparing the size of U.S. current account deficits to the deficits and surpluses of other areas of the world. Table 7.1 shows that since the 1980s, the United States has been absorbing a major share of global savings. Global savings is defined as the sum of current account surpluses; and the use of savings is the sum of current account deficits. The difference between surpluses and deficits is on a net basis and does not reflect gross capital flows. In theory, the difference between global surpluses and deficits should be equal to zero. But in reality, the total does not equal zero because of statistical errors, omissions, and asymmetries in reported balance-of-payments statistics as well as the exclusion of data for international organizations and a limited number of countries.[3]

The past decade has been one where the industrial country group has shown persistent current account deficits. For most of the period, U.S. current account deficits have been large, and the prospect is for these deficits to remain large during the remainder of the 1990s. U.S. current account deficits, which annually exceeded $100 billion in 1985–89, increased again, rising to $109 billion for 1993 and are projected to remain significantly greater than $100 billion for the remainder of the 1990s. Germany, which had large surpluses in 1985–90, became a deficit country in 1991 as a consequence of increased spending associated with reunification with the former

Table 7.1

Balance of Payments on Current Account, 1986–95 (in billions of U.S. dollars)

	1986	1987	1988	1989	1990	1991	1992	1993	1994[a]	1995[a]
Industrial Countries	-34.2	-67.0	-57.0	-84.1	-110.1	-32.1	-43.2	12.1	7.8	8.0
United States	-150.2	-167.3	-127.2	-101.6	-91.9	-8.3	-66.4	-109.2	-140.3	-165.9
Japan	85.8	87.0	79.6	57.2	35.8	72.9	117.6	131.4	133.4	125.7
European Union	47.5	30.2	12.3	1.3	-15.1	-65.5	-67.8	2.4	19.1	30.4
Developing Countries	-46.9	-4.7	-24.9	-16.9	-11.6	-87.9	-67.1	-104.6	-106.2	-100.8
Countries in Transition	6.7	12.5	6.7	-4.1	-17.3	-6.0	-6.6	-6.5	-20.6	-16.7

a. Projection

Source: International Monetary Fund, World Economic and Financial Surveys, *World Economic Outlook, May 1994* (Washington D.C.: International Monetary Fund, 1994), pp. 142 and 152.

East Germany. By 1995, it is projected that the size of this deficit will decline significantly. Japan has continuously been a surplus country. By 1993 these current account surpluses rose to $131.4 billion and are expected to decline only modestly by 1995 and to remain high for a number of years. These surpluses have been a major source of balance-of-payments financing for countries with current account deficits.

The combined deficit of the developing countries for 1983–92 averaged $37.3 billion a year. The combined current account deficit for the group rose sharply in the 1990s—to $104.6 billion in 1993—and is projected to average slightly over $100 billion in 1994–95. Over the decade, the newly industrializing countries of Asia (Taiwan, Korea, Singapore, and Hong Kong) experienced current account surpluses, which were large between 1986–89 but declined to $8 billion by 1993 and are projected to average only $2 billion in 1994–95. The current account deficits for the other Asian developing countries as a group increased significantly and are projected to remain large in 1994–95. Current account deficits rose from $4.5 billion in 1992 to $25.1 billion in 1993 and are expected to average over $27 billion for 1994–95. These increases result from the persistence of large deficits in China, Thailand, Indonesia, the Philippines, and Pakistan. The IMF expects net direct investment and external borrowing in Asia to remain high at about $48 billion in 1994–95 and comprises about one-half of the total flow to developing countries. China is expected to account for one-third of this total. For Latin America, a surge in capital inflows commenced in 1991, and these flows are projected to remain strong in 1994–95. As an outcome of strong economic activity, large current account deficits are projected for Mexico and Argentina (roughly $23 billion and $8 billion, respectively) for 1994–95. It is assumed that these deficits will be financed by private capital inflows.[4] The countries in transition to market economies (the former republics of the USSR and the Central and East European countries) are also expected to require increasing capital inflows in 1994–95. It is projected that current account deficits for countries in transition will rise from $6.5 billion in 1993 to $20.6 billion in 1994 and $16.7 billion in 1995.

The data indicate growing capital requirements for the developing countries and countries in transition. At the same time, U.S. demand for capital is projected to increase in 1994–95. Although demand for foreign capital in the United States declined in 1989–92, the current account deficit in 1993 rose to $109 billion and is projected to rise to $140 billion in 1994 and $166 billion in 1995. Japan remains the only major industrial country with large current account surpluses. After incurring sizable deficits in 1991 and 1992, the European Union showed a small current account surplus of $2.4 billion in 1993, and this surplus is projected to rise to $19 billion in 1994 and $30.4 billion in 1995. The growth in net exports in Europe is expected to have positive impacts on economic growth at the same time that net exports in the United States and Japan are expected to deteriorate, and will roughly offset projected changes for the United States and Japan.

In an attempt to assess medium-term outcomes, the OECD has put together a reference scenario to the year 2000, which is made up of a set of projections for each of the OECD economies.[5] It is emphasized that the scenario is only one of many possible projections and is subject to a wide margin of error. The reference scenario assumes countries steadily adjust toward their stated medium-term fiscal and monetary policy goals, especially those concerned with fiscal balance and low inflation. It is assumed that beyond the forecast period of 1994–95, commodity prices and exchange rates will be basically unchanged. For the United States, GDP growth is projected to slow down in 1996 and 1997 and stabilize at an average of around 2.25 percent until the end of the decade. These projections reflect the tightening stance of monetary policy in 1994–95 in response to projections of robust economic growth through 1995. For Europe and Japan, which are projected to grow more slowly in earlier years, stronger economic growth is projected for 1996–2000, averaging 3 and 3.75 percent, respectively. For the period 1994–2000, inflation rates for the group are projected to be fairly moderate, averaging about 3 percent for the period.

It is assumed that the effects of sustained medium-term growth and committed programs of fiscal consolidation lead to major success in budget deficit reductions. For the United States, the budget deficit is projected to fall to 1.7 percent of GDP (which is much less than the Congressional Budget Office projection of 2.9 percent in the year 2000). For the entire OECD, it is projected that the overall budget deficit declines from 4.2 percent of GDP in 1993 to 1.5 percent in the year 2000.

The OECD reference scenario gives projections for current account balances (see Table 7.2). The U.S. current account is projected to rise from 1.7 percent of GDP in 1993 to 2.1 percent each year during 1994–96, and then decline to 1.9 percent of GDP in 1999 and 2000. The small decline in this percentage after the middle of the decade is associated with a projected slowdown in the rate of economic growth. For the European countries as a group, the current account deficit is projected to improve, rising from a small surplus of 0.3 percent of GDP in 1993 to 0.7 percent in 1994, and then remaining at about 1 percent of GDP over the remainder of the decade. The growth of the surplus for the European countries as a group is expected to be offset by a declining Japanese current account surplus, which falls steadily from 3.1 percent of GDP in 1993 to 1.8 percent by 2000. The decline in Japan's current account surplus is associated with a growth in output in Japan, which starts accelerating in 1995 and rises to over 4 percent a year by the end of the decade.

The projections appear to indicate that if present policies persist, the United States could continue to absorb the major share of OECD current account surpluses for the remainder of the decade. The continuation of U.S.

Table 7.2
Industrial Country Current Account Balances, 1992–2000 (percent of GDP)

	1992	1993	1994	1995	1996	1997	1998	1999	2000
United States	-1.1	-1.7	-2.1	-2.1	-2.1	-2.0	-2.0	-1.9	-1.9
Japan	3.2	3.1	2.8	2.5	2.3	2.1	2.0	1.9	1.8
Germany	-1.1	-1.1	-0.7	-0.2	-0.1	-0.1	0.0	0.0	-0.1
OECD Europe	-0.7	0.3	0.7	1.0	1.1	1.1	1.1	1.0	1.0
Total OECD	-0.2	0.1	0.1	0.1	0.1	0.1	0.1	0.1	0.1

Source: Organization for Economic Cooperation and Development, OECD Economic Outlook, June 1994, (Paris: OECD), p. 28.

demand for foreign capital occurs at the same time that developing countries and countries in transition will be requiring increasing amounts of external financing. The International Monetary Fund has made projections for economic growth and for current account balances of developing countries through 1999.[6] It was assumed that from 1995, nonfuel commodity prices would increase by 1.5 percent a year, world manufacturing prices would increase by 1.6 percent a year, and that exchange rates would remain unchanged in real terms. Given projections for a lack of inflationary pressures in the industrial countries, it was assumed that from 1995 there will be little change in the terms of trade for developing countries. In comparison with 1983–92, total financing flows to net debtor developing countries were projected to increase in 1995–99 because commercial bank lending, particularly to several Latin American countries, has recently resumed, and flight capital continues to return to Latin America.

Based on these assumptions and medium-term projections for industrial countries, the International Monetary Fund projected real GDP growth rates and trade and current account movements for 1994–99 in the developing countries. Growth in real GDP for the group, which was 4.7 percent a year in 1983–92 and 6.1 percent in 1993, is projected to average 5.6 percent in 1994–95 and 6.1 percent in 1996–99. The current account deficit increased from an average deficit of $37.3 billion in 1983–92 to a deficit of $104.6 billion in 1993, and is projected to average $103 billion in 1994–95, before declining to $77.7 billion in 1997 and $42.6 billion in 1999. These projections assume that with strengthening of economic conditions in Europe and Japan, outflows from industrial to developing countries will decline somewhat. To a large extent, the necessity of servicing the debt of those developing countries that are heavily indebted is reflected in the fact that aggregate current account deficits are significantly in excess of the trade deficits.

CAPITAL INFLOWS TO DEVELOPING COUNTRIES AND COUNTRIES IN TRANSITION

Many developing countries have experienced a marked increase in their access to capital markets since the late 1980s. This improvement comes after an extended period when developing countries experienced sharply reduced inflows of foreign capital as a consequence of poor economic performance and uncertain prospects, resulting from the developing country debt crisis of the early and mid-1980s. The projections for the large current account imbalances of the developing countries imply that net capital inflows are expected to continue to be large. The phenomenon of increased capital inflows into Asian developing countries other than the newly industrializing economies started in the late 1980s. For Latin America, the increased inflows commenced in 1990. A 1993 paper on the recent surge in capital inflows into Asian developing countries lists several factors that contributed to surges in capital inflows, summarized as follows:

1. Changes in short-run rates of return including a widening in interest rate differentials.
2. Improvements in the balance of domestic macroeconomic policy, such as a fiscal consolidation that would crowd in investment and net exports at the expense of government consumption.
3. Changes in microeconomic policies, such as a structural reform program that boasts productivity or the opening up of a domestic market to foreigners.[7]

Other factors that have contributed to the surge in capital inflows, especially in Latin America and Asia, have been debt restructuring and reduction that improved creditworthiness; convertibility and policy changes that have improved access to foreign exchange to purchase imported inputs and increased the freedom to remit profits and dividends; the development of domestic capital markets in countries such as Argentina, Chile, Korea, and Mexico that encouraged portfolio capital flows by the reduction of restrictions on foreign holdings; improvement of settlement and clearance procedures; and reduction of taxes and fees on transactions. External factors, particularly the cyclical downturn in economic activity and the decline in interest rates, have also played a role in some cases. Empirical studies suggest that 30–50 percent of the variation in capital flows to developing countries may have been a consequence of external factors. External factors may have played a larger role in Latin America than in Asia.[8]

COMPOSITION OF CAPITAL INFLOWS

The composition of capital flows to developing countries has changed markedly since the 1970s (see Table 7.3). From 1971 to 1981, commercial bank loans contributed a large share of gross capital flows to developing countries, rising from 35.8 percent of all flows to developing countries in 1971–76 to 43.5 percent in 1977–81. Thereafter, the share of bank lending declined, falling to 16.2 percent of all capital flows in 1989–92. This weakness in lending reflected capital constraints on commercial banks arising from problems with domestic loans within the industrial countries, concerns about developing countries' debt problems, and establishment of capital adequacy standards by the Bank for International Settlements.

Official flows (loans and grants) are still an important component, accounting for 40 percent of all capital flows to developing countries; for low income countries, that share is much larger. For instance, in 1989–92, official sources accounted for two-thirds of all flows to Africa.

Between 1977–81 and 1989–92, the share going into foreign direct in-

Table 7.3
Developing Countries: Capital Flows,[1] 1971–92 (in percent of total unless otherwise noted)

	1971-76	1977-81	1982-88	1989-92	1991	1992
Foreign direct investment	10.8	8.5	10.6	17.7	18.8	18.0
Portfolio equity	--	--	--	3.3	4.0	5.8
Bonds	1.4	2.5	3.1	5.7	6.2	10.2
Commercial bank loans	35.8	43.5	27.9	16.2	16.6	9.6
Suppliers and export credits	9.2	10.3	11.7	11.4	9.4	16.1
Official loans	30.9	26.4	35.7	31.9	29.3	28.9
Grants	11.9	8.8	10.9	13.8	15.7	11.4
Total in billions of U.S. dollars	41.2	110.9	125.5	175.3	177.7	218.4
Total in billions of constant dollars[2]	78.1	117.6	117.6	138.0	138.6	167.5

Source: International Monetary Fund, World Economic and Financial Surveys, *World Economic Outlook, October 1993* (Washington, D.C.: International Monetary Fund, 1993), p. 77.

1. Gross flows (excluding short-term loans). These data should be regarded as illustrative of the broad trends of flows to developing countries.

2. Deflated using 1985 = 100 unit value of total imports.

vestment (FDI), equity, and bond financing almost tripled, and such financing has replaced commercial bank lending as a major source of financing. Since the mid-1980s, foreign direct investment flows have increased sharply, especially in Asia and Latin America, and at present account for one-fifth of all flows. As a percentage of global foreign direct investment, the share going to developing countries increased from less than 12 percent in 1987 to 22 percent in 1992. Most of these flows have been concentrated in a few middle income developing countries. Two-thirds of these direct investment flows originate in the United States and Japan. The United States has been the principal supplier of foreign investment for Latin America, and most of this investment has gone into the purchase of existing companies. For Asian developing countries, Japan and the newly industrializing Asian economies have been the main source, and there, foreign investment has been directed toward investment in new establishments. It is noteworthy that in both Asia and Latin America, investment flows have shifted from extractive and manufacturing industries to capital-intensive activities such as telecommunications and transport. These FDI flows have been motivated by the increased role of worldwide production, sourcing, and marketing strategies by multinationals.

Portfolio capital flows to developing countries have also increased sharply since the mid-1980s as a result of changes in domestic policies, the development of domestic capital markets, reduced restrictions on foreign holdings, improvements in settlement and clearance procedures, and reduced taxes and fees on securities transactions. By 1992, equity financing comprised 5.8 percent of all capital flows to developing countries and bond financing made up 10.2 percent. Much of the portfolio capital went to a few middle income countries in Latin America and Asia. Since 1989, more than one-half of these flows have gone to Latin America, and two-thirds of all capital flows to developing countries went to five countries: Argentina, Brazil, Korea, Mexico, and Turkey.[9]

Whereas much of the capital flows to developing countries in the 1970s and early 1980s went to public or quasi-governmental sources, public-sector borrowing has declined and inflows to the private sector account for a larger share of net external financing.

CAPITAL FLOWS TO SEVERAL AREAS

One important factor that has influenced capital inflows to developing countries has been increases in short-term rates of return, including a widening of interest differentials in recent years. In Chapter 6 it was shown that short-term capital flows depend on real interest rate differentials and expected changes in exchange rates. When investors determine the allocation of assets, they compare real interest rate differentials of prospective investments with expected changes in exchange rates between the domestic currency and foreign currency rates. Changes in real interest rate differentials can lead to surges in capital inflows (or outflows). A principal determinant of short-term capital movements to developing countries has been financial trends in the United States, particularly capital inflows to Latin America. For instance, the fall in short-term interest rates in the United States between 1989 and 1993 contributed to the expansion of capital flows into Latin America.

With the passage of time, the rate of return on medium-term and long-term assets becomes subject to greater variability than on short-term investments. It becomes more difficult to predict exchange rate variability, and instruments allowing one to hedge against long-term exchange rate variability are less likely to be available. For the long term, the investor must take into consideration a range of factors that could impinge on the return on investment and the path of the exchange rate. Factors that could affect future returns include prospects for inflation, the cost structure of the economy in relation to its competitors, microeconomic and macroeconomic economic reforms and the resulting structural and stabilization policies, and political stability. It is obvious that political and economic reforms do have the potential to affect capital inflows to developing countries.

An examination of the data for 1991 and 1992 show a marked rise in capital outflows from the United States and Japan and capital inflows into Asia and Latin America. In both cases, it would appear that recession and reduced economic opportunities in the United States and Japan were associated with increased outflows to developing areas. Much of Japan's outflow to developing areas went to Asia. A large part of U.S. capital outflows to developing countries went to Latin America and, since 1990, capital flows to the region have rebounded. From an average of over $8 billion in 1985–89, gross capital inflows to Latin America rose to $24 billion in 1990, almost $40 billion in 1991, and almost $60 billion in 1992. Capital inflows for 1993 were about $50 billion.

While a substantial part of the phenomenon of increased capital flows to Latin America can be explained by economic and political reforms that have recently taken place in these countries, domestic reforms cannot explain all of the inflow. Capital sometimes flowed to countries that did not undertake reforms and did not flow, until recently, to countries that introduced reforms well before 1990. One hypothesis is that some of the renewal of capital flows to Latin America resulted from external factors that can be considered an "external shock" to the region as a whole. It has been argued that a continuing recession, falling interest rates, and balance-of-payments developments in the United States encouraged investors to shift capital resources to Latin America to take advantage of the renewal of investment opportunities and the increase in financial solvency of the region.[10]

Several characteristics of the period of increased capital flows into Latin America stand out. Of the growth in capital flows over the period 1990–92, almost 47 percent was channeled into increased foreign exchange reserves, and the remainder was used to finance widening current account deficits. The growth in reserves represented intervention by the monetary authorities in foreign exchange markets as efforts to sterilize the impact of large capital inflows.

An effort has been made to assess the role of external factors in the inflow of capital into Latin America in 1990–91. Several external factors could have accounted for the increase in capital inflows to Latin America. One factor was the sharp drop in U.S. short-term interest rates that, by reducing debt-service burdens, increased the solvency of Latin American debtors. Returns on other U.S. investments such as real estate and corporate profits also fell. Another important factor was the sharp swing in the U.S. private capital account in 1990–91 in the form of increased outflows and reduced inflows. Foreign direct investment in the United States declined sharply, and purchases of foreign stocks and bonds increased substantially. Like the period 1978–82, U.S. capital outflows played a key role as external impulses that affected the size of capital inflows into Latin America. Similarly, the period of increased capital inflows into the United States in 1983–89 was matched by an increase in capital outflows from Latin America.[11]

The study provided a quantitative assessment of the role of external factors on the accumulation of reserves and on real exchange rate appreciation (two factors that have been closely associated with the recent capital inflows into Latin America). It was shown that there was an important degree of co-movement in reserves and exchange rates across countries that appeared to reflect the effect of a common external shock to Latin American countries, and the degree of comovement across countries increased during the recent capital inflow episode.

It was then hypothesized that a decline in U.S. interest rates, stock market returns, real estate returns, and economic activity (represented by disposable income) could be associated with an increase in the flow of capital to Latin America, which would be partly reflected in an increase in regionwide indexes constructed for reserves and the real exchange rate. Simple, pairwise correlation coefficients for these U.S. variables and each of the two indexes does provide evidence of such a relationship. Another pattern revealed is that the increase in reserves preceded the real appreciation of the exchange rate.

It was also shown that a shock in the form of higher U.S. interest rates could be associated with a permanent decrease in reserves and a real exchange rate depreciation in Latin America. For most of the ten countries in the sample, the response pattern computed supported the hypothesis that an increase in interest rates abroad induced an increased capital outflow from these countries. The implication of this finding is that if external rates of return increase, future capital outflows from Latin America would rise.[12]

The study provided evidence that surges in capital flows between the center and periphery can occur in response to external factors. During 1994 and in February 1995 actions by the Federal Reserve to raise short-term interest rates helped produce an increase in long-term interest rates from about 6 percent to over 7.5 percent. At the same time that U.S. current account deficits were increasing in response to improved economic performance in the United States, major industrial countries were still experiencing recession. As real interest rates rise in the United States, the possibility exists that high real interest rates will lead to capital outflows from (or reduced inflows to) areas such as Latin America, which had been becoming relatively more attractive to investors. In the December 1993 *OECD Economic Outlook,* concern was expressed over whether capital inflows to Latin America would be sustained.[13]

The problem of the sustainability of capital flows to Latin America became apparent in January 1995 when the value of the Mexican peso had fallen by

35 percent in a one-month period. To rescue the Mexican economy and avoid serious financial distress in Mexico, the United States put together a $52 billion aid plan.

Ronald I. McKinnon discussed some of the causes of the crisis.

What caused the Crisis? In large part, the major institutions of international finance—banks in New York, Tokyo and London as well as stock and bond mutual funds (mainly on Wall Street)—which have a lemming-like bent to lend in emerging markets.

A flood of foreign capital can destroy a developing economy by creating a crippling current-account deficit—the difference between what is taken in from exports and what is paid for imports and interest on foreign debt. Foreign investors are also likely to pull their money out in a crisis, further destabilizing the economy.[14]

In 1994, Mexico's current account deficit (its net capital inflow) rose to $29 billion or about 8 percent of GDP. In addition to a large increase in foreign debt, this inflow also had two other adverse consequences. Credit restraints on domestic borrowing were relaxed and the rate of personal saving fell from 15 percent of GDP to 7.5 percent in 1994. Furthermore, the large amount of foreign investment caused an increase in domestic prices, which brought about an overvaluation of the peso and adversely affected Mexican exports.[15] The Mexican case exemplifies the destabilization that can occur when fragile developing economies receive very large infusions of foreign capital.

Another group of countries that in the future could become substantial users of international capital are the Central and East European countries (CEEC) and the newly independent states (NIS) of the former Soviet Union, which are in transition toward market economies. As the transition from socialism proceeds, these economies have been experiencing rising unemployment, high inflation rates, large budget deficits, and (with the exception of the Czech and Slovak Republics) rising current account deficits.

Very large problems face the Russian economy, which has been experiencing hyperinflation, rapidly falling real GDP, and large current account deficits as it attempts to move rapidly toward a market economy and away from a collapsing central planning system. The balance-of-payments problems of Russia as well as the other newly independent states are being driven by available financial assistance. If more external financial assistance were forthcoming, current and projected account deficits could be larger. The financing constraint is severe and hard currency imports are being sharply compressed. The financing constraint has been exacerbated by capital flight from the NIS, estimated at between $5 billion and $15 billion in 1992.[16]

Activities of governments in the region to stimulate economic growth and contain unemployment have been complicated by the necessity of restraining current account and budget deficits. Over the period 1994–95, the need to contain current account deficits is expected to exercise an important influence on economic outcomes. Slow growth in export markets and a high propensity to import should continue to place the current accounts under pressure.[17]

Prospects for growth in these countries will be determined by their ability to successfully undertake economic reforms, but even if the reforms are successful, the financial needs of the region are going to be considerable. In 1990 and 1991, the OECD countries evolved a policy view that initially the opening of export markets would help to meet import financing requirements. Although important barriers to exports from the region remain, the European Union has done much to open markets. In the meantime, short-term lending of international financial institutions—the International Monetary Fund and the International Bank for Reconstruction Development (IBRD)—are expected to help cover financing needs, and it is assumed that later these needs could be met by the inflows of private capital.[18]

Although foreign direct investment flows increased steadily, reaching about $2.5 billion in 1992, they are not expected to grow significantly in 1994–95 and will continue to be concentrated in a few countries, including Hungary and the Czech Republic. In general, with the exception of a few countries, access to world capital markets has been very limited. The OECD has summarized the current situation as follows:

Although foreign direct investment flows have steadily increased since 1990, reaching about $2.5 billion in 1992, they are not likely to grow significantly over the next two years and will be concentrated in a few countries. Slow growth and weak corporate returns in the OECD area will reduce the willingness of firms to invest abroad, while increased contingent trade protection may have lowered the prospective returns. Several countries, such as Hungary and the Czech Republic, have access to the world capital markets and some enterprises in the region have been able to borrow externally. However, there is very likely a limit at this stage to the funds these countries can acquire to finance current account deficits without incurring notably higher interest rates. Other countries such as Poland and Bulgaria have no access at all while trade credit remains limited. For a number of CEECs financing requirements have been filled up till now in large measure by the IMF and the IBRD, but several countries are reaching quota or exposure limits, and repayments will become increasingly important.[19]

The capital flows to the CEEC and the NIS are still limited, even though the need is large. If structural reforms continue and stabilization occurs, private capital inflows would be important for growth in the region. At present, private capital flows to the area remain modest. External official capital flows will be vital during the early stage of the transformation process. During this stage, there are high risks and great uncertainties, and private flows of capital will tend to be limited and are often focused on investments having a high certainty of expected return. To help smooth the initial painful adjustment period, flows of credit from official sources and the international financial institutions tend to dominate the available supply of external resources. The provision of resources that are conditional on countries implementing serious programs of stabilization and reform are considered important at this stage.[20]

International financial institutions—mainly the IMF and the World Bank—have been the principal suppliers of financial assistance to the transition countries. Because the need for orderly adjustment and introduction of currency convertability required more resources than the international financial institutions could provide, lending from the industrial countries within the Group of Twenty-Four (G-24) framework (the OECD countries) complemented the lending of the financial institutions. In 1991–93, these institutions provided a total of $11.6 billion to Albania, Bulgaria, the former Czechoslovakia, Hungary, Romania, and the Baltic states. Private capital and debt relief added another $17.4 billion over the three-year period. To help alleviate the impact of the transition process after the breakup of the former USSR, Russia received a total of $38 billion in official external financing in 1992–93. Of this, $20 billion was provided by bilateral creditors and the European Union, $3 billion came from the IMF and the World Bank, and official debt relief added another $15 billion. In addition, Germany provided a grant of $3 billion to rehouse Russian troops once stationed in the former East Germany, and commercial debt-service relief added another $16 billion.[21]

Asia is an area that has been developing rapidly. The newly industrializing economies of Hong Kong, Korea, Singapore, and Taiwan are generally distinguished from the other developing countries of Asia. They have higher GDPs than other Asian developing economies and have been net exporters of capital. Singapore and Hong Kong have developed as financial centers. Capital flows to Asian emerging markets come substantially from Far Eastern financial centers—Japan and other financial centers.

Table 7.4 shows capital flows to Asian developing countries from 1986 to 1991. As was the case in Latin America, the capital account improvement commenced in 1989, prior to a surge in inflows that began in 1991. For Asian developing countries, direct investment accounted for about 25 percent of the increase in capital flows. In 1990–93 the region received gross FDI inflows averaging $27 billion a year. The main sources for foreign direct investment in Asian developing countries have been Japan and the newly industrializing economies, and foreign direct investment has mainly supplemented fixed capital formation.[22] Long-term and medium-term inflows accounted for a much larger proportion of the inflow than did short-term flows. In 1990–93, inflows of portfolio capital averaged over $10 billion a year. Over the period, much of the capital inflow took the form of reserve accumulations. China has been experiencing rapid economic growth, and it

Table 7.4
Capital Flows to Asia, 1986–91 (billions of U.S. dollars)

	1986	1987	1988	1989	1990	1991
Capital Account, excluding transfers	16.6	14.4	0.0	7.3	19.2	37.5
Medium and long term (net)	11.6	-3.3	6.8	8.9	14.3	21.3
Short term (net)	6.2	15.8	-0.6	0.9	6.8	10.8
Direct investment (net)	5.6	7.6	7.9	7.4	10.7	14.8
Other (residual)	-6.8	-5.7	-14.1	-9.9	-12.6	-9.4
Memorandum:						
Public, publicly guaranteed[1]	26.8	28.6	32.3	31.7	32.1	36.0
Reserve accumulation	23.6	40.7	11.1	8.1	23.1	36.3

Source: Kenneth B. Bercuson and Linda M. Koenig, "The Recent Surge in Capital Inflows to Asia: Causes and Macroeconomic Impact." Paper presented at SEACEN/IMF Seminar, May 14-16, 1993, Seoul, Korea, p. 3a.

1. Gross disbursements, public and publicly guaranteeded debt, *World Bank Debt Tables 1991-92*, adjusted for differences in regional classificationa. Data not available for all countries.

may be expected that private capital flows to China will continue to expand in the future. Since 1992 China has become a large recipient of FDI inflows.

Investors making long-term investment decisions examine factors likely to affect the return on investment. One important factor is the cost structure of the country they are considering relative to its competitors. In a study of three countries—Indonesia, Malaysia, and Thailand—that are developing rapidly and have experienced surges of capital inflows over the past several years, labor earnings relative to the United States, Japan, Korea, and Taiwan were examined. Taking the average of 1980–84 as the base year, it was shown that by 1991 the relative cost of labor had fallen sharply, especially in relation to Korea and Taiwan. Large depreciations against the dollar during the 1980s contributed to the fall in relative labor costs, which provided an important incentive for labor-intensive production to relocate and take advantage of enhanced profit potentials.[23] Fiscal consolidation in these countries, which was important for macroeconomic stability, reduced the risk that inflation would undermine the higher returns resulting from relatively low labor costs. In addition to improving profit potentials, each of these three countries undertook measures to improve access of foreign investors to the domestic market.[24]

THE UNITED STATES AND CAPITAL INFLOWS TO THE REST OF THE WORLD

The short survey of capital flows to the three areas of Latin America, Asia, and the countries in transition raises the probability that capital requirements in those areas will continue to be large.

To a certain extent, large inflows to Latin America in recent years could have partly reflected poor economic performance and low real short-term interest rates in the United States. But a number of countries in Latin America have undertaken economic and political reforms that could help them continue to receive external financing even now that economic conditions in the United States have improved and interest rates have been rising. Furthermore, there are differences from the 1978–82 period when capital inflows to Latin America were also large. First, commercial bank loans comprise a smaller share of capital inflows, and much more new investment consists of foreign direct investment and portfolio investment. This changes the distribution of risk, with private foreign investors now bearing more of the risk. Second, as already noted, a large number of these countries have undertaken changes to produce macroeconomic stabilization and increased privatization. Also, in the earlier period, these economies were primarily export economies, but now a number of them have become significantly more diversified.

Several factors indicate that Latin America will continue to be competitive in global capital markets. Structural and economic reforms have resulted in significantly reduced rates of inflation. This has been aided by the fact that wage increments have been held back. The increasing role of privatization of large companies that formerly were publicly operated has made these firms market oriented.

It has already been noted that external factors can greatly affect capital inflows into Latin America. Most importantly, the economies of Latin America are seriously affected by economic events in the United States, particularly how the Federal Reserve conducts monetary policy. Recession and an easy monetary policy in the United States during the early 1990s made portfolio investment in Latin America more attractive because real short-term interest rates were very low in the United States. Depressed economic activity in the United States would also have helped increase foreign direct investment in Latin America.

The surge of capital inflows into Latin America since 1991 must still be regarded as a short-term phenomenon that was partly caused by low real interest rates in the United States, and it is not possible to know if the size of these flows can be sustained. There is concern that even though the investor base has recently broadened, involvement by mainstream investors in developing country securities is still limited, and there have been reports of investor portfolios becoming saturated. To insure the sustainability of private capital flows to developing countries, it has been suggested that it will be important that the investor base for developing country securities continues to broaden.[25]

Even though the recent Mexican peso crisis may have temporarily hurt investor confidence in the soundness of some of the Latin American economies, several factors increase the likelihood of continued inflows. The substitution of private portfolio capital inflows for commercial bank lending redistributed risk from banks to individual investors. Structural and economic reforms that have helped to stabilize the economies, movements toward privatization of government-run entities, and diversification of the economies help to provide conditions for capital inflows to continue.

The economies of Central and Eastern Europe and the newly independent states have recently begun to make the transition to market economies. Although the Czech Republic and Hungary are attracting private capital, in most of the other countries official inflows by multilateral agencies will be essential. Until investment needs can be met by private domestic savings that will be supplemented by private capital inflows, large official inflows from the international agencies will have to dominate the supply of external resources that will be required to bring about an adjustment from centrally planned economies to capitalistic economies. Resources need to be provided on the condition that countries undertake serious programs of economic stabilization and reform. In addition to an adequate supply of external resources, it is considered to be of critical importance that markets be opened to the exports of transforming economies.[26]

The expansion of competing uses for net international capital comes at a time when there has been a dramatic reversal in the nature of Japanese capital outflows. During the five-year period 1986–90, Japan's cumulative current account surplus amounted to $350 billion, but the cumulative net long-term capital account annual outflow was $532 billion, and over the period Japan supplied an annual average of more than $100 billion in capital to the rest of the world. During 1991 and 1992, the total of Japan's current account surpluses rose to $197 billion, but the net long-term capital export in the two-year period totalled only $9 billion.

It is important to comprehend why the capital export was so large in the second half of the 1980s and how the large gap between the current account surplus and capital export was financed. Three major monetary factors contributed to the large capital export during the second half of the 1980s.[27] First, the very easy monetary policy pursued by the Japanese monetary authorities produced a large interest rate differential between the United States and Japan. Second, after the Plaza Accord in the fall of 1985, the yen appreciated rapidly against the dollar, and with a strong yen, foreign securities and properties were cheap. Furthermore, the strength of the yen reduced the competitiveness of Japanese exports, and outward foreign direct investment in the form of the establishment of subsidiaries abroad occurred. Third, Japanese businesses were able to easily raise funds because of the rapid increase in prices in the Japanese stock market and real estate.

The gap of almost $180 billion between the current account surplus and the long-term capital export between 1986 and 1990 was financed by Japanese banks that engaged in short-term borrowing on the Euromarkets, and over the five-year period the banks' net external short-term liabilities increased by $170 billion. In terms of the capital account, the $532 billion in long-term capital exports has to be balanced against the $170 billion increase in short-term external liabilities. Japanese banks were able to help provide long-term assets internationally by increasing their short-term liabilities and, as such, played a key role in the international maturity transformation.

Several explanations can be given for the rapid decline in Japan's export of long-term capital in 1991 and 1992.[28] One factor was the expansion of foreign investment in Japan, which could have been a result of lower prices for equities and the large appreciation of the yen. Foreign investment also increased because big pension funds in the United States and other countries expanded their strategy of diversifying into non-dollar-denominated securities. Another reason was the fact that the collapse of the Japanese stock market and real estate market would have reduced the ability of Japanese investors to raise low-cost funds for investment overseas. Also, the appreciation of the yen raised the foreign exchange risk of making overseas investments. Finally, Japanese banks, partly as a consequence of the fact that the Bank for International Settlements had installed a system of higher capital adequacy requirements for members, became very conservative. Consequently, private capital outflows ceased, and short-term lending by Japanese banks in the Euromarkets financed Japan's current account surplus. During 1991 and 1992, Japanese banks very rapidly reduced their short-term liabilities in the Euromarkets by $170 billion, and the position of Japanese banking was reduced to its 1985 level.

In terms of balance-of-payments financing, over the two-year period, Japan still exported capital because the reduction in liabilities to the Euromarkets comprised an export of short-term capital. Although it is expected that Japan's current account surpluses will continue to be large during much of the 1990s, it is not expected that Japanese investors will engage in the export of long-term capital to the same degree as in the second half of the 1980s.

Net private foreign investment in the United States amounted to only $12.8 billion in 1993, but the deficiency in capital inflows was made up by net government investment, which nearly doubled to $70 billion. This capital came from foreign central banks, mainly in developing countries, including Brazil, Mexico, Chile, India, and Malaysia. These central banks had increased their holdings of foreign exchange reserves partly as a result of increased investment by Western financial institutions, such as mutual funds and pension funds seeking higher returns than could be found in industrialized countries.[29]

Foreign central banks generally hold a large part of their foreign exchange reserves in the form of U.S. dollar holdings made up of investments in U.S. Treasury securities. These reserves can be used to pay for their countries' imports if the value of exports falls. In addition to keeping the ratio of reserves to imports that they customarily hold to insure themselves an uninterrupted flow of imports, about two dozen central banks in developing countries have greatly increased their foreign exchange reserve holdings in recent years. Many of these central banks have been buying up foreign currencies to sterilize their economies from inflation or an appreciation of their currencies, which would reduce the competitiveness of their countries' exports on world markets.

With current account deficits in excess of $100 billion, the United States is dependent on foreign central banks in developing countries for financing its current account deficits. In such a situation there is pressure to insure that the value of the dollar does not fall precipitously on world markets, and monetary policy has to be watchful that interest rates are kept sufficiently high to encourage inflows of foreign capital.

The demand for foreign capital by both the developing countries and the countries in transition will continue to grow, and there will be a global need for a stable supply of productive long-term capital exports. It is doubtful whether Japan will regain its ability to supply long-term capital within the next few years, given the difficulties being encountered by its financial system. Earlier chapters of this book focused on the need for the United States to increase its domestic saving—both by the federal government and the private sector. If the United States reduced its large dependence on international capital inflows, more capital could be available to meet the needs of the developing nations and the countries in transition toward market economies.

NOTES

1. Charles P. Kindleberger, *International Capital Movements* (Cambridge: Cambridge University Press, 1987), pp. 33–36.

2. Ibid., p. 36.

3. International Monetary Fund, World Economic and Financial Surveys, *World Economic Outlook, October 1993* (Washington, D.C.: International Monetary Fund, 1993), p. 163.

4. IMF, *World Economic Outlook, May 1994*, p. 32. The actual account deficit for Mexico in 1994 was $29.5 billion.

5. Organization for Economic Cooperation and Development, *OECD Economic Outlook*, June 1994 (OECD: Paris, 1994), pp. 26–30.

6. IMF, *World Economic Outlook, May 1994*, pp. 146–47; and *October 1994*, p. 62.

7. Kenneth B. Bercuson and Linda M. Konig, "The Recent Surge in Capital Inflows to Asia: Cause and Macroeconomic Impact." Paper presented at SEACEN/ IMF Seminar, May 14–16, 1993, Seoul, Korea, pp. 2–3. Causes of surges in capital inflows are also discussed in Susan Schadler, Maria Carkovic, Adam Bennett, and Robert Kahn, "Recent Experiences with Surges in Capital Inflows," Occasional Paper 108, International Monetary Fund, 1993, pp. 5–10.

8. IMF, *World Economic Outlook, October 1993*, pp. 75–76; and *October 1994*, p. 53.

9. IMF, *World Economic Outlook, October 1993*, pp. 74–75.

10. Guillermo A. Calvo, Leonardo Leiderman, and Carmen M. Reinhart, "Capital Inflows and Real Exchange Rate Appreciation in Latin America: The Role of External Factors," *International Monetary Fund Staff Papers*, 40, no. 1 (March 1993), p. 109.

11. Ibid., pp. 125–28.

12. Ibid., pp. 128–40.

13. OECD, *OECD Economic Outlook*, December 1993 (Paris: OECD, 1993), pp. 121–22.

14. Ronald I. McKinnon, "Flood of Dollars, Sunken Pesos," *New York Times*, January 20, 1995, p. A29.

15. Ibid.

16. OECD, *OECD Economic Outlook*, June 1993 (Paris: OECD, 1993), pp. 120–21.

17. OECD, *OECD Economic Outlook*, December 1993, p. 116.

18. Ibid., p. 118.

19. Ibid., p. 116.

20. Michael Mussa and Morris Goldstein, "The Integration of World Capital Markets," in *Changing Capital Markets: Implications for Monetary Policy*, paper presented at a symposium sponsored by the Federal Reserve Bank of Kansas City, Jackson Hole, Wyo., August 19–21, 1993, pp. 303–5.

21. IMF, *World Economic Outlook*, May 1994, pp. 75–9.

22. International Monetary Fund, World Economic and Financial Surveys, *Private Market Financing for Developing Countries* (Washington, D.C.: International Monetary Fund), December 1992, p. 31.

23. Bercuson and Konig, "The Recent Surge in Capital Inflows to Asia," pp. 7–9.

24. Ibid., pp. 8–9.

25. International Monetary Fund, World Economic and Financial Surveys, *International Capital Markets, Part II* (Washington, D.C.: International Monetary Fund), August 1993, p. 59.

26. Mussa and Goldstein, "The Integration of World Capital Markets," pp. 303–5.

27. Toyoo Gyohten, "Overview" in Changing Capital Markets symposium, pp. 399–401.

28. Ibid., pp. 402–3.

29. Keith Bradsher, "U.S. Is Attracting New Money Pool," *New York Times*, July 30, 1994, pp. A1 and A4.

CHAPTER 8

Summary and Conclusion

This book has attempted to show the relationship between the development of the U.S. economy into a net importer of capital and the macroeconomic fundamentals that contributed to this change. Although a number of industrial countries incurred large current account deficits in the 1980s and early 1990s and had to import foreign capital, because of its size, the United States had a much greater impact on world capital markets than other countries.

SUMMARY

Changes in Global Capital Markets During the 1980s

The aggregate capital account transactions of the United States increased enormously during the 1980s with the value of total international transactions in securities (bonds and equities) rising from $250 billion to almost $5,500 billion between 1980 and 1989. This huge increment was concentrated largely in bonds rather than equities. Two interesting observations emerge. First, the growth in aggregate U.S. residents' transactions in foreign bonds and equities was much smaller than the growth in foreign transactions in U.S. securities. Second, the increased activity in U.S. securities markets was concentrated predominately in bonds.

Growth in the magnitude of purchases and sales greatly exceeded the growth of capital movements in the 1980s, suggesting that many of the transactions were actually short term and that the relative positions of different countries could have been rapidly reversed. Such transactions are a part of the widening and deepening of international capital markets that occurred during the 1980s.

Aggregate capital flows include all transactions between residents and nonresidents and therefore correspond to "turnover" in financial assets; they do not correspond to gross outflows (or inflows) that come from a country's balance-of-payments figures for gross capital flows. To determine the net capital inflow (or outflow) for a country, gross outflows in the balance of payments are subtracted from gross inflows.

A central concern of this volume is the switch of the United States from being a net exporter of capital to being a net importer. The net inflow of capital on the balance of payments (current account deficit) represents the import of savings from abroad, and these foreign savings make up the difference between total domestic investment and domestic saving.

Although small current account deficits had occurred before, the United States began running large current account deficits in 1983 when the deficit rose to $43.6 billion. Thereafter, it rose continuously, reaching $167.1 billion in 1987, two years after the value of the dollar had peaked after increasing 58 percent between 1980 and February 1985. In a lagged response to the depreciation of the dollar that had commenced in 1985, the current account deficit began to decline in 1988, and fell to $91.7 billion in 1990. In 1991 it fell to $6.9 billion, to a large extent reflecting transfers from U.S. allies during and after the Gulf War. In 1992 and 1993, even though the value of the dollar remained relatively stable, demand for U.S. exports slackened because of weakness in the economies of other industrial countries, and the current account deficit rose to $67.9 billion in 1992 and $103.9 billion in 1993. Because import volume is projected to rise faster than export volume, the deficit is projected to rise to about $170 billion by 1995. Even though Europe and Japan are expected to be recovering from recession by 1995 only moderate economic growth of about 3 percent in Europe and 2.5 percent in Japan is projected.

Because the overall balance of payments must balance, large capital inflows occurred, and in 1987 the United States became a net debtor instead of a net creditor. Inflows of capital that brought about balance-of-payments equilibrium in the United States during the 1980s were provided by both private and public sources. In a number of years, the United States relied on the net inflow of private capital, but during years when private inflows were insufficient, foreign central banks made up the difference by purchasing U.S. government securities.

The large growth of capital inflows into the United States during the 1980s coincided with growing integration into the world economy and structural changes that were occurring in the world financial system.

Liberalization of restrictions on the international movement of foreign exchange and capital as well as cost-reducing technological innovations in financial markets that greatly reduced transaction costs have helped to produce intense competition in the financial systems of major industrial countries. By the early 1990s, domestic financial markets had become more adaptive and international, and segmented financial structures were becoming broader based and integrated. It is argued that competition led to disintermediation from banking systems, especially from wholesale banking, into securitized money and capital markets. Three factors—liberalization, technological innovations in financial markets, and securitization—are structural changes that occurred simultaneously with changes in movements in the U.S. capital account.

Foreign Direct Investment

Although the United States became the recipient of large foreign direct investment inflows in the late 1970s, it was not until 1981 that the inflow of foreign direct investment into the United States exceeded outflows. Between 1981 and 1991, with inflows exceeding outflows, the United States was a net importer of foreign direct investment.

Although the role of foreign direct investment in the U.S. economy grew substantially during the 1980s, these affiliates still played a relatively small role when compared to the size of the U.S. economy. For instance, by 1990, foreign-owned nonbank affiliates produced only 4.4 percent of U.S. GDP and accounted for 5 percent of employment. Even in manufacturing, where foreign direct investment was more important, in 1990 affiliates employed only 10.5 percent of manufacturing employment and accounted for 14.5 percent of sales and 13.5 percent of value added. U.S. affiliates' share of the book value of total assets of all U.S. manufacturing businesses amounted to over 18.6 percent.

During the 1980s, U.S. affiliates of foreign firms played an increasing role in the U.S. economy. Their share in nonbank gross product rose from 2.3 to 3.5 percent between 1977 and 1981, and by 1990 this share had increased to 4.4 percent. U.S. affiliates were important contributors to the growth in output in manufacturing, and their share in gross product of all manufacturing rose from 3.7 to 8.6 percent between 1977 and 1987. This share rose to 11.5 percent in 1990. Affiliates' growth in employment increased faster than for all U.S. nonbank employment and for manufacturing alone. Between 1977 and 1990, employment by nonbank affiliates almost quadrupled, rising from 1.2 to 4.7 million workers, at the same time that employment by all nonbank U.S. businesses rose by a little over one-fourth. As a share of all nonbank employment, the share of affiliates rose from 1.8 to 5.1 percent.

Proponents of inward foreign direct investment cite the benefits to the host country, often arguing that foreign firms are a source of technological change, and therefore contribute to productivity growth. A U.S. Department of Commerce study has shown that in both 1980 and 1987, average gross productivity per employee increased more rapidly for U.S. manufacturing affiliates than in the manufacturing sector as a whole, and that average earnings of workers employed by foreign firms were greater than the average received by all U.S. workers.[1] However, these differences in compensation are largely a result of differences in industrial compensation. A heavy concentration of foreign firms in capital-intensive industries such as petroleum refining and mining raises the average compensation per employee of U.S. affiliates.

Research and development outlays of foreign affiliates can create externalities when the technologies so developed are transferred to the rest of the economy. It has been shown that U.S. affiliates contribute to the technology base of U.S. industry by both the inward transfer of technology from foreign parents and from in-house technology improvements. One indicator of technology inflow is the ratio of R&D expenditures to gross output—the technology intensity of output. In 1987 the technology intensity for U.S. manufacturing affiliates was somewhat greater than for all U.S. manufacturing firms. Another indicator is R&D outlays per worker. Although a comparison of R&D per worker shows outlays per worker in U.S. affiliates in manufacturing are less than for U.S.-owned manufacturing firms, when federally funded R&D expenditures are excluded, outlays per worker in U.S. affiliates become fairly comparable to outlays in U.S.-owned firms. Concerning R&D outlays, the data indicate that U.S. affiliates' behavior is similar to U.S.-owned firms, and that there is no sign of a "headquarters effect," whereby foreign firms undertake a disproportionately large share of their research spending in the home country.

The data show a number of characteristics for export and import behavior of U.S. affiliates. First, the data do show a declining role of exports and imports as a percentage of sales of foreign affiliates. But, when affiliates' merchandise exports and imports are compared to total U.S. merchandise exports and imports, the role of affiliates' imports becomes increasingly significant. For instance, from an average of 31 percent of total merchandise imports in the early 1980s, the affiliates' share rose to 37 percent in 1990 and 1991. However, the share of exports declined somewhat, falling from 27 percent in the early 1980s to an average of over 23 percent in 1989–91. U.S. affiliates engaged in distribution account for the dominant share of exports and imports. For instance, in 1991, wholesale and retail trade accounted for almost two-thirds of affiliates' imports and 53 percent of affiliates' exports. In addition, much of the merchandise trade of U.S. affiliates is with the affiliates' foreign parent groups. In 1987–91, intrafirm trade accounted for about 40 percent of the exports and 75 percent of the imports of all U.S. affiliates. The large share of intrafirm imports reflects the role of many of these affiliates as distributors for their parent companies. A U.S. Department of Commerce study has shown that in 1991, import content (the share of imports) in total purchased inputs was 20 percent, or more than twice the share imported by U.S. parent companies.[2] For manufacturing, the difference between the import content shares for U.S. affiliates and for U.S. parent companies was more modest—16 percent as compared with 11 percent. Edward Graham and Paul Krugman have shown that in terms of imports per worker, U.S. affiliates imported more than twice the amount per worker employed in domestic manufacturing than did domestically owned firms.[3] Had these firms been domestically owned, total U.S. merchandise imports would have been about 4 percent lower than without direct investment, and the equilibrium dollar exchange rate would have been slightly higher.

To explain motivations for foreign direct investment in the United States, the various theories of foreign direct investment were examined in order to comprehend whether this phenomenon can be better explained by factors causing balance-of-payments problems and the reversal of the U.S. capital account during the 1980s, or if factors related to the growth and maturity of foreign-controlled firms and the relative decline of U.S. technological and managerial leadership can better explain this phenomenon.

Theories explaining foreign direct investment can be classified into cost of capital and theory of the firm explanations. According to cost of capital explanations, foreign direct investment occurs because any given cash flow is valued more highly by the foreign firm because it has a lower cost of capital than domestic firms. The experience of the United States during the 1980s had renewed interest in cost of capital explanations. The United States was plunged into the status of a net debtor at the same time that total foreign claims on the United States, including foreign direct investment, greatly increased. One type of cost of capital explanation describes foreign direct investment as an outcome of the existence of imperfections in both foreign exchange and capital markets. Foreign direct investment is viewed as an outcome of the existence of different currency areas and occurs when source-country firms are able to capitalize the same stream of earnings at a higher rate than host-country firms because the market is able to give different capitalization rates to future streams of income that are denominated in different currencies.

Another cost of capital explanation associates changes in the levels of exchange rates with foreign direct investment flows. The desire to engage in portfolio diversification offers another explanation of foreign direct investment.

By the early 1970s, the leading theoretical explanation of foreign direct investment was the industrial organization theory. Even though production abroad entails disadvantages such as additional costs and risks, large oligopolistic firms produce overseas because they possess internal firm-specific (ownership) advantages enabling them to obtain higher profits than domestic firms. Because of these firm-specific advantages, it is more profitable to produce abroad instead of either licensing or producing at home and exporting. These advantages can stem from market imperfections in the goods market, economies of scale both internal and external to the firm, and government-imposed market imperfections.

Another widely accepted theoretical explanation of multinational production is internalization theory. According to the industrial organization theory, there are many firm-specific advantages. Instead of selling or leasing these advantages to other firms, multinationals choose to internalize these ownership-specific advantages across national boundaries within their own organization, either replacing the market or, alternatively, augmenting it. Internalization takes place because of market imperfections and their impact on transactions costs. An explanation that parallels internalization theory is the appropriability theory. According to this theory, the need to appropriate the private returns from investment in information becomes an explanation of foreign direct investment.

John H. Dunning proposed a general theory, the eclectic theory, that integrated much of the existing body of information concerning foreign direct investment.[4] This theory drew upon three areas of economics—industrial organization theory, the Coaseian theory of the firm, and international trade theory.

To serve particular markets, the investing firm must possess net ownership assets that are exclusive or specific to the investing firm. Ownership advantages are of three types—those stemming from exclusive possession of or access to particular income-generating assets, those generally enjoyed by a branch plant as opposed to a separately established firm, and those resulting from geographical diversification or multinationality.

Because of market failure, it may be more beneficial for the firm to bypass the market and internalize its ownership advantages rather than to sell or lease them to other firms. The three main types of market failure that lead to internalization are those arising from risk and uncertainty; those stemming from the ability of firms to exploit the economies of large-scale production, but only in imperfect competition; and those occurring when the transactions in a particular good or service yield costs and benefits external to the transaction, but not reflected in the terms agreed to by the transacting parties. In addition to market imperfections, enterprises may internalize activities because of government intervention in resource allocation.

Whereas ownership and internalization advantages are enterprise-specific, research has shown that location-specific advantages are also important determinants of foreign direct investment. During the 1950s and 1960s, researchers frequently used location theories and international trade theories to explain why multinationals choose to produce in one country rather than in another. Examples of location-specific advantages include prices, quality, and productivity of inputs; government intervention in the forms of tariffs, nontariff barriers, tax rates, foreign investment incentives, and political stability; foreign exchange effects from locating in one country rather than another; the large size of the market in the host country; and psychic closeness of cultures in the host and home countries.

The eclectic paradigm of international production depends on the coming together of ownership-specific advantages, the propensity to internalize these advantages across international borders through managerial control over foreign operations, and the relative attractiveness for production of the foreign location.

It is probable that it was not the movement of the United States into a net debtor position, but rather the growing preeminence of other major nations in the world economy that propelled foreign direct investment growth in the United States in the 1980s. When foreign firms reached maturity, they developed firm-specific (ownership) advantages, including their accumulation of technological and managerial skills. This explanation conforms more to industrial organization explanations than to cost of capital explanations.

The trend toward the United States increasingly becoming a host country for direct investment had begun prior to the chronic current account deficits of the 1980s. First, although smaller than in the 1980s, foreign direct investment in the United States increased significantly during the 1970s, a period during which the U.S. current account deficit was not persistently in deficit. As a result, the share of foreign investment stock in GDP increased continuously, rising from 1.5 percent of GDP in 1973 to 2.2 percent in 1979. By 1991 this share had increased to 7.1 percent. Second, the U.S. net foreign direct investment position has undergone significant change since the 1970s as the United States was increasingly becoming a host country for foreign direct investment. The net foreign direct investment position (the ratio of U.S. direct investment stock abroad to direct investment stock in the United States) fell from more than 4 in 1977 to a little over 1 in 1991.

The Saving Deficiency in the United States

A shortage of U.S. savings has created a situation in which the United States has had to import enormous amounts of foreign capital. Starting in the early 1980s, large federal government budgetary deficits and a declining personal saving rate caused the gross national saving rate to fall from 20.8 percent of GDP in 1977–81 to 14.9 percent in 1993—a drop of almost 6 percent of GDP. Even though the rate of domestic investment declined continuously during the 1980s, falling from an average of 21 percent of GDP in 1977–81 to 15.2 percent in 1991 before increasing to 16.2 percent as the economy began to recover from recession (a drop of 4.8 percent for the period), domestic investment continuously exceeded domestic saving, and the deficiencies were made up by the import of capital from abroad. At the same time, Japan, with its high rates of private and public savings that generated savings surpluses, supplied much of the U.S. capital requirements until 1991. Medium-term forecasts for the United States predict that U.S. savings-investment imbalances and current account deficits will continue to rise in 1994 and 1995 because the United States has made more progress in recovering from recession than the other industrial countries.

It is necessary to consider prospects for raising the U.S. rate of saving. There are three components to the national saving rate: the personal (house-hold) saving rate, the business saving rate, and the government saving rate. Since the early 1980s, the business saving rate has remained fairly constant, but the personal and government saving rates have declined.

Since the 1980s, enormous federal budget deficits reduced the national saving rate and brought about large capital inflows. Government borrowing added excessively to the demand for capital, and for much of the period the real interest rates remained high by historical standards. High real interest rates contributed to a large dollar appreciation in the early 1980s and re-tarded the growth of domestic investment and capital formation.

The American public became increasingly aware of the problem of the large budget deficits during the 1992 presidential elections, and in August 1993 the Clinton administration oversaw the passage of the Omnibus Budget Reconciliation Act of 1993, a major package of revenue increases and spending reductions. In the autumn of 1993 it was estimated that OBRA 1993 would reduce cumulative federal deficits between fiscal year 1994 through 1998 by $433 billion, compared with baseline projections produced in the winter of 1993. Estimates for yearly deficits that were pro-jected in August 1994 show a reduction of the cumulative five-year total by an additional $115 billion. These additional savings result from revised pro-jections of economic growth, a lower overall inflation rate in 1993 than was originally forecast, and technical reestimates.

It has been estimated that more than one-half of the deficit reduction ($278 billion) would come from changes in tax policies that raise revenues— $115 billion in saving would come from revenue measures that restore some of the progressivity of the U.S. federal income tax structure that had been reduced by the Economic Recovery Act of 1981, and the remainder would come from other revenue measures, including higher taxes on gasoline, re-peal of the cap on earnings subject to the Medicare payroll tax, increased taxing of Social Security benefits, raising the corporate income tax, and re-ducing the deductible part of business entertainment.

It was estimated that the remaining $270 billion in budget reduction over the five-year period would come from expenditure reductions, including $122 billion in cuts in mandatory spending: $67 billion from limitations on discretionary spending, and $63 billion from savings on the public debt.

OBRA 1993 reduces the projected size of the federal deficit in 1998 from

$360 billion estimated in the winter of 1993 to an estimated $197 billion. However, the budget agreement must be regarded as only a first step in efforts to reduce the size of the deficit. This is necessary because rising Medicare and Medicaid costs will cause the deficit to grow significantly after 1998, and if current policies are maintained, the deficit is projected to rise to $397 billion in 2004. Furthermore, several factors could retard the amount of deficit reduction that could occur by 1998. Most important, if the rate of growth of real GDP projected to grow by an average rate of 2.7 percent a year during 1994–98 were slower or another recession were to occur, actual federal deficits would be higher than estimated because revenues lower than projected and outlays on categories such as food stamps and unemployment insurance that were higher than projected over the period would affect the deficit. An inflation rate greater than the average rate of about 3 percent that is projected would also affect the deficit. Another factor that could change federal deficits is health care reform. One other outlay that could easily change is the amount spent on servicing the public debt, which was projected at 3.2 percent of GDP by 1998. If inflation is higher than the projection of 3 percent a year, real interest rates greater than projected, and GDP growth slower than projected, net interest on the debt could exceed 3.2 percent of GDP in 1998.

The fastest growing part of federal outlays over the next decade will be mandatory expenditures as opposed to discretionary expenditures. The largest components in mandatory federal expenditures are Social Security, and Medicaid and Medicare, which combined now contribute 54 percent to federal outlays and are projected to rise to 59 percent in 1998 and 63 percent in 2004. By the year 2020, very little could be left for discretionary outlays when many of the baby boom generation reach retirement age if changes are not made in the system of entitlements.

Although federal deficit reduction will increase national saving, saving will not rise by the full amount of the reduction in the deficit because tax increases, by reducing disposable income, will offset some of the improvement in government saving. The Congressional Budget Office estimated that this reduction in disposable income will lower private saving and offset about 30 percent of the estimated reduction in the deficit.[5] The Congressional Budget Office has estimated that allowing for higher taxes, deficit reduction would raise the national saving rate by 1.4 percent of GDP in 1998. A reduction in the deficit would reduce the federal government's borrowing from abroad. It has been estimated that somewhere between 32 and 47 percent of deficit reduction would go toward the reduction of net capital inflows from abroad and would not be available for domestic investment. In conjunction with the reduction in disposable income, the reduction of net capital inflows associated with deficit reduction means that only about 30 percent of the reduction in government borrowing would be available for private investment.

Additional deficit reduction could also be achieved if the economy were to grow more rapidly than the 2.7 percent per annum projected over the 1990s. A plan that was proposed to stimulate the economy by giving $50 billion (about 1 percent of GDP) a year in grants-in-aid for state and local governments to engage in spending increases for education and physical infrastructure, plus restoration of the Investment Tax Credit that served the economy well in 1962–86, could propel the economy toward higher economic growth. If economic growth were to average 4 percent a year until 1998 instead of the 2.7 percent projected by the CBO, revenues could grow by an additional $100 billion, raising the national saving rate by another 0.9 percent a year. Furthermore, smaller deficits would reduce interest payments on the federal debt.

Raising the personal saving rate would increase the national saving rate. A decline of almost 2.0 percent of GDP in personal saving occurred during the 1980s. An examination of some of the theoretical literature on saving could help to assess factors causing a drop in the personal saving rate.

J. M. Keynes in *The General Theory* explained that the ratio of saving to income increases as society becomes richer.[6] This theory of the consumption function fits empirical observations when savings behavior is observed for a given time period, but when averaged over major business cycles, the saving rate for the United States is fairly stable. During the 1950s Milton Friedman's permanent income hypothesis and Franco Modigliani's life-cycle hypothesis were developed to explain this inconsistency.[7] Both of these hypotheses are forward looking; the consuming unit is regarded as having a current income from income and wealth as well as plans and expectations about its future income. Given its vision of future needs, the consuming unit's decisions on current consumption and saving reflect an attempt to achieve an optimum pattern of total consumption over its lifetime.

Friedman's hypothesis makes the simplifying assumptions that life is indefinitely long and that consumers base their expenditures on their perceptions of expected or "permanent" income. The marginal propensity to consume out of permanent income is high, but the marginal propensity to consume out of transitory income is low.

Modigliani in the life-cycle hypothesis assumes that the household has a finite lifetime. As in the permanent income hypothesis, the individual prefers to maintain a stable consumption pattern, but unlike Friedman, Modigliani adds the concept of a "lifetime budget constraint," whereby the household's consumption over a lifetime equals income from work plus income from asset holdings from other sources such as gifts and bequests. Some of the implications that necessarily follow from the life-cycle hypothesis are that the saving rate of a country is independent of per capita income; an individual's life-cycle savings can be consistent with different generational saving rates between countries with identical individual behavior; the aggregate saving rate will be higher the higher is the long-run growth rate of the economy; an economy can accumulate a substantial stock of wealth even if no wealth is passed on by bequests; and the prevailing rate of retirement is the major factor controlling the wealth-income ratio and saving rate for any given growth rate.

The usefulness of the life-cycle hypothesis is affected by a controversy over the role of bequests. According to the life-cycle hypothesis, most of the existing wealth is accumulated because labor income tapers off after retirement, and bequests are not a major source of existing wealth. Modigliani observed that the proportion of existing wealth that has been inherited is not greater than 25 percent and that bequests are important only for those in the very highest income bracket. Although a number of studies find that intergenerational transfers are important in wealth accumulation in the United States, much of the difference between the results of different studies can result from differences defining income and wealth.

The preceding text has discussed two motives for saving: the life-cycle motive, which focuses on the desire of the household to save for retirement, and the bequest motive, which deals with those savings that are accumulated to leave bequests for future generations. A third motive, the precautionary motive, focuses on the desire to save for unforeseen events such as the length of a lifetime, inflation, health emergencies, and unemployment. The precautionary motive can be easily integrated into the life-cycle motive.

A number of factors could have caused the large drop in the U.S. personal saving rate. A very important assumption of the life-cycle hypothesis is that for countries with identical individual behavior, the saving rate will be higher the higher is the long-run growth rate for the economy. Barry Bosworth compared saving rates with long-term growth rates for fifteen industrial countries.[8] Comparing rates of private saving (private saving as a percentage of net domestic product) with rates of economic growth, he found that high saving rates for individual countries coincided with high growth rates for the period prior to the 1973 oil shock; and after 1973 when growth rates for all of the fifteen industrial countries slowed, saving rates declined for all of these countries except for Canada. Probably the most important factor affecting the decline in the private saving rate was the fall in the rate of economic growth following the 1973 oil shock and the acceleration of inflation.

For much of the period 1965–93, personal saving rates appear to have been positively related to large increases in inflation. Despite a secular decline in the U.S. personal saving rate, periods of rapid increase in inflation rates were accompanied by higher personal saving rates. For instance, expectations that the Federal Reserve might react to inflation by tightening monetary policy, which would cause a recession, as well as a loss of confidence in the adequacy of savings to pay for inflated future living costs, may account for the positive relationship between saving rates and inflation.

Economic growth rates can be affected by productivity changes and demographics. With productivity growth, the younger working-age cohorts of the population will have larger lifetime resources than the retired cohorts, and this would make the savings of the younger cohorts larger than for the retired cohorts if people planned their consumption as if they were not anticipating a future growth in income. For the industrial countries, productivity slowed markedly following the 1973 oil shock. For the United States, productivity growth between 1939 and 1973 averaged 3.0 percent compared to an average of 0.9 percent after 1973. Were productivity growth to increase, it is plausible that the U.S. saving rate would also increase.

Two types of demographic changes—the rising percentage of people between the ages of 45 and 64 and the rising percentage of those in retirement—are expected to affect the saving rate. A large increase in the percentage of retirees is expected to occur after the first decade of the twenty-first century, when members of the baby boom generation will begin to reach retirement age. By the late 1990s, many of the workers born in the 1920s and 1930s (a relatively small cohort group) will become retired dissavers at the same time that many of the large group in the baby boom generation will have begun to worry about retirement. The fact that members of the baby boom generation, unlike the generation born in the 1920s and 1930s, have had low propensities to save could have great significance for the U.S. private saving rate. Using the life-cycle hypothesis, one might be able to predict that if this large cohort group would significantly increase its saving as it approaches retirement, the personal saving rate would go up. According to the life-cycle hypothesis, by the mid-1990s, many of this generation will have begun to worry about having enough savings for their retirement and will need to greatly increase their rate of saving.

The standard theories of saving imply that individuals plan for a given amount of wealth for their retirement, and individuals would tend to reduce their saving if the ratio of wealth to disposable income rises. Revaluation of asset values during the rise of real estate values in the 1970s and the stock market boom of the 1980s contributed about three-fourths to the growth in wealth during the 1980s. The wealth-to-disposable-income ratio rose at the same time that the saving rate fell.

During the 1980s, consumers were increasing debt relative to their wealth and disposable income. At the same time that the debt-to-wealth ratio surged and the ratio of household interest payments to disposable income increased, the personal saving rate plummeted. The saving rate increased a little during and after the recession of 1990–91, when consumer confidence fell and consumers reduced spending and borrowing to strengthen balance sheets.

Although the real rate of return on wealth has the potential of affecting the saving rate, both the theory of saving and empirical evidence have been ambiguous about the direction in which the increased returns affect the saving rate. During the early 1980s, high real interest rates and reduced marginal tax brackets raised the fraction of after-tax income that savers could keep, but starting in the mid-1980s, the rate of personal saving fell. By giving households greater access to credit, financial liberalization and deregulation in the 1980s may have been factors contributing to the low rate of personal saving during the second half of the 1980s.

A number of studies of saving that provide additional insight into motivations for saving (including the role of demographics) in the United States are examined.

Robert Mundell argues that as the large junior generation (the baby boom generation) in the United States matures to become net savers, saving will rise, and by the late 1990s and until after the first decade of the twenty-first century when baby boomers retire, there will be excess saving, substantial capital outflows, and current account surpluses.[9]

Michael Boskin and Lawrence Lau also argue that demographics will increase personal saving rates.[10] One focal point in studies by Boskin and Lau is the dependence of U.S. consumption and saving on the age and vintage distribution of resources—as represented by Depression and post-Depression households. It is argued that changes in the age and vintage distribution of household wealth in the United States led to changed patterns of aggregate consumption and saving. Whereas aggregate consumption expenditures grew at an annual rate of 2.89 percent a year in 1950–62, by 1963–80 this growth accelerated to 3.27 percent a year. During the second subperiod (1963–80), the most important sources of growth of real consumption per household were the fall in the share of wealth held by the Depression-vintage households and the age distribution of wealth that, together, accounted for 56 percent of the rate of growth in real consumption per household.

It was concluded that large changes in the distribution of income and wealth in the United States in 1950–80 significantly affected aggregate consumption and saving. The movement of the Depression generation into ages where their saving propensities increased was more than offset by the large post-Depression generation, which had higher propensities to consume. Had the saving rates of the post-Depression vintage been similar to those of the Depression vintage, the personal saving rate would have been more than twice its 1980 level.

In the future, because the share of wealth held by Depression-vintage households has significantly declined, it is not expected that this decline can contribute much to a further drop in the aggregate personal saving rate, and as post-Depression-vintage households age and plan for retirement, their saving rate is expected to rise. Because the younger working group is relatively small compared to the baby boom generation, it is predicted that the saving rate would rise until the end of the first decade of the twenty-first century.

A study by the Brookings Institution that uses microeconomic household survey data is not so optimistic about future increases in the personal saving rate.[11] Referring to the life-cycle hypothesis, the authors examined whether changes in the age structure of the population could have contributed to the decline in the U.S. saving rate. Using consumer expenditure surveys, they found that during the 1980s saving rates declined for almost all age groups and that the evidence did not corroborate the idea that the decline in savings was concentrated in the younger, baby boom generation. Instead of the entry of the large baby boom generation into the labor force, they argued that it was a sharp reduction in saving by middle-aged and older consumers that caused the personal saving rate to fall. Not only did saving rates drop for all age groups, but forecasts indicated that the demographic shift of baby boomers into older age groups would had have only a small impact on future saving rates.

The authors also examined whether the savers who were owners of wealth that had been revalued upward during the 1970s and 1980s contributed to the drop in the saving rate and found no support for the idea that reduced saving in the United States in the early 1980s was concentrated among consumers who were owners of financial assets that had increased in value. However, the large rise in home prices during the 1970s may have helped cause a drop in saving, thereby implying that the wealth effect does affect the saving rate.

Bosworth, in the study cited above, measured the impact of a number of factors on the rates of saving in the industrial countries. As noted above, the most uniform finding was a positive relationship between saving rates and income growth. Inflation also has consistently positive effects on savings. The relationship between demographic factors and saving was also tested. Coefficients were statistically significant for the demographic variable in five countries. Bosworth also empirically tested the relationship between other factors and saving. For the relationship between interest rates and savings, coefficients were statistically significant for only two countries. There was a small but highly significant correlation between government and private saving, indicating some trade-off between government saving and private saving and giving some limited credence to the Barro-Ricardo equivalence theory.

The precautionary motive has also been used to explain saving. Under the precautionary motive, people save for emergencies. Unemployment represents a serious emergency, and pessimism about the possibility of unemployment might affect saving behavior. A study by Christopher Carroll on the "buffer-stock" model of saving gives a central role to unemployment expectations.[12] Carroll argues that consumers hold assets to shield their consumption against unpredictable fluctuations in income. In the model, unemployment expectations are key, and during a cyclical downturn when consumers become more pessimistic about unemployment and uncertain about future income, their target buffer stock increases and they raise saving.

Changes in the expected probability of "bad events" have a major impact on current levels of consumption and saving. The fundamental message provided by Carroll's results is that precautionary saving is important for understanding the cyclical behavior of consumption and saving.

Carroll also applies the results to explain the secular decline in the personal saving rate over the past fifteen to twenty years as well as the low level of consumption in the early 1990s. In the buffer-stock model, the long-run decline in the personal saving rate can be explained by either a fall in the rate of growth or a fall in the target wealth-to-disposable-income ratio. Using the buffer-stock model, it is explained that no more than one-half of the saving rate decline could have been caused by the drop in the growth rate of per capita personal income in the 1980s. It is then explained that declining income uncertainty and relaxation of liquidity constraints may have helped reduce the target wealth-to-disposable-income ratio in the past twenty years. Income uncertainty may have been reduced by the growth in the percentage of two-earner families and the long economic expansion in the 1980s. Carroll then suggests that the low income growth rate and high unemployment rate of the early 1990s could have been instrumental in increasing saving rates by increasing the target ratio of income to wealth.

Policies to Raise the U.S. Saving Rate

Potential policies to raise the saving rate were examined. To raise the public saving rate, measures must be implemented to reduce the deficit beyond the level that it is estimated will result from OBRA 1993. The Congressional Budget Office has estimated that the federal deficit will decline from 3.0 percent of GDP in fiscal year 1994 to a low of 2.3 percent in 1995 and then rise to 2.4 percent in 1998 and 3.6 percent in 2004 if no further deficit reduction measures are implemented. Although discretionary outlays as a share of GDP are projected to decline continuously from 8.2 percent in 1994 to 6.1 percent in 2004, beginning in 1996 the deficit will rise as a share of GDP because of rising Medicare and Medicaid outlays. Policy measures are also needed to help raise the personal saving rate, even though demographic factors may raise this rate.

A program for additional federal budget deficit reduction should involve both spending cuts and revenue increases. Discretionary outlays are estimated to decline from 8.2 percent of GDP in 1994 to 6.1 percent by 2004. It would be difficult for sizable reductions to come from further cuts in these outlays. Further increases in tax revenues and reductions in mandatory outlays will be needed to achieve additional deficit reduction.

Federal revenues averaged 18.6 percent of GDP over 1960–93. It has been estimated that federal revenues will rise to 19.3 percent of GDP in 1995–96, but will then fall to 18.9 percent by 2004. To bring about additional deficit reduction, serious consideration will have to be given to measures to raise additional revenue. Increased excise taxes on alcoholic beverages and cigarettes would be a good source of additional revenues. It is recommended that excise taxes be raised to $1 a pack on cigarettes and $16 per proof gallon on all alcoholic beverages. The Congressional Budget Office has estimated that these two measures could raise over $15 million in additional revenue in 1995 or a total of $76.6 billion in additional revenues over the five-year period 1995–99. In addition to raising revenue, these measures would offset some of the external costs to society from use of these products, including higher health insurance and medical costs. Furthermore, if higher excise taxes reduce consumption of these products, external costs are reduced.

It is strongly recommended that an increase of motor fuel taxes of 10 cents per gallon each year for five years be included in part of an overall energy policy focused on making the United States less dependent on foreign sources of petroleum and reducing pollution. This would raise an additional $42.2 billion of revenue by 1999, or a cumulative five-year addition of $127.3 billion. In addition, some of the external cost imposed on society in the form of pollution and road congestion would be included in the price of gasoline, and less gasoline would be consumed.

A 5 percent national retail sales tax could significantly raise revenue and would help balance the budget. The burden on lower income households could be reduced to about 2.5 percent if tax credits were given to these households. Because a national retail sales tax does have drawbacks, such as incentives for tax evasion and the lack of an effective credit mechanism for taxes businesses pay on their purchases, most countries having general consumption taxes have chosen the value added tax (VAT) over the national sales tax. Substituting a VAT for the present federal income tax would sacrifice the built-in-flexibility of the present tax structure. The pros and cons of substituting the present tax structure with a VAT must be seriously considered. It is proposed that, instead of relying on the sales tax or even a VAT that is regressive and reduces the built-in flexibility of the present progressive income tax structure, serious consideration be given to increasing revenues by further increases of federal income taxes in the higher tax brackets.

A number of other measures are recommended to raise additional revenue. Several of these measures involve repealing indexing of the federal income tax, limiting the deductibility of home mortgage interest, eliminating in most cases the deductibility of home equity loans, and taxing employer-paid health insurance above a certain minimum and other nonretirement fringe benefits. It is recommended that the three highest income tax bracket rates be raised to 33, 38, and 42 percent; and that the alternative minimum tax be raised to 30 percent.

It is also recommended that measures be taken to retard the growth of entitlement spending. Because much of the entitlement spending goes for individuals or households with incomes greater than $50,000, one recommendation considered in Chapter 5 was the implementation of an "affluence test" or "graduated entitlement benefit reduction" for middle- and high-income beneficiaries. It has been recently estimated that reducing entitlement benefits for these recipients could reduce entitlement outlays by about $9 billion in fiscal year 1995 and $190 billion over a five-year period, and that this option would take away an average of one-quarter of the benefits from about one-fifth of all recipients.[13] Making entitlements subject to federal individual income taxes and denying entitlements to high-income recipients are two other possible policy options put forth to address the problem of surging entitlement spending.[14]

The option that makes entitlements subject to federal individual income taxes would tax benefits not attributable to past contributions of recipients. Under this option, entitlements subject to federal income taxes would include 85 percent of all Social Security and Railroad Retirement benefits, 85 percent of the insurance value of Medicare hospital benefits, and the full insurance value of Medicare Supplementary Medical Insurance less premiums paid. Implementing this option during the 1995 tax year would raise $18 billion in additional revenues in fiscal year 1995 and $258 billion over five years. It was estimated that taxes from making more entitlements taxable would average 10 percent of benefits for two-thirds of families receiving entitlements.

The final option would deny entitlements to high-income recipients. This option approximates recent legislative proposals. One such proposal would phase out entitlements at a rate of 50 percent for single people having 1995 nonentitlement income in excess of $100,000 and for couples with nonentitlement incomes in excess of $120,000. When income exceeded these limits by $10,000 or more, all entitlements would be taken away. This proposal would reduce entitlement spending by $4 billion in fiscal year 1995 and $45 billion over a five-year period. Only the richest 1 percent of entitlement recipients would be affected by this proposal.

Because many of the measures recommended above can have contractionary impacts on the economy, it is recommended that some elements of a stimulatory fiscal policy be combined with cutbacks in outlays and revenue increases. It is recommended that a stimulatory fiscal policy be combined with attempts to achieve further deficit reduction.

One such proposal is to let the economy grow its way out of the deficit. Between 1947 and 1979, GDP growth averaged 3.5 percent a year, but between 1980 and 1993, the growth rate averaged only 2.2 percent a year. For 1994–95, the Congressional Budget Office has forecast that real economic growth will average 3.5 percent a year, but this rate is projected to average only 2.2 percent over 1996–99. Because revenues are elastic with respect to growth in GDP, an average growth rate that is in excess of 3 percent a year during 1996–99 would raise additional revenues. In addition, expenditures on unemployment insurance would be lower, and, as a consequence of smaller deficits, interest outlays to service the public debt would grow more slowly.

Growth in the economy affects the deficit. Assuming that real economic growth were 1 percent lower than the annual average of over 2.6 percent projected for 1994–99, it has been projected that by 1999 revenues would be almost $120 billion less than currently projected; changes in outlays (net interest and other) would be about $30 billion greater; and the deficit would be almost $150 billion higher. This means that if annual economic growth were to average 3.2 percent a year over the period 1994–99, instead of the 2.7 percent average now forecast, about $75 billion could be subtracted from the deficit in 1999, leaving a deficit of $156 billion instead of $235 billion.

Low growth rates since 1979 imply that the deficiency of aggregate demand and not low saving has been the principal constraint on the economy. During the 1980s, consumption was high and investment as a fraction of GDP declined. For GDP to grow rapidly, it is necessary for investment to be high. If investment expands, GDP will grow more rapidly, and with higher GDP, savings will rise. Thus, in the Keynesian sense, investment determines saving.

For investment, economic growth, and saving to be high, it is necessary to have a macroeconomic policy mix where investment is encouraged relative to consumption. After the recession of the early 1980s, the real rate of interest was 3 to 4 percent greater than following most other recessions, and the investment rate was less than during previous recoveries. To get the economy back to average growth rates prevailing prior to 1980, what is needed is a policy mix in which monetary policy geared toward keeping real interest rates low is combined with a fiscal policy that encourages investment.

To achieve higher rates of economic growth, it is recommended that a certain amount of federal revenues—for instance, an amount equal to 1 percent of GDP—be directed toward physical and social infrastructure and R&D expenditures. Expenditures on education and training for high-technology developments will be crucial for the skills required in the twenty-first century, and much of the physical infrastructure of this nation is old and falling apart and requires repairs and rebuilding. R&D outlays are needed to keep the United States in the forefront in the twenty-first century. Expenditures on R & D and infrastructure can provide a lot of economic growth in the future. Finally, it is recommended that the Investment Tax Credit be reinstated in order to encourage growth of investment.

Policy options have been suggested to raise the rate of private saving. However, it must be remembered that taxation affects saving basically by changing the after-tax rate of return, and the saving response to changes in the after-tax rate of return has been shown by empirical studies to be basically uncertain. The response to a change in the after-tax rate of return is dependent on the interest elasticity of saving, which depends on the strength of the income and substitution effects. These two effects work against each other, and the outcome is ambiguous. An increase in the real interest rate (or rate of return) makes current consumption more expensive, and the household is induced to postpone consumption (the substitution effect). If the substitution effect were the only effect from the increase in the rate of return, one could state categorically that the increase in the after-tax rate of return would increase saving. But the income effect of an increase in the after-tax rate of return works in the opposite direction, which is to raise consumption now and in the future.

Three possible policy options to increase the level of saving were set forth—a shift from direct to indirect taxation, shifting part of the tax burden from corporations to households, and limiting the deductibility of interest for housing and (indirectly) for consumer credit.

One policy option that studies suggest might raise household saving is to shift from direct to indirect taxation. Many economists have recommended that the United States go toward a value added taxation system. However, unless the consumption tax would be accompanied by rebates or tax credits and exemptions for certain types of purchases, it would have an unfavorable distributional aspect. Furthermore, going to a consumption tax from a progressive income tax system would reduce the built-in flexibility of the present system of taxation in the United States. However, it is recommended that indirect taxation in the form of higher alcoholic beverage, cigarette, and gasoline excise taxes be imposed.

The proposal to shift some of the tax burden from corporations to households is difficult to assess. As it now stands, corporate income taxes represent a declining share of federal revenues in the United States.

As indicated above, it is strongly recommended that the policy of further limiting the deductibility of interest for housing be adopted. The present system of allowing the deductibility of interest payments on mortgages of up to $1 million results in a subsidization of the purchase of expensive homes and a misallocation of resources away from productive investment. Also, households are permitted to deduct interest on up to $100,000 in home equity borrowing, and to the extent that households use the proceeds from these borrowings to purchase consumer goods and services, saving is discouraged. It is recommended that the deductibility of home equity loans be limited to home remodeling and that households be permitted to deduct interest on home mortgages that are no greater than $250,000.

In addition to the three policy options set forth above to increase private saving, it is also recommended that tax benefits related to saving for retirement be extended. Because of low saving in earlier years, baby boomers, many of whom are now in their forties, need to greatly increase their saving for retirement. At present, both premiums paid into retirement funds and the accrued earnings from these contributions are tax exempt until they are paid out at retirement, at which time they are generally taxable at a lower marginal rate than what would have prevailed when the contributor was fully employed. Some evidence exists to show that incentives to save provided by plans such as IRAs, Keogh, and 401k do have a positive effect on saving, and that such plans have not been displacing other savings but are helping to increase wealth in the United States.

Although the preceding focuses on tax incentives to raise saving, it must not be forgotten that the slowdown in the rate of growth in income since the 1970s has consistently been shown to be the principal contributing factor in the decline in the household saving rate. Using policy measures to raise the rate of economic growth back to levels prevailing in the 1950s and 1960s would help to raise private saving and also raise revenues because of the elasticity of the tax system. More rapid economic growth could raise saving rates and help turn the United States into a supplier and not a borrower of global capital.

Capital Flows and Balance-of-Payments Adjustment

This section will examine the process whereby in the present flexible exchange rate system, domestic imbalances cause external imbalances, which result in capital movements that occur as an outcome of the balance-of-payments adjustment process. The exchange rate affects the trade deficit and is itself determined by changes in exogenous macroeconomic variables.

It is assumed that the country operates under a system of flexible exchange rates and that international capital is highly mobile between a given country and the rest of the world. The real exchange rate is dependent on the interest differential between the domestic interest rate and foreign interest rates.

Under the Bretton Woods system of fixed exchange rates (with the exception of the United States, which was the key currency country), countries were not able to run current account deficits over a prolonged period of time. In the 1960s and early 1970s, it was often argued that flexible exchange rates would automatically remove current account imbalances and eliminate the need to hold foreign exchange reserves. Later, with flexible exchange rates and increased mobility of international capital after the removal (or reduction) of capital controls, current account imbalances did not disappear. Instead, countries were under less pressure to pursue contractionary macroeconomic policies to eliminate current account deficits. Saving-investment imbalances could be financed by an inflow of foreign savings.

It is within this climate of flexible exchange rates and increased capital mobility that during the early 1980s the United States pursued a very expansionary fiscal policy at the same time that the Federal Reserve followed a tight monetary policy. An expansionary fiscal policy and high interest rates contributed to large trade balance deficits in two ways. First, in conjunction with the large fiscal expansion during the first half of the 1980s, GDP in the United States grew at a higher rate than for most of its trading partners, and U.S. import growth exceeded growth of its exports. Second, high real interest rates, which raised the value of the dollar, increased the magnitude of the trade balance deficit. The dollar appreciation was very large because high real interest rates plus the federal government's large demand for capital encouraged an inflow of foreign capital. By early 1985, the real value of the dollar had appreciated by about 50 percent, which adversely affected the competitiveness of U.S. exports and caused the demand for imports to increase.

An explanation of the relationship that exists between interest rates and exchange rates in an environment where capital controls have been eliminated helps in comprehending the nature of U.S. capital flow since the early 1980s.

According to the uncovered interest parity condition, exchange rates are dependent on the difference between the domestic and foreign real interest rates. A major determinant of a country's capital account is the real interest rate differential because investors' decisions about investing internationally depend on real interest rate differentials as well as expectations about future changes in exchange rates. It is assumed that investors treat foreign bonds and domestic bonds as perfectly substitutable in their portfolios, that barriers that slow down portfolio adjustment to changes in real returns on assets do not exist, and that expected returns on assets are equalized across countries when they are expressed in common monetary units.

Real interest rate differentials can cause exchange rate changes. For instance, when a country's real interest rate exceeds foreign real interest rates, the actual real exchange rate may appreciate, but investors expect that the country's currency will depreciate in the future. Investors have an idea of purchasing power parity (the long-run equilibrium value of the exchange rate) and when the exchange rate deviates from its long-run equilibrium value, investors expect that, over time, the exchange rate will slowly move back in the direction of long-run equilibrium.

The U.S. exchange rate followed such a pattern in the early 1980s. The contractionary monetary policy pursued by the Federal Reserve Board, which raised real interest rates and the interest rate differential between U.S. and foreign interest rates, continued until mid-1984. Because the dollar had appreciated above its long-run purchasing power parity level, the expectation would then have been that the real exchange rate would depreciate slowly by a certain rate of adjustment (the speed of adjustment) over the next few years until it had reached its long-run equilibrium level, at which point the interest rate differential would have been zero.

The "overshooting" model explains the tendency for an exchange rate to appreciate (or depreciate) away from its long-run equilibrium level. The phenomenon of overshooting occurs because the speed of adjustment to a shock that creates disequilibrium is much faster in the money market than in the market for goods and services. The appreciation of the dollar until 1984 was a classic case of overshooting in response to a monetary tightening by the Federal Reserve. Based on economic fundamentals, it appears that the real appreciation of the dollar should have peaked in July 1984, but because of a speculative bubble phenomenon, the exchange rate appreciated by another 20 percent before it peaked in February 1985.

The Mundell-Fleming model was developed during the 1960s to explain international adjustment to monetary and fiscal policy changes in a system of fixed exchange rates.[15] The revised Mundell-Fleming model referred to here incorporates adjustments for expectations of exchange rate changes and inflation.

The revised Mundell-Fleming model was used to help comprehend the process of adjustment of the U.S. balance of payments to the dollar appreciation of the early 1980s as well as to the large depreciation of the dollar that began in February 1985. In the model, balance-of-payments adjustment involves capital mobility as a response to interest rate differentials. In this model, three relationships—the Keynesian income identity, the equation for money market equilibrium, and the equation for the determination of the exchange rate—simultaneously determine equilibrium in the markets for goods, services, and financial assets. The model is able to show internal and external adjustment to the expansionary fiscal policy and tight monetary policy of the early 1980s as well as to the more expansionary monetary policy during the period 1985–91.

The revised Mundell-Fleming model can help to describe the effects of monetary and fiscal policy during the early 1980s. During much of the period, fiscal policy was highly expansionary and monetary policy was contractionary. According to the Mundell-Fleming model, if there is little or no capital mobility, the increase in interest rates brought about by large government borrowing would significantly crowd out domestic investment. With perfect capital mobility, the higher rate of interest in the United States causes a large inflow of capital, and if there are no expectations of future exchange rate changes, the world real interest rate would rise until it equals the domestic rate. Because of the availability of international capital, the domestic interest rate does not rise as high as it would without capital mobility. The capital flow causes an appreciation of the exchange rate and the trade balance worsens.

In the early 1980s, an expansionary fiscal policy was combined with a tight monetary policy, but beginning in 1985, as part of a serious attempt to bring down the value of the dollar and reduce the trade deficit, monetary policy became expansionary. The impact of monetary expansion can be shown using the revised Mundell-Fleming model. In an open economy with perfect capital mobility, the fall in the interest rate in relation to that of the rest of the world causes an outflow of capital. The domestic currency depreciates, and because foreign interest rates are now greater than domestic interest rates, the currency of the rest of the world appreciates and the domestic trade balance improves at the same time that the trade balance of the rest of the world deteriorates. Even though the value of the dollar declined significantly in 1985–87, because of the J-curve effect, it was not until 1988 that the U.S. current account improved substantially.

The discussion implies a high mobility of international capital to finance current account deficits. But, in 1980, Martin Feldstein and Charles Horioka argued that international capital markets are not well integrated because countries' domestic investment rates do not diverge widely from their saving rates.[16] Regressing ratios of gross domestic investment to GDP on ratios of gross saving to GDP for each OECD country, they found regression coefficients (savings-retention coefficients) not significantly different from one. This appeared to provide evidence of low capital mobility.

Because of large changes in international capital markets, lowered or reduced barriers to international capital flows, and introduction of financial innovations during the 1980s, Feldstein and Philippe Bacchetta compared the experience of the period 1980–86 to results for the 1960s and 1970s and found that the fall in the savings-retention ratio was fairly large.[17] Also, the results appeared to indicate that because of strong institutional links among EEC countries, capital outflows from the individual EEC countries exceeded those of non-EEC countries.

The Feldstein-Horioka hypothesis has been subjected to a number of econometric critiques. One interpretation is set forth by the "policy endogeneity view," which argues that countries adapt their macroeconomic policies in order to prevent the continuation of current account imbalances (saving-investment gaps).

In testing this hypothesis, Lawrence Summers took average budget-deficit-to-GDP ratios for 1973–80 for a cross-section of industrial countries and regressed these averages on the saving-investment gaps averaged over the same period.[18] The regression coefficient was 0.72, implying that each dollar of a country's private saving-investment gap results in the government increasing its budget deficit by 72 cents, and that the endogeneity of fiscal policy can explain much of the correlation between saving and investment.

Tamin Bayoumi also tested the endogeneity hypothesis.[19] When he regressed total saving as a ratio of GNP against investment as a ratio of GNP for 1965–89 and for several subperiods, the results were similar to the Feldstein-Horioka conclusions. However, when private saving as a ratio of GNP was regressed on private fixed investment as a ratio of GNP, the value of the coefficient declined, indicating that private capital was highly mobile, especially after the mid-1970s. Regressions for the period of the gold standard (1890–1913—a period with little government intervention) showed little correlation between saving and investment, implying that the observed postwar correlation between saving and investment reflected government policy and did not indicate structurally low capital mobility.

Jeffrey Frankel observed that the basic problem concerned the definition of capital mobility used, and by some definitions capital was not perfectly mobile.[20] He defined four distinct definitions of capital mobility, listed in ascending order of specificity: the Feldstein-Horioka definition, real interest parity, uncovered interest parity, and closed interest parity.

According to this classification system, the Feldstein-Horioka definition of perfect capital mobility requires that the country's real (inflation adjusted) interest rate be tied to the world interest rate by the criterion that real interest parity holds because, in theory, saving and investment depend on the real and not the nominal interest rate. For real interest parity to hold, not only must the uncovered interest parity condition hold, but ex ante purchasing power parity must also exist.

Frankel then decomposes the real interest differential into a part caused by "political" or country factors (the covered interest differential) and a part due to currency factors, the real forward discount called the currency premium. The covered interest differential, which encompasses all factors having to do with the political jurisdiction in which the asset is issued, captures the barriers to integration of financial markets across national boundaries. The currency premium captures differences in assets in terms of the currencies they are denominated and not in terms of the political jurisdiction in which they are located. The currency premium consists of an exchange risk premium plus an expected real currency depreciation.

The most narrow definition of international capital mobility is related to the political jurisdiction where the currency is issued and would be measured by the variability of the covered interest differential. Frankel showed that the variability for covered interest differentials is smallest for open economies that have low barriers to international capital mobility, and that capital mobility has increased since the 1970s. The results supported the criterion that the covered interest differential is a proper test of financial market integration.

Frankel then shows that the size of the currency premium, which is measured by the "real forward discount," explains why the covered differential criterion gives different results from the Feldstein-Horioka hypothesis showing a high degree of savings retention in industrialized countries. Because real and nominal exchange rate variability exists in a number of industrial countries, a currency premium exists. Here, even if covered interest rates are equalized, differentials in real interest rates are large and the criterion of real interest parity does not hold; therefore, the Feldstein-Horioka definition of capital mobility cannot be achieved.

Two empirical studies that analyzed the balance-of-payments adjustment to the large exchange rate change between 1985 and 1991 then are discussed. The studies by both Lawrence and Cline found that conventional trade adjustment models could fairly well explain movements in the data during that period.

Using several measures of the real effective exchange rate, Robert Lawrence first showed that by 1990, the real value of the dollar had almost returned to its 1980 level, and foreign competitors had lost the relative advantage that they had in the U.S. market when the dollar was stronger.[21]

Lawrence found that conventional models were fairly well able to explain the behavior of the U.S. trade and current account balances up to 1990. First, relative export and import prices responded in a symmetrical manner to the appreciation and subsequent depreciation of the dollar. Second, it was estimated that over the long run, a 1 percent growth of U.S. output coincided with a 2.5 percent increase in the quantity of imports, but a 1 percent increase in foreign demand coincided with only a 1.6 percent increase in the quantity of U.S. exports. These results conformed to the Houthakker-Magee effect, stating that similar rates of growth in the United States and the rest of the world are associated with either a declining trade balance or a continuous real dollar depreciation, and suggesting that rates of growth in the United States that are only 60 percent of those abroad would be required to keep exports and imports growing at the same rate. During the decade of the 1980s, GDP growth in the United States was somewhat lower than GDP growth abroad—30.4 percent over the decade in the United States compared with 34.9 percent abroad. Lawrence points out that with relative prices in 1990 at the same level as in 1980, and with slightly lower growth in domestic output, the trade balance still deteriorated by $80 billion over the decade, measuring the decline in U.S. competitiveness over the decade. He estimated that restoring the trade balance to its 1980 level would have required a depreciation of about 8 percent over the decade, or almost 1 percent a year.

William Cline studied the record of U.S. adjustment to the large imbalances of the 1980s.[22] When comparing actual to predicted outcomes for 1988–90, Cline found that conventional models were able to explain what had happened over the three-year period, especially if they avoided or corrected for the computer pricing problem (the very rapid drop in prices of computers as technology improved). The key finding was that the behavior of the current account conformed to expectations of modelers and policymakers who stressed the impact of the dollar depreciation on current account adjustment in the late 1980s.

Cline then projected the outlook for the current account as of October 1990, and the outlook showed the current account stabilizing in the $100 billion range or at about 1.5 percent of GDP by 1995. The plateauing of the current account deficits at about $100 billion raised two questions. If the Houthakker-Magee asymmetry really held, the forecast of the current account deficit should have shown an increase over the period. The second question referred to the "gap factor," which should have shown an eventual rise in the deficit. The gap factor refers to the fact that by 1987, despite the large reversal of export and import growth rates after the dollar depreciation, imports had risen to a level 64 percent above exports, whereas in 1980 the difference had been only 11 percent. Had external adjustment to the large depreciation of the dollar since 1985 not worked, the projection for the current account deficit in 1995 would have greatly exceeded $100 billion.

Both the IMF and OECD have forecast that the U.S. current account deficit would rise to at least 2.2 percent of GDP in 1994.[23] For 1995, this deficit is forecast at 2.4 percent of GDP. These forecasts assume weak and delayed recoveries from recession in the other industrial countries and fairly substantial growth in the United States, especially in 1994.

It is projected that the U.S. current account deficit will be about 2.4 percent of GDP for most of the 1990s. Although this percentage is below the average of 3.4 percent of GDP experienced for the current account deficit in 1985–87, it is still substantial. Adjustment to the large dollar appreciation and subsequent depreciation of the 1980s has occurred, as reflected in the decline in the current account deficit as a share of GDP. The forecasts for 1994–95 assume that economic growth in the other major industrial countries will continue to be slow, which will retard the growth of U.S. exports and increase external imbalances. However, as of the Autumn of 1994, evidence was increasing that economic recovery was occurring abroad.

To be manageable, it has been argued that the current account deficit should be about 1 percent of GDP. A deficit of this magnitude slows down the accumulation of external debt and, hence, outflows of investment income to service this debt. It also prevents the growth of the deficit in net exports (exports minus imports of goods and services) from exerting a drag on the growth of aggregate demand. Furthermore, pressures on interest rates and the exchange rate would be avoided. In a system of flexible exchange rates without intervention, depreciation of the dollar would result from growing current account deficits unless the Federal Reserve took action to raise the rate of interest. Currently a sizable depreciation of the dollar would have to be countered by increased interest rates because the federal government needs to sell Treasury bills, notes, and bonds abroad to help finance its federal budget deficit and current account deficit.

There is much pessimism concerning the ability to reduce the current account deficit back to zero or even into a surplus, and it is often argued that the dollar will have to undergo a continuous depreciation for the current account deficit to remain at a fairly reasonable level. For instance, Maurice Obstfeld of the University of California has explained the long-term decline in the value of the dollar versus the yen as a consequence of the cost of production in Japan rising less rapidly than in the United States.[24] According to Obstfeld, "the relative cost of a basket of American goods has been going down since 1950. . . . Most people feel that this is related to the relative gains in Japanese productivity." However, there are economists who say that based on the cost of goods in the United States and Japan, the yen is severely overvalued.

A focal point of this book has been the need to demonstrate that measures to raise the U.S. saving rate and reduce the saving-investment imbalance would significantly reduce external imbalances. Additional legislation to reduce federal budgetary deficits would reduce saving-investment imbalances, as would increased saving by the baby boom generation in the second half of the 1990s and first decade of the twenty-first century. If savings were to rise substantially, it is even plausible that the United States could become a net exporter of capital in the next few years.

Global Capital Requirements

Global capital requirements in the 1990s are assessed. During the past decade, the industrial country group had shown persistent current account deficits until 1993, when a small surplus was recorded for the group. Of the two major surplus countries during the 1980s, Germany became a deficit country after reunification with the former East Germany, while Japan's surpluses have continued to grow. The combined current account deficits for the developing countries rose sharply in the 1990s. These countries as well as the countries that are in transition to market economies are requiring an increasing amount of capital inflows.

Projections for current account balances do not show much reduction in capital requirements. For the industrial countries as a group, the overall current account balance as a percentage of GDP is expected to narrow only moderately in the medium term and to show a small surplus. Current account deficits for developing countries as a group are forecast to remain high.

After an extended period when developing countries experienced sharply reduced inflows of foreign capital, since the late 1980s a number of these countries have experienced a marked increase in their access to world capital markets. Factors contributing to this surge in capital inflows include changes in short-run rates of return in developing countries, including a widening of interest rate differentials, improvements in domestic macroeconomic policies and structural reform programs, improved creditworthiness resulting from debt reduction and restructuring, changes in capital and foreign exchange controls, and development of domestic capital markets in countries such as Argentina, Mexico, Chile, and Korea.

The composition of capital inflows to many developing countries has changed markedly since the 1970s. From 43.5 percent of all capital inflows to developing countries in 1977–81, commercial bank loans fell to 16.2 percent of all inflows in 1989–92. Official flows (loans and grants) are still an important component, accounting for 40 percent of all inflows. The share going into foreign direct investment, equity, and bond financing tripled over the period, and such financing replaced commercial bank lending as a major source of financing. Foreign direct investment has increased markedly, and at present accounts for one-fifth of all inflows. Two-thirds originate in the United States and Japan. Portfolio flows to developing countries increased sharply since the mid-1980s. By 1992, equity financing represented 5.8 percent of all capital flows to developing countries and bond financing made up 10.2 percent.

A principal determinant of capital movements in the short term to developing countries has been financial trends in the United States, particularly with respect to capital flows to Latin America. It has been shown that a principal determinant of capital flows to Latin America in 1989–93 was the fall in short-term interest rates in the United States, which increased the solvency of Latin American debtors by reducing debt servicing burdens. At the same time, returns on domestic U.S. investments fell. The sharp reversal in the U.S. private capital account in 1990–91 resembled the 1978–82 period when developments in the U.S. economy played a key role as an external impulse affecting the size of capital flows into Latin America.

The capital requirements of the developing countries will continue to be large. Whereas in the early 1990s, low interest rates and weak economic conditions in the industrial countries helped provide capital at low interest rates to these countries, a key question is the sustainability of these increased inflows to developing countries as industrial countries recover from recession. The situation, however, is different from 1978–82. Many of these economies have been engaged in economic and structural reform programs. Capital flows in the earlier period went largely to public-owned entities, but more recently, a large share of foreign capital has gone to privately owned companies. Increasingly, privatization of public-owned companies has occurred. The economies have become more widely diversified into numerous industrial sectors, and domestic capital markets have emerged in several middle-income developing countries. All of these factors should help sustain inflows of capital into a number of developing countries, even though occurrences such as the sharp increase in Mexico's current account deficit and 35 percent depreciation of the Mexican peso in early 1995 adversely affected capital inflows to emerging markets in the immediate term.

CONCLUSION

This book has focused on macroeconomic explanations for the large U.S. net capital inflows that commenced in the early 1980s and are projected to remain at about 2.4 percent of GDP during the remainder of the 1990s. Although there has been much discussion that loss of competitiveness and unfair foreign trading practices have caused large U.S. trade and current account imbalances, these factors, in themselves, cannot explain why trade and current account deficits became so large during the 1980s and why substantial deficits are projected to continue for the remainder of the 1990s.

The assertion in this book has been that the principal reason for these large external deficits has been a deficiency of national saving in the United States. Here, policy recommendations are focused on raising the national saving rate.

Although the passage of the Omnibus Budget Reconciliation Act in 1993 constituted a milestone in budget deficit reduction, the budget deficit is now projected to rise from a low of 2.3 percent of GDP in 1995 to 3.6 percent in 2004, representing a 1.3 percent reduction in the national saving rate. The main reason for this growth is a projected increase in outlays for entitlements, in particular Medicare and Medicaid. This study recommends that additional federal revenues be raised to cover some of the projected growth in outlays. These tax increases include greater reliance on indirect taxation (higher excise taxes on gasoline, cigarettes, and alcoholic beverages). It is also recommended that more revenue be raised from the personal income tax by raising the higher income tax bracket rates to a minimum of 33 percent, 38 percent, and 42 percent; and that the alternative minimum tax be raised to 30 percent. A number of other measures are strongly recommended, including repealing indexing of the federal income tax, limiting deductibility of home mortgage interest, taxing employer-paid health insurance above a certain minimum, and taxing nonretirement fringe benefits.

It is recognized that revenue increases will not be sufficiently large to eliminate these large deficits. Between 1994 and 2004, discretionary outlays are projected to fall from 8.2 percent of GDP to 6.1 percent, and further reductions in these outlays are not going to be easy. At the same time, mandatory outlays are projected to rise from 11.9 percent of GDP to 14.1 percent. Limiting entitlement spending can be considered fair because many recipients are receiving benefits valued greatly in excess of their contributions, including a reasonable rate of return on their investment. It is also recommended that by 2006 the age to receive maximum Social Security benefits be gradually raised to 68 and the minimum age for receiving reduced benefits be raised from 62 to 65.

Because additional deficit reduction could have contractionary impacts on the economy, it is recommended that cutbacks in outlays and revenue increases be combined with attempts to stimulate the economy and raise economic growth. It is recommended that measures be taken to raise the rate of economic growth to over 3 percent a year for the remainder of the decade. Raising the rate of economic growth could help raise the national saving rate in two manners: it would help the economy grow its way out of the deficit, and it would probably raise the personal saving rate.

A higher rate of economic growth would help the economy grow its way out of the deficit. Revenues are elastic with respect to economic growth, and an average growth rate in excess of present forecasts would raise additional revenues and contribute to lower outlays on items such as unemployment insurance. With smaller deficits, interest outlays to service the public debt would grow more slowly, and because competition by the federal government for domestic capital to finance its deficits would be less, interest rates would be lower.

Studies of saving have consistently shown a positive relationship between economic growth and the personal saving rate. Because higher rates of economic growth are associated with higher rates of personal saving, if the rate of economic growth in the United States increases to the average level of the 1950s and 1960s, the personal saving rate should also increase.

Raising economic growth and the rate of personal saving requires a macroeconomic policy mix that encourages investment relative to consumption. This would require an economic environment favorable to investment, including a monetary policy that attempts to keep interest rates low and a fiscal policy that encourages investment.

During the early 1990s, the Federal Reserve pursued an easy money policy. Following legislation to reduce budget deficits, by the fall of 1993, 30-year Treasury bond rates had fallen to an all-time low of 5.94 percent. Even though economic growth in the first two years following the 1990–91 recession was much lower than after all other postwar recessions, in 1994 and early 1995, the Federal Reserve, concerned about nonexistent inflation, pursued monetary tightening measures. By early 1995, long-term interest rates had risen by 1.5 percentage points. These actions by the monetary authorities are bound to retard future rates of economic growth. Benefits stemming from future deficit reduction legislation and efforts to attain higher economic growth can be achieved only if a guarantee of cooperation from the Federal Reserve can be secured in advance.

It has been proposed that an amount of federal revenues equal to 1 percent of GDP be directed toward expenditures for physical and social infrastructure and R&D activities, and that the Investment Tax Credit be reinstated to encourage investment.

It is also recommended that tax benefits to encourage saving for retirement be expanded. Although evidence is still mixed as to whether such incentives raise net saving, greater efforts need to be made to encourage households that are approaching retirement to raise their saving before they retire.

According to projections, the U.S. current account deficit is expected to remain at about 2.4 percent of GDP for the remainder of the decade, implying that U.S. capital inflows will continue to be large even if, as a share of GDP, they will be lower than during the second half of the 1980s. Because substantial net capital inflows are expected to continue, rising outflows of investment income will result from the need to service the growing foreign debt. In addition, continuous external deficits continue to place a downward pressure on the value of the dollar, making it more and more expensive for Americans to purchase foreign goods at the same time that the value of American goods and services (American resources) become increasingly cheapened on world markets. In other words, Americans will pay more for foreign goods and services at the same time that U.S. resources receive less and less when they are transferred abroad.

It has also been shown that during the 1980s a substantial part of the exchange rate volatility that transpired was not related to economic fundamentals, but was more of a speculative bubble phenomenon. Large exchange rate gyrations contribute to distortions in international competitiveness. It is believed that some degree of monetary policy coordination by the major industrial nations is required to assure that exchange rate volatility is limited. A number of international economists believe that it is possible to limit exchange rate volatility by establishing target zones for exchange rates.

It has been shown that the developing countries of Latin America and Asia and countries that are in transition to market economies are absorbing increasing amounts of world capital. But, instead of exporting capital, it now appears likely that the United States will remain a large importer of capital.

Raising the U.S. national saving rate would help the United States become once again a net exporter of international capital. It is necessary to acknowledge that the recommendations to achieve additional fiscal austerity by raising taxes and reducing entitlements will appear to be a severe step to take. And too many economists have lost sight of the fact that increased investment spending raises the level of income, which in turn raises saving, and that measures to raise investment are vitally important. In conjunction with raising private investment, it is crucial that the United States have good physical and social infrastructure. Much of America's physical infrastructure is outdated and falling apart, and large outlays to repair it will be required. The nation is also in a state of social change, with class divisions becoming larger and more apparent all the time. To remain a society with a middle class that encompasses the vast majority of Americans, many believe that large expenditure outlays on teaching the skills required in the twenty-first century will be required.

NOTES

1. U.S. Department of Commerce, *Foreign Direct Investment in the United States: Review and Analysis of Current Developments* (Washington, D.C.: Government Printing Office, August 1991), pp. 34–35.

2. U.S. Department of Commerce, *Survey of Current Business,* October 1993, pp. 63–65.

3. Edward M. Graham and Paul L. Krugman, *Foreign Direct Investment in the United States,* 2d. ed. (Washington, D.C.: Institute for International Economics, 1991), pp. 69–70.

4. John H. Dunning, "Trade, Location of Economic Activity and Multinational Enterprises: A Search for an Eclectic Approach," in *International Production and the Multinational Enterprise*, ed. John H. Dunning (London: George Allen and Unwin, 1981), pp. 21–45.

5. Congress of the United States, Congressional Budget Office, *The Economic and Budget Outlook: An Update* (Washington, D.C.: Government Printing Office, September 1993), p. 18.

6. John M. Keynes, *The General Theory of Employment, Interest, and Money* (London: Harcourt Brace, 1936).

7. Milton Friedman, *A Theory of the Consumption Function* (Princeton N.J.: Princeton University Press, 1957); Franco Modigliani and R. E. Brumberg, "Utility Analysis and the Consumption Function," in *Post-Keynesian Economics*, ed. K. K. Kurihara (New Brunswick, N.J.: Rutgers University Press, 1954); and A. Ando and Franco Modigliani, "The Life Cycle Hypothesis of Saving: Aggregate Implications and Tests," *American Economic Review*, 53 (March 1963), pp. 55–84.

8. Barry Bosworth, *Saving and Investment in the Global Economy* (Washington, D.C.: Brookings Institution, 1993), pp. 55–61.

9. Robert Mundell, "The Great Exchange Rate Controversy: Trade Balances and the Current Account," in *International Adjustment and Financing: The Lessons of 1985–91*, ed. C. Fred Bergsten (Washington, D.C.: Institute for International Economics, 1991), pp. 189–238.

10. Michael J. Boskin and Lawrence J. Lau, "An Analysis of Post-War U.S. Consumption and Saving," National Bureau of Economic Research Working Papers Nos. 2605 and 2606 (1988); and Lawrence J. Lau, "U.S. Saving Behavior in the Post-War Period," in *World Savings: An International Survey*, ed. Arnold Heertje (Cambridge: Blackwell, 1993), pp. 141–77.

11. Barry Bosworth, Gary Burtless, and John Sabelhaus, "The Decline in Saving: Some Microeconomic Evidence," *Brookings Papers on Economic Activity*, No. 1 (1991), pp. 183–256.

12. Christopher D. Carroll, "The Buffer Stock Theory of Saving: Some Microeconomic Evidence," *Brookings Papers on Economic Activity*, No. 29 (1992), pp. 61–135.

13. Congress of the United States, Congressional Budget Office, *Reducing Entitlement Spending* (Washington, D.C.: Government Printing Office, September 1994), pp. xiii–xv.

14. Ibid., pp. xii–xvi.

15. Robert Mundell: "The Appropriate Use of Fiscal and Monetary Policy Under Fixed Exchange Rates," *IMF Staff Papers*, 9 (March 1962); "Capital Mobility and Stabilization Policy Under Fixed and Flexible Exchange Rates," *Canadian Journal of Economics and Political Science*, November 1962, pp. 475–85; and J. M. Fleming, "Domestic Financial Policies Under Fixed and Under Floating Exchange Rates," *IMF Staff Papers*, 9 (September 1962).

16. Martin Feldstein and Charles Horioka, "Domestic Saving and International Capital Flows," *Economic Journal*, 90 (June 1980), pp. 314–29.

17. Martin Feldstein and Philippe Bachetta, "National Saving and International Investment," in *National Saving and Economic Performance*, ed. B. Douglas Bernheim and John B. Shoven (Chicago: University of Chicago Press, 1991).

18. Lawrence H. Summers, "Tax Policy and International Competitiveness," in

International Aspects of Fiscal Policy, ed. Jacob A. Frenkel (Chicago: University of Chicago Press, 1988).

19. Tamin Bayoumi, "Saving-Investment Correlations; Immobile Capital, Government Policy, or Endogenous Behavior?" *IMF Staff Papers,* 37, no. 2 (June 1990).

20. Jeffrey Frankel, "Quantifying International Capital Mobility in the 1980s," in *National Saving and Economic Performance.*

21. Robert Z. Lawrence, "U.S. Current Account Adjustment: An Appraisal," *Brookings Papers on Economic Activity,* No. 2 (1990), pp. 342–92.

22. William R. Cline, "U.S. External Adjustment: Progress, Prognosis, and Interpretation," in *International Adjustment and Financing,* pp. 15–55.

23. International Monetary Fund, World Economic and Financial Surveys, *World Economic Outlook, October 1994* (Washington D.C.: International Monetary Fund, 1994), pp. 151–53; and Organization for Economic Cooperation and Development, *OECD Economic Outlook* (Paris: OECD, December 1994), p. A1.

24. Cited in Saul Hansell, "A Currency Dragged Down by Twin Deficits," *New York Times,* June 23, 1994, p. D6.

Bibliography

Ackley, Gardner. *Macroeconomics: Theory and Policy.* New York: Macmillan, 1978.

Agmon, T. B. and D. F. Lessard. "Investor Recognition of Corporate International Diversification." *Journal of Finance,* 33, no. 4 (1977): 1049–55.

Aliber, Robert Z. "The Theory of Foreign Direct Investment." In *The International Corporation,* edited by Charles P. Kindleberger. Cambridge, Mass.: M.I.T. Press, 1970.

Aliber, Robert Z. *The Multinational Paradigm.* Cambridge, Mass.: M.I.T. Press, 1993.

Ando, A. and Franco Modigliani. "The Life Cycle Hypothesis of Saving: Aggregate Implications and Tests." *American Economic Review,* 53 (March 1963): 55–84.

Artis, Michael and Mark Taylor. "Abolishing Exchange Control: The U.S. Experience." In *Policy Issues for Interdependent Economies,* edited by A. Courtis and M. Taylor. London: Macmillan, 1990.

Barro, Robert J. "Are Government Bonds New Wealth?" *Journal of Political Economy,* 82 (November/December 1974): 1095–1117.

Bayoumi, Tamin. "Saving-Investment Correlations: Immobile Capital, Government Policy, or Endogenous Behavior?" *IMF Staff Papers,* 37, no. 2 (June 1990): 360–87.

Bercuson, Kenneth B. and Linda M. Konig. "The Recent Surge in Capital Inflows to Asia: Cause and Macroeconomic Impact." Paper presented at SEACEN/IMF Seminar, May 14–16, 1993, Seoul, Korea.

Bergsten, C. Fred and Marcus Noland. *Reconcilable Differences: United States-Japan Economic Conflict.* Washington, D.C.: Institute for International Economics, 1993.

Blecker, Robert A. "Policy Implications of the International Saving-Investment Correlation." Paper presented at the Economic Policy Institute Conference on Saving and Investment, Washington, D.C., April 21–22, 1994.

Boskin, Michael J. and Larry J. Lau. "An Analysis of Post-War U.S. Consumption and Saving." National Bureau of Economic Research Working Papers Nos. 2605 and 2606 (1988).

Bosworth, Barry P. "Institutional Changes and the Efficacy of Monetary Policy." *Brookings Papers on Economic Activity,* No. 1 (1989): 77–124.

Bosworth, Barry P. *Saving and Investment in a Global Economy.* Washington, D.C.: Brookings Institution, 1993.

Bosworth, Barry, Gary Burtless, and John Sabelhous. "The Decline of Saving: Some Microeconomic Evidence." *Brookings Papers on Economic Activity,* No. 1 (1991): 183–256.

Bradsher, Keith. "U.S. Is Attracting New Money Pool." *New York Times,* July 30, 1994: A1 and A4.

Bryant, Ralph. *International Financial Intermediation.* Washington, D.C.: Brookings Institution, 1987.

Buckley, Peter J. "A Critical Review of Theories of the Multinational Enterprise." *Assenwirtschaft,* 36, Heft I (1981): 70–87.

Buckley, Peter J. and Mark Casson. *The Future of the Multinational Enterprise.* New York: Holmes and Meier, 1976.

Buckley, Peter J. and Mark Casson. *The Economic Theory of the Multinational Enterprise.* New York: St. Martin's Press, 1985.

Calvo, Guillermo A., Leonardo Leiderman, and Carmen Reinhart. "Capital Inflows and Real Exchange Rate Appreciation in Latin America: The Role of External Factors." *International Monetary Fund Staff Papers,* 40, no. 1 (March 1993): 108–51.

Carroll, Christopher D. "The Buffer-Stock Theory of Saving: Some Microeconomic Evidence." *Brookings Papers on Economic Activity,* No. 29 (1992): 61–135.

Carroll, Christopher and Lawrence Summers. "Why Have Private Saving Rates in the United States and Canada Diverged?" *Journal of Monetary Economics,* 20 (1987): 249–70.

Caves, Richard E. "International Corporations: The Industrial Economics of Foreign Direct Investment." *Economica,* 38 (February 1971): 1–27.

Caves, Richard, Jeffrey A. Frankel, and Ronald W. Jones. *World Trade and Payments: An Introduction,* 5th ed. Glenview, Ill.: Scott, Foresman Little, Brown Higher Education, 1990.

Cline, William R. *United States External Adjustment and the World Economy.* Washington, D.C.: Institute for International Economics, 1989.

Cline, William R. "U.S. External Adjustment: Progress, Prognosis, and Interpretation." In *International Adjustment and Financing: The Lessons of 1985–91,* edited by C. Fred Bergsten. Washington, D.C.: Institute for International Economics, 1991.

Cline, William R. "Japan's Current Account Surplus." Institute for International Economics, Mimeographed paper, July 1993.

Cline, William. "Macroeconomics and the US-Japan Trade Imbalance." *International Economic Insights,* 4, no. 4 (July/August 1993): 5–8.

Coase, Ronald. "The Nature of the Firm." *Economica,* 4 (November 1937): 1–40.

Congress of the United States, Congressional Budget Office. *Assessing the Decline in the National Saving Rate.* Washington, D.C.: Government Printing Office, April 1993.

Congress of the United States, Congressional Budget Office. *The Economic and Budget Outlook: Fiscal Years 1994–1998.* Washington, D.C.: Government Printing Office, January 1993.

Congress of the United States, Congressional Budget Office. *The Economic and Budget Outlook: Fiscal Years 1995–1999.* Washington, D.C.: Government Printing Office, January 1994.

Congress of the United States, Congressional Budget Office. *The Economic and Budget Outlook: An Update.* Washington, D.C.: Government Printing Office, September 1993, and August 1994.

Congress of the United States, Congressional Budget Office. *Reducing the Deficit: Spending and Revenue Options.* Washington, D.C.: Government Printing Office, February 1993 and March 1994.

Congress of the United States, Congressional Budget Office. *Reducing Entitlement Spending.* Washington D.C.: Government Printing Office, September 1994.

Congress of the United States, Office of Technology Assessment. *Multinationals and the National Interest: Playing by Different Rules,* OTA-ITE-569. Washington, D.C.: Government Printing Office, September 1993.

Dominguez, Kathryn M. and Jeffrey A. Frankel. *Does Foreign Exchange Intervention Work?* Washington, D.C.: Institute for International Economics, 1993.

Dooley, Michael and Peter Isard. "Capital Controls, Political Risk and Deviations from Interest Rate Parity." *Journal of Political Economy,* 88, no. 2 (April 1980): 370–84.

Duisenberg, W. F. and A.H.I.M. Wellink. "Toward an International Saving Policy." In *World Saving: An International Survey,* edited by Arnold Heertje. Cambridge: Blackwell, 1993.

Dunning, John H. "The Determinants of Multinational Production." *Oxford Economic Papers,* 25 (January 1973): 289–336.

Dunning, John H. "Trade, Location of Economic Activity and Multinational Enterprises: A Search for an Eclectic Approach." In *International Production and the Multinational Enterprise,* edited by John H. Dunning. London: George Allen and Unwin, 1981.

Dunning, John H. "Changes in the Structure of International Production in the Last 100 Years." In *The Growth of International Business,* edited by Mark Casson. London: Allen and Unwin, 1983.

Dunning, John H. "Market Power of the Firm and International Transfer of Technology." *International Journal of Industrial Organization,* 1 (1983): 333–51.

Dunning, John H. "The Eclectic Paradigm of International Production: A Restatement and Some Possible Extensions." *Journal of International Business Studies,* Spring 1988: pp. 1–31.

Feldstein, Martin and Charles Horioka. "Domestic Saving and International Capital Flows." *Economic Journal,* 90 (June 1980): 314–29.

Feldstein, Martin and Philippe Bacchetta. "National Saving and International Investment." In *National Saving and Economic Performance,* edited by B. Douglas Bernheim and John B. Shoven. Chicago: University of Chicago Press, 1991.

Fieleke, Norman S. "The USA in Debt." In *International Finance: Contemporary Issues*, edited by Dilip K. Das. London: Routledge, 1993.

"Financing World Growth." *Business Week*, October 3, 1994: 100–3.

"Fixing the U.S. Economy." Statement by 100 economists. National Press Club, Washington, D.C., March 30, 1992.

Fleming, J. M. "Domestic Financial Policies Under Fixed and Under Floating Exchange Rates." *IMF Staff Papers*, 9, no. 3 (1962): 369–79.

Flowers, Edward B. "Oligopolistic Reactions in European and Canadian Direct Investment in the United States." *Journal of International Business Studies*, 7 (Fall/Winter 1976): 43–55.

Frankel, Jeffrey. *The Yen-Dollar Agreement: Liberalizing Japanese Capital Markets*. Washington, D.C.: Institute for International Economics, 1984.

Frankel, Jeffrey A. "Quantifying International Capital Mobility in the 1980s." In *National Saving and Economic Performance*, edited by B. Douglas Bernheim and John B. Shoven. Chicago: University of Chicago Press, 1991.

Frankel, Jeffrey A. "Quantifying International Capital Mobility in the 1980's." In *International Finance: Contemporary Issues*, edited by Dilip K. Das. London: Routledge, 1993.

Frenkel, Jacob and Richard Levich. "Transactions Costs and Interest Arbitrage: Tranquil Versus Turbulent Periods." *Journal of Political Economy*, 85, no. 6 (1977): 1209–26.

Frenkel, Jacob and Richard Levich. "Covered Interest Arbitrage in the 1970s." *Economic Letters*, 8, no. 3 (1981): 267–74.

Friedman, Milton. *A Theory of the Consumption Function*. Princeton, N.J.: Princeton University Press, 1957.

Glickman, Norman and Douglas Woodward. *The New Competitors: How Foreign Investors Are Changing the U.S. Economy*. New York: Basic Books, 1989.

Golub, Stephen. "Is Trade Between the United States and Japan Off Balance?" *Finance and Development*, 31, no. 4 (September 1994): 54–57.

Gordon, Sara L. and Francis A. Lees. *Foreign Multinational Investment in the United States: Struggle for Industrial Supremacy*. Westport, Conn.: Quorum Books, 1986.

Graham, Edward M. and Paul L. Krugman. *Foreign Direct Investment in the United States*, 2d ed. Washington, D.C.: Institute for International Economics, 1991.

Gyohten, Toyoo. "Overview." In *Changing Capital Markets: Implications for Monetary Policy*. Paper presented at symposium sponsored by the Federal Reserve Bank of Kansas City, Jackson Hole, Wyoming, August 19–21, 1993: 399–404.

Helkie, William. "U.S. International Transactions in 1992." *Federal Reserve Bulletin* (May 1993): 379–88.

Hooper, Peter and Catherine L. Mann. *The Emergence and Persistence of the U.S. External Imbalance, 1980–87*. Princeton Studies in International Finance, No. 65. Princeton: Princeton University Press, 1989.

Hymer, Stephen A. *The International Operations of National Firms: A Study of Foreign Direct Investment*. Cambridge, Mass.: M.I.T. Press, 1976.

International Monetary Fund. *Articles of Agreement*. Washington, D.C.: International Monetary Fund, 1968.

International Monetary Fund. *International Financial Statistics,* various issues. Washington, D.C.: International Monetary Fund.

International Monetary Fund. World Economic and Financial Surveys. *International Capital Markets: Developments, Prospects, and Policy Issues.* Washington, D.C.: International Monetary Fund, September 1992.

International Monetary Fund. World Economic and Financial Surveys. *International Capital Markets: Part I, Exchange Rate Management and International Capital Flows.* Washington, D.C.: International Monetary Fund, April 1993, and *Part II,* August 1993.

International Monetary Fund. World Economic and Financial Surveys. *Private Capital Markets for Developing Countries.* Washington, D.C.: International Monetary Fund, December 1993.

International Monetary Fund. World Economic and Financial Surveys. *World Economic Outlook, May 1991, May 1993, October 1993, May 1994,* and *October 1994.* Washington, D.C.: International Monetary Fund, 1991, 1993, and 1994.

Julius, DeAnne. *Foreign Direct Investment: The Neglected Twin of Trade.* Occassional Papers 33. Washington, D.C.: Group of Thirty, 1991.

Keynes, John M. *The General Theory of Employment, Interest, and Money.* London: Harcourt Brace, 1936.

Kindleberger, Charles P. *American Business Abroad: Six Essays on Direct Investment.* New Haven, Conn.: Yale University Press, 1969.

Kindleberger, Charles P. *International Capital Movements.* Cambridge: Cambridge University Press, 1987.

Klein, Lawrence. "The New Administration: First Year Appraisal," Roundtable, Allied Social Science Association, Boston, January 1994.

Knickerbocker, Frederick. *Oligopolistic Reaction and Multinational Enterprises.* Cambridge, Mass.: Harvard Business School, Division of Research, 1973.

Kolhagen, Stephen. "Exchange Rate Changes, Profitability, and Direct Foreign Investment." *Southern Economic Journal,* 44 (1977): 43–52.

Kotlikoff, Laurence J. "Intergenerational Transfers and Savings." *Journal of Economic Perspectives,* 2, no. 2 (Spring 1988): 41–58.

Kotlikoff, Laurence J. and Lawrence H. Summers. "The Role of Intergenerational Transfers in Aggregate Capital Accumulation." *Journal of Political Economy,* 89 (August 1981): 706–32.

Kotlikoff, Laurence T. and Lawrence H. Summers. "The Contribution of Intergenerational Transfers to Total Wealth: A Reply." National Bureau of Economic Research Working Paper No. 1827 (1986).

Krugman, Paul R. *Has the Adjustment Process Worked?* Policy Analysis in International Economics, No. 34. Washington, D.C.: Institute for International Economics, October 1991.

Lau, Lawrence J. "U.S. Saving Behavior in the Post-War Period." In *World Saving: An International Survey,* edited by Arnold Heertje. Cambridge: Blackwell, 1993.

Lawrence, Robert Z. "The International Dimension." In *American Living Standards,* edited by Robert E. Litan, Robert Z. Lawrence, and Charles Schultze. Washington D.C.: Brookings Institution, 1988.

Lawrence, Robert Z. "U.S. Current Account Adjustment: An Appraisal." *Brookings Papers on Economic Activity*, No. 2 (1990): 343–82.

Logue, Dennis and Thomas Willet. "The Effects of Exchange Rate Adjustment on International Investment." In *The Effects of Exchange Rate Adjustment*, edited by Peter B. Clark, Dennis E. Logue, and Richard Sweeney. Washington, D.C.: Department of the Treasury, 1977.

Magee, Stephen P. "Information and the International Corporation: An Appropriability Theory of Foreign Direct Investment." In *The New International Economic Order*, edited by Jagdish Bhagwati. Cambridge, Mass.: M.I.T. Press, 1977.

Makin, John. "Capital Flows and Exchange Rate Flexibility in the Post Bretton Woods Era." Essays in International Finance, No. 103. Princeton, N.J.: Princeton University Press, 1974.

Mann, Catherine L. "U.S. International Transactions in 1993." *Federal Reserve Bulletin*, May 1994: 365–78.

McCulloch, Rachel. "Foreign Direct Investment in the United States." *Finance and Development*, 30, no. 1 (March 1993): 13–15.

McKinnon, Ronald I. "Flood of Dollars, Sunken Pesos." *New York Times*, January 20, 1995, p. A29.

McManus, John. "The Theory of the International Firm." In *The Multinational Firm and the Nation State*, edited by Giles Paquet. Toronto: Collier-Macmillan, 1975.

Meade, James E. *The Theory of International Economic Policy*, Vol. I: *The Balance of Payments*. Oxford: Oxford University Press, 1951.

Modigliani, Franco. "Life Cycle, Individual Thrift, and the Wealth of Nations." *American Economic Review*, 76, no. 3 (June 1986): 297–313.

Modigliani, Franco. "The Role of Intergenerational Transfers and Life Cycle Saving in the Accumulation of Wealth." *Journal of Economic Perspectives*, 2, no. 2 (Spring 1988): 15–40.

Modigliani, Franco. "Introduction." In *World Saving: An International Survey*, edited by Arnold Heertje. Cambridge: Blackwell, 1993.

Mohammed, Azis Ali. "Industrial and Developing Country Policy Linkages." *Finance and Development*, 31, no. 3 (September 1994): 50–53.

Mundell, Robert. "The Appropriate Use of Fiscal and Monetary Policy Under Fixed Exchange Rates, *IMF Staff Papers*, 9 (March 1962), pp. 70–77.

Mundell, Robert. "Capital Mobility and Stabilization Policy Under Fixed and Flexible Exchange Rates." *Canadian Journal of Economics and Political Science*, November 1963: 475–85.

Mundell, Robert. "The Great Exchange Rate Controversy: Trade Balances and the Current Account." In *International Adjustment and Financing: The Lessons of 1985–91*, edited by C. Fred Bergsten. Washington, D.C.: Institute for International Economics, 1991.

Mussa, Michael and Morris Goldstein. "The Integration of World Capital Markets." In *Changing Capital Markets: Implications for Monetary Policy*. Paper presented at a symposium sponsored by the Federal Reserve Bank of Kansas City, Jackson Hole, Wyoming, August 19–21, .1993: 245–313.

Organization for Economic Cooperation and Development. *OECD Economic Out-*

look, June 1993, December 1993, June 1994, and December 1994. Paris: OECD, 1993 and 1994.

Owens, Jeffrey. "Taxations and Savings." In *World Saving: An International Survey,* edited by Arnold Heertje. Cambridge: Blackwell, 1993.

Peterson, Peter G. *Facing Up.* New York: Simon and Schuster, 1993.

Pechman, Joseph A. *Federal Tax Policy.* Washington, D.C.: Brookings Institution, 1983.

Poterba, James, Steven Venti, and David A. Wise. "Targeted Retirement Saving and Net Worth of Elderly Americans." *American Economic Review,* 84, no. 2 (1994): 180–85.

Rugman, Alan M. "New Theories of Multinational Enterprises: An Assessment of Internalization Theory." *Bulletin of Economic Research,* 38, no. 2 (May 1986): pp. 101–17.

Sabelhaus, John. "Deficits and Other Intergenerational Transfers: Restoring the Missing Link." *Challenge,* January/February 1994: 45–50.

Schadler, Susan, Maria Carkovic, Adam Bennett, and Robert Kahn. "Recent Experiences with Surges in Capital Flows." Occasional Paper 108, International Monetary Fund, 1993.

Senner, Madis. "The Grim Shortage of Global Capital." *New York Times,* July 6, 1991: D10.

Summers, Lawrence H. "Tax Policy and International Competitiveness." In *International Aspects of Fiscal Policy,* edited by Jacob A. Frenkel. Chicago: University of Chicago Press, 1988.

Tobin, James. "Life Cycle Saving and Balanced Growth." In *Ten Economic Studies in the Tradition of Irving Fisher,* edited by W. Fellner. New York: John Wiley, 1967.

Tobin, James. "Comments: 'Domestic Saving and International Capital Movements in the Long Run and in the Short Run' by M. Feldstein." *European Economic Review,* 21 (1983): 153–56.

Tobin, James. "Thinking Straight About Fiscal Stimulus and Deficit Reduction." *Challenge,* March 1993: pp. 15–18.

Turner, Phillip. *Capital Flows in the 1980s: A Survey of Major Trends.* BIS Economic Papers, No. 30. Basle: Bank for International Settlements, April 1991.

United States, Council of Economic Advisors. *Economic Report of the President.* Washington D.C.: Government Printing Office, 1991, 1992, 1993, and 1994.

U.S. Department of Commerce, Bureau of Economic Analysis. *Survey of Current Business.* Various issues.

U.S. Department of Commerce, Economics and Statistics Administration. *Foreign Direct Investment in the United States: Review and Analysis of Current Developments.* Washington D.C.: Government Printing Office, August 1991.

Vernon, Raymond. "International Investment and International Trade in the Product Cycle." *Quarterly Journal of Economics,* 80 (May 1966): 190–207.

Vernon, Raymond. "The Product Cycle Hypothesis in a New International Environment." *Oxford Bulletin of Economics and Statistics,* 40 (1979): 255–67.

Index

Action Plan for deficit reduction: defense spending, 106; discretionary spending reduction, 100–101, 105, 106; entitlement spending reduction, 101, 119, 196–97; health care reforms, 101–103, 113–14; investment incentives, 103–104; public investment spending, 100–101, 115; tax increases, 102, 103, 105, 106, 111, 112–13, 117
Age structure, 87–90, 192, 193–194. *See also* Baby boom generation
Agmon, T. B., 42
Aliber, Robert Z., 42–44
Asia, 173–75. *See also* Capital flows
Automatic stabilizers, 108, 124 n.8, 189

Baby boom generation, 83; aging and saving, 87–88, 88–90, 92, 192–94
Bacchetta, Philippe, 140, 203
Balance of payments, United States, 15, 17–23. *See also* Balance-of-payments adjustment; Current account; and United States current account
Balance-of-payments adjustment, 136–39, 145–52; with flexible exchange rates, 145–52; Mundell-Fleming model, 136–39, 202–203; United States, 145–52
Balance-of-payments adjustment, empirical studies: External Adjustment with Growth (EAG) model, 150–51; Helkie-Hooper Cline model, 150–51, 205; Hooper and Mann study, 145–48; Lawrence study, 148–50
Basic balance, 17–18
Bayoumi, Tamin, 142, 203
Boskin, Michael J., 88–90, 193
Bosworth, Barry P., 81, 85, 91–92
Brookings Institution, 90, 193
Buckley, Peter, 46
Buffer-stock model of saving, 92–94, 194–95

Capital account, 13–14, 19, 183; determinants, 133–36; United States, 15–17
Capital controls: liberalization, 23–26, 132, 142, 182–83; Europe, 24; France, 25; Germany, 25; Japan, 25;

United Kingdom, 24; United States, 24

Capital flows, 13–14, 182

Capital flows: Asia, 165–66, 167, 168, 173–75; causes, 174, 168–69, 207, 208; composition of, 166–71, 207; developing countries, 207, 211; Latin America, 165, 167, 168, 169–71, 175–76; 208; Mexico, 170–71, 208; transition economies, 171–72, 176; United States, 17–23

Capital markets: developing country access, 165, 207; global, 181–83; integration, 140; international, 17

Capital mobility, 140–45; capital control reduction, 132, 200; closed interest parity, 143, 204; covered interest differential, 144, 204; currency premium, 144–45, 204; Feldstein-Horioka definition, 140–45, 203; fixed exchange rates, 132; policy endogeneity view, 141, 203; real interest parity definition, 142, 204; uncovered parity definition, 142, 204

Capital shortages, 61–62

Carroll, Christopher D., 92, 122, 194–95

Casson, Mark, 46

Central Europe. See Transition economies

Cline, William, 150–52, 204, 205–206

Coase, Ronald, 46

Consumption: age structure, 83–84, 88–90; bequests, 80, 191; buffer-stock model, 92–93, 194–95; life-cycle model, 78–81, 86–87, 190–91; permanent income, 78–79, 190; precautionary motive, 80, 92–93, 191; theory of consumption, 78–81, 190–91

Consumption tax, 120, 121

Currency risk, 28–29, 144–45

Current account: adjustment theory 145–52, 200–203; balance, 14, 18; developing countries, 162, 207; European Union, 162; Germany, 160–61, 207; industrial country group, 160, 207; Japan, 162, 207; newly in-

dustrializing economies, 162; United States, 18–23, 145, 146–47, 160, 177–78, 182. See also United States: current account

Current account projections: developing countries, 163–65, 207; Europe, 163; industrial countries, 164, 207; Japan, 163; United States, 150–52, 152–55, 165, 188, 205–206, 208, 210; U.S.-Japan bilateral deficit, 153–55

Cyclical patterns, 8

Demographics. See Age structure; Baby boom generation

Dunning, John H., 47–49, 186

Eastern Europe. See Transition economies

Euromarket, 25

European Community (EC), 141

Europe: economic growth, 182; fixed capital formation, 68; investment, 64; saving, 64; saving-investment balance, 64

Exchange rate determinants: interest rate differentials, 133–35, 136–39, 200, 201, 204; price level differentials, 133, purchasing power parity, 134, 201, 204; uncovered interest parity, 133–134, 201

Exchange rate models, 133–34; overshooting model, 135–36, 201–202

Exchange rates, fixed: balance-of-payments adjustment, 131–32, 200, 202; breakdown of fixed exchange rate system, 24; Bretton Woods era, 24, 131–34, 200

Exchange rates, flexible: balance-of-payments adjustment under, 127–31, 132–39, 200, 202–203

Exchange rates, monetary policy coordination for, 211

Excise taxes, 72, 111–12, 116, 196, 209; alcohol, 111, 116, 196; cigarettes, 111, 116, 196; gasoline, 111–112, 117, 196

External adjustment process, 129–31, 136–39

Feldstein, Martin S., 140–41, 203
Feldstein-Horioka definition of capital mobility, 140–45, 203
Firm-specific advantages. *See* Foreign direct investment: theory of the firm explanations; Ownership advantages
Financial disintermediation, 26, 30
Financial market integration, 143
Financial markets: derivative securities, 29–30, 182–83; technological innovations, 28–30
Financial systems, international structural changes, 23–30
Flowers, Edward B., 50–51
Foreign direct investment, cost of capital theories: 42–44, 185; exchange rate changes impact, 49, 185; exchange risk theory, 43, 44; market imperfections, 42; misalignments in exchange rates, 43; portfolio theory, 43, 185
Foreign direct investment, industrial country growth: 51–52; Japan, 51, 55; United Kingdom, 51. *See also* Foreign direct investment, United States
Foreign direct investment measurement, 58–59, n.52
Foreign direct investment, theory of the firm explanations: 44–51, 185–87; appropriability theory, 46–47, 186; eclectic theory, 47–49, 186–87; firm-specific advantages, 44, 45, 48; industrial organization theories, 45, 46, 47–48, 49, 185–87; internalization theory, 47–48, 49, 186, 187; location-specific advantages, 48–49, 186–87; oligopolistic reaction, 49–51; ownership advantages, 47–48, 49, 185–96, 187; product cycle, 49–50; transactions cost, 46, 49, 186
Foreign direct investment, United States: asset ownership, 38, 184; capital intensity, 37, 38, 183; employee compensation, 36–37, 184; employ-

ment, 35–36, 183; gross product share, 34–35, 183; growth, 51–52, 55, 183, 187; host country, 52, 187; inflow, 34, 183; locational advantages, 55–56; ownership advantages, 51, 55; position, 52–55, 187; productivity growth, 36, 184; research and development outlays, 34–38, 184; role in foreign trade, 38–41, 184–85; sales of affiliates, 38; technology transfer inflow, 37–38, 183–184; transfer pricing, 55–56
Frankel, Jeffrey A., 142–45, 203
Friedman, Milton, 78, 190

G-5 countries, 4; foreign direct investment growth, 51; Plaza Accord, 4, 126, 136; policy coordination, 136
G-7 countries, 9; personal saving rate, 9
Germany: current account, 7, 9, 67, 160–62; deficit, 64, 67; personal saving rate, 65; removal of restrictions on capital flows, 25
Glickman, Norman, 56
Global capital mobility and shortages, 6; Latin America, 175–76
Global saving, 160, 175–78; U.S. role, 160, 187
Gold standard period, 142, 203
Graham, Edward, 56

Hooper, Peter, 145–48
Horioka, Charles Y., 140, 203
Household-saving behavior: forward-looking theory, 78–80, 190–91; policy changes to raise, 120–23, 199–200
Houthakker-Magee asymmetry effect, 149, 150, 151, 152
Hymer, Stephen, 45
Hysteresis, 148, 157 n.32

Income effect of a tax, 120–21, 199
Indexing of income tax, 118–19, 196, 209
Interest deduction on home mortgages, 113, 121–22, 196, 199
Interest rates and exchange rates: arbi-

trage, 29; closed interest parity, 143; currency premium, 144–45, 204; political (country) factors, 45, 204; real interest parity, 65–66, 143, 204; real interest rate differentials, 143–44, 201; relationship to capital flows, 168, 170, 201–202, 204; relationship to exchange rates, 133–37, 137–39, 143–45, 200–201; uncovered interest parity, 133–34, 143, 201, 204
Internationalization theory, 4–5, 46, 47–48, 186–87
International banking, 28, Eurocommercial paper facilities, 28; Euronotes, 28; financing, 26–27; note issuance facilities, 28
International Monetary Fund (IMF): exchange and trade restrictions, 23–24; fixed exchange rates, 24
International trade models, 128–31, 146, 148–50, 150–52, 153–55, 204–206

Japan: capital flows, 159, 167, 169, 177–78, 208; current account balance, 6, 7, 9, 162, 176, 177; economic growth, 182; exchange rate, 8, 206; fiscal policy, 9, 63–64; fixed capital formation, 68; monetary policy and capital export, 176–77; monetary policy and exchange rates, 176–77; personal saving, 65; productivity and relative cost, 206; saving-investment balance, 65; saving rate, 9–10, 64–65; 188; U.S.-Japan bilateral trade balance, 8, 9, 154–55
J-curve effect, 5, 8, 139, 152, 156 n.15, 203
Julius, DeAnne, 51

Keynes, John Maynard, 78, 190
Kindleberger, Charles P., 45, 159
Knickerbocker, Fredrick, 49
Kolhagen, Stephen, 43
Krugman, Paul R., 185

Latin America, international capital flows. See Capital flows

Lau, Lawrence, 88–90
Lawrence, Robert Z., 148–50, 185, 205
Lessard, D. F., 42
Liberalization. See Capital controls
Life-cycle model, 78–81, 90, 190–91; age structure, 79, 81, 87–88, 192, 194; bequests under, 80, 87, 191; income growth, 79; saving behavior, 86–87, 192; trade balance effects, 87–88; wealth and saving, 79–80, 84–85
Logue, Dennis, 44
Location-specific advantages, 47–49. See also Foreign direct investment

Magee, Stephen, 46
Makin, John, 42
Mann, Catherine L., 145–48
Marshall-Lerner condition, 139, 156 n.16
Mature creditor, United States, 1, 159, 160
McKinnon, Ronald I., 171
McManus, John, 46
Meade, James, 17
Mexico, 170–71, 176. See also Capital flows
Modigliani, Franco, 78, 80, 120, 190, 191
Mundell, Robert A., 87–88, 193
Mundell-Fleming model: fixed exchange rate case, 136; flexible exchange rate case, 136–39, 202; fiscal policy, 137–39, 202; monetary policy, 139, 202–203; relationship to U.S. balance-of-payments deficit problem, 137–39

National income identity, 127
Newly independent states (NIS), transition economies, 171–72
Newly industrializing economies, 7, 173. See also Capital flows
North American Free Trade Agreement (NAFTA), 55

Obstfeld, Maurice, 206
Oligopolistic reaction, 49–51
Organization for Economic Cooperation and Development (OECD), 68,
140–41, 150, 151, 153, 163, 170,
172, 206
Owens, Jeffrey, 120, 124 nn.19, 25,
220
Ownership advantages, 47–48, 51, 55

Permanent income hypothesis, 78–79,
99
Peterson, Peter, 100. *See also* Action
plan
Phillips curve, 137, 156 n.13
Portfolio investment, 15, 19, 26, 55,
168, 208
Post-Bretton Woods era, 125
Product cycle theory, 49–50
Productivity, 81–83, 191–92
Purchasing power parity, 128, 156 n.4

Retirement: Canada, 122; 401k employer-sponsored plans, 122–23, 200;
individual retirement accounts
(IRAs), 122, 123, 200; Keough
plans, 122–23, 200; saving incentives,
122–23, 199–200
Ricardo-Barro equivalence model, 92,
97 n.42; influence on saving rate, 92;
taxation reduction, 97 n.42
Russia. *See* Transition economies

Saving(s): interest elasticity of, 120–21,
199; precautionary motive, 87, 93,
193–94; projections, 87–88, 89–90,
90–91, 94–95; theory of, 78–81, 86–
87, 92; wealth, 89–90, 91–94;
wealth-income ratio, 84. *See also*
Baby boom generation: Household-
saving behavior; Life-cycle model;
Permanent income hypothesis
Saving(s)-investment balance (SI balance), and external balance, 207; industrial country international
comparisons, 62–68, 188, 207
Saving(s) rates: and bequests, 80, 87;
buffer-stock model, 92, 194–95;

demographics (age structure of the
population), 83, 87–88, 88–90, 90–
91, 95–96, 191–92, 193, 194; deregulation and relaxation of borrowing
constraints, 86, 94, 95, 193; economic growth, 81, 191, 194, 210; financial liberalization, 86; government
saving rates, 91, 92, 194; income
growth, 81, 91, 92; industrial countries, 194, 200; inflation, 85–86, 91,
191, 194; interest rates, 85, 91, 193,
194; private wealth changes, 91, 92,
192–93, 194; productivity growth,
81–83, 191–92; tax incentives to
raise, 120–23, 198–200; unemployment, 93–94, 95, 194–95
Saving-retention coefficient, 140–41,
203
Securitization, 26–27, 183
Speculation, 29, 136
Substitution effect of a tax, 120, 121,
199
Summers, Lawrence, 122, 142, 203

Tobin, James, 141–42
Trade balance, United States, 145–52,
205–206; computer, 148, 151; economic growth, 149–50; energy, 148;
exchange rate changes, 128, 148–49,
205; export prices, 148–49, 205;
"gap factor," 151, 205; Houthakker-
Magee effect, 149, 205; import
prices, 129, 148–49, 205–206; income elasticities, 149, 151, 205;
merchandise, 36–39, 148–49; nonagricultural, 148; noncomputer, 148;
nonenergy, 148; partial equilibrium
factors, 146, 148–50; price elasticities, 149
Transactions costs, 46, 49, 186
Transfer pricing, 55–56
Transition economies, current account
deficits, 171, 176; economic growth,
172; economic reforms, 172; European Union and, 172; International
Bank for Reconstruction and Development, 172; International Monetary

Fund, 172; newly independent states, 171; Russia, 171, 173
"Twin deficits" problem, 129

Unbundling of risk, 26
United States: affluence test for entitlements, 119, 195–96; automatic stabilizers, 108; bilateral trade deficit with Japan, 8, 9, 154–55; budget deficit, 2, 89, 188; budget deficit projections, 114–15, 188–89, 195, 209; budget deficit reduction impact, 73, 75, 106, 189, 197–98; budget deficit reductions, 6–7, 68–76, 188–90; budget deficit reductions and economic growth, 106–8, 115, 190, 197–98; business saving, 76, 188; capital account, 15–17; capital controls, 24; capital formation, 68; capital export, 8; capital import, 4, 5, 7, 10, 18, 182, 188; Clinton administration, 68, 188; consumption growth, 88–89, 193; current account, 2, 6–7, 8, 9, 10, 67, 68, 145, 146–47, 160, 177–78; debtor, 4, 7, 51, 61, 99, 159; Department of Commerce, 17, 18; economic growth, 149, 189, 197–99, 209–210; economic policy, 3; Economic Recovery Tax Act, 3, 5, 117, 188; entitlement spending reduction, 101–102, 119, 196–97; exchange rate(s) 1980s, 126, 132, 201–202; exchange rate overshooting, 136; exchange rate policy, 4–5, 8, 126, 134–35, 136; excise taxes, 111–12, 116, 117, 196–97; federal government discretionary expenditures, 72, 117, 188, 189, 195; federal government mandatory expenditures, 72, 114, 188, 189, 195, 209; federal government revenues, 116–19, 195–96, 209; foreign direct investment (see Foreign direct investment: United States); gross federal debt, 3, 10; income distribution, 118; income tax, 117; income tax

increase recommendations, 118–19, 196; inflation projections, 71–72, 189; infrastructure investment, 8, 115, 198, 210, 211; interest on the debt, 5, 72, 189, 190; interest rates, 8, 73–74, 188, 189, 198; international competitiveness, 2, 3, 4, 78; investment, 64, 198; Investment Tax Credit, 110–11, 190, 210; macroeconomic policy 1980s, 4–6, 126, 146–47; mature creditor, 1, 159–60; Medicaid, 100, 102, 104–105, 116, 189, 195, 209; Medicare, 69, 100, 101–102, 116, 189, 195, 209; monetary policy, 3, 4, 66–67, 198, 210; national investment rate, 9, 10, 64, 75–76, 187; national saving rate, 9, 10, 64, 75–76, 187; Omnibus Budget Reconciliation Act 1990, 117; Omnibus Budget Reconciliation Act 1993, 5, 6, 9, 68–70, 70–72, 100, 114–15, 117–18, 189, 195, 209; private investment rate, 7, 63–64; private saving rate, 9, 76–77, 84–85, 88–89, 93–94, 192, 194; public investment, 115; public investment and projected economic growth, 115, 190, 198; Reagan administration, 3, 4, 7, 136; relationship to global capital markets, 175–76; retirement saving incentives, 122–23, 199–200, 210; revenues and gross domestic product, 8, 116; sales tax, 112–13, 196; saving(s)-investment balance, 2, 7, 114, 187; Social Security, 72–73, 101, 105, 119, 188, 209; structural deficit, 72, 108; tax credit for research and development, 110; trade balance, 7, 132, 200–201; unemployment, 107
U.S.-Canada Free Trade Agreement, 55

Vernon, Raymond, 49

Willet, Thomas, 44
Woodward, Douglas, 56